Consultant reviewer:
Patrick Murray

Discovery

Leaving Certificate Poetry Anthology for Higher and Ordinary Level 2021

Edco
The Educational Company of Ireland

First published 2019

The Educational Company of Ireland
Ballymount Road
Walkinstown
Dublin 12

www.edco.ie

A member of the Smurfit Kappa Group plc
© Kevin McDermott, Simon Coury, Ellen O'Reilly, 2019

ISBN 978-1-84536-830-2

Editor: Jane Rogers
Layout: Graftrónaic
Cover: Slick Fish
Cover Photography: Adobe Stock

All rights reserved. No part of this publication may be reproduced, stored in a retrieval system, or transmitted in any form or by any means, electronic, mechanical, photocopying, recording or otherwise, without either the prior permission of the publisher or a licence permitting restricted copying in Ireland issued by the Irish Copyright Licensing Agency, 63 Patrick Street, Dún Laoghaire, Co. Dublin

Any links to external websites should not be construed as an endorsement by Edco of the content or view of the linked material.

Audio CD

1. 'The Fish' by Elizabeth Bishop
2. 'The Prodigal' by Elizabeth Bishop
3. 'Filling Station' by Elizabeth Bishop
4. 'Child of Our Time' by Eavan Boland
5. 'This Moment' by Eavan Boland
6. 'Love' by Eavan Boland
7. 'The Pomegranate' by Eavan Boland
8. 'The Difficulty that is Marriage' by Paul Durcan
9. 'Parents' by Paul Durcan
10. 'The Tuft of Flowers' by Robert Frost
11. 'The Road Not Taken' by Robert Frost
12. 'Birches' by Robert Frost
13. "Out, Out—" by Robert Frost
14. 'Acquainted with the Night' by Robert Frost
15. 'A Constable Calls' by Seamus Heaney
16. 'The Underground' by Seamus Heaney
17. 'The Pitchfork' by Seamus Heaney
18. 'A Call' by Seamus Heaney
19. 'Spring' by Gerard Manley Hopkins
20. 'Inversnaid' by Gerard Manley Hopkins
21. 'Thou art indeed just, Lord' by Gerard Manley Hopkins
22. 'On First Looking into Chapman's Homer' by John Keats
23. 'La Belle Dame Sans Merci' by John Keats
24. 'Ode to a Nightingale by John Keats
25. 'To Autumn' by John Keats
26. 'Poppies in July' by Sylvia Plath
27. 'The Arrival of the Bee Box' by Sylvia Plath
28. 'Child' by Sylvia Plath
29. 'Meeting at Night' by Robert Browning
30. 'Driving to the Hospital' by Kate Clanchy
31. 'Considering the Snail' by Thom Gunn
32. 'Frogs' by Randolph Healy
33. *Primula veris* by Randolph Healy
34. 'Easter Wings' by George Herbert
35. 'The Glass Hammer' by Andrew Hudgins
36. 'Lament for Thomas MacDonagh' by Francis Ledwidge
37. 'Moonshine' by Richard Murphy
38. 'The Net' by Julie O'Callaghan
39. 'Problems' by Julie O'Callaghan
40. 'Caoineadh Mháire' by Mary O'Malley
41. 'Ozymandias' by Percy Bysshe Shelley
42. 'Jungian Cows' by Penelope Shuttle
43. 'Oranges' by Gary Soto
44. 'Chronicle' by David Wheatley

The following permissions and acknowledgements refer to the audio materials included on the compact disc accompanying printed copies of this book: 'The Fish', 'The Prodigal' and 'Filling Station' by Elizabeth Bishop courtesy of Farrar, Straus and Giroux Ltd. 'Child of Our Time', 'The Pomegranate', 'This Moment' and 'Love' by Eavan Boland, courtesy of Carcanet Press. 'The Difficulty that is Marriage' and 'Parents' by Paul Durcan, courtesy of the poet. 'The Tuft of Flowers', 'The Road Not Taken', 'Birches', "Out, Out-" and 'Acquainted with the Night' by Robert Frost courtesy of Henry Holt & Co. 'A Constable Calls', 'The Underground', 'The Pitchfork' and 'A Call' by Seamus Heaney courtesy of Faber & Faber. 'Poppies in July', 'The Arrival of the Bee Box' and 'Child' by Sylvia Plath courtesy of Faber & Faber. 'Driving to the Hospital' by Kate Clanchy courtesy of Picador. 'Considering the Snail' by Thom Gunn courtesy of Faber & Faber. 'Frogs' and '*Primula veris*' by Randolph Healy courtesy of the poet. 'The Glass Hammer' by Andrew Hudgins courtesy of the poet. 'Moonshine' by Richard Murphy courtesy of Lilliput Press. 'The Net' and 'Problems' by Julie O'Callaghan courtesy of Bloodaxe Books. 'Caoineadh Mháire' by Mary O'Malley courtesy of Carcanet. 'Jungian Cows' by Penelope Shuttle courtesy of David Higham. 'Oranges' by Gary Soto courtesy of Chronicle Books. 'Chronicle' by David Wheatley courtesy of the Gallery Press.

For more information on copyright see page 1.

Foreword

This anthology, which includes all the poems prescribed for the Higher and Ordinary Level English Leaving Certificate Examinations of 2021, has been prepared by experienced teachers of English. Each of the contributors has been able to concentrate on a limited number of the prescribed poets and their work, thus facilitating a high standard of research and presentation.

Guidelines are given which set each poem in context. In addition, each poem is accompanied by a glossary and appropriate explorations, designed to allow the student to find his/her authentic response to the material.

Relevant biographical details are provided for each poet. A list of examination-style questions is provided for each prescribed poet at Higher Level along with a snapshot of the poet's work and a sample examination-style essay to aid revision. A snapshot is provided for all Ordinary Level poems.

Guidelines are included for students on approaching the Unseen Poetry section of the course. There is also advice on approaching the prescribed question in the examination. Students will find the glossary of poetic terms a valuable resource in reading and responding to poetry.

The poetry course for Leaving Certificate English demands a personal and active engagement from the student reader. We hope that this anthology makes that engagement possible and encourages students to explore the wider world of poetry for themselves.

Teachers can access the Discovery for Leaving Certificate Higher and Ordinary Level e-book by registering on www.edcolearning.ie.

Contents

* Denotes a poem included for Ordinary Level English Leaving Certificate

Foreword	iii
Discovery Student CD	vii
Acknowledgements	1
Elizabeth Bishop	2
Biography	3
Social and Cultural Context	5
Themes	6
Timeline	7
The Fish *	8
The Bight	14
At the Fishhouses	18
The Prodigal *	24
Questions of Travel	28
The Armadillo	34
Sestina	38
First Death in Nova Scotia	42
Filling Station *	48
In the Waiting Room	52
Exam-Preparation Questions	58
Snapshot	58
Sample Essay	59
Eavan Boland	62
Biography	63
Social and Cultural Context	64
Themes	65
Timeline	67
The War Horse	68
Child of Our Time *	72
The Famine Road	76
The Black Lace Fan My Mother Gave Me	81
The Shadow Doll	85
White Hawthorn in the West of Ireland	89
Outside History	93
This Moment *	98
Love *	101
The Pomegranate	106

Snapshot	111
Exam-Preparation Questions	112
Sample Essay	113
Paul Durcan	116
Biography	117
Social and Cultural Context	118
Themes	119
Timeline	121
Nessa	122
The Girl with the Keys to Pearse's Cottage	126
The Difficulty that is Marriage	130
Wife Who Smashed Television Gets Jail *	133
Parents *	138
En Famille, 1979	142
Madman	142
'Windfall', 8 Parnell Hill, Cork	144
Six Nuns Die in Convent Inferno	152
Sport *	162
Father's Day, 21 June 1992	168
The Arnolfini Marriage	173
Ireland 2002	178
Rosie Joyce	179
The MacBride Dynasty	187
Exam-Preparation Questions	192
Sample Essay	193
Snapshot	197
Robert Frost	198
Biography	199
Social and Cultural Context	200
Themes	202
Timeline	203
The Tuft of Flowers *	204
Mending Wall	209
After Apple-Picking	214
The Road Not Taken	219

Birches	222
"Out, Out—" *	229
Spring Pools	234
Acquainted with the Night	237
Design	241
Provide, Provide	245
Exam-Preparation Questions	249
Snapshot	250
Sample Essay	251

Seamus Heaney 254

Biography	255
Social and Cultural Context	258
Themes	260
Timeline	261
The Forge	262
Bogland	266
The Tollund Man	270
Mossbawn: Two Poems in Dedication	
(1) Sunlight	275
A Constable Calls *	279
The Skunk	284
The Harvest Bow	288
The Underground *	292
The Pitchfork	297
Lightenings, viii: 'The Annals Say'	301
A Call *	305
Postscript	309
Tate's Avenue	313
Exam-Preparation Questions	317
Snapshot	318
Sample Essay	319

Gerard Manley Hopkins 322

Biography	323
Social and Cultural Context	325
Themes	326
Timeline	327
God's Grandeur	328
Spring *	332
As kingfishers catch fire	337
The Windhover	342
Pied Beauty	347
Felix Randal	351

Inversnaid *	355
No worst, there is none	360
I wake and feel the fell of dark, not day	364
Thou art indeed just, Lord	368
Snapshot	371
Exam-Preparation Questions	372
Sample Essay	373

John Keats 376

Biography	377
Social and Cultural Context	379
Themes	381
Timeline	383
To one who has been long in city pent	384
On First Looking into Chapman's Homer *	387
When I have fears that I may cease to be	392
La Belle Dame Sans Merci *	396
Ode to a Nightingale	404
Ode on a Grecian Urn	414
To Autumn	422
Bright Star	429
Exam-Preparation Questions	433
Sample Essay	434
Snapshot	437

Sylvia Plath 438

Biography	439
Social and Cultural Context	443
Themes	443
Timeline	445
Black Rook in Rainy Weather	446
The Times Are Tidy	451
Morning Song	454
Finisterre	458
Mirror	463
Pheasant	468
Elm	472
Poppies in July *	479
The Arrival of the Bee Box	484
Child *	489
Exam-Preparation Questions	493
Snapshot	493
Sample Essay	494

Ordinary Level poems

Robert Browning — 497
- Meeting at Night — 498
- Exam-Style Questions — 501

Kate Clanchy — 502
- Driving to the Hospital — 503
- Exam-Style Questions — 506

Thom Gunn — 507
- Considering the Snail — 508
- Exam-Style Questions — 511

Randolph Healy — 513
- Frogs — 514
- Exam-Style Questions — 518
- *Primula veris* — 520
- Exam-Style Questions — 524

George Herbert — 526
- Easter Wings — 527
- Exam-Style Questions — 532

Andrew Hudgins — 533
- The Glass Hammer — 534
- Exam-Style Questions — 537

Francis Ledwidge — 539
- Lament for Thomas MacDonagh — 540
- Exam-Style Questions — 544

Richard Murphy — 545
- Moonshine — 546
- Exam-Style Questions — 548

Julie O'Callaghan — 549
- The Net — 550
- Exam-Style Questions — 552
- Problems — 554
- Exam-Style Questions — 557

Mary O'Malley — 559
- *Caoineadh Mháire* — 560
- Exam-Style Questions — 564

Percy Bysshe Shelley — 565
- Ozymandias — 566
- Exam-Style Questions — 569

Penelope Shuttle — 570
- Jungian Cows — 571
- Exam-Style Questions — 573

Gary Soto — 575
- Oranges — 576
- Exam-Style Questions — 580

David Wheatley — 582
- Chronicle — 583
- Exam-Style Questions — 587

Reading Unseen Poetry — 588
- Reading the Unseen Poem — 588
- Possible Ways into a Poem — 589
- Sample Unseen Poems — 592
- Guidelines for Answering Questions on Poetry — 598
- Glossary of Terms — 602
- Poets Examined at Higher Level — 606
- Higher Level Poets at a Glance Revision Charts — 607

Discovery Student CD

Listening to poetry

Discovery is accompanied by a student CD that includes 45 poetry tracks. Each track is read with expression and feeling, which brings the poems on the page to life.

A selection of these poems has been read by the poets, which gives an even greater insight into our understanding of the poems.

The poetry tracks are also available through the *Discovery* interactive e-book on **www.edcolearning.ie**. Click on the 🔊 beside relevant poems throughout the book to hear poems being read aloud.

Track listing

	Title	Poet	Page reference
1	The Fish	Elizabeth Bishop	8
2	The Prodigal	Elizabeth Bishop	24
3	Filling Station	Elizabeth Bishop	48
4	Child of Our Time	Eavan Boland	72
5	This Moment	Eavan Boland	98
6	Love	Eavan Boland	101
7	The Pomegranate	Eavan Boland	106
8	The Difficulty that is Marriage	Paul Durcan	130
9	Parents	Paul Durcan	138
10	The Tuft of Flowers	Robert Frost	204
11	The Road Not Taken	Robert Frost	219
12	Birches	Robert Frost	222
13	"Out, Out—"	Robert Frost	229
14	Acquainted with the Night	Robert Frost	237
15	A Constable Calls	Seamus Heaney	279
16	The Underground	Seamus Heaney	292
17	The Pitchfork	Seamus Heaney	297
18	A Call	Seamus Heaney	305
19	Spring	Gerard Manley Hopkins	332
20	Inversnaid	Gerard Manley Hopkins	355
21	Thou art indeed just, Lord	Gerard Manley Hopkins	368
22	On First Looking into Chapman's Homer	John Keats	387
23	La Belle Dame Sans Merci	John Keats	396
24	Ode to a Nightingale	John Keats	404
25	To Autumn	John Keats	422
26	Poppies in July	Sylvia Plath	479
27	The Arrival of the Bee Box	Sylvia Plath	484
28	Child	Sylvia Plath	489

29	Meeting at Night	Robert Browning	498
30	Driving to the Hospital	Kate Clanchy	503
31	Considering the Snail	Thom Gunn	508
32	Frogs	Randolph Healy	514
33	*Primula veris*	Randolph Healy	520
34	Easter Wings	George Herbert	527
35	The Glass Hammer	Andrew Hudgins	534
36	Lament for Thomas MacDonagh	Francis Ledwidge	540
37	Moonshine	Richard Murphy	546
38	The Net	Julie O'Callaghan	550
39	Problems	Julie O'Callaghan	554
40	Caoineadh Mháire	Mary O'Malley	560
41	Ozymandias	Percy Bysshe Shelley	566
42	Jungian Cows	Penelope Shuttle	571
43	Oranges	Gary Soto	576
44	Chronicle	David Wheatley	583

ACKNOWLEDGEMENTS

'The poems in this book have been reproduced with the kind permission of the publishers, agents, authors or their estates as follows:

'The Armadillo', 'At The Fishhouses', 'The Bight', 'Filling Station', 'First Death in Nova Scotia', 'The Fish', 'In the Waiting Room', 'The Prodigal', 'Questions of Travel', 'Sestina' by Elizabeth Bishop from *The Complete Poems of Elizabeth Bishop* published by Chatto & Windus. Reprinted by permission of The Random House Group Ltd © 1983.

'The War Horse', 'Child of Our Time', 'The Famine Road', 'The Shadow Doll', 'White Hawthorn in the West of Ireland', 'Outside History', 'The Black Lace Fan My Mother Gave Me', 'This Moment', 'The Pomegranate', 'Love' from *Collected Poems* (1995) by Eavan Boland, published by Carcanet Press Limited.

'Wife Who Smashed Television Gets Jail', 'Parents', 'Sport', 'The Girl with the Keys to Pearse's Cottage', 'The Difficulty that is Marriage', 'En Famille, 1979', 'Madman', '"Windfall", 8 Parnell Hill, Cork', 'Six Nuns Die in Convent Inferno', 'Father's Day, 21 June 1992', 'The Arnolfini Marriage', 'Ireland 2002', 'Rosie Joyce', 'The MacBride Dynasty', 'Nessa' by Paul Durcan reprinted with permission of the poet.

'The Tuft of Flowers', 'The Road Not Taken', 'Birches', '"Out, Out"', 'Spring Pools', 'Acquainted with the Night' by Robert Frost from *The Poetry of Robert Frost* edited by Edward Connery Lathem, Copyright © 1916, 1928, 1930, 1934, 1939, 1969 by Henry Holt and Company. Copyright © 1936, 1944, 1956, 1958, 1962 by Robert Frost. Copyright © 1964, 1967 by Lesley Frost Ballantine. Reprinted with permission of Henry Holt and Company. All rights reserved. 'Mending Wall', 'After Apple-Picking', 'Design', 'Provide, Provide' by Robert Frost from *The Poetry of Robert Frost* edited by Edward Connery Lathem, Copyright © 1916, 1928, 1930, 1934, 1939, 1969 by Henry Holt and Company. Copyright © 1936,1944, 1956, 1958, 1962 by Robert Frost. Copyright © 1964, 1967 by Lesley Frost Ballantine. Reprinted with permission of Henry Holt and Company. All rights reserved.

'The Forge' and 'Bogland' from *Door into the Dark* (1969); 'The Tollund Man' from *Wintering Out* (1972); 'Mossbawn: Two Poems in Dedication (1) Sunlight' and 'A Constable Calls' from *North* (1975); 'The Skunk' and 'The Harvest Bow' from *Fieldwork* (1979); 'The Underground' and 'Lightenings viii "The annals say…"' from *Station Island* (1984); 'The Pitchfork' from *Seeing Things* (1991); 'Postscript' and 'A Call' from *The Spirit Level* (1996); 'Tate's Avenue' from *District and Circle* (2006) by Seamus Heaney, published by Faber and Faber Ltd.

'Pheasant', 'Finisterre', 'Mirror', 'Child', 'Morning Song', 'Elm', 'The Arrival of the Bee-box', 'Poppies in July', 'Black Rook in Rainy Weather', 'The Times are Tidy' by Sylvia Plath from *Collected Poems* (1981) published by Faber and Faber Ltd.

'Driving to the Hospital' by Kate Clanchy from *Newborn* 2004, Picador. By permission of the publisher.

'Considering the Snail' by Thom Gunn from *Collected Poems*, Faber & Faber. By permission of the publisher.

'Frogs' and *'Primula veris'* by Randolph Healy from *Green 532: Selected Poems 1983–2000 (2002)*, Salt Publishing. Reprinted with the kind permission of the poet.

'The Glass Hammer' by Andrew Hudgins. Reprinted with the kind permission of the poet.

'Moonshine' by Richard Murphy from *The Price of Stone* (1985). Reprinted with the kind permission of The Lilliput Press.

'The Net' and 'Problems' by Julie O'Callaghan from *Tell Me This is Normal: New and Selected Poems (2008)*, Bloodaxe Books. Reprinted by permission of the publisher.

'Caoineadh Mháire' by Mary O'Malley from *The Boning Hall: New and Selected Poems* (2002). Reprinted by kind permission of Carcanet Press.

'Jungian Cows' by Penelope Shuttle, from *New and Selected Poems*, published by Bloodaxe. Reproduced by kind permission of the poet and David Higham Associates

'Oranges' by Gary Soto from *New and Selected Poems* © 1995, used with permission of Chronicle Books LLC, San Francisco. Visit www.chroniclebooks.com.

'Chronicle' by David Wheatley from *Misery Hill*, 2000. By kind permission of the author and The Gallery Press, Loughcrew, Oldcastle, Co. Meath. By permission of the publisher.

'Blessing' by Imtiaz Dharker from *Postcards from God* (1997), Bloodaxe Books. By permission of the publisher.

'The Envoy' by Jane Hirshfield from *Each Happiness Ringed by Lions: Selected Poems* (2006), Bloodaxe Books. By permission of the publisher.

'Darling' by Jackie Kay from *Darling: New & Selected Poems* (2007), Bloodaxe Books. By permission of the publisher.

'Saint Francis and the Sow' from *Mortal Acts, Mortal Words* by Galway Kinnell. Copyright © 1980, and renewed 2008 by Galway Kinnell. Reprinted with permission of Houghton Mifflin Harcourt Publishing Company. All rights reserved.

While every care has been taken to trace and acknowledge copyright, the publishers tender their apologies for any accidental infringement where copyright has proved untraceable. They would be pleased to come to a suitable arrangement with the rightful owner in each case.

The photographs in this book come from the following sources: Topfoto p2, 198, 254, 322, 376, 438, 497, 502, 526, 565, 570; Alamy p4, 95, 160, 190, 247, 257, 325, 416, 442, 536; Carcanet p62, 559; Rogers Coleridge and White p116; National Gallery p175; Getty p120, 507, 539; Keats House, City of London p408; Randolph Healy p513; Andrew Hudgins p533; Patrick McGree p545; Kim Haughton p549; Carolyn Soto p575; Gallery Press p582.

Elizabeth Bishop
1911–1979

The Fish*	8
The Bight	14
At the Fishhouses	18
The Prodigal*	24
Questions of Travel	28
The Armadillo	34
Sestina	38
First Death in Nova Scotia	42
Filling Station*	48
In the Waiting Room	52

Biography

Early life

Elizabeth Bishop was born in Massachusetts USA on 8 February 1911. While still an infant, her father William, a construction firm executive, died of a condition which affects the kidneys. Her mother Gertrude suffered a complete breakdown following her husband's death and was committed to an asylum in 1916, where she remained until she died in 1934. During this whole time Bishop never visited her mother or saw her again. Poems like 'First Death in Nova Scotia' and 'Filling Station' reflect the lack of a mother – the 'someone [who] loves us all' – in the poet's life.

Nova Scotia, where Bishop lived until she was six.

Bishop was taken to Great Village in Nova Scotia where she had a very happy time with her mother's parents. It seems to have been a simple existence but one where she was cared for, especially by her grandmother; this close relationship is at the heart of the poem 'Sestina'. Bishop was six when her paternal grandparents took her back to Massachusetts to live in a much stricter and more formal home. This enforced move from Nova Scotia affected her deeply and she later commented that it felt like a kidnapping. 'In the Waiting Room' was written about this time and features her paternal aunt, whom Bishop seems to have had little regard for. She then went to live in Boston with her maternal aunt, who introduced her to the work of many poets, including Alfred Lord Tennyson, Robert Browning and Elizabeth Barrett Browning. Here she attended boarding school where she wrote for the school magazine, and then Vassar College, from which she graduated in 1934. She often missed school due to illness.

Bishop considered becoming a composer or a doctor before she became a full-time poet. She rejected music as a career because she was terrified of performing in front of an audience. She painted and travelled around Europe and Africa for a time. Her love of painting and eye for colour and detail are major features of her poetic style, and the musicality and use of sound in her poems reflect her talent for music.

Being orphaned at an early age and moved around between various relatives affected Bishop hugely; she drank heavily at times and suffered from skin conditions like eczema. Poems like 'The Prodigal', 'Sestina' and 'First Death in Nova Scotia' reflect these events.

Adult life and love

Bishop was a lesbian. She lived in New York with her classmate Louise Crane, a lover of jazz music, which led the pair to know the legendary singer Billie Holiday, for whom Bishop wrote 'Songs for a Coloured Singer'. Also at that time Bishop met Maria Carlota Costallat de Macedo Soares (or 'Lota' as Elizabeth would call her), who would later become the love of her life. Crane also encouraged Bishop's love of fishing and introduced her to the delights of Key West in Florida, where the pair bought a house in 1938. 'The Fish' is set here, and the sea is a central image in much of Bishop's work.

> **Gerard Manley Hopkins**
>
> The poet Gerard Manley Hopkins influenced Bishop's work. When she was twenty-one, she published an essay entitled 'Notes on timing in the poetry of Gerard Manley Hopkins'. Her biographer Brett C. Millier says this essay 'contains the seeds of all her later thinking on rhythm in poetry'.

Her first published poems featured in a 1935 anthology called *Trial Balances*, a collection compiled by her great mentor and friend, the modernist poet Marianne Moore. Her first complete collection was *North & South*, published in 1946 to rave reviews. The renowned critic Randall Jarrell said at the time, 'Her work is unusually personal and honest in its wit, perception and sensitivity'.

Her close friend, the poet Robert Lowell, convinced her to accept a Poet Laureate position in the Library of Congress in 1949, a very prestigious job but one she was very nervous about. Lowell was a very successful poet and a huge influence on Bishop. He was seen by many as a voice to represent the nation. In an essay on Bishop, Jonathan Ellis writes, 'she was never the most read or respected at the time. Allen Ginsberg's *Howl* (1956) and Sylvia Plath's *Ariel* (1965) both sold more copies than any of her collections, while Robert Lowell's *Life Studies* (1959) continues to take the critical plaudits as the key work of poetry for most post-World War II readers.'

Bishop's friend Robert Lowell.

Ellis contends that Bishop had as much influence on Lowell's poetry as he did on hers. Certainly, Bishop is a much more well-known poet these days than Lowell. They wrote many letters over the years of their friendship – in fact Bishop was a prolific letter-writer, and several thousand letters survive. The book *One Art* features over 500 of these, selected and edited by Robert Giroux.

In November of 1951 Bishop won a scholarship of $2,500 and decided to travel to South America – a fateful decision, as she met Lota there again and the two became lovers. Bishop made her home in Brazil with Lota, so that a planned two-week holiday lasted fifteen years. Their relationship was a close and loving one. Bishop dedicated her poetry collection *Questions of Travel* to Lota and wrote to Lowell saying, 'I am extremely happy for the first time in my life'. She published *A Cold Spring* in 1955 and won the Pulitzer Prize for Literature the following year.

Later life and death

Elizabeth and Lota became celebrities in Rio de Janeiro, where Lota was very political, and both did a lot of charity work to regenerate parts of Rio and better the lives of children there. For example, they built a complex called Flamingo Park (Aterro do Flamengo) with many amenities for the local children. The park was designed by Lota, who was an architect, and the famous landscape artist Roberto Burle Marx; it was completed in 1965 and is still used extensively today, for example for cycling and athletics events in the 2016 Olympic and Paralympic games.

In 1966 Bishop was invited to be writer-in-residence at the University of Washington. Lota was in Brazil and ill at this time. She came to visit Bishop on 16 September 1967, clearly very unwell (with arteriosclerosis). In the early morning she took a bottle of valium, a drug used to treat anxiety, and slipped into a coma. Lota died on 25 September. Following this Bishop found herself excluded by many of their mutual friends and Lota's family, who blamed the poet for Lota's suicide. Bishop suffered from depression and sought help in psychoanalysis with Dr Ruth Foster, which led to poetry which explored her troubled childhood more openly. She writes about her grief over Lota's death and earlier losses in the poem 'One Art':

'I lost my mother's watch. And look! my last, or
next-to-last, of three loved houses went.
The art of losing isn't hard to master ...

— Even losing you (the joking voice, a gesture
I love) I shan't have lied. It's evident
the art of losing's not too hard to master
though it may look like (*Write* it!) like disaster.'

Working with Dr Foster 'on the origins of her depression and alcoholism' led Bishop to feel that she would have to live with the after-effects of losing her mother always, and be affected by this loss in ever-changing ways. The poetry that came out of that time attempts to put a shape on these tragic events and help Bishop cope and deal with her past. 'Sestina' is a good example of this. It is interesting that though the loss of her mother hovers in the background of many of her poems, 'First Death in Nova Scotia' is the only one on our course where her mother is overtly mentioned.

> **Bishop and Heaney**
>
> **Seamus Heaney came to know Bishop when he replaced her in a teaching position at Harvard University and praised her 'ultimate fidelity to the demands and promise of the artistic event'** – *The Government of the Tongue*. **Bishop developed a warm friendship with Heaney and his wife Marie despite his initial reservations that she would resent him taking over her job.**

In 1969 Bishop published her *Complete Poems* and won the National Book Award for poetry. Her last book, *Geography III* in 1976, was received to great acclaim. 'In the Waiting Room' is from this short collection of only ten poems.

Bishop died of a cerebral aneurysm on Saturday 6 October 1979.

Social and Cultural Context

Spending part of her childhood in Nova Scotia added a dimension to Bishop's life, and **landscape and childhood experiences within a family** were central to her work. Her education in Massachusetts is a factor she shared with other famous poets like Dickinson, Plath, Emerson and Frost. All are poets who used the natural world extensively to convey themes in their work.

A movement called 'Imagism' – where **a central image is key to the theme of the poem** – influenced Bishop greatly, but she didn't align herself to any particular literary movement.

Despite being gay and a very successful and influential woman in her time, she refused to have her work included in women-only anthologies, which showed how forward-thinking she was in terms of equality and moving beyond gender. To be openly gay at this time in a very conservative America was very brave. Without fuss or flourish, Bishop flouted the convention of the very domestic, demure type of woman that US culture and society demanded of her gender – just by simply being herself.

> **The Confessional Poets**
>
> **Bishop is considered by many critics to be one of the 'Confessional Poets'.**
>
> **This refers to poets (including also Sylvia Plath) who place the 'I' at the centre of their poems and often use personas or speakers while the poems deal with private experiences from the life of the poet which are generally negative ones. Plath and Lowell are good examples of this. According to Jonathan Ellis, 'Robert Lowell was godfather to the Confessional Poets.'**

Themes

Travel
Bishop adored travel and wrote about the flora and fauna of places she visited. She was ahead of her time in questioning the ethics of travel and **criticising the harm we sometimes do to the natural world** as we move through it. 'Questions of Travel', 'The Armadillo' and 'Filling Station' are poems which feature this theme.

Nature
Nature itself plays not only a major role in Bishop's imagery, but is also a central theme. 'The Fish', 'The Bight', 'At the Fishhouses' and 'The Armadillo' all focus heavily on aspects of the natural world. Bishop has a very original style when describing nature in her poetry, often using **unusual and striking similes** and **metaphors** which **add vibrancy and interest to her work**, for example comparing fish scales to sequins, hay bales to clouds, or sparks of flaming ash to 'rose-flecks'. Her fascination with nature and her deep love for it permeate her poems, and even in the urban grot of 'Filling Station' she finds time to notice and describe embroidered daisies and a 'hirsute begonia' plant.

Loss, struggle and survival
This is a side of Bishop's poetry that connects her to the 'Confessional Poets'. In 'The Fish' she admires the struggles the fish has survived, while in 'The Prodigal' the main character's resolve to lift his life from its denigrating circumstances is the focus of the poem. In her later poems she explores her experience of being orphaned and her unsettled childhood. Her tone in these poems is often conversational and can almost seem flippant, but the **underlying themes and experiences are often profound**, as in 'Filling Station' and 'First Death in Nova Scotia'.

'At the Fishhouses', 'Questions of Travel', 'Sestina', 'First Death in Nova Scotia', 'Filling Station' and 'In the Waiting Room' are all concerned with Bishop's troubled childhood and her **search for a home**. Bishop returns again and again to childhood experiences in these poignant poems but without a trace of self-pity. There is a **melancholy mix** of nostalgia, loss and pain, combined with an almost **mischievous sense of fun** that is reminiscent of the poetry of Emily Dickinson – 'Why should I be my aunt, / or me, or anyone?' ('In the Waiting Room').

Elizabeth Bishop

Timeline

1911	Born 8 February in Massachusetts; father dies
1916	Mother hospitalised due to mental illness; Elizabeth taken to Nova Scotia to live with maternal grandparents
1917	Taken to live with paternal grandparents and later her aunt Maud in Massachusetts
1930—34	Attends Vassar College, New York
1934	Death of mother
1935	First poem published in an anthology called *Trial Balances*
1938	Moves to Key West in Florida
1942	Meets Lota for the first time through mutual friend Louise Crane
1946	Publishes *North and South*, her first poetry collection; wins Houghton Mifflin Poetry Award
1949	Appointed consultant in poetry (Poet Laureate) at Library of Congress
1951	Wins scholarship which allows her to travel to South America; settles down there with Lota
1955	Publishes second poetry collection, *A Cold Spring*, winning the Pulitzer Prize for Poetry in 1956
1964	Awarded fellowship of the Academy of American Poets
1965	*Questions of Travel* published, her third collection of poetry
1967	25 September, Lota kills herself while visiting Elizabeth in the USA; Bishop moves to San Francisco for a year
1970	Appointed poet-in-residence at Harvard University in Boston
1976	Publishes her final poetry collection, *Geography III*, consisting of ten poems
1977	Close friends and mentors Marianne Moore and Robert Lowell die
1979	Dies in Boston on 6 October
1983	*Complete Poems* published

HIGHER LEVEL

Before you read

Describe an animal in as much detail as you can. Use plenty of adjectives and at least one simile, one metaphor and one instance of personification to bring your description to life. Finish by considering what you might learn from this animal.

The Fish

I caught a tremendous fish
and held him beside the boat
half out of water, with my hook
fast in a corner of his mouth.
He didn't fight.
He hadn't fought at all.
He hung a grunting weight,
battered and venerable
and homely. Here and there
his brown skin hung in strips   10
like ancient wallpaper,
and its pattern of darker brown
was like wallpaper:
shapes like full-blown roses
stained and lost through age.   15
He was speckled with barnacles,
fine rosettes of lime,
and infested
with tiny white sea-lice,
and underneath two or three   20
rags of green weed hung down.
While his gills were breathing in
the terrible oxygen
– the frightening gills,
fresh and crisp with blood,   25
that can cut so badly –
I thought of the coarse white flesh
packed in like feathers,
the big bones and the little bones,
the dramatic reds and blacks   30
of his shiny entrails,
and the pink swim-bladder
like a big peony.
I looked into his eyes
which were far larger than mine   35
but shallower, and yellowed,
the irises backed and packed
with tarnished tinfoil
seen through the lenses
of old scratched isinglass.   40
They shifted a little, but not
to return my stare.
– It was more like the tipping

8 / DISCOVERY: POETRY ANTHOLOGY

of an object toward the light.
I admired his sullen face,   45
the mechanism of his jaw,
and then I saw
that from his lower lip
– if you could call it a lip –
grim, wet, and weaponlike,   50
hung five old pieces of fish-line,
or four and a wire leader
with the swivel still attached,
with all their five big hooks
grown firmly in his mouth.   55
A green line, frayed at the end
where he broke it, two heavier lines,
and a fine black thread
still crimped from the strain and snap
when it broke and he got away.   60
Like medals with their ribbons
frayed and wavering,
a five-haired beard of wisdom
trailing from his aching jaw.
I stared and stared   65
and victory filled up
the little rented boat,
from the pool of bilge
where oil had spread a rainbow
around the rusted engine   70
to the bailer rusted orange,
the sun-cracked thwarts,
the oarlocks on their strings,
the gunnels – until everything
was rainbow, rainbow, rainbow!   75
And I let the fish go.

Glossary

8	*venerable*: deserving respect
9	*homely*: ordinary, plain looking
16	*barnacles*: tiny shellfish that cling to rocks, boats and larger fish, etc.
31	*entrails*: intestines
33	*peony*: a large rose-like flower
40	*isinglass*: a yellowish glass-like substance; the word was originally applied to a gelatine extracted from the swim bladder of certain fish, but is also used for sheets of mica, a semi-transparent mineral
52	*wire leader*: the short piece of wire that links the hook to the fishing line
53	*swivel*: a connecting moveable part that sits between the line and the leader on a fishing line
59	*crimped*: curled from being stretched then broken
68	*bilge*: dirty water that collects in the bottom of the boat
71	*bailer*: metal bucket to scoop the bilge from the boat
72	*thwarts*: the benches for the rower to sit on
73	*oarlocks*: holders for the oars on each side of the boat
74	*gunnels*: top parts of the sides of the boat

Guidelines

'The Fish' is a poem from Bishop's time in Florida where fishing was a favourite pastime. She had caught a Caribbean jewfish. From her first poetry collection *North & South*, it is Bishop's most well-known poem and she came to refer to it as 'That damn fish' due to the number of requests she received for its publication. The poem traces how the speaker's admiration for the fish grows as she examines it more and more closely.

Commentary

Lines 1–21

Our narrator has caught a huge and impressive fish ('tremendous') and is surprised that it puts up no struggle, but just hangs there on the end of her rod. This makes sense later on when we discover the fish has been caught many times before and may not have any fight left. In a **trio of adjectives**, something she often uses, Bishop describes the fish as 'battered and venerable / and homely'. It has suffered, deserves respect and is ordinary looking.

In a quirky simile she compares its tattered skin to peeling wallpaper decorated with roses. It is covered in barnacles and riddled with lice. Strands of seaweed hang from him. This fish has clearly been through a lot. **Bishop is often fascinated with things most people might find uninteresting or ugly**.

Lines 22–33
The narrator notes the sharp blood-red gills and the fish's panic at not being able to breathe. Her **imagination comes into play** as she visualises its insides and compares its 'pink swim-bladder' to a peony – another floral image.

Lines 34–44
Bishop begins to empathise with the fish while at the same time realising the fish does not react to her in the same way. She notices its eyes are different from hers; larger, shallower and yellowed, but they do not return her gaze; rather they just seem to follow the light. She is careful not to personify the fish here.

Lines 45–64
Now she ascribes **human qualities** to him – 'his sullen face'. She notices five hooks embedded in his mouth, indicating that he has escaped capture at least five times before this. She compares these to medals a soldier might win or the beard of a wise old man. The lines are 'crimped from the strain and snap', showing the strength and determination the fish once had. This **contrasts** greatly with the lack of struggle in the fish when Bishop catches it.

Lines 65–76
Noticing these hooks, together with everything else Bishop has observed about the fish, leads her to an epiphany – a moment where she suddenly understands something important. She experiences **a feeling of marvel and wonder, expressed as colour filling up the rusty, cracked boat like a rainbow**. This fish deserves another chance – like her, he is a survivor and has been through difficult and testing times: 'And I let the fish go.'

Themes

Surviving difficulty is a major theme here. The fish has clearly been through many battles and survived, but these hardships have taken their toll. The fish has no resistance left in him, 'He hadn't fought at all'; but despite his lack of struggle Bishop feels that 'victory filled up / the little rented boat'. She is full of **admiration** for the fish; he reminds her of a war hero decorated with medals hanging from his uniform on ribbons. This adds a sense of **honour** to the fish's achievements. Bishop has a **moment of epiphany** at the end of the poem — 'rainbow, rainbow, rainbow!' She suddenly realises that she is like the fish, and deserving of another chance in life.

Loneliness is apparent here also. Bishop seems to be fishing alone and the fish itself is a **solitary figure**. She once wrote to her good friend the poet Robert Lowell, 'When you write my epitaph you must say I was the loneliest person who ever lived' (1948). The poem **reflects her struggle with illness, alcoholism and anxiety**, and the trials of her childhood. Upon starting a new job in the Library of Congress in 1947 she said, 'I have never felt so nervous, like a fish out of water.'

Imagery

> **The fish Bishop caught**
>
> The Caribbean Jewfish, more commonly known these days as the Goliath Grouper, is a large saltwater fish that inhabits shallow tropical waters like those of the Florida Keys, where Bishop fished. It can grow to as large as two and a half metres in length, so it is no exaggeration when Bishop claims that the eye of the fish is larger than hers.

Similes, metaphors and **personification** are all used very effectively by Bishop. Her imagery is also **strikingly original** and **highly imaginative**, for example comparing the skin of the fish to old rose-patterned wallpaper and the barnacles to rosettes, as well as the bladder of the fish to a peony. There is great detail in her description of the fish; she even goes so far as to imagine the intestines and flesh inside the creature: 'coarse white flesh', 'the big bones and the little bones', 'reds and blacks'. Bishop is clearly no stranger to angling and boating and uses **specialised language** – wire leader, swivel, bilge, bailer, gunnels – that lends a real **authenticity** to her account. The boat too is as battered and damaged as the fish; it is 'rusted' and 'cracked'. Bishop seems to appreciate these qualities and values these **signs of resilience and determination**.

Language and form

Alliteration, assonance and sibilance are among the main sound effects Bishop uses. These speed or slow the poem depending on Bishop's level of **concentration or excitement**.

Repetition also conveys excitement: 'rainbow, rainbow, rainbow!' **Trios of adjectives** are a feature of Bishop's style and she uses them to great effect here; 'battered and venerable / and homely' is an example of this. This creates an effect of balance and detail, and is often used in persuasive writing such as advertising and political speeches.

You will also notice some rhyming though there is no formal rhyming scheme. These sound effects help to strike a balance between the speaker sounding poetic and conversational.

The poem is written as one long **narrative**; the narrator is too captivated by the fish to pause for stanzas. The poem moves **from observation to imagination**: Bishop first describes the outer appearance of the fish but then uses her imagination to wonder what his insides might look like. In a real sense this is **what poets do: they observe and describe the world**, but also **connect it, on a deeper level, to their imagination and their personal experiences**. As well as what we know and can see, there are things we cannot know for sure, and we use our imagination to think about these things, a concept Bishop explores further in 'At the Fishhouses'.

> **Fable**
>
> The poem reads very much like a fable. Often in these stories an animal teaches a person an important moral. The structure comprises one long narrative giving us a linear (beginning, middle, end) account of catching the fish. This is a lesson to be learned.

Exam-Style Questions

Understanding the poem

1. How can you tell that the fish does not put up a struggle when caught?
2. 'Battered and venerable / and homely.' What is the poet's meaning in this trio of adjectives? What other trios can you find in the poem? List them.
3. What simile is used to describe the skin of the fish? Do you think this is an effective simile?
4. What else do we learn about the appearance of the fish?
5. In lines 45–64 the poet notices the lines and hooks hanging from the jaw of the fish. Describe them. What two things does the poet compare them to?
6. 'Victory filled up / the little rented boat'. What victory, do you think, is the poet talking about?

Thinking about the poem

1. In your opinion, why does the poet release the fish in the end? Was it the right decision? Why? Discuss in pairs or groups.
2. Choose two of your favourite images from the poem and explain why you chose them.
3. Read Bishop's biography. How might the fish reflect her own life experiences?

Imagining

1. Write Bishop's diary entry **or** a letter to a friend recounting her experience of fishing that day.
2. 'Rainbow, rainbow, rainbow!' Write a short story with this title, in which the main character realises something about life through an encounter with nature.

SNAPSHOT

- A fable
- Highly descriptive
- Speaker learns a lesson
- Poet admires the fish more and more as she looks at it
- Poet has an epiphany – the fish deserves to be set free
- Based on a real event
- Link to 'The Prodigal' – use of animals as a central symbol

> **Before you read**
>
> What would your thoughts and ideas be if you decided to write a poem on your birthday? Where would your setting be and why?

The Bight

On my birthday

At low tide like this how sheer the water is.
White, crumbling ribs of marl protrude and glare
and the boats are dry, the pilings dry as matches.
Absorbing, rather than being absorbed,
the water in the bight doesn't wet anything,   5
the color of the gas flame turned as low as possible.
One can smell it turning to gas; if one were Baudelaire
one could probably hear it turning to marimba music.
The little ocher dredge at work off the end of the dock
already plays the dry perfectly off-beat claves.   10
The birds are outsize. Pelicans crash
into this peculiar gas unnecessarily hard,
it seems to me, like pickaxes,
rarely coming up with anything to show for it,
and going off with humorous elbowings.   15
Black-and-white man-of-war birds soar
on impalpable drafts
and open their tails like scissors on the curves
or tense them like wishbones, till they tremble.
The frowsy sponge boats keep coming in   20
with the obliging air of retrievers,
bristling with jackstraw gaffs and hooks
and decorated with bobbles of sponges.
There is a fence of chicken wire along the dock
where, glinting like little plowshares,   25
the blue-gray shark tails are hung up to dry
for the Chinese-restaurant trade.
Some of the little white boats are still piled up
against each other, or lie on their sides, stove in,
and not yet salvaged, if they ever will be, from the last bad storm,   30
like torn-open, unanswered letters.
The bight is littered with old correspondences.
Click. Click. Goes the dredge,
and brings up a dripping jawful of marl.
All the untidy activity continues,   35
awful but cheerful.

Elizabeth Bishop

Glossary

Title	
	Bight = a wide shallow bay
1	*sheer*: smooth
2	*marl*: soil below water
3	*pilings*: timber posts driven into the ground (e.g. for a fence)
7	*Baudelaire*: French poet (1821–1867); used symbolism extensively
8	*marimba*: a large wooden xylophone-like instrument with an echoing and lively sound
9	*ocher*: pale yellowish-brown colour
9	*dredge*: machine which lifts mud away
10	*claves*: wooden tubes struck against each other as a musical instrument; marimba and claves are both South American instruments used in Latin and jazz music
16	*man-of-war birds*: large tropical seabirds
17	*impalpable*: unable to be felt by touch
17	*drafts*: light air currents
20	*frowsy*: messy and smelly
21	*retrievers*: hunting dogs, a friendly and loyal breed
22	*jackstraw gaffs*: gaffs are hooks to land large fish; they are long and would be stored on a boat pointing upwards; they remind the poet of the thin sticks of wood used in the children's game 'spillikins'
25	*plowshares*: blades of a plough
29	*stove in*: smashed
32	*correspondences*: letters; also associations, connections in the mind between things

Guidelines

From the collection *A Cold Spring* (1955), this poem is set in Garrison Bight in Florida, where Bishop lived with Louise Crane. The poem describes the small messy harbour there with keenly observed detail and unusual metaphors, both common features of Bishop's work. As the mud in the harbour is dredged the **things the poet observes lead her thoughts inwards** to her own life. She wrote to her friend Robert Lowell that the harbour was 'always in a mess … reminds me of my little desk'. This move from **the exterior world to interior thoughts and memories** is often found in her poetry. What a poet observes of the world often **'dredges up' associations and memories** like the action the dredge performs at the harbour.

Commentary

This poem reflects Bishop's love of Florida, South America and jazz music.

Surveying the busy, messy, storm-damaged harbour, Bishop **compares it to her own situation**: she has been through personal storms and survived, perhaps even thrived in the messy chaos of her working life. Despite the ugliness of the scene, the poet takes a positive feeling away from the experience about the harbour and herself: 'All the untidy activity continues, / awful but cheerful.' This quote was, at Bishop's request, carved on her gravestone as her epitaph.

> **Baudelaire and synaesthesia**
>
> Baudelaire used symbolism to link the physical and spiritual worlds and often found unusual comparisons. Bishop imagines him not merely seeing and smelling the gas but hearing it as marimba music also, for Baudelaire experienced synaesthesia, where one sense triggers a response in another, for example hearing music and experiencing it as colours. This effect also occurs in Heaney's poem 'The Skunk', where the smell of his wife on a pillow tastes of wine to the poet.

The subtitle 'On my birthday' may reflect the idea that the poet sees this as a special time to **reflect on her past and present**, though she admitted to Lowell in a letter that it was not actually her birthday at all.

HIGHER LEVEL

Lines 1–15

The tide is out and through the thin layer of water remaining, the poet marvels at how she can see the thick ribbed soil beneath. Despite the seaside setting, everything is dry – the boats, the pilings. It's as if the water is turning to gas in **texture, colour and smell**. The water strangely doesn't dampen anything but rather evaporates as it comes into contact with things. **Sound is evoked** in the regular beat of the dredge, the crashing pelicans (like cymbals) and the suggestion of marimba. There is a veritable orchestra of sound at play here. The energetic efforts of the pelicans seem futile, 'rarely coming up with anything to show for it', yet their 'humorous elbowings' suggest **a spirit of play and fun**. This theme will develop with relation to Bishop's own view of work at the end of the poem. Despite the music, bustle and fun, there is a **creeping tension also**. Danger is alluded to in lines such as 'the gas flame', 'dry as matches' and 'crash / … unnecessarily hard, / … like pickaxes'; this haphazard way of life is not without its risks.

Lines 16–36

Another mechanical simile is used to depict the huge man-of-war birds which open their tails 'like scissors' as they fly on the air currents. Their 'trembling' sustains the underlying atmosphere of tension established in stanza 1. The harbour becomes very busy; 'frowsy sponge boats' come in like retriever dogs that seem eager to please, as if they are playing a game of fetch. Even the fishing gear seems playful, reminding the poet of toys: 'jackstraw gaffs', 'bobbles of sponges'. It is clearly a working harbour, with its wire fence and shark tails drying out to be used in 'the Chinese-restaurant trade'. She surveys the damage storms have wreaked on the 'little white boats … / … stove in.' These remind her of the papers on her desk and as she is thinking this the musicality returns: 'Click. Click. Goes the dredge, / and brings up a dripping jawful of marl', just as her mind has dredged up the image of her correspondence lying unanswered on her desk. Her final thought though seems a cheerful one: she is happy to be productive in this chaotic untidy way of working.

Themes

Often out of chaos comes creativity and productivity – a poem has been created out of the seemingly random group of sounds and images recorded. Perhaps allowing this messiness in how she works and thinks, Bishop can **open her mind to unusual connections and ideas**. This **originality** is part of her style as a poet and gives her a **freedom**. However, there may be dangers in working this way too, as some of the images suggest.

There is an air of **celebration** hinted at in the subtitle ('On my birthday'), but at the same time a suggestion that we should **take stock** of our life and our work. **Exploring and observing** the bight so keenly corresponds to the introspective exploring and observing that the poet is conducting into herself. **Bringing outer observations and experiences to her imagination** and **allowing them to 'correspond' with her inscape** and her life is at the heart of how Bishop's poetry generally works.

Imagery

The overall effect of the imagery is **ugly yet lively**. **Images from nature** – the water, the birds – go **hand in hand with man-made and mechanical objects** like the dredger and the boats. The idea that the marl beneath the water has ribs not only suggests the shaping influence of the tides but also **personifies** the seabed. **Metaphors and similes abound**: the birds are like tools, 'scissors' and 'pickaxes', the smashed white boats remind the poet of her 'torn-open, unanswered letters'. **Colour and sound collide** and a poem filled with energy and vigour results which, like the often fruitless diving of the pelicans, is fun nonetheless.

Elizabeth Bishop

Language and form

The language used by the poet accentuates energy and vigour. There is strength here, and plenty of **lively sound**: 'Pelicans crash / into this peculiar gas … /… like pickaxes'; the 'p', 'c' and 'ck' sounds are harsh and hard like the action being described. The many **hard consonants** reflect the energy and industry of the scene.

More gentle sound effects abound too, like the **long vowels** and sibilance in the lines, 'birds soar / on impalpable drafts / and open their tails like scissors on the curves' and 'frowsy sponge boats'. These lines provide a gentler, sweeter contrast to the harsher sounds in the poem, and together the sound effects have a musical quality to echo the many musical references in the poem.

The poem is written in one continuous list of observations and associations, adding to the statement at the end of the poem that life and work can be 'untidy'.

Questions

1	Write, or draw and label, a description of the scene described by Bishop, including as many of the details she gives us as possible.
2	What senses are evoked in her description of The Bight? Discuss.
3	List and comment on the sounds and sound effects the poet uses.
4	What atmosphere is created by the combinations of sounds and images in the poem?
5	Choose a simile or metaphor which particularly appealed to you; comment on its effect and give a reason for your choice.
6	How is the poet's desk like the damaged boats in the second stanza? Is this a negative comparison?
7	How does the poem move from the exterior world to the poet's interior thoughts? Trace and comment on this in the poem.
8	'Bishop combines a very realistic view of the world around us with highly original and amusing imagery.' Discuss in relation to this poem.
9	What do you learn about the speaker from reading this poem? Try to find three or four adjectives to describe her and back up these ideas with reference to the poem. You may choose from the following list if you wish: optimistic, imaginative, observant, humorous, critical.
10	'The final line changes the poem from something possibly negative to an optimistic vision of life.' Do you agree? Explain.
11	Suggest images and music that you would combine to create an audio-visual accompaniment to a performed reading of this poem.
12	In groups or pairs, choose a character from one of your Paper II texts and suggest a place that would have a special meaning for that person. Describe the place and suggest the memories and thoughts it might evoke for that character.

Before you read

What work might go on at fishhouses? What setting do you think you would find fishhouses in?

At the Fishhouses

Although it is a cold evening,
down by one of the fishhouses
an old man sits netting,
his net, in the gloaming almost invisible,
a dark purple-brown, 5
and his shuttle worn and polished.
The air smells so strong of codfish
it makes one's nose run and one's eyes water.
The five fishhouses have steeply peaked roofs
and narrow, cleated gangplanks slant up 10
to storerooms in the gables
for the wheelbarrows to be pushed up and down on.
All is silver: the heavy surface of the sea,
swelling slowly as if considering spilling over,
is opaque, but the silver of the benches, 15
the lobster pots, and masts, scattered
among the wild jagged rocks,
is of an apparent translucence
like the small old buildings with an emerald moss
growing on their shoreward walls. 20
The big fish tubs are completely lined
with layers of beautiful herring scales
and the wheelbarrows are similarly plastered
with creamy iridescent coats of mail,
with small iridescent flies crawling on them. 25
Up on the little slope behind the houses,
set in the sparse bright sprinkle of grass,
is an ancient wooden capstan,
cracked, with two long bleached handles
and some melancholy stains, like dried blood, 30
where the ironwork has rusted.
The old man accepts a Lucky Strike.
He was a friend of my grandfather.
We talk of the decline in the population
and of codfish and herring 35
while he waits for a herring boat to come in.
There are sequins on his vest and on his thumb.
He has scraped the scales, the principal beauty,
from unnumbered fish with that black old knife,
the blade of which is almost worn away. 40

Down at the water's edge, at the place
where they haul up the boats, up the long ramp
descending into the water, thin silver
tree trunks are laid horizontally
across the gray stones, down and down
at intervals of four or five feet.

Cold dark deep and absolutely clear,
element bearable to no mortal,
to fish and to seals . . . One seal particularly
I have seen here evening after evening.
He was curious about me. He was interested in music;
like me a believer in total immersion,
so I used to sing to him Baptist hymns.
I also sang 'A Mighty Fortress Is Our God.'
He stood up in the water and regarded me
steadily, moving his head a little.
Then he would disappear, then suddenly emerge
almost in the same spot, with a sort of shrug
as if it were against his better judgment.
Cold dark deep and absolutely clear,
the clear gray icy water . . . Back, behind us,
the dignified tall firs begin.
Bluish, associating with their shadows,
a million Christmas trees stand
waiting for Christmas. The water seems suspended
above the rounded gray and blue-gray stones.
I have seen it over and over, the same sea, the same,
slightly, indifferently swinging above the stones,
icily free above the stones,
above the stones and then the world.
If you should dip your hand in,
your wrist would ache immediately,
your bones would begin to ache and your hand would burn
as if the water were a transmutation of fire
that feeds on stones and burns with a dark gray flame.
If you tasted it, it would first taste bitter,
then briny, then surely burn your tongue.
It is like what we imagine knowledge to be:
dark, salt, clear, moving, utterly free,
drawn from the cold hard mouth
of the world, derived from the rocky breasts
forever, flowing and drawn, and since
our knowledge is historical, flowing, and flown.

HIGHER LEVEL

Glossary

3	*netting*: mending fishing nets	
4	*gloaming*: dusk; twilight	
6	*shuttle*: a tool used to repair fishing nets	
10	*cleated*: with anti-slip pieces of wood nailed on	
11	*gables*: ends of a building just under the roof	
15	*opaque*: almost transparent but not quite	
18	*translucence*: transparent enough to see light shining through	
24	*iridescent*: shiny and rainbow coloured	
24	*coats of mail*: armour made of knitted metal worn by medieval knights	
28	*capstan*: machine used to wind up rope	
32	*Lucky Strike*: an American brand of cigarette	
52	*total immersion*: a form of baptism practised by some Christians	
74	*transmutation*: changing from one shape to another	
77	*briny*: salty like sea water	

Guidelines

This poem is from the collection *A Cold Spring* (1955).

As we have come to expect, **Bishop begins with concrete and meticulous description** (of the place, a seal and the sea) and then, prompted by the associations these descriptions produce, **turns her examination inward to explore a more abstract question – what is knowledge?**

She has returned to Nova Scotia **for the first time since her mother's death** in 1934. Some **painful memories** and a deep sense of **loss and alienation** are evident here. The **transformative power of the imagination** is central to this poem.

Commentary

Lines 1–12
The poet sees an old man in the cold dusk mending his nets with a shuttle. Already an air of magic and mystery is introduced: he is 'almost invisible'. The place reeks of fish; there are five fishhouses here and the poet describes them. The image of the planks against the side walls for 'wheelbarrows to be pushed up and down on' echoes the rhythmic movement of the fisherman's shuttle. **Many of our senses**, including smell and sound, **are engaged already**.

Lines 13–25
The poet builds **mystical nuances** into the factual and detailed account of this very ordinary place: 'All is silver'. The detritus of harbour life abounds; the 'lobster pots, and masts' seem translucent. Other workaday objects undergo a similar transformation and become extraordinary: 'big fish tubs' are 'lined / with … beautiful herring scales'; wheelbarrows also covered in scales are iridescent like 'coats of mail', and even the flies glitter with a rainbow of colour. This **recounting** of the ordinary, even ugly, **everyday world being transformed by the poet's imagination** is typical of Bishop.

Lines 26–40
The narrator notices the broken old capstan; it has fallen out of use and seems wounded, with 'stains, like dried blood'. **Human contact** is made through a shared cigarette. The fisherman is an old family friend (possibly a painful association for the poet given her childhood experiences of loss in this place). They discuss the dwindling fish stocks and many details suggest that this man's way of life is under threat, just like the 'black old knife, / the blade of which is almost worn away.' He too is plastered with fish scales – 'sequins'; he has almost become a fish himself. 'Sequins' is a typically humorous choice of image for an old fisherman; **Bishop often injects wry humour into even her saddest poems.**

Lines 41–46

This short stanza **links** the longer sections of the poem effectively – **the ramp** Bishop describes where the boats are dragged down to the water **symbolises the downward path the poet is about to take into her thoughts and imagination, dragging the reader with her**. This area is silver with scales – the whole world of the poem is taking on this shining quality as we are led into **an imaginative experience**. The poet uses **light, colour and depth** to **draw us in**, and our vision is guided simultaneously 'up the long ramp' and down – 'descending into the water'.

Lines 47–66

Plunging with her mind's eye into the sea, Bishop **meditates** upon how she can never truly enter and be a part of its icy chill, for it is an 'element bearable to no mortal' and will not tolerate her presence. She can only imagine how it might feel. Similarly **how can one ever fully enter knowledge or know anything with total certainty? Like the sea, knowledge is fluid and ever-changing**.

A seal appears and seems to know the poet; another gentle touch of humour is present here as she sings him a Baptist hymn. He watches from afar but engages no further; it seems the exchange is rather one-sided compared to the earlier chat with the fisherman. The water is too cold for Bishop to be 'baptised' here. In **another religious image** she notes the 'dignified tall' Christmas trees back on the land awaiting their seasonal felling.

Lines 67–77

Despite her familiarity with this stretch of sea – 'I have seen it over and over' – she cannot complete her knowledge of it. The water is so chill that it burns like fire: 'If you should dip your hand in, / your wrist would ache immediately, / … your hand would burn'. With a detached brutality, the sea rebuffs her quest to know more.

Lines 78–83

Bishop imagines the water's briny taste and **ponders the concept of knowledge**. She fancies that we imagine knowledge would taste and appear like this sea water: 'dark, salt, clear, moving, utterly free'. Knowledge is **not fixed or constant or something humans can control and define**, it is 'flowing, and flown'. It is also 'historical', i.e. **shaped by the lived reality of each person**: Bishop derived her own knowledge 'from the cold hard mouth / of the world, … the rocky breasts' of **childhood pain** and the **absence of a mother**. Perhaps this knowledge is hard for the poet to bear; **nature is personified as cold and unknowable**, **indifferent** to the suffering and history of the humans who inhabit it and who, like the old fisherman, use it to sustain them.

Themes

Nature, **knowledge**, **change** and the **transformative power of the imagination** are all strong themes here. Although we know the world in many ways, we can never know anything completely. Obviously Bishop's own past is a huge theme also; returning to Nova Scotia was bound to produce many **conflicting emotions** for her. From letters written at the time it seems she was quite depressed during this visit, but though she based much of the poem on her actual visit, other parts came to her in a dream.

> **Sea as symbol**
>
> **This poem is a natural progression from 'The Bight' and 'The Fish'. All three use the sea as an important symbol to convey themes of survival and loss. The changing nature of the human world is contrasted with the seeming permanence of an indifferent elemental world exemplified by 'the wild jagged rocks' and 'the dignified tall firs [that] … stand / waiting'.**

Imagery

Factual description combines with dreamlike mysticism to link the themes and imagery of this poem. Bishop typically uses a **multisensory** approach to bring the scene **vividly to life** for the reader: 'The air smells so strong of codfish / it makes one's nose run and one's eyes water.' **Detail is key** for Bishop, from the brand of cigarette to how many feet lie between the tree trunks on the ramp. Details are conveyed with a **cinematic quality** to communicate an **impression** of the 'real world'. **Bishop uses more abstract imagery to make the leap into the imaginative, creative world**: 'an apparent translucence', 'water seems suspended' and 'transmutation of fire' are examples of this.

Language and form

In the first section of the poem Bishop's language is straightforward and almost conversational: 'although it is a cold evening'; but as the poem progresses, the language becomes, like her imagery, more abstract: 'our knowledge is historical, flowing, and flown.'

She uses many **sound effects** in the poem including **softening sibilance**, for example, 'All is silver: the heavy surface of the sea / swelling slowly as if considering spilling over'. The imagery and language combine here to effect **lines of great beauty and impact**. Repetition, **assonance** and alliteration also feature, 'forever, flowing, and 'flowing, and flown' bringing the poem to a wistful conclusion.

Often the poet speaks directly to the reader: 'If you should dip your hand in', creating an **immediacy and engagement**. Long assonant sounds give that background an **air of mystery and yearning**: 'the cold hard mouth / of the world'.

The poem is written in two long irregular stanzas with a short linking stanza. The second longer stanza **delves more deeply** into ideas raised by the descriptions in the first, and comes to its conclusion about how we each arrive at knowledge.

Questions

1. What details make Bishop's descriptions in the first section of the poem particularly vivid and realistic?

2. List the religious references in the poem and offer an opinion as to why Bishop included them.

3. Compare and contrast the two encounters Bishop has in the poem – with the old fisherman and the seal.

4. How is the sea described? What do you think it might symbolise?

5. How is an air of mystery created in the poem? Explore Bishop's language and imagery in your answer here.

6. List two or three sound effects that particularly appealed to you in the poem and comment on the effect you found they had.

7. What images were particularly striking for you and why?

8. What does Bishop learn from the sea? Do you agree with her conclusion in the final six lines? Explain.

9. Which of the following most sums up the theme of the poem for you and why?
    - This is a poem about nature
    - The theme of this poem is knowledge
    - Feeling alienated and out of place is the theme of this poem
    - This poem deals mainly with Bishop's difficult childhood

10. Is there a place that brings back memories or evokes strong emotion in you? Write about this in any format you like (diary entry, personal essay, feature article, poem, etc.).

11. Using Bishop's description and symbolism as a model, create a description of another location, for example a forest, a desert, a city, the moon, the Arctic. Work in pairs or small groups.

HIGHER LEVEL

Before you read

 What do you know about the biblical parable of the prodigal son? In pairs, share your knowledge, research together and present your findings to the class.

The Prodigal

The brown enormous odor he lived by
was too close, with its breathing and thick hair,
for him to judge. The floor was rotten; the sty
was plastered halfway up with glass-smooth dung.
Light-lashed, self-righteous, above moving snouts,
the pigs' eyes followed him, a cheerful stare –
even to the sow that always ate her young –
till, sickening, he leaned to scratch her head.
But sometimes mornings after drinking bouts
(he hid the pints behind a two-by-four),   10
the sunrise glazed the barnyard mud with red;
the burning puddles seemed to reassure.
And then he thought he almost might endure
his exile yet another year or more.

But evenings the first star came to warn.   15
The farmer whom he worked for came at dark
to shut the cows and horses in the barn
beneath their overhanging clouds of hay,
with pitchforks, faint forked lightnings, catching light,
safe and companionable as in the Ark.   20
The pigs stuck out their little feet and snored.
The lantern – like the sun, going away –
laid on the mud a pacing aureole.
Carrying a bucket along a slimy board,
he felt the bats' uncertain staggering flight,   25
his shuddering insights, beyond his control,
touching him. But it took him a long time
finally to make his mind up to go home.

Glossary

Title	*Prodigal*: a person who spends money wastefully and recklessly
1	*odor*: unpleasant smell
10	*two-by-four*: a piece of timber with a cross-section measuring two inches by four inches
20	*companionable*: friendly, getting along together well
23	*aureole*: a halo of light around the head, often shown upon a saint

Elizabeth Bishop

Guidelines

Written in 1951, this poem is from the collection *A Cold Spring* (1955) and takes the form of a double sonnet.

Bishop had a **drinking problem** from her student days and regularly drank herself into such a state that she ended up in embarrassing situations, often having to move on from friends or accommodation out of **shame**. She wrote this poem inspired by an experience in Nova Scotia in 1946, when 'one of my aunt's stepsons offered me a drink of rum, **in the pig styes** at about nine in the morning'.

Commentary

Bishop chooses to set her poem in the sty the Prodigal shares with pigs during the time when he decides to return home. She **identifies with the marginalised alcoholic figure** of the Prodigal, with his **'rock bottom' situation** and **gradual realisation that recovery is possible**. The poem is written in the form of a double sonnet.

Sonnet 1. Lines 1–8

The appalling conditions of the sty are **juxtaposed** with images of beauty and hope in the first sonnet.

The stench of the pigs and their breathing, hair and dung pervade this octave. The Prodigal is at rock bottom and has lost all sense of judgement, so inured is he to his pitiful environment: 'The brown enormous odor he lived by / was too close'. The dung plasters the walls making them 'glass-smooth'. The description moves to a close-up of the pigs themselves, described sympathetically by Bishop as 'Light-lashed', with 'a cheerful stare', yet simultaneously 'self-righteous'. Are they judging the Prodigal and finding themselves to be above him? Although he is sickened by the sow which ate her young (and by his own drinking), he is still desperate for her companionship.

Lines 9–14

Against this degraded, awful existence there are **contrasting moments of beauty and hints at redemption** in the sestet. In the morning, despite his hangover, he notices how 'the sunrise glazed the barnyard mud with red; / the burning puddles seemed to reassure.' The beauty of the sunrise comforts the Prodigal; everything seems a little better in the morning and the Prodigal feels he 'almost might endure / his exile yet another year or more.' The word 'almost' creates doubt here. We see that **he has not faced up to the reality** of his alcoholism yet '(he hid the pints behind a two-by-four)', despite the reality that he has been totally debased and dehumanised by his situation.

Sonnet 2. Lines 15–20

'But' is used to begin sonnet two, a word which negates the conclusion reached at the end of the first sonnet. As night approaches, the Prodigal is less sure he can endure this life much longer. The image of 'the first star' come to 'warn' is ominous, and suggests that the nights were hardest for him, a time when he had to face his demons and his reality. **His isolation is emphasised in contrast to the animals** who are shut away, 'beneath their overhanging clouds of hay', 'safe and companionable'.

Lines 21–28

'The pigs stuck out their little feet and snored'; the farmer's lantern recedes 'like the sun, going away', and the Prodigal is left in darkness, alone and fearful. The sun that brought the Prodigal comfort in sonnet 1 has deserted him. As he carries out his odious chores, 'Carrying a bucket along a slimy board', the erratic flying of the bats brings home to him the **hideousness of his alienation and debasement**. These 'shuddering insights' grip him 'beyond his control'. And yet despite the nightmarish quality of this experience, 'it took him a long time / finally to make his mind up to go home.' This underlines how difficult it can be to begin recovery from something like alcoholism. Home is a last resort. **Home itself is a difficult concept for the poet** who lacked parental love due to her father's early death, her mother's mental illness and the poet's lack of a permanent home in the following years. Note that 'home' doesn't fully rhyme with 'time' at the end of the poem.

Themes

Bishop's alcoholism is clearly a theme here and she draws **strong parallels** between herself and the central character in the poem. Her poetic treatment of him is fair; he is not overly sentimentalised but there is a

compassionate understanding at play. **Redemption and hope** are strong themes. Why might Bishop have used the story and character of the Prodigal rather than write herself into a straightforwardly autobiographical poem? Have you seen her do this elsewhere?

Imagery

Religious imagery abounds in the poem: the Prodigal, the Ark, aureole (aura or halo). Gross and deeply unpleasant images vie with more optimistic ones. The **contrast between light and darkness** is especially symbolic and meaningful. **Images often echo each other** even when the effect is contrasting, for example the dung glazes the sty walls while 'the sunrise glazed the barnyard mud'. The poem is **vivid in its descriptive power and atmosphere**.

Language

Again a **contrast between positive and negative** is very clear in the poet's language: 'cheerful', 'sunrise', 'reassure', 'companionable', 'little feet', 'aureole', 'home'; versus 'brown', 'odor', 'rotten', 'dung', 'ate her young', 'exile', 'dark', 'bats'. These contrasts are at the heart of the poem. Although very descriptive and evocative, the language is straightforward and accessible.

Form

A **sonnet** is a fourteen-line poem made popular by Petrarch and Shakespeare. Sonnet 1 takes the form of a Shakespearean sonnet, made up of three quatrains (four-line sections) and a rhyming couplet (the last two lines). The first eight lines present an issue, the third quatrain offers a deeper meditation on this issue, and the final couplet presents a solution. The terrible state of the Prodigal's life and dwelling is the issue. The description of the farmyard deepens this and provides the reason (the beauty of the sunrise) for the conclusion reached in the couplet, that the Prodigal might be able to survive another year of this.

The second sonnet is less ordered in its structure of form and thought. As night falls there is a sense of crisis; finally the Prodigal feels 'shuddering insights' and reaches a shaky resolution, 'finally to make his mind up to go home'. But **'time' and 'home' do not make a true rhyme** or rhyming couplet as 'endure' and 'more' do at the end of the first sonnet. Why might Bishop have done this? Does it create uncertainty, or suggest that the Prodigal isn't convinced by his decision?

Elizabeth Bishop

Exam-Style Questions

Understanding the poem

1. Describe the living conditions of the Prodigal. What details in particular successfully convey the squalor he lives in?
2. Did you like or dislike the pigs, based on Bishop's description of them? Explain your view.
3. What opinion of the Prodigal did you form in sonnet 1? Support your opinion with quotation and reference.
4. Do you think Bishop is fair in her description of the Prodigal? Explain.
5. How does the atmosphere of the second sonnet differ from the first?
6. Why, do you think, does Bishop use the character of the farmer here? What is his role?

Thinking about the poem

1. In pairs, find images of light and darkness in the poem and comment on their effect. Use a grid to display your examples and ideas.
2. List examples of religious images in the poem and comment upon their effect.
3. Overall does the poem offer a positive or a negative point of view in your opinion? How?
4. What decision is made at the end of the poem and how does the Prodigal feel about this?
5. What, do you think, does the poet reveal about herself, her life and her experiences through the poem?

Imagining

1. Write the letter the Prodigal sends to his father asking if he may come home.
2. In small groups imagine you were to make the poem into a short film. Draft a synopsis of this and / or draw a story board to show how your film would progress. You may also like to choose music or sound effects.

SNAPSHOT

- Double sonnet
- Prodigal's state of mind is conveyed
- Description of animals is realistic and sympathetic
- Images of light and darkness predominate
- Bishop's personal experience parallels the Prodigal
- Complex idea of 'home'
- Religious references

HIGHER LEVEL 2021 / 27

HIGHER LEVEL

Before you read

 Ask and answer these questions with the student beside you: Why do people like to travel? What aspects of travel do you find most enjoyable? Where would you most like to visit in the world and why?

Questions of Travel

There are too many waterfalls here; the crowded streams
hurry too rapidly down to the sea,
and the pressure of so many clouds on the mountaintops
makes them spill over the sides in soft slow-motion,
turning to waterfalls under our very eyes.   5
— For if those streaks, those mile-long, shiny, tearstains,
aren't waterfalls yet,
in a quick age or so, as ages go here,
they probably will be.
But if the streams and clouds keep travelling, travelling,   10
the mountains look like the hulls of capsized ships,
slime-hung and barnacled.

Think of the long trip home.
Should we have stayed at home and thought of here?
Where should we be today?   15
Is it right to be watching strangers in a play
in this strangest of theatres?
What childishness is it that while there's a breath of life
in our bodies, we are determined to rush
to see the sun the other way around?   20
The tiniest green hummingbird in the world?
To stare at some inexplicable old stonework,
inexplicable and impenetrable,
at any view,
instantly seen and always, always delightful?   25
Oh, must we dream our dreams
and have them, too?
And have we room
for one more folded sunset, still quite warm?

But surely it would have been a pity   30
not to have seen the trees along this road,
really exaggerated in their beauty,
not to have seen them gesturing
like noble pantomimists, robed in pink.
— Not to have had to stop for gas and heard   35
the sad, two-noted, wooden tune
of disparate wooden clogs
carelessly clacking over
a grease-stained filling-station floor.
(In another country the clogs would all be tested.   40

Each pair there would have identical pitch.)
— A pity not to have heard
the other, less primitive music of the fat brown bird
who sings above the broken gasoline pump
in a bamboo church of Jesuit baroque: 45
three towers, five silver crosses.

— Yes, a pity not to have pondered,
blurr'dly and inconclusively,
on what connection can exist for centuries
between the crudest wooden footwear 50
and, careful and finicky,
the whittled fantasies of wooden cages.
— Never to have studied history in
the weak calligraphy of songbirds' cages.
— And never to have had to listen to rain 55
so much like politicians' speeches:
two hours of unrelenting oratory
and then a sudden golden silence
in which the traveller takes a notebook, writes:

'Is it lack of imagination that makes us come 60
to imagined places, not just stay at home?
Or could Pascal have been not entirely right
about just sitting quietly in one's room?

Continent, city, country, society:
the choice is never wide and never free. 65
And here, or there . . . No. Should we have stayed at home,
wherever that may be?'

Glossary

11	*hulls*: main bodies of ships
11	*capsized*: turned over in the water
12	*barnacled*: covered with small stony shellfish
20	*the sun the other way around*: the sun seen from the southern hemisphere
22	*inexplicable*: cannot be explained
23	*impenetrable*: cannot be seen through
34	*pantomimists*: people acting in an over-the-top way; actors in a pantomime
35	*gas*: car fuel, gasoline
37	*disparate*: not similar
45	*Jesuit baroque*: ornate seventeenth century architectural style often found in churches in Brazil
51	*finicky*: overly fancy, with lots of small complex detail
52	*whittled fantasies*: wooden items imaginatively carved, e.g. the birdcages in the poem
54	*calligraphy*: the art of handwriting, often ornate and swirled
57	*oratory*: public speaking, e.g. a politician's speech
62	*Pascal*: Blaise Pascal, a French mathematician and philosopher (1623–1662)

Guidelines

This is the title poem in the collection *Questions of Travel* from 1965.

Brazil is the 'here' of line 1, a place Bishop travelled to in November of 1951 intending to stay only two weeks, but where she found herself living for fifteen years with her lover Lota (to whom she dedicated this poetry collection). During this time she wrote to Robert Lowell, saying, 'I am extremely happy for the first time in my life', and the **quirky, upbeat** nature of this poem reflects this. It seems Bishop was a little overwhelmed by Brazil at first, according to the opening section of the poem. It is clear, however, that she comes to love the place, as she admires its churches, birdsong and even the sound of the clogs worn by the locals!

The poet **reflects on the idea of travel** and **wonders why** people want to experience different places and cultures. She is critical of the box-ticking nature of tourism whereby many view a famous sight and move on without really experiencing anything. Bishop concludes in a positive way, having questioned the rights and wrongs of travel and **examined the notion of home**, a **recurring theme in her work**.

Commentary

Lines 1–12
The speaker feels overwhelmed by the Brazilian landscape: the sheer volume of water, the 'crowded streams' becoming waterfalls, then clouds, and the process repeating eternally. Repetition and sibilance in this section emphasise the **weariness the poet feels** and the **repetitive relentless nature of this process**, 'spill over … in soft slow-motion', 'mile-long', 'travelling, travelling'. Mountains are compared to overturned ships. **Boats and water** are **recurring symbols** in Bishop's imagery. The **constant movement** is exhausting.

Lines 13–29
In the persona of a tourist, Bishop wonders whether travel is worth the effort: 'Think of the long trip home.' She wonders if remaining at home and simply dreaming of foreign lands might be better. She asks **eight questions** about travel in this stanza. She **queries the ethics** of watching locals and their customs as if it were a show put on to entertain: 'Is it right to be watching strangers in a play'? She asks whether it is childish to go halfway round the world just to see the sun 'the other way around' or to examine an old building or monument – 'some inexplicable old stonework'. The fact that sights are 'instantly seen' and pronounced 'delightful' clearly irks the poet.

> **Pascal on travel**
>
> 'All the unhappiness of men arises from one single fact that they cannot stay quietly in their own room.'
>
> Pascal

Lines 30–46
The tone calms as the speaker becomes reflective, pondering the sights she has loved and truly savoured, not on the tourist trail. These are the ordinary sights and sounds in Brazil: 'the trees along this road', 'the sad, two-noted, wooden tune / of disparate wooden clogs', 'music of the fat brown bird', 'a bamboo church'. Look at how much **energy and close observation** are contained in these images.

Lines 47–59
The level of **detail** and use of **quirky comparisons** in this stanza really bring the place to life for the reader and Bishop's enthusiasm and humour is infectious, for example in her account of the birdcages which contrast

so much with the clumsy big clogs worn by locals, or comparing the torrential rain to 'politicians' speeches: / two hours of unrelenting oratory'. It is clear that the poet has taken time to truly explore and observe this land, its people and culture, in contrast to the way the 'tourist' persona of the first section approaches their trip.

Lines 60–67

Two stanzas follow written in italics (giving the impression of handwriting in a journal) in which Bishop, as the traveller, asks, 'Is it lack of imagination' that makes people travel? Should we agree with Pascal and stay at home? However, for Bishop the question of travel carries her, as so often her poems do, to **the question of where and what home is**: 'Should we have stayed at home, wherever that may be?'

Is the idea of travel as exotic and exciting for someone like Bishop who never had a fixed home or family life?

Themes

'At the Fishhouses' and 'The Prodigal' also question the **idea of home**. It is clearly a very important theme for Bishop. Perhaps one has to live in a place with a loved one and make it a home to truly appreciate and understand its people and culture. She has clearly fallen for the charms of Brazil and it was to become her home for many years, the most permanent one she ever had.

Travel is a theme also; Bishop had won a scholarship in 1951 enabling her to travel to Brazil. She had also travelled to Europe and around the USA thanks to an inheritance from her father. **Notions of belonging** and of **how we interpret the world** are at play here. There are different, **contrasting and conflicting, points of view** in the poem. Which opinion most closely reflects your own stance on travel, home and belonging?

> ### Baroque
>
> Baroque is a sixteenth-century style of architecture which was highly ornamented and elaborate. When employed by churches it was a powerful statement of the wealth and power of the church. During the seventeenth century, the religious order the Society of Jesus (Jesuits) built churches in this style across Europe and South America. Interiors were busily adorned with stucco, painting and sculpture.

The **beauty of the everyday**, the ordinary, is central: the bamboo church seems to her 'Jesuit baroque', the trees are 'really exaggerated in their beauty,' even the rain and the 'golden' silence afterwards convey this. The **extraordinary nature of the ordinary** is a passion of Bishop's which, she shows us, we can discover if we stop a moment and bring close observation and imagination into play.

> ### Bishop's love of music
>
> 'I am in need of music that would flow
> Over my fretful, feeling fingertips,
> Over my bitter-tainted, trembling lips,
> With melody, deep, clear, and liquid-slow.
> Oh, for the healing swaying, old and low,
> Of some song sung to rest the tired dead,
> A song to fall like water on my head,
> And over quivering limbs, dream flushed to glow!'
>
> Elizabeth Bishop, Sonnet

Imagery

Metaphor, symbolism and simile crowd the poem like the waterfalls of stanza 1 crowd the landscape. As ever with Bishop, the imagery is **carefully detailed and highly evocative**. Nature imagery features heavily: the waterfalls, birds, rain and trees **contrast** with imagery that is of man-made objects like the bird cages, the gas station and the bamboo church. Bishop's quirky originality is particularly strong in this poem. What details would you pick out as the most unusual?

Language and form

Poetic language laden with details and sound effects exists simultaneously with a conversational light-hearted tone. Effective use of sibilance, assonance, repetition and alliteration combine to bring the sights and sounds of Brazil to life – 'wooden clogs / carelessly clacking over / a grease-stained filling-station floor'. The **use of questions is a recurring feature** of Bishop's poetry and this poem is peppered with them, creating a sense of **wonder and fascination**, yet at the same time **uncertainty**.

The poem is made up of four irregular stanzas, the second and third being longer, and then in sharp contrast two regular italicised stanzas which rhyme. Bishop clearly wants these to be very different in form and style. Why might that be?

Questions

1	What picture of Brazil is conveyed to you in stanza 1? Do you find this landscape attractive? Explain.
2	List in your own words the eight questions asked by the poet in stanza 2. In small groups discuss the answers you would give and feed back to the class as a whole.
3	How does the poet's experience of her travels in stanza 3 contrast with that of the tourist persona in stanza 2? Which account do you prefer and why?
4	In stanza 3 choose the sound effects and images which appealed to you most and give reasons for your choices.
5	Write a brief answer to each of the two questions posed in stanza 5, giving your own opinion. Do you think the poet would agree with your answers?
6	'The choice is never wide and never free' (line 65). What does Bishop mean by this, do you think?
7	'Home wherever that may be?' Considering what you have discovered about Bishop's life, especially her childhood, what might Bishop mean here?
8	List the sounds described by the poet in the poem. Do you agree that the poem has a musical quality?
9	'Bishop's poems are full of vivid detailed description, often using quirky and original comparisons.' Analyse 'Questions of Travel' in the light of this statement.
10	What might the cages described in the poem symbolise?
11	What aspects of Bishop's personality are revealed in the poem to the reader?
12	Trace the tone of the poem and how it changes as the poem progresses.
13	Examine the use of personas in the poem. How many different voices do you think the poem contains? Who is speaking in the last two stanzas?
14	'Travel broadens the mind.' Have a class debate on this topic.

HIGHER LEVEL

Before you read

 What customs or traditions can you think of that may be harmful to nature? Research this with a classmate.

The Armadillo

for Robert Lowell

This is the time of year
when almost every night
the frail, illegal fire balloons appear.
Climbing the mountain height,

rising toward a saint   5
still honored in these parts,
the paper chambers flush and fill with light
that comes and goes, like hearts.

Once up against the sky it's hard
to tell them from the stars –   10
planets, that is – the tinted ones:
Venus going down, or Mars,

or the pale green one. With a wind,
they flare and falter, wobble and toss;
but if it's still they steer between   15
the kite sticks of the Southern Cross,

receding, dwindling, solemnly
and steadily forsaking us,
or, in the downdraft from a peak,
suddenly turning dangerous.   20

Last night another big one fell.
It splattered like an egg of fire
against the cliff behind the house.
The flame ran down. We saw the pair

of owls who nest there flying up   25
and up, their whirling black-and-white
stained bright pink underneath, until
they shrieked up out of sight.

The ancient owls' nest must have burned.
Hastily, all alone,   30
a glistening armadillo left the scene,
rose-flecked, head down, tail down,

and then a baby rabbit jumped out,
short-eared, to our surprise.
So soft! – a handful of intangible ash   35
with fixed, ignited eyes.

Too pretty, dreamlike mimicry!
O falling fire and piercing cry
and panic, and a weak mailed fist
clenched ignorant against the sky!   40

Glossary

Title	**Armadillo**: burrowing South American mammal, with bony armour-like skin
3	**fire balloons**: paper lanterns which contain a candle, as the air inside heats, they rise
7	**chambers**: rooms, referring here to the balloon part of the fire balloon; also links to the 'heart' image of line 8
13	**pale green one**: probably Uranus
16	**kite sticks of the Southern Cross**: a cross-shaped constellation in the southern hemisphere
35	**intangible**: cannot be touched
37	**mimicry**: imitation
39	**mailed fist**: the armadillo, when rolled into a protective ball, resembles a glove from a suit of armour

Guidelines

Robert Lowell was a close friend of Bishop and even proposed to her once. He said that this was one of her best poems; it appeared in the *Questions of Travel* collection of 1965.

The setting is Brazil, Rio de Janeiro on 24 June, which is the winter solstice there and the feast day of St John. Traditionally fire balloons were set off at night intended to float towards the saint's mountain shrine; however, many blew off course and landed in the forest wreaking havoc on the flora and fauna there by causing hugely destructive fires. This practice continued in spite of the government making it illegal. In the poem Bishop explores her reactions to this custom, shifting from admiration and wonder at first to outraged horror as the poem progresses.

Commentary

Lines 1–8
As usual Bishop begins with a brief account of what is happening, while providing a **context** for the reader. She **observes** the fire balloon custom rather than participating in it. At first the balloons seem fragile and 'frail' as they climb the 'mountain height'. As the paper balloons expand with heat and become illuminated by the fires within, they appear 'like hearts'. This refers to the red glow but also the pulsating effect of the flame which flickers inside.

Lines 9–20
The balloons rise so high that they seem to join the cosmos. Bishop emphasises those more colourful 'tinted' planets, such as Venus, the planet of love, and Mars, the red planet of war which is often linked to impending violence or catastrophe. The poet is **foreshadowing** the disaster to come. With her reference to 'the pale green one', the narrator endears us with her admission of a lack of complete knowledge, and the **tone is relaxed** and conversational as she admires the trajectory of the balloons; they seem to steer towards the 'Southern Cross'. As the balloons move farther away they abandon the watchers: 'forsaking us'. Then the tone changes dramatically as some balloons are caught by a breeze and blown earthwards.

Lines 21–36
The poet moves from a generalised account to a very specific event – the night before, a balloon had fallen to the ground and 'splattered like an egg of fire'. There is a suggestive **paradox** here: an egg is commonly a

HIGHER LEVEL

symbol of birth and life, but here it brings death and destruction. Extending the egg simile, the first victims of the fire are a pair of 'ancient owls' whose nest has been destroyed. They fly off shrieking in panic, 'their whirling black-and-white / stained bright pink underneath'. In contrast to the 'we' of the poem, a lonely figure appears scuttling out of the undergrowth, 'Hastily, all alone, / a glistening armadillo'. He is 'rose-flecked' with scorching ash and determined to escape – 'head down, tail down'.

Our pity and horror are further engaged as a 'baby rabbit jumped out, / *short*-eared … So soft!' **Through her description of the rabbit, the poet reveals her emotions** concerning the fire: it is a 'handful of intangible ash', and fear shows in its 'fixed, ignited eyes'. The old, the lonely and the young have been displaced, traumatised and harmed.

Lines 37–40

As in 'Questions of Travel' the final stanza is italicised. Here the speaker **rails against the unfairness** of this unnecessary suffering. The balloons' prettiness has deceived her, their captivating charm a cruel ruse: *'Too pretty, dreamlike mimicry!'* In reality they have wrought destruction and doom: *'falling fire and piercing cry / and panic'*. The **language is almost Shakespearean** in this stanza compared to the modern conversational tone of the rest of the poem.

The poet concludes by returning to the image of the armadillo. He rolls into a protective ball, reminding Bishop of a *'weak mailed fist / clenched ignorant against the sky'*. His protest and defiance, and his attempt to survive this situation, are ultimately futile. He will surely die.

Themes

Mankind's disregard for nature is an obvious concern here. Despite the balloons being 'illegal', because of their danger to the landscape, the locals persist in the tradition. The **violence that religion has provoked** continues to be a huge issue in our world today. Do we have the right to cause destruction and death in the name of our beliefs? The **powerlessness** of those who suffer from oppression, and the **loss of home**, could both be seen as themes here**.** The tiny rabbit in particular symbolises this. Its fluffy fur offers no protection; it is totally **innocent and vulnerable**, reduced to 'a handful of intangible ash'. Even the armoured armadillo cannot withstand the onslaught of the flames. All of these animals have **lost their homes**. Like Bishop, the owls are **displaced** and must travel to find somewhere new to settle. The 'whirling' nature of their flight conveys their panic and distress.

On a deeper level Bishop **could be writing about poetry itself**, which is after all a *'pretty, dreamlike mimicry'* of the real world. Is Bishop criticising her own act of writing poetry as a pale reflection of reality, ultimately as powerless to change things as the tiny rabbit? What good can poetry do in the face of violence and injustice? Perhaps the poet sees herself in the armadillo; powerless, without a home and futilely railing against things she cannot change? Is there a more positive alternative interpretation for the ending of the poem?

Imagery

Images of the **balloons, nature and fire** dominate the poem. **Bishop uses adjectives and similes to bring her descriptions alive**: the balloons are like 'hearts' and 'stars', and the smashed balloon is like an 'egg of

Elizabeth Bishop

fire'. As the fire intensifies though, the descriptions become more straightforward, **heightening the immediacy and tension**. Where water has been a central image in Bishop's poems before, fire is the key image here. Perhaps compare Bishop's use of fire here with her use of water in 'The Bight' and 'At the Fishhouses'.

Language and form

The final stanza's **more formal and archaic language** raises the plight of the animals above mere description and hints that the poem's theme has more far-reaching and profound connotations than just a protest against this one traditional custom. It sounds like a **different speaker** is narrating the final lines, and the **two exclamation marks suggest powerful emotion**, for example frustration, anger or despair.

Only this poem and 'The Prodigal' so far have used **regular stanzas**. There are ten quatrains (four-line stanzas) with the last stanza **emphasised** by the use of italics. Every second and fourth line rhyme within each stanza. Why, do you think, does the poet use a stricter, more rigorous structure? Is it perhaps to **contain and shape a very emotional and upsetting experience?** Is it more difficult to write freely about upsetting things? The rhyming scheme falters slightly in stanza 6. Interestingly this is the point at which the fire balloon crashes causing havoc. Does the poet's lack of true rhyme in this stanza ('fell' / 'fire' / 'house' / 'pair') reflect the shock of what she has witnessed?

Questions

1	What information does the poet give us about the setting of this poem?
2	What is the purpose of the fire balloons?
3	How are the balloons described in the first four stanzas? Comment on the imagery used in these descriptions.
4	Where does the poet's tone change and why does this change occur?
5	What consequences do the fire balloons have for the forest and the animals who inhabit it?
6	What, do you think, is the poet saying in the final stanza of the poem? How is this stanza different to the ones before?
7	Why do you think the poet chose 'The Armadillo' as the title of the poem? Choose an alternative title and justify your choice with reference to the poem.
8	In terms of symbols, what might the fire balloons and the forest creatures represent?
9	Identify the sound effects Bishop uses in the poem. List examples and comment on their effect.
10	Why do you think the last stanza is italicised? Is there a new speaker here? Whose voice might this be and what is their position on the events that have unfolded?
11	*Groupwork* In pairs, choose another poem where Bishop uses an animal as a central image, and compare it to this one.
12	How did you feel as you read this poem; what was your overall reaction to it?
13	Write a newspaper article for a tabloid or broadsheet newspaper reporting on the forest fire.

HIGHER LEVEL

Before you read

What are the most typical pictures a young child might draw? Describe and/or draw a typical child's picture.

Sestina

September rain falls on the house.
In the failing light, the old grandmother
sits in the kitchen with the child
beside the Little Marvel Stove,
reading the jokes from the almanac, 5
laughing and talking to hide her tears.

She thinks that her equinoctial tears
and the rain that beats on the roof of the house
were both foretold by the almanac,
but only known to a grandmother. 10
The iron kettle sings on the stove.
She cuts some bread and says to the child,

It's time for tea now; but the child
is watching the teakettle's small hard tears
dance like mad on the hot black stove, 15
the way the rain must dance on the house.
Tidying up, the old grandmother
hangs up the clever almanac

on its string. Bird-like, the almanac
hovers half open above the child, 20
hovers above the old grandmother
and her teacup full of dark brown tears.
She shivers and says she thinks the house
feels chilly, and puts more wood in the stove.

It was to be, says the Marvel Stove. 25
I know what I know, says the almanac.
With crayons the child draws a rigid house
and a winding pathway. Then the child
puts in a man with buttons like tears
and shows it proudly to the grandmother. 30

But secretly, while the grandmother
busies herself about the stove,
the little moons fall down like tears
from between the pages of the almanac
into the flower bed the child 35
has carefully placed in the front of the house.

38 / DISCOVERY: POETRY ANTHOLOGY

Elizabeth Bishop

suggests that will be a recurring feature of Bishop's future. There will be more loss to come

Time to plant tears, says the almanac.
The grandmother sings to the marvellous stove
and the child draws another inscrutable house.

image of the Grandmother singing conveys a sense of life going on amidst sadness and loss

the inscrutable nature of the child's drawing points to the child's ongoing difficulties in coming to terms with the unusual nature of her home life (i.e. a life without a mother or a father)

Glossary

Title	*Sestina*: a poetic form (see below)
4	*Little Marvel Stove*: a brand of solid-fuel stove
5	*almanac*: a calendar that also forecasts the weather and other events on the basis of astrological calculations. For this reason, it was sometimes thought to have magic powers. It also contains jokes
7	*equinoctial*: at the time of the autumn equinox
39	*inscrutable*: cannot be understood

Guidelines

From *Questions of Travel* (1965), and set in Nova Scotia, this is **one of the first poems Bishop wrote exploring her difficult childhood directly**, although she was over fifty when she wrote it. The child deals with past loss as she draws a picture of a house and garden in her grandmother's kitchen, but the **seeds of grief are growing**, and the little girl will have more sadness.

> **Sestina form**
>
> **A sestina is an old-fashioned poetic form consisting of six unrhymed sestets and a seventh stanza of three lines, called an envoy. The same six words end the lines of each stanza, but in a different order each time – 'house', 'grandmother', 'child', 'stove', 'almanac' and 'tears'. The last word in each stanza becomes the end word of the first line in the next. The envoy uses all six words.**

Art therapy today is a recognised way to help children with trauma. The child in the poem uses drawing to express what she has lost and what she longs for – a father and a stable home. The **rigid and difficult structure of a sestina is reminiscent of a nursery rhyme in its repetition**, but the apparent simplicity is deceptive, and requires great skill to accomplish. **The strictness of the form allows Bishop to explore her grief in a contained and manageable way.** Bishop uses a controlled form in a similar way in 'The Armadillo'.

Commentary

Stanza 1
On the surface a cosy scene is described: grandmother and child sit beside the warm stove reading and laughing at jokes from the almanac. Beneath this seemingly happy activity though, there is pain and loss. There is no mother or father. It is raining and the light is fading. The grandmother is 'laughing and talking to hide her tears'. All is not well.

Stanza 2
The child believes the almanac has not only foretold the equinox, but the rain and the grandmother's tears also (she has not been successful in hiding them from the child). In the child's mind the grandmother is the only one who knows what the almanac has foretold. She is at the **centre of this child's world** and is the **holder of all knowledge**. Do you think this is typical of how young children see the adults who are central in their lives? **Comforting everyday routines** soften the sadness: the kettle 'sings' and food is prepared – 'She cuts some bread'. There is a **tension** in the poem **between what is happening on the surface**, and **the emotions which bubble underneath**.

HIGHER LEVEL

Stanza 3
The sorrow grows despite the grandmother's efforts at cosy domesticity: '*It's time for tea now;*' the child, 'watching the teakettle's small hard tears', is well aware of the sorrow that pervades the house. The stove that seemed so cute and toy-like earlier is now menacing, and the 'mad' dance of the kettle's tears might remind us that Bishop's mother had been committed to a mental institution. Outside too a **rain of tears** beats upon the house. **The grandmother's attempts to tidy up reflect the poet's own attempt to impose a rigid order onto this poem**, in an effort to cope with the difficulty of writing about that time. Is imposing order and routine a typical way to cope with difficult circumstances in life?

Stanza 4
The almanac is now hanging open above the child as she draws; it is compared to a bird. The grandmother is clearly upset, shivering with a 'teacup full of dark brown tears', but she perseveres in her efforts to make the house as cheerful and cosy as she can: 'puts more wood in the stove'. Bishop's maternal grandmother was clearly a loving and nurturing presence for the poet, and we know that Bishop was hugely distressed when her deceased father's parents came and abruptly took her away from Nova Scotia.

Stanza 5
The **personification of the household objects** intensifies as they speak to the child: '*It was to be*, says the Marvel Stove', as if the loss of both parents was inevitable. But the almanac, which later sheds tears, answers '*I know what I know*', is this grief? In a heart-breaking image the child draws what so many children draw – a house and garden and 'a man with buttons like tears'. This man is most likely **the poet's father**, **a man she never knew**. He died when she was an infant, the event which triggered her mother's breakdown.

Stanza 6
Even as a child Bishop clearly had the great imagination we see in her poetry. As her grandmother tidies, she draws a flower bed into her picture and fantasises that moons from the almanac drop 'like tears' into it, as if they are watering it. Nature has always been central to Bishop's work. Perhaps the flowerbed symbolises Bishop's future, her growth.

Stanza 7
The almanac says '*Time to plant tears*', implying that more heartbreak and loss may be in store. The child will be ripped from this loving home, but **these experiences will grow into poetry**, which will be Bishop's life. The child continues to create – 'draws another inscrutable house', just as Bishop will continue to create art in the form of literature and painting (she was also a gifted artist). The final image gives some comfort: 'The grandmother sings to the marvellous stove'. The mood has lifted and all is well, for now.

Themes

Childhood, family and loss are central themes. The child acts as children do, drawing pictures and imagining that even household objects come to life, but in many ways the losses suffered by this family have affected the child. The tear-shaped buttons on the man she draws, and her understanding that her grandmother is grieving, convey this. There is a sense too that **the sorrow Bishop endured could not be avoided**. The **inevitability of death and grief** is apparent here: '*It was to be*'. The **comforting power of art and creativity** lift the poem from complete pessimism and melancholy. Music and art comfort the grandmother and the little girl: 'The grandmother sings to the marvellous stove / and the child draws another inscrutable house.'

Elizabeth Bishop

Imagery

Personification is used extensively in the poem. A **child's imaginary inner world brings everyday domestic objects to life**: the almanac is 'clever', the kettle sings and the stove speaks. **Pathetic fallacy**, where the weather mirrors the mood of the poem, is used effectively here too: the rain that beats upon the house reflects the **tears that seem to fall from everywhere** in the poem. The kettle, the tea, the grandmother and even the buttons of the man the child has drawn are tear-shaped. This creates an **overwhelming feeling of sorrow**.

Language and form

The language is simple and repetitive with an almost staccato rhythm, giving the poem **a deceptive air of simplicity** which sounds childlike. Although the child is clearly Bishop, **the poet distances herself from the scene**: 'the old grandmother', 'the child', 'a man'. The poet possibly needs to create this distance in order to cope with the trauma she's undergone while still being honest and objective. The repetition also builds in such a way that the reader comes to expect the words 'Grandmother', 'child', 'stove', 'tears' etc. as the stanzas progress, emphasising the idea of inevitability discussed in 'Imagery' above, but also **giving comfort through steady rhythm**.

Questions

1	This poem was originally entitled 'Early Sorrow'. Why, do you think, was this title chosen and then replaced with 'Sestina' by the poet?
2	What is the tone of this poem? Does it change anywhere? Trace the tone through the poem.
3	The world described by Bishop is seen through the eyes of a young child. Has Bishop created this world effectively? What details worked particularly well to achieve this?
4	Describe the relationship between the two central figures in the poem.
5	Look at the six main words around which the poem is constructed. What meaning or symbolism might each have?
6	Recreate the child's drawing as a simple sketch and write a note explaining what you think it means for the poet.
7	Did you think that the sestina structure of the poem added to its meaning in any way? Why, do you think, did Bishop use this form?
8	This is one of Bishop's most revealing poems. What do you feel you have learned about the poet?
9	What effect does the use of personification have on the poem?
10	'… the child draws another inscrutable house.' What is your understanding of this line in the context of the poem as a whole?
11	Which character in the poem do you feel most sympathy for and why? Look closely at the language used around each character.
12	Write a diary entry where you explore a childhood memory.
13	Work with a partner to create a short dialogue between the grown-up child and her grandmother, where they look back on this time and discuss the issues raised in the poem.

HIGHER LEVEL

Before you read

What poems or songs do you know that deal with the death of a child? How was this sensitive subject handled? For example, you may have studied 'Tich Miller' or 'Mid-Term Break' for your Junior Cycle.

First Death in Nova Scotia

In the cold, cold parlor
my mother laid out Arthur
beneath the chromographs:
Edward, Prince of Wales,
with Princess Alexandra,   5
and King George with Queen Mary.
Below them on the table
stood a stuffed loon
shot and stuffed by Uncle
Arthur, Arthur's father.   10

Since Uncle Arthur fired
a bullet into him,
he hadn't said a word.
He kept his own counsel
on his white, frozen lake,   15
the marble-topped table.
His breast was deep and white,
cold and caressable;
his eyes were red glass,
much to be desired.   20

"Come," said my mother,
"Come and say good-bye
to your little cousin Arthur."
I was lifted up and given
one lily of the valley   25
to put in Arthur's hand.
Arthur's coffin was
a little frosted cake,
and the red-eyed loon eyed it
from his white, frozen lake.   30

Arthur was very small.
He was all white, like a doll
that hadn't been painted yet.
Jack Frost had started to paint him
the way he always painted   35
the Maple Leaf (Forever).

He had just begun on his hair,
a few red strokes, and then
Jack Frost had dropped the brush
and left him white, forever.   40

The gracious royal couples
were warm in red and ermine;
their feet were well wrapped up
in the ladies' ermine trains.
They invited Arthur to be   45
the smallest page at court.
But how could Arthur go,
clutching his tiny lily,
with his eyes shut up so tight
and the roads deep in snow?   50

Glossary

1	*parlor*: a room for receiving guests
3	*chromographs*: coloured copies of pictures
4	*Edward*: a member of the British royal family (1841–1910)
5	*Alexandra*: Edward's wife
6	*King George*: King George V, also a British royal (1865–1936)
6	*Queen Mary*: wife of King George
8	*loon*: a species of water bird which has a crest and dives for food
14	*he kept his own counsel*: he kept his advice and opinions to himself
18	*caressable*: invites touch, you would want to caress it
25	*lily of the valley*: a fragrant winter plant with small white bell-like flowers
28	*frosted*: covered with icing
36	*Maple Leaf*: national symbol of Canada
36	*Forever*: refers to Canada's national anthem at the time, 'Maple Leaf Forever'
44	*ermine train*: long trailing back on a robe or dress trimmed with the fur of an ermine (a white stoat), and worn by royalty
46	*page*: a young boy servant
46	*at court*: in a palace

Guidelines

From *Questions of Travel* (1965). Psychoanalysis had helped Bishop deal with childhood issues such as those raised in 'Sestina'. In this poem, also set in Nova Scotia, Bishop writes about the death of her cousin Arthur. The poet was almost four at the time, and the poem is **written from the perspective of a child**, but this is coloured by an adult's retrospective interpretation.

As in 'Sestina', **ordinary objects in the house take on significance for the child**, and the poem contains a rare direct reference to Bishop's mother.

HIGHER LEVEL

Nova Scotia

Commentary

Stanza 1
The poet's mother has laid out her cousin Arthur in the 'cold, cold parlor'. The **repetition** here emphasises the atmosphere of grief and death that pervades the scene: Arthur is dead, as is the loon which sits stuffed on the table. Family is a central characteristic of the objects described, the pictures of the British royal family and the poet's; the poet's mother, her deceased cousin and his father are all mentioned. (Cousin Arthur's real name was Frank.)

Stanza 2
The loon is depicted as if it is a witness to the scene but keeps quiet out of discretion: 'Since Uncle Arthur fired / a bullet into him, / he hadn't said a word. / He kept his own counsel'. There is a dry if **macabre wit** to this. The loon is described in more detail, it is set on a white marble table resembling an ice-covered lake, and the white feathers of its breast are 'cold and caressable', its eyes of red glass are 'much to be desired'. The speaker seems fascinated with this stuffed bird and longs to touch it. In a macabre association, the body of her cousin is displayed as if it is an ornament, just like the loon.

Stanza 3
As Bishop's mother lifts her up to 'say good-bye' to her cousin, Bishop places the delicate white flower in his hands and notices how pretty his coffin looks; it reminds her of an iced cake, probably referencing the satiny lining the coffin may have had, and the carved painted white wood it was made of. The loon seems to be as impressed by it as the child is, he 'eyed it / from his white, frozen lake'.

Stanza 4

Bishop now goes on to give us a more detailed account of Arthur in his coffin. His tiny stature makes him seem doll-like to her, a comparison that is re-enforced for Bishop by how pale he is, 'all white, like a doll / that hadn't been painted yet.' **In trying to make sense of the scene, the child refers to a familiar image from nature**, the coating of winter frost on leaves: 'Jack Frost had started to paint him'. Using nature to represent and describe aspects of life and death is a technique Bishop uses extensively in her poetry.

Stanza 5

The child now imagines a fairy-tale ending for little Arthur, where the royals in the pictures from stanza 1 welcome him into their gracious world as a page: 'They invited Arthur to be / the smallest page at court', but the child wonders how he could ever get there, given that he seems to be sleeping, and 'the roads [are] deep in snow'. The poem ends on a note of innocent confusion.

Themes

Strong themes in this poem include **death, family and childhood**, and again **the idea of home** surfaces. Bishop has written another biographical poem, a very revealing one. Her family clearly experienced a huge amount of loss and deep sorrow. **Note that she is beginning to name relatives** – 'Arthur', 'Uncle Arthur', 'My mother'. This is a **step towards a more intimate and confessional style**, compared to the distance created in poems like 'Sestina', where the characters are 'The child' and 'The grandmother'. The child seems so comfortable in this home and with the objects around her, compared to her experience 'In the Waiting Room', where the more formal world of Massachusetts is patently unsettling for her.

Making sense of the world through description and unusual comparisons is something Bishop clearly began doing while young, and something she continued to do in her work. In this way, **knowledge and the creation of knowledge** is also a theme (as in 'The Bight'). There is a **tension between what the child knows and does not know**. On the surface it would seem that the child doesn't understand the finality of death, but if we examine the language closely we see there is a **deeper knowledge at play** in words such as 'cold', 'laid out', 'shot', 'white', 'frozen' and 'forever' which hints that the child subconsciously knows more about death than she realises.

The loon

The loon is the official bird of the province of Ontario and is considered a symbol of solitude in this region. It is now a protected species in many areas including the nature reserve of Abraham Lake in Nova Scotia, where this poem is set.

Jack Frost

Jack Frost is the personification of winter in folklore, often depicted as a mischievous, impish figure who brings snow, sleet and ice and is responsible for the pretty intricate lace-like patterns of frost on leaves, windows, etc.

Cousin Arthur

Cousin Arthur's real name was Frank. Bishop renames a relative in her poem 'In the Waiting Room' also — 'Aunt Consuelo' was in fact her Aunt Florence. Even in her most biographical poems, Bishop's need for privacy and the difficulty she had dealing with her traumatic childhood means she changes these factual details. Arthur of course was a famous king of England, according to legend, which fits Bishop's fantasy of her dead cousin being a page at the court of this king.

Imagery

As in the previous poem, **weather mirrors mood** extensively. The **snow and ice outside are brought into the room**, as the child imagines Jack Frost painting young Arthur white in death. **Colour is used symbolically**, white linking death with purity and innocence, and red suggesting death and danger: the loon's eyes are red while Arthur's hair has 'a few red strokes'. Both the loon and Arthur have died before their time.

There is a **surreal quality to the imagery as inanimate objects** – chromographs, stuffed bird – seem to **partake in the drama**. The creativity of a child's inner world is made apparent.

Lily of the valley.

Language and form

Pathetic fallacy

In the poetic technique of pathetic fallacy, nature feels emotion, often reflecting the mood of the speaker. A happy poem may be set on a sunny day, sadness may be deepened with rain, anger with a storm, etc. The wintry weather in this poem emphasises the white of the loon, the coffin and Arthur's cold, pale body. Of course, winter is the season of death, as spring is that of re-birth.

Stream of consciousness

'Stream of consciousness' is a style of writing which seeks to mirror the process of thought. Uninterrupted by dialogue or objective description, it has a free-flowing movement often peppered with surreal, abstract associations that create the effect of a lively dance of thought.

The **unusual juxtapositions** in the poem create a 'stream of consciousness' style, which effectively echoes how a child makes **seemingly random connections** to help make sense of what isn't yet understood. These include describing the coffin as if it is an iced confection, and the comparison of Arthur's deathly pallor to a frosted 'Maple Leaf'. The ending is ambiguous; will Arthur have a happy ever-after? The child thinks so, but sees obstacles to this happy ending. As in 'Sestina', the language is filled with **short lines and repetition**, particularly of key images, **which creates a childlike effect in the tone**.

There are five stanzas of ten lines each and although there are occasional rhymes, there is no regular rhyming scheme. Perhaps Bishop wants to keep the tone informal and conversational. The use of trimeter (three-stressed lines) as the metre of the poem adds to the naturalness of the voice used: 'He was áll whíte, like a dóll'.

The **increasing regularity of form and structure** in Bishop's poetry is something you may have noticed as your study of her work progresses. How might you explain this?

Questions

1	Why, do you think, the poet uses the phrase 'First Death' in the title?
2	List the objects the speaker notices in the parlour. What atmosphere does this description create? What might these objects symbolise?
3	What impressions do you form of the poet's mother, cousin and uncle from the poem?
4	Find examples of how the colours red and white are used in the poem. List and analyse the examples you find, mentioning what you think the meaning attached to them might be.
5	Do you think the poem effectively conveys how a young child might seek to make sense of death? Explain, giving examples.
6	What is the effect of ending the poem on a question, and of the long rhyme at the end? How do these create a sense of closure?
7	Which word best describes the speaker in the poem and why: naïve, confused, imaginative?
8	Why, do you think, does the child create her fantasy for Arthur at the end of the poem? Explain what this fantasy is in your answer.
9	Write about one of the following: the sound effects in the poem OR the imagery in the poem.
10	Compare and contrast this poem to 'Sestina'.
11	How did you respond to this poem? Was it strange, sad, amusing or perhaps something else? Discuss in pairs or groups.
12	How does the poet use repetition in the poem and what is the effect of this?
13	Write Bishop's mother's diary entry for the day described in the poem.
14	Take a memorable event from your childhood and turn it into a fairytale.

HIGHER LEVEL

Before you read

Having read that the title is 'Filling Station', describe the setting that comes to mind. Try to be as detailed as possible.

Filling Station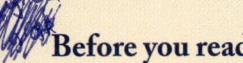

Oh, but it is dirty!
– this little filling station,
oil-soaked, oil-permeated
to a disturbing, over-all
black translucency.   5
Be careful with that match!

Father wears a dirty,
oil-soaked monkey suit
that cuts him under the arms,
and several quick and saucy   10
and greasy sons assist him
(it's a family filling station),
all quite thoroughly dirty.

Do they live in the station?
It has a cement porch   15
behind the pumps, and on it
a set of crushed and grease-
impregnated wickerwork;
on the wicker sofa
a dirty dog, quite comfy.   20

Some comic books provide
the only note of color –
of certain color. They lie
upon a big dim doily
draping a taboret   25
(part of the set), beside
a big hirsute begonia.

Why the extraneous plant?
Why the taboret?
Why, oh why, the doily?   30
(Embroidered in daisy stitch
with marguerites, I think,
and heavy with gray crochet.)

Elizabeth Bishop

Somebody embroidered the doily.
Somebody waters the plant,   35
or oils it, maybe. Somebody
arranges the rows of cans
so that they softly say:
ESSO—SO—SO—SO
to high-strung automobiles.   40
Somebody loves us all.

Glossary

3	*oil-permeated*:	oil has completely soaked into everything
5	*translucency*:	an almost transparent shine
8	*monkey suit*:	overalls
10	*saucy*:	flirtatious in a cheeky or playful way
24	*doily*:	lace-like napkin often placed under plants
25	*taboret*:	a stool without a back or arms
27	*hirsute*:	hairy
27	*begonia*:	a plant with large, blousy flowers
28	*extraneous*:	unnecessary, extra, not required
32	*marguerites*:	daisies
33	*crochet*:	a lacy form of knitting using a small hook
39	*so-so-so*:	Bishop said this was a phrase used to calm horses

Guidelines

From *Questions of Travel* (1965), in this poem we see a **more fun-loving, humorous side** to Bishop. This is something she had hinted at in earlier poems but **this detailed description of a petrol station is particularly playful**, albeit with a poignant message at the end. The poem is set in California where 'gas stations' were becoming an everyday sight. In an allegorical sense, the **filling station may represent the world in general**, and the **importance of home and family as the key to making a disordered and sometimes unpleasant world bearable**.

Commentary

Stanza 1
Bishop speaks as an observer trying to make sense of the strange sights which greet her at the filling station. The tone here seems shocked on the surface, but perhaps the speaker is quite enjoying the grime that covers everything: 'Oh, but it is dirty! / – this little filling station'. The use of 'little' here gives the scene a cosy 'cuteness' and sounds affectionate. Everything appears soaked in oil, and although the speaker says this is 'disturbing', she throws in a jokey, 'Be careful with that match!'

Stanza 2
The poet goes on to describe the men who work there in equally playful terms. It belongs to a father and his sons: 'it's a family filling station'. These men seem happy in their work, the father a little overweight (his overalls cut him 'under the arms'), and the sons are 'quick and saucy' as they assist him. They are 'all quite thoroughly dirty', but the speaker seems to enjoy the energy and bustle of the scene.

Stanza 3
The poet is incredulous as she questions the idea that they live in the station, but concludes they must when she sees the evidence: 'grease- / impregnated wickerwork / … / a dirty dog, quite comfy'. The inhabitants seem quite at home in their grimy environment. The alliterative 'd's of 'dirty dog' sound lively and playful here.

Stanza 4
The only true colour she can see that isn't darkened by an oily layer is provided by some 'comic books'. Perhaps there's a younger child somewhere or perhaps the saucy sons like to amuse themselves with these. The effect is cheerful and devil-may-care. The focus becomes more magnified now as Bishop notices some unlikely

objects. The comics lie on 'a big dim doily / draping a taboret / (part of the set), beside / a big hirsute begonia'. These decorative and inessential items seem at odds with the petrol pumps, overall-clad men and the grease that permeates the filling station. The parenthesis not only shows the **poet's fine eye for detail**, but continues the **good-natured feeling of fun** in the poet's faux horror at what she sees – note the continued alliteration on 'd'.

Stanza 5

The poet pauses to reflect on the objects she has noticed in the last stanza. The repetition of 'why' emphasises her incredulity. Why would anyone bother to add these feminine and decorative touches to this busy, dirty place of work? Someone has even gone to the bother of embroidering daisies onto the doily.

Stanza 6

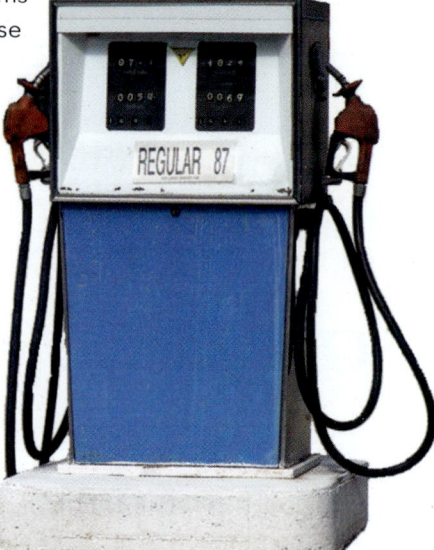

In this touching stanza, Bishop answers the questions she has posed in the previous one. Although the mother is absent from the scene in person, Bishop notices thoughtful touches everywhere. The plant is watered, the doily was embroidered, and the cans arranged uniformly. Bishop jokes that the plant might be oiled rather than watered, and admires the calming sound spelled out by the arrangement of the oil cans. She realises these decorative touches have been executed by an unseen presence in the filling station, a mother-figure, the 'Somebody' who 'loves us all'.

Themes

Family, the **effect of a mother's love** and the **importance of home** are themes in this poem. It is to the poet's credit that she remains very upbeat and cheerful, considering she grew up without her own parents around her, and felt the lack of a mother and a stable home very strongly. It is particularly touching when she asserts 'Somebody loves us all'. The 'us' here includes the speaker, and **perhaps Bishop felt ready to accept that her mother still loved her**, despite her inability to cope with Bishop's father's death and her mother's own subsequent nervous breakdown.

Language and imagery

The punctuation of the poem includes **exclamation and question marks which heighten the emotional reaction the speaker** has to what she notices about the filling station. The language is **deceptively simple and accessible**, and the poem is open to different interpretations. Is it about the presence of a mother making life happy, or is that mother absent and her maternal touches are fading beneath the grime? Is the final line positive and affirming, or sarcastic? The reader must decide.

There is a **contrast** within the imagery; the industrial masculine images of the pumps, the father and sons, cement and oil cans provide a foil for the traditionally feminine touches of the embroidered doily, taboret and plant. What does the covering of oil and grime over everything represent, and why might the comics be of interest? The presence of the contentedly curled up dog adds to the domesticity of this scene.

Elizabeth Bishop

Exam-Style Questions

Understanding the poem

1. Do you think the poet likes or dislikes what she sees in the filling station? Why?
2. Describe the family who lives there.
3. Look at the sibilance (repetition of 's' sounds) in stanza 2 and comment on the effect of this.
4. Why do the decorative touches (the plant, doily, etc.) puzzle the speaker so much?
5. Comment on the phrase 'high-strung automobiles' in the last stanza.
6. 'Somebody loves us all.' What does Bishop mean here? Who is that 'Somebody'? Explain.

Thinking about the poem

1. What word best describes the speaker's personality revealed here and why: nosy, affectionate, playful, sad?
2. Do you agree that the absence of a mother in her own childhood makes Bishop more likely to notice a mother's presence elsewhere? Discuss with reference to this and other poems by Bishop.
3. Which of the following statements best sums up the theme of this poem for you?
   - Everybody is loved by somebody
   - Don't judge by first impressions
   - Life is full of surprises
4. Would you agree that this poem is deceptively casual? Explain your answer.
5. Do you think the final line is a fitting and effective ending to the poem? Explain your answer.
6. Do you agree with the positive, upbeat interpretation of the poem in the commentary or is there another way to read the poem? Perhaps the speaker really is disgusted by what she sees? What do you think?

Imagining

1.  Is this Bishop's most positive poem? Discuss this in groups and feed back your ideas to the class.
2. In general, what touches do you think a mother-figure brings to a home? Is this an outdated idea these days in your opinion?

SNAPSHOT
- Vivid description
- Curiosity of speaker
- Conversational, playful tone
- Looks beyond the surface of things
- Family and home are important themes
- Personality of poet is revealed
- Disapproval and admiration

HIGHER LEVEL 2021

HIGHER LEVEL

Before you read

What do people do to pass the time in waiting rooms? What thoughts and feelings might you have as you sit waiting in one?

In the Waiting Room

In Worcester, Massachusetts,
I went with Aunt Consuelo
to keep her dentist's appointment
and sat and waited for her
in the dentist's waiting room.					5
It was winter. It got dark
early. The waiting room
was full of grown-up people,
arctics and overcoats,
lamps and magazines.						10
My aunt was inside
what seemed like a long time
and while I waited I read
the *National Geographic*
(I could read) and carefully					15
studied the photographs:
the inside of a volcano,
black, and full of ashes;
then it was spilling over
in rivulets of fire.						20
Osa and Martin Johnson
dressed in riding breeches,
laced boots, and pith helmets.
A dead man slung on a pole
– "Long Pig," the caption said.					25
Babies with pointed heads
wound round and round with string;
black, naked women with necks
wound round and round with wire
like the necks of light bulbs.					30
Their breasts were horrifying.
I read it right straight through.
I was too shy to stop.
And then I looked at the cover:
the yellow margins, the date.					35

Suddenly, from inside,
came an *oh!* of pain
– Aunt Consuelo's voice –
not very loud or long.
I wasn't at all surprised;
even then I knew she was
a foolish, timid woman.
I might have been embarrassed,
but wasn't. What took *me*
completely by surprise
was that it was me:
my voice, in my mouth.
Without thinking at all
I was my foolish aunt,
I – we – were falling, falling,
our eyes glued to the cover
of the *National Geographic*,
February, 1918.

I said to myself: three days
and you'll be seven years old.
I was saying it to stop
the sensation of falling off
the round, turning world
into cold, blue-black space.
But I felt: you are an *I*,
you are an *Elizabeth*,
you are one of *them*.
Why should you be one, too?
I scarcely dared to look
to see what it was I was.
I gave a sidelong glance
– I couldn't look any higher –
at shadowy gray knees,
trousers and skirts and boots
and different pairs of hands
lying under the lamps.
I knew that nothing stranger
had ever happened, that nothing
stranger could ever happen.
Why should I be my aunt,
or me, or anyone?
What similarities –
boots, hands, the family voice
I felt in my throat, or even

the *National Geographic*   80
and those awful hanging breasts –
held us all together
or made us all just one?
How – I didn't know any
word for it – how "unlikely"...   85
How had I come to be here,
like them, and overhear
a cry of pain that could have
got loud and worse but hadn't?

The waiting room was bright   90
and too hot. It was sliding
beneath a big black wave,
another, and another.

Then I was back in it.
The War was on. Outside,   95
in Worcester, Massachusetts,
were night and slush and cold,
and it was still the fifth
of February, 1918.

Glossary

Line	Term
1	***Worcester, Massachusetts***: where Bishop lived with her paternal grandparents, after being taken from Nova Scotia
9	***arctics***: overshoes to protect one's shoes from snow and rain
14	***National Geographic***: magazine about different places and peoples, famous for its photography
20	***rivulets***: small streams
21	***Osa and Martin Johnson***: a husband and wife explorer team
22	***riding breeches***: short tight trousers worn for horse riding
23	***pith helmets***: helmets used to protect against strong sun, often worn by explorers
25	***'Long Pig'***: name for a human who is to be eaten by cannibals
95	***The War***: First World War

Guidelines

This is the first poem in Bishop's last collection *Geography III* (1976). The poet remembers a seminal experience at six years old when she was taken to the dentist with her Aunt Florence (called Consuelo here). She disliked Worcester and the formal, distant ways of the family whom she felt had 'kidnapped' her from Nova Scotia. As she looks at photographs in a magazine she becomes **aware of her individuality, but also that she is part of a family and part of the female gender**. It is an important **epiphany** (sudden realisation), yet a **disorienting experience** for her.

Elizabeth Bishop

Commentary

Stanza 1

The poet remembers how as a six-year-old she waited for her aunt at the dentist. It is winter and the locals are dressed appropriately for the weather. She seems to be the only child: 'The waiting room / was full of grown-up people'. Due to the long wait, Bishop reads and looks at the photographs in a *National Geographic* magazine, noting an erupting volcano; the image creates a sense of **foreboding** and the **atmosphere is tense**. She notices an explorer couple in their 'riding breeches, / laced boots, and pith helmets'. As usual **Bishop's eye for detail is precise**. The next image is a shocking one, a dead man hung on a pole ready to be roasted and eaten by a cannibal tribe. The tribe look very strange to the child; 'Babies with pointed heads / wound round and round with string' refers to a custom of binding babies' heads with string to force them to grow into a point. 'Black, naked women with necks / wound round and round with wire' also look strange to Bishop. Some tribes consider long necks on women to be desirable so women have metal rings wound around their necks to extend them. These customs are very alien to the child and shock her; these people look so different to the conservatively dressed adults in the waiting room. The nakedness of the women mortifies her: 'Their breasts were horrifying.' She continues reading then stares at the cover to hide her shame.

> **National Geographic**
>
> **This is the official magazine of the National Geographic Society, first published in 1888, which brought to its readers photography and articles from all over the world, especially concerning nature and anthropology. In those days many parts of the world were still unexplored and readers were fascinated by information and images from other lands and cultures. The magazine is still published and read around the world today.**

Stanzas 2 and 3

She hears a timid cry of pain and thinks it is her aunt whom she has little regard for and is happy to ignore – 'I knew she was / a foolish, timid woman', then has the disconcerting realisation that it is her own 'oh!' she has heard in her aunt's voice, and she realises how much they sound alike. She is struck by this: 'I was my foolish aunt'. She feels faint; this strange moment has unsettled her: 'I – we – were falling, falling'. She tries to steady herself by staring at the magazine cover, noting the date 'February, 1918'. To try and compose herself further she focuses on concrete truths: 'three days / and you'll be seven years old. / I was saying it to stop / the sensation of falling off / the round, turning world'. It is a **moment of epiphany** for the poet as she realises that she is an individual: 'you are an *I*, / you are an *Elizabeth*'. She also realises that she is a women just like her aunt, just like those strange naked women in the magazine: 'you are one of *them*'. She wonders how this could be – '*Why* should you be one, too?' and glances around at the sedate, formally dressed occupants of the waiting room, too nervous to look above their knees. 'nothing stranger / had ever happened' – the moment we realise our individuality is a step on the road to adulthood, and the poet realises how important this moment is.

Bishop **continues to formulate questions**, wondering now about the arbitrary nature of where and what we are born into; that she should be from this repressed society while these tribal women endure painful rituals to be more beautiful is so strange. **She is amazed that humans are the same and yet so different**: 'What similarities / … held us all together / or made us all just one?' **The fact that everyone is an individual yet part of a family, and then a society and culture, is a revelation to her**. Bishop is amazed that she was there at that exact moment to see those photographs and then come to these conclusions and discoveries: 'how "unlikely". . . / How had I come to be here'.

Stanzas 4 and 5

The poet feels dizzy as if she is drowning; she seems to panic, 'sliding / beneath a big black wave, / another, and another'.

She is suddenly okay again; by focusing on the facts of the present she grounds herself: 'The War was on', 'night and slush and cold', 'the fifth / of February, 1918'. However, she is forever changed by a new knowledge that will carry her into adulthood. Mentioning the war shows an awareness of the bigger world outside her childhood concerns, and is a pessimistic note on which to end the poem.

Themes

Childhood and family are themes here. Just as in 'Sestina' and 'First Death in Nova Scotia', Bishop writes **candidly**, using childhood memories to explore incidents from her past. This poem goes beyond her personal life though, to explore **universal themes of individuality, societal customs and traditions, belonging and otherness**. This child who was so shocked by the magazine's content will go on to love travel and write of her experiences of different places and cultures.

The stuffy world of Worcester, Massachusetts is **symbolised by the waiting room** where the 'grown-up people' sit silently dressed head-to-toe in sensible weather-proof clothes: 'arctics and overcoats', 'shadowy gray knees / trousers and skirts and boots'. This is a **massive contrast to the vibrancy and 'otherness' of the wider world beyond**, where volcanoes erupt, cannibals feast, adventurers explore, and naked women and babies change their shape with wire.

Imagery

Vivid description brings the waiting room and the images in the magazine to life for the reader. Bishop creates setting meticulously, **a sense of time and place**, so that the poem is **grounded in reality** and has a cinematic quality to it. In the first three stanzas the imagery is quite straightforward; the only simile is the comparison between the women's necks wound with wire and 'the necks of light bulbs'. The **images become more surreal, reflecting the disorientation Bishop feels**: 'round, turning world / into cold, blue-black space.'

Images of violence and death abound: the erupting volcano, the dead man about to be eaten, the mutilation of babies and women with wire and string. These **contrast sharply with the quiet sedate waiting room** where the poet is embarrassed to see pictures of breasts, and where a small cry of pain might be embarrassing. The images of slush, darkness and war in the final stanza are bleak and pessimistic. These may foreshadow the depression, alcoholism and ill-health that would beset Bishop as she entered adulthood.

Elizabeth Bishop

Language and form

Full of **questions** and **short, clear descriptions**, the language gives **the effect of a child's perspective**, but the **older, wiser voice of Bishop**, now in her fifties, **informs these observations**. The **use of dashes** in stanza 2 onwards **conveys the shock and disorientation** the speaker feels as she thinks about culture, individuality and gender: 'Aunt Consuelo's voice', 'I – we – were falling', 'How – I didn't know any / word for it – how "unlikely"'.

Returning to a familiar structure, Bishop writes in long irregular unrhymed stanzas, with two shorter stanzas completing the poem. The statement of where and when the speaker is, and what is going on in the world, gives the poem a sense of closure: 'Then I was back in it. / The War was on.' The child has recovered her composure. Is she ready to face the world around her and the life ahead of her?

Questions

1	What is the atmosphere in the waiting room? What details in the poem convey this?
2	How does the waiting room contrast with the images in the magazine?
3	How does Bishop feel when she sees the pictures in *National Geographic*? Provide specific points and examples.
4	What, do you think, is the moment that triggers the child's epiphany in the poem?
5	Sum up the questions asked by the poet in the poem. Are they answered? Explain.
6	What images are used to show that the child feels she is losing her grip on reality?
7	How does the child try to recover her composure?
8	Compare this poem to the two others where Bishop recounts childhood memories. In which one, do you think, is she least happy? Why? ('Sestina' and 'First Death in Nova Scotia'.)
9	How might the title be symbolic in the poem? In groups or pairs discuss what a waiting room might represent.
10	Write an account of either the *theme* of this poem OR the *tone* of this poem.
11	Write the speaker's diary entry for that day.
12	Write a composition based on one of the photographs described by Bishop.

Exam-Preparation Questions

1. 'I think geography comes first in my work.'
   To what extent do you agree with Bishop's assessment of her poetry with regard to the poems you have studied by her?

2. 'Elizabeth Bishop's narrative style and her use of conversational language make her poems accessible to the reader.'
   Would you agree with this view?

3. Write the text of a presentation you would give entitled 'Elizabeth Bishop, Home and Away'. Here are some possible ideas you might use:
   - Look at the theme of home in her poetry and how a sense of belonging or not belonging tends to be at the heart of many of her poems
   - Bishop's poems concerning family or the lack of one (NB mother-figure)
   - Poems about travel, unusual customs, different places and experiences

4. A critic once remarked on the 'deceptive casualness' of Bishop's poetry. Do you agree with this assessment of her work?

5. Bishop looks at ordinary things and sees the extraordinary, often finding beauty in what others might consider ugly or banal. Write about how this is true of the poems you have studied.

6. The natural world is celebrated and hugely symbolic in Bishop's poems. Write about how Bishop uses nature in her imagery and suggest what the different aspects of nature you've encountered in her work might symbolise.

7. Analyse the sound effects and references to music in Bishop's poetry.

8. 'Her work is unusually personal and honest in its wit, perception and sensitivity.'
   Do you agree with Randall Jarrell's description of Bishop's poetry?

9. Write about 'observation leading inward and onwards to epiphany' in the work of Elizabeth Bishop.

SNAPSHOT ELIZABETH BISHOP

- Highly descriptive
- Childhood trauma informs outlook and themes
- Nature closely observed and used symbolically
- Variety of forms; sonnets, sestina, lyric, narrative, etc.
- Highly original imagery, especially in terms of comparisons
- Sense of humour evident
- Celebration of the ordinary
- Situation closely observed which often leads to an epiphany
- Confessional poet

Sample Essay

'The poetry of Elizabeth Bishop appeals to the modern reader for many reasons.' Write an essay in which you outline the reasons why poems by Elizabeth Bishop have this appeal. (2002)

In my opinion the modern reader wants a poet with a lively, fresh voice and an original way of looking at the world, someone who isn't afraid to reveal themselves, but who has an ultimately positive and uplifting message for us. I feel Elizabeth Bishop is most definitely that poet. By creating vivid narratives using startling imagery, Bishop not only entertains but educates her audience with her thought-provoking and often wryly humorous poetry.

> *Introductory paragraph addresses question and defines terms, indicating areas that will be developed. Personal response clear by using 'I feel'*

> *Aspects introduced in the opening paragraph are developed*

'The Fish' is a vivid narrative where Bishop uses startlingly original imagery to convey a positive message. She conversationally recounts the tale of catching 'a tremendous fish', noticing that it has survived many battles before: 'from his lower lip / … hung five old pieces of fish-line / … Like medals with their ribbons'. She uses a trio of adjectives as she describes this soldier-like, 'battered and venerable / and homely' fish, in a tone of admiration using unusual and amusing similes: 'his brown skin hung in strips / like ancient wallpaper, / … shapes like full-blown roses'. The assonance here adds to the lively sense of fascination. The more she notices about the creature the more the speaker's mood builds towards an elated epiphany: 'until everything / was rainbow, rainbow, rainbow!' This excited repetition engages the modern reader and leads up to the moment of decision: 'And I let the fish go.' The embattled, exhausted fish is given another chance at life and in this I think the fish represents Bishop herself. She had survived childhood grief, displacement and trauma, and struggles with her physical and mental health, including skin conditions, depression and alcoholism. I like to think that by letting the fish go free, Bishop is symbolically congratulating herself on being a survivor, and extending the message to us, that we all deserve another chance at life. This entertaining fable has taught us a valuable lesson and made us feel we know something of Bishop's personality.

> *Personal response continues*

> *Opening of third paragraph links it with second*

A very similar message is conveyed in 'The Prodigal', where the central character is an alcoholic swineherd living among the pigs he tends. He too gets another chance: 'it took him a long time / finally to make his mind up to go home'. Bishop teaches us that no matter how shameful or debased we have become, redemption is possible. The Prodigal lives in dire conditions – 'the floor was rotten; the sty / was plastered halfway up with glass-smooth dung'; but there is beauty and hope to be seen even here: 'the sunrise glazed the barnyard mud with red'. I find Bishop's original description and ability to see beauty in the most ugly or ordinary things refreshing and lively. Bishop had found herself in many embarrassing situations because of her drinking, and clearly identifies herself with the character of the Prodigal. Even though revealing this side of herself must have been painful for her, the poet can make us smile, for example describing the pigs contentedly sleeping cosily: 'The pigs stuck out their little feet and snored.' This reveals an ultimately optimistic personality and endears the modern reader to her work.

> *The 'modern reader' of the question is kept central to analysis*

'This is the time of year / when almost every night / the frail, illegal fire balloons appear.' In 'The Armadillo', Bishop teaches us about the Brazilian custom of releasing fire balloons on St John's feast day, but goes further to warn about and criticise the terrible harm mankind inflicts on our environment. The balloons often crash to earth, described by Bishop in characteristically unusual and striking imagery: 'It splattered like an egg of fire / … / The flame ran down.' She had admired the beauty of the lanterns, but upon witnessing the harm they inflict she is scathing in her criticism of them: '*Too pretty, dreamlike mimicry! / O falling fire and piercing cry / and panic*'. Her account of the suffering the forest creatures endure is what truly engages the modern reader's emotions: 'a baby rabbit jumped out, / *short*-eared… / So soft! – a handful of intangible ash'. The pair of owls whose nest has been destroyed, and the armadillo himself, rolled into a protective ball yet doomed to die, combine with the rabbit as startling symbols of the damage we needlessly inflict upon the natural world. So far all of these poems have used animals as central images to help the poet convey her message, in this case an environmental one. She loves nature and feels passionately about its preservation. I found I shared wholeheartedly her indignation and empathy.

[Annotation: Linking together the poems discussed so far]

[Annotation: Personal engagement evident in closing sentence]

In later poems Bishop revealed even more about her life, and dealt openly with painful childhood memories. 'Sestina', 'First Death in Nova Scotia' and 'In the Waiting Room' fall into this category. After reading these poems I felt I knew a lot about the poet and understood even more the messages of survival and determination her earlier poetry conveyed. In 'Sestina', Bishop uses this rigid and complex form to explore her childhood confusion at the grief and loss her family had suffered. Bishop's father died when she was an infant and while still a young child her mother was committed to a mental institution, where she was to die without the poet ever seeing her again. Images of tears pervade the poem, but Bishop does create a quietly playful element with the almost cartoon-like personification of domestic objects: 'the child / is watching the teakettle's small hard tears / dance like mad on the hot black stove'. Six key words are repeated in every stanza: 'house', 'grandmother', 'child',' stove', 'almanac' and 'tears'. This repetition emphasises the key symbols and characters while giving the poem a lively childlike rhythm, giving it energy despite the sad subject matter. The ending conveys that life will go on for the child and her grandmother; there is a future for them: 'The grandmother sings to the marvellous stove / and the child draws another inscrutable house.' Bishop offers another valuable lesson of hope, and she conveys her determination to survive by using the demanding structure of a sestina. She wants to understand, to put a shape on her past.

[Annotation: Clear background knowledge of poet's life used to inform analysis]

'First Death in Nova Scotia' is the only poem to directly feature the poet's mother, as she lifts three-year-old Elizabeth up to place a flower into the hand of her dead cousin Arthur. It's another startling poem in terms of the painful memory it describes and the originality of the imagery used to vividly describe the scene. Bishop engages her reader's empathy. A stuffed white loon seems to gaze at Arthur's body echoing the colour of the snow outside, the ermine trim on the clothes of the royal family's pictures, the flower in Arthur's hand and the pallor of Arthur himself. Bishop imagines her little cousin becoming 'the smallest page' at the court pictured in the 'chromographs', conveying effectively how a child's imagination helps them to make sense of confusing and upsetting situations. By using the persona of the child, Bishop reminds us how we thought and felt as children – constantly trying to make sense of an often bewildering world – and does this in a similar way in 'Sestina'. Both poems use a rigid structure laced with repetition to impose an order on the chaotic and traumatic events the poet is dealing with. I felt great sympathy for her here and admired her lack of sentimentality and her skill as a poet. She has developed her style and been

[Annotation: Knowledge of structural aspects of poem used to support observations about content and meaning]

Elizabeth Bishop

Keeping the idea of 'modern reader' from the question central in the answer

more open in her content and mentions her mother directly. This shows a progress in Bishop, and perhaps she is coping better with the awful events of her past. I think seeing a growth and development like this appeals to the modern reader of poetry, allowing them to gain a deeper understanding of the poet and her work.

I feel I have come to know so much about Bishop from reading her poetry, and learned many valuable lessons along the way – that there is always a way forward, another chance to value and preserve nature, to examine the nature of identity and belonging, and more than anything that if we are optimistic, imaginative and keep our sense of humour we can survive anything. Bishop's lively fresh voice, candour and positivity entertain and educate us through vivid and original narratives, offering so much to the modern reader of poetry.

'All the untidy activity continues, / Awful but cheerful.'

I feel this quote sums up Bishop's work and her approach to life beautifully, and I was interested to learn that she chose this as her epitaph. She seems to say to me, 'Don't give up, look at the beauty of life, don't expect it to be perfect, find things to celebrate and deal with the pain as best you can.' It is this message more than anything that means the poems of Elizabeth Bishop appeal to me and so many other modern readers of poetry.

Overall conclusion reached and question addressed again

ESSAY CHECKLIST		Yes √	No ×
Purpose	Has the candidate understood the task?		
	Has the candidate responded to it in a thoughtful manner?		
	Has the candidate answered the question?		
Comment:			
Coherence	Has the candidate made convincing arguments?		
	Has the candidate linked ideas?		
	Does the essay have a sense of unity?		
Comment:			
Language	Is the essay written in an appropriate register?		
	Are ideas expressed in a clear way?		
	Is the writing fluent?		
Comment:			
Mechanics	Is the use of language accurate?		
	Are all words spelled correctly?		
	Does the punctuation help the reader?		
Comment:			

HIGHER LEVEL

Eavan Boland

b.1944

The War Horse	68
Child of Our Time*	72
The Famine Road	76
The Black Lace Fan My Mother Gave Me	81
The Shadow Doll	85
White Hawthorn in the West of Ireland	89
Outside History	93
This Moment*	98
Love*	101
The Pomegranate	106

Eavan Boland

Biography

Personal life

Eavan Boland was born in Dublin in 1944, the daughter of diplomat Frederick Boland and artist Frances Kelly. Because her father's job often took the family abroad, much of Boland's childhood was spent outside Ireland. When she was almost six, the family moved to London, where her father had been made ambassador to the UK. Six years later her father was appointed ambassador to the United Nations and the family moved to New York, which she enjoyed much more than London. On her return to Ireland in her mid-teens Boland completed her secondary school education at the Convent of the Holy Child, Killiney, Dublin. Boland went on to study English and Latin at Trinity College, Dublin. In 1966 she was awarded a first-class degree in English. For a time she was a junior lecturer at Trinity College, but in 1967 she left the academic life, becoming a literary journalist with RTÉ and the *Irish Times* as well as concentrating increasingly on her career as a poet. In 1969 she married the novelist Kevin Casey, and in 1971 they moved to the Dublin suburb of Dundrum at the foot of the Dublin mountains. The couple's two daughters were born within a few years.

> **Boland on her girlhood**
>
> 'In those years of the fifties, in London and New York, I lived, without knowing it, in a time when the profoundest changes were happening: when a radical alteration was getting ready to happen in the way a society saw young girls. And, as a consequence, in the way they saw themselves.'

Poetic life

In 1962, in her first term in Trinity College, Boland published a pamphlet of the poems she had written as a teenager, *23 Poems*. Her first collection to be widely available was *New Territory*, published in 1967. *The War Horse* followed in 1975.

In 1979 she spent three months with her young family in Iowa, USA, where she lectured on the University of Iowa's International Writing Program. This time is remembered in the poem 'Love'. Her next collection, *In Her Own Image* (1980), with its explicitly feminist themes, reflects her exposure to the North American women's movement. In 1980 she was also a co-founder of Arlen House, an Irish feminist press.

Night Feed (1982) and *The Journey* (1986) put Boland's life as a woman at the heart of her poetry. She celebrates domestic life in the suburbs, looking after children and tending the home, and she meditates on her female body and sexuality. The collections *Outside History* (1990) and *In a Time of Violence* (1994) broaden the scope of these issues, exploring the place of women in the past and looking at how myth and history are made and can be remade.

Collected Poems was published in 1995, followed by *The Lost Land* in 1998 and *Code* (titled *Against Love Poetry* in the USA) in 2001. In 2008 *New Collected Poems* was published, followed by *A Woman Without a Country* in 2014.

Boland has also written a number of stimulating prose essays about poetry and the role of the woman poet in society, in particular *Object Lessons* (1995) and *A Journey with Two Maps* (2011). She has been Professor of English at Stanford University in California since 1996, and divides her time between the USA and Ireland.

Social and Cultural Context

Irish history

Eavan Boland has always been keenly aware of her standing in relation to Irish history, and much of her poetry explores that theme. Her childhood was deeply affected by Irish history. Her father's appointment as the first Irish ambassador in London in 1950 was possible only because Ireland had declared itself a republic and outside the British Commonwealth of Nations, thereby taking a critical step in its journey to independent nationhood. Joining the United Nations in 1955 was another significant step, and led directly to the Boland family's move to New York the following year.

For Boland, living abroad meant both becoming detached from her Irish roots and being doubly aware of what they could mean. In London, her red hair and Irish accent drew attention at school at a time when anti-Irish sentiment was common, partly as a result of Ireland's neutral stance during the Second World War. Her Irishness was not something she was able to take for granted, and she felt she needed to claim and relearn it when she came back to live in Dublin as a teenager. She has said of this time, 'I was … unable to name the country I came from. Unable to come from it until I could name it.'

The influence of Yeats

'Yeats is the poet I have loved most,' Boland wrote in an essay in 2000. It was when she got to know the work of W. B. Yeats, reading and rereading his poetry and prose as a teenager newly returned to Ireland, that she found a guide into her Irishness and a sense of belonging in the language he used to evoke Ireland. He got her thinking about Ireland and her relationship with it as a poet. Yeats was very conscious of his role as a national poet in imagining and defining a new Ireland, and although Boland came to resist a lot of what he stood for, he was an important model for what she set out to achieve as a poet. Like him, she wanted to find a **living connection between herself and her country**, and to find a voice that could express it. And although her vision is very different, like Yeats she has shown the ambition and self-belief to carry that project through.

Feminism and the Irish poetic tradition

As an undergraduate in Trinity College, Boland was part of a gifted group of young poets who included Brendan Kennelly, Michael Longley and Derek Mahon. When she became a full-time poet, she was for a time involved in the Dublin literary scene, which was centred on the pubs of the city, in one of which she met Patrick Kavanagh. Soon, however, she began to examine critically the Irish poetic tradition represented by these male poets. She saw that women figured as idealised objects rather than as real women in this primarily 'bardic and male' tradition. In particular, Ireland and Irishness were often represented by female figures such as Kathleen Ní Houlihan, Dark Rosaleen or Mother Ireland. Not only were there precious few women poets, but the lives and interests of real women were outside the usual concerns of poetry. 'I couldn't find my life in poetry,' Boland has said.

Eavan Boland

The influence of the **feminist movement** began to be felt in Ireland in the 1960s and 1970s. Questions about the relationship of gender and power were asked in the field of poetry as well as in the political sphere. For Boland, the discovery of the poems of the American writers Sylvia Plath and, later, Adrienne Rich pointed the way ahead. They offered examples of women writing about their experiences of marriage and motherhood.

Boland has lived at a time of great and rapid change for women in Irish literature, and she has been instrumental in bringing about a shift in focus in Irish poetry in particular. She points out that 'over a relatively short time – certainly no more than a generation or so – women have moved from being the subjects and objects of Irish poems to being the authors of them'.

Boland has said that, for her, feminism has been an enabling perception, but although she calls herself a feminist, she has resisted her poetry being labelled as 'feminist'. She is a woman poet and, as she says, 'Poetry begins where the certainties end … Women writers have struggled to be heard … and it is very important that they are not part of silencing anyone else.' Her autobiographical collection of prose essays, *Object Lessons*, gives valuable insights both into her development as a poet and into her perceptions of the challenges that are faced by female poets in our time.

Classical literature

Boland studied Latin at school and later at Trinity College. The **poetry of Virgil** has been of particular importance to her, especially Book VI of the *Aeneid*, in which Aeneas descends into the underworld; it is central to an understanding of the poem 'Love'. Classical mythology has been a rich source of images and stories for her, notably the story of Ceres and Persephone (see page 108), which is referred to in 'The Pomegranate' and many other poems.

Themes

Women's lives

A major part of Boland's purpose as a poet has been to reclaim the lives of women, both past and present, for poetry. At one level, this has been a matter of writing about the life she leads and the places she knows. For her, she says, the kettle, the baby's bottle, the kitchen 'were parts of my world. Not to write about them would have been artificial'. In the collections *Night Feed* and *The Journey* in particular she explored her life and feelings as a young mother, as a sexual woman and as a poet in suburbia. Unsurprisingly, her poems often touch on the mother–child relationship.

History

Boland has always been interested in her own **relationship with history and nationality**. Perhaps the dominant political fact in Ireland in Boland's young adult life was the Troubles in Northern Ireland, which is central to two of the poems on your course, 'The War Horse' and 'Child of Our Time'. Although there are echoes in later poems she never again dealt directly with contemporary politics. Instead she chose to approach history from the perspective of her own life and experiences. Seeing history in this way means examining critically what history is. Properly

> **Changes**
>
> 'Over a relatively short period of time – certainly no more than a generation or so – women have moved from being the objects of Irish poems to being the authors of them. It is a momentous transit. It is also a disruptive one. It raises questions of identity, issues of poetic motive and ethical direction which can seem almost impossibly complex.'
>
> Eavan Boland, *Object Lessons*

> 'Our present will become the past of other men and women. We depend on them to remember it with the complexity with which it was suffered. As others, once, depended on us.'
>
> Eavan Boland, *Object Lessons*

understood, **history should be a record of the past in its full complexity**, not just the record of wars and taxes and the actions of powerful men. Poetry is capable of reclaiming for history what other written records pass over in silence.

The focus in Boland's poems is increasingly on those who had been left 'outside history' – often, though not always, women. History, she believes, has ignored the lives lived by ordinary women in the past, those whom she terms the 'lost, voiceless, the silent' – women who were victims of the Irish famine, or powerless women like her own grandmother, who died in a fever hospital in Dublin in 1909. Consequently, Boland looks at objects to see what they can tell us about the hidden lives with which they were associated, as in 'The Black Lace Fan My Mother Gave Me' and 'The Shadow Doll'.

Myth

Myth is a frequent preoccupation in Boland's poems. Sometimes it is set against history, as in the poem 'Outside History', where myth seems to be something unreal, as opposed to the real suffering of history. This does not mean, however, that myth is worthless. On the contrary, many of Boland's poems explore myths, and these explorations often find new meanings. 'The Pomegranate' looks at her own relationship with her daughter through the myth of Ceres and Persephone. 'Love' finds a deeper understanding of her relationship with her husband through the myth of Aeneas in the underworld.

A myth is a story that is shared by a culture and that has meaning for that culture. Retelling or reworking a myth can renew its meaning, and Boland is interested in the **ways in which mythic meanings can be made**. 'White Hawthorn in the West of Ireland', for example, looks at how meaning is given to the hawthorn by superstitious stories or her own poetic imagination. Myths can tell the truth and they can distort it. There is always a tension between the myth-making imagination and the world out of which the myths are made. As Boland writes, 'myth is the wound we leave / in the time we have'.

Time and loss

Perhaps because she often looks towards the past, many of Boland's poems deal with the **sense of loss** that the passage of time always brings. Sometimes the loss is part of an inevitable process of growth and change, as in her relationships with her husband in 'Love' or with her daughter in 'The Pomegranate'. Sometimes it is involved with her awareness of what is hidden by the passing of time, such as the relationship of her parents in 'The Black Lace Fan My Mother Gave Me'. Sometimes it has a historical dimension, as in 'The Famine Road' or 'Outside History', where her sense of Ireland's past is filled with loss and suffering; as she has said, the history of Ireland is a history of defeat. Boland notes that her poetry works with the themes of 'time, perception of loss, down-to-earth disappointments or irretrievable segments of human experience'.

Eavan Boland

Timeline

1944	Born in Dublin to diplomat Frederick Boland and painter Frances Kelly
1950	Moves with family to London
1956	Moves with family to New York
1959	Returns to Ireland and attends Holy Child Convent, Killiney
1966	Graduates from Trinity College, Dublin, with a first-class honours degree in English; takes up an academic post at TCD
1967	First collection, *New Territory*, published
1969	Marries novelist Kevin Casey
1975	Second collection, *The War Horse*, published; first daughter, Sarah, born
1978	Second daughter, Eavan Frances, born
1979	Lives for three months in Iowa, USA, attending the International Writing Program
1980	Publishes collection *In Her Own Image*; co-founds Arlen House, Irish feminist publishing company
1982	*Night Feed* published
1986	*The Journey* published
1990	*Outside History* published
1994	*In a Time of Violence* published
1995	Publishes autobiographical essays, *Object Lessons*; publishes *Collected Poems*
1996	Appointed Professor of English at Stanford University, USA
2007	*Domestic Violence* published
2008	*New Collected Poems* published
2014	*A Woman Without a Country* published

HIGHER LEVEL

Before you read

'The War Horse' was written in 1972 against the backdrop of the Troubles. Use the Internet to find out about Bloody Sunday and some of the other things that happened in Northern Ireland in 1972.

The War Horse

This dry night, nothing unusual
About the clip, clop, casual

Iron of his shoes as he stamps death
Like a mint on the innocent coinage of earth.

I lift the window, watch the ambling feather   5
Of hock and fetlock, loosed from its daily tether

In the tinker camp on the Enniskerry Road,
Pass, his breath hissing, his snuffling head

Down. He is gone. No great harm is done.
Only a leaf of our laurel hedge is torn –   10

Of distant interest like a maimed limb,
Only a rose which now will never climb

The stone of our house, expendable, a mere
Line of defence against him, a volunteer

You might say, only a crocus, its bulbous head   15
Blown from growth, one of the screamless dead.

But we, we are safe, our unformed fear
Of fierce commitment gone; why should we care

If a rose, a hedge, a crocus are uprooted
Like corpses, remote, crushed, mutilated?   20

He stumbles on like a rumour of war, huge,
Threatening; neighbours use the subterfuge

Of curtains; he stumbles down our short street
Thankfully passing us. I pause, wait,

Then to breathe relief lean on the sill   25
And for a second only my blood is still

With atavism. That rose he smashed frays
Ribboned across our hedge, recalling days

Of burned countryside, illicit braid:
A cause ruined before, a world betrayed.   30

Glossary

4	*mint*:	imprint, as on a coin
5–6	*ambling … fetlock*:	the hock and fetlock are the lower parts of a horse's back leg; the feather is the long hair on the lower parts of a horse's legs
13	*expendable*:	something that can be done without
15	*bulbous*:	bulging, swollen
22	*subterfuge*:	trick; secret device
27	*atavism*:	the sense of connection with the characteristics and feelings of ancestors
29	*illicit braid*:	'illicit' means against the law; the braid refers to the green ribbon worn as a badge by the nineteenth-century Irish secret society known as the 'Ribbonmen'

Eavan Boland

Guidelines

'The War Horse' was the title poem of the collection Boland published in 1975, but the poem itself had been written in 1972, at a time when the poet and her husband had recently moved to a newly built but still unfinished housing estate in Dundrum, south Dublin. It was also a time of violence in Northern Ireland, which was brought into their living room, in Boland's words, by 'a small television chanting deaths and statistics at teatime'. It is one of the first of her poems that tries to tackle a political theme.

The incident described in this poem is, on the face of it, insignificant: a horse appears in a suburban street, tramples on a garden, and goes away. It is 'nothing unusual', as the first line says, but the poem's title – not just 'The Horse' but 'The War Horse' – alerts us immediately to its undertones of conflict and destruction.

Commentary

Lines 1–9
The beginning of the poem describes the incongruous (out of place) appearance of a horse in a suburban street – first heard in the onomatopoeic 'clip, clop' of the hooves, then seen when the poet opens the window. At first glance, there does not seem to be anything momentous or ominous about the incident. The horse is 'ambling' casually, the 'snuffling' head is unthreatening. In the end, 'No great harm is done.' And yet there is something sinister in the second couplet: with his hooves, the horse 'stamps death' into the ground. It is a dramatic description.

Lines 10–20
These lines consider the harm that has been done, and what it means. At first glance, there is little upset: a torn leaf, a damaged climbing rose plant, a broken crocus. After all, 'we are safe' – 'we' being, first of all, the inhabitants of the street. The question 'why should we care … ?' seems at first to be rhetorical, but the language of the poem prevents us from ignoring its wider implications. The imagery is military and violent: the torn hedge 'like a maimed limb', the rose plant a 'Line of defence' and a 'volunteer', the crocus head 'blown' as if, perhaps, by a bomb. Most strikingly, and disturbingly, the beheaded crocus is seen as 'one of the screamless dead'. Similarly, line 20 likens the damaged plants to 'corpses'.

Notice that they are 'remote', as well as 'crushed' and 'mutilated', just as the maimed limb in line 11 is 'Of distant interest'. The terms the poet uses insist on how the poem is to be understood. Both the violence and the distance speak of the Troubles in Northern Ireland, which were always in the news at that time. That context changes the tone of 'why should we care' into a more urgent and more open one, and the 'we' of the poem is made to encompass not just the residents of the street but the population of Ireland. Understood like this, 'our unformed fear', which the horse's presence conjures up, is perhaps the 'fierce commitment' of the paramilitary groups operating in that conflict.

Lines 21–30
The poem returns to the horse, stumbling on 'like a rumour of war' – a simile that makes the symbolism explicit. The neighbours 'use the subterfuge // Of curtains', closing them to pretend that the horse does not exist. He passes on, and there is a moment of suspense as the poem, like the speaker, pauses at the end of line 24. Her blood 'is still // With atavism'. This word refers to inherited, ancestral characteristics and feelings, and it

describes an emotion that makes the poet connect her present experience with the historical past. The focus of the poem widens, in time and space, as the broken rose plant 'Ribboned across our hedge' brings to mind Ireland's troubled and violent past: 'A cause ruined before, a world betrayed.' The dark past casts an ominous shadow over the present and, perhaps, the future.

Themes and imagery

The poem's themes are conveyed primarily through its images, of which the central one is the horse of the title. Although we are told he is an ordinary Traveller's horse, in the poem he represents a brutal and destructive force. He 'stamps death' (line 3) and is 'huge, / Threatening', 'a rumour of war' (lines 21–22). This rather clumsy creature (we are twice told he 'stumbles') brings an image of war into the domestic order of the suburbs. Notice, too, that the horse is made strange – and so more disturbing – by being described in a fragmented way, through details: we hear his hooves, see his feet and legs, hear his 'breath hissing' (line 8), glimpse his lowered head, then 'He is gone' (line 9).

The rest of the imagery contrasts the **domestic order**, the cared-for garden, with a **vision of violence**, so that the damaged plants become 'mutilated' (line 20) corpses, a decapitated crocus 'one of the screamless dead' (line 16).

The connection – or lack of it – between the peaceful, protected setting and the threatening world elsewhere represented by the horse is the poem's main theme. You can close the curtains, but the violence that lurks not just beyond the country's borders but within its history cannot be completely ignored.

Form and language

The poem's **rhymed couplets create a strong sense of control and order**, like the tidy suburban gardens. But just as the horse disrupts the domestic calm, the poem's **phrasing and line breaks often work against the neatness of the rhymes**. There is enjambment, not just between lines but across stanzas, such as 'his snuffling head // Down' (lines 8–9), 'a volunteer // You might say' (lines 14–15) and 'the subterfuge // Of curtains' (lines 22–23). The effect of these lurches across the lines is a tentativeness and tension in the speaker's voice, an effect that is reinforced by the use of expressions that suggest someone seeking definition or clarity: 'You might say' (line 15); 'But we, we are safe' (line 17).

The accumulation of images and adjectives to describe the scene, on which the poem relies for its effects, can be seen as another manifestation of this **tentative voice**, searching for the right words to use. Look, for example, at the way the rose is described, first as 'expendable', then as 'a mere / Line of defence' and finally as 'a volunteer' (lines 13–14), a word that suggests all the 'volunteer' organisations that have fought in Irish conflicts, from the Irish Volunteers of 1916 to the Ulster Volunteer Force over the course of a century, as well as many others. And in line 20 the damaged plants are 'Like corpses, remote, crushed, mutilated', where each term carries its own particular associations to add to the overall picture.

It is only at the end of the poem that some sense of certainty emerges. The assonance of the long vowels of 'breathe relief lean' in line 25 slows the pace down, and there is a moment of vision that culminates in the final couplet. There, the caesuras (mid-line pauses) create balance and poise in each line, and the strong rhyme underlines the power of the vision: 'Of burned countryside, illicit braid: / A cause ruined before, a world betrayed.' Notice how the power and the balance of these lines are reinforced by the alliteration of harsh 'b' sounds either side of the caesura: '**b**urned … **b**raid' and '**b**efore … **b**etrayed'. The effect is ominous.

Questions

1	What is the first impression we get of the horse? How does Boland create this impression?
2	What is the speaker's attitude to the horse at first? Does that attitude change as the poem progresses?
3	What, do you think, does the horse symbolise?
4	How important is the suburban setting in the poem, in your view? Explain your answer.
5	How does the poet make use of contrast? Find examples from the poem to support your answer.
6	What insights are contained in the poem's final lines, in your view? You might focus in particular on the word 'atavism' and on the connotations of the phrase 'illicit braid'.
7	The poet has referred to 'The War Horse' as her first 'political' poem. What political point is she making? Does it apply to the Irish situation only, or can it be applied to other situations?
8	Choose two images from the poem that you found disturbing or surprising, and say why you found them so.
9	Explore the sounds of the poem – alliteration, onomatopoeia, rhyme, assonance – and explain how they contribute to the poem's meaning.
10	Comment on the poet's use of line and stanza breaks, giving examples from the poem.
11	'We see so much suffering on the news that we learn to ignore it.' Discuss this statement in pairs or groups.
12	In verse or prose, write a description of an animal that conveys the special qualities of that animal.

HIGHER LEVEL

Before you read

What might the title 'Child of Our Time' suggest to you about the poem?

Child of Our Time
For Aengus

Yesterday I knew no lullaby
But you have taught me overnight to order
This song, which takes from your final cry
Its tune, from your unreasoned end its reason,
Its rhythm from the discord of your murder   5
Its motive from the fact you cannot listen.

We who should have known how to instruct
With rhymes for your waking, rhythms for your sleep,
Names for the animals you took to bed,
Tales to distract, legends to protect,   10
Later an idiom for you to keep
And living, learn, must learn from you, dead,

To make our broken images rebuild
Themselves around your limbs, your broken
Image, find for your sake whose life our idle   15
Talk has cost, a new language. Child
Of our time, our times have robbed your cradle.
Sleep in a world your final sleep has woken.

17 May 1974

Glossary

| 5 | *discord*: harsh noise, not harmonious |
| 11 | *idiom*: the way a particular group of people uses a language |

Guidelines

Boland on 'Child of Our Time'

'I wrote it inspired – and I use the word with care – by a photograph I saw two days later on the front of a national newspaper whose most arresting feature was the expression on the face of the fireman who lifted that child, an expression of tenderness as if he were lifting his own child from its cradle to its mother's breast.'

Boland wrote 'Child of Our Time' in response to the bombings that killed 34 people, including several children, in Dublin and Monaghan on 17 May 1974 – the date she placed at the end of the poem. It was first published in the *Irish Times* soon afterwards. Aengus, to whom the poem is dedicated, was the young child of one of the poet's friends and he died from sudden infant death syndrome (SIDS or cot death) around the same time as the bombings.

Eavan Boland

Commentary

Stanza 1
The poem starts very intimately, with the poet ('I') addressing the dead child ('you'), saying that she has been inspired or 'taught' to write the poem ('This song') by the child's death. The sense of shock is indicated by the suddenness of her changed outlook: this has all happened 'overnight'. She thinks of the poem as a lullaby, as if she could still bring peaceful sleep to the child, and explains in detail how its elements have been inspired – its 'tune' from the child's 'final cry', its 'reason' from the unreasonableness of the death ('your unreasoned end'), and so on.

Stanza 2
The second stanza switches from 'I' to 'We', as the poet considers the responsibilities of those who should have looked after the child. The protected, nurtured world of the child is evoked – rhymes and stories and cuddly animals – but these images are undercut by failure: 'We who should have known' how to keep the child safe and secure have failed. The child is dead. The word 'dead' resonates chillingly, isolated by a comma, as the final word of the stanza.

Notice that the second stanza and much of the third is a single sentence, which hinges on the final line of stanza 2: because 'we' did not teach 'you' while you were living, we must 'learn from you' now you are dead.

Stanza 3
The third stanza goes on to state what we must learn. The poem looks to the future and what must change in order to avoid the repetition of senseless deaths like this one. We must 'rebuild' our 'broken images' – our sense of values, perhaps – around the 'broken / Image' of the child's body. We must find 'a new language' – a political dialogue, perhaps – to replace the 'idle / Talk' that led to the child's death.

> **'Careless talk costs lives'**
>
> **The phrase 'whose life our idle / Talk has cost' recalls a British propaganda campaign from the Second World War, which consisted of a series of posters warning against saying things that could be overheard by spies, all with the catchphrase 'Careless talk costs lives'. This was taken up again during the Troubles, when the phrase often appeared on posters or scrawled on walls to intimidate people into being silent about what they knew.**

The poem then returns to the idea of the lullaby. The poet asks (prays?) that, in death, the child may 'Sleep' in a world that has been 'woken' by the shock of that death ('final sleep'), and changed by it. It is a note of desperate hope to set against the grief and outrage at the child's death.

Themes and imagery

The fact that this poem was first published in a national newspaper in response to an event of national importance indicates something very important – and very unusual in Boland's poetry – that **it is a public poem**, addressed to the nation as a whole. The 'We' (line 7) of the poem includes not just parents, but the whole country. The child is the child of 'our time' – the world that 'we' made, the world the child was born into and that failed them. Alongside its tenderness, the poem expresses outrage at the innocent child's death. In that sense **it is a political poem**, but it offers no analysis of the politics that underlie the situation. For example, it does not consider its causes or, in any practical way, its possible solutions. **The poem is a challenge to its readers to respond to what has happened, and to act, in some way, together.**

The emotional impact of the poem comes very largely from its **imagery of childhood**, which we can all relate to and which feels very precious: the nursery rhymes and stories, the cradle and the cuddly toys. These all evoke the innocence of childhood, and so bring home what has been violated in the horror of this child's death.

There are other threads of imagery running through the poem. One central one is the **imagery of teaching and learning**. The adult world has failed the child by not being able to 'instruct' (line 7) the child; instead it 'must learn from you' (line 12) to make a better world, just as the poet has been 'taught' (line 2) to make this poem.

Linked to that is another thread of imagery to do with **music and language**. A lullaby is made out of both words and music; it has 'tune' (line 4) and 'rhythm' (line 5) to set against the 'final cry' (line 3) of the child and the 'discord' (line 5) of their murder. The lullaby is connected in turn to images of **sleep and waking**, both as a natural rhythm in a child's day – 'rhymes for your waking, rhythms for your sleep' (line 8) – and in the metaphorical sense of the final line: 'Sleep in a world your final sleep has woken.'

> **Second thoughts**
>
> Just two weeks after 'Child of Our Time' was published in the *Irish Times*, Boland wrote an essay for the same newspaper in which she rejected the easy, domestic sense of Irish identity and cultural unity that her poem implied: 'there is … no unity whatsoever in this culture of ours. And even more important, I recognise there is no need whatsoever for such unity.'

Finally, it is worth thinking about one other word that has to do with language: 'idiom' in line 11. An idiom is the particular form of a language that a certain group uses, something that identifies you as part of that group. Here, perhaps, the word also suggests the shared values by which a people live. It is this **sense of shared identity** that underpins this poem and that Boland appeals to in writing this poem.

Form and language

'Child of Our Time' is written in **three stanzas of six lines each (sestets)**, where every line rhymes, although there is **no set rhyme scheme**. (The first stanza rhymes *abacbc*. Can you work out the rhyme schemes for the remaining stanzas?) This tight form is matched by a **tightly controlled syntax** (the way the sentences are constructed) that uses parallel phrases and antithesis to bring out the contrasts and paradoxes at the heart of this poem.

The **antithesis** is there in the first stanza, where 'reason' is set against the child's 'unreasoned end' (line 4); in the placement of 'living' and 'dead' in line 12; and it is central to the third stanza, where 'our broken images' contrast with 'your broken / Image' (lines 13–15), and in the play on sleep and waking in the final line. The careful balance of **parallel phrases** reinforces the contrasts in lines 5–6: 'Its rhythm … / Its motive … '. In the second stanza the peaceful image of childhood is reinforced by the lulling movement of matching pairs of phrases: 'rhymes for your waking, rhythms for your sleep'; 'Tales to distract, legends to protect' (lines 8, 10).

You could see this urge to give the poem a clear form and a strong structure as something to set against the overwhelming grief that it is expressing, but also, perhaps, as part of the poet's desire to salvage something poetic from this terrible event, and in a small way to 'rebuild' the nation's 'broken images' (line 13).

Eavan Boland

Exam-Style Questions

Understanding the poem

1. 'Yesterday I knew no lullaby' begins the poem. What has changed since yesterday?
2. How is the world of childhood innocence evoked in the second stanza?
3. What lessons must be learned from the death of the child, according to the poet?
4. In your view, is 'Child of Our Time' an angry poem? Is it a hopeful poem? Is it a regretful poem? Is there another word you would choose? Explain your answers.
5. Boland says that people should 'find for your sake whose life our idle / Talk has cost, a new language' (lines 15–16). What, do you think, is she saying in these lines?

Thinking about the poem

1. Why, in your view, is the child a 'Child of Our Time'?
2. In what ways can this poem be said to be a lullaby? Explain, with reference to the text.
3. A political poem usually seeks to bring about change. Is 'Child of Our Time' an effective political poem, in your view?
4. Comment on the use of either rhyme or antithesis in this poem.

Imagining

1. Imagine you are a young person who has had to leave home because of war. Write a short account of your experiences and feelings.
2. Write out the speech you would make for or against the view that violence can never be justified. Share your views with someone from the group who holds the opposing viewpoint.

SNAPSHOT

- Elegy – poem of lament on someone's death
- Expresses a range of feelings from grief to hope
- Tender images of childhood innocence
- Imagery of language and music
- Imagery of teaching and learning
- Use of antithesis and parallel phrases
- Political poem that does not take sides
- Sense of outrage alongside grief

HIGHER LEVEL

Before you read

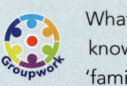 What do you know about 'famine roads'? Share your knowledge in groups or as a class.

The Famine Road

inherently lazy

'Idle as trout in light Colonel Jones,
these Irish, give them no coins at all; their bones
need toil, their characters no less.' Trevelyan's → *arrogant & ignorant*
seal blooded the deal table. The Relief
Committee deliberated: 'Might it be safe,   5
Colonel, to give them roads, roads to force
from nowhere, going nowhere of course?'

    'one out of every ten and then
    another third of those again
    women – in a case like yours.'   10

Sick, directionless they worked; fork, stick
were iron years away; after all could
they not blood their knuckles on rock, suck
April hailstones for water and for food?
Why for that, cunning as housewives, each eyed –   15
as if at a corner butcher – the other's buttock. → *cannibalism – dehumanises them*
                                            – *desperation highlighted*

    'anything may have caused it, spores,
    a childhood accident; one sees
    day after day these mysteries.'

Dusk: they will work tomorrow without him.   20
They know it and walk clear; he has become
a typhoid pariah, his blood tainted, although
he shares it with some there. No more than snow
attends its own flakes where they settle
and melt, will they pray by his death rattle.   25

    'You never will, never you know
    but take it well woman, grow
    your garden, keep house, good-bye.'

'It has gone better than we expected, Lord
Trevelyan, sedition, idleness, cured   30
in one; from parish to parish, field to field,
the wretches work till they are quite worn,
then fester by their work; we march the corn
to the ships in peace; this Tuesday I saw bones
out of my carriage window, your servant Jones.'   35

    'Barren, never to know the load
    of his child in you, what is your body
    now if not a famine road?'

Glossary

1	*trout in light*:	on sunny days, trout tend to get sleepy and inactive
4	*seal*:	wax (usually red) used to close (seal) letters
4	*deal*:	cheap pinewood
17	*spores*:	minute germs or seeds
22	*typhoid*:	deadly disease caught from bacteria in water or food
22	*pariah*:	social outcast
22	*tainted*:	contaminated
25	*death rattle*:	harsh breathing sound made by a dying person
30	*sedition*:	rebellion against authority
33	*fester*:	rot
36	*Barren*:	infertile; unable to have children

Eavan Boland

Guidelines

'The Famine Road' was included in the collection *The War Horse* (1975). It is set against the background of the Great Famine of the 1840s, when over one million people died of starvation and the diseases that accompanied it, and another million emigrated. The poem refers to a Relief Committee (lines 4–5). These committees, which consisted of magistrates, clergy and other prominent citizens, were established by Sir Charles Trevelyan (line 3), Lord of the Treasury, who was responsible for the British government's response to the crisis in Ireland. Through these committees, he organised schemes for famine relief, one of which was building roads in order to give employment to the starving so they could buy food. These so-called famine roads often had no practical purpose and went nowhere. They can still be seen in many places in the west of Ireland. Colonel Jones (line 1) was a British army officer and chairman of the Board of Works, who oversaw the building schemes.

Commentary

Lines 1–7
The first stanza concerns the plans of the Relief Committee, and the first voice we hear is that of Trevelyan in an informal letter of advice to Jones, which is scornful of the laziness of 'these Irish'. The letter's red seal is like blood on the table, foreshadowing the death and suffering that followed from its advice. The second voice we hear is that of a committee member, who has a suggestion: get them to build roads 'going nowhere'.

Lines 8–10
In the three lines of italics that follow we seem to be picking up on a speech mid-sentence, as indicated by the lack of a capital letter at the start. It is hard to know exactly what is being discussed, but the speaker is talking statistics and speaking about women. The reference to 'a case like yours' suggests that it might be a doctor talking to a patient.

Lines 11–16
The focus shifts to what the committee's plans have brought about: the building of a famine road. Although there are no quotation marks here, the description is clipped and cynical, asking cruelly why the workers cannot get their hands bloody if they do not have decent tools, and why they cannot survive by sucking hailstones. The labourers may be ill, but they are called 'cunning as housewives' and accused of looking at each other's bodies as potential meals ('each eyed – / as if at a corner butcher – the other's buttock'). The detachment and contemptuous tone suggest an English observer, an impression that is strengthened by the use of the phrase 'Why for that' (as far as that is concerned), which suggests a rather formal English way of speaking.

Lines 17–19
The voice from the previous tercet (three-line stanza) continues, and it is apparent that the speaker is a doctor talking about some sort of medical problem, whose cause is not clear. The mention of 'spores' connects this part of the poem with the famine, as the fungus that caused potato blight was transmitted by spores.

Lines 20–25
The clipped, cold description of the road-building project picks up again, now focusing on a man who is dying of typhoid – one of the diseases that killed many people during the famine. The speaker paints a bleak picture:

the man is a 'pariah', shunned by the others; he will receive no comfort or care, even though some of the men are related to him ('he shares [his blood] with some there'). They will not even pray with him as he dies.

Lines 26–28

The doctor's voice continues. It is clear that he is male, addressing his patient simply as 'woman', and telling her there is no hope. Though it is not yet clear what the problem is, he shows no compassion, and dismisses her brusquely: 'grow / your garden, keep house, good-bye.'

Lines 29–35

In this stanza we hear the voice of Colonel Jones, mentioned in line 1, as he reports back to Trevelyan on the success (as far as he is concerned) of the road-building project. It has kept the men too busy for rebellion ('sedition'), and he regards it as a success that they work so hard that they can do no more than 'fester by their work'. They become like the bones he sees from his carriage, where he is separated physically as well as emotionally from the lives and deaths of those he is observing. Meanwhile, the corn from the harvest is brought 'to the ships in peace', and transported away from those who need it most, as happened widely during the famine.

Lines 36–38

We hear a different speaker in this final tercet – perhaps the woman talking to herself, perhaps a friend talking to her. Her problem is now made clear: she is 'Barren'. And now the speaker makes the connection with the subject of the main part of the poem in describing her body as 'a famine road' – something useless – because it cannot bear children.

Themes and imagery

A glance at the poem on the page – the short lines in italics between longer stanzas with longer lines – is enough to tell you that the poem consists of **two contrasting elements**. One part deals with the famine of 1847 and the construction of the 'famine roads', the other with a woman who cannot have children. Putting these two elements side by side means that we are asked to **look for the connections between them**.

What, then, do the two elements share? At the simplest level, a comparison is made in the final lines of the poem between the woman's body and the famine road: both are, in their different ways, useless. But there are other levels of similarity. The Irish are observed, discussed, viewed with contempt and dehumanised. The woman is treated offhandedly, dismissively, without compassion. In both cases their experience is regarded as unimportant; it is marginalised. Both the Irish working on the famine road and the barren woman are humiliated and defeated. Neither the Irish nor the woman are given a voice.

> **Boland on her Irishness**
>
> 'Apart from the fact that it connects me with a past, I find it a perspective on my womanhood as well. Womanhood and Irishness are metaphors for one another. There are resonances of humiliation, oppression and silence in both of them and I think you can understand one better by experiencing the other.'

Linking a public disaster with a private grief is daring, and some have questioned whether the analogy is a successful or a justifiable one. Is a woman's childlessness on a par with a great national tragedy? Is the body of a woman really completely useless if it fails to bear a child?

The poem's imagery is dominated by the two central elements of the **famine road** and the **infertile woman**, but there are other

Eavan Boland

aspects worth noting. For example, the way in which the nameless Irish are presented, not as whole people, but as **body parts** (their bones, their knuckles, their buttocks), is one of the techniques that dehumanises them. Notice, too, the way in which **blood** runs through the poem, from Trevelyan's seal to the workers' bloody knuckles to the sick man's 'tainted' blood, suggesting death, but also, perhaps, hinting at the woman's (unmentioned, useless, maybe absent) menstrual blood. Hail in the second main stanza and snow in the third set the emotional as well as the physical **weather** for the poem.

Form and language

It can be hard to find your bearings in reading 'The Famine Road'; we hear **many voices**, none of them sympathetic, and we have to piece together the stories it tells from **fragments**. In contrast, **the poem is tightly bound together by rhyme**. Every line rhymes with at least one other, though some of the rhymes are weak, such as 'him' and 'become' (lines 20, 21), and others strong, such as 'Jones' and 'bones'. The **sense of symmetry and control** is increased by the fact that this rhyming pair both begins and ends the historical element of the poem.

There is a great deal of **internal rhyme** as well, including 'Sick' and 'stick' in line 11. Notice how the effect of this rhyme is extended through the hard 'k' consonants that occur through the opening part of that stanza, in 'worked', 'fork', 'could', 'knuckles', 'rock' and 'suck' (lines 11–13).

The tercets are also linked together by rhyme. Not only do lines 8 and 9 rhyme, but 'yours' in line 10 rhymes with 'spores' in line 17, bridging the gap across stanzas, as if one poem had been interrupted by another. Similarly, 'good-bye' (line 28) makes a half-rhyme with 'body' (line 37), while the final strong rhyme of 'road' with 'load' adds to the feeling that this **final image ties together the poem**, making its theme apparent and bringing us back at last to the title.

The syntax is often condensed and terse in short phrases reduced to the bare bones, such as 'Sick, directionless they worked' (line 11). This style gives the language a flavour that matches the cold detachment of the voices and sometimes suggests the clipped phrasing often associated with upper-class English accents, especially military ones. The **harsh, disjointed effect** is reinforced by the line breaks, which often occur in the middle of a phrase, e.g. 'fork, stick / were iron years away ... could / they not ... suck / April hailstones ... ' (lines 11–14).

The combination of the tight rhyme scheme and uncomfortable, angular phrasing has a distancing effect that suits the **cold detachment** of all the speakers in the poem.

Questions

1	What do we learn about the attitudes of the governing classes to the victims of the famine in the first stanza?
2	What, do you think, might the figures mentioned in the italicised lines 8–10 refer to?
3	What do we learn from lines 11–16 about the conditions of those employed in building the roads?
4	Who, do you think, is speaking in the final tercet (lines 36–38)? Explain your answer.
5	How does the poem succeed in indicating the gradual dehumanisation of the famine victims? Look in particular at the images of body parts.
6	Do you think the poem succeeds in conveying the horror of the famine? Explain your answer.
7	In what ways do the tones of the different speakers resemble one another?
8	Do you find the analogy between the experience of the famine and the childless woman successful? Explain your view.
9	Comment on the poem's use of rhyme and other sound effects (e.g. alliteration, assonance).
10	You have been asked to compile an anthology of poems on the theme of 'women's experiences'. In groups or pairs, discuss whether or not you would include 'The Famine Road'.
11	Imagine you are a member of the Relief Committee set up to deal with the Irish famine. Write three entries from your diary in which you agree or disagree with the attitudes of Colonel Jones, as expressed in the poem.

Eavan Boland

The Black Lace Fan My Mother Gave Me

It was the first gift he ever gave her,
buying it for five francs in the Galeries
in pre-war Paris. It was stifling.
A starless drought made the nights stormy.

They stayed in the city for the summer. 5
They met in cafés. She was always early.
He was late. That evening he was later.
They wrapped the fan. He looked at his watch.

She looked down the Boulevard des Capucines.
She ordered more coffee. She stood up. 10
The streets were emptying. The heat was killing.
She thought the distance smelled of rain and lightning.

These are wild roses, appliquéd on silk by hand,
darkly picked, stitched boldly, quickly.
The rest is tortoiseshell and has the reticent, 15
clear patience of its element. It is

a worn-out, underwater bullion and it keeps,
even now, an inference of its violation.
The lace is overcast as if the weather
it opened for and offset had entered it. 20

The past is an empty café terrace.
An airless dusk before thunder. A man running.
And no way now to know what happened then –
none at all – unless, of course, you improvise:

The blackbird on this first sultry morning, 25
in summer, finding buds, worms, fruit,
feels the heat. Suddenly she puts out her wing –
the whole, full, flirtatious span of it.

Before you read

Objects can often trigger memories and emotions. Discuss with a partner how this can happen and what objects have special meanings for you.

Glossary

2	*Galeries*:	French department store
13	*appliquéd*:	one piece of fabric stitched onto another
15	*reticent*:	uncommunicative, unwilling to speak
17	*bullion*:	gold or silver treasure
20	*offset*:	protected against
25	*sultry*:	hot and humid
28	*span*:	the full spread of the outstretched wing

HIGHER LEVEL

Guidelines

'The Black Lace Fan My Mother Gave Me' is one of a series of poems called 'Object Lessons', part of the collection *Outside History*, published in 1990. It was inspired by a fan that Boland's father had given to her mother when they first met in Paris in the 1930s.

Commentary

Lines 1–12
The poem starts by telling the story of the black lace fan, perhaps a tale that Boland had heard from her parents. The scene is quickly set and the story is told in short, simple sentences. It works rather like a film: the first two stanzas focus on him buying the fan, running late, checking his watch; the next stanza cuts to her, waiting anxiously. The tension is increased by the weather – hot, dry, dark, with the threat of storms. The atmosphere is uneasy, even ominous.

Lines 13–20
The focus of the poem suddenly shifts to a close-up of the fan, leaving the story of that Paris evening unresolved. The poet examines the fan that she seems to have in front of her now, as if to understand its significance. She sees the embroidered roses, 'stitched boldly', hinting at the passion that the lover's gift was meant to symbolise, but perhaps there is also a troubling implication in their being 'darkly picked'.

Eavan Boland

Now she looks at the tortoiseshell, which is 'reticent', suggesting something unspoken or hidden. Looking – or imagining – more deeply, she sees something unsettling: it keeps 'an inference of its violation'. The tortoise from which it came was a living creature, and had to die (be violated) before it could be used to make a fan. She sees the lace on the fan as 'overcast', as if it still carries in itself the oppressive weather of that far-off Paris day.

Lines 21–28

The poet returns to thinking about that day, and specifically about the moments before the meeting happened – the café terrace is empty, as if the woman has already gone, but the man is still running to meet her. We know, of course, that the meeting eventually happened: the fan is the evidence of that. But, in a deeper sense, there is 'no way now to know what happened then'. How can we ever know the truths of other people's lives, especially the love lives of our parents?

Boland imagines it – she improvises – by means of an image: the blackbird spreading its wing. Perhaps it was something she saw in her suburban Dublin garden when she was writing the poem; this is not the evening in Paris, but the first morning of summer, though the weather is 'sultry' on both occasions. Or perhaps the idea came simply from the black fan, which could easily suggest the image of the spread wing. The image is sensual, sexual ('flirtatious') and specifically female: the blackbird is 'she'. It is an indirect way of imagining the sexuality of her parents' relationship.

Themes and imagery

Discussing this poem in her prose book *Object Lessons*, Boland commented on the 'erotic object' in poetry. Conventionally, an erotic object is something given by a man to a woman as a love token, or written about by a man in a love poem to express his desire. She was interested in the object in a different way, and she calls this a 'back-to-front love poem', where **the focus is on the object** rather than on the love of which it is usually a token.

She uses the black lace fan, the central image of the poem, as a way of thinking about male–female relationships in general and about her parents' relationship in particular. She looks not only at the decorated lace, with its embroidery of conventional love symbols in the wild roses, but also at the tortoiseshell that suggests to her something 'reticent' (line 15), unspeaking, but also something violated.

> 'I was aware of my own sense of the traditional erotic object – in this case the black fan – as a sign not for triumph and acquisition but for suffering itself.'
>
> Eavan Boland, *Object Lessons*

It is important to be clear that **there is no single interpretation of the fan's meaning**. The fact that she associates the 'overcast' (line 19) lace with the stormy, ominous weather on that long-ago Paris evening may suggest something about her parents' stormy relationship, but just as there is 'no way' (line 23) for her to know the truth, so we as readers can only pick up on **impressions and associations**.

This is especially true of the striking image of the blackbird with which the poem finishes. It is full of detail – the heat; the buds, worms and fruit the bird finds; the spread wing. We know the poet is thinking about her parents' relationship, so do the buds and fruit suggest fertility – the children the couple went on to have, perhaps? Do the worms imply decay? The word 'flirtatious' (line 28) certainly hints at the sexuality of the relationship. But the image is not commented on, and we are free to understand it in our own way.

HIGHER LEVEL

Form and language

The poem is written in **quatrains (four-line stanzas)**, in which there are occasional hints of rhyme (e.g. 'Galeries' and 'stormy' in the first stanza, 'morning' and 'wing' in the last) but no regular use of it. It is as if the poem is always on the verge of the sense of certainty or comfort that rhyme can give, but never quite achieves it. It is part of **the poem's unsettling effect**.

The first part of the poem is written in short, very plain sentences that keep the underlying passions at a distance and add to the tension of the stormy night. The language becomes more metaphorical in the description of the fan. The syntax is more expansive, with the sentences becoming longer and richer in adjectives, e.g. 'reticent', 'clear', 'worn-out' (lines 15–17), and adverbs, e.g. 'darkly', 'boldly, quickly' (line 14). That expansiveness is present in the final stanza's description of the blackbird, especially in the final line, where the **long vowels** of 'whole' and 'full' and the **consonance of 'f', 'l'** and **'s'** sounds allow us to savour the sensuality of the image.

Questions

1	What sort of atmosphere is created in the first three stanzas? How is that atmosphere created?
2	What impression of the fan do you get from the metaphors and similes used to describe it in stanzas 4 and 5?
3	What, do you think, is conveyed by the metaphor in stanza 6, 'The past is an empty café terrace'? How is the idea developed in the rest of the poem?
4	Explore the image of the blackbird in the final stanza. What associations does it have, and what feelings does it stir? Look carefully at all the words used.
5	What sort of relationship might Boland's parents have had? How might the fan reflect this?
6	What, in your view, is the real subject of the poem? Is it: ■ The mystery of human relationships ■ The workings of memory ■ The emotional power of objects If none of these, explain what you think the poem is about. Give reasons for your choice.
7	Comment on the importance of the weather in the poem.
8	Does it matter to the poem that in reality a female blackbird is brown rather than black? Explain your thinking.
9	Comment on some aspect of the form or language of the poem – for example, rhyme, syntax (sentence structure), sound patterns.
10	In prose or verse, write a short passage about an object that is in some way precious to you or that brings back particular memories.

The Shadow Doll

This was sent to the bride-to-be in Victorian times, by her dressmaker. It consisted of a porcelain doll, under a dome of glass, modelling the proposed wedding dress.

They stitched blooms from ivory tulle
to hem the oyster gleam of the veil.
They made hoops for the crinoline.

Now, in summary and neatly sewn –
a porcelain bride in an airless glamour – 5
the shadow doll survives its occasion.

Under glass, under wraps, it stays
even now, after all, discreet about
visits, fevers, quickenings and lusts

and just how, when she looked at 10
the shell-tone spray of seed pearls,
the bisque features, she could see herself

inside it all, holding less than real
stephanotis, rose petals, never feeling
satin rise and fall with the vows 15

I kept repeating on the night before –
astray among the cards and wedding gifts –
the coffee pots and the clocks and

the battered tan case full of cotton
lace and tissue-paper, pressing down, then 20
pressing down again. And then, locks.

Eavan Boland

Before you read

Read the note under the title and look at the picture of a doll on page 87 before reading the poem. In groups, discuss the thoughts or feelings the information and the image give you.

Glossary

1	*tulle*: fine silk netting	
3	*crinoline*: petticoat stiffened with hoops	
5	*glamour*: romantic attractiveness; also magic spell	
9	*quickenings*: moment in pregnancy when the baby's movements are first felt by the mother	
12	*bisque*: unglazed white porcelain	
14	*stephanotis*: white flower, often used in wedding bouquets	

Guidelines

'The Shadow Doll' is another poem in the sequence 'Object Lessons' from the collection *Outside History* (1990). As with 'The Black Lace Fan My Mother Gave Me', the poet contemplates an object in order to understand what it can tell of lives that are usually forgotten by history. In this case the object is a shadow doll, whose function – to model the wedding dress for the bride-to-be – is explained in the author's note at the start of the poem.

Commentary

Stanzas 1 and 2
The poem starts with 'They' – the anonymous workers, presumably women, who worked for the dressmaker – and the first stanza focuses on how they made the doll's dress, stitching and hemming and making hoops to stiffen the crinoline petticoats. The second stanza presents the finished object, the shadow doll that 'survives its occasion' because although the wedding for which it was made took place long ago, it still exists.

It is important to pay attention to the exact words used and to be open to their various associations: 'stitched' might suggest the idea of stitching someone up in a trap; 'hoops' are also obstacles that people are made to jump through; 'hem' might make you think of being hemmed in somewhere and unable to escape. This sense of restriction and containment is strengthened by the image of the doll imprisoned under its glass dome in 'airless glamour': while 'airless' suggests suffocation, 'glamour' can mean a magic spell. It is as if the doll is a figure from a fairy tale, turned into a toy by a witch's spell – although there is no likelihood here of a handsome prince coming along to break it.

Stanza 3
The focus now is on 'it' – the doll. It is doubly covered, 'Under glass' and 'under wraps', the latter phrase applying to the layers of clothing, but also suggesting secrecy (you keep things under wraps if you want to hide them). The doll may model a bride's dress, but it stays 'discreet', silent and secretive about 'visits, fevers, quickenings and lusts' – words that suggest sex, pregnancy and childbirth. Such areas of the female experience of marriage are not often spoken of in poetry.

Stanzas 4 and 5
Although it is the same sentence that started at line 7, the subject switches now to 'she', the Victorian bride. Boland imagines her looking at the doll and its hard, pale surfaces and seeing herself 'inside it all', as if the lifeless doll is a mirror image of her and reflects her own feelings. She seems 'less than real', like the flowers she will hold at her wedding, not breathing deeply with emotion to make the satin of her dress 'rise and fall'.

Stanzas 6 and 7
Suddenly, and still within the same long sentence, the subject becomes 'I' and the scene switches to the night before the poet's own wedding. Her experience has a lot in common with that of the Victorian bride's: she is surrounded by objects – the cards and gifts, coffee pots and clocks – and seems somewhat bewildered, 'astray among the cards'. The final object, the 'battered tan case full of cotton / lace and tissue-paper' is one that could have come straight from the Victorian era – part of the traditional trousseau of clothes and linens collected by a bride for her new life after her wedding. The image of 'pressing down' resonates with the other

images of restraint, suppression and suffocation throughout the poem, and the brief, almost brutal, final sentence, 'And then, locks', suggests both secrecy and imprisonment. Thus, the final stanza makes all the poem's images of constraint immediate and present, no longer diluted by the distance of history.

Themes and imagery

The main theme of the poem is **the position of women in marriage**. Marriage can mean silence, restriction and submission, but the poem is not really concerned with the mistreatment of women (and there is no male figure in the poem). Rather, it is about what is missing in our perception of women. The shadow doll presents an **image of femininity** that is tidied up, artificial and lifeless; it is silent about the experiences and desires of the real flesh-and-blood woman. It is a symbol of the unexpressed lives of women in the past, but also suggests that little has changed.

Boland wrote that when she started out as a poet, 'I couldn't find my life in poetry'. One of her central concerns as a woman poet was to give voice to the lives, including her suburban domestic one, she felt were not represented in poetry. It is an idea that is particularly important in *Outside History*, the volume that includes several of the poems on your course.

The shadow doll is, of course, the central image of the poem. As well as its associations with constraint, secrecy and suffocation, notice how its **artificiality and lifelessness** are emphasised by all the shades of off-white that are mentioned in describing it: 'ivory', 'oyster', 'shell-tone', 'bisque', even the white flowers of the stephanotis. What other qualities of the doll are important in how you understand it?

Another striking image is that of pressing down and locking the suitcase. What, do you think, does that represent?

Form and language

'The Shadow Doll' is written in **tercets (three-line stanzas)**. There is no regular rhyme or metre, but the lines are of fairly even length, between eight and eleven syllables each. To begin with, the syntax of the poem matches the tercets, and the first two stanzas end with full stops. After that, there is not only enjambment, but the long sentence that comprises most of the rest of the poem also leaps over the stanza breaks, e.g. 'the vows // I kept repeating' (lines 15–16), just as the poet's imagination leaps from the doll to the Victorian bride to herself, making connections.

The language of the poem is precise; one has the feeling that **words have been chosen carefully** for their associations. Although there is a speaker who brings herself into the poem as 'I', the tone is not really

HIGHER LEVEL

conversational. The short phrases in the third stanza, e.g. 'even now, after all, discreet … ' (line 8), have a tentativeness about them, reinforcing the impression of someone who is being careful to say exactly what she means.

There is no showy word music, alliteration or assonance, which means that the few effects the poet uses stand out. The repetition of 'pressing down', especially with the pause created by the line break after 'then' (line 20), underlines the one moment of physical effort in the poem, and the final monosyllabic 'locks', with its hint of onomatopoeia, gives a rather **sinister quality to the end of the poem**.

Questions

1	Who are 'They' in stanza 1?
2	What characteristics of the doll are emphasised in the poem's title and in the first two stanzas?
3	Who is 'she' in stanza 4?
4	What aspects of the Victorian bride's experience does the doll reflect in stanzas 3–5?
5	How would you define the tone of this poem? Is it angry? Regretful? Pessimistic? Accepting? Perhaps you would suggest another term. Give reasons for your choice.
6	Explore the language used to describe the doll in stanzas 2 and 3. Are the implications suggested positive or negative, in your view?
7	Why, do you think, does the poet refer to her own marriage in the last two stanzas?
8	Choose two images that you found particularly interesting from the poem and say why you found them so.
9	Compare 'The Shadow Doll' with 'The Black Lace Fan My Mother Gave Me' in terms of theme and technique. Which poem do you prefer? Why?
10	You wish to include this poem in a short talk entitled 'Introducing Eavan Boland'. Write out the talk you would give.
11	In small groups, discuss the ways in which you think marriage has changed (or not) in modern times and report your opinions to the class.
12	Suggest an alternative title for the poem.

Eavan Boland

White Hawthorn in the West of Ireland

I drove West
in the season between seasons.
I left behind suburban gardens.
Lawnmowers. Small talk.

Under low skies, past splashes of coltsfoot,   5
I assumed
the hard shyness of Atlantic light
and the superstitious aura of hawthorn.

All I wanted then was to fill my arms with
sharp flowers,   10
to seem, from a distance, to be part of
that ivory, downhill rush. But I knew,

I had always known
the custom was
not to touch hawthorn.   15
Not to bring it indoors for the sake of

the luck
such constraint would forfeit –
a child might die, perhaps, or an unexplained
fever speckle heifers. So I left it   20

stirring on those hills
with a fluency
only water has. And, like water, able
to re-define land. And free to seem to be –

for anglers,   25
and for travellers astray in
the unmarked lights of a May dusk –
the only language spoken in those parts.

Before you read

In pairs or small groups, share the superstitions that you know. Are any of them connected with plants? Are any of them particular to Ireland, do you think?

Glossary

Title	*Hawthorn*:	a shrub or small tree that produces a mass of small white flowers in May and early June; often used in hedges, but grows wild throughout Ireland; many superstitious beliefs are connected with it
5	*coltsfoot*:	a yellow flower that resembles the dandelion
6	*assumed*:	took on (like a disguise)
20	*heifers*:	young cows that have not yet had a calf

HIGHER LEVEL

Guidelines

This poem is part of a sequence called 'Outside History', part two of the collection of the same name, published in 1990.

Commentary

Lines 1–4
The poem starts with a journey: 'I drove West'. It is a journey away from ordinary suburban life, signified by 'Lawnmowers. Small talk.' Notice the capital letter on 'West', which would not be used if she was simply going in a westerly direction; 'West' with a capital implies 'the West' – not just another part of Ireland, but a very different place. The fact that the journey happens in a 'season between seasons' adds to the sense of its mysterious significance.

Lines 5–12
Arriving in the West, it is as if the speaker wants to become part of that world – the light that can change so quickly near the Atlantic coast and the flowering hawthorn with all its 'superstitious' associations. The key word is 'assumed', which has the meaning here of taking something on (like a disguise) or even taking something into yourself. That idea is explored further in the next stanza, where she expresses her joyful desire to become immersed in the hawthorn – not just to fill her arms with the flowers, but 'to be part of / that ivory, downhill rush'.

Lines 12–20
The excited rush towards the end of the third stanza is arrested with a 'But', and a contrary impulse is felt, one of caution and superstition. The hawthorn is a sacred bush in folk traditions, and, as is often the way with such things, 'the luck' can cut both ways. In folklore it is unlucky to cut it and, especially, to 'bring it indoors'. She

remembers the stories: 'a child might die' or heifers might get a fever. It is an odd pair of superstitions – one deadly serious, the other faintly comic – as if these are things she has heard but not really understood. Nevertheless, she cannot ignore the threat, and leaves the hawthorn alone.

Lines 21–28

The sixth stanza paints a magical picture of the hawthorn 'stirring' on the hills, comparing it with water and concentrating on its power to transform: it is 'able / to re-define land'. The poet in turn redefines the hawthorn. She imagines an angler or a traveller (like herself, perhaps) in the half-light of dusk being guided by the white flowers of the hawthorn, as if they could speak – as if the hawthorn itself was 'the only language spoken in these parts'. It is a tentative insight, something that might only 'seem to be' the case, but it is a leap of the imagination that has the same exhilarating, transformative power as the hawthorn has on the landscape.

Themes

The sequence 'Outside History', from which this poem comes, is concerned with history, especially Irish history, and what is left out of it. It also looks at myths, and how human beings create them. Through mythological and historical stories we create meaning and lay a claim to the subject of those stories.

> **Myth**
>
> 'myth is the wound we leave in the time we have'
>
> Boland, 'The Making of an Irish Goddess'

There is no simple, single way to interpret this poem, but one way of understanding it might be to think of both the hawthorn and the Irish folk tradition that mythologises it as being **outside the mainstream of history**. This poem gives them a voice.

Another way of looking at the poem is through **the tension between the superstitious myths** that human culture has built around the hawthorn **and the natural object itself**, beyond the reach of human interpretation. The role of the poet in the poem is crucial. Just as folklore appropriates the hawthorn with its superstitious beliefs, so she, in journeying west, 'assumed … / the superstitious aura of the hawthorn' (lines 6–8). She wants to see herself as part of the mythic landscape of the West. But to 'assume' can be dangerous; assumptions are sometimes false assumptions. Perhaps her desire to pick the flowers and become one with them is just as distorting, in its way, as the common superstitions. In the end, her choice is to leave the hawthorn alone and to try to see the power it has in itself, changing the landscape like water. It is not just a thing to be spoken about in poetry or folklore, it is also 'free to seem to be' (line 24), to those like the angler or traveller 'astray' (line 26) among it, a language in itself – 'the only language spoken in those parts' (line 28).

> **Hawthorn as language**
>
> **Notice how the image of the hawthorn as a language picks up on 'fluency' (line 22) – a language can be spoken fluently – and 're-define' (line 24), terms which both have to do with language.**

Imagery

The 'suburban gardens' (line 3) from which the speaker starts, represented by 'Lawnmowers. Small talk' (line 4), are contrasted with the West with its 'Atlantic light' (line 7), and above all with the central image of the hawthorn. The **hawthorn is compared to water** and is given a life of its own, 'stirring' (line 21) as if it could move and even rushing 'downhill' (line 12). Notice, too, that the poet's experience of hawthorn transforming the landscape takes place at an in-between time of year – 'the season between seasons' (line 2), and also an in-between time of day – 'dusk' (see line 27). Why, do you think, do so many of Boland's poems take place at dusk?

Form and language

The poem is written in **unrhymed four-line stanzas** with varying line lengths. This flexibility allows Boland to move from the rather abrupt end-stopped lines of the first stanza to the sense of freedom created by the run-on lines that describe the hawthorn (e.g. lines 9–12). The varied line lengths, and the sometimes jarring line breaks, also help to create a **sense of tentativeness and hesitancy** as she thinks about her response to the hawthorn: 'But I knew, // I had always known / the custom was / not to touch hawthorn' (lines 12–15). Short lines can also focus a particular thought or idea, as when the words 'the luck' are positioned on their own at the start of a stanza (line 17).

The voice of the poem is **intimate**, following the speaker's developing thoughts and imaginings. The language is generally conversational, but there is a strong sense of somebody choosing words carefully, tentatively, and preferring the exact word over the everyday. Think, for example, of the connotations of 'assumed' (line 6) or 'fluency' (line 22), both discussed above.

Questions

1	What sort of environment does the speaker leave behind? How does it contrast with the landscape of the West?
2	What desire does the speaker express in the third stanza? What obstacles does she encounter?
3	Explore the possibilities of meaning implied by the word 'luck' (line 17). What does it suggest about the power of the hawthorn?
4	Why does the speaker decide to leave the hawthorn outside?
5	How does the speaker's mood change as the poem progresses?
6	In what sense does the hawthorn seem to be 'the only language spoken in those parts' (line 28)?
7	Do you think the specific setting of the poem, the West of Ireland, is significant, or could the poem be set anywhere else?
8	Comment on the importance of the time of year and the time of day to this poem.
9	It has been said of Eavan Boland that, while she is a 'poet who works with concrete images', she is also a poet who is 'unafraid of thought'. Discuss this viewpoint with reference to the poem.
10	*Groupwork* — Your group wishes to make a short video based on this poem. Describe the atmosphere you would like to create, as well as the accompanying images and music you would use.
11	'Superstition and folklore are an important part of history.' Write a short paragraph in which you agree or disagree with this statement.

Eavan Boland

Before you read

What do you understand by the phrase 'outside history'? What things could be described as 'outside history'? Make a list, and share it in class.

Outside History

There are outsiders, always. These stars –
these iron inklings of an Irish January,
whose light happened

thousands of years before
our pain did: they are, they have always been   5
outside history.

They keep their distance. Under them remains
a place where you found
you were human, and

a landscape in which you know you are mortal.   10
And a time to choose between them.
I have chosen:

out of myth into history I move to be
part of that ordeal
whose darkness is   15

only now reaching me from those fields,
those rivers, those roads clotted as
firmaments with the dead.

How slowly they die
as we kneel beside them, whisper in their ear.   20
And we are too late. We are always too late.

Glossary

| 2 | *inklings*: hints, suggestions |
| 18 | *firmaments*: skies, heavens (including all the stars in them) |

Guidelines

> **Boland on *Outside History***
>
> 'I think a good few poems in the book are anchored in the conflict between the received version and the unofficial one. So much that matters, so much that is powerful and frail in human affairs seems to me, increasingly, to happen outside history: away from the texts and symmetries of an accepted expression. And, for that very reason, at great risk of being edited out of the final account.'

'Outside History' is the twelfth and final poem in the sequence of the same name from the collection *Outside History* (1990). This collection focuses on one of Boland's constant themes: the lives of those – often, but not always, women – who are not normally noticed in the official accounts, and so exist 'outside history'.

Commentary

Lines 1–6

The poem starts by considering the idea of the outsider: 'There are outsiders, always.' It goes on to think about the stars, and to set up the poem's key contrast between them and human suffering. The stars are 'outside history' because the light we see from them started its journey to us thousands of years ago, a huge distance in time and space from 'our pain'. Who does Boland mean by 'our'? The human race? Or does the fact that she has located the poem in 'an Irish January' imply that she is thinking mainly about Ireland?

Lines 7–11

Boland now focuses on the earthly realm 'Under' the stars, the 'place where you found / you were human' and the 'landscape in which you know you are mortal'. Who is meant by 'you' here? A particular person or people in general?

She also writes of a choice to be made: 'a time to choose between them'. It is not easy to be sure what this choice consists of. Is it choosing between the stars and Earth? Or between the 'place where you found / you were human' and 'a landscape in which you know you are mortal'? The syntax would suggest the latter. In that case, is a distinction being made between 'place' and 'landscape', or between being 'human' and being 'mortal'? Is one more general (any human in any place) and the other more specific (a particular mortal human in a particular landscape)?

Lines 12–18

Now the poem becomes defiantly personal and 'I' is used for the first time: 'I have chosen'. The plain statement, the colon and the stanza break after it all suggest that what follows will be important. The opposition now is between 'myth' and 'history', and the choice is plainly in favour of history. The strong verb 'move' shows positive intent.

The next five lines explain the nature of the choice. It is to be 'part of' the 'ordeal', the suffering, which recalls 'our pain' in line 5. That ordeal is seen as a 'darkness' – not an absence of light but a force in its own right, an inverse image of the starlight at the beginning. The darkness is imagined as reaching the speaker from far away, just as starlight does, and it comes from 'those fields, / those rivers, those roads', images that bring to mind the 'landscape' of line 10. And they are 'clotted' with 'the dead', just as the 'firmaments' – the heavens – are clotted with stars. Who are these dead? There is no simple answer, but the images may recall the famine, which is the subject of another poem in this sequence.

Eavan Boland

Lines 19–21

The final stanza offers another possibility from more recent Irish history. Boland has said that the image here of kneeling down to whisper in a dying person's ear was inspired by a photograph that appeared in all the newspapers in 1988. In Belfast, at a time in the Troubles when feelings were running even higher than usual, two off-duty British army corporals were driving in their car when they strayed into the middle of a republican funeral. They were attacked, stripped and killed. A brave priest came out and knelt beside them to administer the last rites; this was the image in the photograph. Of course, that is only the source of the image, and you do not have to know about it to understand the poem. Consider what this final stanza suggests to you.

Notice that 'I' has become 'we'. In one way, this is a consequence of the poet choosing to identify with a shared history. In another, she is including each individual reader in that 'we' and asking them to acknowledge their own share of that history. We as readers are put at the heart of the poem, a fact that makes the repetition in its final line – 'we are too late. We are always too late' – all the more agonising.

Themes

This poem is hard to pin down, and impossible to reduce to a single, simple interpretation. It is filled with haunting images and arresting ideas, but **much of its power comes from the fact that it retains an element of mystery**, and readers have to find their own meanings in the poem.

The poem can be read in the light of Boland's ideas on **the place of women in history and of women poets in the history of poetry**. The move 'out of myth into history' (line 13) can then be understood as the journey from women being the objects of men's poems to the authors of their own poetry. In Irish poetry especially, women have often had a mythic function, through figures such as Kathleen Ní Houlihan or Róisín Dubh, and one of Boland's lasting concerns has been to find a voice for women in their own right, in their own lives, in the mainstream of history, rather than as symbols. It has to be said, though, that there is no specific mention of gender in this poem. It can be thought of as being about engaging with history in a wider sense – not the history of rulers and treaties, but the history of individual suffering that results from it and is part of it. So much dies and is forgotten with each individual death; perhaps that is why 'We are always too late' (line 21).

> **Boland on Irish history**
>
> 'The Irish experience, certainly for the purposes of poetry, was only incidentally about action and resistance. At a far deeper level … it was about defeat. The coffin ships, the soup queues, those desperate villagers at the shoreline – these things had actually happened.'

Another theme to consider involves **landscape and belonging**. Boland spent much of her childhood living abroad – in London and New York – and has written of how, when she returned to Ireland, she always felt at a distance from her Irishness. This poem can be seen, in part, as her claiming her heritage. The poem is set in 'an Irish January' (line 2) and it is easy to associate the dead in the last two stanzas with images from Irish history, and to see the landscape of fields, rivers and roads as an Irish one. Seeing history as an 'ordeal' (line 14) and a 'darkness' (line 15) is an acknowledgement that much of the Irish story is one of **suffering and defeat**. The statement that this darkness is 'only now reaching me' (line 16) is perhaps the poet's admission of how long it took her to really understand that.

Imagery

Light and dark are important in the poem. On the one hand, there is the light of the stars, cold and distant; on the other, the darkness of history and death, which becomes deeply personal and intimate in the image of kneeling down and whispering in the dying person's ear.

Time and space are important too. The stars are hugely distant in space, and that distance is measured in time – the 'thousands of years' (line 4) it has taken the starlight to reach Earth. The darkness of history travels in time as well, but not in space; the fields, rivers and roads belong to the same 'landscape in which you know you are mortal' (line 10).

Form and language

'Outside History' is written in **unrhymed tercets** (three-line stanzas), with lines of varying length. The form may seem loose, but its existence enables Boland to use the line and stanza breaks to good effect, and to give special focus to particular words and phrases. For example, the key phrase 'outside history' (line 6) is given weight by being given a line to itself at the end of a stanza. In line 9 the word 'and' is isolated between a comma and a stanza break, creating a hesitancy and yet emphasising the fact that a choice has to be made. In contrast, the stanza break after 'I have chosen' (line 12) suggests the determination and importance of that choice.

There is very little in the way of alliteration or other word music in this poem, but **the final stanza builds a strong rhythm**, strengthened by the repetition in the final line, which carries the sense of loss and regret.

Eavan Boland

The language of the poem has a mixture of intimacy and control. The vocabulary is mostly plain, and the voice appears to be conversational, using 'you' and 'I' and 'we'. On the other hand, metaphorical phrases like 'iron inklings' (line 2) remind us that the words are chosen carefully by a poet who is awake to the nuances of meaning they carry, and who is also aware of her responsibilities as a poet. The speaker is not just talking about personal feelings, but her relationship with history and with time. When she says 'I have chosen' (line 12), there is no false modesty about the importance of that choice, and when she writes 'we are too late', that 'we' is more than just you and me; **she is speaking for all humanity**.

Questions

1. What point, do you think, is the poet making when she asserts that 'There are outsiders, always' (line 1)? How is it related to the images of the stars that follow?
2. Who, do you think, is the poet referring to in lines 8–9 when she says 'you found / you were human'? Explain your thinking.
3. What, in your opinion, is the choice referred to in line 11 ('a time to choose between them') a choice between?
4. What, do you think, is the difference between 'myth' and 'history'? Why would the poet choose 'history'?
5. History is referred to as an 'ordeal' in line 14 and is associated with 'darkness' in the following line. What do these words imply about history?
6. What is the effect of the change from 'I' to 'we' in the final stanza?
7. 'And we are too late. We are always too late' (line 21). What is the tone of this line, in your view? What is the effect of the repetition?
8. Do the setting in an 'Irish January' (line 2) and the images of death in the final lines make this a poem specifically about Irish history, or is it universal, or something in between? Explain your answer.
9. Comment on the poem's use of line and stanza breaks.
10. What, in your opinion, is the real subject of this poem? Explain your answer.
11. 'Outside History' and 'White Hawthorn in the West of Ireland' are part of a sequence of twelve poems. What do they have in common? Which of the two poems do you prefer, and why?
12. 'We are always too late.' Write your own poem or story using this phrase as the title.

HIGHER LEVEL

Before you read

Take a moment; stay quiet, listen, look. What is happening around you – what do you see, hear, smell, taste, touch at 'this moment'? And how do you feel about it? (There's no need to share your thoughts.)

This Moment

A neighbourhood.
At dusk.

Things are getting ready
to happen
out of sight.   5

Stars and moths.
And rinds slanting around fruit.

But not yet.

One tree is black.
One window is yellow as butter.   10

A woman leans down to catch a child
who has run into her arms
this moment.

Stars rise.
Moths flutter.   15

Apples sweeten in the dark.

Guidelines

'This Moment' is the first poem in the sequence 'Legends', the second part of the collection *In a Time of Violence* (1994). As the poem's title suggests, it captures a moment in time, a very ordinary moment in many ways, but one that is made radiant by the way it is depicted.

Commentary

The setting is an ordinary suburban neighbourhood. The time is dusk, an in-between time of half-light that soon passes. The information is given in the simplest possible, verbless, sentences.

The next three lines tell us something curious – not that things are happening or even starting to happen, but they are 'getting ready / to happen'. They are 'out of sight'. It is as if it is a play, and the 'Things' are waiting in the wings of the theatre for their moment to come on stage.

Lines 6–7 tell us what those 'Things' are, again in short, verbless sentences: stars, moths, fruit. Line 8 keeps up the suspense, telling us that the moment has not arrived: 'not yet,' The next two lines add details to the suspended scene, in vivid images of colour: the black tree in silhouette, and the yellow window reflecting the low evening sun. Boland's mother was a painter, and these feel almost like painted images.

The next three lines (11–13) are the heart of the poem: the woman catches the running child. They are, as line 13 states, 'this moment'.

The final three lines of the poem return to the 'Things' of lines 6–7, but now there is action, and there are verbs: the stars 'rise'; the moths 'flutter' and the apples 'sweeten'. It is as if they have been released from their frozen suspense by the action of 'this moment', and time has started up again. In theatrical terms, they have been given their cue, and now they are no longer 'out of sight' (line 5) in the wings, but on stage, doing what they were waiting to do.

Themes and imagery

The primary theme of 'This Moment' is the **preciousness of each moment**, even in a very ordinary, domestic setting. The poem implies that the workings of the natural world – stars, moths, fruit – depend on such moments, and the simple, vivid images of the poem make that moment luminous. The most striking of those images is 'One window is yellow as butter' (line 10), which has a sensuous glow that fills and colours the central moment of the poem.

The particular focus is on the mother and child, perhaps the most fundamental of all human relationships, but one which is found relatively rarely in poetry. In choosing this focus, **Boland is placing her life as a mother in a suburban neighbourhood at the centre of the poem**. This achieves one of her main aims in her poetry – to make the ordinary, domestic life she and so many others know a subject for poetry; to 'bless the ordinary, sanctify the common', as she wrote.

And yet it is worth remembering that this poem is taken from a series called 'Legends', in which there are many references to myths and how myths are made. The mother–child relationship could suggest to the reader the Christian Madonna and child, but there are also **hints of the Ceres and Persephone myth**, which Boland explores in 'The Pomegranate' and other poems. In that story, it is only when Ceres is reunited with her daughter that spring can come (see also box on page 108).

Form and language

The **short lines and short sentences create a slow pace**, a sense of suspension, which is reinforced by the gaps between groups of lines. Look at the poem on a page, and you can see that the white space that surrounds the words is part of its effect; it emphasises the slightness and fragility of what the poem describes.

Many of the sentences are without verbs, which adds to the sense of suspended time, so that it feels like time begins again with the simple present-tense verbs of the last three lines.

Exam-Style Questions

Understanding the poem

1	'Things are getting ready / to happen' (lines 3–4). How would the poem be different if Boland had written 'Things are about to happen'?
2	Boland chooses three 'Things' – stars, moths and fruit. Why, do you think, did she choose these three?
3	What is the effect of putting 'But not yet' on an isolated line (line 8)?
4	The poem is called 'This Moment'. What happens at 'This Moment', and how is it made to seem significant?

Thinking about the poem

1	Which of these adjectives best describes the atmosphere in this poem, in your opinion: peaceful, tender, strange? Perhaps you would suggest another word? Give reasons for your choice.
2	Why, do you think, has the poet set this poem at dusk?
3	Comment on the use of the word 'slanting' (line 7).
4	In what ways does this poem resemble a painting? And what does it do that a painting cannot?
5	Eavan Boland has spoken of her desire to 'bless the ordinary, sanctify the common' in her poetry. To what extent does this short lyric succeed in this?
6	Does the fact that this poem comes from a series called 'Legends' affect your understanding of its possible meanings? If so, in what way?

Imagining

1		You have decided to make a short YouTube video of this poem. In groups or pairs, discuss what atmosphere you would try to create by using lighting, music, special effects, etc.
2		Write a short paragraph or poem describing what you see and hear around you at this particular moment.

SNAPSHOT

- Celebrates a particular moment in time
- Suburban setting
- Painterly imagery
- Simple language and short phrases
- Careful use of verbs
- Importance of the mother–child relationship
- Echoes of the Ceres–Persephone story
- Celebrates ordinary experience of women

Eavan Boland

Love

Dark falls on this mid-western town
where we once lived when myths collided.
Dusk has hidden the bridge in the river
which slides and deepens
to become the water   5
the hero crossed on his way to hell.

Not far from here is our old apartment.
We had a kitchen and an Amish table.
We had a view. And we discovered there
love had the feather and muscle of wings   10
and had come to live with us,
a brother of fire and air.

We had two infant children one of whom
was touched by death in this town
and spared: and when the hero   15
was hailed by his comrades in hell
their mouths opened and their voices failed and
there is no knowing what they would have asked
about a life they had shared and lost.

I am your wife.   20
It was years ago.
Our child was healed. We love each other still.
Across our day-to-day and ordinary distances
we speak plainly. We hear each other clearly.

And yet I want to return to you   25
on the bridge of the Iowa river as you were,
with snow on the shoulders of your coat
and a car passing with its headlights on:

I see you as a hero in a text –
the image blazing and the edges gilded –   30
and I long to cry out the epic question
my dear companion:

Will we ever live so intensely again?
Will love come to us again and be
so formidable at rest it offered us ascension   35
even to look at him?

But the words are shadows and you cannot hear me.
You walk away and I cannot follow.

Before you read

What do you expect a poem with the title 'Love' to be about? What images and emotions would you expect to find in it? Write down your thoughts. Then read the poem and see whether any of your expectations are met.

Glossary

1	*mid-western town*:	Iowa City, USA, where Boland attended the International Writing Program at the University of Iowa in 1979
8	*Amish*:	strict Christian sect in the USA; an Amish table would be simple, well-made and unadorned
35	*formidable*:	powerful, even frightening
35	*ascension*:	a sense of uplift

Guidelines

'Love' is the second poem in the sequence 'Legends' from *In a Time of Violence* (1994). The legend or myth that is central to an understanding of this poem is that of Aeneas in Book VI of the *Aeneid* by Virgil. Aeneas visits the underworld and meets the ghosts of his former companions, who are eager to talk to him, but their voices are faint and they cannot communicate.

Commentary

Lines 1–12

'Love' is addressed to the poet's husband, and is set in Iowa, the 'mid-western town / where we once lived'. She is revisiting the city where they and their 'two infant children' (line 13) had spent several months in 1979, and she is looking back on that time. For her, it was a time 'when myths collided', and she uses the legend of Aeneas's descent into the underworld as a way of exploring and expressing her memories and emotions.

Like many of Boland's poems, 'Love' is set at dusk, a time when the outlines of things become blurred and the imagination can take over. Here, it hides the bridge over the river, and the river 'deepens' and becomes, in her imagination, the River Styx, which Aeneas, the 'hero' of line 6, has to cross on his way to the underworld, or 'hell'.

The second stanza remembers the apartment where they lived, in plain and simple phrases, and then, in a wonderful and sensuous image, describes the emotions they experienced there. Love is imagined as a creature with 'the feather and muscle of wings' that had, in a very domestic phrase, 'come to live with us'. This love is perhaps the other of the colliding myths – it is love, not just as an emotion, but as a being, 'a brother of fire and air'. The wings mentioned in line 10 might suggest an angel.

Lines 13–24

The third stanza refers to an agonising experience from that time – one of the children being 'touched by death' (meningitis, in fact). She survived, but the parents must have had to face the real possibility that she would die, and that possibility of death and separation brings the poet back to the Aeneas myth, and the image of his failed attempts to communicate with his dead 'comrades'.

The tone changes in the fourth stanza. It becomes matter-of-fact, as if to keep the trauma of that time at arm's length: 'It was years ago. / Our child was healed.' She calmly assesses her relationship with her husband: 'We love each other still.' The terms are practical rather than romantic, but we do not doubt the truth of what she says. Unlike Aeneas and his companions, 'we speak plainly. We hear each other clearly.'

Lines 25–38

But something is missing from this mature love. There is a sense of loss in her desire to 'return to you / … as you were'. She seems to have a vivid memory of him on the bridge over the river in the snow, lit up by the headlights of a passing car. In her mind the image is 'blazing' and has a mythical quality; he is 'a hero in a text', like an illustration from the *Aeneid*. She has an 'epic question' to call out to him, as if she could speak to that image across the years. The question is about love. Will it ever be as intense again as it was at that time, when love was a palpable presence, like a god, and 'it offered us ascension / even to look at him'? The metaphor suggests that the experience was both powerful and spiritual.

Eavan Boland

Boland knows that her question cannot be answered because she is trying to communicate over impossible distances. She puts herself in the position of Aeneas's companions (she calls him 'my dear companion' in line 32), whose voices cannot be heard. The separation here is not between the living and the dead, but between the present and the past: it is impossible to revive the past or to communicate with it. Nevertheless, the final two lines reflect a sadness that is to do with the present relationship of husband and wife: 'You walk away and I cannot follow' speaks of the separation that, in the end, always exists between individuals, however much they love each other, and hints at the final separation of death.

Themes and imagery

The primary theme of this poem is, of course, love, but although it is relatively unusual for Boland to write about male–female 'romantic' love, this is not a conventional love poem. It **considers different sorts of love and how love changes over time**. The intense love of the young couple, for whom love is like a god who comes to visit, is contrasted with the mature love of a couple who communicate well in a 'day-to-day' way. There is no doubt that they 'love each other still' (line 22), but something has been lost. We might wonder whether the brush with death in their child's illness, and the prospect of separation it represented, had something to do with the change in the couple's relationship.

> **Boland on time**
>
> 'If a poet does not tell the truth about time, his or her work will not survive it. Past or present, there is a human dimension to time, human voices within it, and human griefs ordained by it.'

HIGHER LEVEL

Memory and the passing of time is another of the poem's themes. The past is recalled as a time of great emotional intensity that the present cannot match. Memory can bring the past vividly back to the mind, but it cannot change the present. The result is the sense of loss that pervades the poem.

There are two strands of imagery that help to create the **sense of loss and distance**. One is to do with **light and dark**: the 'dark' and 'dusk' of the poem's opening is contrasted with the 'blazing' (line 30) image of the hero-husband lit up by headlights. The other is to do with **speech**: although the present-day couple 'speak plainly' and 'hear each other clearly' (line 24), there is no such communication between the hero Aeneas and his companions or between the poet in the present and the memory of her husband. The 'epic question' (line 31) cannot be spoken, and 'words are shadows' (line 37).

This brings us to the significance of myth to the poem. Boland has written of myth as 'a beautiful important way of organising the wounded, of bandaging the wounded knee of things'. By looking at personal experience in the light of some of the ancient stories of western culture, Boland connects an individual sense of loss with an epic understanding of death and separation that is the shared property of that culture. In this way, **myths are made relevant to contemporary life, and personal experiences are made universal**, their significance enriched by their association with myth.

Form and language

'Love' is written in unrhymed stanzas and lines of varying length. The stanzas follow a line of thought, and their flexibility allows Boland to change the pace and rhythm to reflect changing ideas. Thus, the short lines 'I am your wife. / It was years ago' (lines 20–21) are blunt and pull back from the melancholy of the previous stanza; the brevity of the final two-line stanza gives it a special emotional force.

The language is plain and direct, although it is able to move from simple statement towards the poetic. But even at its most metaphorical, in the arresting image of 'love had the feather and muscle of wings' (line 10), **the words are simple and unadorned**.

SNAPSHOT

- Meditation on love
- Theme of memory and the passing of time
- Aeneas myth as framework for understanding experiences
- Reveals intimate feelings
- Poem about change and loss
- Desire to recapture the past
- Images of light/darkness; speech
- Moving poem expressing deep emotion

Exam-Style Questions

Understanding the poem

1. What scene is the speaker looking out at in the first stanza of the poem?
2. What is the effect of love, as suggested in the second stanza?
3. Why, do you think, does the speaker make the analogy with the Aeneas myth in the stanza describing the child's illness?
4. How has the poet's experience of love changed over time?
5. How is the speaker's beloved 'dear companion' presented in the fifth and sixth stanzas? Examine the language she uses to describe him.
6. How do the questions the poet asks in the penultimate stanza, and the sense of finality in the couplet at the end, affect the theme and tone of the poem?

Thinking about the poem

1. 'Love' is clearly an autobiographical poem, addressed to the poet's husband. Where in the poem is her love for him most evident?
2. Do you think Boland's use of the Aeneas myth is effective in 'Love'? Give reasons for your answer.
3. This is a poem about memory. In your view, does the poet long for the past?
4. What does this poem tell us about love? Do you find its insights interesting? Explain your response.
5. A company is publishing a book of love poems. You have been invited to choose a poem for publication. Explain why you would or would not choose to include 'Love' in the book.

Imagining

1.  'What is real love?' Have a class discussion on this topic.
2. Write your own poem or prose piece with the title 'Love'. Remember: there are many types of love; your piece does not have to be romantic.

The Pomegranate

The only legend I have ever loved is
the story of a daughter lost in hell.
And found and rescued there.
Love and blackmail are the gist of it.
Ceres and Persephone the names. 5
And the best thing about the legend is
I can enter it anywhere. And have.
As a child in exile in
a city of fogs and strange consonants,
I read it first and at first I was 10
an exiled child in the crackling dust of
the underworld, the stars blighted. Later
I walked out in a summer twilight
searching for my daughter at bed-time.
When she came running I was ready 15
to make any bargain to keep her.
I carried her back past whitebeams
and wasps and honey-scented buddleias.
But I was Ceres then and I knew
winter was in store for every leaf 20
on every tree on that road.
Was inescapable for each one we passed.
And for me.
          It is winter
and the stars are hidden.
I climb the stairs and stand where I can see 25
my child asleep beside her teen magazines,
her can of Coke, her plate of uncut fruit.
The pomegranate! How did I forget it?
She could have come home and been safe
and ended the story and all 30
our heart-broken searching but she reached
out a hand and plucked a pomegranate.
She put out her hand and pulled down
the French sound for apple and
the noise of stone and the proof 35
that even in the place of death,
at the heart of legend, in the midst
of rocks full of unshed tears
ready to be diamonds by the time
the story was told, a child can be 40
hungry. I could warn her. There is still a chance.

Eavan Boland

The rain is cold. The road is flint-coloured.
The suburb has cars and cable television.
The veiled stars are above ground.
It is another world. But what else   45
can a mother give her daughter but such
beautiful rifts in time?
If I defer the grief I will diminish the gift.
The legend will be hers as well as mine.
She will enter it. As I have.   50
She will wake up. She will hold
the papery flushed skin in her hand.
And to her lips. I will say nothing.

Glossary

Line	Term
Title	*Pomegranate*: red fruit filled with seeds that grows in warm climates and ripens in winter
12	*blighted*: diseased; cursed
17	*whitebeams*: a species of tree often planted in city parks and estates
18	*buddleias*: purple-flowered shrubs that attract butterflies
47	*rifts*: openings; tears
48	*defer*: put off

Guidelines

'The Pomegranate' is the third poem of the sequence 'Legends' from *In a Time of Violence* (1994). It comes directly after 'This Moment' and 'Love', and the three poems share certain themes and images. As with 'Love', Boland uses a myth to shed light on personal experience, and refers to a descent into the underworld. The story – or 'legend', as she calls it – that she is concerned with here is that of Ceres and Persephone, which we touched on in looking at 'This Moment'.

Commentary

Lines 1–23

The poem starts by sketching out the myth of Persephone, 'the story of a daughter lost in hell'. For Boland, the story is about love – the mother searching the world for her lost daughter, and about blackmail – the tricking of Persephone by Hades with the pomegranate seeds, which meant that he had a hold over her. She likes the fact that she can 'enter it anywhere'; that different aspects of the story can seem relevant at different times.

Boland spent some of her childhood years in London, where her father was the Irish ambassador. This time is referred to in lines 8–12, where in the 'city of fogs', she thinks of herself as Persephone in the underworld, cut off from her home and feeling exiled. Later, as a mother in a Dublin suburb, she sees herself as Ceres as she searches for her daughter at bedtime – an image that brings to mind the scene in 'This Moment'. It is summer and nature – the whitebeams, the wasps, the buddleias – is flourishing, but as an adult she knows that winter

HIGHER LEVEL

Ceres and Persephone

Ceres is the Roman name for the Greek goddess Demeter, the goddess of agriculture, who was responsible for the fertility of the land and who is also associated with motherhood. Persephone was the daughter of Zeus and Ceres/Demeter. The ancient Greek myth of Persephone is concerned with the cycle of the seasons.

One day Persephone was picking flowers in a meadow when she was seized by Hades, god of hell or the underworld, and carried off on his chariot. He made her his queen, goddess of the lower world. Ceres searched everywhere for Persephone, and the land became barren because of her neglect of it. Eventually Zeus helped Ceres to rescue her daughter from hell, but while Persephone was there Hades had tricked her into eating six pomegranate seeds – eating anything in the underworld usually meant being stuck there forever.

It was finally agreed that she would spend six months of each year on Earth and the other six in the underworld. The spring and summer is when she is on Earth, the autumn and winter when she is in the underworld. In the winter she would be with Hades in the underworld. Each spring she would make the return journey to Earth, bringing renewed life.

will come in its turn; it is 'inescapable', not just for the trees but 'for me'. In mythological terms, it is summer when Ceres and Persephone are together, winter when they are apart (see panel on left). The coming of winter means the separation of mother and daughter.

Lines 24–41

The second section of the poem begins 'It is winter', telling us that not only is it literally winter, but that the mythological winter she foresaw in the previous lines has now arrived. Her daughter has not left the house, but she is a teenager, on the brink of departure, and there is a distance now between mother and child that was not there before. You sense that distance as she watches her child asleep 'beside her teen magazines'. The 'plate of uncut fruit' makes her think of the pomegranate, a fruit that ripens in winter and belongs in the Ceres–Persephone story. Remembering that story, she thinks that if only Persephone had not eaten the pomegranate, she 'could have come home and been safe'. She thinks about the sound of the word 'pomegranate' – the way it contains the 'French sound for apple' (*pomme*) and 'the noise of stone' (granite) – and about the fact that even 'in the place of death, / at the heart of legend', ordinary problems still apply: 'a child can be / hungry'.

Lines 41–53

Turning back to her own daughter, she says, 'I could warn her.' However, she is not in the underworld of the legend, but in a suburb with 'cars and cable television', and the stars may be 'veiled' as in the underworld, but they are 'above ground'. 'It is another world' and the rules of the myth do not necessarily apply. Perhaps her daughter could avoid Persephone's fate. What would she want to warn her daughter about? In terms of the myth, it would be eating pomegranate seeds, but in the modern suburb it might be to do with the dangers of the world beyond, of growing up, of sexuality.

She asks another question: What can a mother give her daughter but 'such / beautiful rifts in time?' The phrase 'rifts in time' conjures up the millennia that have passed since the story of Persephone and Ceres was first told, but also the separations that are repeated from generation to generation, as a mother lets a child pass out of her care to become an adult.

Now the poem switches to the future tense, as she thinks of her daughter's future. She does not want to 'defer the grief' by warning her daughter of the dangers, because that would 'diminish the gift'. The story is the gift; it will be 'hers as well as mine'. 'She will wake up' (the phrase carries overtones of sexual awakening) and will hold the pomegranate, with its 'papery flushed skin', and put it 'to her lips'. The sensual language makes clear the connection between Persephone's fatal action in the myth and the idea of becoming a sexual adult woman. The poet's job, as a mother, is to 'say nothing' – to let her child go, as all mothers must.

Eavan Boland

Themes and imagery

The primary theme of the poem is **the relationship of mother and daughter as the parent prepares to let the child go**, which is a central and inevitable job of parenthood. The poem is filled with the loss that separation brings, with the tenderness of the mother for her child, but also with a joyful sense of the rightness of what is happening.

The underpinning structure of myth is central to how the poem works. The personal narrative is deepened by the ancient legend. It gives the child in London a way of understanding her sense of exile and helps us to see individual experiences, like the separation of parent and child, as part of a universal pattern.

The pomegranate is, of course, the key image in the poem. It has its well-known role in the Persephone legend, in which the fact that it is a fruit associated with winter is important, but Boland teases out other associations. In lines 34–35 she explores the sound of the word, and thinks of the apple, which has its own rich set of mythical

Adam and Eve and the apple

In the story from Genesis, the first book of the Bible, Adam and Eve are the first human beings, living in the garden of Eden. God has forbidden them to eat the fruit of one tree – the tree of the knowledge of good and evil. When they eat an apple from that tree, God curses them and expels them from Eden. They also become aware of their own nakedness, and feel shame for the first time, so the story of the apple and the 'Fall' is also a story about the awakening of sexuality.

HIGHER LEVEL 2021

associations, the most obvious of which is the Adam and Eve story in the Bible. That connection reinforces the association of the pomegranate with sexuality that Boland emphasises in the poem's final two lines: its 'flushed skin' being put 'to her lips'.

Another image that derives from the legend is of the **underworld**, signified several times in the poem by the **starless sky**: the stars are 'blighted' in line 12, 'hidden' in line 24 and 'veiled' in line 44. Along with the dim light of the underworld is the lifeless stone: the 'crackling dust' (line 11), the 'noise of stone' (line 35) and the 'rocks full of unshed tears' (line 38).

Time is a secondary theme of the poem – both the cycle of the seasons and of human life, and also the long timescale that both separates and connects the original tale of Persephone in the underworld and the twentieth-century domestic story. That timescale turns the 'unshed tears' of suffering in the underworld into the 'diamonds' (line 39) they become when the story is told; the image suggests the richness and wisdom of the legend that Boland loves so much. Perhaps that is why she describes her gift of story to her daughter as 'beautiful rifts in time' (line 47).

Form and language

'The Pomegranate' is written in unrhymed lines of fairly even length. There is no regular metre, but you could think of the form as **a free, modern version of blank verse** – the unrhymed iambic pentameter used by Shakespeare, Milton, Wordsworth, Tennyson and many others, including Yeats in 'The Second Coming'. It is a form that is flexible and does not draw attention to itself. It can be used for narrative and reflection, and is good at conveying an easy sense of a voice speaking.

The voice in this poem is direct and quite intimate, with a straightforward 'I' addressing the reader directly, conversationally ('Love and blackmail are the gist of it', line 4), with a little bit of drama, as if she is actually speaking to us in the present: 'The pomegranate! How did I forget it?' (line 28). She controls the syntax carefully, moving, for example, from the long sentence of lines 33–41 ('She put out … hungry') to the short, urgent ones that follow. There is little in the way of striking word music, but what there is has an important function. Notice, for example, the way that 'rifts' in line 47 chimes with 'gift' in the next line, and how both are half-heard in 'grief' in the same line. It is not just decoration: **the meanings of these words in this poem are as closely interlinked as their sounds**.

Eavan Boland

Questions

1	'I can enter it anywhere' (line 7), the speaker says of the myth of Ceres and Persephone. What examples does she give of 'entering' the story?
2	From line 23, the poem becomes more dramatic: we are aware of a particular setting, a time and place. Describe the setting, time and place.
3	What do the images of mother and child in lines 25–27 suggest to you about their relationship at that particular point?
4	Why, in your view, does the poet dwell on the sounds of the word 'pomegranate'?
5	'I could warn her', the speaker says in line 41. Warn her of what? And why, in your own words, does she decide not to warn her daughter?
6	Comment on the meanings of 'beautiful rifts in time' (line 47).
7	What does the pomegranate symbolise in the myth of Ceres and Persephone and how is this reflected in the poem?
8	Would you agree that a sense of loss pervades this entire poem? Explain your answer.
9	What insight does the poem offer us about the mother–daughter relationship?
10	Does the poet blend myth and contemporary life successfully, in your view?
11	'The Pomegranate' is a poem about a mother–daughter relationship. Write a narrative (short story or personal essay) about the relationship between parents and children.
12	Imagine you are the daughter described in the poem, twenty years later. Write a short description of your childhood.

SNAPSHOT EAVAN BOLAND

- Domestic and suburban settings
- Use of myths and legends
- Precise and evocative use of words
- Personal experience reflected
- Themes also public and political
- Feminist concerns
- Voices of the powerless in society
- Lyrical and imaginative descriptions
- Explores family relationships
- Themes of time, loss and memory

Exam-Preparation Questions

1. 'Her personal experience as a wife and mother living in the suburbs is at the heart of the poetry of Eavan Boland.' Would you agree with this view? Explain your answer with close reference to at least three poems on your course.

2. 'In many of her poems, Eavan Boland confronts the violent history of Ireland with honesty but always with compassion.' Discuss this view.

3. In the words of Anne Stevenson, Eavan Boland is a poet who, although she 'works with concrete images', is nevertheless 'unafraid of thought'. Examine Boland's poetry from this point of view.

4. 'A sense of the past pervades Eavan Boland's poetry and she recreates it in an imaginative and dramatic way.' Examine at least three of Boland's poems in the light of this statement.

5. Eavan Boland has said that as a lyric poet she works with themes of 'time, perception of loss, down-to-earth disappointments or irretrievable segments of human experience'. Explore the treatment of these themes in her work.

6. 'Boland makes effective use of symbols and metaphors to explore personal experiences and deliver penetrating truths about society.' To what extent do you agree or disagree with this statement? Support your answer with reference to the poetry of Eavan Boland on your course.

7. 'Boland's reflective insights are expressed through her precise use of language.' Write your response to this statement, supporting your answer with suitable reference to the poetry of Eavan Boland on your course.

8. Discuss the use of myth and legend in the poetry of Eavan Boland, with reference to the poems on your course.

9. Write the text of a talk in which you introduce the poetry of Eavan Boland to a group of students. Your talk might include some of the following points:
   - Her position as one of Ireland's best-known woman poets
   - Her general vision and viewpoint – of history, of women's experience, of the past
   - Her use of language and imagery
   - Her use of myth and legend
   - Her control of language and form
   - The impact her poems make upon the reader

10. 'Although her poems often seem simple and the voice conversational, her use of form and control of language are sophisticated and precise.' Discuss the use of form and language in Eavan Boland's poetry, with reference to the poems on your course.

Sample Essay

'Boland has a way of examining and interrogating an object or an image until it yields unexpected meanings.'

Discuss this statement with reference to the poems of Eavan Boland on your course.

Answer addresses the question immediately

Objects are often important in Boland's poetry, and the idea that they can teach you something is present in the term 'Object Lessons', which Boland used for both a sequence of poems and a book of prose. Many of her poems centre on an object of some sort, sometimes artificial and sometimes natural, as the titles of some of the poems I will be looking at indicate: 'The War Horse', 'The Black Lace Fan My Mother Gave Me', 'The Shadow Doll', 'The Pomegranate', 'White Hawthorn in the West of Ireland'. In all these poems the object is described and imagined from multiple viewpoints, and in each case the examination finishes a long way from where it started, in an unexpected place.

Summary of what the essay will say using some of the terms of the question

Introduces first poem to be discussed

This technique is apparent in 'The War Horse', a relatively early poem that describes the intrusion of a loose horse into a suburban street with its neat gardens. To begin with, the incident is unremarkable, 'nothing unusual', but as Boland describes it, it takes on an increasingly sinister aspect. The horse itself is not at first particularly threatening and is apparently quickly gone, but the most intense focus is on the destruction it leaves behind. Again at first glance there is little to see: 'No great harm is done.' Plants and flowers have been damaged, with the damage to one plant of 'distant interest', but also, shockingly, 'like a maimed limb'. The language and imagery Boland uses make the damage seem both sinister and extreme: the broken head of a crocus is 'one of the screamless dead'; the horse, which seemed to have gone, 'stumbles on like a rumour of war, huge, / Threatening'. In Boland's vision, the whole scene has become a reminder of the violence in Northern Ireland then taking place, and also an image of how people ignore it. But, at the end of the poem, Boland's imagination, digging deeper, finds another layer of historical significance in the devastation. The 'smashed' rose is 'Ribboned across our hedge', calling to mind the outlawed nineteenth-century 'Ribbonmen' and their 'illicit braid'. Thus, a closer examination of the scene, with the poet's searching imagination, makes deeper connections, linking the present-day violence with Ireland's troubled and sometimes violent past: 'A cause ruined before, a world betrayed.'

Short quotations used throughout the essay, incorporated into sentences

Conclusion to first paragraph using the terms of the question

Qualification of the point made in the question's quotation

Boland does not subject the objects she makes poems from merely to intellectual examination and rational interrogation, she also uses the transformative power of the imagination as an essential tool. The role of the poet's imagination is shown even more clearly – and more subtly – in two poems from the sequence 'Object Lessons'. In 'The Black Lace Fan My Mother Gave Me', it is the imagination above all that is required to take the final step that gives the poem its impact. She has looked closely and attentively at the fan – the object in question in this poem – and seen the embroidered wild roses 'darkly picked, stitched boldly', which might suggest the passion of the gift-giver, Boland's father, or of her parents' relationship at that time. She has also examined the

Introduction of second poem connecting it to the point made above

tortoiseshell from which the structure of the fan is made. It suggests 'patience', but also carries 'an inference of its violation'. Similarly, the lace is 'overcast'. These details hint at some of the darker, more disturbing aspects of her parents' relationship, which her close scrutiny of the fan seems to be an attempt to understand. But she acknowledges that there are things that you cannot ever know, things that remain hidden however closely you examine an item, and then she adds 'unless, of course, you improvise'. By this she seems to mean 'use the imagination', and her imagination comes up with the image of the female blackbird spreading its wing – 'the whole, full, flirtatious span of it'. It conjures up some of the sensuality, and specifically female sensuality, that must have been part of her parents' relationship. Her imagination supplies what thought alone cannot reach.

Continued use of short quotations

Striking conclusion to the paragraph

'The Shadow Doll' is perhaps the most clear-cut example of Boland examining an object in order to extract its secrets. The 'porcelain bride in an airless glamour' is suggestive of the status of the Victorian woman for whom it was made to model her wedding dress. It is 'Under glass, under wraps', its silence filled, for Boland, with the female experiences of sex and childbirth that it does not speak of: 'fevers, quickenings and lusts'. Looking more closely, Boland sees the Victorian bride identifying with the artificial doll: 'she could see herself // inside it all, holding less than real / stephanotis'. And then, in a startling shift, Boland's own experience merges with that of the Victorian bride as she waits 'astray among the cards and wedding gifts' on the night before her own wedding. She is no longer a detached observer and now sees herself and her own life in the shadow doll. The 'pressing down' and locking of the poem's final stanza, suggesting oppression and repression, resonate with her own experience, not just that of the Victorian bride. Again, Boland's focus on an object, through the transformative power of the imagination, has taken her and the reader to an unexpected place, and given the object an unexpected meaning.

Introduces third poem using the terms of the question

Returns to the terms of the question

'The Pomegranate' focuses primarily on the myth of Ceres and Persephone rather than on the fruit itself, which plays an important part in that myth. Nevertheless, Boland pays close attention to the pomegranate. It exists in the poem first as fruit on a plate beside her sleeping daughter's bed, and makes a link with the myth she has been describing. By the end of the poem its 'papery flushed skin' is suggestive of the world of adult sexuality that the speaker's daughter is entering into. In between, Boland dwells on the sound of the word 'pomegranate', which contains 'the French sound for apple' (*pomme*) and 'the noise of stone' (granite). This analysis of the pomegranate may seem trivial, but it deepens its role in the poem, bringing out a parallel with the apple in the Biblical story of the Fall on the one hand, and linking with other images of rock and hardness in the poem on the other. Again, Boland's close attention has uncovered an unexpected meaning.

Fourth poem introduced with qualification to the terms of the question

Returns to the terms of the question

Finally, I want to look at 'White Hawthorn in the West of Ireland', where the flowering hawthorn is considered in many lights. It is a joyous element of the natural world that makes the speaker want to be 'part of / that ivory, downhill rush'. From the point of view of superstitious local tradition, it is an object filled with almost magical powers, with 'the luck', which can become a curse if it is treated in the wrong way and brought indoors. The speaker also sees it, in the light of dusk, as a beautiful thing that has a quite different sort of power, that is 'like water, able / to re-define land'. She comes to see it not just as an object to be examined and

Fifth and final poem introduced

defined in words, but as something that itself has the power to define and transform: 'the only language spoken in those parts.' It is hard to pin down the exact meaning of this phrase, but it certainly shifts our perspective as readers: the poem moves from talking about the hawthorn to seeing the hawthorn as a language, the thing that is spoken. The unexpected conclusion that Boland has arrived at here gives the object (the hawthorn) a power that seems to escape all attempts to pin it down and define its meaning.

> Concluding sentence of paragraph returns to the terms of the question

> Final paragraph summarises arguments, but also suggests a qualification to the statement in the question

In conclusion, it is true that many of Boland's poems focus strongly on an object or image, and that she finds meanings in the objects through close examination. At the same time, it is important to recognise that this is not just an intellectual process or scientific deduction. The most unexpected and moving ideas and meanings are reached through the transformative power of the poet's imagination making leaps and odd connections, and seeing deeper than any rational analysis could reach.

ESSAY CHECKLIST		Yes √	No x
Purpose	Has the candidate understood the task?		
	Has the candidate responded to it in a thoughtful manner?		
	Has the candidate answered the question?		
Comment:			
Coherence	Has the candidate made convincing arguments?		
	Has the candidate linked ideas?		
	Does the essay have a sense of unity?		
Comment:			
Language	Is the essay written in an appropriate register?		
	Are ideas expressed in a clear way?		
	Is the writing fluent?		
Comment:			
Mechanics	Is the use of language accurate?		
	Are all words spelled correctly?		
	Does the punctuation help the reader?		
Comment:			

Paul Durcan
b.1944

Nessa	**122**
The Girl with the Keys to Pearse's Cottage	**126**
The Difficulty that is Marriage	**130**
Wife Who Smashed Television Gets Jail*	**133**
Parents*	**138**
En Famille, 1979	**142**
Madman	**142**
'Windfall', 8 Parnell Hill, Cork	**144**
Six Nuns Die in Convent Inferno	**152**
Sport*	**162**
Father's Day, 21 June 1992	**168**
The Arnolfini Marriage	**173**
Ireland 2002	**178**
Rosie Joyce	**179**
The MacBride Dynasty	**187**

Biography

Early life

Paul Durcan was born on 16 October 1944 in the Stella Maris nursing home on Earlsfort Terrace in Dublin. He lived at Dartmouth Square in the capital for a short while before moving to Turlough in County Mayo, a county where both of his parents had roots. He is the eldest of three children, yet he writes very little about his siblings. He has composed many poems about his relationship with his parents. Durcan's father, John, was a teacher and then a barrister before becoming a High Court judge. Durcan got on well with his father until the age of about ten, acknowledging that in those days his father was a great storyteller, but a more distant and difficult relationship soon developed. He had a much more intimate connection with his mother, Sheila MacBride, who also worked in law but gave up her career as a solicitor when she married (as women generally had to do in those days). Durcan felt he often disappointed her but was grateful for the support she gave him.

Durcan was passionate about sport but any ambition to become professional was scuppered by a bone disease he was diagnosed with at the age of thirteen. Colm Tóibín writes that Durcan 'being a writer is always attributed to a long illness he suffered when he was thirteen, but he remembers inspiration stirring at an earlier age'.

In 1956 Durcan was sent to school in Gonzaga College, Dublin, to be educated by the Jesuits there. One teacher in particular was a huge influence on him, Father Joseph Veale, S.J., his English teacher, about whom Durcan has often written and spoken of fondly. Durcan went to UCD briefly in 1962. He met contemporary poets Michael Hartnett and Macdara Woods while he studied law and economics there but he did not stay to get his degree.

Durcan's family had become increasingly concerned about what they saw as erratic behaviour and had him committed to the St John of God psychiatric hospital. So began a two-year period when Durcan was in and out of mental institutions in Ireland and London, receiving treatments such as ECT (electroconvulsive – or electroshock – therapy) and taking prescription medication.

Influences, love and career

In 1965 Durcan left for London with fellow poet and lifelong friend Michael Hartnett, where they worked for Securicor. Durcan had an eclectic mix of jobs, including dishwashing, working for the North Thames Gas Board, working as a clerk on ten pounds a week and being a guide in the Planetarium. During lunch breaks he loved to walk to the Tate Gallery, where he particularly loved to gaze at the Francis Bacon paintings.

Upon his return to Dublin, Durcan went to see the poet Patrick Kavanagh speak in UCD and thought he 'seemed to resemble a caged beast'. This renowned Irish poet was to become a friend, influence, mentor and father-figure to Durcan, who also became great friends with Kavanagh's wife, Katherine. Durcan wrote the foreword to Kavanagh's *Lough Derg*.

In London Durcan liked to look at Francis Bacon paintings in the Tate Gallery

With friend and poet Brian Lynch, Durcan published *Endsville*, his first collection of poetry, in 1967. In the same year, after turning up at a wedding to which he was not invited, Durcan met Nessa O'Neill, the woman he would marry. The poem 'Nessa' recalls the extraordinary passion in the early days of their courtship. He followed her briefly to London but came back to take a job reflecting one of his passions: sport. In November 1967 he was appointed sports sub-editor for an Irish newspaper but walked out after someone made a derogatory remark about one of his heroes, the boxer Cassius Clay (Muhammad Ali). A week later his mother told him the devastating news, 'There's bad news in the paper … Patrick Kavanagh is dead.' Hard hit by this, he returned to London and then went on to Barcelona with Nessa to live for a while. The couple returned again to London and had two daughters, Sarah and Siabhra.

When their daughters were just one and two years old the family moved to Cork. Durcan studied English in UCC until a teacher there told him he had no talent for poetry! He continued to study archaeology and medieval history, graduating with first-class honours. Winning the Patrick Kavanagh Award in 1974 convinced Durcan to become a full-time poet and in 1975 the collection *O Westport in the Light of Asia Minor* was published.

Kavanagh's influence

Durcan said that Kavanagh 'changed everything for me'. He taught Durcan that 'there was nothing that was not fit matter for a poem … and that poetry was most nearly poetry when it was most nearly prose'. This belief is reflected in Durcan's accessible and often conversational style, overwhelmingly favouring free verse and often using colloquialisms.

In 1984 Durcan and his wife split and many of the poems in *The Berlin Wall Café* **(1985) deal with the heartache of this traumatic time.** Durcan felt responsible and said, 'I put the breakdown of our marriage down to my stupidity'. In January 1988 Durcan's father died and the poet began to write the 1990 collection *Daddy, Daddy*.

Besides Kavanagh, other major influences on Durcan were novelists James Joyce, George Orwell and Graham Greene and poets John Keats, T. S. Eliot, Ezra Pound, Emily Dickinson and Robert Frost.

Durcan has become almost as famous for his **dramatic readings of his poetry** as he is for the poems themselves, and people flock to hear him. You can see and hear many of these online and it is worth checking out his collaboration with Van Morrison on the track 'The Days Before Rock and Roll'. Durcan is a member of Aosdána; he's been published in *Magill* and *In Dublin* magazines and has written a column for *The Cork Examiner*.

Social and Cultural Context

Durcan is **keenly interested in Irish political and cultural life** and is often **deeply critical of contemporary Ireland**. He supported Mary Robinson in her successful bid for the presidency and she read a poem of his, 'Backside to the Wind' (a poem about emigration), in her victory speech. He is also a friend and supporter of President Michael D. Higgins and has been very critical of how the media have treated the President.

Political concerns

Durcan has been **outspoken about Irish issues such as emigration, the justice system, financial institutions and how we have failed our youth.** An article in *The Guardian* noted that 'For Durcan, no sacred cow is beyond his satiric reach, which makes him rare in a country where reverential lip-service is so often obsequiously paid to the "great tradition".' An example of this irreverence can be found in 'The MacBride Dynasty', where Durcan debunks the mythical aura that surrounded his great-aunt Maud Gonne MacBride.

The story of Cáit Killann highlights the issue of the forced emigration of our young people in 'The Girl with the Keys to Pearse's Cottage', an issue that crops up again in one of Durcan's couplet poems, 'Ireland 2002'. Inequality in Ireland's patriarchal and flawed justice system is tackled in a darkly comic fashion in 'Wife Who Smashed Television Gets Jail', which also contains a thinly veiled side-swipe at the poet's father. Terry Eagleton summed up Durcan well when he said, 'Like all first-class comedians, he is deadly serious', and Edna Longley has noted that Durcan helps students 'learn that you can be serious about Ireland without being po-faced'.

A pseudo-journalistic style is a common feature of Durcan's work and is very effective for social and political commentary. Colm Tóibín says Durcan became known for 'a certain sort of public poem, with the title like a newspaper headline, a political slogan, a parody or a catchphrase' for example 'Margaret Thatcher Joins IRA'. Here we see Durcan's keen wit, what *The Guardian* called his 'stiletto-sharp and zany observations'.

The Church

Many scandals have rocked the position and perception of the Catholic Church in Ireland in recent decades, but Durcan feels that we have been blinded by these to the good work still done by the men and women on the ground. Nevertheless, he is critical of the larger organisation: 'Irish Christianity was the mother tongue of my soul and it remains the mother tongue of my soul in spite of the institution of the Irish Roman Catholic Church.' Durcan uses many religious references in his poems; see, for example, 'Rosie Joyce' (page 179).

Themes

Personal life

Durcan's **family relationships** are a central theme in a great many of his poems. 'Nessa', 'The Difficulty that is Marriage' and 'Father's Day, 21 June 1992' are three poems that deal specifically with his marriage to Nessa O'Neill, the breakdown of which seems to haunt the poet. We learn a huge amount of autobiographical information from reading Durcan's poetry, although his tendency for hyperbole means we cannot take it for granted that all details are accurate. The poem 'Sport' is an example of this and examines his **father's distant relationship with him** and his **struggles with mental illness**. In 'Parents' and 'Father's Day' he looks at his relationship with his children, while 'The MacBride Dynasty' **takes a wry look at his mother and her distinguished family**. One of Durcan's most positive poems **celebrates the birth of his granddaughter Rosie Joyce**, which he says lifted him from a prolonged bout of depression, from 'the slums of despair'. Durcan has always been very open about his struggles with mental illness, 'I have my troubles and I shall always have them', even when such matters were a taboo subject in Ireland. This openness has brought great comfort to and empathy from fellow sufferers who feel Durcan has championed their hidden pain.

> 'Dear Nessa – now that our marriage is over
> I would like you to know that, if I could put back the clock
> Fifteen years to the cold March day of our wedding,
> I would wed you again.'
>
> 'Hymn to a Broken Marriage'

Art

Durcan is **passionate about the arts**, as we can see from his many references to paintings and painters, most notably in the poems 'Windfall' and 'The Arnolfini Marriage'. He took painting classes and seems to have a deep appreciation for the artists themselves as well as their subjects. Van Eyck, Goya, Van Gogh and El Greco are just some of the artists referenced by Durcan in poems on your course. In 1991, in collaboration with the National Gallery of Ireland, he published *Crazy About Women*, where he wrote poems about a selection of the portraits there. This work led to a similar collaboration with the British National Gallery in 1994, called *Give Me Your Hand*. Both books were very successful.

Connectedness

Connectedness is something a number of commentators and critics have noticed about Durcan's poetry: **connectedness within families, between past and present, between art and life and with our society and culture.**

> **Kavanagh said of Durcan**
>
> 'I've found my successor. I pass my mantle to Durcan.'

Most of Durcan's poems have a **firm sense of place**. Naming places seems very important to him, with Dublin, Cork and Mayo being the setting for many of his works. 'Windfall' and 'Rosie Joyce' are prime examples of this feature, which was something Patrick Kavanagh may have taught the young poet.

Paul Durcan

Timeline

1944	Born in Dublin to John and Sheila Durcan
1956	Attends Gonzaga Jesuit College in Dublin
1962	Drops out of law and economics course in UCD
1963	Forcibly committed to St John of God psychiatric hospital
1965	Goes to London with fellow poet Michael Hartnett
1967	First poetry collection, *Endsville*, published; meets Nessa O'Neill
1968	Marries Nessa; first daughter born
1969	Second daughter born
1970	Durcan and family move to Cork
1971	Studies archaeology and medieval history at UCC
1973	Graduates from UCC with first-class honours
1974	Wins the Patrick Kavanagh Award for poetry
1975	Publishes the collection *O Westport in the Light of Asia Minor*
1984	Marriage to Nessa breaks up
1985	Publishes collection *The Berlin Wall Café*
1990	Wins Whitbread and Irish Times awards for the collection *Daddy, Daddy*
1991	Collaborates with the National Gallery of Ireland on the collection *Crazy About Women*
1994	Publishes *Give Me Your Hand* in collaboration with London's National Gallery
1995	Joint winner of the Heinemann Award
1996	*The Kilfenora Teaboy, A Study of Paul Durcan* is published, edited by Colm Tóibín
2003	Writer-in-residence at UCD
2004	Ireland Chair of Poetry
2007	Publishes *The Laughter of Mothers*
2009	Publishes *Life is a Dream: 40 Years Reading Poems 1967–2007*
2012	Publishes *Praise In Which I Live And Move And Have My Being*
2017	Publishes *Three Great European Poets*

HIGHER LEVEL

Before you read

Think of someone you know with a very forceful personality. What image from the natural world would best describe that individual and why?

Nessa

I met her on the first of August
In the Shangri-La hotel,
She took me by the index finger
And dropped me in her well.
And that was a whirlpool, that was a whirlpool,
And I very nearly drowned.

Take off your pants, she said to me,
And I very nearly didn't;
Would you care to swim, she said to me,
And I hopped into the Irish Sea.   10
And that was a whirlpool, that was a whirlpool,
And I very nearly drowned.

On the way back I fell in the field
And she fell down beside me,
I'd have lain in the grass with her all my life
With Nessa:
She was a whirlpool, she was a whirlpool,
And I very nearly drowned.

O Nessa my dear, Nessa my dear,
Will you stay with me on the rocks?   20
Will you come for me into the Irish Sea
And for me let your red hair down?
And then we will ride into Dublin City
In a taxi-cab wrapped up in dust.
Oh you are a whirlpool, you are a whirlpool,   25
And I am very nearly drowned.

Glossary

2   *Shangri-La*: earthly paradise; originally mentioned in the 1933 novel *Lost Horizon* by James Hilton to describe a mystical, harmonious valley

Guidelines

From the 1975 collection *O Westport in the Light of Asia Minor*, this poem describes the meeting of Durcan and the woman who would later become his wife, Nessa O'Neill, and recalls the heady days of their courtship. It uses water as a central metaphor.

Paul Durcan

Commentary

Stanzas 1 and 2

Durcan's first encounter with his future wife is introduced dramatically. The date here may be significant. The first day of August is the Celtic festival of Lughnasa, often involving matchmaking and visits to holy wells. Durcan tells us that Nessa 'dropped me in her well'. He met her in 'the Shangri-La hotel' in Dalkey, Co. Dublin, and she immediately took control of the relationship. Her forceful personality is conveyed through the verbs used: 'She took me' and 'dropped me'. He is enraptured by her, 'that was a whirlpool', and feels overwhelmed by the force of her passion and intensity, 'And I very nearly drowned'. Note the repeated water imagery which permeates the poem.

> **Wells**
>
> Wells are an important symbol in folklore and often represent a link to Mother Earth, a portal to a mystical world and a source of healing.

Nessa's directness continues with the command 'Take off your pants', implying a sexual relationship has begun. This directness scares him, 'And I very nearly didn't'. Water imagery continues as she invites him to swim with her in the Irish Sea, this time a softer, more polite tone is used, 'Would you care to swim'? (Again there is possibly a sexual connotation here in this surely more metaphorical than literal invitation.) He decides to accept and cheerfully 'hopped into the Irish Sea' with her. He reiterates in the refrain that this experience is a 'whirlpool', emphasising the dizzying pace of their early relationship. Water embodies the mysterious and powerful nature of female sexuality; he is clearly much more inhibited.

Stanzas 3 and 4

The second part of the poem is much calmer and less intense than the first half. It is at first contented and later on subdued. The couple seem exhausted by the experience and both 'fell' into a field beside each other. Now that we are on land, Nessa's strength and energy seem lessened. This change suits Durcan, 'I'd have lain in the grass with her all my life', but 'She was a whirlpool' and cannot be tied down like this. Note that the past conditional 'I'd have' suggests that she would not lie with him there for ever. Also the plaintive 'With Nessa' of line 16 followed by a colon breaks the momentum of the poem and seems to be a moment where the poet reflects and accepts that she will not do this.

> **Whirlpools**
>
> In Greek mythology Charybdis was a female monster, in the form of a whirlpool, which three times daily swallowed masses of water then belched it back out again, creating large whirlpools capable of dragging a ship underwater. Heroes such as Jason and Odysseus are linked to Charybdis.

A yearning tone begins the last stanza with the tender, ballad-like repetition of 'O Nessa my dear'. Durcan is the one offering the invitation this time, but the options he offers are dull and suggest a less than perfect future. She can 'stay with me on the rocks' or travel to Dublin in a 'taxi-cab wrapped up in dust'. 'On the rocks' is a colloquial phrase for something that is in trouble and makes us think of shipwrecks. The dusty taxi is hardly a match for Nessa's 'whirlpool'; the erotic image has been replaced with a staid one suggestive of neglect and decay. It is not surprising then that this red-haired siren finds neither proposition attractive, and the pronouns of the final couplet suggest their separation: 'you are a whirlpool, / And I am very nearly drowned.' The poem ends on this note of resignation and regret; a striking anti-climax given the fierce intensity of its first half. He seems to realise how little he can offer her in terms of sustained passion and excitement.

Themes and imagery

Romantic love and the journey of a romance are themes here. That initial passion and indeed lust in a relationship, she 'dropped me in her well. / And that was a whirlpool' (lines 4–5), will fade in time, and perhaps it will disappear like the offer of a ride in a dusty 'taxi-cab' (line 24). **Land and water** are the contrasting sets of metaphors through which Durcan conveys the different stages of the relationship and the couple's very different personalities.

Nessa is linked to water, she is a 'well', a 'whirlpool' and invites him to swim, a metaphor for sex perhaps. He tries to join her in this world, 'I hopped into the Irish Sea' (line 10) but cannot sustain this and falls into a field, eventually asking her to stay with him 'on the rocks' (line 20). Perhaps they do not belong in each other's worlds and their dream of an earthly paradise is incompatible with their radically different natures. Durcan is generally **self-deprecating** in his poetry and the duller imagery he uses about himself here reflects this. He is very adoring of Nessa, painting her as an enchanting and other-worldly temptress. Do you agree, or is the picture we get of Nessa less than perfect?

Form and language

Like many of Durcan's poems, the style is **anecdotal** and often **euphemistic** and the subject **autobiographical**. (Euphemistic means a word or phrase used to avoid using an explicit or offensive word.) We feel he is chatting to us about his relationship and the use of mainly free verse enhances this effect. The poem is a lyric. The first three stanzas all have a uniform six lines but the final stanza has eight lines; this lengthening slows down the rhythm to reflect the loss of momentum in the relationship. Repetition is widely used and there is some rhyme ('hotel' and 'well' for example), which contribute to a ballad or song-like feel. This and other details make the poem firmly Irish; for example the use of place names, a key feature of Durcan's style, and Nessa's red hair.

> ### Aisling tradition
> This poem relates to the aisling tradition, an ancient Irish poetic tradition centring on a 'dream vision' in which an enchanting female figure beguiles an often naïve or vulnerable young man.

The subtle changes in the refrain are a clever touch and almost imperceptibly affect the inference we might make as the relationship develops. The directness of Nessa's approach – 'She took me by the index finger' (line 3), 'Take off your pants' (line 7) – contrasts sharply with Durcan's much more reticent, 'I fell' (line 13) and 'Will you stay with me … / … come for me' (lines 20–21) and shows us the difference between the two central characters. This contrast also possibly provides an insight into why the relationship eventually broke up.

Paul Durcan

Questions

1	What, do you think, might be important about the date and location of their first meeting? Why include these details? (Further information is available in the Biography.)
2	Durcan specifies that Nessa 'took me by the index finger' (line 3)? Why the index finger?
3	Suggest possible ideas for what Nessa's 'well' and 'whirlpool' might symbolise in stanza 1.
4	What impression do you form of Nessa's character from the first two stanzas? Justify your answer with close reference to the poem.
5	Comment on the verbs the poet uses about himself in the first three stanzas.
6	How does the pace and tone of stanza 3 differ from the previous two? Suggest reasons for this change.
7	The poet wishes that Nessa would lie with him in the grass always in line 15. What might this be a metaphor for?
8	What is the effect of the repetition used at the beginning of stanza 4?
9	There is much metaphorical language in the last stanza. Suggest interpretations for 'on the rocks', 'red hair' and 'a taxi-cab wrapped up in dust'.
10	Trace the subtle changes in the refrain (the last two lines of each stanza). How and why does this change? What is the poet trying to show us here?
11	Analyse the symbolism of land and water in the poem, paying particular attention to the idea of swimming.
12	How would you characterise the relationship described in the poem? You may choose from the following options or supply your own description: unequal, passionate, fulfilling, turbulent. Give reasons for your answer.
13	Imagine you are Nessa. Respond to this poem in the form of an answering poem or letter giving your point of view.
14	In pairs or small groups, research the aisling tradition in Irish poetry. What aspects of 'Nessa' correspond to this genre?

HIGHER LEVEL

Before you read

Research exercise: Emigration has long been a necessity in Ireland. For what reasons have Irish people had to emigrate? What is meant by the term 'diaspora'?

The Girl with the Keys to Pearse's Cottage

to John and Judith Meagher

When I was sixteen I met a dark girl;
Her dark hair was darker because her smile was so bright;
She was the girl with the keys to Pearse's Cottage;
And her name was Cáit Killann.

The cottage was built into the side of a hill; 5
I recall two windows and cosmic peace
Of bare brown rooms and on whitewashed walls
Photographs of the passionate and pale Pearse.

I recall wet thatch and peeling jambs
And how all was best seen from below in the field; 10
I used to sit in the rushes with ledger-book and pencil
Compiling poems of passion for Cáit Killann.

Often she used to linger on the sill of a window;
Hands by her side and brown legs akimbo;
In sun-red skirt and moon-black blazer; 15
Looking toward our strange world wide-eyed.

Our world was strange because it had no future;
She was America-bound at summer's end.
She had no choice but to leave her home –
The girl with the keys to Pearse's Cottage. 20

O Cáit Killann, O Cáit Killann,
You have gone with your keys from your own native place.
Yet here in this dark – El Greco eyes blaze back
From your Connemara postman's daughter's proudly mortal face.

Glossary

Title	*Pearse's Cottage*: Pádraig Pearse built a cottage in Rosmuc, Connemara in 1903 and taught Irish there
9	*jambs*: vertical posts that hold up a door and form part of the door frame
14	*akimbo*: bent outwards, a relaxed and open pose
23	*El Greco*: The Greek; Doménikos Theotokópoulos was a painter, sculptor and architect of the Spanish Renaissance who often used the black and red shades that Cáit Killann wears and who is noted for the dark intensity of his subjects' gaze

Paul Durcan

Guidelines

This poem is from the 1975 collection *O Westport in the Light of Asia Minor* and tackles the theme of **emigration and lost love** by describing the reluctant emigration of a real individual called Cáit Killann, a 'Connemara postman's daughter' (line 24) who looked after the cottage of the executed 1916 leader Pádraig Pearse.

Commentary

Title
Cáit Killann was the caretaker of Pearse's cottage in Rosmuc and would let visitors in to see the former holiday home of one of Ireland's most famous national heroes.

Stanza 1
Like 'Nessa', this poem opens with a speaker reminiscing about meeting a girl whom he fell for immediately. He is very young, only sixteen, when he meets her. Her Mediterranean looks and dazzling smile enchant him. Another attraction is that she is the key-holder to an important national monument: Pearse's summer cottage. It is worth noting here the powerful symbolism of the keys, which could represent the Irish language, Irish national identity, Irish history and also the key to the speaker's heart. To hold the keys to such a special place is an honour and makes Cáit an important and possibly powerful woman.

Stanzas 2 and 3
The speaker now describes the interior and exterior of the cottage itself and the symbolism continues. Its Spartan simplicity is striking, 'bare brown rooms … whitewashed walls', reflecting the ascetic nature of its former occupant. The alliterative contrast of Pearse, at once 'passionate' yet 'pale', is reflected in his photographs and in the house itself. This neglected place, 'wet thatch and peeling jambs' is located in a remote and natural setting on a hillside above a field of rushes. This simple rural idyll is invested with a magical quality of tranquillity, which the speaker has described as 'cosmic' (line 6).

As the speaker gazes at the cottage from the field below, he is 'Compiling poems of passion' – a strange turn of phrase; **one would generally compose poems rather than compile them**. The word sounds business-like, as does the 'ledger-book' he writes them in, which might have been expected to record financial and business transactions. Here Durcan is maybe commenting on one of the reasons why so many people have to emigrate: Ireland has put profits before people.

Stanzas 4 and 5
The poem shifts focus back to Cáit as she sits lingering on the windowsill, tanned and relaxed, 'brown legs akimbo'. There is a slightly uncomfortable element of voyeurism here as she seems not to know she is being observed by this ardent admirer. Cáit is linked to the cosmic nature of the cottage, showing she is in harmony with her home and her culture in her 'sun-red skirt and moon-black blazer'. The alliteration here adds to this harmonious effect. She gazes out onto an alien world in amazement, 'wide-eyed', and perhaps ill-prepared for the enormous upheaval she must face. The reason for her wide eyes is the strangeness of 'Our world'; this world, i.e. modern Ireland, has no future for her and she must emigrate to America. 'She had no choice but to leave her home' and break her link with its historical and cultural past as represented by Pearse's cottage. If our young people have to emigrate and leave behind them ties to our language and history, indeed our national identity, what is to become of us? So much will be lost through our failure to provide economic stability for our youth.

Stanza 6

Again, as in 'Nessa', the last stanza begins with a repeated plaintive call to the female subject of the poem: 'O Cáit Killann, O Cáit Killann'. It is full of regret and yearning. She has left and taken the keys with her. The speaker remains 'in this dark', which is modern Ireland, yet a note of hope is struck as the memory of her eyes 'blaze back' out of the darkness to remind the speaker of an El Greco painting.

The juxtaposition of Cáit's ordinariness as a 'Connemara postman's daughter' with an El Greco painting makes her extraordinary, which comes together in the final phrase, her 'proudly mortal face'. Her passion and pride for her heritage shines through her humble origins. Durcan rues the fact that people like Cáit are betrayed by the avarice of the very culture and nation they adore.

Themes and imagery

Losing love is a theme here; the speaker adores Cáit from afar although it doesn't seem as if she returns or is even aware of his affections. He admires her Mediterranean looks, her 'dark hair … her smile … so bright' (line 2), her 'brown legs' (line 14) and her blazing 'El Greco eyes' (line 23). The fact that she has such a prestigious responsibility in holding the keys to Pearse's cottage is also fascinating for him, and so the theme of a **national identity, history and culture that is threatened by the emigration of young people** becomes important in the poem. Modern Ireland has reneged on the promises of the 1916 Proclamation and is not cherishing its youth as it should. Even poetry is compiled in ledgers, an antithesis to the passionate poetry, freedom fighting and protection of the Irish language to which Pearse devoted himself. Giving the girl an Irish name underlines this and the fact that she is a postman's daughter demonstrates that it is not the rich and powerful who make sacrifices in times of economic need, it is the ordinary people of Ireland who must give up the homes and families they love to try to survive. Like Irish culture, the cottage itself is also in decay, with its 'wet thatch and peeling jambs' (line 9). The beautiful rural setting has a 'cosmic peace' (line 6) about it that contrasts with 'this dark' (line 23) – the state of Ireland today.

Form and language

The poem is written in six quatrains which contain no formal rhyming scheme although some rhyme occurs ('place' and 'face' in stanza 6 for example). This **lack of formality** echoes the naturalistic world Cáit and the cottage inhabit so harmoniously. Comparing Cáit to an El Greco painting elevates her and indeed this relatively simple poem to a piece of art and culture, something the contemporary politicians of Ireland were neglecting.

The **language is straightforward and accessible**, which also complements the simple nature of Cáit's world and the life Pearse embraced. Nevertheless, it is loaded with symbolism, particularly the keys, which have many possible connotations. Repetition, a very common feature of Durcan's poetry, is used as well as alliteration to enhance the lyrical feel of the poem: 'passionate and pale Pearse' (line 8).

Questions

1	What do we learn about Cáit in stanza 1? What details are significant here?
2	Do you think the speaker's age is important in the poem? Explain.
3	What might the 'Keys' of the title symbolise? Explain your answer.
4	Examine the description of the cottage in stanzas 2 and 3. Which elements are ordinary and which are more exotic? What does this contrast illustrate? Is the crumbling nature of the cottage and its setting significant? Why?
5	'with ledger-book and pencil / Compiling poems of passion' (lines 11–12). Analyse these lines. Why, do you think, did Durcan choose the word 'Compiling' and why specify a 'ledger'?
6	What is happening in stanza 4? Is it an uncomfortable stanza to read? Give reasons for your answer.
7	'Our world was strange' (line 17). What is the world Durcan refers to here and how does it differ from Cáit's world? Be specific.
8	What is the tone of the final stanza? What details in the language and imagery establish this tone?
9	What is the effect of the El Greco reference in line 23? Perhaps look at some El Greco paintings online to see if this helps you with your answer.
10	Why, in your opinion, does Durcan mention Cáit's father's profession and location in the last line?
11	What sound effects stand out for you in the poem? Comment on the effect of the ones you have chosen.
12	'The ordinary becomes extra-ordinary in this poem.' Do you agree with this view? Give reasons for your answer.
13	'On a simple level this poem is about a teenage crush, but Durcan elevates this to a poem about history, culture and national identity while criticising modern Ireland in the process.' Discuss this statement with close reference to the poem.
14	Do you know anybody who has emigrated? If not, perhaps a family member does. Why did the person leave? Is it something you would ever consider? Give reasons for your answer. Share your answers with the class.
15	Write a short story entitled 'The Crush'.
16	Imagine you are Cáit Killann. Write the dialogue of a phone conversation you have with your father after your first week in America. Refer to details in the poem as much as you can.

HIGHER LEVEL

The Difficulty that is Marriage

Before you read
Would you rather live for ever on Earth or die and go to paradise or heaven? Give reasons for your answer.

We disagree to disagree, we divide, we differ;
Yet each night as I lie in bed beside you
And you are faraway curled up in sleep
I array the moonlit ceiling with a mosaic of question marks;
How was it I was so lucky to have ever met you?
I am no brave pagan proud of my mortality
Yet gladly on this changeling earth I should live for ever
If it were with you, my sleeping friend.
I have my troubles and I shall always have them
But I should rather live with you for ever   10
Than exchange my troubles for a changeless kingdom.
But I do not put you on a pedestal or throne;
You must have your faults but I do not see them.
If it were with you, I should live for ever.

Glossary

4	*array*: place in a desired, often decorative, order
7	*changeling*: transient, impermanent; also, a child believed to be a fairy child who was left in place of a human child stolen by the fairies
12	*pedestal*: raised platform; also, a position of importance and the subject of unquestioning adoration

Guidelines

This sonnet is from the 1976 collection entitled *Teresa's Bar*. Like the previous two poems, it tackles ideas of losing love and the breakdown of a relationship. Durcan is characteristically honest and open about his relationship with his wife, Nessa, and the poem seems to be **an impassioned and romantic, if unrealistic, plea for their relationship to survive**.

Commentary

Lines 1–4

The poem opens on a series of alliterative 'd' words that form a list of negatives describing the fractious nature of the relationship: 'We disagree to disagree, we divide, we differ'. The staccato effect produced mimics the harsh tones of an argument. Despite the extent of their disagreements, the next three lines are full of tenderness, love and longing. This change in tone is signalled by the word 'Yet'. The couple lie next to each other in bed at night but she seems unreachable, 'faraway curled up in sleep'. The paradox of her proximity while being 'faraway' causes him to ask a series of questions. This idea is beautifully phrased: 'I array the moonlit ceiling with a mosaic of question marks'. Just as a mosaic is formed from many small tiles, the speaker's 'mosaic' is comprised of the questions he longs to ask her. These questions form an imagined work of art which becomes a literal work of art, i.e. this poem.

Lines 5–8

Durcan questions the happy coincidence of their meeting, which is described in 'Nessa'. Did he deserve to be 'so lucky to have ever met' her? He is not a 'brave pagan', suggesting that he holds religious beliefs (including a belief in eternal life after death), but would rather live on this ever-changing planet for ever if it meant he could be with her, his 'sleeping friend'.

Lines 9–14

The dreamy quality of the second quatrain is replaced with a stark admission of his own culpability in the breakdown of their relationship, 'I have my troubles'; nor can he promise to change for the better, 'and I shall always have them'. This statement may refer to Durcan's struggle with mental illness. However, he would love to remain in the relationship and be committed to her always. He repeats the assertion that he would prefer to live for ever in this imperfect secular world than enter the 'changeless kingdom' of heaven even if it meant he would be free from his 'troubles'.

Durcan seems to contradict his assertion that he does not put his beloved on 'a pedestal or throne' immediately when he tells her 'You must have your faults but I do not see them'. The poem ends with his third affirmation that he would live for ever if it could be with her. Repetition in threes is often used by Durcan when describing something of significance (a technique that can be traced back to the work of Homer, who used trilogies to invest an event or description with an added importance and emphasis).

Themes and imagery

The theme of the poem is the **imminent break-up of a marriage**. The reasons for the couple's discord and possible solutions to those issues inform this theme. The wife is unreachable as she sleeps and the image of her 'curled up' (line 3) suggests she is keeping herself from him even in sleep by forming a protective ball. 'Curled up' may also suggest contentment; she is not riddled with the doubts and fears their arguments provoke in him. He clearly idolises her, 'You must have your faults but I do not see them' (line 13), and he also fails to see that he clearly does put her 'on a pedestal or throne' (line 12). Perhaps this adoration and his failure to deal with their issues realistically is at the heart of 'The Difficulty that is Marriage'.

Contrast is used extensively in the poem. For example, he is awake while she is asleep and her perfection is set against his flaws. These contrasts reflect the possibly irreconcilable differences between the couple. **Change and permanence** are themes here too, highlighted by the contrast between this 'changeling earth' (line 7) and 'a changeless kingdom' (line 11). The unrealistic nature of Durcan's suit is further emphasised; how can he live forever here in a changing world? This is impossible.

Form and language

The poem is a **sonnet**, a fourteen-line poem that often deals with love. A sonnet generally consists of either three quatrains (groups of four lines) and a rhyming couplet or an octet (eight lines) and a sestet (six lines). This sonnet is Petrarchan in structure, in other words it has an **octet and sestet** formation. Traditionally the octet presents a situation upon which the speaker then meditates in the sestet. Here, the estrangement of the couple as they lie beside one another yet seem so far apart is the situation that causes the speaker to ask an 'array' (line 4) of questions as to what might be the cause of this estrangement and what might be done to keep the couple together. The sestet seeks to resolve this dilemma and does so here by first acknowledging the reason for their difficulties and proposing the unrealistic scenario that they could live for ever if they were together in this world.

HIGHER LEVEL

As ever with Durcan, **the language is quite accessible yet full of metaphor and symbolism**. The alliteration of the hard 'd' sounds in the first line hints that this couple do not get on. Durcan subverts the phrase 'agree to disagree' to become 'disagree to disagree', which seems even more negative. Repetition is another ever-present facet of Durcan's work and here his wish to live on Earth for ever is asserted three times during the poem. The tone is loving and romantic, 'my sleeping friend' (line 8) and, like the previous poems, full of longing for a love that is a lost cause. It is also **starkly confessional** (honest or open), 'I have my troubles' (line 9), which Durcan often addresses in his more autobiographical poetry. The use of the conditional emphasises this, 'If it were with you, I should live for ever' (line 14). Note the difference if Durcan had said, 'If it *is* with you, I *will* live for ever.' It seems that he knows deep down he is pursuing a love that is already slipping away.

Questions

1	What picture of the couple's relationship is painted in the first quatrain? Comment on the effect of the alliteration used in this section of the poem.
2	What specifically is the speaker doing in line 4? Do you agree that this is a beautifully phrased and effective image? Give reasons for your answer.
3	The speaker is self-deprecating in the second quatrain. Do you agree? Give reasons for your answer.
4	Having read the biography of Durcan on page 117, suggest what he might mean by 'I have my troubles and I shall always have them' (line 9)? Is this an honest admission of culpability or does it reveal a lack of willingness to change for her? Give reasons for your answer.
5	What, do you think, do the 'changeling' (line 7) and 'changeless' (line 11) worlds in the poem represent?
6	What is problematic about the speaker's understanding of the worlds mentioned above? Is Durcan's solution in lines 10 and 11 possible? Give reasons for your answer.
7	What do you identify as the main tone of the poem? Is it loving, yearning, regretful or something else? Give reasons for your answer.
8	What, do you think, might be the actual 'Difficulty that is Marriage' in the title? Give reasons for your answer.
9	Choose the two images in the poem that strike you most and comment on the reasons for your choices.
10	Compare and contrast this poem with 'Nessa'. Look at theme, tone, language and imagery.
11	What effect did the poem have on you? Do you have sympathy for the speaker? Explain with reference to the poem.
12	Imagine you are the speaker's best friend or counsellor. Write the dialogue of a conversation you have with him about the issues raised in the poem, giving him the best advice you can.
13	Durcan asks only one of his 'array' (line 4) of questions directly in the poem. Discuss in pairs what you imagine some of the other questions he has might be.

Paul Durcan

Wife Who Smashed Television Gets Jail

'She came home, my Lord, and smashed in the television;
Me and the kids were peaceably watching Kojak
When she marched into the living room and declared
That if I didn't turn off the television immediately
She'd put her boot through the screen;   5
I didn't turn it off, so instead she turned it off –
I remember the moment exactly because Kojak
After shooting a dame with the same name as my wife
Snarled at the corpse – Goodnight, Queen Maeve –
And then she took off her boots and smashed in the television;   10
I had to bring the kids round to my mother's place;
We got there just before the finish of Kojak;
(My mother has a fondness for Kojak, my Lord);
When I returned home my wife had deposited
What was left of the television into the dustbin,   15
Saying – I didn't get married to a television
And I don't see why my kids or anybody else's kids
Should have a television for a father or mother,
We'd be much better off all down in the pub talking
Or playing bar-billiards –   20
Whereupon she disappeared off back down again to the pub.'
Justice O'Brádaigh said wives who preferred bar-billiards to family television
Were a threat to the family which was the basic unit of society
As indeed the television itself could be said to be a basic unit of the family
And when as in this case wives expressed their preference in forms of violence   25
Jail was the only place for them. Leave to appeal was refused.

Before you read

Do you think television and social media bring families closer together? Discuss your opinions and reasons in pairs or small groups and feed your ideas back to your classmates.

Glossary

2	**Kojak**: 1970s American detective programme, starring Telly Savalas as Kojak, a New York cop who sucked a lollipop while glibly delivering the show's famous catchphrase, 'Who loves ya, baby?'
8	**dame**: American slang for a woman

Guidelines

This poem is from *Sam's Cross* (1978). Durcan adopts a **pseudo-journalistic** (mock newspaper) **style** in this **indictment of Irish family life, the media and the judicial system**. He **uses hyperbole** to depict a ridiculous court case and in so doing presents Ireland as a patriarchal (male-dominated) and Americanised society that punishes women who stand up to or attempt to subvert the status quo. Despite its weighty themes, this poem has a light-hearted and amusing tone. Whether you like or dislike this poem, it is sure to provoke a lively debate!

Commentary

Title
The newspaper headline-style title sets the tone for the rest of the poem. It seems ludicrous that someone would be jailed for smashing a television and it is interesting that 'Wife' is specified rather than, say, a person or a woman. This surreal exaggeration will continue to feature in the poem.

Lines 1–5
The poem opens in the middle of the husband's testimony at a court case; his use of 'my Lord' shows us he is addressing the judge and makes him sound obsequious (fawning or anxious to please). He sets the scene, explaining that he and his children were 'peaceably' watching television in the living room until his wife interrupted them. 'Peaceably' is not an everyday word and sounds more like an adjective from a police report. His use of the verbs 'marched' and 'declared' further reinforce this impression while demonstrating his wife's forceful nature. She has threatened to 'put her boot through the screen' of the television if it is not turned off. Despite the seeming irrationality of her action, it is important to note that the programme he is watching with his children is an inappropriate one as *Kojak* featured strong violence and often very adult themes.

Lines 6–10
When her husband fails to comply with her command the wife makes good on her threat: 'she took off her boots and smashed in the television'. It is significant that the husband makes time in his account to state what was happening in the show at that point. A violent scene is recounted where Kojak callously shoots a woman dead. The husband refers to her as a 'dame', American slang for a woman. His use of this derogatory term demonstrates how immersed and perhaps brainwashed he is by American television, which had invaded Irish popular culture in the seventies and is at odds with his previously quite formal language to the judge. In his excitement at reliving the scene he seems to have forgotten himself momentarily. He notes that Kojak 'Snarled at the corpse' (a very cold and dehumanising term for the deceased), 'Goodnight, Queen Maeve'. There are many interesting things going on here. Kojak's lack of remorse as he kills the woman is emphasised by his 'witty' quip, the unlikely fact that she goes by the same name as the husband's wife and the fact that a strong Irish queen who gained great power and respect in a very male-dominated world is referenced. Surely what the children have just watched on TV is far more violent than the wife's actions? Or does the distance created by the TV screen make it less shocking?

> **Queen Maeve**
>
> Maeve/Medb was a warrior queen in Irish mythology. She features in the epic poem the Táin Bó Cúailnge. She was a strong woman with power and wealth in a very patriarchal world. She insisted she have wealth equal to her husband. She demanded that her third husband, Eochaid Dála, be without fear, meanness or jealousy as she wished to have lovers.

Lines 11–21
The husband's obsession with the show becomes clearer as he reveals that he 'had to bring the kids round to my mother's place', not for the children's protection, seemingly, but to catch the end of the show! In this darkly

Paul Durcan

satirical observation, Durcan highlights our obsession with the media at the expense of our families. He does so in a deeply ironic and subversive manner while managing to make the whole idea amusing for the reader. The following aside in parentheses has the effect of making the husband sound even more sycophantic (anxious to be liked) as he fawningly explains, totally unnecessarily, to the judge, '(My mother has a fondness for Kojak, my Lord)'. Is his mother to blame for his TV obsession?

Upon his return home, he tells the judge, he found his wife had cleaned up the mess and binned the remains of the television. Her motives are then revealed; she wants a relationship with her husband and feels that the television has overtaken them as the parent figure for their children. The TV is what is guiding and educating them. Her comments may have gleaned our sympathy at this point; however, she then proposes what she sees as a better alternative, namely 'talking / Or playing bar-billiards' in the pub, before leaving to go 'back down again to the pub'. So here we have a couch-potato husband and a wife who prefers socialising in bars. It is not an ideal family set-up, but it is an interesting role-reversal for a 1970s couple.

Lines 22–26

The voice now becomes that of a journalist who it seems has been quoting the husband as part of an article. The outcome of the case is reported. 'Justice O'Brádaigh' places the blame for this incident upon the wife and surmises that 'wives who preferred bar-billiards to family television / Were a threat to the family which was the basic unit of society'. Note that **the judge specifies 'wives' rather than 'people' or 'parents'**. This behaviour is inappropriate for women but apparently not for men. In a seemingly absurd but perhaps frighteningly accurate addition to this statement, Justice O'Brádaigh asserts that 'the television itself could be said to be a basic unit of the family'. He sees television as a vital part of family life and the husband receives no reproof for his part in this situation.

Again note the use of the feminine as the judge continues 'when … wives expressed their preference in forms of violence / Jail was the only place for them'. We are not surprised on one level as the title has told us as much, but the biased and warped sense of righteous indignation of the judge is clearly misogynistic. The harshness and finality of her sentence is emphasised by the **legalistic and journalistic terminology** of the ending: 'Leave to appeal was refused.'

Maeve does not get to tell her side of the story. Like Queen Maeve in *Kojak*, she has been silenced by the law. In this is pseudo-journalistic style, we see a reporting of the facts without any overt editorialising; however, the absence of Maeve's input is a glaring omission. We are left to draw our own conclusions.

Themes and imagery

A **deeply dysfunctional family** is at the heart of the poem and Durcan exploits his **exaggerated and improbable cautionary** (warning) **tale** of their situation to highlight some social issues in contemporary Ireland. On the surface it seems we are told not to let our children watch violent TV shows and not to neglect them by frequenting bars; however, there is more to this poem than first meets the eye. Like much of Durcan's work, it is **deceptively simple**. First there is a criticism of the misogynistic nature of the media and our judicial system. 'Wives' are punished if they lash out or drink, but the ineffectual husband is not reprimanded at all. A woman is killed on screen in cold blood and disrespected further by a throwaway quip. A past where women could be the strong and ruthless ones has disappeared. **Criticism of the Americanisation of our culture** is also implicit here when the husband refers to the murdered woman as a 'dame' (line 8). Durcan seems to be questioning what has happened to our values, our culture and how we raise our children.

HIGHER LEVEL

As in 'Nessa' and 'The Difficulty that is Marriage', the poem features a relationship between a strong woman and a weaker man and addresses the issue of marital discord, albeit in more exaggerated terms. We sense the wife's exasperation here: the TV is clearly an issue for her and she takes action by destroying it after fair warning. The husband, however, seems relatively unaffected, hurrying to his mother's house so as not to miss the end of the show. Also his comments to the judge are meek and fawning, 'My mother has a fondness for Kojak, my Lord' (line 13).

The poem's imagery is **violent**: the shooting dead of the woman in *Kojak* and the wife's aggressive destruction of the TV. It works with the language (see below) to emphasise the strong themes in the poem.

Form and language

The poem is **a satire written in free verse as a faux** (fake) **newspaper article**. Headline-style titles are a feature of Durcan's work, as we will see again later in 'Six Nuns Die In Convent Inferno'.

Durcan skilfully combines different registers (types of language) to create the layers of text and subtext that convey the damning picture of modern Ireland highlighted above. 'Whereupon' (line 21), 'peaceably' (line 2) and 'my Lord' (line 1) are **legalistic** and formal phrases in the poem that emphasise the courtroom setting. The American influence is seen in the summary of the *Kojak* episode and the husband's use of 'dame' (line 8). We also encounter more **colloquial** language such as 'has a fondness for' (line 13). And finally the poem is framed by **pseudo-journalistic** language in the title and in the final phrase, 'Leave to appeal was refused'.

The language used against women in the poem is dismissive and **misogynistic** (anti-women), and the voices that get to speak directly are male. Maeve's words are quoted through her husband. The anger and vitriol aimed at women in the poem is striking from Kojak's quip, 'Goodnight, Queen Maeve' (line 9), to the judge's harsh sentence, 'Jail was the only place for them' (line 26). However, it must be noted that Maeve is not a model parent either, and that the judge and the wife are named but the husband is not. Why might this be?

SNAPSHOT

- Free verse
- Darkly humorous, satirical
- Social commentary
- Themes of justice, family, media, misogyny
- Dominated by male voices
- Legalistic and pseudo-journalistic language
- Written as a spoof newspaper article
- Reference to Ireland's mythical past
- Different registers
- Violent imagery

Paul Durcan

Exam-Style Questions

Understanding the poem

1. In bullet points, list what happened in the couple's home, according to the husband.
2. Explain what happens in the *Kojak* episode. Is this appropriate viewing for children, in your opinion? Explain.
3. Why did the husband say he 'had to bring the kids' to his mother's house (line 11)?
4. What is the wife's explanation for her actions (lines 16–18)? Was she justified, in your opinion?
5. What does the wife suggest as a better way to spend time as a family? Do you agree with her? Give reasons for your answer.
6. Explain the judge's take on this incident. Give your opinion on his comments and ruling.

Thinking about the poem

1. List the different voices we hear in the poem and say which, if any, are direct. Discuss the tone and gender of each one.
2. Whose side are you on by the end of the poem? Why? Debate this as a class.
3. Did you find this poem disturbing, funny or ridiculous? Choose one of these adjectives (or offer an alternative) and justify your choice with close reference to the poem.
4. What is Durcan's message here? Whom or what is he criticising? You may offer a number of answers.
5. Comment on the effect of the verbs in the poem.
6. Durcan's father, John, was a judge and the two had a difficult relationship. How, do you think, may this background have influenced the poem? Refer closely to the poem in your answer.

Imagining

1. Write this story as a tabloid article with a suitable headline.
2. Imagine you are one of the children. Write the statement you have given to the police about the incident. Mention how you felt as well as recounting what happened.

HIGHER LEVEL

Before you read

'The Generation Gap' – what issues cause division or distance between parents and their children? Discuss in pairs or small groups.

Parents

A child's face is a drowned face:
Her parents stare down at her asleep
Estranged from her by a sea: —
She is under the sea
And they are above the sea: 5
If she looked up she would see them
As if locked out of their own home,
Their mouths open,
Their foreheads furrowed –
Pursed-up orifices of fearful fish – 10
Their big ears are fins behind glass
And in her sleep she is calling out to them
Father, Father
Mother, Mother
But they cannot hear her: 15
She is inside the sea
And they are outside the sea:
And through the night, stranded, they stare
At the drowned, drowned face of their child.

Guidelines

This poem comes from the 1978 collection *Sam's Cross*. It was written when Durcan's daughters were young and deals with the distance between a sleeping child and her anxiously watching parents. Family issues, most notably estrangement, abound in Durcan's work.

138 / DISCOVERY: POETRY ANTHOLOGY

Paul Durcan

Commentary

Lines 1–5
The matter-of-fact title leaves us ill-prepared for the shock of the metaphor in the first line: 'A child's face is a drowned face'. This bold statement remains enigmatic (puzzling) even at its repetition at the end of the poem. We learn that the child is asleep and her parents are gazing worriedly down at her. This scenario is conveyed to us through a third-person speaker, which further emphasises the theme of distance and estrangement. The speaker tells us this distance between the parents and child is a sea that separates them and seems to have broken the bond between them. To the parents it seems that their daughter is lost, sleep-drowned in this sea. She is in the sea and they are above it.

Lines 6–10
The observer imagines that if the child opened her eyes she would perceive her parents as fish pressed up against a screen of glass, their mouths agape and with worried expressions, 'Their foreheads furrowed'. They seem 'locked out' of where they belong, 'their own home'. Durcan has switched the imagery somewhat to have the parents as the sea-dwellers, the 'fish'. Are they fish out of water or fish in a different body of water? The glass suggests some sort of tank. Could this represent a window? Perhaps to a hospital room or an incubator? Or perhaps it is purely metaphorical to represent the gulf between them. The parents are described almost comically; they could be animated characters in a child's cartoon with their fin-like ears and gaping mouths: 'Pursed-up orifices of fearful fish – / Their big ears are fins behind glass'.

> Compare this poem with 'Love' by Eavan Boland in relation to parenthood and coping with the illness of a child. Look at the use of water in the imagery of both poems.

Lines 11–19
The sleeping child is not at peace either. Like her anxious parents, she seems panicked by the situation and calls out for them in her sleep. Her anxiety is clear in the repetition used: 'Father, Father / Mother, Mother'. But the invisible barrier remains and they cannot pierce her dream-state to know her need for them: 'they cannot hear her'. Both parties remain in their separate physical and psychological states. The parents are outside, above and awake, while the child is under, inside and asleep. What links them, though, is a desperate need for each other and a deep anxiety. The parents' vigil – they watch her 'through the night' – leaves them feeling 'stranded', a word that encapsulates the powerlessness any parent feels when their child needs them and they are unable to help. The shocking metaphor of the first line is repeated twice in the last line as they continue to stare helplessly down 'At the drowned, drowned face of their child'.

Themes and imagery

Distance and estrangement are major themes here, symbolised by the sea. The use of balance and contrast in the imagery emphasises that the parents and child are in different realms but are united by their worry and need for each other, 'She is under the sea / And they are above the sea' (lines 4–5). **The sea is a recurring metaphor in Durcan's poetry** and here his depiction of the parents as fish gazing at a submerged child they cannot reach effectively conveys the estrangement at the heart of the poem's anxiety.

HIGHER LEVEL

Form and language

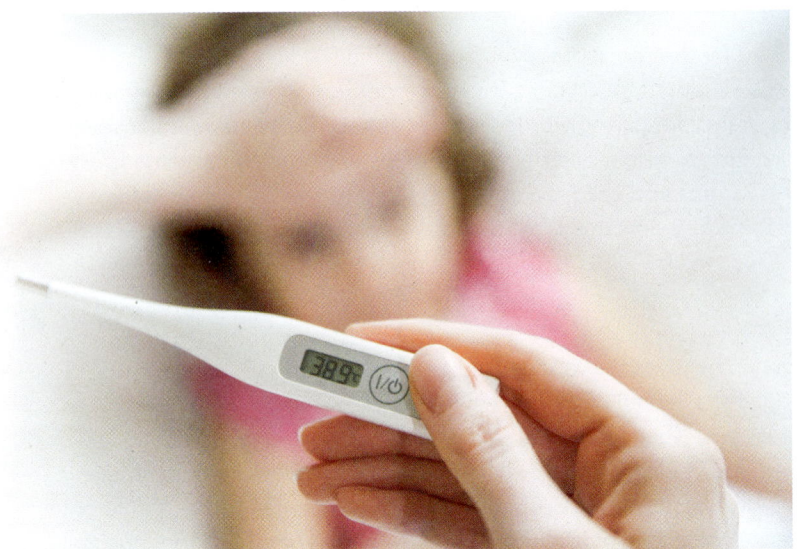

The **hypnotic effect** of the repetition in the poem, the short lines and brief, stark statements combine to produce a trance-like result. This effect perfectly conveys how a parent worriedly watching over a child (possibly an ill one or one they feel estranged from?) feels; they are in a bubble, they can think of nothing else. The repetition used throughout the poem conveys the prolonged suffering of the child and her parents. The exhaustion of the parents in their vigil is apparent in the final line lengthened by repetition, 'At the drowned, drowned face of their child'.

The sibilance, for example, 'She is inside the sea. / And they are outside the sea' (lines 16–17) has a plaintive effect, a **feeling of quiet suffering**. The alliteration in lines like 'foreheads furrowed – / … orifices of fearful fish' (lines 9–10) speeds up the rhythm, conveying the panic the parents feel.

The visual break in the child's imagined cry for her parents at lines 13 and 14 is the climax of the poem emotionally. There is an almost resigned note to the rest of the poem as the parents are left stranded and staring down at her helplessly. The lack of progress or resolution at the end of this free-verse lyric leaves a chilling effect and the absence of hope or solace makes for uncomfortable reading in this surreal and nightmarish poem.

SNAPSHOT

- Theme of distance and estrangement
- Free verse lyric
- Helplessness and worry of parents
- Unsettling effect of the opening and ending
- Mood of anxiety
- Enigmatic
- Sea is a central image
- Repetition
- Family issues explored
- Surreal, nightmarish quality

Paul Durcan

Exam-Style Questions

Understanding the poem

1. What, do you think, does the first line mean? What effect did it have on you? Was it surprising, strange, shocking …? Give reasons for your answer.
2. Briefly describe the tableau depicted. In other words, if the scene described in the poem were a painting or photograph, what would you see?
3. What are the parents compared to? How is this achieved?
4. What emotions are the parents and the child feeling? What words and images in the poem convey this?
5. What is meant by the words 'Estranged' (line 3) and 'stranded' (line 18) in the context of the poem? Are they linked in any way? Give reasons for your answer.
6. What is the child conveying when the speaker imagines she calls out to them in lines 13 and 14?

Thinking about the poem

1. What does the sea represent in the poem? Where are the parents and child in terms of this sea?
2. Why, do you think, are the parents compared to fish in the poem?
3. What might the glass (line 11) represent, in your view? Explain your answer.
4. What effect does the repetition in the poem have? Give examples.
5. Apart from repetition, identify another sound effect in the poem that struck you and explain the reason for your choice.
6. What is the main theme of this poem, in your opinion? Give reasons for your answer and back these up with evidence from the poem as a whole.

Imagining

1. Discuss the poem in pairs and suggest another metaphor the poet might have used instead of the sea to represent the distance between parents and child. Justify your choice.
2. Write a dialogue or short story, inspired by the poem, exploring what has happened to the family and what happens next.

HIGHER LEVEL

Before you read
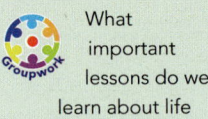 What important lessons do we learn about life in childhood? Discuss this idea in pairs and come up with a list.

En Famille, 1979

Bring me back to the dark school – to the dark school of childhood:
To where tiny is tiny, and massive is massive.

Glossary
Title *En Famille*: a French term meaning with one's family, at home

Madman

Every child has a madman on their street:
The only trouble about our madman is that he's our father.

Guidelines
Durcan's **couplet poems** are one of his most well-known forms. They tend to be **pithy, direct and thought-provoking**. These two poems focus on some **darker aspects of childhood and family life**.

Commentary

'En Famille, 1979'
Durcan's nostalgic opening, 'Bring me back', seems to yearn for the past; however, this yearning quickly becomes bleak and seems twisted when the past he longs to return to is characterised as 'the dark school of childhood'. He seems to feel that his childhood years were ones where he learned hard or unsettling lessons. Perhaps this refers to his difficult relationship with his father. The poem 'Sport' deals with this topic in more detail. What Durcan does seem to appreciate about the past is how simple it was. You knew where you stood, it was a more black-and-white world, a place 'where tiny is tiny, and massive is massive'. This longing for a simpler time is strange as this time was 'dark' for the speaker. Why would one long to revisit a troubled childhood? Perhaps it is still a more attractive option than the current situation? What lessons might this 'dark school' have taught the older and troubled Durcan?

'Madman'
This single-word title may refer to Durcan's father or perhaps to Durcan himself. It is, on the surface, a funny poem; however, it has a more troubling truth at its core. Durcan reports that he was often beaten and verbally abused by his ambitious and prominent father, Judge John James Durcan. His father was instrumental in Durcan being sectioned against his will into a mental institution as a very young man. The initial assertion seems general enough, almost glib, 'Every child has a madman on their street'. Then, like 'En Famille, 1979', a much darker notion stops us in our tracks, 'The only trouble about our madman is that he's our father'. This strange combination of darkness, autobiographical honesty and humour is at the heart of Durcan's style. Whether the madman is generic, himself or his father, we are disarmed by his directness and by, as Brendan Kennelly said of Durcan, his 'manic confidentiality'.

Paul Durcan

Themes and imagery

Both couplets are dark in their theme: 'the dark school of childhood' in 'En Famille, 1979' is further darkened by the idea that as a child Durcan's father seemed to be a 'madman' regarded as such by the whole street. Durcan's childhood seems to have been a bleak place. Despite having siblings, he writes little or nothing about them and concentrates instead on his parental relationships. The idea of a school being dark rather than filled with the light of learning is also intriguing and unsettling.

Durcan seems to yearn for the past despite its bleakness. He longs for simplicity and deals with painful memories with a **surface levity** and **insouciance** (indifference). Contrast and reversal are built in, 'where tiny is tiny, and massive is massive', he writes in 'En Famille, 1979'. What does 'tiny' represent? The powerlessness of a child in the face of an angry and violent parent, perhaps? Durcan leaves this up to the reader. A funny, joke-like poem about a mad father, 'Madman', is another example of the **reversals of expectations and conventions** achieved by this poet.

Form and language

Couplets are a popular form for Durcan, but generally in poetry couplets rhyme. Durcan prefers free verse, which lends an immediacy, accessibility and authenticity to his poetic voice. The **frankness** of what he is conveying is emphasised, but we do not feel Durcan is feeling sorry for himself or expecting our sympathy. It is a characteristically Irish thing to deal with difficult issues through a **dark sense of humour** and in doing so Durcan avoids sounding needy or sentimental. Indeed, 'Madman' sounds like it could be the set-up and punchline to a joke. Both poems make use of carefully chosen and timed repetition to great effect. Consider, for example, the phrase 'to the dark school – to the dark school of childhood' in 'En Famille, 1979'. We pause at the dash and so the repeated phrase 'dark school' is given time and weight for the reader. There is plenty of alliteration in this couplet as well, making the language of such a short poem very rich in sound.

Questions

1	Describe the tone of each poem. Choose from the list that follows or suggest your own ideas: humour, nostalgia, yearning, anger. Give reasons for your answers.
2	Comment on the title of each poem and suggest an alternative title for each. Justify your choices.
3	Examine childhood as a central theme of each poem.
4	Do you agree with Durcan that 'Every child has a madman on their street'? If so, why? If not, then why, do you think, does Durcan say this?
5	Which of the two couplets did you prefer? Explain with reference to both poems.
6	Comment on the imagery in each couplet. Which has the most striking imagery? Give reasons for your answer.
7	Analyse the use of repetition in each poem and the effects the repetition produces.
8	Why, do you think, does Durcan opt for free verse rather than rhyming couplets?
9	Revisit the 'Before you read' exercise and turn some of your suggestions into couplets of your own.

HIGHER LEVEL

Before you read
What photographs are most treasured by your family? What specific events are depicted? Why are these memories the most treasured?

'Windfall', 8 Parnell Hill, Cork

But, then, at the end of day I could always say –
Well, now, I am going home.
I felt elected, steeped, sovereign to be able to say –
I am going home.
When I was at home I liked to stay at home;　　　　　　　　　　5
At home I stayed at home for weeks;
At home I used sit in a winged chair by the window
Overlooking the river and the factory chimneys,
The electricity power station and the car assembly works,
The fleets of trawlers and the pilot tugs,　　　　　　　　　　　10
Dreaming that life is a dream which is real,
The river a reflection of itself in its own waters,
Goya sketching Goya among the smoky mirrors.
The industrial vista was my Mont Sainte-Victoire.
While my children sat on my knees watching TV　　　　　　　15
Their mother, my wife, reclined on the couch
Knitting a bright-coloured scarf, drinking a cup of black coffee,
Smoking a cigarette – one of her own roll-ups.
I closed my eyes and breathed in and breathed out.
It is ecstasy to breathe if you are at home in the world.　　　　20
What a windfall! A home of our own!
Our neighbours' houses had names like 'Con Amore',
'Sans Souci', 'Pacelli', 'Montini', 'Homesville'.
But we called our home 'Windfall'.
'Windfall', 8 Parnell Hill, Cork.　　　　　　　　　　　　　　　25
In the gut of my head coursed the leaf of tranquillity
Which I dreamed was known only to Buddhist Monks
In lotus monasteries high up in the Hindu Kush.
Down here in the dark depths of Ireland,
Below sea level in the city of Cork,　　　　　　　　　　　　　30
In a city as intimate and homicidal as a Little Marseilles,
In a country where all the children of the nation
Are not cherished equally
And where the best go homeless, while the worst
Erect block-house palaces – self-regardingly ugly –　　　　　　35
Having a home of your own can give to a family
A chance in a lifetime to transcend death.

At the high window, shipping from all over the world
Being borne up and down the busy, yet contemplative, river;
Skylines drifting in and out of skylines in the cloudy valley;　　40

Paul Durcan

Firelight at dusk, and city lights;
Beyond them the control tower of the airport on the hill –
A lighthouse in the sky flashing green to white to green;
Our black-and-white cat snoozing in the corner of a chair;
Pastels and etchings on the four walls, and over the mantelpiece   45
'Van Gogh's Grave' and 'Lovers in Water';
A room wallpapered in books and family photograph albums
Chronicling the adventures and metamorphoses of family life:
In swaddling clothes in Mammy's arms on baptism day;
Being a baby of nine months and not remembering it;   50
Face-down in a pram, incarcerated in a high chair;
Everybody, including strangers, wearing shop-window smiles;
With Granny in Felixstowe, with Granny in Ballymaloe;
In a group photo in First Infants, on a bike at thirteen;
In the back garden in London, in the back garden in Cork;   55
Performing a headstand after First Holy Communion;
Getting a kiss from the Bishop on Confirmation Day;
Straw hats in the Bois de Boulogne, wearing wings at the seaside;
Mammy and Daddy holding hands on the Normandy Beaches;
Mammy and Daddy at the wedding of Jeremiah and Margot;   60
Mammy and Daddy queueing up for *Last Tango in Paris*;
Boating on the Shannon, climbing mountains in Kerry;
Building sandcastles in Killala, camping in Barley Cove;
Picnicking in Moone, hide-and-go-seek in Clonmacnoise;
Riding horses, cantering, jumping fences;   65
Pushing out toy yachts in the pond in the Tuileries;
The Irish College revisited in the Rue des Irlandais;
Sipping on an orange *pressé* through a straw on the roof of the Beaubourg;
Dancing in Père Lachaise, weeping at Auvers.
Year in, year out, I pored over these albums accumulating,   70
My children looking over my shoulder, exhilarated as I was,
Their mother presiding at our ritual from a distance –
The far side of the hearthrug, diffidently, proudly.
Schoolbooks on the floor and pyjamas on the couch –
Whose turn is it tonight to put the children to bed?   75

Our children swam about our home
As if it were their private sea,
Their own unique, symbiotic fluid
Of which their parents also partook.
Such is home – a sea of your own   80
In which you hang upside down from the ceiling
With equanimity, while postcards from Thailand on the mantelpiece
Are raising their eyebrow markings benignly:
Your hands dangling their prayers to the floorboards of your home,
Sifting the sands underneath the surfaces of conversations.   85

The marine insect life of the family psyche.
A home of your own – or a sea of your own –
In which climbing the walls is as natural
As making love on the stairs;
In which when the telephone rings   90
Husband and wife are metamorphosed into smiling accomplices,
Both declining to answer it;
Initiating, instead, a yet more subversive kiss –
A kiss they have perhaps never attempted before –
And might never have dreamed of attempting   95
Were it not for the telephone belling.
Through the bannisters or along the bannister rails
The pyjama-clad children solemnly watching
Their parents at play, jumping up and down in support,
Race back to bed, gesticulating wordlessly: 100
The most subversive unit in society is the human family.

We're almost home, pet, almost home …
Our home is at …
I'll be home …
I have to go home now …   105
I want to go home now …
Are you feeling homesick? …
Are you anxious to get home? …
I can't wait to get home …
Let's stay at home tonight and …   110
What time will you be coming home at? …
If I'm not home by six at the latest, I'll phone …
We're nearly home, don't worry, we're nearly home …

But then with good reason
I was put out of my home: 115
By a keen wind felled.
I find myself now without a home
Having to live homeless in the alien, foreign city of Dublin.
It is an eerie enough feeling to be homesick
Yet knowing you will be going home next week;   120
It is an eerie feeling beyond all ornithological analysis
To be homesick knowing that there is no home to go to:
Day by day, creeping, crawling,
Moonlighting, escaping,
Bed-and-breakfast to bed-and-breakfast;   125
Hostels, centres, one-night hotels.

Paul Durcan

>Homeless in Dublin,
>Blown about the suburban streets at evening,
>Peering in the windows of other people's homes,
>Wondering what it must feel like   130
>To be sitting around a fire –
>Apache or Cherokee or Bourgeoisie –
>Beholding the firelit faces of your family,
>Beholding their starry or their TV gaze:
>Windfall to Windfall – can you hear me?   135
>Windfall to Windfall ...
>We're almost home, pet, don't worry anymore, we're almost home.

Glossary

3	***steeped, sovereign***: both colloquialisms for 'lucky'
10	***pilot tugs***: small boats that guide much bigger ones in and out of harbours
13	***Goya***: Francisco José de Goya (1746–1828), a Spanish artist
14	***Mont Sainte-Victoire***: mountain in southern France, painted by Paul Cézanne
28	***Hindu Kush***: mountain range in Pakistan and Afghanistan
61	***Last Tango in Paris***: steamy 1972 film that depicts a tragic love affair
68	***pressé***: French term for juice
73	***diffidently***: modestly, humbly
78	***symbiotic fluid***: symbiotic means a mutually and equally beneficial relationship in nature; by adding 'fluid' Durcan is referencing 'amniotic fluid', which is the nurturing fluid in the womb
82	***equanimity***: calmness
83	***benignly***: kindly, compassionately
86	***psyche***: the mind, consciousness
91	***metamorphosed***: changed completely
121	***ornithological***: concerning the study of birds
132	***Apache, Cherokee***: Native American tribes
132	***Bourgeoisie***: middle class; conservative and materialistic

Guidelines

This poem is from *The Berlin Wall Café* (1985). Like 'Nessa' and 'The Difficulty that is Marriage', this poem is a meditation on Durcan's marriage and its break-up. The tone is often confessional and full of regret and longing. The poet's love of his home and family life in Cork dominate.

Commentary

Title

'Windfall' is a term denoting an unexpected piece of luck, often financial, that originally comes from fruit trees shedding their ripe fruit in windy weather. Calling their house this suggests the couple felt lucky to have such a lovely home.

Lines 1–19

Durcan reflects that no matter what troubles he has had he was once in a position to say 'now, I am going home' (line 2). We immediately infer that he can no longer say this from the conditional 'I could' in the first

> **Francisco José de Goya**
>
> Goya was a Spanish artist whose paintings, particularly the later ones, often portrayed their subjects bleakly. Here, Durcan references a painting of the Spanish royal family where Goya inserts an image of himself in a dark mirror. Perhaps with this reference Durcan is reminding us that the artist is always present in their creations and has a duty to depict the world truthfully. The painting in question is dark and full of menacing shadows.

line. Thus, the poem is infused with regret and at the same time with great fondness. These contrasting emotions dominate the poem. The poet uses colloquialisms to show how lucky and happy he once felt being able to say this; he was 'steeped, sovereign' (line 3). He loved staying at home in his 'winged chair by the window' (line 7) for weeks on end, gazing out upon the busy scene beyond. His life was like a dream of a life that is a dream to live, and he enjoys watching the busy river. 'The industrial vista' (line 14) reflected in the river reminds him of a Goya painting and of Mont Sainte-Victoire, a mountain which the artist Cézanne loved to paint. A cosy domestic scene is described: he sits with his children on his knees 'watching TV' while his wife knits on the sofa, smoking and drinking coffee. Note that even here his wife is distant, sitting apart from him and engaged in a different activity. He recollects, 'I closed my eyes and breathed in and breathed out' (line 19), savouring the preciousness and perfection of the moment. Note the repetition of 'home' in this section, fixing this as the central theme of the poem.

Lines 20–37

Mentioning home for an eighth time in the poem so far, Durcan tells us that breathing in one's beloved home is 'ecstasy' (line 20). He lists the names of the houses of their neighbours, all suggesting peace and blissful contentment: 'Con Amore' – with love, 'Sans Souci' – without a care, 'Pacelli' – little peace, 'Montini' – little mountain (lines 22–23). 'Pacelli' and 'Montini' were also family names of two popes. The idea of peace continues as Durcan compares the sense of tranquillity his home provides him with to the utter contentment of Buddhist monks meditating amid lotus flowers in monasteries on the Hindu Kush.

Durcan moves on to wider issues and a criticism of some aspects of the 'dark depths of Ireland' (line 29) follows. Have you noticed Durcan referring to Ireland as 'dark' in other poems on your course? Here, he compares Cork city to the southern French city of Marseilles in terms of its intimacy and its 'homicidal' nature (line 31). Durcan criticises Ireland's lack of success in fulfilling the 1916 Proclamation's promise that all children will be 'cherished equally' (line 33). This inequality is further emphasised as he laments that the 'best' of people are homeless while 'the worst' build garish, ostentatious 'block-house palaces' reflecting their own arrogance and self-importance, 'self-regardingly ugly' (lines 34–35). He says that being able to put a roof over your family's head gives a person a legacy, 'A chance in a lifetime to transcend death' (line 37). Perhaps the safety and protection offered by a home is the most valuable thing one can provide for one's family, in Durcan's view. The mention of homelessness here foreshadows Durcan's fate later in the poem.

Lines 38–75

After an account of the evening skyline, Durcan depicts his home's interior: the family cat is 'snoozing' (line 44) on a chair, the walls are covered in art and any remaining space has been filled up by books and photograph albums. These albums record the changes and important events in this family's life, 'adventures and metamorphoses' (line 48), including pregnancies, baptisms, school photos, teenage years, communion and confirmation days and family holidays at home and abroad. Like Durcan's own poetry, they record the transient nature of family life, and the huge changes and important events common to all families. Likewise, the books and the art on the walls reflect the interests and passions of this couple.

Paul Durcan

Durcan has 'pored over these albums' (line 70) and added to them over the years, his children have too, but his wife remains distant, 'diffidently, proudly' (line 73). A note of tension is introduced as, surveying the floor and couch littered with schoolbooks and pyjamas, someone asks, 'Whose turn is it tonight to put the children to bed?' (line 75). Who, do you think, is asking this question? It breaks the hypnotic effect of the list of photographs.

Lines 76–101

As in 'Nessa' and 'The Difficulty that is Marriage', the sea is used symbolically to convey the safe and mutually beneficial environment of the family home. The children swim in its 'unique, symbiotic fluid' (line 78) and the parents enjoy the privilege of this 'private sea' (line 77) also. Home is 'a sea of your own' (line 80); like the amniotic fluid of the womb it nurtures and protects us from the world outside. Home is where you can do as you wish, 'hang upside down from the ceiling' (line 81), but it can also be a place of discord. In lines 85–86, 'Sifting the sands underneath the surfaces of conversations. / The marine insect life of the family psyche', perhaps Durcan is commenting on how the couple read into what the other is saying, looking for a subtext, for something unsaid that may rankle, and that often these things are petty, niggling, inferred slights.

Durcan's mental health issues may be hinted at when he mentions 'climbing the walls' (line 88), and the passion and intimacy of the couple is conveyed in the anecdotes about 'making love on the stairs' (line 89) and kissing while ignoring a ringing telephone as their children watch through the bannisters. It is as if the couple are like children, playing mischievously while the real children watch supportively.

Line 101 is enigmatic: 'The most subversive unit in society is the human family.' Durcan shows us that we never know what goes on behind closed doors in family homes, where people can truly be their weird and wonderful selves without having to adhere to societal norms. Of course, there is a darker side to this and we know that Durcan's childhood home life with his father was often an unhappy one.

Lines 102–113

The list of incomplete phrases much used by so many of us reflect a lifetime's worth of conversations between couples and family members. The absolute necessity and comfort of the institution of the family home is emphasised in this tender and poignant section of the poem, 'We're nearly home, don't worry, we're nearly home …' (line 113).

Lines 114–126

The turning point of the poem comes next and explains the poet's use of the conditional and past tenses back at lines 1–3. With an abrupt change of tone and pace Durcan admits, 'But then with good reason / I was put out of my home' (lines 114–115). He compares this experience to being a tree 'By a keen wind felled' (line 116). This image brings the title and the name of the poet's now former home back to mind. Home has lost its connotations of safety and comfort and he must move to the 'alien, foreign city of Dublin' (line 118). He is now homeless like those he had previously pitied (line 34). The cosy domesticity of his home with its river view, books, photographs and art has been lost to a nightmarish life 'creeping, crawling' (line 123) between temporary accommodations. Deep loneliness, which defies 'ornithological analysis' (line 121), is the pervading effect here. Durcan is lost and bereft in this harsh place, perhaps like a bird out of its nest.

Lines 127–137

'Homeless in Dublin' (line 127), Durcan continues the felled tree idea of line 116, being blown about the streets by a wind of loneliness like a **desultory leaf** (lacking purpose/enthusiasm). As with the image of estrangement in 'Parents', he is now on the outside looking in at scenes of cosy domesticity. He notes that sitting round a fire at the end of the day is common in so many cultures, 'Apache or Cherokee or Bourgeoisie' (line 132). The playful internal rhyme here is at odds with the deeply sad nature of the subject matter.

The final lines are like an SOS call to his former home, 'Windfall to Windfall – can you hear me?' (line 135). The repetition of this emphasises its plaintive effect. A phrase from line 102 is repeated here, 'We're almost home, pet', but sounds hollow and tragic in its yearning for reassurance.

Themes and imagery

Home and the protection, safety and love it provides is central to the poem. Durcan's constant repetition of the word 'home', his long descriptions of aspects of his home and, most starkly, his desolation at losing his home combine to make this the dominant theme. It is possible that Durcan didn't ever feel deserving of a home and so perhaps there was almost a sense of inevitability to his losing it. 'Windfall', the name they chose to give to their Cork home, suggests unexpected, even undeserved luck. He tells us early on he felt 'steeped' (line 3) to ever be able to say he was going home. The imagery used underlines this, the idea of the home as a 'private sea' (line 77), where the safety and love within its walls allows those within to swim about in a totally nurturing and protected environment. The internal rhyme of 'Such is home – a sea of your own' (line 80) reinforces the harmonious feeling described.

Form and language

This long narrative lyric is at once accessible and also surreal. Eamonn Grennan describes how Durcan's everyday 'uncomplicated language' is transformed and energised by metaphor, citing the example of Durcan's use of the sea in this poem. To compare the comfort and protection of home to the sea is straightforward enough, but with Durcan there is 'a gradual thickening of metaphor' as he attempts to express emotional truths. The extension of the sea metaphor to compare it to a womb-like fluid is then twisted further in lines 85–86: 'Sifting the sands underneath the surfaces of conversations. / The marine insect life of the family psyche', demonstrating Durcan's ability to transport a simple and accessible comparison into a far more textured and abstract one.

The poem is full of allusions to places, artworks, artists and memories and utilises lists repeatedly, which is another feature of many Durcan poems.

Questions

1	What is the effect of Durcan's use of the conditional and past tenses in the opening of the poem (lines 1–3)?
2	What do we learn about Durcan's home life and the home itself in this poem? Why does he mention 'home' so much?
3	How is Durcan's wife portrayed in the poem?
4	Look at the description of Cork in lines 7–14 and compare and contrast this with the description given in lines 30–43.
5	Comment on Durcan's extensive use of place names. What effect do they have on the poem? Have you seen Durcan use place names in other poems? Write about this, comparing the effects achieved.
6	What is Durcan's opinion of modern Ireland, judging by lines 31–35?
7	List the events portrayed in the family photographs described in the poem (lines 49–69). Why, do you think, did Durcan choose these particular events? What picture do they give us of his upbringing and family? Do any match the list you made in the 'Before you read' exercise?
8	Describe and explain the water metaphor in lines 76–80.
9	How are the roles of the parents and children reversed in the poem (see lines 91–101)? Which of the two parents seems most childish to you and why?
10	Comment on the effect of the 'home' section (lines 102–113). Why, do you think, did Durcan include this section in the poem?
11	How does the Dublin section (lines 114–137) contrast with the rest of the poem? What picture of Dublin is presented here?
12	What, do you think, does Durcan miss most about home as suggested in this Dublin section? Provide evidence for your answer.
13	How did reading the final three lines of the poem make you feel? Explain.
14	What are the main themes addressed in the poem and how are they conveyed?
15	Research the paintings mentioned by Durcan in the poem, then write a descriptive passage, poem or short story based on one or more of them.
16	What do you see from your window at home or in school and how does this view make you feel? Model your description on Durcan's description of Cork.
17	'The most subversive unit in society is the human family' (line 101). Discuss in pairs or small groups whether you agree with Durcan's statement, giving reasons and examples.

Six Nuns Die in Convent Inferno

To the happy memory of six Loreto nuns who died between midnight and morning of 2 June 1986

I

We resided in a Loreto convent in the centre of Dublin city
On the east side of a public gardens, St. Stephen's Green.
Grafton Street – the paseo
Where everybody paseo'd, including even ourselves –
Debouched on the north side, and at the top of Grafton Street, 5
Or round the base of the great patriotic pebble of O'Donovan Rossa,
Knelt tableaus of punk girls and punk boys.
When I used to pass them – scurrying as I went –
Often as not to catch a mass in Clarendon Street,
The Carmelite Church in Clarendon Street 10
(Myself, I never used the Clarendon Street entrance,
I always slipped in by way of Johnson's Court,
Opposite the side entrance to Bewley's Oriental Café),
I could not help but smile, as I sucked on a Fox's mint,
That for all the half-shaven heads and the martial garb 15
And the dyed hair-dos and the nappy pins
They looked so conventional, really, and vulnerable,
Clinging to war paint and to uniforms and to one another.
I knew it was myself who was the ultimate drop-out,
The delinquent, the recidivist, the vagabond, 20
The wild woman, the subversive, the original punk.
Yet, although I confess I was smiling, I was also afraid,
Appalled by my own nerve, my own fervour,
My apocalyptic enthusiasm, my other-worldly hubris:
To opt out of the world and to 25
Choose such exotic loneliness,
Such terrestrial abandonment,
A lifetime of bicycle lamps and bicycle pumps,
A lifetime of galoshes stowed under the stairs,
A lifetime of umbrellas drying out in the kitchens. 30

I was an old nun – an agèd beadwoman –
But I was no daw.
I knew what a weird bird I was, I knew that when we
Went to bed we were as eerie an aviary as you'd find
In all the blown-off rooftops of the city: 35

Before you read

Think of a current event that is prominent in the media. Imagine you are centrally involved in this and write a personal account of your experience.

Scuttling about our dorm, wheezing, shrieking, croaking,
In our yellowy corsets, wonky suspenders, strung-out garters,
A bony crew in the gods of the sleeping city.
Many's the night I lay awake in bed
Dreaming what would befall us if there were a fire: 40
No fire-escapes outside, no fire-extinguishers inside;
To coin a Dublin saying,
We'd not stand a snowball's chance in hell. Fancy that!
It seemed too good to be true:
Happy death vouchsafed only to the few. 45
Sleeping up there was like sleeping at the top of the mast
Of a nineteenth-century schooner, and in the daytime
We old nuns were the ones who crawled out on the yardarms
To stitch and sew the rigging and the canvas.
To be sure we were weird birds, oddballs, Christniks, 50
For we had done the weirdest thing a woman can do –
Surrendered the marvellous passions of girlhood,
The innocent dreams of childhood,
Not for a night or a weekend or even a Lent or a season,
But for a lifetime. 55
Never to know the love of a man or a woman;
Never to have children of our own;
Never to have a home of our own;
All for why and for what?
To follow a young man – would you believe it – 60
Who lived two thousand years ago in Palestine
And who died a common criminal strung up on a tree.

As we stood there in the disintegrating dormitory
Burning to death in the arms of Christ –
O Christ, Christ, come quickly, quickly – 65
Fluttering about in our tight, gold bodices,
Beating our wings in vain,
It reminded me of the snaps one of the sisters took
When we took a seaside holiday in 1956
(The year Cardinal Mindszenty went into hiding 70
In the US legation in Budapest.
He was a great hero of ours, Cardinal Mindszenty,
And any of us would have given our right arm
To have been his nun – darning his socks, cooking his meals,
Making his bed, doing his washing and ironing). 75
Somebody – an affluent buddy of the bishop's repenting his affluence –
Loaned Mother Superior a secluded beach in Co. Waterford –
Ardmore, along the coast from Tramore –
A cove with palm trees, no less, well off the main road.
There we were, fluttering up and down the beach, 80

Scampering hither and thither in our starched bathing-costumes.
Tonight, expiring in the fire was quite much like that,
Only instead of scampering into the waves of the sea,
Now we were scampering into the flames of the fire.

That was one of the gayest days of my life, 85
The day the sisters went swimming.
Often in the silent darkness of the chapel after Benediction,
During the Exposition of the Blessed Sacrament,
I glimpsed the sea again as it was that day.
Praying – daydreaming really – 90
I became aware that Christ is the ocean
Forever rising and falling on the world's shore.
Now tonight in the convent Christ is the fire in whose waves
We are doomed but delighted to drown.
And, darting in and out of the flames of the dormitory, 95
Gabriel, with that extraordinary message of his on his boyish lips,
Frenetically pedalling his skybike.
He whispers into my ear what I must do
And I do it – and die.
Each of us in our own tiny, frail, furtive way 100
Was a Mother of God, mothering forth illegitimate Christs
In the street life of Dublin city.
God have mercy on our whirring souls –
Wild women were we all –
And on the misfortunate, poor fire-brigade men 105
Whose task it will be to shovel up our ashes and shovel
What is left of us into black plastic refuse sacks.
Fire-brigade men are the salt of the earth.

Isn't it a marvellous thing how your hour comes
When you least expect it? When you lose a thing, 110
Not to know about it until it actually happens?
How, in so many ways, losing things is such a refreshing experience,
Giving you a sense of freedom you've not often experienced?
How lucky I was to lose – I say, lose – lose my life.
It was a Sunday night, and after vespers 115
I skipped bathroom so that I could hop straight into bed
And get a bit of a read before lights out:
Conor Cruise O'Brien's new book The Siege,
All about Israel and superlatively insightful
For a man who they say is reputedly an agnostic – 120
I got a loan of it from the brother-in-law's married niece –
But I was tired out and I fell asleep with the book open
Face down across my breast and I woke
To the racket of bellowing flame and snarling glass.

The first thing I thought was that the brother-in-law's married niece 125
Would never again get her Conor Cruise O'Brien back
And I had seen on the price-tag that it cost £23.00:
Small wonder that the custom of snipping off the price
As an exercise in social deportment has simply died out;
Indeed a book today is almost worth buying for its price, 130
Its price frequently being more remarkable than its contents.

The strange Eucharist of my death –
To be eaten alive by fire and smoke.
I clasped the dragon to my breast
And stroked his red-hot ears. 135
Strange! There we were, all sleeping molecules,
Suddenly all giving birth to our deaths,
All frantically in labour.
Doctors and midwives weaved in and out
In gowns of smoke and gloves of fire. 140
Christ, like an Orthodox patriarch in his dressing gown,
Flew up and down the dormitory, splashing water on our souls:
Sister Eucharia; Sister Seraphia; Sister Rosario;
Sister Gonzaga; Sister Margaret; Sister Edith.
If you will remember us – six nuns burnt to death – 145
Remember us for the frisky girls that were,
Now more than ever kittens in the sun.

II

When Jesus heard these words at the top of Grafton Street
Uttered by a small, agèd, emaciated, female punk
Clad all in mourning black, and grieving like an alley cat, 150

He was annulled with astonishment, and turning round
He declared to the gangs of teenagers and dicemen following him:
'I tell you, not even in New York City
Have I found faith like this.'

That night in St. Stephen's Green, 155
After the keepers had locked the gates,
And the courting couples had found cinemas themselves to die in,
The six nuns who had died in the convent inferno,
From the bandstand they'd been hiding under, crept out
And knelt together by the Fountain of the Three Fates, 160
Reciting the Agnus Dei: reciting it as if it were the torch song
Of all aid – Live Aid, Self Aid, Aids, and All Aid –
Lord, I am not worthy
That thou should'st enter under my roof;
Say but the word and my soul shall be healed. 165

Glossary

3	*paseo*: pedestrian street; or in Spanish, an evening stroll
5	*Debouched*: came out from; emerged
7	*tableaus*: scenes that look like a picture (a 'freeze-frame' effect)
15	*martial garb*: military clothing; uniforms
20	*recidivist*: repeat offender (often used for criminals who reoffend)
23	*fervour*: intense feeling or belief
24	*hubris*: extreme arrogance; excessive pride
29	*galoshes*: shoes worn over one's own shoes to protect them from water
32	*daw*: colloquialism for a fool (from the jackdaw)
34	*aviary*: large enclosure for a collection of birds
45	*vouchsafed*: given or granted as a favour
47	*schooner*: type of ship
48	*yardarms*: ends of the crossbeam of a ship's mast
70	*Cardinal Mindszenty*: leader of the Catholic Church in Hungary who was persecuted by the communist government and who found refuge in the US embassy in Budapest
76	*affluent*: wealthy
87	*Benediction*: Roman Catholic ceremony where the host is displayed in a special stand
97	*Frenetically*: in an agitated manner
115	*vespers*: evening prayers
118	*The Siege*: a history and analysis of the Jewish state of Israel from the birth of Zionism and its founders on, written by politician and historian Conor Cruise O'Brien
120	*agnostic*: someone who believes that it is not possible to know whether God exists
129	*social deportment*: knowing the correct and mannerly way to act in social situations
141	*Orthodox patriarch*: bishop of the Greek or Russian Orthodox Church
149	*emaciated*: wasting away through lack of food
151	*annulled*: invalidated; cancelled (often refers to a marriage being dissolved because it has not been consummated)
152	*dicemen*: street performers; Thom McGinty, a well-known mime artist on Grafton Street, was known as 'The Diceman'
161	*Agnus Dei*: lamb of God (a prayer)

Guidelines

This is another poem where, like 'Wife Who Smashed Television', Durcan **uses a headline-style title and adopts a persona**. The voice adopted here is that of one of six nuns who died in a fire in their convent in Dublin city centre. Here, Durcan stays with this voice for the duration of this long and at times surreal narrative. Note also the use of digression, even during some of the most dramatic parts of the poem, and consider the effect produced as you read the poem.

Commentary

Title

The headline-style title refers to a real event, a 1986 fire in a convent in Dublin city centre. According to the *LA Times*, the victims, ranging in age from sixty to eighty-three, were 'asleep in a dormitory on the top floor of the four-storey Loreto Secondary School when the fire broke out'. The dedication or subtitle sets the precedent for the many paradoxical and quirky details we will encounter in the poem. 'To the happy memory' seems an odd choice of phrase for such a tragedy, but all will be revealed! The date and the detail of the nuns' order (Loreto) adds authenticity to the piece. Durcan uses the same technique in poems like 'Father's Day, 21 June 1992' and 'Ireland 2002'.

Paul Durcan

Part I

Lines 1–62

As the narrative opens the nun tells us warmly and conversationally where she lived and how she loved to stroll round the city centre, often passing groups of punks with their 'half-shaven heads and the martial garb' (line 15). Contrary to their aggressive image the nun perceives these punks as 'conventional' and 'vulnerable' (line 17) as she scurries past them to go to Mass. Indeed, she sees herself as far more rebellious; she is the 'delinquent', the 'wild woman' (lines 20–21) because she has dropped out of or abandoned the conventional, secular world to live a cloistered and unusual existence. This choice, she feels, is 'subversive' (line 21) and the loneliness of this life is, for her, 'exotic' (line 26). Durcan goes against conventional ideas and preconceptions of religious life and turns our expectations inside out with descriptions such as this.

> **Punks**
>
> Punks or punk rockers enjoy punk music (mainly fast and aggressive anti-establishment songs) and dress in an unconventional manner (typically having extreme hairstyles, multiple piercings and wearing heavy make-up, metal chains and torn clothes decorated with zips and safety pins).

She may be a 'beadwoman' (line 31), using rosary beads to count prayers, but she is no fool, 'daw' (line 32). She extends this ornithological image, referring to herself as a 'weird bird' (line 33) and the convent as an 'aviary' (line 34). She knew that should the convent catch fire she would not survive, 'We'd not stand a snowball's chance in hell' (line 43). Imagery of hell will reappear later on.

> **Beatniks**
>
> Beatniks were people who participated in a social movement of the 1950s and early 1960s that stressed artistic self-expression and the rejection of conventional society.

The next metaphor compares the convent to a ship that the nuns maintain. Another compound word is used to compare the nuns to beatniks, 'Christniks' (line 50), stressing the conscious 'opting out' from conventional society that nuns choose. She offers a simplistic explanation of the life a nun chooses; to follow a 'common criminal' (line 62) from Palestine who died two millennia ago, leaving behind the chance of lovers, marriage or children, which is 'the weirdest thing a woman can do' (line 51).

Lines 63–108

The fire is introduced here, the chaos of which **incongruously** (not in harmony, out of place) reminds her of a beach holiday the nuns took, where they scampered 'hither and tither' (line 81); now they cheerfully scamper 'into the flames of the fire' (line 84) – yet another juxtaposition that may surprise the reader. The nun is reminded of the story of Cardinal Mindszenty, who was a hero to these nuns and went into hiding the same year as their holiday. They would have loved to mend his clothes, do his laundry and cook for him – the typical domestic duties that a 1950s wife would have performed for her husband. The bishop's wealthy 'buddy' (line 76) owns this beach. Could this be a veiled criticism of the Church?

She recalls a spiritual moment during Benediction that connects the memory of the beach holiday to her view of Christ, whom she says 'is the ocean / Forever rising and falling on the world's shore' (lines 91–92). The sea is often connected with love and family in Durcan and, of course, nuns see themselves as 'brides of Christ'. Twisting the water metaphor ever further, Christ as an ocean becomes a wave of flame during the fire in which the nuns rejoice, 'We are doomed but delighted to drown' (line 94). She imagines Gabriel, the archangel who announced to Mary that she would give birth to Christ, cycling up to her and giving her instructions as this surreal, bizarre account of the fire unfolds. In a touching comment she pities and praises the firemen who will have to deal with the blaze and its aftermath, 'Whose task it will be to shovel up our ashes and shovel / What is left of us into black plastic refuse sacks' (lines 106–107). This image is graphic; its harshness reflected in the hard alliteration of 'c' and 'ck' sounds. Is this disrespectful and unnecessary or does it strengthen the impact of the poem?

Lines 109–147

Mundane musings are juxtaposed with the intense drama of the fire, adding extra layers of interest to the poem. She feels 'lucky' (line 114) to have lost her life so unexpectedly, calling the experience 'refreshing' and feeling 'a sense of freedom' (lines 112–113). On the evening of the fire she had forgone bathing in her rush to read a book about Israel and is surprised that its agnostic author had such an 'insightful' (line 119) take on religious events there. This book lies open on her chest as she sleeps and the fire rages round her like an angry beast, 'bellowing flame and snarling glass' (line 124). The nun notes with some distaste that her 'brother-in-law's married niece' (line 125), from whom she borrowed the book, has left the expensive price tag on the cover in a brash attempt to show off. We might be reminded of 'Windfall', where Durcan finds the ostentatious houses of the wealthy to be 'self-regardingly ugly'. The mundane digression about the book adds a surreal and darkly comic quality to this section of the poem as the fire is so dramatic and arresting. Her first thought on waking to the blaze is that this woman will not get her book back! Again consider Durcan's juxtaposition of incongruities here and his motives for including such details.

The fire consumes their flesh as people who receive communion eat the Eucharist; thus, the experience is a sacred one for her. The blaze is likened to a dragon that she affectionately caresses. Another contrasting image

Paul Durcan

ensues where the convent is like a labour ward in which the nuns give birth to death and Christ (possibly the fireman) douses their souls with water. Giving birth to death is surely the ultimate paradox and is made all the stranger by the fact that nuns are chaste. The nun asks that we remember them as 'frisky girls' and 'kittens in the sun' (lines 146–147). Movingly, the dead nuns are named.

Part II

In a dream-like section Jesus seems to have heard the tragic news from an 'emaciated, female punk' (line 149) dressed in black as if mourning the nuns. (The tragedy had a huge effect on the country, especially the capital, which almost came to a standstill for the funeral.) This punk is 'grieving like an alley cat' (line 150). Jesus is 'annulled with astonishment' (line 151), which is a puzzling turn of phrase, at the faith he encounters in the people who live on society's margins in Dublin. What might Durcan be trying to convey here? Jesus praises the punks and the street performers for their faith and we return to St Stephen's Green, as mentioned at the start of the poem, where it seems that the six nuns gather at the statue of the Three Fates to pray for help for the world. Here, Durcan references charity concerts for famine (Live Aid) and for the unemployed in Ireland (Self Aid) and the nuns pray for those with Aids and for all who need help.

The poem ends on a respectful and religious note as the nuns finally pray, using the traditional prayer before communion, that they will be welcome in heaven and hope to be worthy of this, 'Say but the word and my soul shall be healed' (line 165). This ends a startlingly upbeat and imaginative treatment of a real and tragic event.

> **The dead**
>
> Six elderly nuns who slept in a dormitory on the top floor of the convent at the back of the building died in the fire. Eucharia was very unsteady on her feet, Rosario was from Youghal, Seraphia was a brilliant science and maths teacher, Gonzaga had a form of dementia, Edith from Tipperary worked in the laundry and had a reputation for being extremely kind and Margaret was very quiet and shy. All six were former teachers and are buried in Rathfarnham.

> **Three Fates**
>
> These were ancient Greek deities of destiny, life and death. One sister held a ball of twine (birth), the next measured the length of the twine (the duration of one's life) and the third sister cut the twine (death). The central concept is the inevitability of one's fate and the idea that our lives are predetermined.

Themes and imagery

Durcan **subverts the conventional** view of nuns as being conservative and reserved by presenting us with a compassionate, funny powerhouse of positivity and joy. The nun's unwavering faith, along with the surprisingly weird portrayal of religious figures such as Jesus and Gabriel, ensures that religion is a major theme but it is not presented in any version we have seen before. **Religion is subversive**, it is rebellious and it is fun, the nuns scamper on a beach, they are 'frisky girls' and 'kittens in the sun' (lines 146–147). Their rebellion echoes that of their hero Cardinal Mindszenty, who stood up to the communist regime in Hungary. Comparisons of the nuns to birds, 'we were as eerie an aviary as you'd find' (line 34) and sailors 'sleeping at the top of the mast / Of a nineteenth-century schooner' (lines 46–47) imply a freedom about their lifestyle, which is one that others often perceive as restrictive.

Fire and water are key images in the poem. The sea is an important metaphor in many of Durcan's poems and the nun likening the fire to a frolic on a beach is typical of the **zany contrasts and juxtapositions** that crowd this poem. The image of the fire as a dragon might seem an obvious one, but the nun strokes it as if it were a beloved pet, 'I clasped the dragon to my breast / And stroked his red-hot ears' (lines 134–135). The fire consuming the nuns as if they were the Eucharist is yet another startling comparison and one that many religious people might find irreverent. Is Durcan trying to shock or provoke with such imagery and language?

Form and language

This long narrative poem weaves real events, places and people with a surreal, surprising and imaginative consciousness – that of the nun. The voice of the nun is an incredibly engaging one. Her sunny disposition and passion radiate from the page even in the most unlikely situation, 'Isn't it a marvellous thing how your hour comes / When you least expect it?' (lines 109–110). This **conversational tone** is something that grabs the reader from the start. Real places (St Stephen's Green, Ardmore), real people (Cardinal Mindszenty, Conor Cruise O'Brien) and current events (Live Aid, Self Aid) help to ground this fanciful poem in reality. They combine with the use of colloquial and religious language to make a very abstract work accessible to us. The sombre prayer at the end of the poem brings a solemn tone to its closing and reminds us that the nuns are ultimately deeply spiritual people with absolute faith in an afterlife in the presence of their God.

Paradox, contrast and subversive ideas abound in the poem. The punks are 'conventional, really, and vulnerable' (line 17), the nuns are 'wild' (line 21) women and 'Christniks' (line 50) who give 'birth to our deaths' (line 137). The message is: do not take anything at face value; it is our perception that creates the world around us and colours it. The nun certainly perceives the world in her own unique way; the fire for her is welcome, as is death.

'The Three Fates' in St Stephen's Green in Dublin.

Questions

1. What picture of 1980s Dublin emerges from this poem?

2. The nun feels that she is far more rebellious than the punks. How does she convey this? Do you agree with her? Give reasons for your answer.

3. What do we learn about the nuns and their lives here? Did any details surprise you? Explain why or why not.

4. The speaker is very positive about her death. How is this viewpoint conveyed to us and why might the nun feel this way?

5. Why include seemingly random details like the beach holiday, the book and the cardinal during the sections describing the fire?

6. How is the fire itself described in the poem (lines 63–147)? Analyse and comment on the metaphors used. Which ones struck you most and why?

7. What phrases stood out to you most in the poem? Choose two or three that you found intriguing or surprising and discuss the reason you chose them and the reactions they provoked in you.

8. What three adjectives would you use to describe the character of the nun? Justify your choices with close reference to the poem.

9. Do you agree with Ruth Palin that 'Most women in Durcan are disappointed except the nun'? Discuss with reference to at least two other poems by Durcan on your course.

10. If there is a message or a moral to the nun's story, what might it be? Give reasons for your answer.

11. Imagine you are Durcan's editor. Write the text of an e-mail you send him where you express some concerns about his handling of this incident and suggest some changes, omissions and/or additions, giving reasons for your suggestions.

12. Write a tabloid or broadsheet article about this event using the title as your headline (you might wish to change the headline to suit if you opt for a tabloid article).

13. There are many details in the poem you might like to find out more about (e.g. Cardinal Mindszenty, punks, the Diceman, Conor Cruise O'Brien's book, the charity concerts, the statue of O'Donovan Rossa or of the Three Fates). In pairs or small groups, divide the items that interest you between your classmates, investigate and present your findings briefly afterwards.

Sport

There were not many fields
In which you had hopes for me
But sport was one of them.
On my twenty-first birthday
I was selected to play
For Grangegorman Mental Hospital
In an away game
Against Mullingar Mental Hospital.
I was a patient
In B Wing.
You drove all the way down,
Fifty miles,
To Mullingar to stand
On the sidelines and observe me.

I was fearful I would let down   15
Not only my team but you.
It was Gaelic football.
I was selected as goalkeeper.
There were big country men
On the Mullingar Mental Hospital team,   20
Men with gapped teeth, red faces,
Oily, frizzy hair, bushy eyebrows.
Their full forward line
Were over six foot tall
Fifteen stone in weight.   25
All three of them, I was informed,
Cases of schizophrenia.

There was a rumour
That their centre-half forward
Was an alcoholic solicitor   30
Who, in a lounge bar misunderstanding,
Had castrated his best friend
But that he had no memory of it.
He had meant well – it was said.
His best friend had had to emigrate   35
To Nigeria.

Paul Durcan

To my surprise,
I did not flinch in the goals.
I made three or four spectacular saves,
Diving full stretch to turn   40
A certain goal around the corner,
Leaping high to tip another certain goal
Over the bar for a point.
It was my knowing
That you were standing on the sideline
That gave me the necessary motivation –
That will to die
That is as essential to sportsmen as to artists.
More than anybody it was you
I wanted to mesmerise, and after the game
Grangegorman Mental Hospital   50
Having defeated Mullingar Mental Hospital
By 14 Goals and 38 points to 3 goals and 10 points –
Sniffing your approval, you shook hands with me.
'Well played, son.'
I may not have been mesmeric
But I had not been mediocre.
In your eyes I had achieved something at last.
On my twenty-first birthday I had played on a winning team
The Grangegorman Mental Hospital team.   60
Seldom if ever again in your eyes
Was I to rise to these heights.

Glossary

27	*schizophrenia*: mental disorder characterised by disturbances in thought (e.g. delusions), perception (e.g. hallucinations) and behaviour
32	*castrated*: removed the testicles from

Guidelines

This poem is from the 1990 collection *Daddy, Daddy*, which contained many poems exploring the complex and often fractious relationship between Durcan and his father, John. It was written following his father's death. Durcan was a keen sportsman and hoped for a career in sport until a bone disease put an end to such dreams in his early teens. He was in and out of mental institutions for a time and this poem recounts a match he played when a patient on one such hospital's Gaelic football team, a premise that readers of the poem often find darkly amusing.

HIGHER LEVEL

Commentary

Lines 1–14

The speaker addresses his father directly, ruefully acknowledging that his father had not had many ambitions for his son but had hoped that sport might be one area where his son might achieve something. There is a sense that Durcan felt he was a failure in his father's eyes but still strove to get his approval. The pun on 'fields' in the first line is a clever one, at once referring to the pitch on which the match will be played and also suggesting the many areas his father did not feel his son would excel in. The fact that he had some hope for his son in the 'field' of sport motivates his father to drive 'Fifty miles' to 'stand / On the sidelines and observe me'. In line 11 Durcan uses the phrase 'all the way' as if this relatively short journey is considered an onerous trek by his father. We get the sense that this is not a close, supportive or loving relationship and the clinical, detached phrase 'to observe me' reinforces this impression.

The speaker reveals he is a patient 'In B wing' and is playing for his hospital's team, 'Grangegorman Mental Hospital'. This information is given in a matter-of-fact way without explanation or preamble; such forthrightness is characteristic of this poet. Calling this institution a 'Mental Hospital' might seem inappropriate today but was the terminology used at the time. He is playing a team of patients from Mullingar Mental Hospital. Durcan has not revealed whether this match ever really took place but the details given as the poem unfolds lend the account an authenticity regardless. It is poignant that this is how Durcan is celebrating his twenty-first birthday.

Paul Durcan

Lines 15–36

The speaker fears letting his father down as much as his own team-mates in this match, where he is in goal against a formidable team. Their appearance makes them sound like Neanderthals, 'gapped teeth, red faces, / … frizzy hair … / over six foot tall' and possibly the most intimidating factor, all three full forwards are 'Cases of schizophrenia'. To prove just how intimidating and unpredictable these opponents may be, Durcan digresses to tell us an anecdote about one of them: 'their centre-half forward' is 'an alcoholic solicitor' who during a row in a bar castrated his best friend but does not remember the incident. His friend, possibly too embarrassed or traumatised to stay in Ireland, has emigrated to Nigeria. Why does Durcan digress here? What is the effect this anecdote is intended to have on us? It is bizarre, darkly comic and perhaps intended to shock. It is worth noting that the veracity of the tale is in question as was the 'fact' that the opposing team's full-forward line were all schizophrenics. These details are hearsay: 'I was informed' and 'There was a rumour' cast doubt in our minds and portray these institutions as hotbeds of gossip.

Lines 37–55

In the face of the various challenges posed by the intimidating opposition, the speaker is surprised at his own excellent performance. He 'did not flinch in the goals' and seems bursting with pride at his achievements that day: 'I made three or four spectacular saves'. Amazed at his own fearlessness he relates to us, in the manner of a sports commentator, the details of his performance: 'Diving full stretch to turn / A certain goal around the corner' and 'Leaping high to tip another certain goal / Over the bar for a point'. He feels he possesses the killer instinct, 'That will to die', that makes a great artist or sportsperson and concedes that it was his father's presence there that brought this 'will' out in him: 'it was you / I wanted to mesmerise'. The level of detail makes us feel we were there and his excitement, pride and enthusiasm are infectious. After a resounding victory, '14 Goals and 38 points to 3 goals and 10 points', Durcan's father is less than gushing in his praise for his son: 'Sniffing your approval, you shook hands with me.' This is surely quite a formal gesture and his father's words of approval are equally reticent, 'Well played, son', but perhaps it is the word 'son' that has meant so much to Durcan.

> **'That will to die'**
>
> **Brendan Kennelly noted this characteristic in Durcan's poetry, 'his hypnotic repetitions of what other poets would hardly dare utter once' which give Durcan's poetry its air of audacity.**

Lines 56–62

The speaker admits that perhaps he overdid his self-praise earlier, 'I may not have been mesmeric'. However, he knows that he certainly 'had not been mediocre' because, in his father's eyes, he 'had achieved something at last' by being on the winning team in this match. This is a bittersweet moment; on the one hand he is jubilant but on the other he admits that it was an isolated incident and would probably not be repeated: 'Seldom if ever again in your eyes / Was I to rise to these heights.' We are pleased for Durcan but perhaps saddened that he received so little warmth or encouragement from his distant father. It is also sad that this is how he spent his twenty-first birthday. Nevertheless, the concept of the match is quite amusing, making this a very emotional poem on a number of levels.

Themes and imagery

This poem is about **Durcan's quest to achieve his father's approval** and touches on his **struggles with mental illness**. There is melancholy here but also pride as Durcan is glad his father was there to see him do well. His father's presence motivated him, 'It was my knowing / That you were standing on the sideline / That gave me the necessary motivation' (lines 44–46). Peggy O'Brien notes that 'Durcan manages to cut his father down to size and give him at the same time a sweet kiss on the cheek'. Durcan handles a subject few people would discuss openly at the time, mental health, alongside admitting how distant his father was and how much he craved his father's approval. He does so **without sentimentality or self-pity, using humour and hyperbole to disarm and charm the reader**.

Durcan's friend Brian Lynch asked Durcan about his time in Grangegorman, 'How do you stand it?' To which Durcan replied, 'It's better than living at home', yet he also told Lynch that he felt 'incarcerated' in St Patrick's (another psychiatric hospital) during his time there.

Form and language

The poet addresses his father directly, 'You drove all the way down' (line 11), as he recalls a single instance when he felt something approaching approval from his father. He adopts a similar style in 'Rosie Joyce'. Here, **the tone is not quite accusatory but it is certainly not warm or affectionate**, 'There were not many fields / In which you had hopes for me' (lines 1–2). The free verse of this conversational narrative lends itself to Durcan's direct and often anecdotal style, 'There was a rumour / That their centre-half forward / Was an alcoholic solicitor' (lines 28–30).

Durcan's excitement and penchant for **pseudo-journalistic language** is clear in lines 37–55 as he relates his performance during the game to us in a style worthy of a newspaper's sports section: 'Diving full stretch to turn / A certain goal around the corner' (lines 40–41).

SNAPSHOT
- Father–son relationship
- Comic and tragic elements
- Autobiographical
- Confessional
- Addresses father directly
- Accessible
- Anecdotal
- Mental illness
- Estrangement

Exam-Style Questions

Understanding the poem

1. What, do you think, does Durcan mean in the opening lines: 'There were not many fields / In which you had hopes for me / But sport was one of them'?
2. What efforts had his father made to attend the match? Comment on the effect of the verb 'observe' at the end of stanza 1.
3. What was the poet 'fearful' of in stanza 2?
4. Describe the players on the opposing team. What is the effect of this description? Is it comic, shocking, intimidating? Give reasons for your choice.
5. Describe the details of the match as revealed in the third stanza of the poem.
6. Outline the content of the rumour that has circulated about the other team's centre-half forward (stanza 3). Why, do you think, does Durcan include this in the poem?
7. 'To my surprise' (line 37). What surprises Durcan here? Give specific details.
8. How does Durcan's father react to his win? What does this reaction tell us about their relationship?
9. What is your understanding of the lines, 'I may not have been mesmeric / But I had not been mediocre' in the final stanza? Do you agree with Durcan's assessment of his performance? Explain.
10. What effect did this event seem to have on Durcan and his father's relationship, taking the last two lines of the poem into account?

Thinking about the poem

1. This poem is at once comic and tragic. Do you agree with Bruce Woodcock that Durcan displays 'agonising humour and tortured affection' towards his father in this poem? Give reasons for your answer.
2. What overall picture of the relationship between father and son emerges in the poem?
3. 'That will to die' (line 47). What, do you think, does Durcan mean by this phrase? Do you agree that great sportspeople and artists need this quality? Can you think of any examples?
4. Is the last stanza of the poem positive or negative, in your opinion? Identify the tone of the poem in this section and highlight the details that suggest this.

Imagining

1. Imagine you are a sports journalist writing about the match. Write either the dialogue of an interview you conduct with Durcan after the game or an article about the match designed to appear in the sports pages of a newspaper.
2. Imagine you are Durcan's father. Write your diary entry after you return home following the match.

HIGHER LEVEL

Before you read

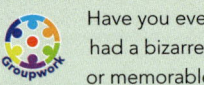 Have you ever had a bizarre or memorable encounter with a stranger? Share your stories of this.

Father's Day, 21 June 1992

Just as I was dashing to catch the Dublin–Cork train,
Dashing up and down the stairs, searching my pockets,
She told me that her sister in Cork wanted a loan of the axe;
It was late June and
The buddleia tree in the backyard   5
Had grown out of control.
The taxi was ticking over outside in the street,
All the neighbours noticing it.
'You mean that you want me to bring her down the axe?'
'Yes, if you wouldn't mind, that is –'   10
'A simple saw would do the job, surely to God
She could borrow a simple saw.'
'She said she'd like the axe.'
'OK. There is a Blue Cabs taxi ticking over outside
And the whole world inspecting it,   15
I'll bring her down the axe.'
The axe – all four-and-a-half feet of it –
Was leaning up against the wall behind the settee –
The fold-up settee that doubles as a bed.
She handed the axe to me just as it was,   20
As neat as a newborn babe,
All in the bare buff.
You'd think she'd have swaddled it up
In something – if not a blanket, an old newspaper,
But no, not even a token hanky   25
Tied in a bow round its head.
I decided not to argue the toss. I kissed her goodbye.

The whole long way down to Cork
I felt uneasy. Guilt feelings.
It's a killer, this guilt.   30
I always feel bad leaving her
But this time it was the worst.
I could see she was glad
To see me go away for a while,

168 / DISCOVERY: POETRY ANTHOLOGY

Glad at the prospect of being 35
Two weeks on her own,
Two weeks of having the bed to herself,
Two weeks of not having to be pestered
By my coarse advances,
Two weeks of not having to look up from her plate 40
And behold me eating spaghetti with a knife and fork.
Our daughters are all grown up and gone away.
Once when she was sitting pregnant on the settee
It snapped shut with herself inside it,
But not a bother on her. I nearly died. 45

As the train slowed down approaching Portarlington
I overheard myself say to the passenger sitting opposite me:
'I am feeling guilty because she does not love me
As much as she used to, can you explain that?'
The passenger's eyes were on the axe on the seat beside me. 50
'Her sister wants a loan of the axe …'
As the train threaded itself into Portarlington
I nodded to the passenger 'Cúl an tSúdaire!'
The passenger stood up, lifted down a case from the rack,
Walked out of the coach, but did not get off the train. 55
For the remainder of the journey, we sat alone,
The axe and I,
All the green fields running away from us,
All our daughters grown up and gone away.

Guidelines

This extended narrative poem, from the collection *A Snail in my Prime* (1993), meditates upon Durcan's ailing marriage by relating an anecdote to us. Durcan has dated the title, perhaps ironically as nowhere in the poem do his family members seem to acknowledge or celebrate Father's Day.

Commentary

Stanza 1

The speaker rushes to get to a taxi waiting outside his home so that he can catch the Cork train on time but is delayed by a strange request, or demand, from his wife: he is to take an axe on the train with him for her sister, who has a buddleia tree in need of taming. The speaker is already feeling uneasy and self-conscious, he seems to think the neighbours are watching the taxi nosily, 'the whole world inspecting it', and this tension increases as a minor argument ensues. He clearly does not want to bring the axe and pleads, 'surely to God /

She could borrow a simple saw'. But his wife is firm; she insists that her sister wants the axe. The speaker is further alarmed to be handed the bare axe with no bag or cover for it, 'not even a token hanky'. In a quirky simile he compares the axe to 'a newborn babe, / All in the bare buff'. The poet gives up, 'decided not to argue the toss'. Note the use of colloquial language here as if we are a friend he is chatting to. His affection for his wife is clear though: 'I kissed her goodbye.'

Stanza 2

Anxiety and guilt hang over the speaker 'The whole long way down to Cork'. He realises that he often feels like this 'leaving her' but the feeling is worse than usual this time. Part of this reaction may be because she seemed so happy to see him leave, 'Glad at the prospect of being / Two weeks on her own'. He ponders the things she will enjoy about his absence: having the bed to herself, not having to witness his eating habits (like eating spaghetti with a knife and fork) and not having to endure his clumsy attempts to seduce her, ('my coarse advances'). His admissions here suggest a relationship in trouble and a wife seeking time apart. He recalls a happier time when she was pregnant and the fold-up settee 'snapped shut', trapping her. Just like their exchange about the axe earlier, she remained calm and assured, 'not a bother on her', while he was much more emotional, 'I nearly died'.

Stanza 3

The speaker's worry about his relationship overwhelms him, causing him to blurt out to a fellow passenger on the train, 'I am feeling guilty because she does not love me / As much as she used to, can you explain that?' To any stranger this alone would be disconcerting; however, to make things worse, the passenger has spied 'the axe on the seat beside'. The dark comedy of the situation continues as the poet attempts to explain, saying, as if it is the most logical and obvious thing in the world, 'Her sister wants a loan of the axe'. Perhaps to put an end to the awkwardness between them, or because he cannot stop himself blurting out random information to this passenger, he announces the approaching stop, 'Cúl an tSúdaire!' – Portarlington. The passenger takes the opportunity to move; he takes his 'case from the rack' as if he's getting off the train but instead moves to another carriage. Would we blame him? The speaker is clearly desperate to communicate with someone but his estrangement from those around him only deepens. He is left alone with the axe – he describes it as if it is a friend, a companion, 'we sat alone, / The axe and I' – and with his thoughts, which now focus on the couple's two daughters who are 'grown up and gone away'. The speed of their growing up and departure is likened to the speed with which 'the green fields' he can see from the train's window are speeding past, 'running away from us'. 'Us' here could suggest he and the axe as well as the speaker and his wife. The speaker realises that with the departure of their children the bond between him and his wife has diminished. It is a poignant ending.

Themes and imagery

The axe seems symbolic of their impending split and the fact that it is stored behind the settee rather than, for example, shut away in a shed seems to imply that this split is imminent – the axe is at hand. The settee itself symbolises domesticity, their life together and maybe happier times. The fact that Durcan must take the axe with him might suggest that the split is in his hands, it is his fault: as he says in 'Windfall', 'But then with good reason / I was put out of my home: / By a keen wind felled'. 'Felled' here reminds us of the purpose of the axe, to deal with a tree that had got 'out of control'. Is the speaker's family tree about to be cut back also? The simile used to describe the axe links it to the later mention of pregnancy; it is 'As neat as a newborn babe, / All in the bare buff' (lines 21–22). This simile takes all of the menace out of the axe; it seems vulnerable and meek. Is the poet transferring his own qualities onto the axe? He acquiesces quite readily to his wife's demand that he take the axe to Cork on the train and clearly does not want to split up with her, 'I kissed her goodbye' (line 27), telling us 'I always feel bad leaving her' (line 31). He knows or feels that this distance growing between them is his fault, 'It's a killer, this guilt' (line 30). His repetition of 'two weeks' in lines 36–41 while listing all the things his wife will enjoy about his absence shows us he is well aware of the trouble his marriage is in. In 'The Difficulty that is Marriage' Durcan acknowledges, 'I have my troubles and I shall always have them' but wishes to remain with her: 'If it were with you, I should live for ever.' Here, however, Durcan seems less hopeful and there seems less to hold the couple together now that their children have grown up and left home, which we see in the poignant but beautiful image of the train speeding past the green fields. This poem, like 'Rosie Joyce', involves a journey that is metaphorical as well as physical as the poet explores the changing dynamics of family.

> **Similes**
>
> Similes are relatively rare in Durcan's poetry and this has been attributed to a conversation he had on a plane to Moscow where he commented to a friend that the mountains looked like tents to which his friend, Anthony Cronin, replied 'would you ever stop saying that things look like things' and Durcan it seems took his advice!

Form and language

Like 'Windfall', the disintegration of a marriage amid memories of happier times is at the centre of this narrative poem. Its three sections deal first with the awkward conversation between the speaker and his wife, then with his misgivings about their relationship, especially now that their daughters are all 'grown up and gone away' (line 59), and finally with the train journey itself where he fails to communicate with his fellow passenger and is left alone with the axe to ponder the loneliness ahead. His awkward attempt at conversation with another passenger provides much comedy as well as **pathos** for the reader.

HIGHER LEVEL

Questions

1	Look at the conversation between the speaker and his wife in the first stanza of the poem. What is revealed about the personalities of Durcan and his wife and about their relationship here?
2	Why is the speaker self-conscious, in your opinion, about the taxi waiting outside?
3	Durcan supplies specific details in the first section of the poem including place names and the name of the taxi company as well as the species of tree. Why, do you think, does he do this and what is the effect achieved?
4	What does the axe symbolise, in your opinion? Think about the relationship described. What might be the significance of having the axe behind the settee?
5	What extended simile does Durcan use to describe the axe? What reaction did this provoke in you? Explain.
6	Why, do you think, does the poet feel guilty and worried in lines 28–41?
7	Why tell the anecdote about his wife being trapped in the settee? What might Durcan be trying to convey here?
8	There is an uncomfortable and quite comic exchange between the speaker and the stranger on the train. What aspects of this section (lines 46–54) were uncomfortable or comic?
9	What is Durcan conveying in the final four lines of the poem? What do you feel is the tone here?
10	What is the significance of the title in the context of the poem as a whole?
11	Which of the following options do you feel is the main theme of the poem: marital breakdown, loneliness, the passing of time, or perhaps there is another theme you have identified? What details and techniques in the poem best conveyed this theme to you?
12	Imagine you are the passenger on the train. Write your diary entry for that evening.
13	In pairs, choose either the speaker and his wife or the speaker and the passenger on the train. Write an extended version of the exchange between them, inspired by the poem, as a short drama including stage directions about body language, facial expressions, tone of voice, etc. Act this out in class.

Paul Durcan

Before you read

Study in detail the painting of the Arnolfini couple by Dutch artist Jan van Eyck on page 175 and consider the items featured in the painting, for example the bed, the window, the shoes, the chandelier, the dog, the broom, etc. What might each symbolise?

The Arnolfini Marriage

After Jan Van Eyck

We are the Arnolfinis.
Do not think you may invade
Our privacy because you may not.

We are standing to our portrait,
The most erotic portrait ever made,   5
Because we have faith in the artist

To do justice to the plurality,
Fertility, domesticity, barefootedness
Of a man and a woman saying 'we':

To do justice to our bed   10
As being our most necessary furniture;
To do justice to our life as a reflection.

Our brains spill out upon the floor
And the terrier at our feet sniffs
The minutiae of our magnitude.   15

The most relaxing word in our vocabulary is 'we'.
Imagine being able to say 'we'.
Most people are in no position to say 'we'.

Are you? Who eat alone? Sleep alone?
And at dawn cycle to work   20
With an Alsatian shepherd dog tied to your handlebars?

We will pause now for the Angelus.
Here you have it:
The two halves of the coconut.

Glossary

7	*plurality*: state of being more than one
15	*minutiae*: tiny details
15	*magnitude*: great size or importance

HIGHER LEVEL

Guidelines

From the 1994 collection *Give Me Your Hand*, 'The Arnolfini Marriage' takes a subversive and wry look at a famous portrait. The collection was commissioned by the National Gallery in London, following a similar collection that Durcan, a passionate art lover, had worked on in Ireland where he wrote companion poems for a selection of portraits. These poems were published alongside images of the paintings themselves. In an essay called 'Prime Durcan: A Collage', Eamonn Grennan commented that these painting poems bring 'normally hidden voices to articulate life'.

Commentary

Title
The Arnolfini Marriage is a famous portrait by Jan van Eyck painted in Bruges, Belgium in 1434. The couple depicted are wealthy Italian merchants. Although the woman appears to be pregnant, some experts say that the bunching of fabric at the front of her dress signified wealth and status and was just the fashion of the time. Durcan imagines what the couple are communicating to the viewer in their stance and through the items on display.

Stanzas 1 and 2
The stern, proud image of this couple is echoed in their confident declaration of their name, 'We are the Arnolfinis.' 'We' is repeated often in the poem and is a central concept – the power of being able to declare that you are a couple. Their stern and condescending command follows, 'Do not think you may invade / Our privacy because you may not.' On first viewing the painting we may disagree with their assertion that it is 'The most erotic portrait ever made', but they explain that this is because of their 'faith in the artist', they trust him completely to convey the aspects of their relationship that make it so perfect and passionate. The setting is, after all, their bedroom. This idea of the artist reflecting their values is literally conveyed in the painting as he is reflected (along with a second figure) in the mirror behind the Arnolfinis. Art reflects life and life reflects art.

Stanzas 3 and 4
The next two stanzas contain a litany of the details the artist is going to record faithfully for them, repeating the phrase 'To do justice to' three times. They trust him implicitly to record the key aspects of their marriage. First, their 'plurality' is symbolised by their holding hands in the portrait; two are as one. 'Fertility' is the next concept represented in her bulging stomach and the image of St Margaret, the patron saint of childbirth, on the bedpost. The third is 'domesticity', symbolised by the brush hanging from the bed. The last concept is 'barefootedness', which we can see in the shoes casually thrown aside as the couple stand together in their bedroom. Many of these details show us that this couple are not as formal as they might first seem. These four concepts combine to sum up what their marriage truly is, 'a man and a woman saying "we"'.

Stanza 4 singles out their bed, a powerful symbol of marriage, and calls it the 'most necessary furniture', emphasising the importance of physical love in marriage. The mirror behind them is referenced in the line 'To do justice to our life as a reflection'. The Arnolfinis reflect for the viewer the values and joys of married life just as the poem reflects the painting, and the artist reflects himself in the painting just as Durcan reflects himself in the poem.

Stanzas 5 and 6

This so far quite straightforward poem takes a surreal turn at the line, 'Our brains spill out upon the floor'. What might the couple mean here? Is it that the sharp intelligence of the pair (one commentator called their expression 'chillingly intellectual') pervades the atmosphere of the room, that theirs is a chiefly cerebral relationship and this informs all other parts of their marriage? Even their terrier, a dog famed for its loyalty and cleverness (like its owners, perhaps), can sense every detail of the importance of its masters, 'The minutiae of our magnitude'. Their 'magnitude' or power and status come from their union and the strength of this is reflected in the repetition of 'we' in stanza 6. The speakers pause to meditate on this pivotal word and feel that those who can say 'we' are extremely lucky. Or are the Arnolfinis still speaking here? It is unclear. The tone has relaxed somewhat: 'The most relaxing word in our vocabulary is "we"'. Certainly it sounds as if the voice is the Arnolfinis – their condescension continues when they declare, 'Most people are in no position to say "we".'

Stanzas 7 and 8

The spotlight is turned to the reader of the poem, to the poet or perhaps to the viewer of the painting, 'Are you? Who eat alone? Sleep alone?' These seemingly general staccato questions become very specific indeed and we may feel that a particular individual is being addressed. Could this be the poet himself? 'And at dawn cycle to work / With an Alsatian shepherd dog tied to your handlebars?' The individual described here seems an epitome of loneliness, a pathetic figure when compared with the self-assured confidence in the togetherness of the painting's subjects.

> **The Angelus**
>
> The Angelus is as much a cultural as a religious reference. The daily Angelus broadcast on RTÉ One is RTÉ's longest-running programme. It is one minute for silent reflection at twelve and six. The name comes from a Catholic prayer which, like the poem, 'Six Nuns Die', references the angel Gabriel, 'The Angel of the Lord declared into Mary: And she conceived of the Holy Spirit'.

The poem ends on a bemusing note with what seems to be an almost glib, dismissive, throwaway ending to an initially stern and serious poem. Durcan begins with a characteristically religious allusion as he echoes a television or radio announcer: 'We will pause now for the Angelus.' Durcan then sums up the poem enigmatically: 'Here you have it: / The two halves of the coconut.' Why a coconut? To juxtapose the serious and steady tone and subject of the poem so far with something that sounds silly? To introduce levity? To suggest something hard to crack? We also must ponder what is meant by 'two halves' here, and whose voice we are hearing. Is it still the Arnolfinis? Perhaps these two halves are the husband and wife in the portrait, or the artist and his subjects, or the couple and the lonely figure described near the end, or the poem and the painting, or the poet and the reader. There are many possibilities and the ambiguity at the end leaves it up to the reader to decide. The modern and seemingly random details (the bicycle and Alsatian, the Angelus, the coconut) certainly contrast strongly with the austere world of the Arnolfinis.

Themes and imagery

Marriage is a clear theme here, and the confidence and assuredness that being in a marriage can bring, 'We are the Arnolfinis' (line 1). Of course the converse of this is **being alone** as represented by the solitary figure near the end of the poem who has only an 'Alsatian shepherd dog tied' to his 'handlebars' (line 21) for company. Also **the role of the artist** is a less obvious theme here, with the term 'artist' including not just the painter but also the poet. This is most present in the idea of **reflection**. The image of the mirror in the painting highlights this; the mirror reflects the artist (who is not alone, another figure is present). If we take it that the lonely lifestyle in the poem could reflect Durcan's life following the break-up of his marriage, he is reflecting his present situation and mourning his past one as a married man.

The bed is a key image both in the painting and in the poem and the fact that the painting's setting is the couple's bedroom reflects the importance of intimacy and privacy in the Arnolfinis' relationship. Some things are none of our business and every married couple has an intimacy that is not for anyone else to know.

Form and language

The speakers address us in a very direct manner, 'Do not think you may invade / Our privacy' (lines 2–3). Repetition is used to emphasise the safety and power that being a couple can bring, particularly in the word 'we', which is repeated seven times. 'Our' is also repeated in the poem; in fact it is repeated eight times, just as there are **eight unrhymed tercets** in the poem as a whole. The personal pronoun 'you' is also repeated in the poem. The effect of this is to emphasise the contrast between a most fundamental difference – us and you. The confident togetherness of the couple highlights the loneliness of the figure in the seventh stanza of the poem, 'you? Who eat alone? Sleep alone?' (line 19). This ordered and balanced form is different from Durcan's much longer narrative about love and relationships, 'Windfall'. Although the poem is written in free verse there is a little internal rhyme; the most notable example being in stanza 3 to further emphasise the importance of the word 'we' – 'plurality, / Fertility, domesticity, ... / ... saying "we"'.

'Standing to' is an interesting phrase in line 4 and sounds almost militaristic, as if they are 'standing to' attention. They sound serious and highly engaged here. The artist has their full attention.

The solemnity of the couple's voice is subverted in the poem by quite **bizarre observations** and seemingly random interjections, 'brains spill out upon the floor' (line 13) is a prime example of this and may have us scratching our heads for context. The TV announcer-like voice that interrupts, saying 'We will pause now for the Angelus' (line 22), is another example. Perhaps its purpose is to tell us that the Arnolfinis have revealed all they are going to and we should not expect to know any more. This is typical of Durcan, who likes to surprise the reader and subvert our expectations whenever possible.

Paul Durcan

Questions

1	What declaration and command make up the first stanza? What tone of voice can you identify here? Which details of this stanza led you to this conclusion?
2	Looking at the portrait on which the poem is based, do you agree with the Arnolfinis that it is erotic? Explain why or why not.
3	What do the couple have faith in the artist to do (stanzas 3 and 4)?
4	List and explain the four important concepts to do with marriage outlined in stanzas 3 and 4. What details in the painting reflect these?
5	Why do you think the Arnolfinis say that their bed is 'our most necessary furniture' in line 11? Which details previously mentioned in the poem relate to this statement?
6	'To do justice to our life as a reflection' (line 12). What do the couple mean by this, in your view? How is the concept of 'reflection' central to the poem as a whole?
7	Stanza 5 is quite a strange one. What is your opinion of the possible meaning of this stanza? It may help to share ideas with a classmate.
8	'We' is an important word and concept in this poem. Examine its significance in the poem as a whole.
9	How does the figure described in the seventh stanza contrast with the Arnolfinis?
10	The last stanza is quite ambiguous. Why does Durcan mention the Angelus? What are the 'two halves' he is talking about? Keep in mind there may be more than one possibility here.
11	Is the speaker in the poem just the Arnolfinis speaking as one or are there other voices present? If so, where and how did you identify them?
12	Where else have you seen Durcan tackle the subject of marriage in his poetry on your course? Choose two or three poems and compare and contrast their treatment of this subject with this poem.
13	Imagine you could interview Durcan about this poem. What four questions would you ask him about it and why?
14	In pairs or small groups, find another portrait of a couple (perhaps in an art book or online) and write down what the couple seem to be saying about themselves through their portrayal in the painting.

HIGHER LEVEL

Ireland 2002

Before you read
What was the Celtic Tiger? Research this period in Ireland's recent history. What led to its end?

Do you ever take a holiday abroad?
No, we always go to America.

Guidelines

Like 'En Famille, 1979' and 'Madman', this is **a couplet poem**. In a very brief space it manages to entertain, to comment on wealth during the Celtic Tiger period (namely our rampant spending), and to suggest that America is like a home to the Irish because of our long history of migration there.

Commentary and themes

Celtic Tiger

'Celtic Tiger' was a way of referring to Ireland during the late 1990s and early 2000s when the economy grew and became successful very quickly: many people spent freely and invested heavily, and property was vastly overvalued. When the economy crashed, it caused huge unemployment, many people lost their homes and emigration rose sharply.

Sounding like an overheard snippet of conversation, this couplet poem not only tackles the extravagant spending of the Irish during the Celtic Tiger period but also touches on the theme of the diaspora, of Irish emigration. The idea that America does not seem as if it is 'abroad' to the second speaker might reference the crazy consumerism of the Celtic Tiger period in Ireland. Many people travelled to the USA several times a year to shop. It could also allude to the huge numbers of Irish migrants living in America, who made it their home because of economic necessity in the past. 'The Girl with the Keys to Pearse's Cottage' also deals with this phenomenon.

Form and language

This is another of Durcan's couplets where he manages to pack many possible meanings, themes and ideas into this very brief form. It sounds almost like the set-up and punchline to a short joke, yet it is a **social commentary on greed, materialism, the Americanisation of Irish culture and language and Ireland's long history of emigration.**

Questions

1	What point, do you think, is Durcan making in this poem?
2	What is the tone of each speaker in this couplet?
3	Compare and contrast this with the other two couplet poems by Durcan on your course.
4	Write a short dialogue that continues this conversation.

Rosie Joyce

I

That was that Sunday afternoon in May
When a hot sun pushed through the clouds
And you were born!

I was driving the two hundred miles from west to east,
The sky blue-and-white china in the fields
In impromptu picnics of tartan rugs;

When neither words nor I
Could have known that you had been named already
And that your name was Rosie –

Rosie Joyce! May you some day in May
Fifty-six years from today be as lucky
As I was when you were born that Sunday:

To drive such side roads, such main roads, such ramps, such roundabouts,
To cross such bridges, to by-pass such villages, such towns
As I did on your Incarnation Day.

By-passing Swinford – Croagh Patrick in my rear-view mirror –
My cell phone rang and, stopping on the hard edge of P. Flynn's highway,
I heard Mark your father say:

'A baby girl was born at 3.33 p.m.
Weighing 7 and a ½ lbs in Holles Street.
Tough work, all well.'

II

That Sunday in May before daybreak
Night had pushed up through the slopes of Achill
Yellow forefingers of Arum Lily – the first of the year;

Down at the Sound the first rhododendrons
Purpling the golden camps of whins;
The first hawthorns powdering white the mainland;

The first yellow irises flagging roadside streams;
Quills of bog-cotton skimming the bogs;
Burrishoole cemetery shin-deep in forget-me-nots;

Paul Durcan

Before you read

Ask your grandparents how they felt when they heard you had been born. If you are not in a position to do this, perhaps ask your parents about your grandparents' reaction to this event.

The first sea pinks speckling the seashore;
Cliffs of London Pride, groves of bluebell,
First fuchsia, Queen Anne's Lace, primrose.

I drove the Old Turlough Road, past Walter Durcan's Farm,
Umbrella'd in the joined handwriting of its ash trees;   35
I drove Tulsk, Kilmainham, the Grand Canal.

Never before had I felt so fortunate.
To be driving back into Dublin city;
Each canal bridge an old pewter brooch.

I rode the waters and the roads of Ireland,   40
Rosie, to be with you, seashell at my ear!
How I laughed when I cradled you in my hand.

Only at Tarmonbarry did I slow down,
As in my father's Ford Anglia half a century ago
He slowed down also, as across the River Shannon   45

We crashed, rattled and bounced on a Bailey bridge;
Daddy relishing his role as Moses,
Enunciating the name of the Great Divide

Between the East and the West!
We are the people of the West,   50
Our fate to go East.

No such thing, Rosie, as a Uniform Ireland
And please God there never will be;
There is only the River Shannon and all her sister rivers

And all her brother mountains and their family prospects.   55
There are higher powers than politics
And these we call wildflowers or, geologically, people.

Rosie Joyce – that Sunday in May
Not alone did you make my day, my week, my year
To the prescription of Jonathan Philbin Bowman –   60

Daymaker!
Daymaker!
Daymaker!

Popping out of my daughter, your mother –
Changing the expressions on the faces all around you –   65
All of them looking like blue hills in a heat haze –

But you saved my life. For three years
I had been subsisting in the slums of despair,
Unable to distinguish one day from the next.

III

On the return journey from Dublin to Mayo 70
In Charlestown on Main Street
I meet John Normanly, organic farmer from Curry.

He is driving home to his wife Caroline
From a Mountbellew meeting of the Western Development Commission
Of Dillon House in Ballaghadereen. 75

He crouches in his car, I waver in the street,
As we exchange lullabies of expectancy;
We wet our foreheads in John Moriarty's autobiography.

The following Sunday is the Feast of the Ascension
Of Our Lord into Heaven: 80
Thank You, O Lord, for the Descent of Rosie onto Earth.

Glossary

Line	
6	*impromptu*: not planned in advance
15	*Incarnation*: becoming flesh; a spirit or soul (often a god) taking on human form
20	*Holles Street*: a Dublin maternity hospital
39	*pewter*: dull grey metal that is a mixture of tin and usually lead
46	*Bailey bridge*: portable, pre-fabricated bridge developed by the British during the Second World War for military use
68	*subsisting*: supporting oneself on a very basic, minimal level
79	*Feast of the Ascension*: celebrates the Catholic belief that Jesus rose into heaven, normally held forty days after Easter

Guidelines

This poem was written to celebrate and commemorate the birth of Durcan's granddaughter Rosie in 2001. He had been suffering from depression for quite a while before her birth and here he records how this joyous event lifted him out of his depressed state, giving him solace and renewed hope. The poem was published in Durcan's 2004 collection *The Art of Life* and takes place over the course of a car journey the poet made from Mayo to Dublin and back, where news of Rosie's birth infuses the places he passes through with extra beauty and joy.

HIGHER LEVEL

Arum lilies.

Commentary

Part I

Durcan tells his granddaughter that she was born on a hot May Sunday. He addresses her directly, much like he does with his father in 'Sport'. Durcan recalls that he drove across Ireland that day, 'two hundred miles from west to east'; the weather was beautiful, 'sky blue-and-white china', which brought picnickers out into the fields. He did not know that she had already been named Rosie. Durcan hopes that when she is his age, 'Fifty-six years from today', she feels as lucky as he does right now upon hearing of her birth. He feels blessed to be driving through such a beautiful landscape and lists the sights on his journey: 'roads … ramps … roundabouts / … bridges … villages … towns'. He calls the day of her birth 'Incarnation Day', as if she is a deity that has been made flesh and blood. In stanza 6 the poet revisits the moment he heard of her arrival into the world, 'My cell phone rang … / I heard Mark your father say: / "A baby girl was born … "'. The poet had pulled over to the side of the road to take the call 'on the hard edge of P. Flynn's highway'.

> **P. Flynn's highway**
>
> Pádraig Flynn was a government minister and this new road was in his constituency. Durcan's tone seems to be mocking here using the Americanism 'highway' to describe the fancy new road.

Part II

Lines 22–39

Now follows an extensive list of many wildflowers, shrubs and trees adorning the Irish landscape as Durcan continues his journey east. The beauty of a variety of Irish flora is intensified by his joy at Rosie's arrival (note that she has been given a floral name). Arum lilies are slender trumpet-like creamy flowers, rhododendrons are large shrubs with blousy purple blooms growing beside 'whins' or yellow thorny gorse bushes that remind the poet of tents, 'golden camps'. He uses a pun to describe how water-loving tall irises, often called flag irises, mark the location of streams and rivers, 'flagging roadside streams', while spiky and fluffy bog-cotton looks like quills and tiny blue forget-me-nots grow in a 'shin-deep' carpet in 'Burrishoole cemetery'. Note the joy and reverence involved in this careful naming of flora and places. This is something of a tribute to Durcan's friend and mentor, the poet Patrick Kavanagh. Seaside plants, small ground-hugging varieties like sea pinks and London Pride are listed next as the scenery changes, then purple-pink fuchsia shrubs, groves of bluebells and white, frothy, delicate Queen Anne's Lace, which grows in hedgerows all over Ireland. Primroses, tiny butter-yellow clusters of flowers, and ash trees lead Durcan into Dublin by the banks of the Grand Canal. Every size, shape, colour and habitat conveys the beauty and infinite variety of the Irish landscape as the poet traverses the country.

In Dublin, Durcan once again remarks on his luck, he feels 'fortunate' to be there. In an image half-borrowed from Patrick Kavanagh, Durcan notes the beauty of the canal bridges, which he compares to 'an old pewter brooch' adorning the water of the Grand Canal.

> **Kavanagh's canal**
>
> After a serious illness Patrick Kavanagh recuperated by the banks of Dublin's Grand Canal and saw it transformed into a place of renewal and rebirth, describing it with child-like excitement, much like Durcan's tone in 'Rosie Joyce'. Look up Kavanagh's canal poems for examples of this.

Lines 40–57

Durcan has travelled this epic journey to be with his granddaughter, her breathing like a 'seashell at my ear', and rejoices in his first time holding this tiny miracle, 'How I laughed when I cradled you in my hand.' This new family member and the journey taken to meet her puts Durcan in mind of his father and a journey they took in his father's 'Ford Anglia' when Durcan was very young. Like Moses parting the Red Sea in the Bible story, Durcan's father notes that the River Shannon is the 'Great Divide' between the east and west of Ireland. During the journey they 'rattled and bounced on a Bailey bridge' (a legacy of the British occupation). Division has been a large and troubled part of Ireland's history and Ireland is still a divided island, but Durcan hopes and prays that Ireland will never be 'Uniform', a homogenous nation lacking in difference and variety. The different flowers and plants mentioned previously become symbolic here of the beauty and vitality that difference brings.

Durcan's thoughts focus even more sharply on family now and he sees that all the different landscapes and people of Ireland are linked. They are family: all rivers are sisters to the Shannon and all mountains their brothers. Their 'family prospects' are the flora, 'wildflowers' that 'geologically' are the people of the land, its children. Perhaps Durcan sees Rosie as a flower who has grown from the landscape of his family. Our landscape and people are infinitely connected and this transcends the petty squabbles of politics and division, 'There are higher powers than politics'. It seems he wishes a world of tolerance and acceptance for his new granddaughter.

Lines 58–69

Durcan now references a popular radio programme of the time, which was presented by Jonathan Philbin Bowman and which in its 'Daymaker' section invited the public to get in touch about something or someone who had made their day. For Durcan, this is obviously Rosie and a whole stanza is given to a simple yet joyous repetition ascribing this title to her, 'Daymaker! / Daymaker! / Daymaker!'

Her birth is described as if it is a surprise: 'Popping out of my daughter'. It has spread happiness to 'the faces all around you' who, in a link to Durcan's metaphor in stanza 19 about mountains being brothers, are described as 'blue hills in a heat haze'. The lovely soft alliteration of the 'h' sounds here reflects the happy effect of her birth on those connected to Rosie, 'Changing the expressions'.

She has not only made his day but also 'my week, my year'. It is as if she were a 'prescription' for his depression, which he had been suffering from for 'three years'. Comparing his previous state to 'slums of despair', he feels he has only been 'subsisting', barely getting through the days, before Rosie's birth. This is the darkest part of the poem and the imagery of 'slums' is in sharp contrast to the idyllic imagery of nature in much of the poem. The transformative power of birth, of new life, brings new hope to the poet and transforms the world around him. Quite simply, Rosie has 'saved my life'.

Part III

Having met and held his granddaughter, Durcan returns to Mayo and meets a friend, John Normanly, on the main street in Charlestown. They chat through his friend's car window about an autobiography they have read. This ordinary, everyday conversation takes on an almost sacred quality. It soothes Durcan, 'lullabies of expectancy', and their exchange is like a blessing of holy water, 'We wet our foreheads'. The final stanza is a prayer of thanksgiving to God for Rosie and Durcan notes that one week from her birth, 'the Descent of Rosie onto Earth', is the Feast of the Ascension. It is as if he feels these two events are connected, as if Rosie is a deity come to Earth, something sacred to be celebrated and venerated.

Themes and imagery

The central image is of a journey, a physical one across Ireland to see Rosie and return home, but also a metaphorical one from the 'slums of despair' to total joy: 'How I laughed when I cradled you in my hand' (line 42). **The weather** from the beginning tells us the mood of this poem is as bright and sunny as the hot Sunday afternoon in May on which the poem is set. The sunshine reflects the jubilant mood of this proud and excited grandfather as he sets out to meet his brand new granddaughter. **Family** is a key theme here. Rosie's birth adds to Durcan's family and the journey to see her reminds him of a journey with his father in their 'Ford Anglia half a century ago' (line 44). He mentions his daughter and her husband, Mark. Durcan even ascribes familial relationships to the rivers and mountains of Ireland, 'There is only the River Shannon and all her sister rivers // And all her brother mountains and their family prospects' (lines 54–55). Here Durcan pauses to embrace a wider theme, **the division that has plagued Ireland's history**, but he sees a brighter future for Rosie, 'There are higher powers than politics' (line 56), and hopes for a more united country yet one that embraces diversity, 'No such thing, Rosie, as a Uniform Ireland / And please God there never will be' (lines 52–53).

Religion is also a theme here and is woven into the language and imagery of the poem. In line 15 Rosie's day of birth is called 'Incarnation Day' and capitalised as if it were a religious feast. This corresponds with the mention of 'the Feast of the Ascension' in the final stanza and elevates a relatively everyday event, the birth of a child, to a sacred occasion, which of course to those closest to the child, it is! Durcan can see Croagh Patrick in his 'rear-view mirror' (line 16) when he gets the phone call about his granddaughter's birth. This is one of the most important religious and pilgrimage sites in Ireland and Durcan's journey is a similar pilgrimage, a kind of sacred road trip. It is as if he is travelling to see a saint, 'Thank You, O Lord, for the Descent of Rosie onto Earth' (line 81). Again, note the capitalisation here.

At the core of the poem lies a most simple and universal truth; how we feel affects how we perceive the world around us. **Positivity transforms our surroundings**, making the everyday sights we see extraordinarily beautiful. Birth brings renewal and perhaps redemption for all concerned, as we see in Durcan's prayer of thanksgiving in the final stanza. The idyllic imagery of nature also brings **serenity** to the poem, reflecting Durcan's release from his depression, while **the names of places and people ground the poem in reality**.

Form and language

Free verse allows a very **accessible and conversational tone** as befitting a poem directed at a child and helps create the **sense of childlike excitement and wonder**, which is the strongest mood in the poem. The 27 tercets impose some order on this **heartfelt and touching lyric**, allowing Durcan to marshal his thoughts and ideas. Further structure is imposed in the division of thought into three parts. Part I is the journey to Dublin and news of Rosie's birth. Part II continues the journey, memories of Durcan's father emerge and the variety and beauty of Ireland's changing landscape is celebrated as an extension of the hope and joy Rosie has brought. Part III follows Durcan back across the country to Mayo, a changed man as even everyday conversations are now infused with hope and redemption, 'We wet our foreheads in John Moriarty's autobiography' (line 78).

Litany is an effect in Durcan's language and here we see an aspect of it in the prayer-like lists and invocations the poem contains, particularly regarding the places Durcan mentions and the plants and flowers he notices along the way. The **lists of flowers, place names and people** in this and many other poems is like a blessing; naming them is a sacred thing and elevates ordinary everyday things to an extraordinary level. This central feature of Patrick Kavanagh's work has been so influential for Durcan and many other Irish poets.

Repetition is rarely absent in a Durcan poem. One of the most striking examples here is the ecstatic repetition of 'Daymaker!' three times standing alone as a stanza in its own right (lines 61–63). The exclamation marks add to the feeling of exultation. Since Homeric times, trilogies or triplets imbued a subject with a special importance and reverence so it is no wonder Durcan employs them here to celebrate Rosie's 'Incarnation Day' (line 15). This display of exuberance precedes Durcan's admission that he has been severely depressed for three long years; the reference to 'slums' here is the only negative image in the poem, representing the doldrums of despair that Durcan had been merely 'subsisting' in before Rosie's arrival (lines 67–68).

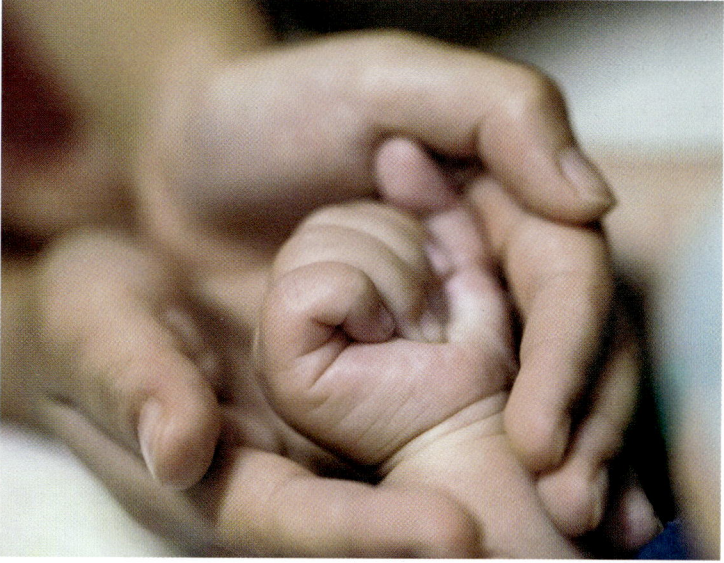

HIGHER LEVEL

Questions

1	What is the poet doing in Part I of the poem and what does he notice around him? Describe his mood in this section also.
2	Who is the poet addressing here; how do you know and what is the effect of this?
3	Describe the poet's journey in Part II (stanzas 8–13). Which images and phrases appeal to you most here? Give reasons for your choices.
4	'seashell at my ear' (line 41). What does Durcan mean by this? What is he saying to Rosie in this stanza? How does this stanza bring the first part of the poet's journey to an end?
5	What does Durcan hope for Ireland in Rosie's future (stanza 18)? Why, do you think, does he mention division and uniformity in relation to Ireland?
6	Stanza 19 personifies the Irish landscape. How does Durcan achieve this and why, do you think, has he chosen to do so at this point in the poem? How is this related to the themes of the poem? Explain.
7	'Daymaker!' Explain what Durcan means by this in stanza 21 and the effect achieved by the repetition and punctuation.
8	How has Rosie's birth affected Durcan and those around her (stanzas 22 and 23)? Comment on Durcan's imagery here.
9	In Part III, how has Rosie's birth transformed Durcan's interactions with others?
10	Look at the detail: the names and information Durcan packs into the first three stanzas of Part III. Does this add to or take away from the mood of the poem in your opinion? Give reasons for your answer.
11	Find as many examples of religious language and imagery as you can in the poem and speculate on Durcan's reasons for including these. Does this affect the tone and theme?
12	Nouns abound in this poem (people, places, plants, etc.). Why does Durcan do this? What other poems have you studied where Durcan uses this technique and was the effect similar or different? Consider at least three other poems in your answer.
13	What were your feelings as you read the poem and why? Did you note any similarities between how Durcan reacted to his granddaughter's birth and the responses you encountered in the 'Before you read' assignment? Explain.
14	Is this the most positive poem of those you have studied by Durcan? Give reasons for your answer.
15	Imagine a similar poem but one that records a journey to and from a funeral. What details would you change in the language and imagery to reflect the change of theme and mood?
16	Divide your class into groups and assign each a number of stanzas to set music and images to. Collate your work at the end to produce a collaborative audio-visual version of the poem.

The MacBride Dynasty

What young mother is not a vengeful goddess
Spitting dynastic as well as motherly pride?
In 1949 in the black Ford Anglia,
Now that I had become a walking, talking little boy,
Mummy drove me out to visit my grand-aunt Maud Gonne   5
In Roebuck House in the countryside near Dublin,
To show off to the servant of the Queen
The latest addition to the extended family.
Although the eighty-year-old Cathleen Ní Houlihan had taken to her bed
She was keen as ever to receive admirers,   10
Especially the children of the family.
Only the previous week the actor Mac Liammóir
Had been kneeling at her bedside reciting Yeats to her,
His hand on his heart, clutching a red rose.
Cousin Sean and his wife Kid led the way up the stairs,   15
Sean opening the door and announcing my mother.
Mummy lifted me up in her arms as she approached the bed
And Maud leaned forward, sticking out her claws
To embrace me, her lizards of eyes darting about
In the rubble of the ruins of her beautiful face.   20
Terrified, I recoiled from her embrace
And, fleeing her bedroom, ran down the stairs
Out onto the wrought-iron balcony
Until Sean caught up with me and quieted me
And took me for a walk in the walled orchard.   25
Mummy was a little but not totally mortified:
She had never liked Maud Gonne because of Maud's
Betrayal of her husband, Mummy's Uncle John,
Major John, most ordinary of men, most
Humorous, courageous of soldiers,   30
The pride of our family,
Whose memory always brought laughter
To my grandmother Eileen's lips. 'John,'
She used to cry, 'John was such a gay man.'
Mummy set great store by loyalty; loyalty   35
In Mummy's eyes was the cardinal virtue.
Maud Gonne was a disloyal wife
And, therefore, not worthy of Mummy's love.
For dynastic reasons we would tolerate Maud,
But we would always see through her.   40

Paul Durcan

Before you read

What do you know about Major John MacBride and Maud Gonne? Research these famous Irish historical figures from whom Durcan is descended.

HIGHER LEVEL

Guidelines

This poem was published in 2007 in the collection *The Laughter of Mothers*, which celebrated Durcan's relationship with his mother, Sheila MacBride Durcan, to whom he was far closer than his father. Sheila's uncle was the famous soldier Major John MacBride, the husband of Maud Gonne. Durcan is fascinated by these important historical and literary figures. Major John MacBride was shot for his part in the rebellion of 1916. Maud Gonne was an ardent supporter of this cause. She was an activist, actress, suffragette and founder of the nationalist group 'The Daughters of Ireland'; she was also the muse of the poet W. B. Yeats and turned down more than one marriage proposal from him. Maud is the main subject of this poem, which centres on Durcan's visit with his mother to Roebuck House to see her when he was a young boy.

Commentary

Lines 1–8

Yeats on ageing

'What youthful mother, a shape upon her lap
Honey of generation had betrayed,
And that must sleep, shriek, struggle to escape
As recollection or the drug decide,
Would think her son, did she but see that shape
With sixty or more winters on its head,
A compensation for the pang of his birth,
Or the uncertainty of his setting forth?'

In this stanza from 'Among School Children' W. B. Yeats asks whether any young mother upon seeing her son as an old man would think the pain of his birth worth the effort.

Durcan asks a rhetorical question suggesting that any young mother would defend her family's honour like 'a vengeful goddess' should that family's ancestors or pride be brought into question: 'Spitting dynastic as well as motherly pride'. The opening here is unusually formal for Durcan, who tends to begin his poems in a far more accessible and conversational fashion. He is clearly mimicking the voice of W. B. Yeats, for whom Gonne was a muse and an obsession. Durcan recalls travelling in his father's 'Ford Anglia', a vehicle also mentioned in 'Rosie Joyce', to the rather grand sounding 'Roebuck House' to visit Gonne. A 'walking, talking little boy' is how Durcan describes himself, and his youth is emphasised by his use of the term 'Mummy' throughout. It seems he is to be shown off to Gonne as 'The latest addition to the extended family', which is 'The MacBride Dynasty' of the title. Durcan, possibly sardonically, refers to Gonne as a 'servant of the Queen', a reference to her autobiography, which bore this title. Of course Gonne was anything but and spent her days trying to recruit young men to fight the British – alluded to by Yeats in the poem 'No Second Troy': 'that she would of late / Have taught to ignorant men most violent ways'. So far perhaps Gonne is the 'vengeful goddess' of line 1, but Durcan's mother may also be, as we will soon see.

Lines 9–14

Cathleen Ní Houlihan

A mythical figure in Irish folklore, she personified Ireland and urged young men to martyr themselves to free her four green fields (the four provinces). Yeats wrote an eponymous play about this character especially for Gonne to play the title role. Yeats was completely besotted with Gonne and also wrote many poems about her.

Now eighty years old, Gonne's beauty has faded and she has 'taken to her bed', but her part in Irish literature and history is noted by Durcan when he refers to her as 'Cathleen Ní Houlihan'. She clearly still revels in this attention and adoration as evidenced by the visit the week before of the famous actor Micheál Mac Liammóir, who 'Had been kneeling at her bedside reciting Yeats to her, / His hand on his heart, clutching a red rose.' This anecdote reflects not only the adoration Gonne was accustomed to but also the theatrical and rarefied circles she remained part of.

Paul Durcan

Lines 15–25

'Cousin Sean [MacBride] and his wife Kid [Catalina Bulfin] led the way': using these familiar familial terms shows us that Durcan is an insider in this family, his relationship with and view of this powerful and famous clan is an intimate one and very different from that of the Irish general public. When young Durcan encounters the aged Gonne, his reaction is extreme and markedly opposite to Mac Liammóir's fawning attentions. He runs from her, 'fleeing her bedroom' and out of the house, 'Terrified' at this reptilian creature 'sticking out her claws / To embrace me, her lizards of eyes darting about / In the rubble of the ruins of her beautiful face.' This harsh imagery effectively conveys the terror the small boy feels. The phrase 'her beautiful face' reminds us that Gonne had been a famous beauty, compared by Yeats to Helen of Troy with 'beauty like a tightened bow', but she has now become wizened and old. How must she have felt at his reaction? Affronted? Upset? His Uncle Sean runs after him and brings him for a walk to placate him.

Lines 26–34

Sheila MacBride Durcan's reaction is an interesting one. She is a 'little but not totally mortified', suggesting a hint of **schadenfreude** (joy at another's discomfort) about the incident, perhaps enjoying the discomfort of Gonne whom 'She had never liked … because of Maud's / Betrayal of her husband, Mummy's Uncle John'. Yeats suggested that MacBride had molested Gonne's daughter, Iseult, but the only charge a Paris divorce court substantiated was that he had been drunk once. The MacBride family raised the molestation allegation in court to have his name cleared. Many thought that Yeats was being vindictive as he was jealous of MacBride. Gonne moved to Paris with the children until John was executed in 1916 for his part in the Rising. She then returned to Ireland.

> **Seán MacBride**
>
> This former IRA chief-of staff later won the Nobel Peace Prize, continuing the family 'dynastic' tradition of political activism and involvement. He worked for peace around the world and helped found Amnesty International.

'Mummy's Uncle John' is a telling phrase. Durcan is clearly influenced by his mother's loyalties and seems to use his mother's words as he waxes lyrical about his famous great-uncle. Although the 'most ordinary of men', suggesting humility, he was clearly extraordinary in her eyes, 'most / Humorous, courageous of soldiers, / The pride of our family'. He recalls his grandmother Eileen similarly rhapsodically speaking about him: 'John was such a gay man.' How can Maud – who had had two children with a married man before marrying John, who divorced him amid accusations of abuse, abandoned him and took his son to France, while all the time being very publicly wooed by Yeats – possibly be anything but tolerated by this tight-knit family for whom loyalty 'was the cardinal virtue'? Durcan states it boldly, unequivocally, 'Maud Gonne was a disloyal wife'. Why do the family 'tolerate Maud', why bother to visit her? 'For dynastic reasons' – so the outside world will see only loyalty and accord within this powerful family; but the truth is known by the family members, 'we would always see through her'.

Themes and imagery

Debunking misconceptions and accepted norms is something Durcan sees as a duty in his poetry and here he does this with his family on a private level but also on a public level, debunking the mythology of Gonne, Yeats and MacBride through this childhood anecdote.

Family, loyalty and betrayal dominate the poem thematically. Loyalty in particular is emphasised and repeated in the poem. Is Durcan being as disloyal as Gonne in revealing this picture of his family behind closed doors? It is worth noting that Durcan's mother gave up a promising career in law when she married Durcan's father

HIGHER LEVEL

Maud Gonne.

and supported him in his political and legal ambitions despite how abusive and difficult he could be to live with, especially for her son Paul. She was a loyal wife, as her family's status and the social mores of the time demanded. Maud was not such a loyal wife. She had committed the 'cardinal' (line 36) sin, 'Betrayal of her husband' (line 28). This public and political woman, so mythologised by Yeats and his ilk, is perceived very differently by her in-laws. She is tolerated because of her connection to the 'MacBride Dynasty' but, through Durcan's words (channelling those of his mother and grandmother), she is seen as vain and affected. The references to both her 1938 autobiography and her role on the Abbey stage seem mocking in tone, 'the servant of the Queen' (line 7), 'Cathleen Ní Houlihan had taken to her bed' (line 9). Durcan seems to poke fun not only at Gonne but also at himself in the repetition of 'Mummy', making him sound a little precocious (Mummy was quite an English term for mother and not used commonly in Ireland at that time). And also at his mother, 'Mummy was a little but not totally mortified' (line 26). Perhaps even the perfect, saint-like view the family hold of John MacBride is lampooned gently, 'most / Humorous, courageous of soldiers, / The pride of our family' (lines 29–31). This pride must have been a difficult thing for Gonne to live with while her part in the fight for Irish independence and for prisoners' and women's rights is ignored. An outspoken female activist was not seemly in an important family like this in Ireland at the time, unlike the honour of being related to a martyred freedom fighter like Major John MacBride. However, Durcan is not overly cruel or unfair to any party and allows the reader to evaluate all sides of this family dynamic for themselves.

The picture we get of this family is one of a façade: 'To show off' (line 7) and 'we would tolerate Maud' (line 39) are two phrases from the beginning and ending of the poem that convey how important it was for this dynasty to portray a sense of family relationship and loyalty, which in reality was not there, 'She had never liked Maud Gonne' (line 27). In running away, 'fleeing her bedroom' (line 22), is Durcan symbolically **rejecting all of this affectation and pretence**? He certainly achieves this in this revealing autobiographical poem about a fascinating family.

Form and language

Apart from the very Yeats-like opening, a **sardonic** (mocking) mimicry of his poetry about Gonne, the language is **conversational and anecdotal**. The lack of stanzas, rhyme or any sustained metrical pattern adds to this effect.

The world created by the imagery and language in Durcan's poem is one of **privilege**. Gonne's home sounds grand, 'Roebuck House' (line 6), and has a 'wrought-iron balcony' (line 23) and a 'walled orchard' (line 25). Durcan's use of the word 'Mummy' and the famous visitors to Gonne, 'the actor Mac Liammóir' (line 12), add to this air of privilege. Most striking in terms of imagery is the aged Gonne herself; once beautiful, she is now like a crumbling building, 'the rubble of the ruins of her beautiful face' (line 20). Durcan could have just used either 'rubble' or 'ruins', so using both emphasises strongly how wrinkled and old she now is. The alliteration here slows the line and gives us time to take in the import of the phrase. Gonne has 'claws' and 'lizards of eyes' (lines 18–19), putting the reader in mind of an ancient reptilian creature.

Questions

1. Who are the members of the 'MacBride Dynasty' alluded to in the poem? What does the word 'Dynasty' suggest about them? Is the title sarcastic, in your opinion? Explain.

2. What do the first two lines mean, in your opinion? How do they differ in style and tone from the rest of the poem? Who is represented here by the 'young mother'?

3. How is Maud Gonne depicted physically and in terms of personality in the first twenty lines of the poem?

4. Is Durcan's reaction to Gonne purely spur-of-the-moment or do you suspect it may be coloured by his mother's opinion of her? Give reasons for your answer.

5. 'Mummy was a little but not totally mortified' (line 26). Why was 'Mummy' not 'totally mortified'? Do you think she may have enjoyed Gonne's discomfort?

6. Why had Durcan's mother 'never liked Maud Gonne' (line 27)?

7. How is Gonne's ex-husband Major John MacBride depicted?

8. Examine how loyalty and betrayal are themes of the poem. The commentary may guide your answer by explaining some of the reasons why the MacBrides might have considered Gonne disloyal.

9. What other themes can you identify in the poem? How are these themes conveyed to you through the language and imagery of the poet?

10. What is the effect of Durcan's repetition of the word 'Mummy' throughout the poem? What other examples of repetition can you find in the poem and what is their effect?

11. Considering the poem as a whole, is Durcan cruel or unfair to Gonne? Is his mother? Does Gonne have your sympathy? Explain your answers with close reference to the poem, but you may also include details from the commentary and your own research.

12. Analyse the final four lines of the poem. What meaning and tone do you detect within them?

13. You might, having read the poem, like to continue your research into 'The MacBride Dynasty' or those connected to them such as Yeats and Mac Liammóir. Write a short piece on one (or more) of the people mentioned. This will further inform your understanding of the poem and its context.

14. Imagine you are Maud Gonne. Write two diary entries: the first after the visit from Mac Liammóir and the second following the visit of Durcan and his mother a week later.

15. In a similarly anecdotal style write about an incident from your childhood that reveals something about your family history.

Exam-Preparation Questions

1	'Even at their most apparently revelatory, there is a reticence at the heart of the poems indicative of deep respect for their subjects, which permits the reader to be involved, but never in an uncomfortably voyeuristic way.' Do you agree with this assessment from *The Guardian* of Paul Durcan's poetry in the light of the poems you have studied on your course?
2	Family is a major theme in Paul Durcan's work. What picture of Durcan's family life emerges from his poetry through his language and imagery?
3	*The Irish Times* dubbed Paul Durcan 'the most playful poet in Ireland'. Does your experience of studying Durcan's poetry support this view? Explain with close reference to at least five poems on your course.
4	Discuss the poetry of Paul Durcan in the light of the following statement from Fintan O'Toole: 'Durcan's Ireland is a place at once real and absurd. For all the comic invention, all the dark exploration of his work, Durcan is above all a great realist.'
5	'Powerful emotions explored through startling imagery – this is what the reader of Paul Durcan's poetry will encounter.' Discuss.
6	Imagine your school has decided to invite Paul Durcan to speak about his poetry on your Leaving Certificate course. Write the letter of invitation you would send him, outlining why he has been invited, what it was about his poetry that made the students want to hear him speak and what questions the students would like him to answer about his work. Ensure your letter is full of close reference to the poetry you have studied.
7	Would you agree that the women in Paul Durcan's poetry are strong-willed and often let down by the men in their lives?
8	'Durcan, who makes a fetish of excess, repeats and repeats and repeats' – Peggy O'Brien. Examine Durcan's use of repetition as a poetic technique in the poetry you have studied by him on your course.
9	UCD's citation on Paul Durcan remarks that 'his forensic scrutiny of hypocrisy, his relentless self-questioning, his unique blend of the real and the fantastic' are important features of his work. Analyse the poetry of Durcan in the light of this statement.
10	'Undemanding grammatical and syntactical forms, which put no impediments between utterance and understanding.' Is Durcan's poetry too accessible? Discuss.

Paul Durcan

Sample Essay

'Powerful emotions explored through startling imagery – this is what the reader of Paul Durcan's poetry will encounter'. Discuss.

[Annotation: Quote/idea introduced that will reappear in the conclusion to demonstrate structure and planning]

'that was a whirlpool, that was a whirlpool, / And I very nearly drowned.' Paul Durcan's use of metaphors and symbols to express strong feelings is encapsulated in this quotation from 'Nessa', which conveys the passionate and overwhelming nature of falling madly in love. He is adept at expressing powerful emotions such as regret, love, estrangement, joy and heartbreak, using striking imagery to capture the attention and imagination of the reader. I have noticed that he uses accessible language and a conversational, sometimes even confessional, tone to relate anecdotes, memories and events that provide an insight into the man. These reveal details about his life, his emotions and his values. His use of original and startling imagery also reveals his skill as a poet. As Dr Eve Patten said, he is 'a poet of love, eroticism and loss. His striking metaphors and dislocating images, meanwhile, result in a poetry which is extraordinarily visual and frequently surreal.'

[Annotation: Personal response demonstrates engagement with the poet's work]

[Annotation: Show time and effort has been taken to research poet]

The dizzying excitement of his passionate relationship with his wife is the subject of Durcan's poem 'Nessa'. He recalls that he met her 'In the Shangri-La hotel, / She took me by the index finger / And dropped me in her well'. In this poem, and many others, Durcan uses water as a key image to convey his emotions. His use of water (wells, sea, swimming, etc.) here is startling in its intensity and originality. Water represents the passionate sexual relationship he has with Nessa. It seems to be one he can barely keep up with. She dropped him 'in her well'. She 'is a whirlpool' and tells him 'Take off your pants' as she invites him to hop 'into the Irish Sea'. Water here represents potent female sexuality. Like the subject of an aisling poem, she is a flame-haired temptress: 'let your red hair down'. Durcan, however, is brutally honest about himself here, something fellow poet Brendan Kennelly characterised as 'manic confidentiality', and admits he finds it hard to keep up with Nessa: 'I very nearly drowned'. The imagery Durcan uses to describe his side of the relationship pales dramatically beside Nessa's 'whirlpool'. He wants her to lie in the grass beside him, and asks her to 'stay with me on the rocks' and to 'ride into Dublin City / In a taxi-cab wrapped up in dust'. These images seemed so drab and lacklustre to me when compared with the heady eroticism offered by this strong woman. I felt that for Durcan to be so honest and self-deprecating was admirable. As we shall see, this contrast between the two foreshadows the later distance between the couple and the eventual break-up of their marriage. He hints at this again in 'The Difficulty that is Marriage', when he lies awake next to his sleeping wife and tells her 'I array the moonlit ceiling with a mosaic of question marks'. This beautiful image relates clearly the estrangement between these two and his feeling of helplessness at the situation. One of the things I like most about Durcan is his skill in using striking and revealing imagery like this to convey honestly the feelings he experienced. He offers an astonishingly frank access to his life experiences, far more than other poets I have studied. His confessional style pulls no punches and he admits finally, 'I am very nearly drowned'. This refrain, though subtly changed as the poem progresses, is repeated at the end of each

[Annotation: Question addressed, with explanation and book-up of assertion]

[Annotation: Personal response]

stanza. Repetition is a key feature of Durcan's poetry and often emphasises significant emotions and events.

> Reference to language and style

'Parents' is another poem where water is an important and effective metaphor repeated to convey powerful emotions and, as the quote in the introduction states, is 'extraordinarily visual and frequently surreal'. The emotions conveyed here are estrangement and worry as the parents gaze at the face of their sleeping child. The poem's opening contains a dramatic metaphor, startling the reader: 'A child's face is a drowned face: / Her parents stare down at her asleep / Estranged from her by a sea'. Again we have water to symbolise at once love and distance. The parents feel they are 'behind glass' as they desperately wish to reach their daughter, but 'She is under the sea / And they are above the sea'. The anxiety they feel is expressed by representing them as 'fearful fish' with 'foreheads furrowed'. I found this metaphor highly original, totally surreal and almost cartoonish. The parents' worry is compounded by a striking image of helplessness: 'through the night, stranded, they stare'. This vigil is characterised almost as a shipwreck or abandonment of some kind through the image of being 'stranded', and they are given no solace or comfort as the repetition of the last line (echoing the first) shows us: 'the drowned, drowned face of their child'. I felt for Durcan and his wife here, his imagery and the strong emotions conveyed engaged my sympathy as again Durcan admits to failing somehow, to being helpless.

> Personal response

When Durcan wrote 'Father's Day, 21 June 1992' his daughters had 'grown up and gone away' and the speed of this progression he likens to a train journey where 'the green fields' fly by the windows, 'running away from us'. This metaphor effectively captures how quickly time passes and how you cannot be as close to your children when they are adults as you were when they were small. In 'Windfall', for example, Durcan tells us his children used to sit on his lap as they watched television and pored over photograph albums and he again uses water symbolically to characterise the safety and protection of the family home as a 'private sea, / Their own unique, symbiotic fluid / Of which their parents also partook', coining this surreal idea in the phrase, 'Such is home – a sea of your own'. Taking a metaphor and twisting it so that a sea becomes like the amniotic fluid of the womb, a 'symbiotic' one, is typical of Durcan, who often stretches a metaphor as far as he can to convey the complexity and multi-textured nature of emotion and experience. We rarely just feel happy or sad. Life isn't that simple and Durcan conveys this so effectively when he uses imagery in this way. I was struck that he could suggest safety, happiness, birth, nurturing and love in this one developing metaphor and it makes his admission that 'with good reason / I was put out of my home' all the more tragic. Again, I learned a little more about this man and his life in the process.

> Deep appreciation of poet's style and technique

> 'Windfall' is very rich in emotion and imagery and it is a pity to see so little of it discussed here

It is the axe in 'Father's Day' that is the startling image and again encapsulates love and loss. It is a simple, if bizarre, anecdote in which Durcan recounts how his wife made him take an axe on the train to Cork for her sister because 'The buddleia tree in the backyard / Had grown out of control'. This was one of my favourite poems by Durcan as I found the premise immediately engaging and amusing, but as always with Durcan when he is being funny he is often at his most serious. The axe, in a rare simile and using fun alliteration, is 'As neat as a newborn babe, / All in the bare buff'. This image is not only amusing but I find it striking that something generally representing destruction and violence could be compared to the most vulnerable and

> Reference to style and language

least threatening thing imaginable. The incongruous juxtaposition works perfectly. The axe for me represents the impending break-up of the marriage and Durcan knows it is coming. His wife is relieved to see the back of him: 'Two weeks of having the bed to herself, / Two weeks of not having to be pestered / By my coarse advances'. Again we see repetition used effectively, this time to convey her relief. Durcan is typically self-deprecating while wryly humorous, even mentioning that she will be glad not to have to watch him 'eating spaghetti with a knife and fork'! The imagery here is again of estrangement and yet it is clear he loves her: 'I kissed her goodbye' and 'I always feel bad leaving her'. The axe, even though it represents the split to come, is something he also seems fond of, 'we sat alone, / The axe and I', perhaps because it still links him to her, it is something that he can do for her as he tells a disconcerted fellow passenger on the train, 'I am feeling guilty because she does not love me' and 'Her sister wants a loan of the axe'. So he is not just estranged from his daughters but from his wife too and he has only the axe for company by the end. The raw emotion here startled me, as did the quirky and original imagery, and again Durcan lets us into the most important and painful memories and experiences with openness and an admirable lack of self-pity or sentimentality.

Appreciation of characteristic voice of poet

Quotation used effectively here

The poems discussed so far have explored Durcan's adult life but the emotions and images associated with his childhood and early twenties are just as powerful in tone and image. The couplets 'En Famille, 1979' and 'Madman' and the lyric poem 'Sport' are good examples of this. 'En Famille, 1979' begins with a mood of yearning, 'Bring me back', but this emotion is soon compounded by a darker feeling as the speaker wishes to be brought back to 'the dark school of childhood'. I am startled by this image, which is seemingly at odds with the emotion of longing expressed. Why describe childhood as a dark school? Does this mean it is a place where hard lessons were learned? We know that Durcan's relationship with his father was a very difficult one. It seems the speaker took some comfort in the certainty that seemed to exist in this childhood place, 'To where tiny is tiny, and massive is massive'. A clue to this strange contrast of image and emotion can be witnessed in another of Durcan's couplet poems to reference his childhood. In 'Madman' Durcan may also be referring to his difficult relationship with Judge John Durcan, his powerful and demanding father: 'Every child has a madman on their street: / The only trouble about *our* madman is that he's our father.' Again here the tone and imagery seem at odds. The couplet sounds like the set-up and punchline to a joke and yet something more serious and sinister lies beneath through the imagery of his own father as a madman. Some critics have argued that Durcan may be assuming the voice of his own children here and referencing himself as the 'madman'. As he admits in 'The Difficulty that is Marriage', 'I have my troubles and I shall always have them', an allusion to his struggle with depression. These couplet poems certainly explore powerful emotions through startling imagery despite their brevity.

Poet's use of contrast discussed with relevance to the question

Knowledge of poet beyond poems themselves

Appreciation of different interpretations of the poem

Durcan's struggles with mental illness and the fractious nature of his relationship with his father are explored in more detail in the arresting and darkly entertaining poem 'Sport'. This poem had a deep impact on me. Again there is a certain levity at the surface in the mood that belies the dark pain and estrangement underneath as he tells us an anecdote revealing how much he longed for his father's approval and how rarely he received it. The mood of the poem as it opens is

HIGHER LEVEL

confessional and direct as he speaks to his father, admitting, 'There were not many fields / In which you had hopes for me / But sport was one of them'. Durcan's father had him forcibly committed to a psychiatric hospital as a very young man and Durcan was in and out of such institutions for years. He relates the story of a match his hospital, Grangegorman, played against a similar team from Mullingar: 'I was a patient / In B wing.' His father had driven down 'to stand / On the sidelines and observe me'. I find the imagery and language here very telling. The word 'sidelines' characterises the distance between him and his father, and there is a cold and almost scientific detachment in the word 'observe'. Despite Durcan's amusing description of his opponents and a surreal tale of one of them castrating his own best friend, both darkly amusing sections of the poem, it is a very sad poem and the feeling again of estrangement is very clear. Even though Durcan puts in a stellar performance, 'I made three or four spectacular saves', his father's reaction is less than enthusiastic: 'Sniffing your approval, you shook hands with me. / "Well played, son."' Even the tiny detail of the comma before the word 'son' shows the reticence and lack of warmth in his father's response and yet this was one of the only times Durcan felt his father's approval: 'Seldom if ever again in your eyes / Was I to rise to these heights.' The emotion here is again a longing for approval and recognition. The contrast between Durcan's attempt to 'mesmerise' his father, 'It was my knowing / That you were standing on the sideline / That gave me the necessary motivation', and his father's lacklustre reaction was the strongest image and conveyed Durcan's mix of emotions, pride and disappointment very effectively.

[Margin note: This point could have been backed up with closer reference and quotation]

[Margin note: Close reading of poem evident]

[Margin note: Question fully addressed and discussed]

The final poem I am going to discuss in terms of Durcan's powerful emotions being explored through startling imagery is another poem dealing with family relationships and Durcan's childhood, 'The MacBride Dynasty'. Durcan's mother, Sheila MacBride Durcan, was a relative of Major John MacBride, a martyred hero of the 1916 Rising. The poem reminisces about a visit of Durcan and his mother to see MacBride's ex-wife Maud Gonne. Of course Gonne was an activist during the Rising herself and more famously a muse to the poet W. B. Yeats. The image that struck me most here is the description of Maud Gonne and young Durcan's reaction to her. She is like a reptile. Her once famously beautiful face is ravaged by time: 'sticking out her claws / To embrace me, her lizards of eyes darting about / In the rubble of the ruins of her beautiful face.' She is used to being feted and adored as the visit of the 'actor Mac Liammóir' earlier in the poem shows: 'She was keen as ever to receive admirers'. However, young Durcan, at that time merely a 'walking, talking little boy', is horrified at this aged creature and runs from the room terrified. Durcan's imagery here and his masterful storytelling convey effectively the tragedy of ageing. I could not help but pity Gonne, bedridden and ancient. I felt Durcan conveyed his fear effectively too, 'Terrified, I recoiled from her embrace'. The word 'recoiled' put me in mind of a snake coiled in its lair and related cleverly to the reptilian description of Gonne. Again Durcan explores powerful emotions through startling imagery and I feel it is the added element of stories and events from the poet's life woven through this that makes him one of my favourite Leaving Certificate poets.

[Margin note: Question continues to be central to answer]

[Margin note: Imagery linked to theme]

Water, mosaics, axes, madmen, Gaelic matches, ruins, lizards – whatever the image, Durcan finds a way to make it at once relatable, representative exactly of the emotion he wishes to convey and yet always surprising and original. You may notice that the poems I have chosen to discuss all relate to Durcan's family. These are the poems that engaged me most as I felt I was learning so much about him and he is a genuinely fascinating character. I feel the variety and intensity of emotion and imagery 'was a whirlpool' of discovery and imagination that I will happily dive into and explore for many years to come.

[Margin note: Enthusiasm and appreciation is clear and the 'whirlpool' reference brings the answer full circle to demonstrate planning and closure]

ESSAY CHECKLIST		Yes √	No ×
Purpose	Has the candidate understood the task?		
	Has the candidate responded to it in a thoughtful manner?		
	Has the candidate answered the question?		
Comment:			
Coherence	Has the candidate made convincing arguments?		
	Has the candidate linked ideas?		
	Does the essay have a sense of unity?		
Comment:			
Language	Is the essay written in an appropriate register?		
	Are ideas expressed in a clear way?		
	Is the writing fluent?		
Comment:			
Mechanics	Is the use of language accurate?		
	Are all words spelled correctly?		
	Does the punctuation help the reader?		
Comment:			

SNAPSHOT PAUL DURCAN

- Accessible language
- Autobiographical
- Repetition and lists
- Free verse
- Uses anecdotes and digression
- Couplets
- Headline-style titles
- Use of dates and place names
- Dark humour
- At once realistic and surreal
- Family relationships
- Water is a key symbol
- Names of people

HIGHER LEVEL

Robert Frost

1874–1963

The Tuft of Flowers*	204
Mending Wall	209
After Apple-Picking	214
The Road Not Taken	219
Birches	222
"Out, Out—"*	229
Spring Pools	234
Acquainted with the Night	237
Design	241
Provide, Provide	245

Robert Frost

Biography

Early life

Although Robert Frost is always associated with New England in the eastern United States, where he lived for most of his life, he was born in San Francisco, on the west coast, in 1874. His father, Will, was an adventurer, a drinker and a gambler, who was always trying to make something of himself; from him, Robert inherited a tough-minded independence of thought and a sense of adventure. His mother, Belle, was a rather other-worldly woman, whose intense spirituality was passed on to her son, even though the adult poet steered clear of organised religion of any sort.

His father died of tuberculosis when Frost was eleven, leaving the family very poor, so Belle took them across the country to live with her parents in Massachusetts. Robert attended Lawrence High School, where he was an excellent scholar, especially in Latin, but the years after leaving school were unsettled. He quit his undergraduate studies at Dartmouth College after only two months, and took up a succession of jobs – mill worker, journalist, schoolteacher and farmer – looking for something that would suit him but always wanting to be a poet.

In 1895 he married his high-school sweetheart and rival for academic honours, Elinor White, but his restlessness continued. He spent some time as a student at Harvard but did not like the rigid structure of university life. Then, in 1900, the Frosts bought, with his grandfather's help, a farm in Derry, New Hampshire. They grew apples and raised chickens, and although Frost was not the most dedicated farmer, he liked the life and it gave him time to work on his poetry. He laid the foundations of his career as a poet, working close to the land, taking long walks in the woods and fields, and getting to know the local rural people. He found subjects and metaphors for his poetry, and a voice in which to write.

Meanwhile, children had been coming along. The eldest, Elliott, died from cholera in 1900 when he was only three years of age, and the youngest, Elinor, died soon after she was born in 1907. In between there were three daughters – Lesley, Irma and Marjorie – and a son, Carol. They were schooled at home, a task that Frost enjoyed. The farm brought in little money, so he supplemented his income with teaching. The farm was sold in 1911. The next year they took a big decision to move to England, at least for a while. For Frost, this was a matter of choosing poetry over teaching. He wanted to be at the heart of the English-language literary scene, and at the time that meant London.

Poetic life

In London Frost, for the first time in his life, found himself among other poets, and found himself accepted and admired as a poet himself. He met two other Americans, Ezra Pound and T. S. Eliot, who were also making their way in the English literary world, as well as W. B. Yeats, whose poetry Frost had long admired. This was a hugely important time for Frost. His first two volumes of poetry were published in England – *A Boy's Will* (1913) and *North of Boston* (1914). By the time he returned to the USA in early 1915, with the First World War under way, he discovered that his books had been noticed and reviewed back home, and he was already something of a success.

Frost never looked back as a poet. His career went from strength to strength as collection followed collection and his reputation grew. He went back to farming but was offered teaching jobs – at Amherst College,

Dartmouth, the University of Michigan and, later, Harvard – which would make him financially secure. Frost was torn between farming, which produced little income but gave him the time to write and live in an environment that encouraged his poetry, and teaching, which he threw himself into with enthusiasm but which took up his time and exhausted his energies.

As Frost became more famous, the offers from colleges became more generous and his duties less taxing. He did not feel able to turn them down. He also gave 'readings' of his poems (although he usually spoke them from memory) all over the country. He attracted huge audiences and charmed them with his poems and his witty off-the-cuff comments and digressions. His readings were always something of a performance. He played the role of a plain-speaking, hard-minded Yankee farmer, a man of the people; however, the man behind the mask was a good deal more complicated and, in many ways, darker, as some of his poems suggest.

Frost was prone to bouts of depression, often followed by illness, especially when he over-exerted himself with teaching, travelling and reading. Moreover, while his fame grew and he became something of a national cultural icon, his family life remained dark and difficult. Three of his four surviving children had mental health problems, and Robert and Elinor did all they could to support them, financially and emotionally. So it was a terrible blow when Marjorie, who had always been troubled, died from complications following childbirth in 1934, just when it seemed she had settled down and found some happiness in her life. In 1938 Frost's devoted wife, Elinor, who had always been a vital support, died of a heart attack. Then in 1940 his only surviving son, Carol, who had never found his way in life, died by suicide. A few years later Irma had to be taken to a psychiatric hospital, where she spent the rest of her life.

Frost's reputation as a poet kept growing. His collections won the Pulitzer Prize for poetry – the top literary award in America – a record four times, and he was given more than forty honorary degrees. By the last decades of his long life, he had become an institution – the greatest living American poet, whose books sold tens of thousands of copies. He looked the part, with his big head, his shock of white hair and his bushy eyebrows, and he enjoyed playing it. He read his poem 'The Gift Outright' at the inauguration of President John F. Kennedy in 1961, and the next year, aged eighty-eight, he visited the Soviet Union and met the Soviet leader, Nikita Khrushchev, with whom he had a frank discussion about East–West politics.

He died in Boston, Massachusetts, on 19 January 1963.

Social and Cultural Context

Modernism

Frost lived at a time when the world was changing fast. The most important aesthetic movement during his maturity was modernism. The modernist movement in the Arts reacted against the confident certainties of the nineteenth century. In painting, modernists rejected representational naturalism in favour of cubism or abstraction. In music, modernists rejected the traditional system of key signatures that had been the foundation of Western music for centuries. In poetry, modernists rejected traditional forms and metres. The guiding principle in all cases was the instruction of US poet Ezra Pound to 'Make it new!'

Frost got to know Pound in London in 1913. London was the centre of activity for modernist poetry at the time, and Pound was the driving force. He championed Frost's poetry, even though Frost was working in a different

Robert Frost

style. Other modernist American poets, notably T. S. Eliot, were living and working in London, and Frost met them all.

Frost, however, was not a modernist. Of his contemporaries, he loved the poetry of W. B. Yeats, whom he met – and was highly praised by – in London in 1913. He also admired Thomas Hardy. Like both of them, Frost opted to use **rhyme and traditional metre**, and could not see the point of so-called free verse. He compared writing it to playing tennis with the net down.

While the modernists were primarily poets of the city, Frost was first and foremost a **rural poet**, with his roots in the New England countryside, which he wrote about all through his career. As he wrote in an early notebook, '**Locality gives art**.' And where the modernists were often obscure and difficult to read, their poems full of allusions, Frost wanted to be understood, and although he was a very learned man and his poems are often complex and subtle, they are not difficult on a superficial level.

The sound of sense

The fact that Frost used traditional forms does not mean that he was out of date or an imitator. Far from it. He worked hard to master his craft and was an **excellent technical poet**. He was confident of that long before he had any recognition as a poet. As he wrote to his friend John Bartlett in 1913: 'To be perfectly frank with you I am one of the most notable craftsmen of my time. That will transpire [become evident] presently.'

He believed in the importance of the conversational speaking voice in poetry, as you can tell from reading any of his poems. This was not a new idea – the Romantic poets in the late eighteenth century had called for poetry written in 'the language of men' – but Frost has his own refinement of the principle, which he called **'the sound of sense'**. He believed that the unit of sense was the sentence – not just as a grammatical entity but as a sound: 'A sentence is a sound in itself on which other sounds called words may be strung.' He said that you could best hear the sound of sense by listening to people talking from behind a door, when the words could not be heard, but the patterns of sound they made could be.

It is not necessary to understand the details of Frost's theory to appreciate that his main concern was to reproduce in his poems the authentic sound of a person speaking. This speaking voice is then held in creative tension with the metre of the verse; see also the discussion on page 202.

American culture and politics

The story of Frost's career as a poet is interesting for the light it throws upon cultural attitudes in America. His success can be partly explained by the way he deliberately built up a public persona of himself as a typical Yankee: a plain man living in rural New England, a man for whom the hard work of farming was a real inspiration. Poems such as 'Mending Wall' and 'After Apple-Picking' reflect this image of his life.

Biographers and critics have discussed the extent to which this persona was real or invented. They point out that he was a distinguished teacher and intellectual. His poems are not the simple 'nature' poems that they seem to be on the surface. As he said himself, 'I'm not a nature poet. There's always something else in my poetry.' But he continued to play a role that appealed to the public, as an essentially American poet rooted in rural values. Caribbean poet Derek Walcott described him as 'the icon of Yankee values, the smell of woodsmoke, the sparkle of dew, the reality of farmhouse dung, the jocular honesty of an uncle'.

HIGHER LEVEL

Frost's best poems were always subtler, darker and more interesting than his public image might have suggested, and yet the reading public who bought his books may well have responded to something simpler. In the twentieth century the American way of life became increasingly urbanised and remote from the rustic idylls that Frost's poems seem to depict, for example in 'Birches'. It may be that **nostalgia** played a part in the public acclaim of Frost. He became a cultural icon. During the Second World War 50,000 copies of one of his poems were distributed to US troops stationed overseas to boost morale.

The great events Frost lived through, including two world wars and one 'cold war', have left relatively little trace in his poems. He was strongly supportive of the Allies in the First World War and surprisingly lukewarm about the Second, but neither event is a strong presence in his poems. As noted above, he read his own poem at Kennedy's inauguration, and was very eager to meet Khrushchev, but contemporary politics was not often his theme. Although later poems like 'Provide, Provide' see him taking a stance in response to American politics, the truths expressed in metaphors derived from rural life were more powerful than topical observations. It is no coincidence that the poem that was read as a comment on the Cold War, 'Mending Wall', was written fifty years before the Berlin Wall was built.

Themes

Rural life

Frost spent many years as a farmer, so it is no surprise that most of his poems have **rural settings**. Although he is sensitive to the beauties of the natural world, he knew it above all as a place of work. In the poems on your course we hear about mending walls, picking apples, making hay ('The Tuft of Flowers'), tending cows ('Birches') and sawing logs ('"Out, Out—"'). Frost wrote about the **practical business of rural labour** as no other poet has done, and he knew intimately the trees and flowers, streams and pools that he wrote about. But he did not write about these things just for their own sake. The poems explore the human soul, human relationships, the poetic imagination and the transience of all things, using his observations of **rural life as metaphors** or as starting points for meditations on broader subjects.

Design

Frost's mother was a deeply religious person, and although Frost avoided organised religion, he read widely in philosophy and theology, and his poetry makes it clear that he was always on a spiritual quest. Although the idea of God (or gods) is rarely addressed directly, many of his poems **question the nature and structure of the universe**. At its most benign, as in 'The Tuft of Flowers' or 'Birches', this leads to a moral vision encompassed in a memorable phrase: 'Men work together … / Whether they work together or apart'; 'Earth's the right place for love'. In darker poems, the universe can seem to be in the grip of a sinister power: the trees that 'darken nature' by destroying the 'flowery waters' in 'Spring Pools', the saw that leaps out at the boy's hand in '"Out, Out—"', even the mysterious force that topples the walls in 'Mending Wall'. That vision is stated most clearly and chillingly in 'Design', in which Frost contemplates the 'design of darkness to appall'.

Poetry and the imagination

Although Frost was a farmer for many years, the main work of his life was as a poet. It is not surprising, then, that he wrote about that work, as well as rural labour, in his poems. When he does so, he does so indirectly, in a metaphorical way that may not be apparent on first reading, but which colours the whole poem. He stated, for example, that 'The Tuft of Flowers' contains a 'definition of poetry'; 'Spring Pools' uses a metaphor from nature to explore the creative and destructive processes of the imagination; 'After Apple-Picking' and 'Birches' both contain metaphors that reflect on Frost's creative life as a poet.

Robert Frost

Timeline

1874	Born in San Francisco, USA
1885	Father dies; family moves to New England
1892	Graduates from Lawrence High School; briefly attends Dartmouth College
1895	Marries Elinor White
1896	Birth of first child, Elliott
1897–99	Attends Harvard University
1900	Elliott dies; family move to farm in Derry, New Hampshire
1912	Moves to England, hoping for literary success
1913	Publishes first book of poems, *A Boy's Will*
1914	Publishes second collection, *North of Boston*
1915	Returns to America, settling on a farm in Franconia, New Hampshire
1916	Publishes *Mountain Interval*
1917	Begins teaching at Amherst College
1920s	Divides time between farming, teaching and public readings
1923	Publishes *New Hampshire*, which won the first of his four Pulitzer Prizes for poetry
1928	Publishes *West-Running Brook*
1930	Publishes *Collected Poems*; elected to the American Academy of Arts and Letters
1934	Daughter Marjorie dies, aged 29
1936	Publishes *A Further Range*
1938	Wife, Elinor, dies
1940	Son Carol dies by suicide, aged 38
1942	Publishes *A Witness Tree*
1947	Publishes *Steeple Bush*
1961	Reads his poem 'The Gift Outright' at the inauguration of President John F. Kennedy
1962	Visits Russia on a goodwill mission for the US Department of State; publishes *In the Clearing*
1963	Dies in Boston, survived by two of his six children

HIGHER LEVEL

Before you read

 The events of this poem take place during haymaking, at a time when the job was done using tools that had stayed much the same for hundreds of years. Find out what you can about old-fashioned haymaking and the tools that were used, and share your knowledge in class.

The Tuft of Flowers

I went to turn the grass once after one
Who mowed it in the dew before the sun.

The dew was gone that made his blade so keen
Before I came to view the leveled scene.

I looked for him behind an isle of trees;   5
I listened for his whetstone on the breeze.

But he had gone his way, the grass all mown,
And I must be, as he had been – alone,

'As all must be,' I said within my heart,
'Whether they work together or apart.'   10

But as I said it, swift there passed me by
On noiseless wing a bewildered butterfly,

Seeking with memories grown dim o'er night
Some resting flower of yesterday's delight.

And once I marked his flight go round and round,   15
As where some flower lay withering on the ground.

And then he flew as far as eye could see,
And then on tremulous wing came back to me.

I thought of questions that have no reply,
And would have turned to toss the grass to dry;   20

But he turned first, and led my eye to look
At a tall tuft of flowers beside a brook,

A leaping tongue of bloom the scythe had spared
Beside a reedy brook the scythe had bared.

The mower in the dew had loved them thus,   25
By leaving them to flourish, not for us,

Nor yet to draw one thought of ours to him,
But from sheer morning gladness at the brim.

The butterfly and I had lit upon,
Nevertheless, a message from the dawn,   30

That made me hear the waking birds around,
And hear his long scythe whispering to the ground,

And feel a spirit kindred to my own;
So that henceforth I worked no more alone;

But glad with him, I worked as with his aid,   35
And weary, sought at noon with him the shade;

And dreaming, as it were, held brotherly speech
With one whose thought I had not hoped to reach.

'Men work together,' I told him from the heart,
'Whether they work together or apart.'   40

Glossary

3	*keen*:	sharp-edged
6	*whetstone*:	stone used for sharpening tools
18	*tremulous*:	quivering, trembling
23	*scythe*:	curving, sharp-edged blade with a long, upright handle, used for cutting grass

Guidelines

'The Tuft of Flowers' was first published in *A Boy's Will* (1913), Frost's first book of poetry, where it is not the only poem about mowing and haymaking. In this poem, the speaker is turning cut grass, probably with a fork.

Commentary

Lines 1–10
These lines set the scene. The speaker has come to turn the grass to help it dry in the sun. He is aware that someone must have been working in the same place earlier, 'in the dew before the sun', to mow the grass with a scythe, but there is no sign of him now. He is an absence rather than a presence, although the speaker looks and listens for him. So the speaker is alone, as the mower had been, and he finds a lesson or moral in this: we are all alone, 'Whether [we] work together or apart'.

Lines 11–24
The speaker's thoughts are interrupted by the appearance of a butterfly, which is flying about 'bewildered' because it is looking for the flowers that were there yesterday, but have since been cut down with the grass.

The speaker sees it flying 'round and round' a flower that 'lay withering on the ground', then it flies away and comes back again. Notice how the word 'tremulous' suggests a nervous emotional state as well as the fluttering of the butterfly's wings, as if the butterfly were almost human.

'I thought of questions that have no reply,' the speaker says. What questions might those be? What mood does the line suggest the speaker is in? He tells us he would have gone back to his task, but the butterfly 'led my eye' towards a 'tuft of flowers' that had been left untouched by the mower – 'A leaping tongue of bloom the scythe had spared' – beside a brook.

Lines 25–40

Brimming over

The phrase 'at the brim' (line 28), which refers to the position of the flowers at the side of the brook, also suggests an emotional overflowing – something brimming over. Compare this use of the word 'brim' with lines 37–38 of 'Birches' (page 222), where the idea of overflowing is more explicit: 'With the same pains you use to fill a cup / Up to the brim, and even above the brim.'

The last part of the poem considers the flowers. The mower has spared them, the speaker thinks, out of love – not as a deliberate gift, 'not for us', or to make others think of him, but from 'sheer morning gladness', a spontaneous impulse. Notice that when the speaker says 'us', he means himself and the butterfly; he thinks of them as companions involved in the same enterprise. This is made clear in line 29: 'The butterfly and I had lit upon … '.

The speaker decides that what they have 'lit upon' is 'a message from the dawn': they are being told something that they must interpret. For the speaker, what they are being told has to do with kinship and connections. Seeing the tuft of grass, and realising that it has been left there by someone with the same sort of feeling for the natural world as himself, it is as if he can hear the dawn chorus of the 'waking birds' and the sound of the mower's scythe, and he can sense 'a spirit kindred to my own'. Now he no longer feels that he is working alone, but that the mower is a companion, with whom he can communicate, hold 'brotherly speech'.

The final couplet reverses the gloomy formula from earlier in the poem. Now he believes, and tells his imagined companion 'from the heart', that 'Men work together … / Whether they work together or apart'. The poem has moved from a sense of everybody being alone to a sense of nobody really being alone.

Themes and imagery

Psyche and the butterfly

Psyche is the Greek name for the soul or the spirit, and also a figure from Greek mythology, a beautiful princess who was loved by Cupid. Psyche and the soul were associated with the butterfly, and often depicted as a butterfly. Frost knew his classical mythology very well, so perhaps the butterfly in this poem is a sort of spirit guide for the speaker.

Frost said that this poem is **'about fellowship'**. The main movement of the poem is **from isolation towards companionship**, which the speaker finds with the mower, even though he is not actually present – and also, perhaps, with the butterfly.

The poem belongs to a long tradition of **nature** poems in which nature is seen not just as a source of delight, but also as a teacher of lessons about the human world. The **role of the butterfly** is interesting in this regard. The butterfly belongs naturally to the setting in the field, but for the speaker it is a guide, as if it is deliberately leading him to the tuft of flowers, and so to the lesson he can learn from it. In this respect, the poem **resembles a fable**, a story featuring animals that has a moral or lesson. Do you think it is significant that in classical mythology the butterfly was associated with Psyche, or the soul?

Frost also said of this poem that it contained a **'definition of poetry'**. Perhaps he was thinking of the butterfly as poetic inspiration, leading the poet towards an image (the tuft of flowers) from which a harmonious vision of the world could be drawn. Less fancifully, the poem can be read as a description of the way in which a poet relates to other poets, especially those in the past. Although each poet works alone, he or she is always **working within a tradition of poetry**, in which other poets have written poems that inspire and influence that poet. In the same way, the speaker in 'The Tuft of Flowers' is inspired by the beauty left behind by the mower, a person he neither saw nor heard but whom he recognises as 'a spirit kindred to my own' (line 33). The imagery supports the notion that words are more important to the poem than may seem obvious at first glance: Frost writes of 'questions' (line 19), 'a message' (line 30), 'brotherly speech' (line 37). Even the flowers are described in a way that brings speech to mind: 'A leaping *tongue* of bloom' (line 23).

Form and language

'The Tuft of Flowers' is written in **rhyming couplets**, a form whose frequent rhymes suggest the harmony of the poem's vision, which is much more optimistic than that in many of Frost's poems. In a poem about **making connections** with others, the rhymes themselves embody those connections; you hear and feel them as you read the poem.

The language of the poem is generally **conversational**, and you get a sense of someone speaking to you and telling you a story in a fairly straightforward way. This is an early poem, however, and Frost became more assured in the way he used ordinary language as he matured as a poet. Here there are some slightly artificial, **'poetic' turns of phrase** that belong to conventional poetic diction rather than everyday speech: the inversion of 'swift there passed me by' (line 11), 'o'er night' (line 13), 'of yesterday's delight' (line 14) are all examples. Can you find others? How would you 'translate' these phrases into ordinary language?

SNAPSHOT

- Peaceful rural setting
- Beautiful images of nature
- Initial feelings of loneliness
- Butterfly as messenger or guide
- Realisation of human companionship
- Poem teaches a lesson
- Poem about poetry
- Rhyming couplets

Exam-Style Questions

Understanding the poem

1. Where and when does the poem take place? How would you describe the setting: peaceful, lonely, bleak? Perhaps you would suggest another word. Explain your answer.
2. Describe the mood of the speaker in the first ten lines.
3. What does the speaker realise when he sees the tuft of flowers?
4. In your own words, what is the 'message from the dawn' (line 30)? Explain your answer in as much detail as you can.
5. What is the speaker's mood at the end of the poem?

Thinking about the poem

1. What is the role of the butterfly in the poem? How does the language in which it is described help to create that role?
2. Why, in your opinion, does the speaker refer to the previous mower as a 'spirit kindred to my own' (line 33)?
3. Do you agree with the view suggested in the guidelines that the poem is about writing poetry? Give reasons for your answer.
4. 'A leaping tongue of bloom the scythe had spared' (line 23). Comment on the image of flowers as a 'leaping tongue'. Do you find it an effective image?
5. Comment on *either* the language *or* the form of the poem.

Imagining

1. Write a story or poem in which you realise that somebody has been at a particular place before you. It could be anyone and any place.
2. From your imagination, but using what you have learned from reading the poem, write a description of the speaker of 'The Tuft of Flowers'. Try to capture his character as well as his appearance. (Or, if you think it appropriate, *her* character.)

Mending Wall

Something there is that doesn't love a wall,
That sends the frozen-ground-swell under it
And spills the upper boulders in the sun,
And makes gaps even two can pass abreast.
The work of hunters is another thing: 5
I have come after them and made repair
Where they have left not one stone on a stone,
But they would have the rabbit out of hiding,
To please the yelping dogs. The gaps I mean,
No one has seen them made or heard them made, 10
But at spring mending-time we find them there.
I let my neighbor know beyond the hill;
And on a day we meet to walk the line
And set the wall between us once again.
We keep the wall between us as we go. 15
To each the boulders that have fallen to each.
And some are loaves and some so nearly balls
We have to use a spell to make them balance:
'Stay where you are until our backs are turned!'
We wear our fingers rough with handling them. 20
Oh, just another kind of outdoor game,
One on a side. It comes to little more:
There where it is we do not need the wall:
He is all pine and I am apple orchard.
My apple trees will never get across 25
And eat the cones under his pines, I tell him.
He only says, 'Good fences make good neighbors.'
Spring is the mischief in me, and I wonder
If I could put a notion in his head:
'*Why* do they make good neighbors? Isn't it 30
Where there are cows? But here there are no cows.
Before I built a wall I'd ask to know
What I was walling in or walling out,
And to whom I was like to give offense.
Something there is that doesn't love a wall, 35
That wants it down.' I could say 'Elves' to him,
But it's not elves exactly, and I'd rather
He said it for himself. I see him there,
Bringing a stone grasped firmly by the top
In each hand, like an old-stone savage armed. 40
He moves in darkness as it seems to me,
Not of woods only and the shade of trees.
He will not go behind his father's saying,
And he likes having thought of it so well
He says again, 'Good fences make good neighbors.' 45

Robert Frost

Before you read

'Good fences make good neighbors' is a phrase that occurs twice in 'Mending Wall'. This, or something like it, is a saying in many cultures. What does it mean? In what ways is it true? In what ways is it, perhaps, untrue? Discuss in groups or as a class.

Glossary

4 *abreast*: side by side and facing the same way

HIGHER LEVEL

Guidelines

'Mending Wall' is the opening poem from *North of Boston* (1914), the collection that made Robert Frost's name. The collection's title refers to the area of New England where Frost lived after his father's death, an area to the north of the city of Boston that includes Vermont, New Hampshire and parts of Massachusetts. Much of it is rough farming country, and this is where Frost farmed from 1900 until 1911, in Derry, New Hampshire. The poems draw on the experience of a working farmer, and are populated by the country people of that region.

Commentary

Title
The poem's title indicates the situation it describes: mending the wall between two farms. It is a meditation on the nature of walls and the impulses that make people want to build them or tear them down; live with them or without them; love them or distrust them.

Lines 1–11
The poem starts by considering the gaps in walls that make mending them necessary, and suggests in the first line, 'Something there is that doesn't love a wall'. There is a clear sense of a person thinking and speaking, somebody who knows walls and how the gaps in them can be made. He knows the holes are not caused by hunters tearing them down to get 'the rabbit out of hiding', but by something mysterious. Although he mentions the action of freezing and thawing, 'the frozen-ground-swell', it feels significant that 'No one has seen them made or heard them made'. Perhaps that is why it feels to him as though there is an unknown force at work.

Lines 12–22
If there are gaps in the wall, they need to be mended and this section of the poem describes how this is done. The speaker meets up with his neighbour, who owns the land on the other side of the wall, to walk along the line of the wall, repairing it as they go. Although they work together, there is a separation to the process, 'We keep the wall between us as we go', and each repositions the stones on his own side: 'To each the boulders that have fallen to each.' They 'have to use a spell to make them balance', as if the wall could be held up only by a sort of magic and always wanted to fall apart. There is a playfulness to this idea too, and the speaker describes their work as a 'kind of outdoor game'.

Lines 23–35

Now the speaker considers the purpose of the wall, or rather its lack of purpose: 'There where it is we do not need the wall'. His neighbour has pine trees, he has apples, and he jokes with the neighbour that his apple trees will never cross the wall 'And eat the cones under his pines'. The neighbour replies, 'Good fences make good neighbors.' But the speaker, feeling mischievous, does not want to let him get away with a cliché. He points out that that may be true where there are cows to keep apart, 'But here there are no cows.' He questions the nature of walls, what they are 'walling in or walling out', and the possibility that they might 'give offense'. What, in other words, does it mean to put a wall between yourself and somebody else? Is it always a good thing? He repeats, this time to his neighbour, the line that begins the poem: 'Something there is that doesn't love a wall'.

Lines 36–45

The final section of the poem focuses on the neighbour's reaction to the speaker's thoughts. The speaker gives a striking image of the man as he sees him, a stone in each hand, 'like an old-stone savage armed', as if he is something out of prehistory, a Neolithic caveman. This impression of something brutal and uncivilised is strengthened by the 'darkness' the speaker sees surrounding him, which is 'Not of woods only and the shade of trees'. In other words, it is a spiritual darkness of some kind. He does not want to think any more deeply about the matter: 'He will not go behind his father's saying'. And he repeats what his father has told him: 'Good fences make good neighbors.'

Themes and imagery

The wall itself is, of course, the central image of 'Mending Wall'. First of all, it is a real thing. Frost had plenty of experience of repairing walls in his life as a farmer, and although we should be wary of saying that the speaker in the poem is simply Frost himself, he was certainly drawing on that experience in writing the poem. But the wall is also a metaphor. It is something that separates people, and the debate in the poem is over whether that is a good thing or not.

The neighbour says, twice, **'Good fences make good neighbors'** (lines 27 and 45). What does that saying imply? Is it that if people (or countries) stick to themselves, keep to the established rules and do not intrude on one another, they will get on better? People often talk about respecting someone's boundaries or making those boundaries clear. Are walls and rules the best way to make them clear? Perhaps the poem's one simile throws some light – or, rather, darkness – on this old saying. The man who says it (the neighbour) is pictured 'like an old-stone savage', moving 'in darkness' (lines 40–41), implying that for the speaker it is an **ancient and outmoded attitude**.

The other repeated phrase is **'Something there is that doesn't love a wall'** (lines 1 and 35). The speaker questions whether walls are always needed, and suggests that by 'walling in or walling out' (line 33) something vital can be lost. Like 'The Tuft of Flowers', this poem is about **human connections**. Just as the speaker in 'The Tuft of Flowers' is made glad by discovering an unexpected fellowship with another, so in 'Mending Wall' the speaker's instinct is in favour of breaking down walls so as not to deny fellowship with another human.

> **International walls**
>
> Although 'Mending Wall' is set on a New England farm, its consideration of the walls and boundaries that divide people can be applied to many situations, including political ones. The building of the Berlin Wall to divide the Communist-controlled sectors of Berlin from the Western-controlled ones in 1961 made the central metaphor of Frost's poem seem especially relevant to international politics, and when Frost himself visited the Soviet Union the following year, he read the poem to a large gathering of Russian writers and intellectuals.

We have to be cautious about declaring what a poem is 'saying'. Remember that it was the speaker who set the process of wall-mending in action by going to his neighbour to fix a day for the job. He has **contradictory feelings**; all the while he is expressing his doubts about the wall, he is building it. Contradictory impulses of this sort are often found in Frost's poems. Readers can make up their own minds about what they might mean.

Form and language

'Mending Wall' is written in **unrhymed iambic pentameters** – lines with five stresses, alternating unstressed and stressed syllables. That, at least, is the underlying form. In fact, the language and the rhythms of the poem are **always natural, close to a conversational speaking voice, and specifically the voice of a New England farmer**. Frost believed in using what he called **'the sound of sense'** in poetry. In essence, that is the natural way of using words, not just in the individual words but in the ways in which sentences are put together, to create the effect of a natural speaking voice. But, as he knew, that was not the whole job. In verse there is always a tension between the natural rhythms of spoken English and the metre in which a poem is written. In Frost's words: '**if one is to be a poet he must learn to get the cadences** [music of the verse] **by skilfully breaking the sounds of sense with all their irregularity of accent across the regular beat of the metre.**'

Very rarely in good verse do you find a line that fits neatly and exactly into the **metre** of an iambic pentameter or any other metre. You can see this by looking closely at any lines of verse. Start from the beginning of 'Mending Wall', for instance, and you can see that the first line is not regularly iambic. Try reading it with the stresses arranged according to the strict iambic pentameter, like this: 'Something there ís that doésn't lóve a wáll'. It doesn't sound natural. For a start, the natural stress comes on the first syllable of 'something'; 'is' probably doesn't need a full stress; and the other stresses do not feel equal in strength, with 'love' requiring a stronger stress than the others. If we use the mark ´ to stand for a full stress and ˘ to stand for a lesser stress, then we might read the first line something like this: 'Sómething there ĭs that dŏesn't lóve a wáll'. Different readers will hear a given line slightly differently but over the course of a poem they will always be aware of the underlying metre giving the whole thing unity, and so will be sensitive to the ways in which the actual lines of verse vary from the strict metre. This helps the poet to achieve specific effects.

Look, for example, at how the poem's single simile is made all the more striking and disturbing by the way in which it breaks the metre. In line 40 the natural stresses fall something like this: 'In eách hánd, like an óld-stóne sávage ármed'. The paired stresses on 'each hand' help to create the idea of a pair of things – a pair of stones in a pair of hands – but also disrupt the iambic metre in a way that suggests the brutality of the image. This impression is reinforced by the strong stresses of the second part of the line, three in a row on 'óld-stóne sávage', and their effect is increased by the assonance of long vowels in 'old-stone'.

Questions

1. 'Something there is that doesn't love a wall' (lines 1 and 35). How, according to the poem's speaker, do walls get broken down?

2. Describe how the speaker and his neighbour go about repairing the wall.

3. What difference of opinion exists between the speaker and his neighbour about the wall?

4. What 'notion' (line 29) does the speaker want to put into his neighbour's head?

5. Based on evidence from the poem, what sort of person is the neighbour?

6. What, in your view, is the real theme of the poem? Explain your answer.

7. How would you describe the tone of voice of the speaker? What words or phrases help to create that tone of voice, in your opinion?

8. What details from the poem suggest that the writer knew well the rural life he was describing?

9. 'Oh, just another kind of outdoor game, / One on a side. It comes to little more' (lines 21–22). Do you think Frost sees mending the wall as 'just another kind of outdoor game'? Give a reason for your answer.

10. Compare this poem to any other poem by Frost that you have studied as part of your course.

11. Is the saying 'good fences make good neighbours' true, in your opinion? Write an essay, poem or story in which you make clear your opinion.

12. You are Frost's neighbour. Write an entry in your diary in which you describe mending the wall and give your opinion of your neighbour, Robert Frost.

HIGHER LEVEL

Before you read

Have you ever worked so long and hard at something physical and repetitive that you still seem to be doing it as you fall asleep? Or have you ever had the sensation of still being at sea after getting off a boat? Discuss your experiences in class or in groups.

After Apple-Picking

My long two-pointed ladder's sticking through a tree
Toward heaven still,
And there's a barrel that I didn't fill
Beside it, and there may be two or three
Apples I didn't pick upon some bough. 5
But I am done with apple-picking now.
Essence of winter sleep is on the night,
The scent of apples: I am drowsing off.
I cannot rub the strangeness from my sight
I got from looking through a pane of glass 10
I skimmed this morning from the drinking trough
And held against the world of hoary grass.
It melted, and I let it fall and break.
But I was well
Upon my way to sleep before it fell, 15
And I could tell
What form my dreaming was about to take.
Magnified apples appear and disappear,
Stem end and blossom end,
And every fleck of russet showing clear. 20
My instep arch not only keeps the ache,
It keeps the pressure of a ladder-round.
I feel the ladder sway as the boughs bend.
And I keep hearing from the cellar bin
The rumbling sound 25
Of load on load of apples coming in.
For I have had too much
Of apple-picking: I am overtired
Of the great harvest I myself desired.
There were ten thousand thousand fruit to touch, 30
Cherish in hand, lift down, and not let fall.
For all
That struck the earth,
No matter if not bruised or spiked with stubble,
Went surely to the cider-apple heap 35
As of no worth.
One can see what will trouble
This sleep of mine, whatever sleep it is.
Were he not gone,
The woodchuck could say whether it's like his 40
Long sleep, as I describe its coming on,
Or just some human sleep.

Glossary

12	*hoary*: white with frost
20	*russet*: reddish-brown colour
22	*ladder-round*: rounded rung of a ladder
40	*woodchuck*: North American rodent that hibernates during winter

Robert Frost

Guidelines

Like many poems in the collection *North of Boston*, 'After Apple-Picking' was written in England in 1913, but it draws on Frost's life as a farmer in New Hampshire, where he grew apples. The language of the poem is not difficult, but its logic imitates the hallucinatory state of mind that you sometimes get at the edge of sleep when you have worked very hard and are very tired.

Commentary

Lines 1–8
At the beginning of the poem, the speaker is reflecting on how he left everything at the end of a long day spent picking apples. There is a sense of something not quite finished or not quite achieved – the unfilled barrel and a few apples unpicked – but there is also a sense of striving for something: the ladder is pointing towards heaven, as if he has been reaching for something perfect or ideal. But the picking is finished, 'I am done with apple-picking now', and not just for the day but for the year, we suspect. The picking of apples begins in early autumn and can go on until the beginning of November, and it is clear that the cold weather is here now. It is the time of year when the harvest finishes and winter takes over. For the speaker, the 'scent of apples' represents 'Essence of winter sleep'. The end of line 8 makes it clear that the speaker himself is almost asleep, probably reflecting on the day from his bed: 'I am drowsing off.'

Lines 9–17
The speaker remembers the way the world appeared when he looked at it through 'a pane of glass' this morning. It becomes clear that this 'glass' must have been ice, as he 'skimmed' it 'from the drinking trough', and later 'It melted, and I let it fall and break.' The distorting view through the ice gave his vision a 'strangeness' that he cannot get rid of, even now in bed.

Lines 14–15 are confusing: 'I was well / Upon my way to sleep before it fell'. Either he is remembering looking through the ice and is almost asleep before the memory has finished playing in his mind, or in some way he has been falling asleep all day. Either way, the distorting vision through the sheet of ice resembles the way he relives the day in his dreams. That may be the implication when he says, 'I could tell / What form my dreaming was about to take'.

Lines 18–36
This section of the poem describes the speaker's hallucinatory half-dream state. The apples are 'Magnified'; they 'appear and disappear' and every speck of colour is vivid. His senses are overwhelmed – not only sight but touch, as he feels still 'the pressure of a ladder-round', and balance: 'I feel the ladder sway as the boughs bend'. His hearing is also involved, and he hears 'the rumbling sound / Of load on load of apples coming in'.

The sense of overload continues: 'I have had too much / Of apple-picking'. The speaker is not just tired but 'overtired' – a state in which proper sleep is impossible in spite of exhaustion. The sense of frustration or anxiety that often goes along with this state is implied by what he is overtired with: 'the great harvest I myself desired.' He has got what he wanted and yet he is not at peace. The paradox is made more pointed by the rhyme of 'overtired' and 'desired'. The harvest may have been wanted but it was also a burden – so many fruit ('ten thousand thousand', or ten million apples, which is hyperbole) to look after and 'not let fall'. Any apples that fell ('struck the earth') went to be juiced for cider 'As of no worth'.

HIGHER LEVEL

Lines 37–42

Then, rather enigmatically, the speaker says, 'One can see what will trouble / This sleep of mine'. It is not obvious what will in fact 'trouble' his sleep, but presumably it has to do with those fallen apples, as if he has failed them. As at the beginning of the poem, there is a sense of imperfection – of failing to achieve what might have been achieved. The speaker is not sure what sort of sleep he will have. Will it be like the woodchuck's winter hibernation ('Long sleep'), which must have started already as the woodchuck is 'gone'? Or will it be something more ordinary, 'just some human sleep'? It is not clear which he would prefer.

Themes and imagery

On one level, 'After Apple-Picking' is about exactly what the title suggests: **the state of exhaustion and obsessive semi-dreaming that comes after long and repetitive physical labour**. There is no doubt that Frost knew the work of apple-picking and the feelings that went with it, and anybody who has done work of this sort will recognise the state of mind that often follows. You are almost too tired to sleep and cannot get the experiences of the day out of your mind, and the day repeats itself as confused hallucination at the edge of sleep. The speaker can see the apples as if magnified, can hear them rumbling in the barrels, and can feel himself as if he is still swaying in the breeze among the branches, the rungs of the ladder pressing into his feet. As a portrayal of this dream-like and yet troubled state of mind, 'After Apple-Picking' is impressive and powerful. Whatever else it may be 'about', **readers respond to the mood it creates**, of troubled tiredness and the desire for peaceful sleep.

> **Frost on metaphor**
>
> 'Poetry provides the one permissible way of saying one thing and meaning another. People say, "Why don't you say what you mean?" We never do that, do we, being all of us too much poets. We like to talk in parables and in hints and in indirections.'

One theme that runs through the poem is the **striving for perfection** that any human task can involve, and the **failure to achieve it**. The first image of the poem encapsulates that idea: the ladder points 'Toward heaven'

Robert Frost

(line 2), but the barrel is unfilled and 'two or three' (line 4) apples are left unpicked on the tree. The apple-picker's job of looking after every apple is an impossible one to do perfectly. Some will fall and go to the 'cider-apple heap' (line 35), and that fact will 'trouble' (line 37) his sleep. Is that why the speaker is 'overtired / Of the great harvest I myself desired' (lines 28–29)?

> **The Fall**
>
> **The imagery of apples and the idea of falling call to mind the Bible story of Adam and Eve in the Garden of Eden and the Fall of Man. Do you think there may be a connection between the impossibility of human perfection and the idea of original sin suggested by the biblical story?**

Another way of interpreting 'After Apple-Picking' is to see it, as the biographer and critic Jay Parini does, as being about the **poet's imagination**. In his half-asleep state, the speaker is bombarded by images of his day's work, transformed in his imagination. The image of the sheet of ice is crucial here. Looking through the ice transforms the world and gives it a 'strangeness' (line 9), just as the poet's imagination transforms reality. In this reading, the harvest of apples stands for the harvest of poems that Frost was reaping in England when he wrote this, grown from the seeds that had been sown in his years of farming in New Hampshire. They are to be cherished and handled with care, although there is still regret and anxiety concerning the poems that have not been written or not been considered good enough – those consigned to the cider-apple heap.

Form and language

The form of 'After Apple-Picking' is unique among Frost's poems. Although the metre is basically iambic, and many of the lines are iambic pentameters, Frost **varies the line lengths**: the first line has six beats, while others, especially in the second half of the poem, are shorter. Rhyme, too, is used in an irregular away. Every line rhymes but the **patterns of rhyme are unpredictable**. Sometimes the rhymes come thick and fast, as in lines 14 to 16, where three lines in a row rhyme together. At other times there is a greater gap between rhymes, the largest of which leads up to the final rhyme on 'sleep'. In the poem where sleep is always coming on and where the word is mentioned six times, the rhyme we know must come after 'cider-apple heap' in line 35 finally arrives in line 42 with a sense of completion. The varied rhymes and line lengths help to create a mood that can be **intense** and **dream-like**, but which never lets us relax. It has the power to cast an uneasy spell over the reader.

The poem's powerful, almost hypnotic, quality comes from Frost's **masterly control over language**. Although the imagery of 'After Apple-Picking' is often very vivid, as the speaker's imagination is working overtime, the language itself is always close to plain **conversational** speech and the voice is that of an educated farmer: 'Magnified apples appear and disappear, / Stem end and blossom end, / And every fleck of russet showing clear' (lines 18–20). The image is hallucinatory, but it is described in plain terms with **precise vocabulary**; this is a man who knows his apples.

> **The Great Harvest**
>
> During his time in England in 1913 Frost wrote many poems that were based on his experiences in the years he farmed in Derry, New Hampshire. These poems form the core of his first two published collections, *A Boy's Will* and *North of Boston*. It was a very prolific period for Frost.

HIGHER LEVEL

Questions

1. Describe the speaker's state of mind in lines 1–26 of this poem.
2. Is there a point in the poem at which the speaker falls asleep, in your opinion? If so, where? Give reasons for your view.
3. 'One can see what will trouble / This sleep of mine' (lines 37–38). What, in your opinion, will trouble the speaker's sleep? Do you think it is clear or uncertain?
4. In your opinion, which would the speaker prefer: the woodchuck's 'Long sleep' (line 41) or 'just some human sleep' (line 42)? What, do you think, is the difference between the two?
5. What impression does the poem give you of the speaker? Explain your answer with reference to the text.
6. Is it significant that the speaker has been picking apples and not some other fruit? In your response you might remember the biblical story of the Tree of Knowledge and the Garden of Eden.
7. Would you agree that there is a contrast between the poetic imagery and the everyday language of the poem? Give reasons for your answer.
8. How does Frost create the dream-like atmosphere of the poem?
9. Explore the sound patterns of assonance, consonance and rhyme throughout the poem and say what effect they had on you as a reader.
10. The poem has been called a 'lyric idyll'. The word 'idyll' suggests a happy, ideal situation. Comment on this description and say whether you think the mood of the poem is entirely happy.
11. If you were asked to choose your favourite poems of Robert Frost, would you include this one among them? Give reasons for your answer.
12. You have been asked to make an audio-visual presentation to accompany this poem. In groups, decide what music, sounds and images you would use.

Robert Frost

The Road Not Taken

Two roads diverged in a yellow wood,
And sorry I could not travel both
And be one traveler, long I stood
And looked down one as far as I could
To where it bent in the undergrowth;   5

Then took the other, as just as fair,
And having perhaps the better claim,
Because it was grassy and wanted wear;
Though as for that, the passing there
Had worn them really about the same,   10

And both that morning equally lay
In leaves no step had trodden black.
Oh, I kept the first for another day!
Yet knowing how way leads on to way,
I doubted if I should ever come back.   15

I shall be telling this with a sigh
Somewhere ages and ages hence:
Two roads diverged in a wood, and I—
I took the one less traveled by,
And that has made all the difference.   20

Before you read

Do you find it hard to make decisions? Why, or why not? Do you have any advice about making decisions? Discuss in pairs or small groups.

Glossary

1	*diverged*: went in different directions
5	*undergrowth*: bushes, ferns, etc. growing beneath taller trees in a wood

Guidelines

'The Road Not Taken' was first published in *Mountain Interval* (1916). It was probably written in England in 1914, so the setting is perhaps an English wood in autumn when the leaves are yellow. It is a poem about choices, and Frost wrote it for and about his friend Edward Thomas, who always had regrets about choosing the wrong path.

Commentary

Stanzas 1–3

The first line presents the situation: 'Two roads diverged in a yellow wood'. There is a choice to make, and some indecision over it: 'long I stood'. Lines 4–5 describe one 'road', which here might be best thought of as a woodland path rather than a road for motor vehicles. This is the 'road not taken' of the poem's title, because in stanza 2 the speaker tells us that he took the other road. It had 'the better claim' because it had not been much used. But the speaker immediately casts doubt on that claim, stating: 'the passing there / Had worn them really about the same'.

HIGHER LEVEL

The opening of stanza 3, continuing the sentence from stanza 2, again emphasises the similarity of the paths – they 'both that morning equally lay' covered in fallen autumn leaves that had not been 'trodden black' – i.e. turned black by being walked on. The speaker says he 'kept the first for another day', thinking he would come back to explore the other path some time, but knowing how one thing leads to another, 'way leads on to way', he realises he probably won't come back to that first path. The poem's title makes sure that the idea of an untaken path, like a missed opportunity, haunts the poem. Might the other path have been a better choice?

Stanza 4

The final stanza, especially its final two lines, is what readers tend to remember best about the poem. It seems to lead to a neat moral that appeals to people who think of themselves (as most people do) as individualists who like to do things their own way rather than follow the crowd: 'I took the one less traveled by, / And that has made all the difference.' In fact, the speaker has admitted in the previous stanzas that the two paths were 'really about the same', so the statement that 'I took the one less traveled by' contradicts what has gone before. Why?

Notice that the speaker is thinking ahead, to what he will say in a distant future: 'I shall be telling this … / … ages and ages hence'. He is thinking of himself as an older man telling a story to an audience, and telling it 'with a sigh'. Is that a sigh of regret or of satisfaction, or something else? He sees himself falsifying what actually happened – changing it for the sake of a good story. The idea of taking the road 'less traveled' might seem an appropriate one for a poet – a sign of courage and of faith in his vocation. But we have to remember what we have already been told: there was no road 'less traveled by'. Is the poet poking fun at himself?

Themes and imagery

It is easy to state the primary theme of the poem: **choices**. The central metaphor of the diverging paths encapsulates the idea of choosing. This choice has to be made with limited information as the speaker cannot see further up the first path than to 'where it bent in the undergrowth' (line 5). Once the choice is made, there is no going back: 'way leads on to way' (line 14). The idea that making the more unusual choice, taking the road 'less traveled by' (line 19), can make 'all the difference' (line 20), although what many readers take from the poem, is at odds with what the rest of the poem suggests.

The **apparent simplicity** of the poem is misleading. There is a great deal of **subtlety and wit** beneath the surface. We have already noted the apparent contradiction contained in the poem. How, then, are we to interpret it?

On one level, it may be a comment on **memory** and the way we understand our lives **retrospectively** (looking back on what we have done). A choice which at the time was hard to make and felt like a toss-up becomes, looking back, something fatal, and seems to have 'made all the difference' (line 20), whereas in fact a different choice might have led to a similar result. We tell ourselves (and others) stories about our lives to give them

Robert Frost

shape, so perhaps Frost is making a sly comment about how we remember things selectively to give our lives the neatest shape. Thus, in the final stanza the speaker looks knowingly into the future, 'ages and ages hence' (line 17), when he has turned a simple choice into the key moment in the myth of his own life. Frost, especially as he got older, liked to play up to his own image as a plain-speaking New England farmer. It was a partial truth that went down well in public – his own myth of himself.

The origins of the poem give us an important clue as to how it should be read. The poem was written with Edward Thomas in mind. It was a **playful rebuke** to Frost's friend, who always regretted the choices he made. Frost was teasing him, although Thomas, when he read the poem, did not really get the joke. Nor did many others. When Frost read it to a college audience the poem was 'taken pretty seriously' in spite of the fact that Frost said he did his best 'to make it obvious that I was fooling'. Although different readers will always take different things from poems, any considered reading of 'The Road Not Taken' should take into account its **humour**.

Form and language

The language of 'The Road Not Taken' is **simple**, **descriptive** and **direct**. It has a strong sense of the speaking voice, with **casual phrasing** such as 'Though as for that' (line 9) and with hesitation that sounds rather like someone **pausing for dramatic effect**: 'Two roads diverged in a wood, and I— / I took the one less traveled by' (lines 18–19). At the same time, this speaking voice is fitted into a **disciplined pattern** of five-line stanzas rhyming *abaab*. The basic metre is the iambic tetrameter, although Frost often adds extra unstressed syllables to vary the rhythm (e.g. 'iň ă yéllŏw wóod'). Despite the tight structure, the form is unobtrusive, and has an ease that complements the simple language, tempting the unwary reader to ignore the subtleties of what the poem is saying.

Questions

1	In your own words, how did the two roads appear to the speaker?
2	Trace the speaker's train of thought as he makes his decision.
3	How does the speaker imagine himself 'ages and ages hence' (line 17)? Why, do you think, does he tell the story 'with a sigh' (line 16) and who is he telling it to?
4	'And that has made all the difference' (line 20). What might the speaker mean here? Do you think he is happy about the choice he made?
5	'Two roads diverged in a yellow wood' (line 1). Comment on the poem's setting.
6	'Frost seldom wrote about nature for its own sake.' Write a short paragraph in which you discuss this statement with reference to 'The Road Not Taken'.
7	Frost himself said he was 'fooling' in this poem. Is this how you read it? Explain your answer.
8	Can you understand why this is a well-loved poem in America and elsewhere? Explain your answer.
9	With a partner, discuss suitable music and images to accompany a reading of this poem. Share your ideas with the class and be prepared to explain/defend your choices.
10	Write your own poem, or a story, about making a choice and the consequences of that choice. It can be about yourself or someone else.

HIGHER LEVEL

Before you read

 Look at the photograph of bending trees opposite. Do you recognise the trees? How, do you think, did they get this way? Do you have any emotional response to the image? Discuss in pairs or small groups.

Glossary

9	*crazes their enamel*: makes networks of small cracks in the hard coats of ice on the birches
13	*dome of heaven*: see box on page 224
14	*bracken*: large ferns
43	*considerations*: things that have to be taken into account or taken care of

Birches

When I see birches bend to left and right
Across the lines of straighter darker trees,
I like to think some boy's been swinging them.
But swinging doesn't bend them down to stay
As ice storms do. Often you must have seen them   5
Loaded with ice a sunny winter morning
After a rain. They click upon themselves
As the breeze rises, and turn many-colored
As the stir cracks and crazes their enamel.
Soon the sun's warmth makes them shed crystal shells   10
Shattering and avalanching on the snow crust—
Such heaps of broken glass to sweep away
You'd think the inner dome of heaven had fallen.
They are dragged to the withered bracken by the load,
And they seem not to break; though once they are bowed   15
So low for long, they never right themselves:
You may see their trunks arching in the woods
Years afterwards, trailing their leaves on the ground
Like girls on hands and knees that throw their hair
Before them over their heads to dry in the sun.   20
But I was going to say when Truth broke in
With all her matter of fact about the ice storm,
I should prefer to have some boy bend them
As he went out and in to fetch the cows—
Some boy too far from town to learn baseball,   25
Whose only play was what he found himself,
Summer or winter, and could play alone.
One by one he subdued his father's trees
By riding them down over and over again
Until he took the stiffness out of them,   30
And not one but hung limp, not one was left
For him to conquer. He learned all there was
To learn about not launching out too soon
And so not carrying the tree away
Clear to the ground. He always kept his poise   35
To the top branches, climbing carefully
With the same pains you use to fill a cup
Up to the brim, and even above the brim.
Then he flung outward, feet first, with a swish,
Kicking his way down through the air to the ground.   40

Robert Frost

So was I once myself a swinger of birches.
And so I dream of going back to be.
It's when I'm weary of considerations,
And life is too much like a pathless wood
Where your face burns and tickles with the cobwebs   45
Broken across it, and one eye is weeping
From a twig's having lashed across it open.
I'd like to get away from earth awhile
And then come back to it and begin over.
May no fate willfully misunderstand me   50
And half grant what I wish and snatch me away
Not to return. Earth's the right place for love:
I don't know where it's likely to go better.
I'd like to go by climbing a birch tree,
And climb black branches up a snow-white trunk   55
Toward heaven, till the tree could bear no more,
But dipped its top and set me down again.
That would be good both going and coming back.
One could do worse than be a swinger of birches.

HIGHER LEVEL

Guidelines

Frost considered 'Birches' one of his finest poems, and many of his readers agree. It was written in England in a burst of creativity in 1914, but is based on his experiences in rural New England where, as a boy, he had learned to 'swing' birch trees by climbing carefully to the very top of the tree and then using his weight to bring himself and the treetop all the way back down to the ground. It was a trick he taught his own children, but the adult poet sees far more in it than a childhood game. 'Birches' was published in *Mountain Interval* (1916).

Commentary

> **Dome of heaven**
>
> **Many ancient cultures imagined Earth as flat, and the sky – or the heavens – as a dome or series of domes rising over it. The domes over many great churches, cathedrals and mosques represent those heavens. Some traditions imagined that the dome was made of crystal. In others, the inner dome was the one with the stars and the sun embedded in it. Either way, Frost's image presents a beautiful catastrophe: the glories of the heavens glittering on the ground.**

Lines 1–20

Frost starts in a conversational way, remarking that the sight of birch trees bent over makes him imagine that a boy has been swinging them. It is a moment of nostalgia for his own childhood because he knows that really only ice storms bend trees like that. The next fifteen lines comment on that phenomenon. They show a wonderful eye for detail in describing the process of the ice clicking and cracking in the wind, then falling in fragments to the ground in the sun. This description clearly comes from close observation, and Frost has a wonderful way of finding the extraordinary in the actual, culminating in the image of the 'heaps of broken glass', as if 'the inner dome of heaven had fallen'.

The birches remain bent, 'arching in the woods / Years afterwards'. It is an acute observation of the natural world. Frost brings it to life with a surprising and sensual image that indicates much more than a dry scientific understanding: the trees are 'Like girls on hands and knees that throw their hair / Before them over their heads to dry in the sun'. The speaker later dismisses all this as just 'matter of fact about the ice storm' (line 22), but he is being sly: his observations may be factual but the tone is full of wonder.

Lines 21–40

Now the speaker goes back to where he started – the idea of the boy swinging birches. The speaker has an emotional attachment to the idea of swinging birches: 'I should prefer to have some boy bend them'. He pictures that boy, a loner living and working on his father's farm, 'Whose only play was what he found himself, / Summer or winter, and could play alone'. As a boy, Frost had spent happy times on his uncle's farm in New Hampshire, so it is not hard to see this boy as a version of Frost's younger self.

The speaker imagines what the boy would have had to do in order to bend all those birches, one by one: 'riding them down over and over again / Until he took the stiffness out of them'. He is seen as a conqueror who has 'subdued his father's trees'. Whether or not he is challenging his father, he is certainly asserting his own power. Then we are told about the technique that he has learned through practice – the patience to climb to the very top of the tree before 'launching out'. Frost finds a precise, apt and evocative metaphor for his climbing skill; he uses 'the same pains you use to fill a cup / Up to the brim, and even above the brim'. Although the image is accurate – you can, because of surface tension, fill a cup slightly above its brim – it suggests the almost magical quality of the act. Next he describes the climax: the release of energy as the boy flings himself out and down to the ground.

Lines 41–59

Now the speaker explores the personal and metaphorical aspects of swinging birches. He used to do it, he says, and dreams of doing it again. But as an adult its meaning has changed for him. He no longer thinks of it in terms of asserting his power, but sees it as a form of escape. The mood hits him 'when I'm weary of considerations', by which he seems to mean that the world is getting him down. He describes this state in terms of walking in 'a pathless wood', with the inconveniences and irritations of struggling through the low branches and the cobwebs that hang from them. His reaction is to wish for relief by means of temporary escape: 'I'd like to get away from earth awhile'. But he makes it very clear that this is not a death wish: he wants to 'come back to it and begin over', if only because, for all its imperfections, 'Earth's the right place for love'.

He is pulled in two directions. He wants to get away from his day-to-day troubles, but does not want to give up his human connections. Swinging a birch tree is his image for those opposing desires: he can climb '*Toward* heaven', and all that is perfect and ideal, but always the laws of gravity will make the tree bend and set him back down in the real world. 'That would be good both going and coming back,' he says. It is a perfect metaphor to reconcile his opposing desires and have it both ways. But he is not going to get too self-indulgent about it. The final line is a wry understatement from a practical man: 'One could do worse than be a swinger of birches.'

Themes

All the themes of the poem cluster around its central image, which is also the title of the poem: 'Birches'. For the speaker, it is all about **swinging birches**, and what that notion means to him. He uses it as a **metaphor to express his conflicted feelings about life** – his desire to escape its 'considerations' (line 43) and yet his commitment to it, and to human love. From his point of view, all the 'matter of fact about the ice storm' (line 22) is a digression from the main point.

But if that were really the whole point of the poem, the section on the ice storm could have been left out. There is more going on in the poem than the speaker intends. Although that speaker closely resembles Frost, in his voice and in his attitudes, it is Frost the poet who controls the monologue and shapes the poem. In many ways, the poem is *about* **the speaker's complicated relationship with the world**.

The speaker's world-weariness contrasts with the energy of the boy who swings birches and conquers his father's trees, showing his mastery of his environment. Frost was about forty when he wrote 'Birches', and there

HIGHER LEVEL

is a strong sense of **nostalgia**, of an older man looking back on his youth, when the world seemed simpler and his purpose clearer. It is a theme that is not directly discussed, but which informs and enriches the whole poem.

Looking back often brings a **sense of regret or loss**, which is present even in the first few lines of the poem, where the speaker says he would 'like to think' (line 3) the bent birches are the result of a boy swinging them. Perhaps that regret is also present in the description of the birches bent down by the ice storm: 'once they are bowed / So low for long, they never right themselves' (lines 15–16). Like the birches, the speaker is weighed down by the world. Even his description of himself swinging a tree in the poem's final lines is coloured by the fact that he was 'once … a swinger of birches' (line 41) and his desire to be one again is a 'dream' (line 42). His birch-swinging days are over.

Imagery

Imagery drawn from the **natural world**, especially the woods, underpins any metaphorical interpretation of this poem. Frost's intimate knowledge and close observation of the rural New England environment is apparent throughout the poem. Even the speaker's state of mind when he is 'weary of considerations' (line 43) is described using the imagery of the woods in which the poem is set.

The **delight in detail** is one of the most striking things about Frost's treatment of the natural world, and one of the great joys of 'Birches'. In a poem that seems torn between pessimism and optimism, the sheer beauty of the description of the trees affected by the ice storm and the glorious image of the ice fragments, as if 'the inner dome of heaven had fallen' (line 13), override, for most readers, any sense of loss or regret that might be present. It tells us that, however troubled he may sometimes be, the speaker's spirit is alive and **awake to the world**. Even the bent trees, which could be objects of pity, are transformed into things of wonder and beauty by the image that describes and rejuvenates them: 'Like girls on hands and knees … ' (lines 19–20).

> **Facts**
>
> Frost believed in the importance of a detailed understanding of the real world as a basis for, not an alternative to, the imagination. A line in an early Frost poem states, 'The fact is the sweetest thing that labor knows'. The line contained, according to Frost, 'a definition of poetry'.

Another way of seeing the image of swinging birches – reaching upwards towards the heavens but always returning to the ground – is as a **metaphor for writing poetry**. Poetry, too, reaches towards heaven and matters of the spirit, but is rooted in the details of the real world. The two are connected, not separated, and poetry is interested in finding these connections. There is also something in the image of the boy learning, by long practice, how to swing a birch that suggests the labours of a poet gradually mastering the craft of poetry writing. That may seem fanciful, but it is because Frost creates his images so vividly that they can take on such a range of metaphorical significances, the details of which can vary from reader to reader.

Form and language

'Birches' is written in **blank verse** – unrhymed iambic pentameters. The metre is not strictly adhered to, but is varied and sometimes played against to allow the voice of the speaker to be heard naturally. Look, for example at lines 10–11: 'Soon the sun's warmth makes them shed crystal shells / Shattering and avalanching on the snow crust—'. It is completely unnatural to emphasise every second syllable in accordance with the metre, but the iambic pattern can be heard in the first of those lines, slowed down by the double emphasis and long syllables of 'sún's wármth'. In the second line the iambic metre has almost completely disappeared in the string of short, unstressed syllables of 'sháttĕrĭng ănd ăvălănchĭng'. The effect here is to suggest the rapid, chaotic movement of the fragments of ice. You can find other examples of how Frost **varies the rhythm** by reading and speaking the verse for yourself.

The language of the poem is **conversational**. There is a strong sense of a man talking to someone (whether the reader or another). He addresses that other directly, 'Often you must have seen them' (line 5), and interrupts himself after being side-tracked: 'But I was going to say … ' (line 21). He is a plain-speaking country man and although he notices the beauty in things and comes up with wonderful images, the language in which he expresses himself is essentially straightforward. It may be fanciful to think that the heavens have fallen to Earth, but there is nothing fanciful about the language he uses to say it: 'You'd think the inner dome of heaven had fallen' (line 13).

Nevertheless, there is plenty of **subtle word music**. Look, for example, at the hard 'c' sounds and the 's' and 'z' sounds in lines 7–9: 'They click upon themselves / As the breeze rises, and turn many-colored / As the stir cracks and crazes their enamel.' Or at the burst of energy you get from the alliteration and double stresses of 'Then he flúng oútward, féet fírst, with a swísh' (line 39). Again, you can find many more examples.

Questions

1	'I like to think some boy's been swinging them' (line 3); 'I should prefer to have some boy bend them' (line 23). Why this preference? What does it tell you about the speaker?
2	What did you learn about the speaker from his description of the results of the ice storm (lines 5–20)?
3	What picture did you get of the boy in lines 23–40? Why does he want to swing birches?
4	Comment on the image in lines 36–38: 'climbing carefully / With the same pains you use to fill a cup / Up to the brim, and even above the brim.'
5	Why does the speaker say, 'May no fate willfully misunderstand me' (line 50)? What is he afraid will happen? What does he want to happen?
6	'That would be good both going and coming back' (line 58). Explain what the speaker means by this.
7	In what way does the swinging of birches take on a metaphorical significance? Where in the poem does this occur? What is the first lesson a boy learns from swinging birches, for example?
8	Does the poem invite a number of further metaphorical readings as it progresses? What readings, in your opinion? Explain your answer.
9	'The poem enacts the desire to escape, to move beyond the here and now of the real world to the world of the imagination.' In what lines is this most evident?
10	Frost once said that poetry 'begins in delight and ends in wisdom'. Does this remark help you to appreciate the theme and mood of 'Birches'?
11	What did you learn about the speaker from the way in which he uses language?
12	Some commentators note the hidden sexual energy of 'Birches'. Where, if anywhere, can you identify it? What, if anything, does it add to the poem?
13	Imagine you are the boy in the poem. Write a paragraph about your life and what swinging the birches means to you.
14	Write – or draw or paint, if you can do it that way – a portrait of the speaker in the poem, bringing out the sort of man he seems to you.

"Out, Out—"

Robert Frost

Before you read

'"Out, Out—"' tells the story of a fatal accident on a farm. Is that the sort of topic that you expect poetry to deal with? What tone do you expect such a poem to have?

The buzz saw snarled and rattled in the yard
And made dust and dropped stove-length sticks of wood,
Sweet-scented stuff when the breeze drew across it.
And from there those that lifted eyes could count
Five mountain ranges one behind the other   5
Under the sunset far into Vermont.
And the saw snarled and rattled, snarled and rattled,
As it ran light, or had to bear a load.
And nothing happened: day was all but done.
Call it a day, I wish they might have said   10
To please the boy by giving him the half hour
That a boy counts so much when saved from work.
His sister stood beside them in her apron
To tell them 'Supper.' At the word, the saw,
As if to prove saws knew what supper meant,   15
Leaped out at the boy's hand, or seemed to leap—
He must have given the hand. However it was,
Neither refused the meeting. But the hand!
The boy's first outcry was a rueful laugh,
As he swung toward them holding up the hand,   20
Half in appeal, but half as if to keep
The life from spilling. Then the boy saw all—
Since he was old enough to know, big boy
Doing a man's work, though a child at heart—
He saw all spoiled. 'Don't let him cut my hand off—   25
The doctor, when he comes. Don't let him, sister!'
So. But the hand was gone already.
The doctor put him in the dark of ether.
He lay and puffed his lips out with his breath.
And then—the watcher at his pulse took fright.   30
No one believed. They listened at his heart.
Little—less—nothing!—and that ended it.
No more to build on there. And they, since they
Were not the one dead, turned to their affairs.

Glossary

1	*buzz saw*:	circular machine saw
2	*stove-length*:	cut to the right size to fit in a stove
6	*Vermont*:	state in New England, USA
19	*rueful*:	wry, sorrowful, apologetic
28	*ether*:	an anaesthetic
34	*affairs*:	activities; things that have to be done

HIGHER LEVEL

Guidelines

'"Out, Out—"' was first published in *Mountain Interval* (1916). It is set on a farm like Frost's, from where many mountain ranges are visible. The poem is based on a real incident, a calamity that happened on a neighbouring farm in which a boy died from shock following an accident with a machine saw.

Commentary

Title
The poem's title echoes a speech from Shakespeare's *Macbeth*: 'Out, out, brief candle! Life's but a walking shadow'. The speech is a moving comment on how short and meaningless life is. It might make the reader think about the similarities and differences between the lives of a young country boy and a king.

Lines 1–9
The first section of the poem sets the scene. There are elements of rural beauty: the view of the mountain ranges and the smell of the wood. But the dominant element in this scene is the buzz saw. It is noisy, discordant, disturbing. It is the central figure in the scene, and it is active. Notice the active verbs that are associated with it: 'snarled' and 'rattled', 'made' and 'dropped'.

The people are only there by implication: they are 'those that lifted eyes'. We have to assume they are too busy to look about them, whoever they are. There is work to be done. It is a routine day – 'nothing happened' must mean nothing out of the ordinary had taken place – and it is almost over.

Lines 10–18
We are introduced to the boy, who is evidently the one operating the buzz saw. He is working, and would have appreciated half an hour off. His sister also seems to have been working: she has her apron on, and has presumably been cooking supper as well as announcing it. The adults, however, remain shadowy figures, referred to only as 'they' and 'them'. We never know how many or who they are.

Then the accident happens. If the saw was active at the beginning, it now seems to be conscious, or even positively malevolent: 'the saw, / As if to prove saws knew what supper meant, / Leaped out at the boy's hand, or seemed to leap—'. The last phrase keeps the intentions ambiguous. Frost encourages this further in the suggestion that the boy 'must have given' his hand. In any case, 'neither refused the meeting'. It is as if it was fated.

Lines 19–27

Now we are told of the reaction to the accident. The boy's 'rueful laugh' suggests an almost humorous, ironic acceptance of what has happened. His gesture is pathetic and appalling in its futility: 'holding up the hand, / Half in appeal, but half as if to keep / The life from spilling.'

The next moment is crucial: 'Then the boy saw all'. He is 'old enough to know' and understand the significance of his accident. 'He saw all spoiled': he knows that without two good hands he is of limited use on a farm, which relies on everybody pulling together to get all the work done. That is why he appeals, hopelessly, to his sister not to let the doctor cut his hand off. He needs it. It matters to his future, to the farm's future and to the family's future. But it is too late: 'the hand was gone already.'

Lines 28–34

The poem moves rapidly to its bleak conclusion. The boy is anaesthetised, 'And then—' something horrifying and unexpected happens. Frost refers, oddly, to 'the watcher at his pulse'. This might well be the doctor, but it could also be the father or mother or another. It is deliberately left obscure. Again, the faceless 'They' 'listened at his heart', but in one line it is all over: 'Little—less—nothing!—and that ended it.'

The final two lines are perhaps the most chilling in the poem. 'No more to build on there' might refer to the boy's heartbeat, but it is also about his role on the farm. He cannot be part of its future – as a worker, or even as the future owner. As for 'they' – the others, the adults who are still alive – they have 'affairs' to get on with.

Themes and imagery

Frost's worldview in '"Out, Out—"' feels very far away from that in 'Birches'. If the latter was life-affirming and humane, this is **bleak** and **pessimistic**. It is a poem in which the rural world that Frost writes about with such love and understanding is seen as a far from idyllic place. The poem highlights the **economic reality of life in a poor farming community**. We see a boy 'Doing a man's work' (line 24) because that is what is required on the family farm. To do this, he needs to have full use of his hands. Without them, even before he dies, there is nothing to 'build on' (line 33). There is no sentimentality in the acknowledgement of this fact. That is why 'they' go straight back to what they have to do. You can see this as cruel, indifferent, practical or realistic. It is up to readers both to understand and to respond in their own way.

As in 'Birches', there is a **contrast between the children's world and the world of the adults**. The adults in the poem are shadowy figures referred to merely as 'they' and 'them' throughout. It is only the boy and his sister who are vividly present. The boy is 'a child at heart' (line 24) but does not have the opportunity to be a child. Where the boy in 'Birches' was free to play, this boy has to work. He realises straight after the accident that all is 'spoiled' (line 25). He knows that he will not be able to do his bit for the running of the farm. Is there even a sense that his death is an acceptance of the fact that he is now essentially redundant?

A related theme is the **threat that mechanisation poses to rural life**. The buzz saw is a central character and does the terrible damage that is depicted in the poem. Machines like this were relatively new on New England farms when the poem was written. You could see the saw as the villain that is destroying the rural harmony.

There is a suggestion in this poem, in the way that the accident seems almost fated – 'Neither refused the meeting' (line 18) – of a **malign providence**. This was a view that Frost, who was prone to bouts of depression, often toyed with. It is an idea that he takes up in 'Design'.

HIGHER LEVEL

There is very little metaphorical language in '"Out, Out—"'. It is **a tale simply told**. The one image that stands out is that of the buzz saw, which is seen as something more than an inanimate machine. It becomes an active participant in the drama, with a half-animal, half-machine existence, snarling and rattling. Both those verbs are used three times, reminding us of its threatening presence. At the critical moment, it even seems to take on a will of its own, leaping out at the boy's hand. Does it personify the cruel destiny that seems to govern the poem?

Form and language

'"Out, Out—"' is written in **blank verse**, with all the freedom regarding **metre** that Frost's poetry usually demonstrates. A line like 'And the saw snarled and rattled, snarled and rattled' (line 7) cannot be read in a strict iambic (di-dum) rhythm, but that metre is always felt in the poem, and individual lines get their effects from how they pull against it. The fact that the line above fights with the iambic rhythm emphasises the dangerous energy of the buzz saw.

The speaker is not personalised, but he tells the story in a **New England voice** we have come to recognise from Frost's poems. There is always a strong sense of a person speaking, even in fragmented sentences: 'But the hand!' (line 18); 'So.' (line 27); 'And then—' (line 30). He has a sense of the **dramatic**, and how to conjure it in few words: 'Little—less—nothing!— and that ended it' (line 32).

The language contains nothing fanciful, except perhaps the portrait of the buzz saw. One of the most interesting things is what is *not* said. **No emotions are described** at all, and, in a somewhat sinister way, the adults are always kept at a distance by using a neutral 'they' or 'them' or even 'the watcher' (line 30).

You can find alliteration, assonance and onomatopoeia if you look, but this is not a poem where the effects are striking. Nevertheless, it is worth noting Frost's craft at the key moment in the poem, when the boy 'saw all spoiled' (line 25). The assonance of 'saw' and 'all', the repetition of 's' and 'l' sounds, and the three consecutive stresses on long vowels that the words demand **slow down the rhythm** at this point and put strong emphasis on this crucial phrase.

Robert Frost

Exam-Style Questions

Understanding the poem

1. Describe the place where the poem is set.
2. Tell the story of the poem in your own words.
3. How does the speaker portray the buzz saw?
4. What did you learn from the poem about the lives of the boy and his sister?
5. 'Then the boy saw all—' (line 22). What, in your opinion, did he see?
6. 'And they, since they / Were not the one dead, turned to their affairs' (lines 33–34). What impression is created by these final lines?

Thinking about the poem

1. How does the poet prepare us for the tragedy from the beginning?
2. What impressions of country life do you get when you read this poem?
3. Comment on the portrayal of the adults in the poem.
4. 'Neither refused the meeting' (line 18). What, in your opinion, are the implications of this phrase? Is it important in the poem?
5. Which of the following words best describes the tone of the poem, in your view: cruel, unfeeling, sympathetic, practical? Explain your choice.

Imagining

1. Write the diary entry of the boy's sister in which she records her experiences and feelings on the day the accident happened.
2. You are a reporter for the local newspaper in Vermont. Write a report of the accident.
3.  Your class wants to make a short film based on the poem. In pairs or groups, discuss the sort of atmosphere you would create, and say what music, sound effects and images you would use.

SNAPSHOT

- Tells a tragic story
- Contrast between beautiful setting and tragic incident
- Conveys harshness of country life
- Focuses on the children
- Detached tone
- Disturbing final lines
- Readers respond differently

HIGHER LEVEL

Before you read
What images and feelings do you associate with springtime? Would you expect these to be evident in a poem entitled 'Spring Pools'?

Spring Pools

These pools that, though in forests, still reflect
The total sky almost without defect,
And like the flowers beside them, chill and shiver,
Will like the flowers beside them soon be gone,
And yet not out by any brook or river,   5
But up by roots to bring dark foliage on.

The trees that have it in their pent-up buds
To darken nature and be summer woods—
Let them think twice before they use their powers
To blot out and drink up and sweep away   10
These flowery waters and these watery flowers
From snow that melted only yesterday.

Glossary

2	*defect*: flaw
6	*foliage*: leaves
7	*pent-up*: held back, ready to burst open

Guidelines

'Spring Pools' is the opening poem of the collection *West-Running Brook*, first published in 1928. Its position at the beginning of the book means that it sets the tone for the volume, and also encourages the reader to look at the poem closely in order to understand why it was placed there. The description of transient forest pools that the surrounding tree roots suck dry to feed the trees' spring growth is rich with metaphorical meaning.

Commentary

Stanza 1
The first stanza is a single sentence. Although the images may be tranquil and delicately beautiful, the core of the sentence is 'These pools … / … / Will … soon be gone'. These are the spring pools of the title – the result of melting snow, as we are later told in line 12 – and they are transient (only there for a short while). The pools

reflect 'The total sky almost without defect' because the nearby trees are not yet in leaf. There is a sense of fragility both in the pools and in the flowers beside them, as they 'chill and shiver'. The last two lines of the stanza explain why the pools will disappear; they are not drained by a river but sucked up by the roots of the trees that surround them.

Stanza 2

The second stanza – again a single sentence – focuses on the trees, and the potential in the 'pent-up buds' to flourish and, with the shadow cast by their foliage, 'darken nature'. It is an unusual way of looking at 'summer woods'. The speaker warns them to 'think twice' before they do what they inevitably will do, and 'blot out and drink up and sweep away / These flowery waters and these watery flowers'. It is a heartfelt plea, but it is futile. The trees flourish by sucking up the water from the pools and their shade will stop other flowers growing. The final line impresses on us how transient things are by reminding us that the pools come from 'snow that melted only yesterday'.

Themes and imagery

On one level this is a poem about the **transient beauty of nature**. The spring pools and the flowers beside them last only a short time. They are born from the winter snows and are destroyed by the summer growth. Their very transience makes their fragile beauty seem all the more precious, which is why the speaker urges the trees to 'think twice' (line 9) before destroying it. The trees, on the other hand, are **threatening**, with their 'dark foliage' (line 6) and their ability to 'darken nature' (line 8); they have the 'powers / To blot out and drink up and sweep away' (lines 9–10).

The transience of things in the natural world is apt to remind the reader of the transience of human life, and the **element of loss** that any change inevitably brings. Just as the flourishing of the strong summer trees means the loss of the fragile beauty of the pools, so, for example, the growth of a child to full maturity involves the loss of innocence and the special beauty of childhood.

But, as so often in his poems, **Frost is also writing about poetry itself**. For him, water is often seen as the source of inspiration. The pools that reflect the sky are also reminiscent of a classical image of **art as a reflection of nature**. Frost, as a fine classical scholar, would have been very conscious of this. But if we follow his metaphor through, what he is saying is hard to pin down. If the pools of water stand for inspiration, the 'foliage' (line 6) they bring on must be poems. The 'pent-up buds' (line 7) certainly suggest creative power, but the fact that the trees 'darken nature' (line 8) suggests that their power is a dangerous one. The poetic imagination transforms its raw material in a way that can be destructive (it can destroy a peaceful vision of the world) and also creative (it can create a vision that is both beautiful and frightening).

That is one way of looking at it. A slightly different way is to think of the delicate beauty of the 'flowery waters and … watery flowers' (line 11) as the pristine idea or inspiration that a poet has, which, when it is transformed into an actual poem, loses some of the perfection that it had in the imagination.

You might notice that the pools, trees and flowers in this poem are not particularised. Frost was a true countryman in his knowledge of the different sorts of plants, and in other poems he is very specific about which flower or tree he is thinking of. Here, however, the fact that he is not describing a particular place so much as a **pattern of relationships** makes it all the easier to see the possible metaphorical significances of his imagery.

Form and language

'Spring Pools' is one of Frost's most **finely crafted** poems. It comprises two **matching stanzas** of six lines and one sentence each, both rhyming *aabcbc*, in subtly varied iambic pentameters. The syntax is not simple but it is clear; the language is measured and precise. Together they ensure **clarity of thought** and **concision of expression** in order to create a clear image that feels appropriate to the still, reflective pools. The **idea of reflection is carried into the form**, with its intricate rhymes and mirroring phrases: 'like the flowers beside them' is doubled in lines 3 and 4; the two halves of line 11 mirror each other: 'These flowery waters and these watery flowers'. There are no obvious verbal fireworks in the poem, but to get an idea of Frost's inconspicuous craftsmanship, compare line 11 with the one before it. Line 10 has a series of double stresses that push against the iambic metre and suggest the power of the trees: 'blót oút and drínk úp and swéep awáy'. The many unstressed syllables of the next line suggest a contrasting delicacy: 'Thĕse flówĕrў wátĕrs ănd thĕse wátĕrў flówĕrs'.

Questions

1	How is the beauty of the spring pools suggested in the early lines of the poem?
2	What irony is there in the manner in which their beauty will soon be destroyed?
3	How are the trees portrayed? Why are they associated with darkness (lines 6 and 8)?
4	What does the final line add to the poem in terms of meaning or mood?
5	Describe the mood or atmosphere of the poem.
6	How do the sound patterns of the poem – rhyme, rhythm, assonance, repetition – contribute to the mood of the poem?
7	In your view, is the poem purely concerned with the natural world, or does it have a relevance to human life? Give reasons for your answer.
8	Compare the attitude to nature implied in this poem with that in 'The Tuft of Flowers'.
9	Imagine that you have been commissioned to take a photograph to be displayed beside this poem on a website. Describe what you would include in your photo. What lighting would you use? What mood or atmosphere would you try to convey?
10	'The destructive power of nature.' Write a poem or a story that uses this title as its starting point.

Robert Frost

Before you read

What comes to mind on reading the title 'Acquainted with the Night'? Consider all the possible implications of both the key words, 'acquainted' and 'night'.

Acquainted with the Night

I have been one acquainted with the night.
I have walked out in rain—and back in rain.
I have outwalked the furthest city light.

I have looked down the saddest city lane.
I have passed by the watchman on his beat   5
And dropped my eyes, unwilling to explain.

I have stood still and stopped the sound of feet
When far away an interrupted cry
Came over houses from another street,

But not to call me back or say good-by;   10
And further still at an unearthly height
One luminary clock against the sky

Proclaimed the time was neither wrong nor right.
I have been one acquainted with the night.

Glossary

| 12 | *luminary*: luminous; light-giving |
| 13 | *Proclaimed*: announced publicly |

Guidelines

'Acquainted with the Night' is unusual among Frost's poems in having an urban setting. It was written when Frost was living in the town of Ann Arbor and teaching at the University of Michigan. The 'luminary clock' in the poem was, according to the poet, in the tower of the Washtenaw County Courthouse, which he would often pass during the night-time walks he liked to take when he could not sleep. The poem was published in *West-Running Brook* (1928).

Commentary

The title and first line of the poem set its tone, but it is not a simple one. Night means darkness; it might suggest depression or the dark night of the soul, and then again it might just be night. The word 'acquainted' is interesting too. It suggests familiarity, but a degree of detachment as well; after all, an acquaintance is not a friend. The tense used adds to that sense of detachment: 'I have been' is not as strong or as specific as either 'I am' or 'I was'. The poem uses that tense throughout, putting a slight distance between the speaker and his own experiences. He is not describing a particular night so much as a continuing state of mind.

Rain and darkness dictate the melancholy mood. Even the city lanes are sad. Human contact is avoided: the speaker has 'passed by the watchman', refusing eye contact. There is something of a mystery here: what is it that he is 'unwilling to explain'? There is mystery too in the 'interrupted cry' that stops him in his tracks. It is at one remove from him, 'from another street', and has nothing to do with him: 'not to call me back or say good-by'. This sense of separation from the world seeps into the way language is used. When he 'stood still and stopped the sound of feet', those feet were presumably the speaker's own, but he stops them as if they were separate from himself.

There is a surreal quality to the 'luminary clock' 'at an unearthly height'. It is hard not to think of the moon, especially as the word 'lunar' (meaning 'to do with the moon') is contained in 'luminary', and might itself lead to thoughts of lunacy. But it is a clock, although it shines like the moon. It, too, is detached from the speaker and suggests the indifference of the world towards him. Its message, that 'the time was neither wrong nor right', is mysterious. The speaker seems to be dislocated in time as well as space.

The final line of the poem repeats the first with a finality that is heightened by the completion of the rhyming scheme. There has been no change or development – just the elaboration of this one dark mood.

Form

The poem is fourteen lines long, and so could be regarded as a sonnet, but it is not structured in any of the traditional sonnet forms. Instead there are **four tercets** (three-line stanzas) **and a couplet**, using only four rhymes altogether in the pattern *aba, bcb, cdc, dad, aa*. This pattern closely resembles what is known as **terza rima**, a form invented by the Italian poet Dante, who used it in his *Inferno*, which is about a descent into hell.

Perhaps the most striking thing about this poem is the spell that it casts with its **powerful, insistent rhythms** and its tight network of **end-rhymes**. There is something **claustrophobic** about the atmosphere they create. Frost himself said that the poem was 'written for the tune'. You could see all its melancholy imagery as an extension of **the atmosphere created by the poem's music**.

The first four lines are all complete sentences, all end-stopped. All start 'I have … ' and there is an extra repetition in line 2: 'out in rain—and back in rain'. The fifth line follows the same pattern, even though that sentence continues into the following line. These **repeated patterns** create a sense of **downbeat monotony**.

Lines 6–13 are allowed to breathe a little more freely, with longer clauses and enjambment between the lines, most strongly between lines 12 and 13. Even this longer sentence reinforces the speaker's isolation: 'But not to call me back or say good-by' (line 10); 'Proclaimed the time was neither wrong nor right' (line 13). The final line returns to the beginning and reasserts the original pattern, unchanged.

Robert Frost

Themes and imagery

In this poem Frost touches on the theme of **urban alienation** – the sense of separation from other human beings and from the environment – that is often found in the work of modernist poets such as T. S. Eliot. The speaker is alone, isolated, avoiding human contact, in an urban setting that is dark with night and bleak with rain. The images that the city throws up are mysterious and unsettling: a disembodied cry from an uncertain place; the clock that shines from 'an unearthly height' (line 11). Notice also the **contrast of darkness and light** throughout, picked out in the first rhyme: 'night' and 'light' (lines 1 and 3).

And yet it is possible to read the mood of this poem as one of **resignation** rather than of despair or depression. There is **no direct expression of emotion** in the poem. There is no self-pity. Is there even a sense of achievement or pride in the speaker's acceptance of his solitary role, especially in a line like 'I have outwalked the furthest city light' (line 3)? Different readers will form different impressions.

It may be that in this poem we **glimpse some of Frost's darker thoughts** – the thoughts that surfaced in his frequent bouts of depression. The critic Lionel Trilling referred to Frost as 'a tragic poet whose work conceived of a terrifying universe'. Poems such as 'Acquainted with the Night', 'Design' and 'Provide, Provide' would bear out this perception of Frost's vision.

Language

Although the word 'I' begins every sentence and half the lines in this poem, we do not get the strong sense of the speaker's personality that we do in poems like 'Birches' and 'Mending Wall'. In part, this is because the poem does not adopt the conversational style of much of Frost's poetry. Instead its **language has a somewhat deadpan neutrality**: 'I have walked out in rain—and back in rain' (line 2). The odd, dislocating effect of 'I have stood still and stopped the sound of feet' (line 7) has been discussed above. The line with which the poem opens and closes has something of the same quality. As well as the detachment of the tense and the word 'acquainted' discussed earlier, the fact that he says 'I have been *one* acquainted with the night' rather than 'I have been acquainted with … ' puts him at a slight remove from himself. It is not the most natural of expressions.

Questions

1. In your opinion, what is the poet suggesting when he says that he has been 'acquainted with the night'?
2. How is the indifference of the city suggested in the imagery of the poem?
3. What, in your opinion, does the image of the clock contribute to the poem?
4. Seven of the poem's fourteen lines begin with 'I'. Write a paragraph commenting on the effect of this.
5. Describe the theme and mood of the poem, and the impact they have on you.
6. How does Frost use the form of the poem, especially rhyme and rhythm, to contribute to its impact?
7. Comment on the language of the poem and how this contributes to its effect.
8. Do you find this poem different in tone from other poems by Frost on your course? Explain your answer.
9. Imagine you are the 'watchman on his beat' (line 5). Write a paragraph on the person who passed you by and would not look you in the eye.
10. Your class has been asked to make a short film to accompany a reading of this poem. In small groups, describe how you would use sound effects, lighting and music to create an appropriate atmosphere.

Robert Frost

Before you read

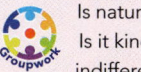

Is nature cruel? Is it kind? Is it indifferent? Contribute your views to a class discussion on these questions.

Design

I found a dimpled spider, fat and white,
On a white heal-all, holding up a moth
Like a white piece of rigid satin cloth—
Assorted characters of death and blight
Mixed ready to begin the morning right,   5
Like the ingredients of a witches' broth—
A snow-drop spider, a flower like a froth,
And dead wings carried like a paper kite.

What had that flower to do with being white,
The wayside blue and innocent heal-all?   10
What brought the kindred spider to that height,
Then steered the white moth thither in the night?
What but design of darkness to appall?—
If design govern in a thing so small.

Glossary

2	*heal-all*	type of plant in the mint family, once used for medicinal purposes; usually the flowers are violet-blue
3	*satin*	shiny, silky material; often used to line coffins
4	*blight*	disease
11	*kindred*	related; of the same family
12	*thither*	to that place; there
13	*appall*	literally, 'to make pale'; to horrify

Guidelines

'Design' was first published in *A Further Range* (1936), although Frost wrote the first version of the poem about twenty-five years earlier. Frost often wrote drafts of poems that he took up and polished many years later. One consequence of this is that his work shows relatively little development or change over the many decades of his career as a poet, as he was often returning to the same sources of inspiration. 'Design' is a sonnet, with a conventional division between the first eight lines (octave) and the last six (sestet).

HIGHER LEVEL

Commentary

Lines 1–8 (octave)
The poem starts by describing the three elements of the scene: a spider on a heal-all flower holding a moth – all are white. They are described as 'characters of death and blight'. Why? Presumably the spider has caught and killed the moth. Its being described as 'dimpled' and 'fat' might suggest the speaker's disgust, but it is the whiteness that is striking. White is an unusual colour for a spider and, as we later learn (see lines 9–10), abnormal for the heal-all. Although white is often associated with purity and innocence, the absence of colour also implies absence of life. In many ancient cultures, and today in countries such as China, India and Ethiopia, white rather than black is the colour associated with death and funerals.

There seems to be something perfect in their wrongness or malevolence. They are 'ready to begin the morning right' – the word 'right' is heavily ironic – and are mixed like 'the ingredients of a witches' broth'. Lines 7 and 8 restate and elaborate the central image: the 'snow-drop spider', the flower 'like a froth' and the dead moth the spider carries 'like a paper kite'. Those comparisons seem harmless, charming, playful, and yet the poem has already established their deeply sinister quality.

Lines 9–14 (sestet)
It is conventional in a sonnet for the sestet to develop the material of the octave. Here, the sestet questions the origins of the miniature scene previously described. Although the word is not used, the real question the speaker asks is why. Why was the heal-all white when it is usually blue and, ironically, 'innocent'? Why was the 'kindred spider' on top of it? (We might wonder why the word 'kindred' is used; is it because they have a family resemblance by both being white, or is there a suggestion of a conspiracy?) Why had the moth flown there?

Perhaps, however, the questions are better expressed as 'What force brought about all these things?' The answer – or the suggestion of an answer – is given in line 13: 'What but design of darkness to appall?' The implication is that there was a deliberate 'design' on the part of some dark force to 'appall' – meaning both 'horrify' and 'make pale'. What can have done something so perfectly horrible, the speaker asks, but a malign (ill-wishing) fate?

And then the final line gently undermines, or questions, this logic: 'If design govern in a thing so small.' In other words, if this is not too insignificant a matter for a malign fate to bother with. Or perhaps it is meant to imply that design (whether for good or evil) might have nothing to do with it – that it was just a strange accident. It is as if the speaker wants to cast doubt on everything they have said in the rest of the poem, in case they are taken too seriously. Perhaps they just want to lighten the mood; after all, they are only talking about a spider, a moth and a flower.

Themes

The title of the poem declares its theme: design. **Design in nature** is a subject that has interested theologians and philosophers for many centuries. The traditional view of design in nature is that it is a benign, harmonious thing, and the idea that the natural world is evidence of the existence of a benign creator goes back at least as far as the ancient Greeks. The medieval philosopher Thomas Aquinas put forward the so-called 'argument from design' as a rational proof of the existence of God. He argued that the fact that natural objects are perfectly fitted for what they do, and interact in harmony, demonstrates that they must have been fashioned by God.

In this sonnet, Frost turns that idea on its head. He speculates that the force that governs nature may in fact be evil. It is a **dark view of the universe**, and although he is careful in the final line that he should not be taken too seriously, it was a view that appealed to him. He came across it in the works of Henri Bergson and William James that he read as a young man. It suited his temperament, which could often be dark, and perhaps it appealed to his sense of humour as well.

Diabolical design

The philosopher William James, brother of novelist Henry James, suggested that if God had created each living thing for a particular purpose, then that purpose must be an evil one: 'To the grub under the bark the exquisite fitness of the woodpecker's organism to extract him would certainly argue a diabolical designer.'

Imagery

Whiteness dominates the imagery of 'Design', but there is always an **ambiguity or doubleness** to it. Whiteness usually implies purity, but here it is associated with 'death and blight' (line 4), and the 'white piece of rigid satin cloth' (line 3) suggests the lining of a coffin. Frost reminds us of the potential innocence of the white objects – the 'snow-drop spider' (line 7), the 'froth' of a flower (line 7), the moth like a child's 'kite' (line 8), but at the same time they are described as 'the ingredients of a witches' broth' (line 6). It is, in contrast, the everyday 'wayside blue' heal-all that is called 'innocent' (line 10).

Form and language

'Design' is a very **tightly woven sonnet**. It follows the Petrarchan model, with the octave rhyming *abba abba*, but the sestet introduces only one more rhyming sound, rhyming *acaacc*, so that there are only three rhyme sounds altogether. It is a poem in which **the octave contains observation and precise description, the sestet considers meaning, using questions and giving an answer**. It has, in other words, a **strong logical structure**, and the rhymes both mirror and help to create that structure. Perhaps, too, the tight structure mirrors the horrible neatness of the all-white scene of death.

The metre used is the **iambic pentameter**, and although Frost takes fewer liberties with it here than in some poems, it is flexible enough to allow a natural speaking voice to come through.

The language and syntax of the poem reflect the intricacy of the form and argument. Language is used precisely while still being **colloquial**. The choice of words pays attention to **word origins and associations**. For example, the original sense of 'appall' (make pale) enriches its meaning in line 13 of this poem that considers whiteness. The word 'characters' (line 4) contains the sense of written characters or letters, reinforcing the idea that the scene described is a sort of message to the viewer/reader.

The voice in the poem is not characterised in the way it is in poems like 'Birches' and 'Mending Wall', but there is a strong sense of a mind at work. In the sestet especially, you get a sense of the speaker's emotions as he asks questions.

Questions

1	Explore the imagery of the octave, paying special attention to Frost's use of the colour white and the connotations of his similes.
2	Having considered the imagery, how would you describe the tone of the octave?
3	How are the octave and the sestet linked together? Structurally, a sonnet is often said to move from 'sight to insight' (i.e. from description to contemplation). In what way might this be true of 'Design'?
4	What emotions are conveyed in the sestet?
5	What point is the speaker making in the poem's final line, in your opinion?
6	What vision of nature is suggested by this poem? How does it compare with that expressed in 'The Tuft of Flowers' or 'Spring Pools'?
7	The critic James Dickey has said that the best of Frost's poetry has to do with 'darkness, confusion, panic, terror'. Do you think this comment is relevant to 'Design'? Give reasons for your answer.
8	Do you think 'Design' is a well-made poem? Explain your answer.
9	Do you agree with the view of the world expressed in 'Design'? Write a paragraph giving your opinion, with reasons for your views.
10	Write your own poem or prose account of something you have observed in the natural world, explaining what you saw and expressing how it made you feel.

Robert Frost

Provide, Provide

The witch that came (the withered hag)
To wash the steps with pail and rag,
Was once the beauty Abishag,

The picture pride of Hollywood.
Too many fall from great and good   5
For you to doubt the likelihood.

Die early and avoid the fate.
Or if predestined to die late,
Make up your mind to die in state.

Make the whole stock exchange your own!   10
If need be occupy a throne,
Where nobody can call *you* crone.

Some have relied on what they knew;
Others on being simply true.
What worked for them might work for you.   15

No memory of having starred
Atones for later disregard
Or keeps the end from being hard.

Better to go down dignified
With boughten friendship at your side   20
Than none at all. Provide, provide!

Before you read

Have you ever been given advice about how to live your life? Was it good advice or not? Share your answers in pairs or small groups. Then see what you think of the advice given in 'Provide, Provide'.

Glossary

1	*hag*: ugly old woman	
2	*pail*: bucket	
3	*Abishag*: allusion to the biblical story of Abishag, a beautiful girl who came to attend the dying King David (I Kings 1:3)	
8	*predestined*: determined beforehand; fated	
9	*in state*: surrounded by the ceremony that goes with power	
12	*crone*: withered old woman	
17	*Atones*: makes up for	
20	*boughten*: something bought (rather than something naturally acquired)	

Guidelines

'Provide, Provide' appeared in the collection *A Further Range* (1936). The poet Derek Walcott speculated that the poem had its origin in Frost's childhood experience. When his father died at the age of thirty-four, Frost's mother had exactly eight dollars left to pay for her husband's funeral; the remaining family then crossed the United States to live with his mother's relatives. Frost had an anxiety about money for the rest of his life. When faced with the choice between the peace and quiet to write and the financial rewards of a paid teaching job or poetry reading, he almost always chose the latter so that he knew he would be able to provide for himself and his family.

Commentary

Stanzas 1–2
The first six lines establish the dilemma that the poem explores: however famous or beautiful you are, fame and beauty do not last. Frost makes the point by means of an image of a 'withered hag' who is washing the steps, a lowly task. That, he says, was once 'the beauty Abishag, // The picture pride of Hollywood'. Abishag is a renowned beauty from the Bible, but by making her a Hollywood star Frost is effectively saying that things have always been this way.

Stanzas 3–5
What can you do then to avoid this fall? With sarcastic exaggeration that covers a hard core of truth, Frost gives his advice: either 'Die early' (while you still have your looks) or make sure that you 'die in state', surrounded by wealth and power. And how do you do that? Simple! Be very rich: 'Make the whole stock exchange your own!' Alternatively, 'occupy a throne' so that you have enough power to ensure that you will be treated well and 'nobody can call *you* crone'.

The fifth stanza steps back to present another tentative possibility. Wisdom and goodness have worked for some and 'What worked for them might work for you.' The key word is 'might'. Given what we have already been told, it does not sound like much to rely on, and is certainly no guarantee.

Stanza 6
This stanza reiterates the poem's first point: the memory of past glories ('having starred' recalls 'the picture pride of Hollywood') does not help when you have been forgotten, and does not make old age and death ('the end') any easier.

Stanza 7
The final stanza draws a depressing conclusion. Money can buy you dignity and 'boughten' friends are better than none at all, so you had better make sure you have money: 'Provide, provide!' Clearly he means provide for yourself by making provision for your own end, rather than provide anything for others.

Themes

There is no ambiguity about the poem's theme, nor about the advice the speaker appears to be giving: **look after yourself by making money**. 'Provide, Provide' is both the poem's title and its take-away message. Nevertheless, there has been a great deal of disagreement among readers and critics about what the poem is *really* saying. This is largely a matter of how you judge the tone of the poem (see below).

Robert Frost

The historical context of the poem, however, sheds some light on where Frost's thoughts might have been when he wrote it. He was opposed to President Roosevelt's so-called New Deal policies, which he felt went against traditional American principles of self-reliance. He wrote this poem soon after the New Deal came into operation, and it can be read as a **response to those policies** and to those who supported them. Its message that you should provide for yourself is a direct rebuff to the New Deal policies of providing financial help to the needy. Sometimes when he read the poem in public he would add, as a quip at the end of the poem, 'Or somebody else'll provide *for* you!'

Tone

The **hard-bitten, humorous, cynical tone** of the poem, and of the advice the speaker gives, is unmistakable, and is highlighted and **reinforced by the sharp rhymes**. The humour is not gentle, and the tone has often been described as sarcastic, but it is worth thinking about whether that is really the case. Certainly there is comic exaggeration in the advice to either take over the stock exchange or 'occupy a throne' (line 11), never mind to 'Die early' (line 7). It is not serious advice, and cannot really be followed, but does it hide a serious intent? Is Frost mocking the American tradition of self-help, and mocking himself as someone who often seems to embody it, or does he mean what he says?

Interpretations usually rest on the final triplet, and the cynical advice to have 'boughten friendship' (line 20) rather than none. For some readers, this is genuine advice, however bleak: all you can do is make yourself as comfortable as you can, and that means making money. For others, there is a deeper message. Since the alternative to a lonely and undignified old age and death is merely the companionship of false friends, it just goes to show that all attempts to provide for yourself are futile. **No real comfort is available.**

The New Deal

In the 1930s the United States went through the Great Depression, following the Wall Street Crash of 1929. In response to widespread unemployment and poverty, President Franklin D. Roosevelt introduced financial relief for the poor and unemployed, as well as a scheme of public works and financial regulation, beginning when he took office in 1933. This was known as the New Deal.

End of life

After reading this poem in public in 1961, as an old man, Frost commented on it with these words: 'The worst part of life is the end. You can't keep the end from being hard, not the state – nobody but God.' What light, do you think, does this comment throw on the poem?

HIGHER LEVEL 2021 / 247

HIGHER LEVEL

According to poet and critic Randall Jarrell, this poem is a subtle description of how the 'wisdom of this world … demonstrates to us that the wisdom of this world isn't enough'. There is no level of material success or social status that will save you from the brute realities of life.

Imagery

The only real image in this poem is the one at the start: the old, withered woman washing the steps. It is there to make a point and to warn you what life can do to you. It is the starting point of a poem that **works by argument and rhetoric rather than imagery**.

Form and language

'Provide, Provide' is written in lines of four beats (tetrameters), which rhyme in groups of three. These are known as **rhyming triplets** (rather than the more common couplets), and with their **strong rhythm** and strong rhymes have an energy which is essentially **comic**. The form has plenty of what Frost called 'tune', and gives a simple pleasure in the **bold rhymes coming thick and fast**.

The language is **plain and direct**, as if the speaker is addressing a public meeting and enjoying the effect his words are having on the audience: 'Make the whole stock exchange your own!' (line 10). The poem was written at the height of Frost's fame, when he was well used to addressing large rooms or theatres full of people. In it we hear the **public-speaking voice** of Frost, or at least the voice of a person who is used to hearing his own voice in public.

Questions

1	What advice does the speaker give to anyone who wishes to avoid the fate of people like Abishag? In what tone is the advice given?
2	Does the tone of the poem change as it progresses? Explain your answer.
3	What significance might there be in the fact that Frost does not use the first person 'I' in the poem?
4	Comment on lines 13–15, ending 'What worked for them might work for you.' What is the tone of this triplet?
5	Randall Jarrell described this poem as 'an immortal masterpiece'. What qualities of the poem might have led him to this conclusion?
6	Would you agree that the view of life expressed in 'Provide, Provide' is darkly cynical? Give your response to this poem and to the speaker's advice.
7	Imagine you are one of the people listening to the speaker in this poem. Write an imaginary account of the event – the setting, the listeners, but above all the speaker and how he (or she) came across. What sort of person might the speaker be?
8	The poem is unlike most of Frost's other poems. Would you include it in a personal selection of Frost's poems for an anthology? Explain your answer.

Exam-Preparation Questions

1. Write an introduction to a short collection of poetry chosen from the poems of Robert Frost on your course. You are free to choose whichever poems you wish when answering this question. Some possible areas for discussion include:
- His themes: nature and what we can learn from it about human experience, etc.
- What his poems reveal about him as a person – his poetic voice
- His use of language, in particular his use of metaphor
- His choice of traditional forms in which to write
- The emotions underlying his best poems

You must support the points you make with relevant quotation or reference to the poems on your course.

2. In your opinion, what qualities of Robert Frost's poetry made him one of the most popular and best-selling poets of twentieth-century America?
Possible points include:
- His themes, while personally expressed, have a universal appeal
- His language is attractive and accessible
- His images and phrases are vivid and memorable
- His imagery is rooted in the American landscape and experience
- He appeals to the reader both intellectually and emotionally
- The reader can always gain some insight or learn some lesson from his poems

Always support the points you make with relevant quotation or reference.

3. W. H. Auden described the characteristic voice of Robert Frost's poems as 'always that of the speaking voice, quiet and sensible'. Examine this statement in the light of your reading of Frost's poems.

4. 'Many of Robert Frost's poems begin with straightforward description and move towards meditation and commentary.' Discuss this view.

5. 'It begins in delight and ends in wisdom.' This is how Frost described the process of composing a poem. How far might this reflect the imaginative structure of a typical Frost poem?

6. 'In his poems Robert Frost sees the beauty of nature, but there is also an awareness of its menace.' Do you agree with this view?

7. 'Robert Frost seldom describes nature merely for its own sake. He uses it also as analogy for human and even artistic concerns.' Discuss this statement with reference to the poems on your course.

8. Robert Frost said of his poetry that it provided a 'momentary stay against confusion'. To what extent might this statement illuminate the feelings behind the poems on your course?

9. 'Frost's simple style is deceptive and a thoughtful reader will see layers of meaning in his poetry.' Do you agree with this assessment of Robert Frost's poetry? Write a response, supporting your points with the aid of suitable reference to the poems on your course.

10. 'Frost communicates rich insights into human experience using language that is both accessible and appealing.' Discuss this statement, supporting your answer with reference to the poems by Robert Frost on your course.

SNAPSHOT ROBERT FROST

- Said that 'poetry begins in delight and ends in wisdom'
- Rural setting of poems is attractive to readers
- Writes about nature, but not merely for its own sake
- Poems can often be read metaphorically
- Writes about artistic creation and the power of the imagination
- Language of poems is accessible and memorable
- Voice in poems 'always that of a speaking voice, quiet and sensible'
- Theory of 'the sound of sense'
- Poems reveal his personality
- Shows an awareness of the darker side of life
- Uses traditional metres and rhythms

Robert Frost

Sample Essay

The critic James Dickey has said that the best of Frost's poetry has to do with 'darkness, confusion, panic, terror'. Another critic, Lionel Trilling, spoke of him as a 'terrifying poet'. How do you respond to these views? Support your answer with reference to the poems by Robert Frost on your course.

Immediately addresses the terms of the question

The public image Robert Frost cultivated and projected at hundreds of public readings throughout his long career was anything but 'terrifying'. With his shock of white hair, his Yankee voice, his humour and homespun philosophy, he perfected the reassuring image of himself as a wise country man, a trusted uncle and a national treasure. His books sold in numbers that few books of poetry have ever achieved, and I doubt that too many of the people who bought them would have responded with 'darkness, confusion, panic, terror'. Nevertheless, I have to agree, at least in part, with the views of Dickey and Trilling in so far as I find many of Frost's poems to have a darker side, as this essay will show.

Gives a personal response to the question

Offers a counter-argument to the quotes in the question

First it is important to note that Frost's poetry is not always dark. Indeed, there are plenty of poems in Frost's collections that I find deeply reassuring in their view both of the natural world and of human relationships. An example of such a poem is 'The Tuft of Flowers', where the speaker who goes out to 'turn the grass' alone finds evidence that the mower who had cut it earlier that day had seen the beauty in a tuft of flowers and, 'from sheer morning gladness', left it to flourish. From that moment he recognises 'a spirit kindred to my own' and feels the other man's presence beside him. He draws the moral: 'Men work together … / Whether they work together or apart.' It is a consoling, not a terrifying, vision, making this poem a counter-argument to the views expressed in the question.

Introduces the first poem to be discussed

Discussion of first poem ends by returning to the terms of the question

Next paragraph reconsiders the question and develops the argument

It is true, however, that not all Frost's poems are quite so reassuring. Even in his best and best-loved poems, which show a wonderful appreciation of the beauty of the natural world and have a positive message about human relationships, there are often darker forces beneath the surface. In 'Birches', for example, whose touching and comforting conclusion is that 'Earth's the right place for love', the speaker's memories of swinging birches are brought to mind when he is in a dark mood: 'It's when I'm weary of considerations, / And life is too much like a pathless wood'. He wants to escape his troubles: 'I'd like to get away from earth awhile'. Even though he insists he does not want to leave it for good, and his image of swinging a birch tree includes a return to the ground, there is an impulse to escape the troubles of life, perhaps a suicidal impulse. We know that Frost went through periods of depression throughout his life, and this poem gives us just a glimpse of what troubled him. There are other disconcerting elements in the poem. For example, the image of the young boy swinging his father's trees, 'riding them down over and over again / Until he took the stiffness out of them, / And not one but hung limp, not one was left / For him to conquer'. For me, there is an element of anger here, and suppressed sexuality, hinting at darker energies the poem's reassuring conclusion does not entirely contain.

HIGHER LEVEL

Third poem is introduced with a link to the previous paragraph

In 'Mending Wall', too, there is a pervasive sense of threat and dark energies at work. Not only is the neighbour like an 'old-stone savage' who 'moves in darkness', but there is the force that breaks apart the wall, the 'something' that 'doesn't love a wall', and which is left mysterious: 'I could say "Elves" to him, / But it's not elves exactly'. This element of uneasy uncertainty in the poem is important to its overall effect. It is part of what makes it more than a debate about whether walls are good or bad things.

Has the student discussed this poem sufficiently?

If 'Mending Wall' hints at a malevolent force in nature, 'Design' confronts that possibility head on. Its depiction of the white spider, white flower and white moth may seem perfectly innocent in itself, but it strikes the speaker in the poem with horror. For him, the little scene is almost perfect in its wrongness. The heal-all should not be white; the 'fat' spider should not be on top of it. He sees the trio as 'Assorted characters of death and blight', and their whiteness as sinister and morbid. This may sound like an overreaction, but there is no doubting the reality of the speaker's horror. The sestet of the sonnet asks in exasperation for an explanation of what brought this about, and concludes: 'What but design of darkness to appall?' This is more than an unhappy accident, the speaker seems to be saying: it is evidence of a malevolent power in nature. As if horrified by his own conclusions, the speaker pulls back from the brink in the final line, and lightens the mood – 'If design govern in a thing so small' – but Frost has presented us with a chilling vision that cannot be so easily dismissed.

Quotations are incorporated into the discussion

Just as 'Design' turns the ancient 'argument from design' for the existence of God on its head, so 'Spring Pools' inverts the conventional view of the natural world. Where we might expect the speaker to revel in the beauty of the 'summer woods', in this poem they are seen to 'darken nature'. They are a threat to the spring pools of the title, and the speaker urges them to 'think twice before they use their powers'. Enchanted by the beauty of the transient pools and the flowers that grow beside them, he is appalled at the idea that they will soon be gone. It is the transitory nature of their frail beauty rather than that beauty itself that most strongly strikes him. There is even a sense of panic at the thought of what will be destroyed to enable other things to grow. This thought, of course, has resonances with the idea of human mortality, so perhaps it is the fear of death that is at the bottom of these emotions.

Smooth transition effectively links the poems

Introduces a new idea that will link with the next paragraph

Note the link

The fear of mortality, and of the old age that precedes it, is powerfully present in 'Provide, Provide', which offers cynical and ironic advice about how to prepare for that eventuality. It offers little comfort. The solutions it proposes for those who fail to 'Die early' – 'Make the whole stock exchange your own!'; 'occupy a throne' – are effectively impossible; they are comic exaggerations. The alternative to loneliness in old age is 'boughten friendship', which is not real friendship at all. In effect, the poem is saying that no source of comfort is worth anything, no attempt to 'provide' can succeed. It is a dark, bleak view of the world, fuelled by the fear of old age and death. The combination of that dark vision and the comic panache with which Frost sets it out in swashbuckling triplets makes this poem at once shocking and delightful.

Final poem is introduced

Death haunts many other Frost poems, including '"Out, Out—"', which is about the accidental death of a farm boy. One of the best things about the poem is the way in which Frost captures the different stages of the boy's responses to his accident: denial in his 'rueful laugh', confusion in the way he turns to the adults holding up his hand, and the panic that comes

252 / DISCOVERY: POETRY ANTHOLOGY

with the growing realisation of what this will mean to him – 'He saw all spoiled', and his desperate plea to his sister – 'Don't let him cut my hand off'. His subsequent death is sudden, unexpected and shocking, but there is no sentimentality in how the family or Frost treat the death, and no outpouring of emotion. This is a clear-sighted portrayal of a rural farming economy, and the death of the boy is an economic fact. There is no time to mourn because there is work to be done. For some readers this is too cruel, but I think the remarkable thing about the poem is that Frost neither shies away from this reality nor comments on it. The darkness, confusion and panic are observed and acknowledged, but they are also put in perspective, as facts of existence.

Refers again to terms used in the question

Frost's ability to see clearly and coldly may in itself seem terrifying to some readers, but I do not find that his poetry is overwhelmed by the terror. Frost's poetry is not all dark, but darkness is certainly a crucial element of it. It is something Frost knows about and can work with in his poetry, and his poems are often made richer by embracing it, as highlighted in this essay. Frost did not take easily to speaking in front of large numbers of people, and the mask he created for himself over decades was hard won. He had to conquer his fears and insecurities, just as he coped with depression and the grief and guilt that came with family tragedies. Terror was familiar to him. In his own words, 'I have been one acquainted with the night.'

Gives personal response

Conclusion returns to a general discussion of the question, suggesting a qualification

Final paragraph returns to a topic covered in the introduction, tying up the threads

A striking final sentence

ESSAY CHECKLIST		Yes √	No ×
Purpose	Has the candidate understood the task?		
	Has the candidate responded to it in a thoughtful manner?		
	Has the candidate answered the question?		
Comment:			
Coherence	Has the candidate made convincing arguments?		
	Has the candidate linked ideas?		
	Does the essay have a sense of unity?		
Comment:			
Language	Is the essay written in an appropriate register?		
	Are ideas expressed in a clear way?		
	Is the writing fluent?		
Comment:			
Mechanics	Is the use of language accurate?		
	Are all words spelled correctly?		
	Does the punctuation help the reader?		
Comment:			

Seamus Heaney
1939–2013

The Forge	262
Bogland	266
The Tollund Man	270
Mossbawn: Two Poems in Dedication	
1 Sunlight	275
A Constable Calls*	279
The Skunk	284
The Harvest Bow	288
The Underground*	292
The Pitchfork	297
Lightenings, viii: 'The Annals Say'	301
A Call*	305
Postscript	309
Tate's Avenue	313

Seamus Heaney

Biography

Seamus Heaney was born on 13 April 1939, on a farm called Mossbawn, in south County Derry. Heaney was the eldest of the nine children (two girls and seven boys) born to Margaret and Patrick Heaney. Patrick Heaney farmed fifty acres and also worked as a cattle dealer. When Heaney was fourteen, the family moved from Mossbawn to a nearby farm that his father inherited from an uncle. The death of Christopher Heaney, the poet's young brother, was a factor in this move.

Home and school

The Heaneys were a close and loving family. The poems Heaney wrote about his aunt ('Mossbawn: Two Poems in Dedication: 1. Sunlight') and parents ('The Harvest Bow', 'The Pitchfork') reflect the quality of family life. He was raised as a Catholic and steeped in the traditions and rituals of his religion. The family was nationalist in outlook. Heaney was educated at the local primary school in Anahorish, attended by both Catholic and Protestant children. In 1951, he won a scholarship to St Columb's College in Derry, about forty miles from his home. St Columb's was a Catholic college, with a distinguished roll of past pupils including John Hume, joint winner of the 1998 Nobel Peace Prize, and the writers Seamus Deane and Brian Friel. Heaney's early years at St Columb's were marked by homesickness, but as he moved up the college his talent was recognised and nurtured by a number of teachers, particularly Sean O'Kelly, who shared his enthusiasm for the poetry of Hardy, Wordsworth and Hopkins. A summer spent in the Gaeltacht deepened Heaney's interest in, and love of, the Irish language.

University and early influences

Heaney won a scholarship to Queen's University, Belfast, where he studied English Literature and Language, graduating with a first class honours degree in 1961. During his time in St Columb's and Queen's, Heaney remained deeply attached to his home place, and to the values and traditions of his parents. This attachment is evident in his first collection of poems, the much-acclaimed *Death of a Naturalist* (1966). Heaney had read the poetry of Robert Frost while a student at Queen's, and Frost's autobiographical poems about life in a farming community pointed the way forward for Heaney's own writing.

Although he was offered the chance to do further study at Oxford, Heaney decided to train as a teacher, demonstrating the influence of his rural ancestors who, in Heaney's words, were not illiterate, but not literary. Moreover, Heaney's sense of duty dictated he should pay back his parents for the support they had given him throughout his education, so he took a job teaching in a secondary school in Ballymurphy, Belfast. The principal teacher was Michael McLaverty, the short-story writer, who introduced Heaney to the work of Patrick Kavanagh. At about this time, 1962, Heaney began to write poems in a serious way, and the poetry of Kavanagh, like that of Frost, influenced the direction and style of his work. Heaney wrote, 'Kavanagh gave you permission to dwell without cultural anxiety among the usual landmarks of your life.'

> **Education Act**
>
> **The system of scholarships, introduced by the Education Act of 1947, allowed the children of small farmers and the urban working class, like Seamus Heaney, to attend university for the first time. The influence of these students was particularly noticeable in the civil rights movement of the late 1960s.**

Heaney wrote about rural life.

Early success

In August 1965, Seamus Heaney married Marie Devlin, a teacher and writer. In the following year, the London publishers Faber & Faber published his first collection of poems, *Death of a Naturalist*. The book was acclaimed by reviewers, and Heaney was awarded a number of prestigious literary awards. These awards, and the favourable reaction to *Death of a Naturalist*, contributed to Heaney being appointed lecturer in English at Queen's University, Belfast in 1966. He also began to write for magazines in England, and make broadcasts for the BBC. And, in July, the Heaneys' first child, Michael, was born.

Situation in Northern Ireland

At the time Seamus Heaney became a public figure, the situation in Northern Ireland was growing tense and dangerous. The civil rights movement, campaigning for equality of treatment for Catholics, met with fierce resistance from extreme Protestant loyalist groups and from the police force (RUC). In October 1968, the year in which the Heaneys' second son, Christopher, was born, the first major, violent clash occurred in Derry. Television coverage of the incident, in which the RUC baton-charged peaceful marchers, was greeted with shock and outrage. The following months were marked by periodic violence and sectarian clashes. In August 1969, there were clashes between Catholics and Protestants in what became known as 'The Battle of the Bogside'. Many Catholics feared that they would be driven out of their homes. When the British Army entered Derry, they were welcomed as protectors by the Catholic community of the city. However, relations between the Catholic community and the army quickly deteriorated and five months later the Provisional IRA was formed in Dublin and soon began their bombing campaign, which intensified throughout 1971. As a Catholic nationalist, Seamus Heaney was affected by the violence and the events in Northern Ireland. He had taken an active part in the civil rights movement, and wrote about the fears of Catholic nationalists living in a state dominated by Protestant loyalists.

America

In the early 1970s, Seamus Heaney taught at the University of California for a year. There, he read the poetry of Robert Lowell, William Carlos Williams and Gary Snyder. These writers opened his mind to the possibility of a looser form of poetry than the kind he had been reading and writing. Heaney's time in America coincided with student protests against American government policies in Vietnam, and he saw how poetry could become 'a force, almost a mode of power, certainly a mode of resistance'. This insight shaped the direction of his future writing.

Seamus Heaney

Move south

Seamus Heaney returned to Northern Ireland in September 1971, during the week in which internment without trial was introduced. The situation depressed him; there was fear in the air and the army was on the streets: to Heaney it felt like martial law was in place. January 1972 saw the 'Bloody Sunday' killing of thirteen civil rights protesters by the British Army. Not surprisingly, Heaney resigned from his job at Queen's University Belfast. He moved south to Glanmore, a secluded spot in Wicklow. Threats from loyalist extremists played some part in his decision. However, it was the general feeling of oppression within Northern Ireland that he sought to escape. The period in Glanmore was one of domestic happiness. In 1973, the Heaneys' daughter, Catherine, was born. Many of the poems written during this period, including a sequence of sonnets, are love poems, which celebrate Heaney's marriage to Marie Devlin ('The Skunk'). Following the move to Wicklow, Heaney, with the encouragement of the poet Ted Hughes, began work on 'The Tollund Man' and related bog poems. Archaeological work on the Viking settlement in Dublin fuelled Heaney's interest in the culture of Northern Europe, first stirred by P. V. Glob's book, *The Bog People*. This book offered Heaney ideas on how his poetry might address the historical situation in Northern Ireland. The result was the collection *North*, published in 1975, in which Heaney wrote about the division between the two communities in the North, and the pressure of history upon the present ('A Constable Calls', 'The Tollund Man').

> **Bloody Sunday**
>
> On Sunday 30 January 1972, thirteen unarmed men were shot dead and seventeen wounded by the Parachute Regiment of the British Army, following a march organised by the Northern Ireland Civil Rights Association against internment without trial.

This book earned lavish praise from reviewers in Ireland, England and America. In the same year as *North* was published, Heaney was appointed to the English department of Carysfort Teacher Training College, where he worked for a number of years until he gave up his post to become a visiting professor at Harvard University in Boston. (He replaced Elizabeth Bishop. The two became friends in the short time they knew each other.) This full-time employment gave him the financial security to buy a house and, in 1976, he and his family moved to Sandymount in Dublin. For the rest of his life, he divided his time between living in Dublin and living in America and England, where he taught and lectured at Harvard and Oxford.

Mural commemorating Bloody Sunday, Derry, 30 January 1972.

In 1980, Heaney became a director of Field Day. Field Day began as a theatre company, but it soon expanded to become a forum for vigorous debate on cultural and political issues in Ireland. Heaney's writing contributed to that debate from a mainly nationalist, Catholic perspective. The years 1980 and 1981 were turbulent years in Northern Ireland: the hunger strikes, staged by republican prisoners in support of their demands for political status, brought relations between the Irish and British governments to a low point. Francis Hughes, one of the prisoners to die on hunger strike, was a neighbour of the Heaneys. The poems in Heaney's 1984 collection, *Station Island*, face up to the complexities of the situation and the feelings called out in him by the events in the North.

> **Hunger strikes**
>
> In 1981, ten IRA prisoners starved themselves to death in a dispute with the British government over their status. The families of two of those who died were known to the Heaneys. Heaney, although not an IRA supporter, attended the wake of one of the hunger strikers, Thomas McElwee.

Grief and joy

Heaney's next collection of poetry, *The Haw Lantern* (1987), is dominated by a sense of loss and grief as the poet mourns his mother, who died in 1984. And many of the poems in *Seeing Things* (1991) commemorate his father ('The Pitchfork'), who died in 1986. However, the late 1980s were marked by joy as well as grief. Heaney's journeys to America brought him into contact with many writers, including a number from Eastern Europe, and there is a palpable sense of freedom in his writing in this period ('Lightenings, viii: "The Annals Say"'). The 1990s were marked by increasing international recognition which culminated with the award of the Nobel Prize for Literature in 1995. The prize is often awarded to writers at the end of their career, but Heaney produced some of his finest work after receiving the award. His 2006 collection, *District and Circle*, won both the T. S. Eliot Prize and the Irish Times Poetry Now Award. The collection is notable for poems which respond to the attacks on the World Trade Centre in New York on 11 September 2001 and the bombing of the London Underground in July 2005. Other poems such as 'Tate's Avenue' look back in time. In 2010, Heaney published *Human Chain*, his twelfth collection. This was awarded the Forward Poetry Prize and the Irish Times Poetry Now award.

Death

In August 2013, Heaney was hospitalised in Dublin for treatment of a swelling to the artery. After his departure for the operating room he sent a text to his wife, Marie, which included the words, 'Noli timere' – 'Be not afraid'. The poet died shortly afterwards. At the time of his death he was, without question, one of the most admired and loved poets writing in English.

Social and Cultural Context

The social and political context in Northern Ireland was part and parcel of Seamus Heaney's inheritance and his poetry. Heaney was **steeped in the history of division**, in the family stories of sectarian assassinations in the 1920s, the murder of his cousin Colum McCartney in the 1970s, and the death of his neighbour Francis Hughes on hunger strike. He addressed this reality in his poetry; throughout these notes, you will find references to key moments in 'The Troubles' from a Catholic, nationalist perspective, including the civil rights marches of the late 1960s, the Bloody Sunday shootings in Derry in 1971, the sectarian murders of the 1970s and the hunger strikes. A major achievement of Heaney is that, **while he sought to face up to his responsibilities as a writer, his work is not overwhelmed by the enormity of the events to which it responds**. However, it is equally true that while his later work was marked by a lightness of spirit, Heaney questioned his own impulse to take flight and to ignore the demands of his community.

Poetic influences

One of the most interesting features of Heaney's search for an adequate poetic response to the pressure of public events is the range of poets who inspire him. Having trained as a teacher and having taught trainee teachers, Heaney is open to the idea of **learning from others**, and **his poems and essays borrow from and refer to a wide range of writers**. When Heaney began to write, and before he was aware of contemporary writers, the main influences on him were the works of Wordsworth and Hopkins. The subjects of *The Prelude*,

Seamus Heaney

Wordsworth's long, autobiographical poem, which charts the poet's childhood and his relationship with nature, are reflected in the themes of Heaney's first collection *Death of a Naturalist* (1966). As in Wordsworth, **there is little separation between the poet and the persona of the poems**, while the influence of Hopkins is especially evident in the rhythms and forceful diction of the early poems.

Patrick Kavanagh was an important influence, who, Heaney said, gave him permission to write about his own place. And the manner in which Kavanagh **bridged the gap between the ordinary and the sacred** has been taken up by Heaney in his later work. John Montague provided further examples of **how the local might serve the universal** in poetry and, through him, Heaney was led to the tradition of *dinnseanchas* – poems and tales which relate to the original meaning of place names. As Heaney delved into the Gaelic tradition, he also looked to other sources such as Greek myths and Northern or Norse rituals and sagas. From an early stage in his career, he showed a liking for a form that goes beyond the single poem, and his collections contain linked poems and poetic sequences.

The political and the transcendent

Following the example of early twentieth-century poets like T. S. Eliot, Heaney used classical poems as reference points for the present. His poems do not stand alone but draw strength and power from other poems. Thus, for example, both Virgil and Dante are presences behind many of the poems in which Heaney addresses the dead. Heaney admired the **mix of the political and the spiritual** in the work of both poets, and he tried to achieve a similar balance in his own. It was also the **balance between the practical and the poetic** that drew Heaney to the ancient Irish annals. Elsewhere, Heaney found inspiration and encouragement in the work of writers from Eastern Europe, who wrote in difficult and dangerous political circumstances.

From all these writers celebrated by Heaney, he draws the single lesson expressed thus in his essay *The Government of the Tongue* (see right).

Part of the excitement of reading Seamus Heaney is the way in which he leads you from the parish of Anahorish in County Derry outwards in space and time, making **connections with kindred spirits, both living and dead**, so that he verifies for us Patrick Kavanagh's belief that the local is universal. And it is impossible not to feel attracted to a poet who speaks of **poetry as 'an agent of possible transformation**, of evolution towards that more radiant and generous life which the imagination desires'.

Heaney on Patrick Kavanagh

'Kavanagh walked into my ear like an old-style farmer walking a field. He had that kind of ignorant entitlement, his confidence contained a mixture of defiance and challenge. You were being told that you would never hit your stride if you didn't step your own ground, and would never hit the right note if you didn't sound as thick as your own first speech.'

Eastern European writers

Heaney has stated his affinity with Eastern European writers: 'Eastern European poetry … was nurture, but it was also injunction: it enjoined you to be true to poetry as a solitary calling, not to desert the post, to hold on at the crossroads where truth and beauty intersect.'

Paradox of poetry

'Here is the great paradox of poetry and of the imaginative arts in general. Faced with the brutality of the historical onslaught, they are practically useless. […] In one sense the efficacy of poetry is nil – no lyric has ever stopped a tank. In another sense, it is unlimited. It is like the writing in the sand in the face of which accusers and accused are left speechless and renewed.'

Seamus Heaney, *The Government of the Tongue*, 1968

Themes

Seamus Heaney's poetry changed over the years. His early work is concerned with giving a faithful description of nature and reality, his middle work addressed the Northern Ireland situation, and his later work is playful and spiritual. Heaney's poetry **celebrates family** and grieves for the loss of loved ones. He is a poet of love, marriage and death. His work celebrates **farming and the link between that craft and the craft of poetry**. He explores the **relationship between childhood and adulthood**, as well as the **relationship between the past and the present**, especially in relation to the violence between the two communities in the North during the Troubles.

Heaney's poetry has always had a **documentary** quality, a **looking-back and a taking-stock**. However, his later poetry expresses a **delight in the marvellous and the miraculous**, the mystery and otherness of the world, including the mystery of death and the absences left by the dead. Poetry itself is, for Heaney, the means through which **ordinary life is acknowledged, enriched and elevated**. Poetry offers a kind of compensation for the sorrows of the world. It is the place where the dead are given an afterlife. Throughout his career, his poetry shows a **delight in words, their sounds and textures**.

In a review of Heaney's prose collection, *The Redress of Poetry* (1995), the reviewer referred to Heaney's character and its 'general benevolence'. And it is the generous, life-affirming vision of the poetry that is impressive and memorable. Heaney might well have been writing about his own work when he said: 'We go to poetry to be forwarded in ourselves.'

> **Phases in a writer's life**
>
> Heaney spoke of phases in a writer's life — the starting out, the taking stock (at around thirty), and the new freedom of later life: 'I believe the three phases turn out to be cyclic, that there are renewed surges of endeavour in your life and art, and that in every case the movement involves a pattern of getting started, keeping going and getting started again. Some books are a matter of keeping going; some — if you're lucky — get you started again. *Seeing Things* was a new start.'

Seamus Heaney

Timeline

1939	Born on 13 April on Mossbawn farm, south County Derry
1944	Attends Anahorish national school
1951	Wins a scholarship to St Columb's College in Derry, where he boards for six years
1957	Begins his studies in Queen's University, Belfast
1965	Marries Marie Devlin
1966	Publication of first collection, *Death of a Naturalist*; birth of first child, Michael
1968	Birth of second child, Christopher
1969	*Door into the Dark* published; visits United States for the first time
1972	Moves south to live in Wicklow; *Wintering Out* published
1973	Birth of third child, Catherine; travels to Jutland
1975	Publication of *North*
1979	Publication of *Field Work*; visiting lecturer in Harvard University
1984	Publication of *Station Island*; mother dies
1986	Father dies
1987	Publication of *The Haw Lantern*
1991	Publication of *Seeing Things*
1995	Awarded the Nobel Prize for Literature
1996	Publication of *The Spirit Level*
1998	Elected as Saoi by Aosdána, the highest award that can be bestowed on an artist in Ireland
2006	Publication of *District and Circle*; wins the T. S. Eliot Prize and Irish Times Poetry Now Award
2006	Suffers a minor stroke; cuts back on public engagements
2009	Public celebrations to mark his 70th birthday
2010	Publication of twelfth collection *Human Chain*; wins the Forward Prize and Irish Times Poetry Now Award
2013	Dies on 30 August in Dublin; buried in County Derry, near the graves of his mother and father

HIGHER LEVEL

Before you read

Share your knowledge of the craft of blacksmithing with the class. If there is a forge in your locality, tell your classmates about it.

The Forge

All I know is a door into the dark.
Outside, old axles and iron hoops rusting;
Inside, the hammered anvil's short-pitched ring,
The unpredictable fantail of sparks
Or hiss when a new shoe toughens in water.   5
The anvil must be somewhere in the centre,
Horned as a unicorn, at one end square,
Set there immovable: an altar
Where he expends himself in shape and music.
Sometimes, leather-aproned, hairs in his nose,   10
He leans out on the jamb, recalls a clatter
Of hoofs where traffic is flashing in rows;
Then grunts and goes in, with a slam and a flick
To beat real iron out, to work the bellows.

Glossary

Line	
Title	*Forge*: a blacksmith's workshop
3	*anvil*: the heavy iron block on which the blacksmith hammers metal into shape
4	*fantail*: the sparks make a shape like a fan
7	*unicorn*: a mythical creature, usually represented as a white horse, with a spiralled horn on its forehead
9	*expends himself*: uses up all his energy
11	*jamb*: the side part of a door frame
12	*flashing*: signalling; speeding
14	*bellows*: device with two handles that blows air into a fire

Guidelines

'The Forge' comes from Seamus Heaney's second book, *Door into the Dark* (1969). The title of the collection is taken from the first line of the poem. The door into the dark is the door into the forge, but metaphorically, it is **a door into mystery**, particularly the **mystery of poetry** and **the imagination**.

The poem uses the forge and the work of the smith as **symbols** for writing. **The poet, like the blacksmith, uses his skill to create well-made objects.**

Words are doors

'When I called my second book *Door into the Dark* I intended to gesture towards the idea of poetry as a point of entry into the buried life of the feelings [...]. Words themselves are doors' Seamus Heaney

Seamus Heaney

Commentary

Title and line 1
The title of the poem recalls the young Heaney's fascination with the local forge: 'I was thinking of Barney Devlin's forge at Hillhead, on the roadside, where you had the noise of myth in the anvil and the noise of the 1940s in the passing car.' In both classical and modern literature, artistic creativity is associated with the figure of the smith.

The first line of the poem encapsulates the way the poem hovers between memory and imagination. It suggests that as a young boy the poet was attracted to the mystery of the forge, with its door opening into a dark interior. Now, as a poet, he is interested in using words to **explore the dark**, the inner place of imagination and feeling where poetry begins.

> **Heaney on 'the dark'**
>
> 'I thought of "the dark" as a … positive element … in which poetry originates. The phrase "door into the dark" comes from the first line of a poem about a blacksmith, a shape maker, standing in the door of the forge … There's also the usual old archetype of the dark as something you need to traverse in order to arrive at some kind of reliable light or sight of reality.'

Lines 2–5
The poet describes the outside of the forge, the bits of rusting metal from old cart wheels. The imagery suggests that the axles and iron hoops belong to a different era. If the outside of the forge suggests decay, the inside (lines 3–5) suggests energy and excitement. The anvil sings to the blacksmith's hammering. Sparks fly and the hot metal hisses as it is cooled in water. Glimpsed from the doorway, the forge is an exciting and stimulating place.

Lines 6–9
Lines 6–9 concentrate on the anvil, the centre of the forge. The dark interior means that the anvil is not visible and this adds to its sense of mystery. Its shape is likened to the horn of the mythical unicorn. But the mythical is countered by its heaviness, such that it is immoveable. The anvil is now described as an altar where the priest/blacksmith uses up all his energy, and his hammer, as it beats metal into shape, makes music.

Lines 10–14
The last five lines of the poem describe the blacksmith, 'leather-aproned, hairs in his nose', coming to the door of the forge to look out on the world. The suggestion is that the blacksmith looks back fondly to a time when people used horses for transport and has little time for the traffic 'flashing in rows'. The blacksmith's grunt (line 13) suggests his dismissal of the modern world; he turns his back on it. There is defiance in the way he slams the forge door behind him and sets to work, doing what blacksmiths have done for centuries – beating out metal.

Theme and imagery

Poetry
The poem moves between detailed physical description of a real forge and a real blacksmith, and the idea of the smith as a mythic figure, who, on the **altar of creativity**, makes art. The blacksmith and his craft are presented as symbols of poetry and the poet. At the time of writing this poem, Heaney spoke of poetry as something that lies in the darkness of memory and the subconscious (the forge), waiting to be discovered. When the discovery is made, **the poet applies the traditional techniques of poetry to fashion the poem.**

HIGHER LEVEL

To speak of technique is not to take the magical or sacred qualities away from the art of the smith or the art of the poet. In the mind of the boy, the 'I' of the poem, there is something mysterious and sacred in the transformations which take place in the forge. Indeed, the central symbol of the poem, the anvil, is described as an altar and linked to the horned unicorn, symbols of the sacred and the mysterious respectively.

Traditional crafts

While the poem dwells on the mysteries of creation, it is also laments the passing of traditional crafts. The smith is a heroic but doomed figure, out of place in a

changing world, upon which, in disgust and defiance, he turns his back and continues his craft. The poem praises the smith's dedication to his craft and sets him up as a **timeless, exemplary figure**. Interestingly, 'The Forge' ends with the poet still outside the door. The smith retires into the darkness as if he has escaped the modern world, or as if the poet's younger self has not yet entered the world of the forge where, in the dark interior, the smith works the magic of creation. The ending opens out a range of possible interpretations.

Form and language

'The Forge', as a celebration of the traditional craft of the blacksmith, is, appropriately, written in a **traditional form, the sonnet**, though the poem is looser in organisation than more traditional sonnets. The opening line has ten syllables, as in a Shakespearean sonnet. The poem falls into two parts: the first eight lines of the poem (octave) focus on the forge and its mysteries; the last six lines (sestet) focus on the smith himself.

> ### The smith
>
> **In both classical and modern literature, artistic creativity is associated with the figure of the smith. In classical literature were Hephaestus, who crafted the armour of the gods, and Daedalus, who designed the Labyrinth at Knossos to house the Minotaur. Shakespeare describes the imagination as 'the quick forge and working-house of thought', and Heaney also admired Hopkins' poem 'Felix Randal'. In James Joyce's *A Portrait of the Artist as a Young Man*, Stephen Dedalus (note the surname) declares that he is going 'to forge in the smithy of my soul the uncreated conscience of my race'.**

'The Forge' is remarkable for the **effects Heaney achieves in the use of consonants**, and **short, strong-sounding words** (dark, ring, sparks, grunts, slam, flick, beat) which give a **muscularity to the language**, in keeping with the energy and noise of the smith's work. The **rhymes and half-rhymes** in the poem mirror the music of the hammer striking the anvil. In the poem, the strength of the consonants and the effort required in giving voice to their sounds imitate the energy and forcefulness of the smith's work.

Questions

1. Based on the description of the inside of the forge (lines 3–5), what impression do you form of the blacksmith and his art?
2. How does the description of the outside of the forge (line 2) compare with the description of the inside?
3. What details in Heaney's description of the blacksmith are most striking?
4. Based on the last five lines of the poem, what kind of person do you imagine the blacksmith to be?
5. Trace the imagery of light and sound in the poem. What do they suggest about the art of the smith? Explain your answer.
6. At the centre of the poem are the images of the altar and the horned unicorn. What is the significance of these images for the theme of the poem?
7. The poem ends with the contrast between the traffic and the blacksmith's traditional craft. What is the effect of this contrast?
8. The poem is written in the present tense. What is the effect of this?
9. a) Give three examples of words which, in your view, capture the strength and energy of the blacksmith and his work.
   b) Give an example of an image that is connected with sight; one that is connected with hearing; and one connected to the imagination.
10. Taking the forge and the blacksmith as standing for the poet and his work, what does the poem say about the process of making a poem?
11. Which of the following is closest to your reading of the poem?
    - This is a poem about the process of writing poetry
    - This is a poem written in celebration of a local craftsman
    - This is a poem about boyhood fascination
    - This is a poem about the pleasure of memory

    Explain your choice, considering each point of view in your answer.
12. If you were asked to nominate a person as an example of skill, artistry and imagination, whom would you choose? In pairs or groups, explain your choice.
13. Compare this poem with 'Bogland' and 'Lightenings, viii' for variations on Heaney's exploration of the art of making poetry.

Before you read

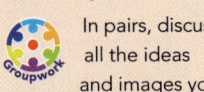

In pairs, discuss all the ideas and images you associate with the words 'bog' and 'bogland'. Consider the extent to which these words have a positive or negative connotation for you. You might return to your discussion when you have studied the poem and considered Heaney's meditation on bogland.

Bogland

for T. P. Flanagan

We have no prairies
To slice a big sun at evening –
Everywhere the eye concedes to
Encroaching horizon,

Is wooed into the cyclops' eye   5
Of a tarn. Our unfenced country
Is bog that keeps crusting
Between the sights of the sun.

They've taken the skeleton
Of the Great Irish Elk   10
Out of the peat, set it up
An astounding crate full of air.

Butter sunk under
More than a hundred years
Was recovered salty and white.   15
The ground itself is kind, black butter

Melting and opening underfoot,
Missing its last definition
By millions of years.
They'll never dig coal here,   20

Only the waterlogged trunks
Of great firs, soft as pulp.
Our pioneers keep striking
Inwards and downwards,

Every layer they strip   25
Seems camped on before.
The bogholes might be Atlantic seepage.
The wet centre is bottomless.

Glossary

1	*prairies*:	the vast areas of grassland in the central plains of North America
2	*slice*:	cut. The distant horizon cuts the sinking sun in half
3	*concedes*:	gives way to
5	*cyclops' eye*:	the Cyclops is a one-eyed giant in Greek mythology
6	*tarn*:	a small mountain lake; the word comes from Old Norse
10	*Great Irish Elk*:	skeletons of huge deer were found preserved in the bogs
12	*crate*:	Heaney compares the skeleton of the elk to a crate or container made of slats
20	*coal*:	coal is what the bog will eventually become ('its last definition'), but it will take millions of years for this to happen
23	*pioneers*:	settlers in previously unknown, wild or unclaimed territory

Seamus Heaney

Guidelines

'Bogland' is the final poem in Seamus Heaney's collection *Door into the Dark* (1969). It is widely regarded as one of Heaney's most important early poems, a poem which suggests new possibilities for the direction of the poet's writing. This is what Heaney himself said about the origins of the poem:

> 'We used to hear about bog butter, butter kept fresh for a great number of years under the peat. Then when I was at school the skeleton of an elk had been taken out of a bog nearby and a few of our neighbours had got their photographs in the paper, peering out across its antlers. So I began to get an idea of the bog as the memory of the landscape, or as a landscape that remembered everything that happened in it and to it … Moreover, since memory was the faculty that supplied me with the first quickening of my own poetry, I had a tentative unrealised need to make a congruence between memory and bogland and, for want of a better word, our national consciousness. … At that time, I had … been reading about the frontier and the west as an important myth in the American consciousness, so I set up – or rather, laid down – the bog as an answering Irish myth.'

'Bogland' is one of the first poems in which Heaney speaks as a representative of his nationalist community.

> **The prairies**
>
> The prairies or Great Plains were the vast areas of open grasslands in the central part of America. The prairies were sacred to many American tribes, including the Sioux, Blackfoot, Crow, Cheyenne and Apache, and home to herds of buffalo. In the second half of the nineteenth century, the railways brought many white settlers, moving westward from their original settlements along the east coast. From the perspective of the settlers, the opening of the prairies was a great adventure. For the American tribes, it ensured the destruction of their way of life.

Commentary

The poem consists of a series of statements.

Statement 1: Lines 1–6
The poem begins with the poet speaking on behalf of the Irish race: 'We have no prairies …' The speaker compares Ireland to America. On the prairies the eye can travel across great distances to the furthest horizon, to where the sun sets. In contrast, in Ireland, the horizon advances towards you, or the eye is drawn to small lakes in the hills.

> **Poem as response**
>
> Heaney's poem reads like a response to 'In Praise of Prairie' by the American poet, Theodore Roethke. In that poem, Roethke writes that 'Horizons have no strangeness to the eye'. In another line he states, 'Here distance is familiar as a friend'.

Statement 2: Lines 6–8
The comparison between Ireland and America continues. In Ireland, the unfenced country is bog, which develops a hard layer on its soft turf between periods of sunshine.

Statements 3 and 4: Lines 9–15
The speaker informs the reader about items recovered from the bog in a preserved state: a Great Irish Elk and hundred-year-old butter.

Statements 5 and 6: Lines 16–22
According to the speaker, the bog itself is like butter, and gives way under foot. Millions of years will pass before it is changed into coal. That is why it is only the soft, waterlogged trunks of trees that will be dug out of the bog.

HIGHER LEVEL 2021

Statement 7: Lines 23–26
The speaker makes an implied comparison between the American and Irish pioneers. In America, because of the vast prairies, the pioneers spread across the land into unclaimed and uninhabited territory. Because of the bog, Irish pioneers strike inwards and downwards (as opposed to onwards and upwards), and every layer they uncover seems previously inhabited.

Statement 8: Line 27
This is the only statement in the poem that is less than definite. The speaker wonders if the water in the bogholes might be seepage from the Atlantic Ocean.

Statement 9: Line 28
The poem concludes with the declaration that the wet centre of the bog is bottomless.

Theme and symbolism

'Bogland' turns on a comparison between the American prairies and Irish bogs. As the poem presents it, the American pioneers moved across empty spaces of the prairies but, in Ireland, pioneers explore downwards. The word 'pioneer' suggests **adventure and discovery**: the adventure of **poetry**; the adventure of **discovering your past and your national identity** by **cutting down through the layers of bog**. According to the poem, the bog is generous: it **preserves and returns the past to us**, in the form of ordinary, domestic gifts (butter) and traces of the marvellous (the elk). The bog is also **soft and accommodating**.

'Bogland' is not simply a landscape poem. The landscape it describes is both the natural landscape of Ireland but also a **cultural/visionary landscape**. Thus, the poem is **poised between the literal and the symbolic and the reader must constantly shift between the two**.

The memory of the race
Heaney offers the bog as a symbol for Ireland, for Irish history, and for the **memory and unconscious** of the Irish race. To dig the bog, by 'striking / Inwards and downwards', is to search into the bottomless centre of Irish history. Although not stated explicitly in this poem, it is clear that the action of digging the bog is seized by the poet as a symbol of his work as a poet. For the poet, the bog is a symbol which seems inexhaustible, whose 'wet centre is bottomless'. The last line of the poem comes from the warning given by older people to keep children away from the bog. It is presented here with the force and excitement of illumination, as if the poet has gained an unexpected insight, which he offers to the reader with confidence and certainty. There is no bottom to the well of imagination. Indeed, the whole poem is delivered with a remarkable air of assurance and confidence. Seamus Heaney **speaks on behalf of the race** ('We have no prairies'; 'Our unfenced country'; 'Our pioneers keep striking'), with no hint of self-consciousness.

In 'Bogland', Heaney sets out to establish his **own poetic myth**, and does so with a confident excitement. What is most notable is the way that the bog, and the work associated with it, is treated as a **metaphor**. This is carried forward in Heaney's poetry.

Seamus Heaney

Form and style

'Bogland' is written in seven four-line stanzas, with many short lines ('Every layer they strip').

There is no formal rhyme scheme but there are many instances of **slant or half-rhyme** ('skeleton'/'elk', 'peat'/'crate', 'years'/'here'). **The form is loose and yielding, mirroring the softness of the bog.** In 'Bogland' there is a new spareness in Seamus Heaney's poetic language and a **direct way of speaking**. The poem consists of nine sentences, each one a statement. This lends an air of certainty and authority to the speaker, as in the opening line, 'We have no prairies'.

Questions

1	What contrast does the poem establish between the American prairies and the bogs of Ireland?
2	In the poem what qualities are ascribed to bogland? Is it, for example, sinister, dangerous, generous, barren, shallow …? Explain your answer.
3	How does the bog work as: a) a symbol of Irish history, and b) a symbol of the imagination of the poet? In your view, is it a successful symbol? Explain your answer.
4	How would you describe the tone(s) of the poem? In making your answer, consider the poet's use of the communal pronouns 'Our' and 'We', and the declarative statements of the poem.
5	The poem has a sense of excitement and possibility about it. Where, in your view, is this excitement most evident?
6	Speaking of the poem, Seamus Heaney said, 'From the moment I wrote it, I felt promise in 'Bogland'. What, do you think, did he mean by this?
7	What kind of person do you imagine the speaker of the poem to be?
8	The poem speaks of the bog melting and opening underfoot. Select two examples where the short line and/or the sounds of the poem also melt and open.
9	In pairs, read the poem aloud to each other. As you listen, write down all the words and phrases which you find memorable. Based on this selection, discuss the themes and concerns of the poem.
10	Which of the following statements is closest to your understanding of the poem? ■ The poem is about the difference between an American outlook and an Irish outlook ■ The poem is about the relationship between the past and the present in Ireland ■ The poem is about the relationship between memory and poetry ■ The poem is about the importance of symbols in understanding experience Explain your choice, considering each point of view in your answer.
11	Write your own text (poem, monologue, paragraph, essay, etc) on the idea of the Irish as people of the bog.
12	The poet James Simmons has suggested that Heaney's poetry is stuck in the past. Based on this poem, is this a fair criticism?
13	What differences and similarities can you see in the ideas on poetry and poetry-making in 'Bogland', 'The Forge' and 'Lightenings, viii'?

Before you read

This is the official museum website for the Tollund Man: http://www.tollundman.dk. When you have visited it, write your own response to the Tollund Man.

The Tollund Man

I

Some day I will go to Aarhus
To see his peat-brown head,
The mild pods of his eye-lids,
His pointed skin cap.

In the flat country near by 5
Where they dug him out,
His last gruel of winter seeds
Caked in his stomach,

Naked except for
The cap, noose and girdle, 10
I will stand a long time.
Bridegroom to the goddess,

She tightened her torc on him
And opened her fen,
Those dark juices working 15
Him to a saint's kept body,

Trove of the turfcutters'
Honeycombed workings.
Now his stained face
Reposes at Aarhus. 20

II

I could risk blasphemy,
Consecrate the cauldron bog
Our holy ground and pray
Him to make germinate

The scattered, ambushed 25
Flesh of labourers,
Stockinged corpses
Laid out in the farmyards,

Tell-tale skin and teeth
Flecking the sleepers 30
Of four young brothers, trailed
For miles along the lines.

Seamus Heaney

III
Something of his sad freedom
As he rode the tumbril
Should come to me, driving,   35
Saying the names

Tollund, Grauballe, Nebelgard,
Watching the pointing hands
Of country people,
Not knowing their tongue.   40

Out there in Jutland
In the old man-killing parishes
I will feel lost,
Unhappy and at home.

Glossary

1	*Aarhus*: a city in Jutland, Denmark
3	*pods*: shells or husks for peas and beans
4	*skin cap*: leather hat
12	*the goddess*: Nerthus, a goddess of the earth and fertility
13	*torc*: necklace made of metal, usually bronze or gold
14	*fen*: bog or marshy land
16	*kept*: preserved
17	*trove*: treasure buried in the earth
18	*Honeycombed workings*: the turfcutters dig out many small sections of the bog
21	*blasphemy*: the act of insulting sacred things
22	*cauldron*: large metal pot
24	*to make germinate*: to cause to sprout or grow
27	*Stockinged corpses*: the image comes from a photo of a farmer's family who had been shot in reprisals by the Black and Tans during the War of Independence, 1919–1921
31	*four young brothers*: refers to an incident from the sectarian troubles of the 1920s in which four brothers were killed by Protestant paramilitaries. According to Heaney, their bodies were 'trailed along the railway lines, over the sleepers as a kind of mutilation'.
34	*tumbril*: a farm cart of the kind used during the French Revolution to bring condemned prisoners to the guillotine
37	*Tollund, Grauballe, Nebelgard*: place names in Jutland

Guidelines

'The Tollund Man' comes from Seamus Heaney's third collection *Wintering Out* (1972). Like many of the poems in the collection, 'The Tollund Man' was written in response to the violence and murders in Northern Ireland. The book *The Bog People* provided Heaney with an imaginative framework for thinking about the violence in his home place. Heaney tells us that:

'It was chiefly concerned with preserved bodies of men and women found in the bogs of Jutland, naked, strangled or with their throats cut, disposed under the peat since early Iron Age times. The author P. V. Glob argues convincingly that a number of these and, in particular, The Tollund Man, whose head is now preserved near Aarhus in the museum at Silkeburg, were ritual sacrifices to the Mother Goddess, the Goddess of the ground who needed new bridegrooms each winter to bed with her in her sacred place, in the bog, to ensure the renewal and fertility of the territory in the spring. Taken in relation to the tradition of

> Irish martyrdom for that cause whose icon is Cathleen Ni Houlihan, this is more than an archaic barbarous rite: it is an archetypal pattern. And the unforgettable photographs of those victims blended in my mind with photographs of atrocities, past and present, in the long rites of Irish political and religious struggles.'

Seamus Heaney draws **a parallel between the Tollund Man, the victim of a ritual killing in Iron Age Jutland, and political killings in contemporary Ireland**, which he compares with the **archetypal pattern of making sacrifices to the Mother Goddess** (in this case, **Mother Ireland**). In trying to make sense of the present troubles, Heaney searches the past, and finds not only a long history of barbaric rites, but a recurrence of ancient patterns.

Commentary

Section I
'The Tollund Man' opens with the speaker making a declaration of intent to go to Aarhus, in Jutland, to see the preserved body of the Tollund Man. The man had been hanged and his body placed in the bog, as a 'Bridegroom to the goddess'. The bog has preserved the body, which takes on, for the speaker, the qualities of a saint. Once there, the poet says that he will stand a long time in contemplation (line 11). The opening sections give a detailed description of the preserved head of the Tollund Man, and the circumstances of his death.

Section II
In the second part of the poem, the speaker expands on the idea of the Tollund Man as a saint. He says he could risk blasphemy by making holy the bog and praying to the Tollund Man to make something good grow or germinate from the broken and scattered bodies of the victims of sectarian violence in the North.

Section III
In the third part of the poem, the speaker imagines himself driving through Jutland, en route to Aarhus, in a country where he does not speak the language. He imagines experiencing some of the feelings of the Tollund Man as he rode in the cart, to his death. In the country of Iron Age murder, the poet imagines he will feel lost, but also, unhappily, at home.

Themes

Religion
The poem was written in response to photographs of the Tollund Man. The poem is written out of the **awe** and **fascination** provoked by the images. The entire poem has a religious feel to it and operates as a **kind of prayer**. The first part announces the speaker's intention to go on a pilgrimage to view the sacred figure of the Tollund Man, who has experienced a kind of resurrection from his burial place in the bog. The second part invokes the Tollund Man's power. The third part imagines how the speaker will feel when he goes to Jutland.

Iron age killings and contemporary violence
In the movement from the past to the present and from Jutland to Ireland, in part two of the poem, there is a **compacting of both time and space**. The poem brings into relation the victims of political atrocities in the North, and the Iron Age Tollund Man. However, whereas the Tollund Man was forewarned of his death and, perhaps, was even a willing sacrifice, the four brothers had their bodies broken and shredded. Contemporary

violence denies its victims the dignity that Heaney sees in the Tollund Man. In contemplating an appeal to the Tollund Man, 'to make germinate / The scattered … flesh of labourers', Heaney searches to find some way of translating the deaths of these victims of savage, sectarian hatred into a positive, generative force, to **confer meaning and value on the deaths of local men**.

Recognising the nature of home
In the final part of the poem, the poet identifies with the Tollund Man, imagining himself retracing the final journey of the bridegroom to the goddess. The poet's **imagined sense of disorientation**, evident in the strange place names and the implied threat in the pointing hands leads him to an epiphany: he realises that to travel to Jutland would be to encounter **his own desolate, disconsolate sense of home**. And implicit in this desolation is the poet's desire for home – that is, Ulster – to be other than what it is.

Dangerous myth or consolation?
'The Tollund Man' is a remarkably accomplished poem by any standards, but critics have raised questions about its achievement. Does the poem represent a refusal to confront the reality of violence in the North? Heaney asks these questions of himself. He admits that **he found it easier writing about a victim of 2,000-year-old violence than a local, contemporary incident**:

> 'The barman at the end of our road tried to carry out a bomb and it blew up. Now there is of course something terrible about that, but somehow language, words didn't live in the way I think they have to live in a poem when they were hovering over that kind of horror and pity. They just become inert. And it was in these victims made strangely beautiful by the process of lying in bogs that somehow I felt I could make offerings or images that were emblems.'

Seamus Heaney wants the Tollund Man to stand as an **emblem or symbol**, and in the poem the Tollund Man achieves a kind of beauty. Is it dangerous to suggest that the victims of ritual killings achieve a kind of beauty, or is there something consoling in this idea?

Imagery

At the centre of the poem is the image of the Tollund Man preserved in the bog, and returned to us after thousands of years as a **kind of sacred ancestor**. The bog is personified as a goddess and the poet uses sexual imagery to describe **his burial as a kind of consummation** (lines 12–16). Another set of imagery describes the victims of sectarian/political violence in graphic terms, their flesh scattered and defiled. In the final section, the speaker pictures himself driving through Jutland. The place names suggest the foreignness of the place. The **image of the journey** is one frequently used by Heaney, as in 'Postscript', 'The Pitchfork', 'The Underground' and 'Lightenings, viii'.

Form and language

The poem is written in four-line stanzas. The short line allows for **subtle changes of pace and tone**. The **underlying tone of sadness** of the opening stanza, the long vowel sounds, the half-rhymes ('peat'/'head', 'mild'/'lids'); the alliteration ('peat', 'pod', 'pointed') and consonance ('mild', 'pods', 'lids') sets the dominant tone of the poem.

HIGHER LEVEL

Questions

1	Summarise in a few sentences what the poem is about.
2	What, in your view, is the tone of the first stanza? How is this tone achieved?
3	The Tollund Man was a bridegroom to the goddess. What kind of bride was she? Look particularly at the images in stanzas 3 and 4 of the first section of the poem.
4	Where is the identification of the Tollund Man as a kind of sacred ancestor most evident in the poem?
5	Why is the bog described as a cauldron (line 22)?
6	The poet considers calling on the Tollund Man 'to make germinate' the murdered victims of sectarian violence in the North. What kind of germination, do you think, might the poet have in mind? Explain your answer.
7	In your view, what does the phrase 'sad freedom' suggest about the bridegroom/victim?
8	What are the differences between the death of the Tollund Man and the deaths of the four brothers referred to in the second section of the poem? Explain your answer.
9	What, in your opinion, does the Tollund Man represent? Is he, for example, a Christ-like figure, whose death and bizarre resurrection offers a kind of hope? Explain your answer.
10	The poet identifies closely with the Tollund Man's experience. Does the poet make the same identification with the victims of contemporary violence? Explain your answer.
11	The poem ends with a kind of revelation. What, in your opinion, has the poet gained from his imaginary pilgrimage to Jutland?
12	Some critics argue that the poem's linking of the sectarian violence in the North to the ritual killings in Jutland offers an excuse to murderers. Do you agree with this point of view? Discuss in groups.
13	Here are three views of the poem. Discuss the extent to which each view corresponds to your own view of the poem. ■ The theme of the poem is religious pilgrimage ■ The poem is a meditation on violence in society ■ 'The Tollund Man' is a personal poem about public events
14	Does the analogy between the violence in the North and the ritual killings in ancient Jutland help you understand, in any way, the violence in the North during the Troubles? Explain your answer.

Mossbawn:
Two Poems in Dedication

for Mary Heaney

1 Sunlight

There was a sunlit absence.
The helmeted pump in the yard
heated its iron,
water honeyed

in the slung bucket   5
and the sun stood
like a griddle cooling
against the wall

of each long afternoon.
So, her hands scuffled   10
over the bakeboard,
the reddening stove

sent its plaque of heat
against her where she stood
in a floury apron   15
by the window.

Now she dusts the board
with a goose's wing,
now sits, broad-lapped,
with whitened nails   20

and measling shins:
here is a space
again, the scone rising
to the tick of two clocks.

And here is love   25
like a tinsmith's scoop
sunk past its gleam
in the meal-bin.

Seamus Heaney

Before you read

In pairs, discuss the images you would choose to suggest the security and warmth of home. Return to your discussion after you have read the poem.

Glossary

Title *Mossbawn*: Heaney's childhood family home
dedication *Mary*: the poet's aunt, unmarried sister of his father, Patrick; Mary lived with the family in Mossbawn

7	*griddle*: flat iron pan used for baking
21	*measling*: becoming red from the heat, like the rash from measles
25	*love*: one of the few occasions in Heaney's poetry when the word 'love' is used
28	*meal-bin*: a container for storing meal (flour); also used for animal feed

HIGHER LEVEL

> **Heaney on Mossbawn**
>
> 'Our farm was called Mossbawn. Moss, a Scots word probably carried to Ulster by the planters, and bawn, the name the English colonists gave to their fortified farmhouses … Yet … bán is the Gaelic word for white. So might not the thing mean the white moss, the moss of bog-cotton?'

Guidelines

'Sunlight' is the first of two poems under the collective title 'Mossbawn', which open the collection *North* (1975). The poem, set in the poet's childhood home, stands outside many of the poems in *North* which deal with the violence of the conflict in Northern Ireland. In 'Sunlight', Heaney paints a portrait of the farmyard and kitchen, with the poet's aunt as the central human figure.

Commentary

Lines 1–9

The first nine lines recreate a scene from the poet's childhood – the empty farmyard bathed in sunlight. The yard is transformed by the glow of the sun (and the poet's memory), so that the 'water honeyed / in the slung bucket'. The references to warmth – the iron of the pump heating up, the sun as griddle cooling off – prepares for the change of focus in the poem to the aunt baking in the kitchen.

Lines 10–16

The poet paints a warm, tender portrait of his aunt at work. The stove itself seems to respond to the aunt, sending out 'its plaque of heat', where she stands in a 'floury apron'.

Lines 17–21

As the description continues, the change in tense – 'Now she dusts … / now sits …' – places the aunt in a continuous present. The ordinary, domestic chore of baking is described with a painter's eye: the aunt 'dusts the board / with a goose's wing'; fingernails are whitened; shins redden from the heat. The image might be from a painting by Vermeer and has a timeless quality.

> **Heaney on his Aunt Mary 1**
>
> 'Mary had white hair and a fair rosy face; she stood still and straight while her hands did all the work at the bakeboard and the kitchen filled with the fragrance of the baking bread.'

Lines 22–28

The space named in the second-last stanza (line 22) is not only the space where the scones will rise, but the space where Heaney can pause and **celebrate the love shown by his aunt for his family**, a love **enacted every day in her domestic routine**. It is the **space that allows the final thought to grow and blossom**, as the poem opens out emotionally at the end:

> 'And here is love
> like a tinsmith's scoop
> sunk past its gleam
> in the meal-bin.'

Just as the scoop is hidden in the meal, so his aunt's love is **hidden but constant, as is the memory of her**, sunk in the poet's consciousness, but brought to light now in loving remembrance.

Seamus Heaney

A Constable Calls

Before you read

As a class, brainstorm the likely circumstances in which a local Garda might call to your house, and discuss the welcome he or she would receive.

His bicycle stood at the window-sill,
The rubber cowl of a mud-splasher
Skirting the front mudguard,
Its fat black handlegrips

Heating in sunlight, the 'spud' 5
Of the dynamo gleaming and cocked back,
The pedal treads hanging relieved
Of the boot of the law.

His cap was upside down
On the floor, next his chair. 10
The line of its pressure ran like a bevel
In his slightly sweating hair.

He had unstrapped
The heavy ledger, and my father
Was making tillage returns 15
In acres, roods, and perches.

Arithmetic and fear.
I sat staring at the polished holster
With its buttoned flap, the braid cord
Looped into the revolver butt. 20

'Any other root crops?
Mangolds? Marrowstems? Anything like that?'
'No.' But was there not a line
Of turnips where the seed ran out

In the potato field? I assumed 25
Small guilts and sat
Imagining the black hole in the barracks.
He stood up, shifted the baton-case

Further round on his belt,
Closed the domesday book, 30
Fitted his cap back with two hands,
And looked at me as he said goodbye.

A shadow bobbed in the window.
He was snapping the carrier spring
Over the ledger. His boot pushed off 35
And the bicycle ticked, ticked, ticked.

Glossary

Title: *Constable*: the constable is a member of the Royal Ulster Constabulary

8	*the boot of the law*: suggests that the law is administered in an oppressive way
11	*bevel*: a line or an edge left by the band of the constable's cap
25	*assumed*: took on, felt
30	*the domesday book*: in 1068 William I ordered a survey of the value and ownership of the land of England. The Domesday Book recorded the result of this survey. In the poem, the phrase is used to refer to the official record of crop returns, registered by the constable. The word 'Domesday' also refers to The Last Judgement, or any other day of reckoning

HIGHER LEVEL

Guidelines

'A Constable Calls' is the second poem in a sequence of six called 'Singing School'. These poems are autobiographical, describing key moments in the poet's life which helped define him as a poet and a citizen from the Catholic community, in a sectarian state. The poems in 'Singing School' concern **fear and power**. In 'A Constable Calls' Heaney conveys the **sense of implicit threat** felt by the young boy in the official visit of the constable. The poem shows the alienation of the Catholic, nationalist community from the agents of the state.

Royal Ulster Constabulary (RUC)

From the beginning of the Northern Ireland State in the 1920s until the establishment of the Police Service of Northern Ireland in 2001, the RUC was the police force in Northern Ireland. The RUC had a predominantly Protestant membership and was seen as pro-loyalist. Unlike the Gardai, the members of the RUC were armed. When the civil rights movement started in the North in the late 1960s, the RUC used excessive force in breaking up marches.

Commentary

Lines 1–8
The poem opens with a description of the constable's bicycle, leaning outside against a window-sill. In **precise language**, the individual parts of the bike are described. The choice of words suggests that the observer is not simply recording what he sees but is responding in a negative way. The scene is from the past.

Lines 9–16
The speaker observes the scene indoors. The cap of the policeman was lying on the floor. It had left a mark in the constable's sweating hair. In the fourth stanza, the observer speaks directly about the constable ('He had unstrapped / The heavy ledger'). Lines 13–15 make clear what was happening and where it was happening. The observer's father was making tillage returns to the local constable. The constable had called to the family home.

Lines 17–20
The opening line of the fifth stanza sums up the situation in three words: 'Arithmetic and fear.' The poet looking back captures what the young boy felt at the time. Lines 18–20 describe the young boy's fixation with the constable's gun in its holster.

Lines 21–27
The curt exchange between the boy's father and the constable is recorded. The boy remembers something that his father has not reported: 'a line / Of turnips'. He feels guilty at this omission and imagines the jail, 'the black hole', where he or his father might be sent.

Heaney on being Catholic in Derry

'Even though there was no sectarian talk or prejudice at home, there was still an indignation at the political status quo. We knew and were given to know that Ulster wasn't meant for us, that the British connection was meant to displace us.'

Lines 28–36
The narrator describes the policeman preparing to leave. His actions are deliberate: he fixes his baton, closes the ledger and puts on his cap. The observer says that the constable looked at him as he said goodbye. The final four lines describe the policeman getting on his bicycle and cycling away. The final three words capture the tension and pressure of the entire visit.

Seamus Heaney

Themes

Power and control

In the poem, the father is obliged to give an account of his crop returns. This relatively minor matter is used by the poet to suggest the many ways in which the nationalist community was called to account by a police force which they **regarded as oppressive**. In 'Sunlight', the aunt's presence evoked warmth and security, but here the **constable's presence is enough to cause fear, doubt and guilt in the young Heaney**.

The constable would have been a neighbour of the Heaneys, but there is no sense of this visit having a social dimension. The constable is not offered tea or a drink, although he is sweating. There are no pleasantries. **The interaction takes the form of an interrogation**, with a minimum exchange of words. The only words spoken by the constable are a series of questions. The only word spoken by the boy's father is the monosyllabic 'No'.

> **Heaney on his parents' attitude to sectarianism**
>
> 'My mother … had a critical, disaffected attitude, but my father tended to sail through many of those aggravations as if he didn't notice.'

Menace

The young boy, the narrator, is fascinated by the constable's gun. His fascination turns to dread when his father fails to mention a line of turnips, and the boy, feeling like an accessory to a crime, pictures a fearful place of punishment 'in the barracks'. Even as the policeman cycles away, the sounds of the bicycle, as it 'ticked, ticked, ticked', carry menace – the menace of an explosive timing-device. This is in **high contrast with 'Sunlight'**, where the ticking of the clocks, as the aunt waits for the scones to rise, **creates a space for love**.

HIGHER LEVEL

> **Heaney on being an Ulster Catholic**
>
> 'When I began to write in 1962 … I was a graduate with a job, a self-respecting adult of sorts, but I was still subject to the … Northern Ireland reminders that I'd better mind my Fenian manners. The B-Special Constabulary were on the roads at night. The anti-Catholic speeches were still being delivered by Unionist leaders on the Twelfth of July.'

Language and imagery

The poem works by way of detailed descriptions. The bicycle of the constable is first described, in the opening stanzas, in precise, cold language: 'rubber cowl of a mud-splasher / … fat black handlegrips'. The elements of the bicycle are associated, by **clever word play**, with the character of the constable and with the power of the police to arrest and use force. The phrase 'handlegrips' suggests handcuffs, and the gleaming 'cocked back' dynamo brings to mind a gun ready to fire. The phrase 'the boot of the law', when read in the context of 1969 and the violence done on the civil rights marchers by a Protestant constabulary, gains an **emotional force**. When the focus of the poem switches indoors, the constable remains **an impersonal, indistinct presence**. The parts of his uniform are described so that **the man, like his bicycle, seems composed of separate, inanimate pieces**.

The **harsh 'ck' sounds** and the **clipped 't' and 'd' sounds** in the first two stanzas, which are picked up in the final stanza, contribute to the cold, impersonal nature of the descriptions. Heaney uses **plosive 'p' and 'b' sounds** and alliteration to create a sense of heaviness and threat. While the descriptions might be impersonal, they are not objective. They convey the attitude of the observer to the constable as much as they convey a sense of the constable or his position in the community.

The image in the final line, the ticking of the bike as the constable cycles away, with its repetition and the harsh 'ck' sounds, bring the poem to a **tense close** that suggests an impending explosion.

Form of the poem

The poem is written in four-line stanzas and composed in **short, concise phrases** such as 'the boot of the law'. The **short lines help to build the tension** in the poem. There is no regular rhyming scheme in the stanzas and this creates an impression of **control without harmony**, which matches the theme of the poem. The poem has a short-story quality, the relationship between two communities dramatised in one small incident.

SNAPSHOT

- A snapshot from the poet's autobiography
- Themes of fear and power
- Personal memory that speaks of the experience of a whole community
- Constable intrudes into the private world of the family
- Constable described in terms of his uniform and equipment
- Descriptions are cold and impersonal
- Harsh sounds
- Feelings of guilt, alarm and dread
- Ominous last line

Seamus Heaney

Exam-Style Questions

Understanding the poem

1. How do you imagine the young boy felt when the constable arrived at the house?
2. On the evidence of the poem, what kind of man do you imagine the constable to have been?
3. What kind of welcome did the constable receive from the narrator's family?
4. 'I sat staring at his polished holster.'
   What does this tell us about the boy?
5. What was the purpose of the constable's call?
6. What caused the young boy to feel guilty?

Thinking about the poem

1. Select two words or phrases from the first two stanzas of the poem that are suggestive of threatening violence. Explain your choice.
2. Does the poem allow the reader room to sympathise with the constable or is he definitely the 'baddie' in the story? Explain your answer.
3. 'And the bicycle ticked, ticked, ticked.'
   What is the effect of the last three words of the poem, particularly in the context of Northern Ireland?
4. Here are three statements about the poem. Which one is closest to your reading of the poem? In groups or pairs, discuss your choice.
   - The poem is about a small boy's fear
   - The poem is about the Troubles in Northern Ireland
   - The poem is about ordinary people's fear of the law

Imagining

1. Turn the events described in the poem into a short story, written as first-person narrative, in the voice of the young boy.
2. You are asked to make a film of the poem. Describe the atmosphere you would create and the images, music and sounds you would use to create it.
3. You are the young boy in the poem. It is twenty years later and you are studying to become a journalist. You go to the home of the retired constable and interview him about this incident. Write the script of the interview.

HIGHER LEVEL

Before you read

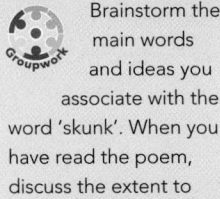 Brainstorm the main words and ideas you associate with the word 'skunk'. When you have read the poem, discuss the extent to which any of these associations are present in 'The Skunk'.

The Skunk

Up, black, striped and damasked like the chasuble
At a funeral mass, the skunk's tail
Paraded the skunk. Night after night
I expected her like a visitor.

The refrigerator whinnied into silence.　　　　　　　5
My desk light softened beyond the verandah.
Small oranges loomed in the orange tree.
I began to be tense as a voyeur.

After eleven years I was composing
Love-letters again, broaching the word 'wife'　　　　10
Like a stored cask, as if its slender vowel
Had mutated into the night earth and air

Of California. The beautiful, useless
Tang of eucalyptus spelt your absence.
The aftermath of a mouthful of wine　　　　　　　　15
Was like inhaling you off a cold pillow.

And there she was, the intent and glamorous,
Ordinary, mysterious skunk,
Mythologized, demythologized,
Snuffing the boards five feet beyond me.　　　　　　20

It all came back to me last night, stirred
By the sootfall of your things at bedtime,
Your head-down, tail-up hunt in a bottom drawer
For the black plunge-line nightdress.

Glossary

1	*damasked*: damask is a reversible fabric with a design woven into it. Like damask, the skunk's tail is reversible – it has markings on the underside
1	*chasuble*: the outer vestment worn by a priest when saying mass, usually with a decorative design in a different colour from that of the chasuble itself. At a funeral mass, the chasuble is white with black markings
8	*voyeur*: a person who derives pleasure or excitement from watching, often secretly, others undress or engage in sexual acts
10	*broaching*: opening, as in opening a bottle of wine
11	*stored cask*: suggests a valuable wine or spirit kept in storage
12	*mutated*: changed
19	*Mythologized*: turned into a myth
22	*sootfall*: soundless fall

Seamus Heaney

Guidelines

'The Skunk' comes from Seamus Heaney's fifth collection of poetry, *Field Work* (1979). This collection has a number of poems which deal in personal terms with the Troubles, remembering friends and family of Heaney who were murdered in Northern Ireland. *Field Work* also contains a number of poems in which Seamus Heaney speaks in a natural, conversational voice about himself and his wife. 'The Skunk' is one of these marriage poems.

Commentary

'The Skunk' is a poem about the poet's love for his wife. It is a poem about the **daily habit of love**, a **playful poem** that combines irony and humour with genuine affection and love. It is also a poem that could not have been written without a **sense of trust** in the love between husband and wife.

> **Heaney on Marie 1**
>
> 'I met her in October 1962 and the next month I published what I consider to be the first poem where I was in earnest … Everything happened quickly and at the same time – the development of our relationship, the entry into poetry, the marriage itself. Inside three years. One excitement quickening the other.'

Stanza 1
The poem begins with an old memory from when the poet lived in California, opening with the startling image of a skunk's tail held high. The tail is compared to the black and white vestments worn by a priest at a funeral mass. Night after night the poet expected the skunk to appear in the garden 'like a visitor'.

Stanza 2
In the house each evening the speaker waits for his visitor. It is a quiet house; the noise of the refrigerator is compared to the neighing of a horse. The light from the desk casts a soft light beyond the verandah. There are small oranges on the orange tree in the garden. In this quiet atmosphere the poet describes himself as feeling as 'tense as a voyeur'. It is a **humorous, if risky, comparison**, linking the coming of the skunk to erotic feelings in the speaker.

> **Heaney on Marie 2**
>
> 'Marie has always been a buoyant spirit. There's a terrific readiness about her. She has this great combination of spontaneity and staying power.'

Stanzas 3 and 4
There is a change of focus: the speaker tells us he had been writing love letters to his wife for the first time in eleven years. Suddenly the word 'wife' – with 'its slender vowel' – takes on a special meaning. It seems as if everything in his surroundings – the night air, the fragrant smell of the eucalyptus trees, the taste of wine – is filled with **her invisible presence**.

Stanza 5
The poet brings us back to the speaker waiting for the skunk to visit; and she is suddenly there, not five feet from the speaker. Adjectives such as 'intent and glamorous, / Ordinary, mysterious' indicate an association for the poet with his feelings for his wife and their marriage.

Stanza 6
The speaker explains to his wife that the memory of the skunk came back to him as she undressed and searched in a bottom drawer for her black nightdress. The erotic charge of the moment brings back the memory of the love and desire he felt for her when he was separated from her during his time in California.

Themes and imagery

Married love

This is a poem about a husband's love for his wife and the erotic love at the heart of marriage.

> **Heaney on showing poems to Marie**
>
> 'Marie had a good sense of what rang true. No matter what she'd actually say, I always knew what she felt … I don't think there was any nervousness [in showing Marie 'The Skunk']. There was a playful element in the poem, after all, and a definite serious engagement. It was about a skunk … but it was also about the transatlantic cable that connected us.'

The theme of the poem is **absence** and the **effect of absence upon the lover**, a sophisticated version of the theme 'absence makes the heart grow fonder'. The distance between the poet and his wife serves to bring her more sharply into his focus. She fills his consciousness as, away from home, he writes her love letters. **Through her absence, the poet rediscovers and reclaims her**, realising how much he prizes and values her. **To say the word 'wife' is to release her presence into the air around him.** The bedroom scene, in which the poet's wife adopts a 'head-down, tail-up' posture as she searches for her nightdress, becomes a symbol for the nature of erotic intimacy in marriage. It is **an intimacy that is affectionate, sometimes comic, and stirring**.

The poem conveys **the sacred mystery at the heart of an ordinary marriage**. Through the image of priestly vestments, in the first stanza, and in the magical effect of saying the word 'wife', described in stanzas three and four, he causes her spirit to be present in the atmosphere and the objects around him. There is an echo of the sacramental in the lines:

> 'The aftermath of a mouthful of wine
> Was like inhaling you off a cold pillow.'

The imagery clearly draws on Heaney's Catholic upbringing and **likens the mystery of marriage to the mysteries of the Eucharist**. The black nightdress of the final line echoing the chasuble in the first, represents a vesting in preparation for the mysteries of married love.

Form and language

The poem is written in unrhymed four-line stanzas. Heaney uses lines of different length and enjambment (run-on lines) to create a conversational tone. The language is **carefully considered and phrased**, as in the line, 'Tang of eucalyptus spelt your absence'. The line is perfectly balanced; the long vowels and the clusters of consonants ('ta_ng_', 'eucaly_pt_us', 'spe_lt_') create a **sensuous** atmosphere. The effect is to create a poem that is **warm and affectionate in tone and rhythm**, but is **simultaneously highly wrought and carefully fashioned**. In contrast to the tension and pressure conveyed in the short lines of 'A Constable Calls', the long lines of this poem reflect an attitude that is **relaxed and playful**.

The **metaphors** in 'The Skunk' **are enriched by many brilliant choices of words and phrases**. 'Sootfall' (line 22) is a notable example. The word captures the gentle noise of the clothes falling to the ground. It also picks up on the colour black which features throughout the poem. For the critic Neil Corcoran, 'sootfall' also contains the idea that the falling clothes are worn and soiled by everyday living. The speaker is 'stirred' (line 21) by the fall of these clothes, a stirring that is all the more authentic for being caused by such a real undressing. The

Seamus Heaney

phrase 'a stored cask' (line 11) is also noteworthy. It suggests something valued, precious and mature. For the poet, his relationship with his wife contains these qualities.

> **Heaney on advice from a friend**
>
> 'In his wisdom, as poet and psychologist, he advised us that all would be well provided we never let six weeks pass without seeing each other. And we never did.'

Questions

1	What causes the poet to think about the skunk that used to visit his garden in California?
2	What words and phrases in the poem establish the setting as being outside Ireland?
3	a) In the first stanza, the skunk's tail is compared to the priest's chasuble at a funeral. Explain the comparison. b) Identify other unusual images in the poem. What, in your view, is the effect of these images?
4	In the second stanza, what is the effect of the speaker describing himself as 'tense as a voyeur'?
5	The poet/speaker recollects a period of absence from his wife. How does the poem suggest that, despite this absence, the poet was aware and mindful of her?
6	a) In what way, do you think, might the word 'wife' be like a 'stored cask'? b) Do you think Seamus Heaney gives the word 'wife' a romantic and erotic charge? Explain your answer.
7	In the poem, the poet's wife is identified with the skunk. a) What, in your view, are the risks involved in this identification? b) Do you think the poem overcomes them? c) The critic Christopher Ricks suggests that the comparison of his wife to a skunk reveals Heaney's trust in the love between them. Would you agree? Explain your answer.
8	The skunk is described as 'glamorous'. Do you think this is an apt description? Is there any other animal you would associate with glamour? Explain your answer.
9	Comment on the use of 'sootfall' in the final stanza.
10	Read back over the poem. Identify the images that have a religious or magical association. Bearing these in mind, what, in your view, is the poem saying about the nature of marriage?
11	'"The Skunk" is a poem that is full of humour, affection and love.' Give your view of this assessment of the poem.
12	Imagine how the poet's wife felt when she read 'The Skunk'. Imagine then the poet's children reading the poem. Discuss, in pairs or groups.
13	Write a short piece of prose or poetry in which you describe the quiet of a house at night. You can use stanza two of this poem as your inspiration.

HIGHER LEVEL

Before you read

This poem is about an object which has no monetary value but is priceless to the poet. As a class, discuss family keepsakes (photos, objects) which are much loved and treasured.

The Harvest Bow

As you plaited the harvest bow
You implicated the mellowed silence in you
In wheat that does not rust
But brightens as it tightens twist by twist
Into a knowable corona,   5
A throwaway love-knot of straw.

Hands that aged round ashplants and cane sticks
And lapped the spurs on a lifetime of game cocks
Harked to their gift and worked with fine intent
Until your fingers moved somnambulant: 10
I tell and finger it like braille,
Gleaning the unsaid off the palpable,

And if I spy into its golden loops
I see us walk between the railway slopes
Into an evening of long grass and midges,   15
Blue smoke straight up, old beds and ploughs in hedges,
An auction notice on an outhouse wall—
You with a harvest bow in your lapel,

Me with the fishing rod, already homesick
For the big lift of these evenings, as your stick   20
Whacking the tips off weeds and bushes
Beats out of time, and beats, but flushes
Nothing: that original townland
Still tongue-tied in the straw tied by your hand.

The end of art is peace   25
Could be the motto of this frail device
That I have pinned up on our deal dresser—
Like a drawn snare
Slipped lately by the spirit of the corn
Yet burnished by its passage, and still warm.   30

Seamus Heaney

Glossary

1	*harvest bow*: a bow made from straw worn in one's lapel at the fair to celebrate the end of the harvest	
2	*implicated*: in this poem, 'implicated' has the meaning of intertwined or woven	
2	*mellowed*: calm and relaxed	
5	*corona*: a circle of light like that which surrounds the sun or the moon	
6	*love-knot*: originally, harvest bows were love tokens	
8	*lapped*: wrapped. The spurs are held in place by cloth that is wrapped around the legs of the birds	
8	*spurs*: spikes on the back of the legs of cock birds	
8	*game cocks*: a bird that is bred and trained for cock fighting	
9	*Harked*: paid attention to	
10	*somnambulant*: as in a state of sleep-walking	
12	*Gleaning*: gathering or understanding	
12	*palpable*: that which can be touched or felt by hand	
17	*An auction notice on an outhouse wall*: the notice announces the auction of Mossbawn, the family home where Heaney spent his childhood	
20	*the big lift*: the lift to the spirit; the emotional life	
22	*flushes*: rouses or startles (game birds) so that they fly up from the ground	
25	*The end of art is peace*: a line from a poem by Coventry Patmore, popular Victorian poet	
28	*a drawn snare*: a trap that has been activated	
29	*Slipped*: slipped free from; escaped	
29	*spirit of the corn*: the spirit that makes the corn germinate each year	

Guidelines

The poem is addressed to the poet's father and comes from the collection *Field Work* (1979). In 1972, at the height of the troubles, Heaney moved to Glanmore in Co. Wicklow. This was the year of Bloody Sunday, when thirteen marchers were shot dead by British soldiers at a civil rights march in Derry. In 'The Harvest Bow' there is a sense of **the poet looking to the example of his father to draw inspiration and hope**. Another Heaney poem, 'Digging', demonstrates how his father provides the poet with an example that he wishes to follow.

Commentary

Lines 1–10

The poem begins with the poet remembering his father making the harvest bow. In the son's eyes the father wove his 'mellowed' silence into this 'throwaway love-knot of straw'. The poet recalls the hands that made the harvest bow: the hands of a cattle dealer who carried a stick or a cane; the hands of an unsentimental countryman who enjoyed cock fighting. Now they work 'with a fine intent', weaving the stalks of wheat into a little bow.

Lines 11–24

The poem moves to the present, with the poet holding the harvest bow and 'reading' it like a blind person might read braille. As the poet looks through the loops of the bow, he remembers an evening from childhood, walking with his father, who wore a harvest bow and carried a stick. The walk took place as the family farm was about to be sold. The poet suggests that his father's feeling about the original family home were **tied into the harvest bow rather than spoken aloud** (lines 23–24).

> **Moving house**
>
> **The notice of auction (line 17) is a reminder of the move made by the Heaneys from Mossbawn, the family home, after the death of the poet's younger brother Christopher, an event commemorated in 'Mid-Term Break'. The sale of the house marked the end of the poet's childhood. As the auction draws near the young Heaney already feels 'homesick' (line 19).**

Lines 25–30
In the final stanza the poet considers the significance of the bow, now placed on the dresser in his family home. The description of it as 'still warm' brings to mind the treasured domestic atmosphere of 'Mossbawn 1. Sunlight'.

Themes and symbols

Love for his father
The poem is one of the many that Seamus Heaney wrote about his father. The portrait of Patrick Heaney presented in the poem is among the most affectionate to be found in Heaney's writing. The poet's father emerges as a man who is strong, robust and unsentimental. He is a man who has 'lapped the spurs on a lifetime of game cocks', or strode with his stick 'Whacking the tips off weeds and bushes'; a man 'tongue-tied', who expressed himself in action; a man who mellowed in silence and whose hands, as he plaited the straw, were his means of self-expression.

Exemplar
As with many of the craftsmen celebrated in Heaney's poetry, the father in 'The Harvest Bow' becomes an exemplar, **a model, teaching the poet how an artist or craftsman can express himself through his work**. The father's hands, harkening 'to their gift', worked with a 'fine intent' (line 9). There is an understanding between the father and the son, not reached through words but expressed by the harvest bow, which Heaney fingers and reads 'like braille, / Gleaning the unsaid off the palpable'. Thus the poet translates what he has read in the harvest bow into words, which he, in his turn, **fashions or plaits and weaves into a poem**.

The harvest bow is a symbol of the love between the father and the son. It is a **'love-knot'** which joins them. Holding it in his hands, and looking through 'its golden loops', the poet sees the evenings he shared with his father – the boy walking towards his future ('already homesick / For the big lift of these evenings'), the father walking by the remnants of his past. The bow celebrates the gathering in of the harvest, and the **gathering in of the father–son relationship**. The harvest bow may be lifeless, 'the spirit of the corn' having slipped away from it, but it retains its warmth and is enriched by the spirit of the man who gave it life.

Spirit of the corn
The harvest bow is an emblem of agricultural labour and love of the land. The spirit of the corn is not only the spirit of bountiful nature, but it is also the patient spirit of agriculture – of the human being working the soil. As such, the harvest bow represents a strength of continuity and inheritance that is free of the pressures of tribal loyalties and communal strife. It is a symbol of rural rituals tied to the land.

Art and peace
The motto which opens the final stanza, 'The end of art is peace', expresses, among other things, the peace and harmony between father and son, arrived at through their respective arts. The motto also suggests that the aim or purpose of art is the creation of peace, though the double meaning can be read to suggest that peace, as in peace of mind, may bring artistic inspiration to an end. The motto has wider and larger significance when read in the context of the political situation in Northern Ireland.

Seamus Heaney

Form of the poem

The poem itself represents a poetic plaiting and weaving. It is a carefully structured and textured creation in six-line stanzas of near-rhyming couplets ('rust'/'twist', 'loops'/'slopes', 'peace'/'device'), with **internal rhymes and repetitions** – 'brightens as it tightens twist by twist'. The son follows his father's example by **weaving together sound and images** into a tightly woven creation. At the same time, the **long lines and enjambment create a conversational effect**.

> **Heaney on 'The Harvest Bow'**
> 'I remember discovering a shape and then realising that it could be built on, and relishing the whole gradual, cumulative effect. But the texture of 'The Harvest Bow' is richer than many of the other poems in *Field Work*.'

Questions

1. Explain as clearly as you can what a harvest bow is.

2. a) From the evidence of the poem, what kind of man was Heaney's father?
   b) What parts of his personality are represented by the plaiting of the harvest bow?

3. a) What, in your view, are the implications of the phrase, 'mellowed silence' (line 2)?
   b) What does the phrase suggest to you about the relationship between father and son?

4. 'Gleaning the unsaid of the palpable.' What does the poet glean from touching the harvest bow? Do you think family heirlooms or keepsakes can tell us about the person who owned or made them? Explain your answer.

5. What, do you think, do the images of stanzas 3 and 4 say about the closeness and distances between father and son? Explain your answer.

6. Write a note on the phrase 'the spirit of the corn' and its relationship to the themes of the poem.

7. *'The end of art is peace.'* Discuss, in pairs or groups, the significance of this motto for:
   - The father
   - The relationship between father and son
   - The poet
   - The North

8. Explain your understanding of the image of the drawn snare which concludes the poem.

9. Like the harvest bow, which it celebrates, the poem is a tightly made structure. Describe the stanza form and the variety of rhyme used in the poem.

10. 'The harvest bow, the "frail device" woven by the father, becomes a rich and complex symbol within the poem.' Discuss this statement.

11. 'I was already homesick for the big lift of those evenings …'
    Writing in the voice of the poet (or in your own voice) write a poem or prose piece inspired by the above line.

HIGHER LEVEL

Before you read

 Try to find some atmospheric images based on the idea of 'under ground'. Discuss all the ideas, real and imaginary, associated with 'underground'.

The Underground

There we were in the vaulted tunnel running,
You in your going-away coat speeding ahead
And me, me then like a fleet god gaining
Upon you before you turned to a reed

Or some new white flower japped with crimson   5
As the coat flapped wild and button after button
Sprang off and fell in a trail
Between the Underground and the Albert Hall.

Honeymooning, moonlighting, late for the Proms,
Our echoes die in that corridor and now   10
I come as Hansel came on the moonlit stones
Retracing the path back, lifting the buttons

To end up in a draughty lamplit station
After the trains have gone, the wet track
Bared and tensed as I am, all attention   15
For your step following and damned if I look back.

Glossary

Title	*The Underground*: the London train system (the Tube) which operates through tunnels under the ground
2	*going-away coat*: the coat worn by a bride when leaving on her honeymoon
3–4	*… a fleet god gaining / Upon you before you turned to a reed*: an allusion to the story of Pan and Syrinx
5	*japped*: an Ulster Scots word meaning spattered or splashed
8	*Albert Hall*: the Royal Albert Hall, in the fashionable South Kensington area of London; one of the most famous concert venues in the world
9	*honeymooning*: a honeymoon is, traditionally, the holiday taken immediately after a wedding and is associated with harmony and happiness
9	*moonlighting*: doing something by the light of the moon. The word has a host of interesting associations related to dangerous, secret or illegal activities undertaken in the night
9	*the Proms*: a season of summer concerts of classical music held at the Albert Hall. 'Prom' is an abbreviated form of 'promenade', a walk or stroll associated with display and dressing up. Today a promenade concert is one in which some of the audience stand. On the last night of the Proms, many of the audience attend in fancy dress
11	*Hansel*: 'Hansel and Gretel' is one of the fairy tales collected by the Grimm brothers
15–16	*all attention / For your step following and damned if I look back*: the line echoes the story of Orpheus and Eurydice

Seamus Heaney

Guidelines

The poem comes from the 1984 collection *Station Island*, a book concerned with questions of guilt, and the public responsibility of the poet. While many of the poems in the collection are severe and self-admonitory, 'The Underground' is an exception – it is a **playful, celebratory love poem** recalling a dash to a concert in the Albert Hall during the Heaneys' honeymoon in London, and captures the energy and excitement of the newly-weds. Here is Heaney's own account of the poem:

London Underground

Speaking of 'District and Circle', a sequence of poems set in the London underground, Heaney talks of the dreamlike or nightmarish quality of travelling on the Tube – how 'the underground/underworld/otherworld parallels come into play'. He also refers to the 'awareness of the mythical dimensions of all such journeys underground, into the earth, into the dark.'

'… we're into this next book at a run, heading up and away. I liked it because it seemed to have both truth to life and truth to love.'

Commentary

Lines 1–8

The poem opens with the poet addressing his wife, recalling the dash they made from the vaulted tunnel of the London Underground to the Albert Hall. As they ran, the buttons of her going-away coat fell off. The poet compares their dash to a Greek legend.

Lines 9–10

The poet fills in the background: the couple were on their honeymoon and were late for the Proms concert. There is a change of tone in line 10: clearly time has passed and something has changed between the 'There' which opens the poem and the 'now' which concludes line ten.

Lines 11–16

The poet describes himself as Hansel retracing the path they made on their honeymoon. Now the journey ends in a draughty station after the trains have all gone. He is tense, listening for his wife's footsteps behind him. Is he too stubborn to look back for her, or is he realising that now they are married, he must trust that she is following him?

Pan and Syrinx

Pan was the Greek god of shepherds, fields and woods. With the hindquarters, legs and horns of a goat, he was associated with fertility and spring. The amorous Pan pursued the beautiful wood spirit Syrinx. Fleeing him, she called to her sisters, the spirits of the river, to save her, and they transformed her into a reed, just as Pan was about to seize her. From this reed, Pan made musical pipes upon which he played sad and sweet melodies.

Hansel and Gretel

Hansel and his sister Gretel were the children of a poor woodcutter. Facing starvation, the children overheard their stepmother urge their father to abandon them in the woods. The children gathered pebbles from the garden and laid a trail as they were brought deep into the woods. In the moonlight, they found the pebbles and retraced the path home.

Themes

A love poem

Although it is a love poem, Heaney does not use the word 'love' (he rarely does in his poetry). The poem ends unconventionally, with the male persona waiting for his beloved who is following behind but 'damned if I look back'. It is not a conventional end to a love poem but it may have the truth to life that Heaney refers to in his comments on the poem. The love described in the poem is composed of many elements: desire, pursuit, excitement, escape, change, silence, complication and perseverance.

> **Orpheus and Eurydice**
>
> Orpheus was a Greek musician and poet with the power to charm any creature, even moving stones to tears. He visited the underworld, land of the dead, to plead for the return of his wife, Eurydice. His music moved Hades and Persephone, rulers of the underworld, to allow Eurydice to return with him, on condition that Orpheus walk ahead of her and not look back until they reached the upper world. However, in his anxiety and love, on reaching the border of the two worlds Orpheus looked behind him, and Eurydice was lost to him forever.

On the run

Interestingly for a poem which describes a honeymoon, 'The Underground' is about emerging from the underground only to return to it, or somewhere very similar: 'a draughty lamplit station'. The honeymoon described in the poem is defined by **pursuit and flight**. The couple described in the poem seem constantly on the run, with neither the young husband nor young wife at rest or together. **One pursues the other or one leads and the other follows.** In this poem of flight and return there is an erotic tension in the first two stanzas as the speaker, 'like a fleet god' (line 3), pursues his beloved, and another kind of tension, possibly that between being a husband and a poet, in the last stanza where the 'I' of the poem strides ahead of his wife and refuses to look back. Does he fear he will lose her if he does, as Orpheus lost his wife? Is he obliged to trust that she is following, as he listens for her step? Certainly the distance between 'There' in line 1 and the 'now' in line 10 seems immense, and the placing of the word 'die' in line 10 seems to bring the honeymoon and the sense of togetherness to an abrupt stop.

Open and closed

As in 'Postscript' and 'The Pitchfork', 'The Underground' describes the persona of the poet caught between the excitement and energy of a moment and a more cautious and clenched way of encountering the world.

> **Heaney on Orpheus**
>
> 'But in the end, the "damned if I look back" line takes us well beyond the honeymoon. In this version of the story, Eurydice and much else gets saved by the sheer cussedness of the poet up ahead just keeping going.'

The honeymoon is **all rush and excitement**. The final stanza well beyond the honeymoon presents the persona of the poem as guarded and closed. The lesson of encountering the world off guard is one that the poet learns again and again, as in 'The Pitchfork' ('the opening hand') and 'Postscript'. In 'A Call', the **impulse to open the heart is suppressed** and the declaration of love never leaves the poet's lips.

Seamus Heaney

Imagery and classical allusions

The poem reminds us of one of Heaney's poetic methods: he takes a memory from ordinary life and overlays it with **classical allusions**, so that the story of the young honeymooners is **enlarged and takes on greater significance**. In this poem the young honeymooners' race through the London Underground is linked to the classical lovers Orpheus and Eurydice and their journey from the underworld, and also to the story of the God Pan and the nymph Syrinx. There is humour and ingenuity in Heaney's use of classical allusions. Orpheus, for example, was chief among poets and musicians and his journey to the Underworld in pursuit of his beloved wife is one of the most famous of all classical love stories. We can see the parallel with Heaney's poetic persona, full of love for his new wife, racing through the underground en route to a concert of classical music. The god Pan, renowned for his lusty passion and linked to fertility and spring, is often seen in the company of Eros, the god of love and romance.

Form and language

The poem is written in four four-line stanzas with a variable rhyming pattern. As with all of Heaney's poems, there are **all kinds of rhymes and half-rhymes echoing through the poem**. The **first two stanzas proceed at a break-neck pace**, with only two commas to slow the headlong rush. The energy of the poem and the excitement of the young couple caught in the series of actions is described with a present participle, 'running', 'speeding', 'gaining', 'honeymooning', 'moonlighting'. There is also a hint of erotic abandonment in the use of the word 'wild' and the image of the buttons not simply falling but springing from the flapping coat. The final rhyme of 'track' and 'back' provides a sense of ending and also catches something of the stubborn character of the poem's narrator.

SNAPSHOT

- Playful, celebratory poem
- Energy and excitement reflected in language of poem
- True to life in description of love
- Love as desire, pursuit, escape, silence, perseverance
- Ordinary moment described in terms of ancient tales and classical stories
- A love poem without the word 'love'
- Not a conventional ending
- Persona presented as attentive but stubborn

Exam-Style Questions

Understanding the poem

1	In a couple of sentences, tell the story of the poem.
2	Look at the images of flight and pursuit in the poem. Who leads and who follows in the course of the poem?
3	Look at the use of personal pronouns in the poem ('I', 'me', 'You', 'we', 'Our'). What do they tell you about the relationship between the poet and his wife?
4	How is the energy and excitement of the newly-weds captured in the first nine lines of the poem? Refer to language, imagery and sounds in your answer.
5	In a couple of sentences say what you think is the theme of the poem.
6	In the poem there are allusions to the story of Orpheus and Eurydice; Pan and Syrinx; and Hansel and Gretel. Did these add to your enjoyment of the poem? Explain your answer.
7	How would you characterise the relationship described in the last six lines of the poem? Explain your answer.
8	From your reading of the poem, which of the following statements best describe the personality of the speaker? ■ He is romantic ■ He is stubborn ■ He is determined Explain your choice.

Thinking about the poem

1	Select your favourite image, line, phrase or sequence in the poem and say why you have chosen it.
2	Discuss the possible meanings of the statement: 'Our echoes die in that corridor' (line 10).
3	Select one stanza from the poem. Comment on the music and rhythm of the stanza.
4	'The love described in the poem is characterised by energy and an erotic charge though not by harmony and togetherness.' Give your response to this assessment of the poem.

Imagining

1	Write a short (3–6 lines) poem in the voice of the 'You' of the poem, spoken in the 'draughty lamplit station'.
2	Rewrite the poem leaving out all the classical and fairy tale allusions. What is lost and gained in doing so?
3	Your class is compiling an anthology of love poems. In pairs, make a case each for including or omitting 'The Underground' from the selection, and debate the decision.

Seamus Heaney

The Pitchfork

Before you read

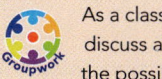

As a class, discuss all the possible uses and misuses of a pitchfork. Now read to see if Seamus Heaney goes beyond what you might expect to find in a poem with this title.

Of all implements, the pitchfork was the one
That came near to an imagined perfection:
When he tightened his raised hand and aimed high with it,
It felt like a javelin, accurate and light.

So whether he played the warrior or the athlete   5
Or worked in earnest in the chaff and sweat,
He loved its grain of tapering, dark-flecked ash
Grown satiny from its own natural polish.

Riveted steel, turned timber, burnish, grain,
Smoothness, straightness, roundness, length and sheen.   10
Sweat-cured, sharpened, balanced, tested, fitted.
The springiness, the clip and dart of it.

And then when he thought of probes that reached the farthest,
He would see the shaft of a pitchfork sailing past
Evenly, imperturbably through space,   15
Its prongs starlit and absolutely soundless –

But has learned at last to follow that simple lead
Past its own aim, out to an other side
Where perfection – or nearness to it – is imagined
Not in the aiming but the opening hand.   20

Glossary

Title	***Pitchfork:***	a long-handled fork with a number of steel prongs used for tossing hay or other loose material like dung. The word can also refer to a tuning fork. Heaney plays upon both meanings in the poem
6	***chaff:***	fine cut hay or straw used as animal feed or bedding. The word can also refer to the dry outer casing of grain which is also used as animal feed. Traditionally, the chaff was separated from the grain by tossing the grain into the air
12	***the clip and dart:***	the pitchfork has taken on the qualities of the actions performed with it – trimming or clipping the hay or tossing it swiftly
13	***probes:***	spacecrafts that travel through space to gather scientific information

HIGHER LEVEL 2021

HIGHER LEVEL

> **Heaney on saving hay**
>
> 'My heyday in the hay was when I was in my mid- to late-teens, home from college, enjoying the camaraderie of the neighbours, the freedom of the holiday. And it would always be happening in sunshine, because you couldn't work at hay unless you had good weather.'

Guidelines

'The Pitchfork' comes from the 1991 collection *Seeing Things*. It is a collection that has many poems which 'credit marvels'. It is also a collection that celebrates and mourns the poet's father, Patrick Heaney, who died in 1986. The poet worked on 'The Pitchfork' and a companion piece, 'The Ashplant', in the house where his father was dying. The opening poem of the collection is a translation of the *Aeneid*, Book VI, in which Aeneas asks permission to go to the underworld to meet his dead father.

Commentary

> **Heaney on handling a pitchfork**
>
> 'I loved handling the fork and the rake, their lightness and rightness in the hand, the perfect suitedness to the jobs they had to do. It meant that the work of turning a swathe, for example, was its own reward; angling the shaft and the tines so that the hay turned over like a woven fabric – that was an intrinsically artistic challenge. Tasty work, as they say. Using the pitchfork was like an instrument. So much so that when you clipped and trimmed the head of a ruck, the strike of the fork on the hay made it a kind of tuning fork.'

Stanzas 1 and 2
The poem opens with a statement. As often with Heaney, it is like we have come into the middle of a conversation. The speaker states that of all the farm implements the pitchfork was one which came closest to 'an imagined perfection'. When the 'he' of the poem held it above his head, it felt like a javelin. He tells us that 'he' loved the polished grain of the handle, whether he used it in play, as a warrior or athlete, or in work.

Stanza 3
The third stanza is a brilliant description of the physical qualities of the pitchfork and the feel of the implement in the hand.

Stanzas 4 and 5
The speaker tells us that when the 'he' of the poem thought about spacecraft exploring the farthest reaches, he saw in his mind's eye the pitchfork sailing silently through space, its prongs lit by the stars. And he has learned to follow the lead of the pitchfork, way out beyond 'its own aim', to where perfection is imagined not in aiming but in opening the hand and letting go.

Themes

Commemoration
The poem is one of commemoration, celebrating the poet's father through one of the farm implements associated with him. **The poem works by indirection**; there is no direct address to his father or mention of him in the poem. It is likely that the 'he' referred to on five occasions in the poem relates to the poet's younger self. Yet it is impossible to read the poem, and the collection from which it comes, without relating it to the poet's father. (Some critics believe the 'he' is the poet's father, and the poet commemorates him by depicting him as a perfect craftsman, a skilful warrior and javelin thrower, **like a hero from classical mythology**.)

The pitchfork, like other objects in Heaney's poetry – spade, ashplant, trowel, hammer, cane – speaks of **masculine strength and solidity**, and is associated with the men in his family as well as with friends and neighbours. Like the harvest bow, in the poem of the same name, the pitchfork is linked to his father, and **the open hand** of the last line of the poem **may well refer to the poet letting his father go**, letting his soul sail free in the afterworld. Equally it could refer to the father preparing to **let go his hold on life and set sail into the afterworld**.

> **'Digging'**
>
> **The first poem in Heaney's first collection,** *Death of a Naturalist*, **was a celebration of the skill of his father and grandfather in handling farm implements. 'By God, the old man could handle a spade. Just like his old man.'**

The art of poetry

As in many of Heaney's poems, 'The Pitchfork' is **a sophisticated meditation** on the art of poetry. With line 2, 'an imagined perfection', the poem is not saying that the pitchfork was perfect but it came closest to what the young poet imagined perfection to be. In its **suitedness to the task**, the pitchfork, the tuning fork, works as a **symbol for the kind of poetry Heaney wants to write**. It is **rooted in the earth** and in the ordinary things of a farm, yet it is **capable of flight** through the air, probing the empty spaces with its metal prongs.

The poem also reveals Heaney's attitude to real working objects and the ordinary lives of the people, like his father and grandfather, who used them. In mixing the description of ordinary farm work with fanciful visions, **the real sits side by side with the marvellous**. The pitchfork belongs to the real world of measurement, weight and balance, but it also belongs to the imagined world of visions, wonders and miracles, serving as **both farm implement and poetic tuning fork**. At the heart of the poem is the **desire to translate, to transform**.

Openness and generosity

The poem concludes with an admission that the 'he' of the poem has learned 'at last' to follow the lead of the pitchfork/spaceship as it sails 'Past its own aim, out to an other side' (line 18). This is a **lesson in acceptance and trust**, both in relation to life and the work of poetry. The concluding image of the 'opening hand' represents an openness to experience and **a willingness to follow the imagination wherever it leads**. In 'The Pitchfork', that willingness leads to a calm floating through space. In an interview about the poem, Heaney quoted the Polish poet, Czeslaw Milosz: 'Open the clenched fist of the past.' 'The Pitchfork' is a poem that looks forward with an open hand, while remaining rooted in the past.

Imagery and symbolism

Although the poem was written around the time of his father's death, 'The Pitchfork' has a playful quality. Heaney **takes a farm implement from his childhood and projects it into a dream world**, turning it into a rich and beautiful symbol. In Heaney's poem 'Crossings', the poet's father is associated with Hermes, the 'god of fair days, stone posts, roads and crossroads', and a guide to souls journeying to the otherworld. The poem concludes:

> '… Flow on, flow on
> The journey of the soul with its soul guide
> And the mysteries of dealing-men with sticks.'

The imagery in 'Crossings' resonates with the imagery of the pitchfork sailing soundlessly through space, travelling out beyond this world, mirroring his father's soul travelling in an imagined afterlife, a placeless heaven. In 'The Pitchfork' **Heaney improvises a vision of eternity from a farm implement** he and his father both loved and handled with skill, an image of eternity for a generation raised on *Star Trek*. This fantasy element lends surprise and delight to a poem of commemoration.

Form

The poem is written in four-line stanzas. There is a pleasing mixture of sensuousness and lightness to the language that mirrors the qualities of the pitchfork. Indeed, line 12 of the poem ('The springiness, the clip and dart of it') might well serve as a description of the poem itself, with its **consonance, precise sounds, repetitions and balanced vowels**.

The language which describes the physical quality of the pitchfork reveals not only Heaney's **power of observation**, but **a genius for precise, balanced language**. However, it is lines 14–16, which capture the weightless, soundless flight of the pitchfork, that reveal Heaney's genius in matching sound and rhythm to meaning:

> 'He would see the shaft of a pitchfork sailing past
> Evenly, imperturbably through space,
> Its prongs starlit and absolutely soundless –'

Doctrine of True Presence
This doctrine of Catholicism, where the bread is simply the bread but is also something other-worldly and wonderful – the body and blood of the Saviour – allows the marvellous to radiate from a real object.

Questions

1. Consider the ways in which a pitchfork might be used by an athlete, a warrior and a farmer. Do you think it is an interesting symbol, as developed in the poem?
2. What was your reaction to the image of the pitchfork sailing through space? Did you find it amusing, silly, thought-provoking, moving? Explain your answer.
3. Make a selection of three or four of your favourite words, phrases or images from the poem and say why you chose them.
4. The third stanza is a brilliant listing of the physical qualities of the pitchfork. Comment on the stanza in detail, noting the patterns of sound which give the stanza its spring and dart.
5. Who, in your opinion, is the 'he' referred to in the poem? Is it Heaney's younger self, his father, or a combination of both? Explain your answer.
6. 'In choosing to write about the pitchfork, Heaney is celebrating both his farming background and his father. Here, as elsewhere in his poetry, Heaney makes the ordinary into something extraordinary, visionary and poetic.' Give your response to this view of the poem.
7. In interviews Heaney referred to the final image in the poem, the opening hand, as representing a generous and unclenched attitude to life. Have a class discussion on the circumstances, personal, social, or political, that might facilitate or hinder the development of such an attitude.
8. Give your response to the afterlife as imagined by Heaney in the poem.
9. Do you like the fact that the meaning of the poem cannot be paraphrased in a simple way? Explain your answer.
10. Think of an object or keepsake associated with a loved one who has died and write a commemorative piece using the object as a starting point.

Seamus Heaney

Before you read

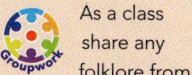
As a class share any folklore from your area — stories that contain the mysterious, magical or supernatural.

Lightenings

viii: 'The Annals Say'

The annals say: when the monks of Clonmacnoise
Were all at prayers inside the oratory
A ship appeared above them in the air.

The anchor dragged along behind so deep
It hooked itself into the altar rails   5
And then, as the big hull rocked to a standstill,

A crewman shinned and grappled down the rope
And struggled to release it. But in vain.
'This man can't bear our life here and will drown,'

The abbot said, 'unless we help him.' So   10
They did, the freed ship sailed, and the man climbed back
Out of the marvellous as he had known it.

Glossary

1	*annals*: The Annals of Clonmacnoise	
1	*Clonmacnoise*: the monastery of Clonmacnoise was one of the most important monasteries in early Christian Ireland. Founded in 548 by St Ciaran, it flourished until the sixteenth century and was renowned as a place of learning. Many manuscripts were written there	
2	*oratory*: a small chapel	
3	*A ship*: in Anglo-Saxon poetry, there are references to a ship that transports the souls of the dead from this world to heaven	

Guidelines

The poem comes from the collection *Seeing Things* (1991). It is one of a sequence of forty-eight, twelve-line poems. Most of these poems derive from dreams, visions, old stories or quotations. The sequence is divided into four sections, each with twelve poems. The section from which this poem comes is called 'Lightenings'. Lightenings are **moments of vision, insight or illumination when the actual flows into the visionary**.

Heaney on the title 'Lightenings'

'The title arrived by accident when I found a dictionary entry that gives it to mean a flaring of the spirit at the moment before death. And there were the attendant meanings of being unburdened and illuminated, all of which fitted what was going on as the first poems got written.'

The Annals of Clonmacnoise, in which the story of the ship appears, was originally written in Irish, but survives now only in an English translation dating from the seventeenth century. The annals were early quasi-historical records kept by monks in various monasteries, detailing notable events in a given year, such as the death of an important person – for example, the abbot of the monastery, eclipses of the sun or similar natural phenomena, as well as miracles and other marvellous happenings. The annalists recorded events without comment or any effort at interpretation. In a matter-of-fact way, the wonders of the world were listed alongside mundane happenings.

In some respects, the annals provide Heaney with an example to follow – an example of how the commonplace and the visionary might exist side by side. Here is Heaney's account of the story:

'The story was unforgettable: it's there in Kenneth Hurlstone Jackson's *A Celtic Miscellany*, but the version I have is a bit different because I misremembered some of the details. In the original, the boat's anchor "came right down to the floor of the church", whereas I have it hooking on to the altar rails – somehow it enters miraculously through the roof and the crewman shins down a rope into the sanctuary.'

'The story has the "there-you-are and where-are-you" of poetry. A boat in the air, its crewman on the ground, the abbot saying he will drown, the monks assisting him, the man climbing back, the boat sailing on. The narrative rises and sets, the magic casement opens for a moment only and the marvellous occurs in a sequence that sounds entirely like a matter of fact. The crewman is a successful Orpheus, one who goes down and comes back with the prize, which is probably what gives the whole episode its archetypal appeal.'

Commentary

Lines 1–3
The opening stanza tells us that the annals report that a ship appeared in the air above the monks as they prayed in their chapel.

Lines 4–12
The anchor of the ship dragged along behind and got stuck in the altar rails. As the ship came to a halt, a crewman climbed down the rope and tried to release the anchor. The abbot said to the monks that the man would drown unless they helped him. So the monks did help and the ship sailed on. The last two lines tell us that the man climbed back into the ship, out of a world that to him seemed marvellous.

Seamus Heaney

Themes and imagery

A lightness of being

Station Island (1984), the collection which preceded *Seeing Things*, was written during a turbulent period in the North, and conscience and civic responsibilities are recurrent themes. In comparison to *Station Island*, *Seeing Things* is characterised by a lightness of being, a freeing of the poet's spirit. While the poems in the collection deal with truth, they also **celebrate mysteries**. **'Lightenings, viii' brings together contrasting elements**: the life of prayer and the life of action; the religious and the secular; a world that is earth-bound and one that floats free. The contrasts are **captured in the images of weight, strain, anchorage, release, buoyancy and flight**. And amid these images of restraint and freedom, there is the desire of the imagination to loosen the binds of this world and float away.

Perspective

'Lightenings, viii' suggests that **the marvellous is ultimately a matter of perspective**. For the sailor, the monks at prayer represent the marvellous while, for them, it is the ship sailing through the air that is marvellous. The ship itself is symbolic. It hints towards Anglo-Saxon poetry that contains many references to a ship that brings the souls of the dead from this world to a world elsewhere.

> **Beowulf**
>
> Heaney's 1987 collection *The Haw Lantern* contains a translation from the Anglo-Saxon epic poem 'Beowulf', describing the placing of King Scyld in the ship of death and the launching of the ship on the sea. The journey appears as a magical adventure, whose ultimate destination is unclear and uncertain.

Tolerance and acceptance

In 'Lightenings, viii', the earth-bound experience of the monks and the flight of the sailors are linked. The ship cannot continue its journey without the assistance and permission of the monks. Read symbolically, the poem suggests that the high-flying imagination is dependent upon commonplace experience. Read in the light of the political situation in Northern Ireland, the abbot, another exemplary figure in Heaney's poetry, preaches a doctrine of tolerance and understanding which translates into an act of genuine friendship: '"This man can't bear our life here and will drown," / The abbot said, "unless we help him."' The crewman is saved by goodwill and commonsense. The crewman is a supernatural being, a spaceman, but the abbot acts out of a spirit of neighbourliness, with **an open hand**. And the poem itself, in offering the story of the ship, invites its readers to show the same openness as that demonstrated by the abbot.

Poetry as vehicle of harmony

Interestingly, Seamus Heaney speaks of 'Lightenings, viii' in the context of **the division and contradiction involved in being born in Northern Ireland**, and the **role of poetry as a vehicle of harmony – as a means of imagining a totally inclusive future**. He quotes with approval the historian Roy Foster statement that 'the notion that people can reconcile more than one cultural identity may have much to recommend it.' Heaney goes on to say:

> 'Whatever the possibilities of achieving political harmony at an institutional level, I wanted to affirm that within our individual selves we can reconcile two orders of knowledge which we might call the practical and the poetic; to affirm also that each form of knowledge redresses the other and that the frontier between them is there for the crossing. All of which is implicit in this short poem.'

HIGHER LEVEL

Form and language

The poem is written in four three-line stanzas (tercets). Heaney said this about the form of the poem:

'The 12-line form felt arbitrary but it seemed to get me places swiftly. So I went with it, a sort of music of the arbitrary that's unpredictable, and can still up and catch a glimpse of the subject out of the blue. There's a phrase I use, "make impulse one with wilfulness": the wilfulness is in the 12 lines, the impulse is in the freedom and shimmer and on-the-wingness.'

As befits the telling of a traditional tale, the **long lines and long vowel sounds create an unhurried, conversational feel to the poem**. Here is the **voice of the storyteller**, claiming an authority that goes beyond his personal authority. The tone of the poem is simple and matter-of-fact. The **marvellous is presented as the ordinary**.

Questions

1	Having read the poem, see if you can retell the story to a classmate, without hesitation.
2	Why, do you think, does Heaney begin the poem with 'The annals say …'?
3	Identify the contrasting elements brought together in the poem. How, in your view, do the contrasting elements relate to the theme of the poem?
4	In your view, what does the final line of the poem suggest about the nature of the marvellous? Explain your answer.
5	What, do you think, is the effect created by the long line employed in the poem?
6	a) In your opinion, what virtues does the abbot possess? b) What example does he offer to the poet and to the reader?
7	Writing of the poetry of Patrick Kavanagh, Heaney declared: 'When he writes about places now, they're the luminous spaces within his mind.' How, in your view, might this statement be applied to 'Lightenings, viii'?
8	Heaney said that the poem was 'a kind of image of poetry itself'. In your view, what image of poetry does it offer?
9	Although concerned with a visionary experience, examine how the verbs used by Heaney root the poem in the physical world.
10	Write your version of the story, adding any details which you think will enhance its qualities.
11	Discuss the extent to which the internet and social media encourage belief in the marvellous and the miraculous.

Seamus Heaney

Before you read

With a partner, discuss the best and worst kind of phone calls you might have to make.

A Call

'Hold on,' she said, 'I'll just run out and get him.
The weather here's so good, he took the chance
To do a bit of weeding.'
                    So I saw him
Down on his hands and knees beside the leek rig,   5
Touching, inspecting, separating one
Stalk from the other, gently pulling up
Everything not tapered, frail and leafless,
Pleased to feel each little weed-root break,
But rueful also . . .   10
                    Then found myself listening to
The amplified grave ticking of hall clocks
Where the phone lay unattended in a calm
Of mirror glass and sunstruck pendulums . . .

And found myself then thinking: if it were nowadays   15
This is how Death would summon Everyman.

Next thing he spoke and I nearly said I loved him.

Glossary

5	*rig*: ridge, the leeks are planted in ridges	
10	*rueful*: feeling sorrow or regret	
14	*pendulums*: the swinging levers that mark time in a clock	
16	*Everyman*: Everyman is the central character in a late 15th century English morality play of the same name. God sends Death to summon Everyman to come before Him to give an account of his life	

HIGHER LEVEL

Guidelines

'A Call' comes from *The Spirit Level* (1996), Heaney's first collection after he received the Nobel Prize for literature. It is a book published in the poet's middle age and is concerned with keeping going, with maintaining a level spirit. The title of the collection suggests, on the one hand, a poetry that is airy and free floating, and on the other, a questioning of that impulse – a measuring of the spirit; a taking-stock; a self-examination. The poems in *The Spirit Level* move back and forth between earth-bound realities and airiness. In this poem the lift to the spirit comes from hearing the voice of the beloved after the dreaded thought of the loved one's absence through death.

Commentary

Lines 1–5
The poem describes what was once a common experience in a time before mobile phones: a caller waits for a loved one to come to the phone. As he waits, he can hear the faint background noises of the house. The poem opens with the dramatic, 'Hold on' and we are immediately brought into the middle of the scene. The person answering the phone asks the caller to wait while she runs out to get 'him', most likely the poet's father. The line break after the word 'weeding' (line 3) signals a shift in the poem's perspective.

Lines 6–10
The narrator imagines the loved one on his knees, weeding. The three dots, or ellipsis, at line 10 indicate a shift in the poem as well as a sense of space and time.

Lines 11–14
The narrator is back in the present moment, listening to the hall clocks through the phone. Skilfully, the poet draws us in and we too become aware of the silence.

Lines 15–16
What fills the silence is the imagining of the phone call as Death's summons. In a brilliant shift, the phone call is re-imagined as a contemporary version of Death summoning Everyman. In *Everyman*, God sends Death to bring Everyman before Him to give an account of his life.

Final line
The final line of the poem – 'Next thing he spoke and I nearly said I loved him.' – is separated from the rest of the poem, and conveys the relief of the narrator.

Theme and imagery

Love
'A Call' is a poem about the **fragility of life and the love we have for those closest to us**. **The themes are developed through the imagery.** In describing his father, Heaney returns to the imagery of the first poem in his first collection, 'Digging', when the poet describes his father handling a spade with vigour. That physical strength has diminished. Now the gardener is described as 'touching', 'inspecting' and 'separating' the plants. The **use of the word 'frail'** and the **image of the root breaking** suggest that the gardener is as fragile as the

Seamus Heaney

weeds he pulls. The adjectives 'pleased' and 'rueful' capture the mixture of pleasure in the work and sorrow at causing a living thing to cease to be. The activity of weeding serves as a reminder to both gardener and narrator of the fragile hold we have on life, **the constant threat posed by mortality to the living roots of family**.

Death

The centre of the poem (lines 11–14) is **filled with absence and silence**. The placing of the word 'grave' casts a shadow on everything that follows. The narrator imagines the empty hall and a mirror which reflects nothing but sunlight. As he waits for his father to come, he is conscious of the empty space and his father's absence. The **ticking of the clocks** is a reminder of the time left to his father, and from here it is a short imaginative leap to *Everyman*. The reference to the medieval morality play evokes a world in which there were constant reminders of death and the judgement of God which would follow it. These death reminders feature not only in literature but in religious and secular art. Heaney's gift, here and elsewhere, is to take a thoroughly modern object, in this case a phone, and an equally modern activity – making a phone call – and relate them to the medieval or the ancient world, reminding us that **the modern world is not so distant, after all, from the world of the middle ages**. Like our medieval ancestors we are faced with the mystery of death and the human emotions which surround it.

Regret

The phone call made by the poet in the late twentieth century brings to mind the call that will soon summon his beloved father to death. The choice of the word 'thinking' (line 15) is interesting. It is more guarded, more cautious, more distancing than words like 'feeling' or 'fearing' that could also have been chosen. The last line ('Next thing he spoke and I nearly said I loved him.') has

> **Strong silent father**
>
> In his poem 'The Stone Verdict' from the 1987 collection *The Haw Lantern*, Heaney refers to his father's 'old disdain of sweet talk and excuses', and his 'lifetime's speechlessness'.

a double effect of allowing us to hear words that were not spoken. It shows the middle-aged narrator **shielding himself from feeling**. Here, as in other poems we are studying, the **poet notes his own tendency to be guarded**, though openness is celebrated in both 'Postscript' and 'The Pitchfork'. The line also succeeds in suggesting something of the character of the gardener. In other poems, Heaney has described his father as a silent man who was stoical in the face of life's ups and downs. The last line reveals the taciturnity the son has inherited from the father. There is a **gentle irony** in the fact that a **poem on the subject of a phone call is filled with silence**. In the poem 'Album', in Heaney's final collection, he regrets that he never embraced his father when his father was well.

Form and language

The poem is laid out in **irregular stanzas**, which **mirror the progression of thought**. As in a sonnet, the **connecting words** 'So', 'Then', 'And', and 'Next' mark this progression. **This organisation creates the dramatic tension and the relief felt in the final line.** The layout, the line length and the absence of rhyme give the poem **the appearance of a text from a play**, in keeping with the *Everyman* theme.

The language of the poem has an unfussy naturalness about it that masks the verbal patterns, the assonance and consonance, and the weight and balance in the phrasing. The language of lines 11–14, as the narrator listens to the clocks, emphasises the tension. The **careful choice and placing of words** with **long vowels** and **clear consonants slows everything down** so **we hold our breath with the narrator**, and **listen as he listens**. Elsewhere in the poem the sense of immediacy is created by the use of **present participles** (-ing verbs): weeding, touching, inspecting, separating, listening, thinking.

Exam-Style Questions

Understanding the poem

1. What thoughts go through the narrator's head as he waits for his father?
2. What picture do you form of the poet's father?
3. What does the last line of the poem suggest about the relationship between the two men?
4. What does the word 'here' in line 2 tell us about the back story of the poem?
5. How does the poet picture the gardener in lines 5–10?
6. What are the fears and the tension which govern the third stanza of the poem?
7. 'The final line is marked by feelings of relief and love.' Do you agree with this reading of the line? Explain your answer.

Thinking about the poem

1. As the poet waits for his father to come to the phone, he hears the ticking of 'hall clocks' (line 12). What does the ticking of the hall clocks symbolise in the context of the poem? Explain your answer.
2. 'The amplified grave ticking of hall clocks' (line 12). Comment on the effect of the word 'grave' and its position and importance in the poem.
3. Consider the word 'thinking' in line 15. Suggest why the poet chose to use it.
4. How is the movement of thought reflected in the shape of the poem on the page? Explain your answer.
5. Look at the final line of the poem: 'I nearly said I loved him.' In your view, is the poem stronger or weaker for having no direct declaration of love?

Imagining

1. Writing in the voice of the poet (or in your own voice) write a poem or prose piece inspired by the following line? 'Were I to have embraced you and told you I loved you, I would have said …'
2. 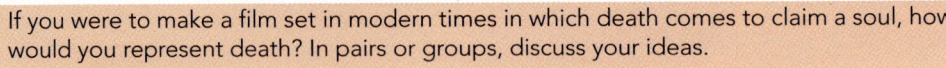 If you were to make a film set in modern times in which death comes to claim a soul, how would you represent death? In pairs or groups, discuss your ideas.

SNAPSHOT

- Dramatic opening
- Moves from action to remembering
- Further movement from remembering to thoughts of death
- Amplified silence at the centre of the poem
- Relief at sound of father's voice
- Language plain and unfussy
- Relates the modern phone call to the Medieval summons of Death
- Guarded feeling at end

Seamus Heaney

Before you read

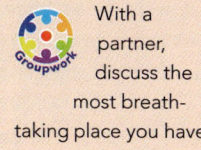

With a partner, discuss the most breath-taking place you have ever travelled to.

Postscript

And some time make the time to drive out west
Into County Clare, along the Flaggy Shore,
In September or October, when the wind
And the light are working off each other
So that the ocean on one side is wild   5
With foam and glitter, and inland among stones
The surface of a slate-grey lake is lit
By the earthed lightning of a flock of swans,
Their feathers roughed and ruffling, white on white,
Their fully grown headstrong-looking heads   10
Tucked or cresting or busy underwater.
Useless to think you'll park and capture it
More thoroughly. You are neither here nor there,
A hurry through which known and strange things pass
As big soft buffetings come at the car sideways   15
And catch the heart off guard and blow it open.

Glossary

Line	Term
Title	**Postscript**: something added as an afterthought
2	**the Flaggy Shore**: portion of the Atlantic shoreline near Kinvara County Clare, where the flat slabs of Burren limestone run right to the sea
8	**earthed lightning**: the white swans look like lightning which has struck the surface of the lake
11	**Tucked or cresting**: some of the swans have tucked in their heads so that they rest on their bodies; some have their necks extended, while others have their heads underwater
15	**buffetings**: gusts of wind which push or knock against the car

HIGHER LEVEL

The swans

The playwright Brian Friel and his wife, Anne, were close friends of Seamus and Marie Heaney. In visiting Mount Vernon, they were recalling another literary friendship, that between Lady Augusta Gregory and the poet W. B. Yeats. The swans mentioned in the poem bring to mind the swans in Yeats' poem 'The Wild Swans at Coole', written when he stayed with Lady Gregory in her home at Coole Park in South Galway, about fifteen miles from the Flaggy Shore.

Guidelines

'Postscript' is the final poem in the collection *The Spirit Level* (1996), published after twenty-five years of violence in the North had ended with a ceasefire in 1994. 'Postscript' reads like a small moment of happiness after the storm of public discord. It is also a poem written in middle age and shows **an awareness that life is constantly changing**. The poem was written after a trip made by Heaney and his wife, Marie, and the playwright Brian Friel and his wife, Anne. This is how Heaney describes it:

'[The poem] came from remembering a windy Saturday afternoon when Marie and I drove with Brian and Anne Friel along the south coast of Galway Bay. We had stopped to look at Mount Vernon, Lady Gregory's summer house – still there, facing the waters and the wild; then we drove on into this glorious exultation of air and sea and swans. There are some poems that … leave you with a sensation of having been visited, and this was one of them. It excited me, and yet publishing it in the *Irish Times* was, as much as anything else, a way of sending a holiday postcard – a PS of sorts – to the Friels.'

The poem is a record of the sightseeing drive as well as the rich afterthoughts of the drive. It captures the real journey and the sense of mystery and reward to which it gave rise. **Like many of Heaney's poems, it is not a poem that can be tied to a single meaning**. As Heaney says in the poem, 'Useless to think you'll park and capture it'.

Commentary

Lines 1–11
The first eleven lines, written as **one sentence**, consist of advice to 'make the time to drive out west / Into County Clare, along the Flaggy Shore, / In September or October'. This is the time of year, the speaker says, when the wind and the light create memorable effects on the ocean and the inland lake with its flock of swans.

Lines 12–16
The second sentence of the poem makes a simple statement: it is useless to think that you will park your car and capture the experience more thoroughly. The next and final sentence elaborates, in an elusive and mysterious way, on this impossibility, They suggest that **the experience is poised somewhere between the physical and the spiritual**, and has the power to touch the heart.

Themes of the poem

Pleasure of driving
Reading 'Postscript' is like overhearing the end of a conversation in which someone offers advice to a friend (or a tourist) to take a car journey along the west coast of Clare, and describes the beauty of the landscape, the changing light and the feelings it will inspire, especially in September or October. So one theme of the poem is the pleasure of going for a coastal drive in a place of great natural beauty in Irish weather. But there's more. It's about the **feelings caused in us by natural beauty and a changing landscape, the way these can move us and make us question our place in the world**. The poem suggests that it is impossible to capture or snatch from time the important and profound experiences of life – they hurry through us and we hurry through life.

Seamus Heaney

Flux

The journey described in the poem is a **dramatic** one, with the wild sea on one side and a lake on the other, on which a flock of swans appear like 'earthed lightning'. Like a painter, **the speaker appreciates the interplay between the light and the wind**, the way the wind whips up foam on the ocean and ruffles the feathers of the swans. Like everything else in this landscape the swans seem powerful, with 'fully grown headstrong-looking heads'. The world described in 'Postscript' is a world in flux, **caught between wild things and settled things, between things earthed and things in flight**. In the last line the speaker links the drive out west along the Flaggy Shore with a profound moment when the heart is surprised and open to experience. (Is there an implication that the speaker's heart is often guarded and not open to the world?) Some critics see the whole poem as **symbolising the way poetry brings you to places that are neither here nor there**, but exist between the physical world and the world of art.

Passing of time

Seamus Heaney wrote 'Postscript' in middle age. For some readers, the poem is about getting older. It is about realising that you are poised between earth and sky, that **the self is a hurry through which life passes**, and that there is no escape from the time and change. Paradoxically, the poem attempts to capture the immediate experience more thoroughly, and preserve the moment from the ravages of time.

Imagery and symbolism

Like all journey poems, 'Postscript' **can be read in a metaphorical way**, with the journey symbolising the journey through life and the journey of the poet. It focuses especially on a moment when we seem to be 'neither here nor there', but exist on the edge of things, just as the car travels in the space between the land and the sea and is blown off balance. Therefore, the observation that it is 'Useless to think you'll park and capture it' might well be read as the speaker's philosophy that **life cannot be controlled or commanded**, because **our hearts can always be blown open by the surprising and unexpected in our lives**. (This is reminiscent of the 'opening hand' at the end of 'The Pitchfork'.)

The swans – 'earthed lightning' – can be seen as symbolising poetry itself, an elemental force that connects earth and sky. The shore also has symbolic resonance, standing as the boundary between land and ocean, earth and heaven.

Heaney has spoken of imagining a phase in a writer's life which might involve 'solitary wandering at the edge of the mighty waters'. These remarks might lead you to read the poem in a new light.

Form

The poem has **a sonnet-like structure**. The opening eleven lines, written as one sentence, describe an experience and the last five lines, containing two sentences, reflect on it. The opening 'And' sets a conversational tone and the entire poem, written in blank verse, proceeds **as if we are overhearing a conversation**. However, the alliteration, consonance and internal rhymes create **a rich pattern of sounds**. As the poem moves to its emotional climax, the final thought is expressed in simple and powerful words: 'And catch the heart off guard and blow it open.' Indeed the whole poem is written with great confidence and assurance.

Questions

1	a) What advice does the speaker give to the would-be traveller? b) Does the speaker make a good job of promoting the West of Ireland and the wild Atlantic? Explain your answer.
2	'Useless to think you'll park and capture it' (line 12). Explain, as clearly as you can, what the 'it' is that is so hard to capture.
3	The poem is rich in description. Select two images which you think are particularly effective and explain your choice.
4	The first eleven lines of description are written as one sentence. What effect is created by this?
5	The poem reads like the advice of a wise man on how to lead your life. What is the wisdom that the speaker offers?
6	'A hurry through which known and strange things pass.' In the overall context of the poem, what, do you think, is the meaning of this line, and what does it say about the nature of the self?
7	'Catch the heart off guard.' a) What does this phrase tell us about the speaker of the poem? b) What are the things in life that have the power to catch the heart off guard?
8	The poem recalls a car trip through the Burren. Comment on the symbolism of the car journey and the landscape through which the travellers pass.
9	Which, if any, of the following statements are closest to your own view of the poem? ■ It is a poem about the power of nature to take our breath away ■ It is a poem about how life passes us by in an instant ■ It is a poem about being open to experience ■ It is a poem about the power of poetry to capture the mysteries of life
10	'The poem is written in ordinary language which seems to take flight and lifts off, just as the car seems to lift off as the wind catches it sideways.' Do you agree with this statement? Support your answer by reference to the poem.
11	Describe a place you know which has the power to lift the spirits and explain, in as much detail as you can, why this is so.
12	'Other than saying, "I was there" most photos and selfies fail to capture the special quality of important and profound moments in our lives. Even when we take a photo, the moment remains elusive.' In pairs or groups, give your response to this statement in the context of the poem.
13	'Postscript' is a memory poem, a postcard sent to friends after a memorable day driving along the coast of Clare. Write your own memory poem, recalling a special day in your life, associated with a particular place.

Seamus Heaney

Tate's Avenue

Not the brown and fawn car rug, that first one
Spread on sand by the sea but breathing land-breaths,
Its vestal folds unfolded, its comfort zone
Edged with a fringe of sepia-coloured wool tails.

Not the one scraggy with crusts and eggshells   5
And olive stones and cheese and salami rinds
Laid out by the torrents of the Guadalquivir
Where we got drunk before the corrida.

Instead, again, it's locked-park Sunday Belfast,
A walled back yard, the dust-bins high and silent   10
As a page is turned, a finger twirls warm hair
And nothing gives on the rug or the ground beneath it.

I lay at my length and felt the lumpy earth,
Keen-sensed more than ever through discomfort,
But never shifted off the plaid square once.   15
When we moved I had your measure and you had mine.

Glossary

Title	
Title	*Tate's Avenue:* a street in Belfast near the university
3	*vestal*: virginal or chaste. The word derives from Vesta, the Roman Goddess of the hearth and the household; the Vestal Virgins kept the sacred flame in the temple dedicated to the goddess
4	*sepia-coloured*: brown, like the colour in early photographs
7	*Guadalquivir*: one of the great rivers of Spain that flows through Andalusia. The cities of Seville and Córdoba are along the Guadalquivir
8	*corrida*: bullfight

HIGHER LEVEL

Guidelines

'Tate's Avenue' comes from the 2006 collection *District and Circle*. District and Circle are both lines on the London Underground system. Two trains on the Circle line were bombed in the attack of 7 July 2005, killing fourteen people. This attack and the attack on the World Trade Center in September 2001 influence some of the poetry in the book. Many of the poems are elegies or are set in the afterlife. Other poems circle back to the district of Heaney's childhood and cover the same ground explored in his first collection, *Death of a Naturalist*, published forty years earlier. 'Tate's Avenue' comes out of the poet's relationship with his wife, Marie, whom he met in Belfast in 1962 when both were completing their studies and starting out on their teaching careers. **The development of the relationship is traced through describing three rugs used by the young couple** that mark different stages in their life together.

> **On the Heaneys' early relationship**
>
> 'Marie and I had started to see each other just about the time of the folk revival. Marie was a very true singer so we moved about for a while with a crowd of other young teachers, scouring the parties.'

Commentary

Stanza 1
The first of the three rugs recalled in the poem is a 'brown and fawn car rug'. It is not the rug he wants to describe but it is associated with the early, chaste stage of their relationship. This rug is associated with car trips to the seaside.

Stanza 2
The 'scraggy' rug of the second stanza is an altogether different one. This rug is more used and more bohemian. The setting is Spain, and the references to food and wine suggest excitement and passion.

Stanza 3
And it is to Belfast that the poem turns in the third stanza. This is 'locked-park Sunday Belfast', a world away from the excitement of the time recalled in stanza 2. Although the two who occupy it are aware of each other, 'nothing gives on the rug'.

Stanza 4
In the final stanza the pronouns 'I' and 'You' appear for the first time. The narrator tells us he never shifted once, and when eventually they moved, they each had the other's measure.

Themes and imagery

> **Remembering Tate's Avenue**
>
> '"Death of a Naturalist" I wrote in one of the flats on a Sunday afternoon, after lying out in the sun with Marie and her flatmates at the back of the place they had in Tate's Avenue. The dead heat in their little back garden …'

Stages in a love relationship
The brown and fawn car rug of stanza 1 refers to an early stage in the relationship. Everything about the description suggests **care and caution**. The use of the adjective 'vestal' suggests the newness of the rug and the **chasteness** of the relationship. The rug does not breathe sea air but the tamer breaths of land. The

image of the comfort zone fringed with 'sepia-coloured wool tails' suggests neatness and order rather than the wildness of young passion. The impression is created of a **relationship that is formal, careful and virginal**.

A different stage is described in stanza 2. Here there is a sense of abandonment and intoxication: the intoxication of exotic food and drink, and the danger, passion and sexuality invoked by the Spanish setting ('the torrents of the Guadalquivir') and the reference to the *corrida*. The couple have moved from the safety and chastity of the first stanza to something more **wild, exciting and passionate**. The *corrida* represents a difference in the way life is lived and understood from the culture of Belfast.

> **Heaney on the corrida**
>
> '**The choreography in the ring and the surge and response of the crowd with the music going on and on just carried you away. And your focus stayed tight on the man and the bull. There was something hypnotic about the cloak-work, something even vaguely Satanic about that black crumpled-horn killing-cap on the matador's head …**'

The relationship described in stanzas 3 and 4 belongs to an earlier phase of the relationship than that described in stanza 2. The reference to 'locked-park Sunday Belfast' suggests a puritanical culture and an **atmosphere of suppression and inhibition**, far removed from the wild romanticism of Spain. A prison-like sense of curtailment and drabness is suggested in the description of the 'walled back yard, the dust-bins high and silent'. It is against this backdrop that the young couple play out a love game or test. The rug is spread on the hard unyielding ground and, intent on reading, nothing is given away by the reader to the one observing. The phrase 'nothing gives' suggests a battle of wills in which neither party is willing to concede or yield an inch. In erotic terms, the phrase suggests that there will be no yielding of the 'soft' feminine to the 'hard' masculine.

In the final stanza the pronouns 'I' and 'You' appear for the first time. Now the 'I' stretches out on the rug and feels 'the lumpy earth'. He is, we are told, 'keen-sensed'. Though uncomfortable he is not prepared to move, to give up his place on the rug beside her. Instead, he persists and stakes a claim to the territory. When eventually the pair move, nothing is said, but things are understood. No one will be taken for granted in this relationship and both will bring determination and stubbornness to it.

Grounded love

Interestingly, the final stanza of the poem is firmly rooted on 'the lumpy earth'. This is not love as a flight of fantasy, but something altogether more grounded and careful, **love as a measuring up, as an equal match**. If the rug itself symbolises love, then **love is a patch of ground to be marked out and defended**. The fact that nothing external happens and nothing is said seems to intensify the erotic frisson between the young lovers.

Belfast love

From the poem it is clear that love is influenced by where you come from and where you are. In the poem 'Tollund', which is set in Jutland in a landscape that looks like the familiar landscape of Co. Derry, the persona describes himself and his beloved standing 'footloose, at home beyond the tribe'. In Belfast, with its locked gates, there is no escape from the tribe. In Belfast, lovemaking becomes a version of 'no surrender' and 'not an inch'.

> **Heaney on a good poem**
>
> '**Each poem is an experiment … The image I have is from the old cartoons: Donald Duck or Mickey Mouse coming hell for leather to the edge of a cliff. Skidding to a stop but unable to halt, and shooting out over the edge. A good poem is the same, it goes that bit further and leaves you walking on air.**'

Form

'Tate's Avenue' is written using the same four four-line stanza that is found in 'The Underground'. The first three stanzas are composed of single sentences. The final stanza is composed of two sentences; the second forms the last line and gives the poem **a strong concluding statement**. Like so many of Heaney's poems, it is richly patterned with half-rhymes ('never'/'measure'), assonance ('spr_ea_d', 'br_ea_ths'), alliteration ('_l_ay', '_l_ength', '_l_umpy') and consonance ('drun_k_', 'loc_k_ed', 'par_k_', 'bac_k_'). Here as elsewhere in his poetry, **Heaney delights in the shape and sound of words.**

> **Heaney on the erotic in poetry**
>
> '[The erotic belongs in poetry] but the problem is, how to get it in. It's present – in an abstinent kind of way – in a *District and Circle* poem like "Tate's Avenue".'

Questions

1	Place the three rugs in order, according to the stages of the relationship.
2	What impression of the rug (and the relationship between the couple who shared it) do you form from stanza 1? What words and details influence your impression?
3	The rug described in the second stanza suggests an altogether different phase of the lovers' relationship. What words and details strike you as particularly revealing?
4	Use three carefully considered adjectives to characterise the love described in stanza 2.
5	The third stanza moves the poem to Belfast. What impression of the city is conveyed in this stanza? Identify the keys words and phrases in creating this impression.
6	'And nothing gives on the rug or the ground beneath it.' Would you agree that the relationship between the young lovers reflects an attitude of 'No surrender' and 'Not an inch'.
7	How does the last stanza convey the stubbornness of the persona of the poem?
8	'The idea of love that emerges from the poem is one of measuring up and finding each equal to the other.' Comment on this view of the poem.
9	'It is clear from "Tate's Avenue" that love and the way you behave as lovers are related to where you are. This is a Belfast poem.' Comment on this interpretation of the poem.
10	Examine one stanza and note how Heaney uses alliteration, consonance and assonance to create the music of the poem.
11	Based on the last stanza of the poem, write a short dialogue between the young lovers that captures the quality of their relationship.

Seamus Heaney

Exam-Preparation Questions

1. 'In Heaney's poetry we encounter contrasting female and male presences in a world that is, by turns, familiar and reassuring, and violent and unnerving.' Give your view of this assessment of Heaney's poetry.

2. 'Heaney's poetry is constantly engaged in finding images for the processes of the imagination and for poetry itself.' Discuss.

3. 'Seamus Heaney's poetry is rich in imagery and metaphor and expressed in a sensuous language.' Discuss this statement, supporting your answer with reference to the poetry of Seamus Heaney on your course.

4. 'In his poetry, Seamus Heaney seeks to find a balance between the demands of his social conscience as a Northern nationalist, and the freedom of his imagination.' Discuss this statement, supporting your answer with reference to the poetry of Seamus Heaney on your course.

5. 'I no longer wanted a door into the dark, I wanted a door into the light.' Discuss Seamus Heaney's poetry in terms of poems of darkness and poems of light. You should refer to both the themes and imagery found in the poetry of Heaney on your course.

6. Heaney's poetry is populated with exemplary figures from whom he learns. Give examples of three figures from the poems you have studied, outlining their importance to the poet.

7. Do you agree with the view that history and memory – personal, familial, racial – lie at the heart of Heaney's poetry? Support your opinion with reference to the poems by Seamus Heaney on your course.

8. 'Many of Heaney's poems explore relationships: relationships of love; relationships of conflict; the relationship between the real and the imagined; and the relationship between the past and the present.' Discuss this statement, supporting your answer with reference to the poetry of Seamus Heaney on your course.

9. The citation for the Nobel prize refers to 'an authorship filled with lyrical beauty and ethical depth which brings out the miracle of the ordinary day and the living past'. Point to examples of Heaney's poetry where these qualities are to be found. Explain your choices.

10. 'What I find appealing in the poetry of Seamus Heaney.' Write an essay in which you outline the appeal that Heaney's poetry has for you. Some of the following might be included:
    - Heaney's skill as a poet
    - The themes – personal, familial and national
    - The attachment to his home place
    - The careful attention Heaney pays to the actual, and his delight in the visionary and marvellous
    - The memorable lines and images that stay with you

    Support your answer with reference to the poetry of Heaney on your course.

HIGHER LEVEL

11 Write an introduction to the poetry of Seamus Heaney for readers new to his work. Your answer should include:
- The themes and concerns of his poetry
- Heaney's use of language and your response to it

Some of the following might also be included in your answer:
- The importance of exemplary figures in his poetry
- The marriage poems and the relationship they describe
- The metaphors for poetry
- The question of the response to the pressure of public events
- The relationship between the real and the imaginary

Support your answer with reference to the poetry of Heaney on your course.

12 Seamus Heaney remains one of the most popular poets in the English-speaking world. Why, do you think, is this so? You could consider some of the following in your answer:
- While often dealing with his home place, his poetry has universal appeal
- Detailed descriptions of the real flow into flights of imagination
- The personality of the poet revealed in the poems
- The celebration of love and family
- His courage in speaking as a representative of his people
- His delight in the sounds and shapes of words
- The hopefulness of his poetry

Support your answer with reference to the poetry of Heaney on your course.

SNAPSHOT SEAMUS HEANEY

- Mossbawn is childhood Eden
- Celebrates the rural, the local, and traditional crafts
- Celebrates exemplary figures – Aunt Mary and his father
- Public poems address violence and conflict in Northern Ireland
- Private world familiar and reassuring – public world violent and unnerving
- Speaks as representative of his community
- Roots of poetic language found in childhood experience
- Descriptive language, strong rhythms and rich sound patterns
- Themes of memory and excavation of the past
- Love poems playful, celebratory and unsentimental
- Poetry rooted in the ordinary world – imagination flies beyond it
- Contrasting images of weight and flight
- Classical allusions deepen everyday experiences
- Poetry is hopeful and uplifting

Seamus Heaney

Sample Essay

'Seamus Heaney's poetry moves between earth-bound realities and flights of poetic fantasy.' Discuss this view of Heaney's poetry, supporting your answer with references to the poems by Heaney on your course.

I think Seamus Heaney's poetry does move between 'earth-bound realities' and 'flights of fantasy'. However, it can be argued that it is only in his later writing that his poetry breaks free of earth-bound realities and takes flight.

Answer addresses the task straight away

Seamus Heaney's father farmed fifty acres in County Derry and also worked as a cattle dealer. He was a man of the earth, and the earth and the soil are central to Seamus Heaney's poetry. After primary school, Heaney won a scholarship to St Columb's College, Derry, and there he came to love English literature and the literature of the Greeks and Romans. The mixture of a love of ordinary things and a love of literature is reflected in many of Heaney's poems, where the poet uses his poetry to celebrate the life he knew as a child.

Answer gives brief note on poet's background to help make its case

Take the example of his early poem 'The Forge'. What could be more real and down-to-earth than a detailed description of the local forge with its 'old axles and iron hoops rusting', where 'real iron' is beaten out? The young poet sees music in the solid objects and celebrates the music of ordinary life when he writes of 'the hammered anvil's short-pitched ring'. The poem is a celebration of a traditional craft and is written in a traditional form: the sonnet. The figure of the blacksmith in his leather apron, with 'hairs in his nose' is as earth-bound a figure as they come. The language of the poem, with its alliteration and consonant sounds, suits the description of the blacksmith as a strong, masculine figure: 'Then grunts and goes in, with a slam and a flick'.

This paragraph introduces first poem to be discussed

The discussion keeps the terms of the question in focus

Uses short quotations to support points

For the poet, the blacksmith's anvil becomes an altar, a magical object 'Horned as a unicorn'. Upon this altar the blacksmith beats out iron and 'expends himself in shape and music'. In other words, the blacksmith symbolises the poet, who takes the raw material of life and beats it into the shape and music of poetry. The door of the forge, 'a door into the dark', symbolises the young poet entering through the door of words into the darkness of the imagination. At this early stage of his career, Heaney places his faith in describing real things in carefully shaped and musical poems. He is happy to stay earth-bound, though the image of the unicorn is an early indication of the visionary qualities which characterise his later poetry.

In concluding the discussion of the poem, the answer goes back to the terms of the question

Another early, earth-bound poem, 'Bogland' makes the association between the earth and the imagination. When Heaney was at school, the skeleton of an elk had been taken out of the bog near his home. This skeleton, and the stories he had been told of butter buried for 'More than a hundred years', made him think of the bog as the memory of the landscape. To recover the past you dig 'Inwards and downwards'. The last line of the poem – 'The wet centre is bottomless' – suggests that the young poet realises that just as there is no bottom to the bog, there is no bottom to the well of imagination, especially when the imagination explores the past of his childhood and his community. The final

Introduces second poem

Throughout the answer, short quotations are integrated into the argument

HIGHER LEVEL 2021

HIGHER LEVEL

> **The candidate returns to the key phrases and ideas in the question**

line of the poem suggests a poetry rooted in the soil, though it must be dug up by the imagination. What greater contrast could there be between poetry imagined as digging into the soil and poetry imagined as taking flight?

> **Introduces third poem into answer**

'Mossbawn 1: Sunlight' is another poem dealing with the real. Like a painter painting a life portrait, Heaney paints a domestic scene and places his much-loved aunt in the centre. The portrait is warm and affectionate, filled with images of light and heat, and while the beautiful last stanza is written with love, the image is of a love half-buried:

> 'And here is love
> like a tinsmith's scoop
> sunk past its gleam
> in the meal-bin.'

The scoop is sunk and stuck in the meal-bin, just, as it can be argued, Heaney's imagination is stuck in the real.

> **Concludes one line of argument**

> **Makes reference across poems**

'The Pitchfork' is a poem that recalls the poet's youth in Co. Derry, when he learned to handle a pitchfork. In many ways it is a poem that goes back to 'The Forge' in its celebration of a farm implement made of beaten metal and wood.

To the young poet, the pitchfork was an implement of work and play. Holding it, he could imagine himself as a warrior or an athlete:

> 'When he tightened his raised hand and aimed high with it,
> It felt like a javelin, accurate and light.'

The poem sets out to capture the physical quality of the pitchfork in a series of descriptive words and phrases:

> 'Sweat-cured, sharpened, balanced, tested, fitted.
> The springiness, the clip and dart of it.'

> **Having established one line of argument, the answer now introduces a different line**

However, the centre of the poem is inspired by the image of the pitchfork in flight through the air. On this occasion the imagination does not stay rooted in the earth but sails beyond it into space. The pitchfork becomes a space probe sailing 'Evenly, imperturbably through space, / Its prongs starlit and absolutely soundless'. It is a beautiful and striking image. Here we can see the poet's imagination take flight and leave the earth-bound realities behind. In the poem, the visionary and the marvellous take over from the real and the earth-bound. At the end of the poem, Heaney seems to offer himself some advice on how his poetry might develop. He tells himself he has to let the poem travel wherever it is bound. The 'opening hand' which concludes the poem suggests a willingness to follow the imagination where it leads. In this poem it leads far out into space on a soundless flight through starlight.

> **The argument is developed in the paragraph. Concludes with a strong image**

> **The final poem supports the new line of argument**

Another poem which celebrates the imagination in flight is 'Lightenings, viii: "The Annals Say"'. The poem comes from a collection entitled *Seeing Things*. The title hints at the theme of visions and marvels which lie at the heart of 'The Annals Say'. It is a poem written in a light-hearted way and the lightness allows the poem and the imagination to

320 / DISCOVERY: POETRY ANTHOLOGY

Seamus Heaney

rise and take flight. The poem gives an account of an incident recorded in the Annals of Clonmacnoise, in which the monks of Clonmacnoise were disturbed at prayer by a ship sailing above their heads through the air. Heaney tells the story in a matter-of-fact way describing how 'The anchor … / hooked itself into the altar rails'. A crewman 'shinned and grappled down the rope' and the abbot orders the monks to assist the sailor. The ship is released 'and the man climbed back / Out of the marvellous as he had known it'. The poem brings together a world that is earth-bound and one that floats free. The contrast between these two worlds is captured in the images of anchorage, on the one hand, and release on the other.

> There is a good deal of summary in this paragraph, so a clear point has to be made in the final sentences

In the poem, the earth-bound monks and the flying sailors are linked. The ship cannot continue its journey without the assistance of the monks. Reading the poem as a metaphor for Heaney's poetry, we could say that the poem suggests that the high-flying imagination is dependent upon earth-bound realities. However, these realities do not weigh the imagination down and the poem delights in the wondrous quality of the story it tells.

> The concluding comments sum up the argument made throughout the essay

In this poem the imagination takes flight, though it does not lose sight of the earth and the same may be said of all Heaney's poetry: there are dizzying moments of flight and lightness but the earth remains always in view.

ESSAY CHECKLIST		Yes ✓	No ✗
Purpose	Has the candidate understood the task?		
	Has the candidate responded to it in a thoughtful manner?		
	Has the candidate answered the question?		
Comment:			
Coherence	Has the candidate made convincing arguments?		
	Has the candidate linked ideas?		
	Does the essay have a sense of unity?		
Comment:			
Language	Is the essay written in an appropriate register?		
	Are ideas expressed in a clear way?		
	Is the writing fluent?		
Comment:			
Mechanics	Is the use of language accurate?		
	Are all words spelled correctly?		
	Does the punctuation help the reader?		
Comment:			

HIGHER LEVEL

Gerard Manley Hopkins

1844–1889

God's Grandeur	328
Spring*	332
As kingfishers catch fire	337
The Windhover	342
Pied Beauty	347
Felix Randal	351
Inversnaid*	355
No worst, there is none	360
I wake and feel the fell of dark, not day	364
Thou art indeed just, Lord	368

Gerard Manley Hopkins

Biography

Gerard Hopkins was born in Stratford, close to London, on 28 July 1844. He was the eldest of nine children. The family was prosperous: his father, Manley Hopkins, had been Consul-General to the Hawaiian Islands and he owned a company that insured against ship wrecks. He was also a writer and a poet. His mother, Catherine Smith, was the daughter of a wealthy physician. She was highly educated and well read in German literature and philosophy. An aunt who lived with the family was a musician and painter, and she encouraged her nephew in both of these arts for which he showed a precocious talent, as he did for languages. Gerard was not the only talented member of his family: two of his brothers became professional artists. The household was a religious one. The family was Anglican, and one of Gerard's sisters became an Anglican nun.

When Hopkins was eight, the family moved from Stratford to Hampstead in North London. Stratford was suffering from the effects of industrial development and Gerard and Catherine wanted their children to grow up in a healthy environment. As a young boy, Gerard loved to climb trees. He had a love of nature all his life.

Hopkins attended a prestigious grammar school; past students included the famous writers Samuel Coleridge, Charles Lamb and Thomas De Quincey. Hopkins was not physically strong but he had tremendous courage and spirit and he was academically gifted. His talent for words and writing were clear from an early age. What was also clear was his remarkable willpower and his willingness to endure hardship. On one occasion, to prove a point, he abstained from all liquids for a week until his tongue went black and he collapsed.

An inscription of a Hopkins quotation in Edinburgh.

His studies and vocation

In 1863, Hopkins won a scholarship to Oxford University. There he met Robert Bridges and the two became lifelong friends, keeping up a correspondence right up to the time of Hopkins's death in 1889 and Bridges prepared and edited the first edition of Hopkins's poetry in 1918. At Oxford Hopkins was tutored by the art critic Walter Pater, who also became his friend.

At the time, the university was a hotbed of ideas; many of the students were influenced by ideas from the German philosophers Kant, Hegel and Marx, and were turning away from religion. The Anglican Oxford Movement was an attempt to stem the tide of secular ideas by presenting a fervent, intellectual defence of religion. Hopkins was drawn to the Oxford Movement and to one of its founder members, John Henry Newman. Newman had been converted to Catholicism and after some soul-searching, Hopkins followed his example. Hopkins had a stubborn and wilful streak but he was willing to submit to the authority of Rome. Initially, his conversion caused a rift with his parents, who were loyal and devout Anglicans. However, they had a deep love for their son and the rift was soon healed.

Robert Bridges

Bridges was born in the same year as Hopkins, but lived forty-one years longer than his friend. Their friendship was conducted mainly through letters, in which they exchanged opinions on philosophy, religion, poetry and politics.

Joins Jesuits

Hopkins enjoyed university and was a brilliant student. His sketchbooks, diaries and poems from this period show his love of nature, his gift for friendship and a serious and intense personality. A sonnet from this time, 'Myself Unholy', reveals a tendency to judge himself harshly. In 1868, a year after graduating from Oxford, Hopkins joined the Society of Jesus, whose members are called Jesuits. In a gesture that shows the severity of his personality, he destroyed all his poetry in order to devote his life to God. The training to become a Jesuit is long, rigorous and disciplined. However, it was during this training that he experienced some of the happiest days of his life. For three years (1874–1877), he studied theology at St Beuno's college in North Wales. He loved Wales; he loved the people, the countryside and the Welsh language. He was particularly struck by the rich sound patterns of Welsh poetry. At St Beuno's his Superior encouraged him to write a poem commemorating the death of five nuns who had drowned in a shipwreck. The poem 'The Wreck of the Deutschland' incorporates the alliteration, assonance and internal rhymes he found in Welsh poetry, and set Hopkins on his writing journey. The poem was turned down by the editors of the Jesuit magazine but, encouraged by his Superior, Hopkins continued to write and produced ten sonnets which show a delight in the world and a view of nature as a sign of God's energy and beauty in the world. These sonnets include: 'God's Grandeur', 'Spring', 'The Windhover' and 'Pied Beauty'. For the rest of his life, Hopkins wrote religious poetry and made his writing part of his religious vocation, though he was careful to avoid publication.

> **Sensitive Hopkins**
>
> **Hopkins was extremely sensitive to environment. From Liverpool, he wrote to Bridges: 'I take up a languid pen to write to you, being down with diarrhoea and vomiting, brought on by yesterday's heat …'**

Hopkins was ordained in 1877. For four years he held several posts, including one in the parish of Leigh, a small industrial, 'smoke-sodden' town in Lancashire. The people needed a priest and Hopkins fell in love with them. It is likely that 'Felix Randal' was written after the death of one of his parishioners in Leigh. After Leigh, he was transferred to a parish in a slum district of Liverpool, which he called a 'hellhole'. Hopkins was overwhelmed by the degradation caused by industrialisation, and the baseness of both the people and the life they lived. In Liverpool he was fatigued, dispirited and depressed, and lost the ability to write. However, he worked as hard as he could and was conscientious in his duty.

In preparation for his final vows in the Jesuits, Hopkins spent most of 1882 studying and reading. He wrote: 'my mind … is more at peace than it has ever been and I would gladly live all my life … in seclusion from the world and be busied only with God.' But the Jesuits did not live in seclusion. Instead, in 1884 Hopkins was appointed Professor of Greek at University College Dublin.

Hopkins in Dublin 1884–1889

Hopkins was not happy in Ireland. He found Dublin dirty and grim. His colleagues at the university did not know what to make of this eccentric, patriotic Englishman. His accommodation at St Stephen's Green was dilapidated and rat-infested. He considered the professorship an honour but it came with a huge examination load. 'It is killing work,' he wrote, 'to examine a nation.' The sickness and depression to which he was prone increased during his time in Dublin and became, in his own words, 'constant and crippling'. He went on to say, 'when I am at the worst … my state is much like madness'. Out of this personal anguish he wrote six sonnets in 1885, collectively known as the 'terrible sonnets' or 'the sonnets of desolation'. Among them are 'No worst,

Gerard Manley Hopkins

there is none' and 'I wake and feel the fell of dark'. Hopkins struggled on. He felt an increasing conflict between his impulse to write and his religious duties. Four years after writing the terrible sonnets, on 17 March 1889, Hopkins wrote of his frustration and his loss of poetic inspiration in 'Thou art indeed just, Lord'. It was one of the last poems he wrote. Three months later, he fell ill with typhoid. On 8 June he was given the sacrament of the sick. As he received it he was heard to say, 'I am so happy'. He died soon afterwards and was buried in the Jesuit plot at Glasnevin Cemetery in Dublin. At the time of his death his poetry was known only to family members and some friends.

Social and Cultural Context

Hopkins lived through **a time of change** in economics, politics, arts, religion and science. Darwin's *On the Origin of Species* had been published in 1859. *The Communist Manifesto* had appeared in 1848. Dickens published *Hard Times* in 1854. Many intellectuals **challenged traditional beliefs**, including belief in God. Child labour, poor housing and health care, infant mortality, and the damage caused to the environment by industrialisation were all indicators of a society in turmoil.

Hopkins is buried in Glasnevin Cemetery, Dublin.

As a priest working in parishes in Lancashire and Liverpool, Hopkins would have been conscious of the **inequality in society**. He witnessed the desperate poverty and appalling living and working conditions of the poor. His experiences led him to make the half-serious statement that he was a Communist, in a letter to his friend Robert Bridges in 1871. He believed it 'a dreadful thing' that so many lived 'a hard life without dignity, knowledge, comforts, delight, or hopes in the midst of plenty – which plenty they make'. He was also aware of **the consequences** for both workers and the environment of **the industrial revolution**.

Science and religion

As an intellectual Hopkins was aware that more and more people were turning to science to find the meaning of life. And the world that science described had little place for God. The publication of Darwin's *On the Origin of Species* in 1859 marks a moment in history when scientific truths began to replace religious ones. For Hopkins, **the advances in science and art did not threaten his religious belief** – they reinforced it. He believed that **any close examination of nature revealed the grandeur of a Divine creator**. To perceive and appreciate beauty in nature was, for Hopkins, to discover the presence of God, as in the poem, 'As kingfishers catch fire'. For Hopkins, nature was charged or 'electrified' with the power of God. The uniqueness of every living thing in every moment expressed the purpose and creativity of God. Hopkins's concepts of '**inscape**' (the **unique quality of an object**, its 'thisness') and '**instress**' (the **energy which holds** this uniqueness together and the effect of the uniqueness of an object upon the beholder; the **internal excitement** of the beholder) were **ways of describing God's presence**. In Hopkins's mind, science could describe nature and explain natural phenomenon, but it was religion which understood the purpose and meaning of nature. For him, **nature was the expression of God in the world**. When Hopkins saw beauty in nature – as in a kingfisher, or a falcon in flight – he felt motivated to love and serve God.

The inscape and instress of poetry

Hopkins brought his ideas on inscape and instress into his writing. He believed that each poem should have its own **unique set of qualities, held together by the energy of the artist**. He disliked the repetitive and tame rhythms and metres used by many of his contemporaries. He believed that poetry should draw strength from the rhythms of speech. He wanted the freedom to create particular rhythmic effects to suit the uniqueness of the object or experience described in each of his poems. He wanted his poems to **sound dynamic and dramatic**. Hopkins devised the term '**sprung rhythm**' for his system. The basic idea was that each line of a poem should have a fixed number of stresses per line rather than a fixed number of syllables. The effect is to create **a feeling of energy and forward motion**. However, what gives a Hopkins's poem its unique quality is inscape, **the total pattern of sound**, not just its rhythm. He used rhyme, both at the end of lines (end rhyme) and within lines (internal). He was fascinated by vowel music and alliteration. Influenced by Welsh-language poetry, he created **complex patterns of vowel sounds and alliteration**. Hopkin also sought out Anglo-Saxon words to breathe life and vitality into his poems. He used **compound adjectives** ('dapple-dawn-drawn' in 'The Windhover', for example) combined with alliteration and internal rhyme. Just as Hopkins believed God shapes things into unique forms and patterns, **he used his energy to shape each poem into its unique form**.

> **Duns Scotus**
>
> Hopkins worried whether his thoughts and ideas were compatible with religious thinking. Then, in 1872, during his training with the Jesuits, he discovered the writing of a medieval English Friar, Duns Scotus. Scotus maintained that it was the unique combination of qualities (size, texture, colour, shape, movement and so on) which give a thing its individual identity. This essence, this 'thisness' is what defines the reality of every object in nature. After studying Scotus, Hopkins felt able to celebrate the particularity and variety of nature and to celebrate the Creator whose spirit and energy moulds things into their unique patterns and forms.

Themes

Hopkins's poetry expresses **his love of God and God's creation**. When Hopkins looks upon the beauty of nature, he sees the **creative power** and **grandeur** of God ('The Windhover', 'Spring', 'Pied Beauty', 'God's Grandeur', 'As Kingfishers Catch Fire'). In some of the poems he contrasts the creative power of God with the destruction and smearing of the beautiful earth by humankind ('God's Grandeur'). Hopkins's poetry expresses his consciousness of sin and its corrupting influence ('Spring'). This is countered by the power of Christ to redeem and save sinners ('Spring', 'Felix Randal', 'The Windhover'). And just as Hopkins's love of God can lead to outpourings of joy and ecstasy in his poetry, **his religious doubt and depression can lead to outpourings of despair** ('No worst, there is none', 'I wake and feel the fell of dark'). Hopkins's frustration and personal unhappiness are expressed in 'Thou art indeed just, Lord'.

Gerard Manley Hopkins

Timeline

1844	Born on 28 July in Stratford, Essex to High Anglican parents
1852	Family move to Hampstead
1854	Attends Highgate Grammar School
1863	Attends university at Oxford
1866	Follows John Henry Newman into the Catholic Church
1867	Graduates with a first-class degree in Classics
1868	Enters the Jesuit order
1874–7	Studies theology and learns Welsh in North Wales
1876	Writes 'The Wreck of the Deutschland'; poem rejected by a Jesuit journal
1877	Ordained a priest; writes some of his best poems, including 'Pied Beauty', 'The Windhover' and 'God's Grandeur'
1879	Spends three months in a parish in a small town in Lancashire
1880	Writes 'Felix Randal'; spends two years in a parish in the slum area of Liverpool
1882	Spends a year studying and reading before final vows
1884	Appointed Professor of Greek at University College, Dublin
1885	Writes his 'terrible sonnets'
1889	Dies in Dublin of typhoid fever
1918	Robert Bridges, poet and friend of Hopkins, publishes an edition of Hopkins's poems
1967	First complete edition of Hopkins's works is published

HIGHER LEVEL

Before you read

Using a good dictionary, look up the different meanings of the word 'grandeur'. In your view, how many of these meanings could apply to God?

God's Grandeur

The world is charged with the grandeur of God.
It will flame out, like shining from shook foil;
It gathers to a greatness, like the ooze of oil
Crushed. Why do men then now not reck his rod?
Generations have trod, have trod, have trod;   5
And all is seared with trade; bleared, smeared with toil;
And wears man's smudge and shares man's smell: the soil
Is bare now, nor can foot feel, being shod.

And for all this, nature is never spent;
There lives the dearest freshness deep down things;   10
And though the last lights off the black West went
Oh, morning, at the brown brink eastward, springs –
Because the Holy Ghost over the bent
World broods with warm breast and with ah! bright wings.

Glossary

1	*charged with*: filled with the energy of, as in a charge of electricity
2	*foil*: gold or silver in sheet form; when shaken the foil gives off flashes of light like lightning
3	*like … oil*: like the ooze of oil from crushed olives
4	*reck his rod*: heed or care about God's authority; in the Bible, the rod is often a symbol of God's power, anger and just punishment; on other occasions it symbolises God's guidance; *reck* = pay heed to
5–6	*Generations … toil*: the earth has been polluted by the weary routine of generations of workers
6	*seared*: dried up, withered, scorched
6	*bleared*: blurred, e.g. by tears or inflammation
8	*nor can … shod*: by wearing shoes, people no longer have a direct connection with the soil
11	*the last lights*: the setting sun
13–14	*the Holy Ghost … bright wings*: while the world is 'bent' in sleep, the Holy Ghost, like a dove, broods over it

Gerard Manley Hopkins

Guidelines

This is one of the ten sonnets which Hopkins wrote at St Beuno's in North Wales in 1877, during one of the happiest periods of his life. The poem contrasts the destructive effect of human activity on the earth with the regenerative power of nature. Here as in 'Spring', 'Pied Beauty' and 'The Windhover', Hopkins **celebrates the divine energy that flows through nature and manifests itself in the beauty of the natural world**. In a meditation, Hopkins wrote, 'All things … are charged with love, are charged with God and if we know how to touch them give off sparks and take fire …'

> **Hopkins describing St Beuno's**
>
> 'The house stands on a steep hillside, it commands the long-drawn valley of the Clwyd to the sea … opposite it is Snowdon and its range … The air seems to me to be very fresh and wholesome.'

Commentary

In 'God's Grandeur', Hopkins presents two contrasting worlds: the world of nature made by God, unspoiled and beautiful; and the degenerate, ugly world that is the result of generations of human activity.

Lines 1–8

The poem opens with the natural world, shot through with the splendour of its creator. The world is like an electric battery, fully charged with the divine energy that keeps it in being and sustains it. The second line tells us that God's grandeur 'will flame out, like shining from shook foil'. The image here, as Hopkins explained to his friend, the poet Robert Bridges, is of the glinting of gold leaf or tinsel. In line 3 we have another image of the traces left by God's grandeur on the natural world ('like the ooze of oil'). Here, the oil oozes from crushed olives. Hopkins had the Old Testament in mind when he used this image – olive oil symbolised power and kingship as well as priesthood.

Line 4 ('Why do men then now not reck his rod?') introduces a firm moral tone into the sonnet. Hopkins is asking why human beings pay no attention to God's authority and anger. The lines that follow explain why God might be angry. Through their various activities, generations of people have converted a beautiful world into a place 'seared with trade' and 'bleared, smeared with toil'. The planet 'wears man's smudge and shares man's smell'. This sonnet identifies Hopkins as an environmentalist before the term came into use.

Lines 5–8 reflect Hopkins's experience as a priest in Lancashire: 'I was yesterday at St Helens, probably the most repulsive place in Lancashire… The stench of sulphuretted hydrogen rolls in the air, and films of the same gas form on railing and pavement.' In line 8 we find a reminder of industrial man's divorce from nature: 'nor can foot feel, being shod.' The foot in a shoe is no longer in direct contact with the earth, an image of the separation of mankind from the natural world.

Lines 9–14

The final six lines of the sonnet take over where the first three left off, and reintroduce a celebratory, optimistic note. The despair expressed in lines 5–8 gives way to consolation. In spite of all the grimness created by mankind ('And for all this'), nature possesses the power of renewal. The key here is line 10: 'There lives the dearest freshness deep down things'. This is a reference to the undying life forces that are constantly at work renewing the face of the earth.

HIGHER LEVEL

Lines 11–12 ('And though the last lights … / eastward, springs') convey an image of the dark night giving way to a bright morning in the east. In the final two lines, Hopkins identifies the source of the constantly renewed life of nature. This is the Holy Ghost, the great spiritual power that broods over Earth with 'bright wings'. In the New Testament, the Holy Spirit is represented as a dove.

What Hopkins writes in the final two lines of the sonnet is a distinct echo of Milton's treatment of the same theme in *Paradise Lost*, where the Holy Spirit has a similar function:

> 'Thou from the first
> Wast present, and with mighty wings outspread
> Dove-like satst brooding on the vast Abyss
> And mad'st it pregnant'

This in turn is based on the account of Creation in the *Book of Genesis*: 'and darkness was upon the face of the deep, and the Spirit of God was moving over the face of the waters'.

Theme and imagery

The main theme of the poem is that the world is filled with the grandeur of God and sustained by divine energy. The presence of God in nature is shown in two ways. One is sudden and brilliant as when foil is shaken and gives off flashes of light, like lightning. The other is more gradual and accumulative, as when oil is crushed and gathers into a thick pool. **The poem contrasts the brilliance of God's presence with the way in which humans have defaced Earth**, leaving it smeared and soiled. The images of human activity suggest the monotony and soul-destroying nature of work in industrial England. It is not only nature but humans, too, who are 'bleared, smeared with toil'. The poem concludes with **a series of hopeful images**. The first is the sense of renewal with the arrival of morning light. The second is the image of the Holy Ghost, the embodiment of divine energy and power, hovering in a protective way over the world, as a mother bird hovers over a nest. It is this image which draws the **ecstatic 'ah!'** of the last line of the poem.

Form and language

'God's Grandeur' is a Petrarchan sonnet – that is, it is divided into an octave (eight lines) and a sestet (six lines) with a tight rhyming scheme, in which only four rhymes are used. The pattern is *abbaabba cdcdcd*. **The strict formal structure acts as a counterbalance to the passion and excitement** that the poem expresses. Though there are many end-stopped lines, the poet uses enjambment (running-on of a phrase or thought from one line to another) to great effect: 'like the ooze of oil / Crushed' (lines 3–4) throws the emphasis onto the verb by holding it back until the next line, and so adds to the force of the physical action of 'Crushed'. In a different way, the enjambment in the final four lines, together with the interjected 'Oh' and 'ah!', give a **breathlessness** to the joy that is being expressed.

Gerard Manley Hopkins

As you read the poem aloud, you will notice that Hopkins chooses **plain, simple words, mostly of one syllable**, rather than unfamiliar or learned ones. The following words from the poem all have their origin in Old English or in the Anglo-Saxon elements of Middle English: world, God, will, shook, gathers, greatness, ooze, reck, rod, trod, smeared, smell, bare, foot, shod, spent, dearest, freshness, deep, down, things, though, last, lights, black, west, went, morning, brown, brink, eastward, springs, Holy Ghost, broods, warm, breast, bright, wings.

Hopkins uses alliteration in every line of this poem. For example, the first three lines contain 'grandeur of God', 'shining from shook foil', 'gathers to a greatness' and 'ooze of oil'. This gives vigour and emphasis to what he has to say.

Another common feature of Hopkins's style is his use of **internal rhyme**. For example, 'rod' at the end of line 4 rhymes with the treble 'trod' in line 5.

Questions

1	'God's Grandeur' is based on a contrast. Identify this contrast and explain how Hopkins develops it.
2	Comment on the effect of the word 'charged' in line 1.
3	What is the effect of placing 'crushed' at the start of the fourth line?
4	a) Comment on the verbs chosen by Hopkins to describe human work and its effect in the world: 'trod', 'seared', 'bleared', 'smeared'. b) Discuss the portrayal of humans in the poem and the effect of their presence on the earth.
5	'Nature is never spent' (line 9). Explain your understanding of this statement.
6	What kind of God is contemplated in the poem?
7	What is the role of the Holy Ghost in the poem?
8	Identify four interesting words or phrases from the poem and describe their impact.
9	'In the poem Hopkins shows his love of God but also his disgust for humanity.' Discuss.
10	Some critics suggest that it is easy to differentiate between Hopkins the poet and Hopkins the priest in reading the poem. Do you agree?
11	In pairs, discuss how this poem might be used by the 'save the planet' movement.
12	Write your own poem contrasting the beauty of the planet with the destruction caused by human activity.

HIGHER LEVEL

Before you read

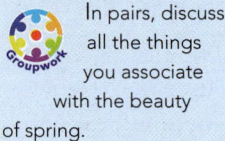

In pairs, discuss all the things you associate with the beauty of spring.

Spring

Nothing is so beautiful as Spring –
When weeds, in wheels, shoot long and lovely and lush;
Thrush's eggs look little low heavens, and thrush
Through the echoing timber does so rinse and wring
The ear, it strikes like lightnings to hear him sing;   5
The glassy peartree leaves and blooms, they brush
The descending blue; that blue is all in a rush
With richness; the racing lambs too have fair their fling.

What is all this juice and all this joy?
A strain of the earth's sweet being in the beginning   10
In Eden garden. – Have, get, before it cloy,
Before it cloud, Christ, lord, and sour with sinning,
Innocent mind and Mayday in girl and boy,
Most, O maid's child, thy choice and worthy the winning.

Glossary

2	*weeds, in wheels*: 'weeds' here refers to wild flowers; the long shoots turn over and over as they grow out – Hopkins may have had blackberry stems in mind
3	*look little low heavens*: the blue eggs with their black spots remind him of the sky studded with stars
4	*rinse*: purify
4	*wring*: squeeze and twist; in this case also evoking 'ring' as a bell
9	*juice*: the sap of life, the joyful fruitfulness
10	*strain*: echo, reminder or symbol
11	*Have, get*: claim for yourself
11	*it*: the innocent mind of youth (line 13)
11	*cloy*: induce a feeling of distaste or nausea as a result of indulging in food or drink that is too rich or too sweet
13	*Mayday*: A spring festival, celebrated on the first day of May, for Catholics, it is a day of special devotion to Mary and celebrates her purity
14	*maid's child*: Christ, the son of the Virgin Mary
14	*worthy the winning*: worth winning

Gerard Manley Hopkins

Guidelines

This is another of the sonnets Hopkins composed in 1877 while studying theology in North Wales at St Beuno's. It was written in May. He was attracted to the **sonnet form** because it **allowed him to combine precision** (necessary because its brevity demanded this) **with freedom**. The sonnet remained **his favourite poetic form**. The poem celebrates the loveliness of spring and relates it to the Garden of Eden and the innocence of humankind before the Fall. The poem also expresses a bleak view in relation to the effects of sin on the innocence and purity of children.

Commentary

The sonnet is **divided clearly into an octave (eight lines) and a sestet (six lines)**. In the octave, Hopkins describes an experience of the countryside in spring. He celebrates the hedgerows and the meadows and their varied beauties. The **tone is enthusiastic** and the **language is fresh and vivid**. The final six lines take the poem in an explicitly religious direction. For Hopkins spring is an echo of the sweet purity of life in the Garden of Eden before the Fall. The poem ends with an urgent plea to Christ to preserve the youthful, spring-like innocence of girls and boys.

> **From a Hopkins sermon**
>
> '… the boy or girl, that in their bloom and heyday, in their strength and health give themselves to God and with fresh body and joyously beating blood give him glory, how near he will be to them …'

The octave

The entire octave (lines 1–8) conjures up a world of beauty, joy, movement, colour and happy innocence. Nature is untroubled and enjoying itself: the weeds 'shoot long and lovely and lush'; a thrush's eggs resemble 'little low heavens'; and the song of the thrush echoing through the woods, with its bell-like clarity and pure sound, affords an almost mystical experience: 'it strikes like lightnings to hear him sing'. The pear tree dazzles in the sun. The branches brush the blue of the sky as it rushes towards the earth. The emphasis is on the carefree state of all natural things ('the racing lambs too have fair their fling').

The sestet

The sestet reflects on the natural world depicted in the octave. The fresh beauty of spring is an echo for Hopkins of the lost innocence 'of the earth's sweet being in the beginning / In Eden garden', when humanity was still free from original sin. From line 11 to the end of the poem, **spring becomes a symbol** of the youthful innocence of children ('Innocent mind and Mayday in girl and boy'). There is, as Hopkins sees it, a second Fall when sin takes away this innocence, when the innocence of children becomes 'sour with sinning'. This is why he asks Christ to protect the innocence of children in the springtime of their lives, when they are not tainted by the world. If Christ answers Hopkins's fervent plea in lines 11–14, the effect will be the preservation of innocence, at least in the case of the young. Thus, in a sense, Hopkins is asking Christ to reverse the original Fall, which involved the corruption of Adam and Eve and the loss of Eden.

Hopkins took a pessimistic view of human nature. He saw how people were confirmed in their 'sinful' ways. In 1880, he wrote, 'And the drunkards go on drinking, the filthy … are filthy still …'.

> **'The Fall'**
>
> In Catholic teaching, Original Sin is the sin inherited by all humankind from Adam because he disobeyed God's command not to eat from the Tree of Knowledge. Adam's disobedience is called 'the Fall' because he fell from a state of grace and innocence.

Themes and imagery

Vitality of spring

The poem **celebrates the loveliness, energy and vitality of spring**. The **colourful descriptive language** reveals Hopkins's sympathy with nature and his **painter's talent for close observation**. The imagery strives to capture the movement, sounds, colours, shapes, texture and luxuriousness of the countryside in spring. The shoots of the wild flowers curl forward in graceful wheels. The imagery next focuses on the little sky of the thrush's eggs (line 3) before zooming out later in the poem (lines 7–8) to take in the wide expanse of blue sky.

The song of the thrush striking the ear is compared to lightning, like the 'flame out' in 'God's Grandeur'. The reference to lightning is taken up in the description of the 'glassy' pear tree, which suggests the light catching the leaves and blossoms of the tree so that they glint like jewels. The **sense of abandon** is caught in the use of 'fling' to describe the lambs as they frisk about. In the first eight lines, the senses are overwhelmed. Even the blue of the sky (lines 7–8) seems to be rushing to the earth. The effect is dizzying.

Innocence and sinfulness

As in almost all of Hopkins's other poems, the impulse behind 'Spring' is primarily religious. And this impulse becomes clear in the sestet. Here the **themes of innocence and sinfulness** are introduced. The springtime of the year reminds Hopkins of the springtime of the world before the sin of Adam and Eve caused them to be expelled from the Garden of Eden and lose their original innocence. Hopkins is downcast when he thinks of the effects of sin on the innocence and purity of children, who are close to the original innocence of Eden. It is the contrast between the beauty of spring and the sickening effects of sin ('cloy', 'sour') which leads to the urgent prayer to Christ to claim the mind of young people before they become corrupted. The innocent mind of youth is symbolised in the freshness of 'Mayday'. **Hopkins uses a simple but telling metaphor** to suggest the loss of innocence, **making the physical a reflection of the spiritual** in the reference to 'cloy', 'cloud' and 'sour'. The idea here is that the innocent mind, like a health-giving drink, is sweet at the beginning, but can, with time, turn sour, in this case 'with sinning'. The reference to Christ as 'maid's child' recalls the child Jesus and his Virgin mother, both symbols of purity in Catholic teaching. It suggests that the innocence of youth will be particularly prized by Christ.

> **'Maid's Child'**
>
> In Catholic teaching, Jesus was conceived by the Holy Spirit, without the agency of a human father. In the Gospel of Luke, Mary is informed by the angel Gabriel that she will conceive a child and answers: 'Behold the handmaid of the Lord.'

Gerard Manley Hopkins

Language

The first eight lines of the poem convey with tremendous emotion and energy the **unique qualities** (the inscape) of different features of the hedgerow and meadows around him. Hopkins uses **alliteration, long vowels and sweet sounds** to describe the weeds growing in lush abundance: 'When weeds, in wheels, shoot long and lovely and lush'. The poem shows Hopkins **pushing language to its limits**. The thrush is said to 'rinse and wring' the ear in a phrase whose **sound and meaning combine** to convey an intense experience. The phrase carries strong religious overtones. 'Rinse' suggests purification by holy water, while 'wring' is a play on words, suggesting both the strong impact of the thrush's song and the clear, bell-like quality of its sound.

Hopkins makes generous use of **alliteration** ('blooms', 'brush', 'blue', for example) and **run-on lines** to give the **effect of the energy associated with spring**. Lines 7 and 8 provide a good example: 'that blue is all in a rush / With richness'. The energy is also conveyed in the **strong nouns and verbs**: shoot, rinse, wring, strikes, leaves, blooms, brush and the -ing of: echoing, descending, racing. There is a tone of ecstasy throughout the first eight lines as the **rhythm rushes forward**. The rhymes 'lush', 'thrush', 'brush' and 'rush' express the **sensuousness** of spring.

There is a **slower, more meditative feel** to the beautiful words which run across lines 9–10. Here the alliteration, assonance, half-rhyme and repetition create a quiet, harmonious and sweet-sounding, **prayerful tone**. In lines 11–12, the music of the poem takes on a jarring, abrupt rhythm, with the **repeated use of the comma**, creating a staccato effect. The alliteration ('cloy' and 'cloud', 'sour' and 'sinning') and the strangled sound of the verb 'get' suggest the poet's **physical revulsion** from the sins which will sour the innocent children. The order of the words in the final two lines suggest the poet's anguish, though the sounds of the poem are harmonious once again.

Exam-Style Questions

Understanding the poem

1	Do you agree with Hopkins when he says, 'Nothing is so beautiful as Spring'?
2	Describe as clearly as you can the way the loveliness of spring affects the poet (lines 1–8).
3	What, in your view, do the weeds, the eggs, the thrush, the pear tree and the lambs all have in common?
4	How does he describe the sky in lines 6–8?
5	How would you answer the poet's question, 'What is all this juice and all this joy?'
6	Why does the springtime remind the poet of 'the beginning / In Eden garden'?
7	What are the poet's fears and wishes for the 'Innocent mind and Mayday in girl and boy'?
8	a) Why does Hopkins refer to Christ as the 'maid's child'? b) What does Hopkins ask Christ to do for the children of the world?

Thinking about the poem

1. Do you think the religious turn in the poem, in the sestet, works?

2. One critic suggests that the voice in the sestet of the poem (lines 9–14) is not in harmony with the voice of the octave (lines 1–8). Comment on the two voices, and explain why you agree or disagree with the critic.

3. Which of these three statements is closest to your understanding of the poem?
   - The poem is about the loveliness of spring
   - The poem is about the corruption of humanity
   - The poem is about the power of Christ

   Explain your choice, considering each statement in your answer.

4. 'Hopkins is too pessimistic in his view of humanity and too optimistic in his view of nature.' Discuss, in pairs or groups.

Imagining

1. Describe an occasion (real or imagined) when it seemed the blue of the sky was rushing towards you. Use 'Spring' as a model in choosing your words and phrases to describe the experience.

2. You are making a short film to accompany a reading of the poem. Describe how you would use images, colour and sound effects to convey the mood of the poem.

SNAPSHOT

- A sonnet
- Impressive alliteration
- Original imagery
- First eight lines describe
- Final six lines reflect; they are a prayer
- Contrast in tone between octave and sestet
- Close, accurate observation of nature
- Spring as the season of innocence
- Lively and energetic

Gerard Manley Hopkins

Before you read

'This is me.' 'I am what I am.' 'I am what I do.' As a class, discuss the idea of being true to yourself and having your own identity. What is a person's true self? Now read Hopkins's thoughts on individuality and selfhood.

As kingfishers catch fire

As kingfishers catch fire, dragonflies dráw fláme;
As tumbled over rim in roundy wells
Stones ring; like each tucked string tells, each hung bell's
Bow swung finds tongue to fling out broad its name;
Each mortal thing does one thing and the same: 5
Deals out that being indoors each one dwells;
Selves – goes itself; *myself* it speaks and spells,
Crying *Whát I do is me: for that I came.*

Í say móre: the just man justices;
Kéeps gráce: thát keeps all his goings graces;   10
Acts in God's eye what in God's eye he is –
Christ. For Christ plays in ten thousand places,
Lovely in limbs, and lovely in eyes not his
To the Father through the features of men's faces.

Glossary

1	*kingfishers*	a kingfisher is a small bird with brilliantly coloured feathers
1	*dragonflies*	a dragonfly is an insect with colourful, transparent wings
1	*As kingfishers … flame*	Hopkins is describing the flash of the sun on the wings of the kingfisher and dragonfly
2	*tumbled … wells*	this line describes the stones of line 3
3	*tucked*	an old form of 'plucked'
4	*Bow*	the thick metal area at the mouth of the bell; the clapper strikes the bow and causes it to 'fling' out its unique sound
6	*Deals out*	gives expression to
6	*indoors each one dwells*	which dwells inside each one; *indoors* = inside
7	*Selves*	Hopkins coins the verb 'selves'. It means 'goes its own way', becomes completely itself. The subject of the verb is 'Each mortal thing' in line 5
9	*justices*	acts justly and reveals his innermost spiritual nature
10	*Keeps grace*	observes God's will
12	*plays*	acts

Guidelines

The poem is undated and is not mentioned in any of Hopkins's letters. It is the clearest expression of Hopkins's view of the world, as influenced by Duns Scotus, the medieval philosopher who maintained that each thing in nature had a unique individuality which defined its reality. Hopkins follows Scotus's example, **praising the uniqueness of each thing in creation** and declaring its true purpose is **to be itself**. This is a standard sonnet consisting of an octave (eight lines) and a sestet (six lines), with a change of thought and emphasis after the octave.

Commentary

The sonnet resembles a **hymn** in which the uniqueness of each created thing is affirmed. Moreover, Hopkins asserts that it is the **purpose of each created thing to be itself**. Hopkins was influenced by the fourteenth-century British philosopher, Duns Scotus, who emphasised the distinction between the created world and the uniqueness of each individual thing within the world. Scotus used the Latin word *Haecceitas*, usually translated as '**thisness**', to describe the uniqueness of each thing. Hopkins believed that this word corresponded to his own word '**inscape**'. In the act of being itself, of expressing its uniqueness, **each thing gives glory to God**.

The octave lines 1–4

The first four lines of the poem give examples of how everything in nature **expresses its inner identity**, its inscape, in ways that are unique to itself. A kingfisher diving into a river or a dragonfly skimming the surface of the water express their unique identity in ways that dazzle, as their wings catch the sun. Stones tumbling down a well **'ring' out or proclaim** their identity in their own way. A plucked string gives out a distinctive note; a ringing bell fling's out its sound like a signature.

The octave lines 5–8

Having given his examples, Hopkins now expresses **his theory or principle of selfhood** as it relates to mortal or living things. All living things have a unique identity, but they also share a **common purpose** (line 5). That purpose is **to give expression** ('Deals out') to the uniqueness that lies within (line 6). They give expression to their inner identity in their actions and all they do. Lines 7–8 state that each mortal or living thing becomes completely itself ('Selves'); proclaims itself ('speaks and spells') and, by being, declares its purpose on Earth (*for that I came*).

Gerard Manley Hopkins

The sestet lines 9–14

In the sestet Hopkins focuses his attention on human beings: 'Í say móre: the just man justices; / Kéeps grácë: thát keeps all his goings graces'. Hopkins believed that humans are born with certain potential qualities or personalities. So, for example, a person might be born 'just'. However, in order to make this quality become real, **the person must choose to act in a just way**. It is only when 'the just man justices' (line 9) that he becomes fully himself, as God wishes him to be and made him to be. In becoming fully himself, the just man **keeps the favour or grace of God** and all his action (goings) are marked by God's grace. The last four lines develop this idea further. When a just man acts according to his inner nature in the sight of God, **God sees him for what he is** – Christ, because Christ lives in those who live good lives. According to Hopkins, God sees Christ in the limbs and eyes of men, and Christ looks through their features 'To the Father'.

> **'Justices'**
> The phrase 'the just man justices' echoes the words spoken by Jesus to John the Baptist in the gospel of Matthew (Chapter 3: Verse 15): 'For so it becomes us to fulfil all justice.'

The references to 'Lovely in limbs' and 'lovely in eyes' (line 13) suggest that spiritual goodness impacts on the physical loveliness of the person. In a sermon, Hopkins spoke of how Christ's divinity was reflected in his body:

> 'In his body, he was most beautiful. … I leave it to you, brethren, then to picture him … in his bearing how majestic, how strong and yet how lovely and lissom in his limbs, in his look how earnest, grave but kind.'

Themes and imagery

Unique identity

According to Hopkins, everything in nature strives to express its unique identity and in doing so gives glory to God and is charged with God's grandeur. When Hopkins writes in line 8, '*for that I came*', he means that the purpose or mission of each thing is to be fully itself. As a priest and theologian, Hopkins believed that each thing in nature, by becoming itself, glorified God the creator. In a sermon Hopkins preached that all things in nature 'make him [God] known; they tell of Him; they give Him glory'. **In the sestet he turns to humanity.** Human beings are more individualised and distinctive than anything else in the world. For Hopkins, the man who acts justly realises his deepest and truest identity, and in doing so **becomes one with the body of Christ, and lovely in the sight of God**.

> **'All things glorify God'**
> Hopkins wrote, 'All things glorify God but they do not know it. The birds sing to him, the thunder speaks of his terror, the lion is like his strength … they are something like him, they make him known …'

Free will

Hopkins distinguishes between humankind and the rest of creation. All non-human objects give glory to God by being what they are. However, they do this in an unconscious way. **Humans are the only beings in God's creation who have the power to accept or reject the will of God.** A stone expresses itself ('Selves') as it tumbles down a well, but it cannot be other than what it is. It cannot refuse its identity, as ordained by God. When a 'just man' chooses to live his life in accordance with God's will, it pleases God. For Hopkins, the human being who lives a life of grace, who lives as God desires, lives in Christ and Christ in him and is therefore lovely in the sight of God.

Line 8 of the sonnet is an echo of the words of Jesus in the Gospel of John: 'For this was I born, and for this I came into the world; that I should bear witness to the truth' (John 18:37). Hopkins's invocation of Christ's words

> **Charged with love**
>
> In his notes, Hopkins wrote: 'All things therefore are charged with love, are charged with God, and if we know how to touch them give off sparks and take fire, yield drops and flow, ring and tell of him.'

reminds us that in doing what they were created for – in expressing themselves and their purposes – all things in creation, but especially human beings, bear witness to the truth of God the Creator.

Painter and musician

Hopkins was a **painter and a musician** and this is reflected in the imagery he used. **He loved the way some surfaces threw off brilliant flashes of light and colour as they were lit by the sun.** The imagery which describes this phenomenon is itself exciting: the kingfishers 'catch fire'; the dragonflies 'dráw fláme'. **His ear was attuned to the different sounds** around him. A stone, a bell and stringed instrument all have their unique signature, their way of announcing their uniqueness through sound. The idea that God sees Christ in the body of the just person follows the teaching of St Paul, who wrote: 'I live, now not I; but Christ lives in me.'

Language

The sonnet is written in Hopkins's **sprung rhythm**, with **five stresses per line**. The rhyming scheme is conventional with the octave rhyming *abbaabba* and the sestet rhyming *cdcdcd*. The energy and particularity of the examples chosen from nature (the kingfishers, dragonflies and stones) are each described in language that has its own soundscape and **unique combinations of echoing sounds**. Compare, for example, the combination of sounds in the first four words of the opening line – 'As kingfishers catch fire', with the sounds in the last three: 'dragonflies dráw fláme'. The words used to describe the stones falling down the well have a **musical and onomatopoeic quality**: tumbled, rim, roundy, ring. Notice how in line 13 ('Lovely in limbs, and lovely in eyes not his'), describing the loveliness of the humans in whom Christ lives, the alliteration and repetition, the long vowel sounds, and the soft 's' and 'l' sounds all combine to create a sound that is pleasing and lovely in itself.

> **Hopkins on sprung rhythm**
>
> 'Why do I employ sprung rhythm? Because it is the nearest to the rhythm of prose, that is the native and natural rhythm of speech, the least forced, the most rhetorical and emphatic of all possible rhythms …'

Elsewhere, the poem features some **daring experiments** with language and syntax. For example, Hopkins uses the accumulated words 'tumbled over rim in roundy wells' as an adjective to describe stones. In lines 3–4, there is internal rhyme and half-rhyme, which subtly imitates the sound of bells, an effect best appreciated when the lines are read aloud; notice **how the sound echoes** across the following groups of words: 'ring', 'string' and 'fling'; 'hung', 'swung' and 'tongue'. This kind of internal rhyme was a feature of the Welsh poetry that Hopkins studied during his time in North Wales.

The **syntax of the poem** (its ordering of words) is often **so condensed that the meaning is both rich and difficult to unravel**. (All the complex thought of the poem is contained in just two sentences.) In line 6, for example, 'that being indoors each one dwells' is a compressed way of saying 'the essence that lives (dwells) inside each mortal thing'. **Hopkins often makes nouns function as verbs**, as in line 7, where 'Selves' is used to mean 'becomes completely itself'. Another example is in line 9, 'the just man justices', where the use of 'justices' as a verb expresses the idea that the actions of a just man reveal his just nature.

Gerard Manley Hopkins

Questions

1	How do kingfishers catch fire and dragonflies draw flame?
2	Hopkins describes a ringing bell as finding its tongue 'to fling out broad its name' (line 4). What does he mean?
3	'What I do is me: for that I came.' (Line 8) What, according to the poem, is the purpose of every mortal thing?
4	'The just man justices.' Discuss the meaning of this memorable statement.
5	According to the last four lines of the poem, how does the just man appear to God?
6	How does Hopkins distinguish between human beings and natural things in relation to his theme of selfhood?
7	Discuss the theme of celebration in the poem.
8	'For Hopkins, each human being is made in the image of Christ and it is his or her purpose to reflect Christ back to God.' Discuss this statement in relation to the poem.
9	'The poem suggests that everything in creation is unique to itself.' Do you agree with this reading of the poem?
10	Hopkins uses language in an original way in an effort to convey the beauty, energy and mystery of creation. Select some examples of words and phrases that strike you as original. Explain your choices.
11	Comment on the resemblances between this sonnet and 'God's Grandeur'. What differences can you discover?
12	'Hopkins comes across as a person of great sensitivity and conviction.' Based on this sonnet, do you agree with this view of the poet?
13	*Groupwork* — Working in groups, create a rap-style version of the poem, using percussive sounds to bring out the musical qualities of the poem.
14	Select four things from nature and write a poem celebrating their unique qualities.

HIGHER LEVEL

Before you read

 As a class, discuss the concepts of heroism, beauty, sacrifice and supreme achievement, and the figures who embody these qualities for you. Now examine how these ideas are incorporated into 'The Windhover'.

The Windhover

To Christ our Lord

I caught this morning morning's minion, king-
dom of daylight's dauphin, dapple-dawn-drawn Falcon, in his riding
Of the rolling level underneath him steady air, and striding
High there, how he rung upon the rein of a wimpling wing
In his ecstasy! then off, off forth on swing,   5
As a skate's heel sweeps smooth on a bow-bend: the hurl and gliding
Rebuffed the big wind. My heart in hiding
Stirred for a bird, – the achieve of, the mastery of the thing!

Brute beauty and valour and act, oh, air, pride, plume, here
Buckle! AND the fire that breaks from thee then, a billion   10
Times told lovelier, more dangerous, O my chevalier!

No wonder of it: shéer plód makes plough down sillion
Shine, and blue-bleak embers, ah my dear,
Fall, gall themselves, and gash gold-vermillion.

Glossary

Title	*Windhover:* a kestrel or small hawk. As the name suggests, the windhover can stay suspended in the air for long periods while looking for prey	
1	*caught:* saw (caught sight of)	
1	*minion:* follower, servant	
2	*dauphin:* prince, the heir to the throne	
2	*dapple:* marked with spots or splashes of colour	
2	*drawn:* attracted; also drawn or outlined	
2	*Falcon:* note the capital letter. Falcon is a French-derived word	
4	*rung upon the rein:* a metaphor from horse-training, where a horse is held at the end of a long rein and made to circle as if in a ring. In falconry, the verb 'ring' means to rise in spirals. The image suggests that the kestrel is pivoting on the point of a wing as he banks or spirals	
4	*wimpling:* beautifully pleated, fluttering, rippling	
6	*bow-bend:* wide arc	
7	*Rebuffed:* mastered, pushed back	
8	*achieve:* perfection	
9	*here:* in my heart and/or in this bird	
10	*AND:* in Hopkins, the capitalised 'AND' seems to mean, 'and as an inevitable result'	
11	*chevalier:* knight on horseback; pronounced to rhyme with 'here' and 'dear'	
12	*plód:* hard work; 'shéer plód' may be a pun on 'ploughshare'	
12	*plough:* ploughed land	
12	*sillion:* furrow; a word Hopkins coins from the French word, *sillon*	
14	*gold-vermillion:* royal colours in coats of arms; vermilion is a rich red colour	

Gerard Manley Hopkins

Guidelines

The poem was written at St Beuno's in North Wales and was dated 30 May 1877. In a letter to a friend, Hopkins described it as 'the best thing I ever wrote'. The title comes from a local name for a kestrel, and reflects the bird's remarkable ability to hover in the wind. There was a display of stuffed birds at the college which included a kestrel. The inscription for the exhibit included the name 'windhover'. The bird, hovering in the air, makes a **distinctive cross shape**. The subtitle, 'To Christ our Lord' was added later to emphasise the religious significance of the poem. 'The Windhover' is the most discussed of all Hopkins's poems because of the **richness and ambiguity of the language** and the relationship between the octave and the sestet.

Commentary

The poet recalls watching a kestrel flying through the dawn sky. He was deeply moved by the strength, skill and beauty of the bird as it **mastered the air and the wind**, performing the most difficult exercises with ease and total control. The **poet's thoughts move from the falcon to his own heart and to Christ**. The falcon's beauty and skill may be great, but the beauty and achievement of Christ are a billion times greater, as is the achievement of those who serve God faithfully, though this beauty may be hidden from view. While the language may be difficult, the structure of the sonnet is straightforward. **The first eight lines, written in the past tense**, are **devoted to the windhover**, and the **final six, written in the present tense, concern Christ and the poet himself as the servant of Christ**.

The octave lines 1–8

As in most sonnets, the first eight lines of this poem set the scene. The poet was up at dawn and caught sight of the windhover, or falcon. In these eight lines, we find the poet concentrating on the skill, power and majesty of the bird. He **marvels** at its control of the air, its swift, graceful movements and its ability to overcome the forces that would hinder its passage. The poet sums up all this in a few words: 'the achieve of, the mastery of the thing!'

The sestet lines 9–11

In the second part of the poem, Hopkins reflects on **the meaning of the experience** he has described in the first eight. 'Brute beauty' (line 9) describes the **unselfconscious, instinctive, physical beauty** of the bird which also, however, gives off **flashes of divine beauty**, like every natural thing. However great these qualities are, they are 'a billion / Times told lovelier' in Christ, whose divine energy, glory and splendour breaks from him like fire. (It is generally agreed that 'my chevalier' in line 11 is Christ, and that the 'thee' of line 10 refers to Christ. However, the 'thee' could also refer to Hopkins's own 'heart in hiding'.)

The sestet lines 12–14

The phrase 'No wonder of it' means that it is not surprising that the 'lovelier' fire of God's beauty has broken forth. After all, **humble, everyday actions can produce sudden, unexpected beauty**, as the plough shines from being polished by the earth it turns over. In the same way, the dull embers of a fire can break open to reveal 'gold-vermilion' sparks.

Christian ideas behind the poem

The Christian framework within which Hopkins wrote may help you in understanding his intention in writing 'The Windhover'. For example, Hopkins describes **the fire that breaks from Christ** (or from the heart of Christ's follower) as **'dangerous' as well as lovely**. Behind this is the idea that the **service of God** can involve the Christian in doing God's will without question, which **can often mean danger and suffering**, as it did for Christ. Hopkins stresses the **link between suffering and spiritual achievement**. The **language and imagery of the final two lines** of the poem **invokes Christ's suffering and death**. Christ's greatest work for mankind was to offer himself on the cross as a sacrifice. The 'blue-bleak embers' can be seen as his suffering and death and apparent failure at the end of his life. 'Fall, gall themselves, and gash' suggests the **physical torment** of Christ as he carried the cross and was crucified. Vermilion is the colour of blood, which is also gold, or precious,

because, for Christians, Christ's blood redeemed the world. From his suffering and apparent defeat, the true splendour of Christ is revealed to the world, 'the blue-bleak embers' of death breaking open to reveal their 'gold-vermillion' splendour.

Another idea behind the poem is that the follower of Christ, like Christ himself, often leads a humble, plodding or even bleak life. However, this **life can suddenly be charged with the power of God and can flame out**, so that what may seem hidden, obscure or commonplace from the outside, conceals a spiritual and divine beauty within. In a sermon Hopkins described the poverty and hardship of Christ's life, which he believed must also be lived by his followers: 'poor was his station, laborious his life, bitter his ending: through poverty, through labour, through crucifixion his majesty of nature shines.'

Theme and imagery

The main theme of the poem is that the natural beauty and achievement of the kestrel is only a faint reflection of the spiritual splendour of Christ, whose power and energy are 'a billion / Times told lovelier, more dangerous', and the followers of Christ share in this spiritual splendour even if their lives seem unremarkable from the outside. The theme is elaborated through **a series of striking images**.

The **images relate to the bird, to Christ and to the poet himself**; and because the bird is charged with the grandeur of God, and the follower of Christ shares in Christ's life, the **imagery can transfer from one to the other**. The opening of the poem contains **a succession of comparisons**: the windhover is presented as a royal bird ('Falcon'), as the faithful servant of the morning ('minion'), as a prince and heir to the daylight ('dauphin').

Next he a is masterful horseman and a graceful skater; his strength and skill ('hurl and gliding', line 6) overcome the attack of the wind. These images along with the reference to 'chevalier' (line 11), invoke the world of the royal court and princely knights. If the windhover is **a prince of the natural world**, Christ is the **prince of the spiritual world**. All of the qualities of the bird come to symbolise Christ, the poet's chevalier: royalty, valour, pride and beauty.

As in other poems by Hopkins, there are **images of hiding and sudden revelation**. Against the glamour, freedom and exhilaration of the bird, the poet's life seems hidden ('My heart in hiding', line 7) and plodding (line 12). Contrasted with these notions of obscurity and dullness are the images of fire (line 10) and the **transformation** of the 'blue-bleak embers' (line 13) into the beautiful colour combination of 'gold-vermillion'.

The images of buckling, falling, galling and gashing relate to the suffering and death of Christ on the cross.

Language and rhythm

The **rhythm and movement of the lines**, allied to the **impressive patterns of sound**, capture the kestrel's **freedom, energy and mastery of the air**, and the poet's reaction to what he saw. Notice the **range of punctuation, which controls the ebb and flow** of the poem: the four exclamation marks, the difference between the fragmented punctuation and the free-flowing lines, between the sudden stops mid-line and the enjambment. Listen out for the rhymes, alliteration and assonance. (In the first two lines alone, there are eleven alliterative words.) Remarkably, the rhyming scheme of 'king', 'wing', 'swing' and 'thing', and the closely allied 'riding', 'striding', 'gliding' and 'hiding', does not sound monotonous because of the punctuation and enjambment. Read the poem aloud and **notice how the lines rise and fall**. Note also the **onomatopoeic** qualities of some words and phrases. In line 5, for example, the sound and rhythm of 'then off, off forth on swing' suggests the **swooping flight** of the falcon. The very sound of 'Rebuffed the big wind' mirrors the meaning of the words.

Hopkins uses **noun-adjective combinations in a highly original way**. The most extreme example is 'rolling level underneath him steady air'. Here, the first five words are to be read as a single adjectival phrase qualifying 'air'.

On nearly every line there are **interesting word choices**, for example the use of 'caught' (line 1) rather than 'saw'; 'caught' is a more dynamic word; it dramatises the moment when the poet saw the bird. It also introduces the **theme of freedom** – there is no way that the timid, duty-bound priest can catch the free, magnificent bird. Consider 'drawn' (line 2): the windhover is attracted or lured by the dawn. However, it also suggests that the bird is drawn or outlined by the dawn light and so is visible to the observer. (References to painting and writing recur in Hopkins's poems – the plume of line 9 can be read as an oblique reference to his own writing, which glorifies God.)

> **French and Anglo-Saxon Words**
>
> The title of the poem, 'The Windhover', is an interesting example of a compound word or *kenning*, found in Anglo-Saxon poetry. However, this is the only poem of Hopkins which contains so much French vocabulary – 'minion', 'dauphin', 'chevalier', 'sillion', 'vermillion' – and draws much of its imagery from the world of Norman/French chivalry. By line 2, the Anglo-Saxon 'windhover' has become the French 'Falcon', the only upper case noun in the poem.

The most interesting word in the poem is 'Buckle!' in line 10. Here the **meaning is so concentrated that it is neither possible nor useful to identify a single meaning**. There are three ways of interpreting it: (a) bring together, fasten, fuse; (b) prepare for battle; (c) collapse, crumple, buckle under pressure, surrender. There is an argument that the word contains all these meanings.

HIGHER LEVEL

Questions

1	a)	Identify the four titles given to the kestrel in the title and opening lines of the poem.
	b)	What is the effect of these titles?
2		How does the poet convey the control and beauty of the kestrel's movements?
3		What do the words 'hurl' and 'gliding' suggest about the bird in flight?
4		Where in the poem is the sense of breathless excitement most evident?
5		Explore the variety of meaning in the phrase 'my heart in hiding', as it relates to Hopkins's life, purpose and ambition.
6		In what way did the sight of the kestrel stir the heart of the poet?
7		Look at the six nouns used in line 9 to summarise the qualities displayed by the kestrel. Explain your understanding of each.
8		Consider the possible meaning of the three words 'here', 'Buckle!' and 'thee' (lines 9–10).
9		The Windhover is used as a symbol of Christ. What relationship do you see between them? What have they got in common?
10		Why, do you think, might Hopkins, Jesuit and student for the priesthood, consider Christ his chevalier (or consider himself Christ's chevalier)?
11		How might Hopkins consider the achievement of Christ and the achievement of a follower of Christ to be more lovely and dangerous than that of the kestrel?
12		The windhover embodies beauty. Look at the images of emerging beauty in the final three lines of the poem. How do these images relate to the life of Christ and the life of a follower of Christ?
13		How do the movement and rhythm of the poem help to convey its meaning? Discuss the significance of alliteration in this regard.
14		Hopkins added the dedication 'To Christ our Lord' some time after he composed the poem. Without this dedication, would you be able to recognise this sonnet as a Christian poem? If so, which words or expressions would allow you to do this?
15		What words that the poet uses suggest that this is a love poem?
16		In this sonnet we encounter the natural speech of a person under the stress of excitement. Mention some of the elements that make the poet's language sound natural and true to life.
17		Working in small groups, devise a reading of the poem that does justice to its dynamic qualities.
18		Write an account of an encounter with a natural phenomenon that was so impressive that it felt like a spiritual experience.

Gerard Manley Hopkins

Before you read

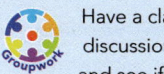 Have a class discussion and see if you can agree on what in the world deserves to be praised and glorified?

Pied Beauty

Glory be to God for dappled things –
For skies of couple-colour as a brinded cow;
For rose-moles all in stipple upon trout that swim;
Fresh-firecoal chestnut-falls; finches' wings;
Landscape plotted and pieced – fold, fallow, and plough;   5
   And áll trádes, their gear and tackle and trim.

All things counter, original, spare, strange;
Whatever is fickle, freckled (who knows how?)
With swift, slow; sweet, sour; adazzle, dim;
He fathers-forth whose beauty is past change: 10
          Praise him.

Glossary

Line	Term	Definition
Title	*Pied*	formed of different colours, like a magpie
1	*dappled*	marked with spots or splotches of colour
2	*couple-colour*	of two colours
2	*brinded*	brown with streaks of another colour
3	*rose-moles all in stipple*	rose-coloured markings spotted with black
4	*Fresh-firecoal chestnut-falls*	Hopkins liked to think of chestnuts being as bright as coals of fire
5	*plotted and pieced*	patchwork effect given by the pattern and variety of fields
5	*fold, fallow, and plough*	these are fields devoted to grazing ('fold'), unused fields ('fallow') and cultivated fields ('plough')
6	*trádes*	occupations
6	*gear and tackle and trim*	equipment appropriate to the trade; 'tackle' generally refers to rigging for a ship, while 'trim' can refer to outfits or fittings
7	*counter*	contrasting
7	*spare*	unique or rare
8	*fickle*	liable to change
9	*adazzle*	glittering, sparkling
10	*fathers-forth*	generates, creates

HIGHER LEVEL

Guidelines

The poem is dated Summer 1877, and was written at St Beuno's. This was the year in which Hopkins emerged fully as a poet. Within a few months he wrote some of the poems for which he is best known, among them 'God's Grandeur', 'Spring', 'The Windhover' and 'Pied Beauty'. These are celebratory poems which express delight in the beauty of nature and in a world 'charged with the grandeur of God'. They are **hymns of praise** to God and to the world marked by his presence.

John Ruskin

Art critic John Ruskin (1819–1900), who had a great influence on Hopkins, believed that the kinds of beauty found in nature were signs of God's presence. He argued that the experience of natural beauty prompted a desire to love and serve God. He encouraged artists to look in nature for fresh evidence of the ceaseless working of the divine power for glory and for beauty. Ruskin believed it was the role of the artist to open the eyes of others to the beauty of the world, and suggested that artists should focus on what distinguishes the individual of any species.

Commentary

Standard sonnets have fourteen lines, but this poem has ten lines plus two words. **Hopkins called this experimental form a 'curtal sonnet'.** It is constructed, as Hopkins explained, 'in **proportions** resembling those of the sonnet proper, namely, 6 + 4 instead of 8 + 6, with however a half line tail piece'.

St Ignatius, the founder of the Jesuits, summed up the philosophy of the order in two mottoes: '*Ad majorem Dei gloriam*' (For the greater glory of God) and '*Laus Deo semper*' (Praise to God at all times). In Jesuit schools there was a tradition that students wrote these mottoes at the beginning and end of each piece of work. **The sonnet follows the Jesuit tradition, by employing shortened versions of the motto at its beginning and end.**

Lines 1–4
The poem begins with a prayer glorifying God for the variety of the created world. It then goes on to give examples of this variety, moving from the sky to the water, and then to earth. Animals, fish, birds and trees are mentioned. The examples come in a rush, in quick succession.

Lines 5–6
Hopkins introduces the variety in human activity, first in relation to agriculture, where the fields have a patchwork quality, and then in relation to working trades, summarised in three words: 'gear and tackle and trim'.

Lines 7–9
These lines summarise the qualities Hopkins admires in dappled things. He likes the fact that they stand out; he likes the contrast which runs in great variety throughout nature.

Lines 10–11
Hopkins clearly identifies the unchanging and eternal God as the source from which flows all the changeable beauty of nature. In the final line Hopkins sings God's praise.

Gerard Manley Hopkins

Theme and imagery

God's glory found in nature

The glory of God is to be found in the **variety and diversity** of nature, and in the work of humans. All good things come from God and it is our duty to praise him. In this poem the presence of humans is not detrimental to nature; human activity fits the pattern of the variety in nature.

Both 'dapple' and 'pied' suggest a **diversity in patterns of colour and texture**. This visual diversity of the first five lines gives way to more general qualities of diversification and difference, to **a celebration of the unique and original** (line 7) and to the **principle of similarity and contrast** which adds such variety to the world (lines 8–9). Line 10 introduces the greatest contrast of all: between an eternal God, whose beauty is unchanging, and the constantly changing beauty of the world. Note how **Hopkins uses a present tense verb ('fathers-forth') to suggest that God's creative activity is never ending**, and how **the poem begins and ends with God**. It is the creative power of God which gives unity and harmony to the diversity of dappled things.

Movement and change

Notice how **nature in the poem lives in movement and change**. The 'couple-colour' of the sky is a passing thing. The chestnuts fall, the finches fly, the trout swim. The 'Fresh-firecoal' provides **an instance of energy which spends itself as it burns**. As for the landscape, what is 'fold' (grazing land) one year is fallow the next, and 'plough' (cultivated land) after that. All trades, with 'their gear and tackle and trim', are constantly in the process of **making and changing the world**.

Form and language

Hopkins's sonnets about nature have **a two-part structure**. In the **first part the poet describes a scene**, while the **second part places this scene in a religious context, and extracts a lesson from it**. 'Pied Beauty' – a shortened, 'curtal' sonnet – works in a similar way. The first six lines celebrate the varied wonders of God's creation, while the next four sum up the general qualities he appreciates in 'dappled things', and identifies and praises God for the ever-changing beauty of the world, whose own beauty is eternal.

The language of the poem is **dynamic, suggesting urgent activity and ongoing life and movement**. Hopkins **breaks up conventional syntax** and **multiplies associations between things** with bewildering rapidity. The lists of things ('Fresh-firecoal chestnut-falls; finches' wings') and qualities ('swift, slow; sweet, sour; adazzle, dim') come thick and fast. It is noteworthy that the **sound** of every quality word ('brinded', 'freckled', 'sweet', 'sour', 'adazzle', 'dim') **suggests the qualities they name**. The punctuation – with its dashes, commas, semi-colons, full stops and the colon of line 10 – helps create the sense of excitement and forward movement. The overall effect is to make us feel **as if the things which language lays out in space and time** and in order of succession (in the first 9 lines), are **really happening simultaneously**.

HIGHER LEVEL

Questions

1	What do the first and last lines of the poem tell you about Hopkins's purpose in writing the sonnet?
2	Hopkins compares the coloured sky to a 'brinded' cow. Do you think it is an amusing or successful comparison?
3	List all the 'dappled' things mentioned in the poem. How many are natural and how many are made by human activity?
4	How does Hopkins convey a sense of movement and change in nature?
5	What does Hopkins mean when he says that God's beauty is 'past change'?
6	There is a paradox (a seeming contradiction) in the relationship between Hopkins's God and the created universe. Comment on this.
7	How does this poem differ from the other Hopkins sonnets you have studied? Comment on this difference.
8	'In "Pied Beauty" there is an elaborate pattern of sound (assonance, alliteration and rhyme) and punctuation which enhances the meaning of the poem.' Discuss.
9	This has been described as a visionary poem. Would you agree?
10	In your own words, outline the main idea expressed by Hopkins in this poem. Are you convinced by what Hopkins is claiming here?
11	How are humans presented in this poem? Compare and contrast the presentation of humans in this poem with their presentation in 'God's Grandeur'.
12	*Groupwork* Based on this poem and the others written at St Beuno's in 1877 ('God's Grandeur', 'Spring', 'The Windhover') and 'As kingfishers catch fire', what kind of man do you imagine Hopkins to have been? In pairs or groups, discuss.
13	Using 'Pied Beauty' as a model, write a short piece (poetry or prose) urging people to open their eyes to the beauty of the world.

Gerard Manley Hopkins

Felix Randal

Felix Randal the farrier, O is he dead then? my duty all ended,
Who have watched his mould of man, big-boned and hardy-handsome
Pining, pining, till time when reason rambled in it and some
Fatal four disorders, fleshed there, all contended?

Sickness broke him. Impatient, he cursed at first, but mended   5
Being anointed and all; though a heavenlier heart began some
Months earlier, since I had our sweet reprieve and ransom
Tendered to him. Ah well, God rest him all road ever he offended!

This seeing the sick endears them to us, us too it endears.
My tongue had taught thee comfort, touch had quenched thy tears,   10
Thy tears that touched my heart, child, Felix, poor Felix Randal;

How far from then forethought of, all thy more boisterous years,
When thou at the random grim forge, powerful amidst peers,
Didst fettle for the great grey drayhorse his bright and battering sandal!

Before you read

What, do you think, are the special qualities that are needed to work with the sick and the dying? Imagine how you would cope if you had a duty of care to people who were close to death. Read the poem in light of your thoughts on the subject.

Glossary

Line	Term	Meaning
Title	*Felix Randal*	the farrier's real name was Felix Spencer; he died in 1880, aged thirty-one
1	*farrier*	blacksmith who specialises in the shoeing of horses
3	*pining*	wasting away due to pain and upset
3	*when reason rambled in it*	when Felix lost the full use of his mind
4	*Fatal four disorders*	four illnesses, all of which were fatal
4	*fleshed*	took hold in his body
4	*contended*	fought (to kill Felix)
6	*anointed*	given the Sacrament of the Sick, part of the last rites of the Catholic Church, where the priest blesses the sick person with holy oils and prays for them
6	*heavenlier heart*	a more religious outlook; a heart ready to accept God's will
7	*our sweet reprieve and ransom*	Holy Communion
8	*Tendered*	brought or offered, but also with the meaning of acting in a tender way
8	*all road ever*	in whatever way he may have; this is a dialect expression from Lancashire in the north-west of England
9	*us too it endears*	sick people grow fond of the priests who minister to them in their illnesses
11	*child*	in a spiritual sense, with also the suggestion that sickness has made him as helpless as a child
12	*How far ... years*	when you were fit and strong, thoughts of sickness and death were far from your mind
12	*boisterous*	noisy and energetic
13	*random*	built of stones of irregular shapes and sizes; also suggests a carefree attitude
13	*peers*	fellow blacksmiths
14	*fettle*	fix, prepare; also the suggestion that farrier and horse are 'in fine fettle', i.e. healthy and well
14	*drayhorse*	large, strong horse used to pull heavy loads
14	*sandal*	horseshoe

HIGHER LEVEL

Guidelines

The sonnet was written in Liverpool in April 1880. Hopkins worked in Lancashire for three months at the end of 1879. There he tended to one of his sick parishioners, a local farrier. The poem begins at the end of the story with the news of the death of Felix Randal. As a priest, Hopkins takes consolation in the fact that he helped the once powerful man to make his peace with God. He reflects how ministering to the sick creates a close bond between priest and patient, and how moved he was by the plight of his parishioner, his spiritual child. The poem concludes with an image of the blacksmith in his prime, when he had no thought of the sickness that was to befall him.

Commentary

The sonnet is clearly divided into two parts: octave and sestet. As in Hopkins's other sonnets the first is primarily descriptive, the second reflective.

> **Communion**
>
> **Hopkins believed that Holy Communion ('our sweet reprieve and ransom') commemorates and re-enacts the sacrifice Christ made on Calvary. Christ's death is believed to have freed or ransomed the human race from the effects of sin and death and opened the door to eternal life.**

The octave lines 1–8

In the first four lines, Hopkins sketches the circumstances of Felix Randal's decline and death. We learn some essential things about the farrier: we are told of his magnificent build and hardy-handsome appearance ('his mould of man, big-boned and hardy-handsome'), and his fatal illness. Lines 2–4 describe the physical decay of the once powerful Felix Randal. However, the story of Felix is told from Hopkins's perspective as a priest. From line 1 the emphasis is on his duty as a priest to comfort the sick, so lines 5–8 describe the spiritual acceptance that Felix developed ('a heavenlier heart', line 6), after initially cursing God for the sickness that befell him. Hopkins traces the change in Felix to when he brought him Holy Communion ('our sweet reprieve and ransom') and gave him the Sacrament of the Sick ('Being anointed and all'). In line 8 Hopkins turns with a sigh ('Ah well') from his memories of Felix to the present and offers prayer for the soul of the departed.

The sestet lines 9–11

In line 9, Hopkins reflects on the **sympathy and fondness that is established between a sick person and those who care for them**. But instead of the poem continuing in a more general way, Hopkins paints a personal and touching picture of his care of Felix Randal and the **emotional effect** of the experience. As a priest he had spoken and prayed words of comfort ('My tongue had taught thee comfort'); with his hands he had blessed and comforted the farrier ('touch had quenched thy tears'). But his own heart had been touched by the man's suffering and he refers to Felix as 'child', a term that suggests both a spiritual relationship and a feeling of **tenderness**. Had the poem ended here, it would have been a touching poem about the relationship between a priest and a dying man. But it doesn't.

> **Farrier**
>
> **A farrier is a blacksmith who specialises in shoeing horses. The trade of the farrier flourished in industrial towns: most heavy goods were transported on carts pulled by teams of heavy dray horses.**

The sestet lines 12–14

Instead Hopkins paints a vivid picture of the blacksmith in his prime, before there was any thought of sickness. The final three lines of the poem, which are **splendid, forceful and musical**, offer an impressive contrast to what has gone before. There is a sense

352 / DISCOVERY: POETRY ANTHOLOGY

of celebration in the final two lines, as the dominance of Felix in his mastery of his craft ('powerful amidst peers') is invested with an almost **mythic quality**. He is a figure like Hercules in his strength and power. The exclamation mark which ends the poem lends an air of **triumph and awe**.

Themes

The poem has a number of **interrelated themes**. The first is **sickness and death** and how illness can weaken the strongest of men. The second is **the comfort that religion can offer** to those close to death. The third theme relates to **Hopkins in his role as priest**; Hopkins finds **consolation** in knowing that his priestly care helped his parishioner to make peace with God before his death. Underlying the poem is the Catholic belief that the **sacraments**, here the Eucharist, or Holy Communion, and the Sacrament of the Sick, can reconcile sinners to God.

The **poem turns on the contrast between strength and weakness**; how the powerful and physically huge blacksmith is reduced to a tearful child by sickness and pain.

Language and form

This is a **Petrarchan sonnet** and follows a standard pattern of rhyme, *abbaabba ccdccd*. In addition, there are **internal rhymes**. In line 1, 'dead then' is a half-rhyme with 'ended'. In line 5, 'cursed' and 'first' are set side by side, while in line 9, 'endears' rhymes with itself. In the final line, 'grey' and 'dray' chime off each other. Hopkins uses alliteration and **alliterative phrases** throughout the poem ('big-boned', 'heavenlier heart', 'reprieve and ransom', 'tears that touched', 'bright and battering'). The use of heavy alliteration and the presence of six stresses in every line create a sense of **solidity and urgency** in a poem about a strong and powerful man.

Felix Randal was a blacksmith and Hopkins uses both **dialect phrases and older words** ('farrier', 'all road ever he offended', 'random', 'fettle') to suggest a craft which has existed for centuries.

'How far from then forethought of' in line 12 is an example of Hopkins's **daring use of language**. He **inverts normal word order** and omits some words, but still conveys his meaning. The 'random grim forge' in line 13 is an expression typical of Hopkins, conveying more than one meaning. It suggests that the dark forge where Felix worked was built of stones of irregular shapes and sizes, and thus constructed in a 'random' fashion. But the phrase also carries the hint that in his carefree days, Felix had been unthinking, or random, in his thoughts. However, it is not only in complex uses of language where Hopkins's genius is apparent. The verb 'tendered' (line 8) preceded by the use of 'our' (line 7) perfectly captures the sense of care and tenderness that Hopkins brings to his duties as a priest. The closeness between the priest and the sick man is conveyed in the use of the pronouns 'my' and 'thy', with their internal rhyme, and the **beautifully balanced** phrases 'thy tears' and 'my heart' (line 11).

Arguably, the most impressive use of language is in the **magnificent final line**, 'Didst fettle for the great grey drayhorse his bright and battering sandal!' Here, **meaning is reinforced by the soundscape** and the choice of words. The powerful rhythm, strong alliteration ('great'/'grey', 'bright'/'battering') and assonance (the 'ay' sounds in 'great grey dray') enact the hammer-blows delivered by Felix on the anvil, and the sounds of the horse's shoes as they batter the ground, while the verb 'fettle' and the onomatopoeic adjective 'battering' work perfectly.

Questions

1	What, do you think, is the tone of the first line of the poem? ■ Relieved ■ Sad and upset ■ Cold and indifferent Explain your answer. Is this the dominant tone of the poem?
2	How are the strength and power of the healthy Felix conveyed?
3	How did Felix Randal react to his sickness?
4	What role did Hopkins play in tending to the sick and dying Felix Randal? How was he affected by the experience?
5	Explain as clearly as you can why the Holy Communion is referred to as 'our sweet reprieve and ransom' in line 7.
6	Does the speaker see the illness of Felix as an unqualified disaster? Explain your answer.
7	What is the effect of the final line of the poem on our perception of Felix Randal?
8	Why is the sandal of the last line described as 'bright and battering'?
9	'The theme of the poem is the comfort that religion brings to the sick and dying.' Discuss.
10	The language of the poem is original and exciting. Choose three examples of this and show how they work.
11	From the evidence of the poem, do you think Hopkins was proud of his achievement as a priest in ministering to his sick parishioner?
12	Imagine you are Hopkins. Write a letter to your mother in which you tell her about your parishioner who died, and share your thoughts and feelings on his death.
13	You are invited to make a backing track to accompany a reading of the poem. In groups discuss the sounds and music you would use to enhance the poem. If possible, create the track.

Gerard Manley Hopkins

Inversnaid

Before you read

 Do you have a favourite wild place? What is it about it that inspires you? Share your thoughts with a partner. Now read 'Inversnaid'.

This darksome burn, horseback brown,
His rollrock highroad roaring down,
In coop and in comb the fleece of his foam
Flutes and low to the lake falls home.

A windpuff-bonnet of fawn-froth   5
Turns and twindles over the broth
Of a pool so pitchblack, fell-frowning,
It rounds and rounds Despair to drowning.

Degged with dew, dappled with dew
Are the groins of the braes that the brook treads through,   10
Wiry heathpacks, flitches of fern,
And the beadbonny ash that sits over the burn.

What would the world be, once bereft
Of wet and wildness? Let them be left,
O let them be left, wildness and wet;   15
Long live the weeds and the wilderness yet.

Glossary

Title	*Inversnaid*: a small village on Loch Lomond in the Scottish Highlands, famous for its waterfall	
1	*darksome*: mixture of 'dark' and 'handsome'	
1	*burn*: Scots word for stream	
2	*rollrock*: describes the river's path, a rocky, rolling path	
2	*highroad*: the path or course of the river	
3	*coop*: enclosed hollow where the water is hemmed in by rocks	
3	*comb*: the fast-flowing water combs over the stones	
4	*Flutes*: forms channels; also the sound made by the stream	
5	*windpuff-bonnet of fawn-froth*: the windblown foam on the pool at the foot of a waterfall; the foam is a fawn colour and sits on the water like a hat	
6	*twindles*: a word coined by Hopkins, probably combining 'twists', 'dwindles' and 'twitches'; another possible meaning is 'dwindling into twins' (i.e. dividing itself in half)	
6	*broth*: seething water	
7	*fell-frowning*: frowning in a sinister way; a fell is also a mountain	
8	*rounds*: surrounds; murmurs	
9	*Degged*: sprinkled	
10	*groins*: folds or curved edges, e.g. where the legs meet the body	
10	*braes*: steep banks	
10	*brook*: stream	
11	*Wiry heathpacks*: clumps of heather	
11	*flitches*: ragged clumps	
12	*beadbonny ash*: the ash tree, with its pleasing (bonny) red berries (looking like beads)	
13	*bereft*: deprived	

Guidelines

The poem was written in September 1881. Writing to a friend towards the end of his life, Hopkins wrote: 'I could wish I were in the Highlands. I never had more than a glimpse of their skirts. I hurried from Glasgow one day to Loch Lomond. The day was dark and partly hid the lake, yet it did not altogether disfigure it but gave it a pensive or solemn beauty which left a deep impression. I landed at Inversnaid … for a few hours.' The visit to Inversnaid was a fleeting one but Hopkins's notebooks have many references and notes on waterfalls and streams in other wild places.

Commentary

The poem describes a stream in the Highlands of Scotland. The first stanza describes the brown stream flowing rapidly and falling over a waterfall to the lake below. The second describes the froth on the surface of a dark whirlpool on the path of the stream. The third describes the gentle landscape on the upper part of the stream. In the final stanza, the poet **wonders what would become of the world** if it were deprived of such wet and wild landscapes, and pleads for them to be retained.

The poem has two main aspects: one is a celebration of the wild beauty of the Scottish Highlands; the second is the **verbal music and word play** that Hopkins uses to capture the landscape. In this, as in his other work, **Hopkins captures the uniqueness of each thing he describes**. Throughout the poem **sound, rhythm, movement and description work together to paint a fresh, original and precisely accurate picture** of what is being described.

Stanza 1
The first stanza is a description of a stream (a 'burn') rushing down a hillside over its rocky, rolling riverbed. The water is rushing at such a pace that the stream is topped with foam. The river bed has many stones and pools so that the flow of water is sometimes checked in hollows ('coop', line 3), or the water combs its way over and through protruding stones and obstacles. The sense of line 4 is that the foamy water forms channels ('Flutes') until it flows over a low waterfall into the lake below. In the first stanza, the **energetic surge of the stream is emphasised in the strong alliteration** ('burn, horseback brown', 'rollrock highroad roaring') and the music of the stream is reflected in the **repetition of the musical 'r' sound**.

Stanza 2
The second stanza describes the brown-coloured suds in a 'pitchblack' whirlpool on the stream's path. The froth sits on the surface of the pool like a bonnet. The water in the pool is described as 'broth', suggesting it is thick and brown from the peat soil of the mountain. In this whirlpool, the froth twists and turns on the surface of the twirling water. In lines 7–8, the pool is described as so black and so menacing ('fell-frowning'), and its swirling water as so powerful, that even Despair itself would drown here. (Another way of reading the line is that the energy of the swirling water overcomes despair.)

Stanza 3
The third stanza is a piece of landscape painting describing the upper part of the stream, now called a 'brook', and its banks. This stretch of water, being a 'brook', is a gentler stretch of water. The 'groins of the braes' are the narrow folds that the brook passes through on this part of its journey to the lake. Here the banks are

Gerard Manley Hopkins

sprinkled with dew, which creates the kind of dappled effect celebrated by Hopkins in 'Pied Beauty'. The 'heathpacks' are clumps of heather, while the 'beadbonny ash' depicts the bright berries of the rowan tree that is common in the Highlands. The landscape here is dotted with the splotches and flecks of colour so loved by Hopkins. What is notable in these lines is Hopkins's understanding of **how a variety of strong consonant sounds suggests the range of colour in the scene**.

Stanza 4

Whereas the first three stanzas are purely descriptive, the final stanza **reflects on the value** of what the poet has seen at Inversnaid, and wonders what would happen if the world was deprived of such places. A lover of nature, Hopkins pleads that such areas 'Of wet and of wildness … be left', noting that the world needs 'the weeds and the wilderness yet'.

Themes

The poem expresses **a deep appreciation of the wilderness**, away from the influence of humans. Hopkins was much concerned with what he called 'the decline of wild nature', and having experienced the depressing and poisonous atmosphere of industrial Britain, he delighted in the wildness, remoteness, peace and unspoiled beauty of places like Inversnaid. The wilderness symbolised for Hopkins what he described in 'God's Grandeur' as 'the dearest freshness deep down things'. Hopkins regarded wilderness as **nature in its purest form**. Hopkins was always able to find spiritual meanings in nature, although 'Inversnaid' is one of the few poems in which God is not mentioned. However, the flowing stream in the Highland wilderness has spiritual overtones. For Hopkins, it signifies the **waters of healing and rebirth** so often mentioned in both Old and New Testaments.

The poem is an exercise in the kind of word painting that Hopkins loved. The emphasis is placed on the colour, texture and movement of the stream and the surrounding nature. Interestingly, there is darkness in the imagery at the heart of the poem, depicting a 'pool so pitchblack' it can round 'Despair to drowning'.

Language and form

The poem is written in a four-line, rhyming stanza and has the quality of a **Scottish folk song**, no more so than in line 12: 'And the beadbonny ash that sits over the burn'. The four verses are packed with **alliteration**: 'fleece of his foam' (line 3), 'Degged with dew' (line 9), 'flitches of fern' (line 11), 'wet and wildness' (line 14); **vowel music**: in line 9, 'Degged with dew, dappled with dew', we move from 'e' to 'i' to 'u', and then from 'a' to 'i' to 'u'; **internal rhyme**: 'comb' and 'foam' (line 3); **repetition, personification, compound words**: 'rollrock' (line 2), 'heathpacks' (line 11), 'beadbonny' (line 12); **dialect words**: 'burn' (line 1), 'braes' (line 10); and **archaic words**: 'rounds' with the sense of 'whispers' (line 8). The soundscape of the poem, with its strong, clear-sounding words, mirrors the energy, movement and sound of the rushing stream. Hopkins uses the pronoun 'his' instead of 'its' in referring to the stream (line 2); the **personification of the rushing water** gives effect to the idea of **a living stream**.

Exam-Style Questions

Understanding the poem

1	In stanza 1, what words and phrases capture the energy of the gushing stream?
2	'… and low to the lake falls home'. Describe what is happening at the end of stanza 1.
3	a) Describe the water in the whirlpool of stanza 2. b) What is the mood of this stanza?
4	Read stanza 3 in your best Scottish accent and enjoy the music of the language.
5	What does the poet wish for in the final stanza? How does he emphasise this wish?

Thinking about the poem

1	Comment on Hopkins's playful and experimental use of language in the poem in phrases such as 'flitches of fern'. Select your favourite example.
2	What does the scene depicted in the poem mean to Hopkins, and why?
3	Show how rhythm and movement contribute to the effect of the poem.
4	What, do you think, is the main point of the poem?
5	This poem differs in one respect from the other nature poems by Hopkins you have read on the course. Comment on this difference.
6	Hopkins believed in the value of wild and natural landscapes. How important do you consider them to be? Discuss your opinions in groups or pairs.
7	'Hopkins was both energised and thrown into anxiety by his visit to Inversnaid.' Discuss.

Imagining

1	Write a short poem or prose piece in response to the title 'In Praise of Wilderness'. If possible, make a recording of your piece. Consider what images, sounds and music you would use in making a film to accompany it.
2	What, do you think, attracts tourists to the Wild Atlantic Way tourist trail? Would Hopkins have understood the attraction? Share your thoughts with your class.

SNAPSHOT

- Poet's love of the Scottish Highlands
- First three stanzas are descriptive, and create pictures
- Last stanza reflects on the value of wild nature and pleads for it to be left alone
- Lively rhythm and movement
- Constant alliteration
- One of the few poems by Hopkins where God is not mentioned

Gerard Manley Hopkins

The Terrible Sonnets

'No worst, there is none' and 'I wake and feel the fell of dark' are two of a series of sonnets which Hopkins wrote in Dublin in 1885. Along with the later 'Thou art indeed just, Lord', these are known as the 'dark' or 'terrible sonnets', or 'the **sonnets of Desolation**'. These poems reveal Hopkins in **a mood of black depression and facing despair, weighing up the alternatives of death and madness**. They were written after a prolonged bout of psychological torment in which he imagined himself barely out of Hell. The causes of this torment were multiple, and **the sonnets reflect years of frustration**.

In Dublin Hopkins was overcome by the drudgery and boredom involved in marking large numbers of examination scripts at University College, Dublin, but his career as a university professor was merely the culmination of a **life marked by disappointed hopes**. During his working life, as he remarked, he had done nothing 'but do without, take tosses, and obey'. His eccentric manner had undermined his gifts as a preacher; he was a scholar who had produced no important work; he was a lover of beauty who was obliged to minister for years in ugly slums; he was a poet whose work was not recognised in his lifetime; and a priest whose varied talents were never fully made use of. His often poor health left him with impaired energy. He was a patriotic Englishman forced to live in a country (Ireland) whose 'unlawful' politics he despised. Above all these circumstances, **his fanatical devotion to duty tended to make him too hard on himself**. One commentator suggests that his action displayed 'a destructive ruthlessness with himself'. In the depths of despair, **he allowed himself little comfort and sought little outside help**, relying instead on his own willpower to carry him through. By willpower alone he tried to overcome his feelings of loss, frustration and despair and act as a true servant of God. The strain of this effort caused him great suffering and personal anguish.

HIGHER LEVEL

Before you read

 In pairs, speculate on the circumstances and state of mind of a person who describes their situation as the worst possible, as Hopkins does at the outset of this sonnet.

No worst, there is none

No worst, there is none. Pitched past pitch of grief,
More pangs will, schooled at forepangs, wilder wring.
Comforter, where, where is your comforting?
Mary, mother of us, where is your relief?
My cries heave, herds-long; huddle in a main, a chief –   5
woe, wórld-sorrow; on an áge-old anvil wince and sing –
Then lull, then leave off. Fury had shrieked 'No ling-
ering! Let me be fell; force I must be brief'.

O the mind, mind has mountains; cliffs of fall
Frightful, sheer, no-man-fathomed. Hold them cheap   10
May who ne'er hung there. Nor does long our small
Durance deal with that steep or deep. Here! creep,
Wretch, under a comfort serves in a whirlwind: all
Life death does end and each day dies with sleep.

Glossary

1	*No worst, there is none*:	compare Edgar in King Lear: 'The worst is not / So long as we can say "This is the worst"'
1	*Pitched past pitch of grief*:	made blacker than black (*pitch* = black); or thrown farther than grief can throw (*pitch* = throw); or beyond any measurable pitch of sound (a musical analogy)
2	*pangs*:	sudden pains, physical or emotional
2	*schooled*:	trained, conditioned
2	*forepangs*:	previous pangs
2	*wring*:	distress or torture (*wring* = twist)
3	*Comforter*:	the Holy Ghost
4	*Mary*:	to many Catholics, Mary is the 'Comforter of the Afflicted'
5	*cries heave, herds-long*:	his cries of distress go on and on like the bellowing of herds of cattle
5	*main*:	wide expanse, as of an ocean; principal part
8	*fell*:	cruel and swift in the infliction of pain
10	*fathomed*:	measured (the depth of something); *fathom* = unit of depth in water
10	*Hold them cheap*:	dismiss or underestimate them
11	*ne'er*:	never
12	*Durance*:	the human ability to endure; short for endurance

Gerard Manley Hopkins

Guidelines

The poem was written in Dublin sometime in 1885. 'No worst, there is none' is the most despairing of the Terrible Sonnets. The poem might justly be described as **an uncensored look into the depths of Hopkins's soul**. In a letter to his friend he described how these poems came to him 'like inspirations unbidden and against my will'. He also described his state as one 'of a continually jaded and harassed mind'.

Commentary

The structure of the sonnet is clear. The eight lines of the octave (lines 1–8) describe the **intense mental agony** of a man in deep spiritual desolation and depression. The six lines of the sestet (lines 9–14) offer a general reflection on what has been described in the octave.

The octave

The theme is announced in the first sentence – 'No worst, there is none': there is no bottom limit to this suffering; the poet declares he has been thrown beyond all measure of grief. In line 2, Hopkins suggests that the suffering he will experience in the future will be worse than what has gone before; the new torments ('pangs') have been taught by the previous ones ('forepangs'), so his mind and soul will be tortured all the more ('wilder wring'). In the face of such horror, the speaker looks in vain for help and comfort from the Holy Spirit (the 'Comforter'), repeating the question, 'where?' (line 3). He next turns to the Virgin Mary ('mother of us') for relief (line 4). These pleadings remain unanswered and it is clear that Hopkins feels cut off and alone in his torment.

> **The Furies**
>
> The reference to 'Fury' comes from Greek myth and drama. The Furies were spirits from the underworld who punished those who had committed a crime. They were a continuous, tormenting presence, devoid of human sympathy and relentless in their desire to punish. They are sometimes regarded as the embodiment of a tortured conscience, never letting the person escape their predicament.

Lines 5–8 use **a series of disconnected images** to convey his suffering. Echoing Psalm 130 ('Out of the depths, I cry unto thee, O Lord'), line 5 describes his cries of despair. His cries 'heave' or come forcefully from his chest, suggesting the physical side of his distress. He associates his cries with the ungainly heaving movement of a line of cattle ('herds-long') as they move one behind the other. Next he thinks of his cries huddling together like a herd in a great expanse ('huddle in a main'). 'Huddle' suggests **fear and unease**. The word 'main' also brings in an image of his cries crowding together in an ocean of sorrow. In line 6 there is the suggestion that his personal torment forms part of a greater 'wórld-sorrow', presumably that of a sinful world, or perhaps a world in which the faithful feel abandoned by God? He now compares his cries to the sound of iron being beaten on an anvil. The iron seems to wince or flinch as it rings out, just as the poet's soul cries out as it is beaten on the 'áge-old' anvil of suffering. For some commentators the image of 'wince and sing' suggests the soul of the faithful person singing God's praise, in the depths of their suffering.

In lines 7–8, there is a **temporary respite** from torment. Just as the sounds of a violent storm can 'lull' and 'then leave off', so his cries settle. This lull seems to follow the intervention of 'Fury' (line 7), a vengeful spirit whose shriek, echoing in the poet's tormented mind, speaks of sudden and cruel punishment: '"Let me be fell; force I must be brief"'. Interestingly, the word 'lingering' is broken in two at the line break. Does this suggest that the poet is somehow hanging on to his own despair?

HIGHER LEVEL

The sestet

The tone of the final six lines of the sonnet is more subdued and less agitated than that of the first eight. The sestet comments on the octave; it is a **grim reflection** on the ways in which human beings can be exposed to terror and intense suffering. Hopkins uses the image of a mountain climber confronted with the prospect of plunging into an unmeasured abyss to suggest the horror of a mind's plunge into deep despair. In lines 10–11 ('Hold them cheap / … hung there'), Hopkins is saying that only those who have never experienced the depths of despair that he has ('ne'er hung there') may make light of the terrors that he is describing ('hold them cheap'). In the next sentence (lines 11–12), he is saying that even those like himself who have reached the depths of despair are not able to endure its horrors for long. Human endurance ('Durance') is small or limited in such cases.

In the final lines the sonnet offers 'a comfort [that] serves in a whirlwind' (line 13), a phrase which suggests that when someone is in such a state of desperation as the one the poem describes, any means of sheltering from it is better than none. In this instance, the comfort is sleep, or death: 'all / Life death does end and each day dies with sleep' (lines 13–14).

For Hopkins, though, this thought can scarcely have been consoling. Each day may die with sleep, but given what we have learned from the poem the next day will probably yield new horrors.

Theme and imagery

The theme of this poem is **mental and spiritual torment**. The poem expresses this torment in a **profound** way. The poet is **overcome by feelings of desolation and abandonment**. In the octave, he uses a series of disconnected images to convey his cries of despair, moving from images of a herd of cattle to the sound of metal being beaten on an anvil, to the shrieking of a Fury. The randomness of the imagery suggests a mind **desperately searching for an adequate means to express his torment**. Little wonder that Hopkins drew on the imagery of Shakespeare's *King Lear*, which explores the themes of mental anguish and madness, as well as Greek legend, to convey the horror of his experience. The opening words of the poem, 'No worst, there is none', echo those of Edgar (*King Lear*), upon seeing his blind father: '… the worst is not / So long as we can say, "This is the worst."' In lines 9–10 of the poem, the imagery of cliffs and mountains is similar to that in Act 4, Scene 6 of *King Lear*, where Edgar leads his blind father in imagination to the cliffs of Dover and gives him a vivid description of the dizzying fall. The phrase 'no-man-fathomed' – echoes Edgar's 'So many fathoms down precipitating'. Turning away from the 'steep or deep' (line 12), the poet seeks any shelter in a whirlwind. The reference to 'Wretch' echoes Lear's speech in the storm: 'Poor naked wretches, wheresoe'er you are / That bide the pelting of this pitiless storm …' (Act 3, Scene 3). The shelter brings to mind the hovel found for the tormented Lear by his servant, Kent. The final line of the sonnet echoes a line from Shakespeare's *The Tempest*: 'Our little life is rounded with a sleep' (Act 4, Scene 1). The effect of these allusions is to add weight to the poem.

In the sonnet there is an overriding sense that despair is associated with **falling, plunging or being thrown** into darkness, a personal version of the First Fall, when sin tainted the 'Innocent mind and Mayday in girl and boy', as Hopkins says in 'Spring'.

Language and form

The poem is a Petrarchan sonnet, with an octave and sestet and rhyming *abbaabba cdcdcd*. In traditional sonnets, many of the lines begin with an unstressed syllable. Here, line 4 ('Mary'), line 10 ('Frightful'), line 13

Gerard Manley Hopkins

('Wretch') and the last line ('Life') **all begin with a stressed syllable, adding an emphatic and unrelenting quality** to the poem, an effect also achieved by the **heavy alliteration** – 'Pitched past pitch' (line 1), and the brilliant use of consonant sounds – 'h', 'w', 'f', for example – which **embody the physical effort involved in saying the words of the sonnet**. Compared to the nature sonnets, **the diction is simpler and more straightforward** and there are **no compound or unusual words**. There is **compression** and the use of words which have **multiple meanings**, such as 'pitch' in line 1. 'Pitch' is used to convey the sense of being thrown or cast forcefully beyond any normal level of suffering. The nerves of the speaker are like a musical instrument set to an unbearably high pitch. 'Pitch' also conveys complete darkness, as in 'pitch black'. The word is also used to describe the high-pitched shrieks of a person overwhelmed by suffering.

Questions

1	Consider what it means to be 'Pitched past pitch of grief' (line 1).
2	In lines 3–4, the speaker asks two questions. What is the answer to these questions?
3	What is the effect of the verb 'heave' in line 5?
4	What is the effect of the speaker personifying the voice in his mind as a Fury?
5	Comment on the imagery of the mountains and the cliffs in the sestet. Do you think it is effective?
6	What is the nature of the relief from the torment of despair, as described in the last two lines of the poem?
7	How does Hopkins suggest that the spiritual and mental torments he records here are not peculiar to himself?
8	What image of human life emerges from the poem?
9	Hopkins was a deeply religious man. What help does he get from his religious faith here?
10	What lines in the poem best convey the intensity of the poet's torment through the use of sound, rhythm and word choice?
11	Having read the poem, do you understand the cause of the suffering described so vividly by Hopkins? Explain your answer.
12	Which of the following statements is closest to your view of the poem? ■ The Hopkins who emerges from this poem is a person of immense courage ■ The Hopkins who emerges from this poem is a person obsessed with himself ■ The Hopkins who emerges from this poem is a person who suffers intolerable torment Explain your choice, referring to all three statements in your answer.
13	Using the title, 'No worst, there is none' as a source of inspiration, write a monologue in which a person, real or imagined, speaks of their situation.
14	In groups, identify a text (poem, novel, play, autobiography, film) which paints a convincing and powerful portrait of a person in a state of desolation.

HIGHER LEVEL

Before you read

Darkness, insomnia, nightmares, unheard cries for help, hell, bitterness, self-disgust. In pairs, discuss the kind of text where you would expect to find these elements.

I wake and feel the fell of dark, not day

I wake and feel the fell of dark, not day.
What hours, O what black hours we have spent
This night! what sights you, heart, saw; ways you went!
And more must, in yet longer light's delay.
With witness I speak this. But where I say   5
Hours I mean years, mean life. And my lament
Is cries countless, cries like dead letters sent
To dearest him that lives alas! away.

I am gall, I am heartburn. God's most deep decree
Bitter would have me taste: my taste was me;   10
Bones built in me, flesh filled, blood brimmed the curse.
Selfyeast of spirit a dull dough sours. I see
The lost are like this, and their scourge to be
As I am mine, their sweating selves; but worse.

Glossary

1	*fell*: a word with a variety of meanings: as a noun it means the hairy skin of an animal, a hill, bitterness; as an adjective it means cruel, fierce, malevolent	
2	*black hours*: the hours of darkness and despair before morning	
5	*witness*: good reason, personal experience	
7	*dead*: here, undelivered or unanswered	
9	*gall*: bitter liquid from the gall bladder, associated with bitterness of spirit	
9	*decree*: law	
12	*Selfyeast of spirit*: the poet imagines his spirit as a yeast which sours the body	
13	*The lost*: the damned souls in hell	

Guidelines

The poem is undated but was most likely written in 1885, during Hopkins's time in Dublin. It is the darkest of the 'terrible sonnets', taking up where 'No worst, there is none' leaves off, with the speaker waking from sleep. But where 'No worst …' ended in sleep, this poem ends in a version of hell.

Gerard Manley Hopkins

Commentary

This sonnet is an expression of Hopkins's **spiritual and mental crisis** and of his struggle to overcome it. He **enacts** this struggle rather than merely describing it, and **involves the reader intimately** in it. In the process, he **strains and stresses language** to achieve a remarkable intensity of expression. Sometimes the language is so compact that meaning is obscured ('And more must, in yet longer light's delay', 'Selfyeast of spirit a dull dough sours'). In a sense, **words are not adequate to express what Hopkins is feeling**: the terrible consciousness that God, the ultimate source of meaning in his life, is too far away to hear his cries of distress. The sonnet divides itself into two distinct parts. The first part, consisting of the eight opening lines (the octave), are mainly devoted to a description, and enactment, of the speaker's terrifying, tortured state of mind. The second part, consisting of the remaining six lines (the sestet), is mainly reflective, as the speaker wonders why he has been chosen by God to suffer so intensely, and compares his state to that of souls condemned to endure the pains of Hell for eternity.

The octave

The first four lines of the sonnet show the speaker suffering symptoms which are characteristic of despair and depression. The speaker wakes in darkness, long before daybreak, and is haunted by despairing thoughts until it is time to rise. Waking is accompanied by the perception of the **darkness as a malevolent, menacing element**: 'the fell of dark'. Here, **'fell' is both an adjective and a noun**. As an adjective it means 'having evil intent or purpose'; as a noun it is the hairy skin of a wild beast, an image of nightmarish horror. The night has been marked not by refreshing sleep, but by 'black hours' filled with terrifying visions of repulsive things. To add to the miseries already endured, the speaker knows there will be further hours of self-torture before he faces another comfortless day ('And more must, in yet longer light's delay').

The extent of the speaker's misery is further emphasised in lines 5–6: 'But where I say / Hours I mean years, mean life'. Hopkins's bouts of depression increased both in intensity and in length as he grew older. Thus, each episode, like the one described in the sonnet, seemed like an **eternity** of suffering and horror, extending intolerably both into the past and into the future, taking over his entire life. In lines 6–8, the speaker comes to the heart of his suffering: **the experience of being cut off entirely from God and thus from all spiritual comfort**. His 'countless' cries for God's help are not being answered. God, i.e. 'dearest him', is so far away that he cannot, or does not wish to, answer the sufferer's pleas, which are like 'dead letters'. Interestingly, Hopkins expresses no anger towards God, still referred to as 'dearest him'.

The sestet

In the sestet, the opening sentence ('I am gall, I am heartburn') presents an image of the speaker's sense of his torment. Gall is a bitter substance produced by the liver; heartburn is a form of indigestion caused by stomach acids; both can leave a bitter taste in the mouth. These physical ailments are symbolic of Hopkins's bitter state of mind. They also suggest that his entire being, his body as well as his mind, was in pain during his bouts of depression. In 1888, he noted that 'that body cannot rest when it is in pain, nor the mind be at peace as long as something bitter distils in it and aches'.

He seeks an explanation for his sufferings and bitter frustration in a mysterious ('most deep') decree issued by God at his (Hopkins's) birth, which laid down that he would be doomed to taste bitterness in his life, or that he himself would be the taste of bitterness ('my taste was me'). It is **a haunting image of self-loathing**. The 'curse' of line 11 is the curse of Adam, the curse of original human sinfulness. In Hopkins's eyes, it is his sinful nature that is the origin of his unbearable spiritual and mental suffering and his physical distress. He sees the curse as having taken effect at his birth and as being part of his very nature – his bones, flesh and blood.

In line 12 ('Selfyeast of spirit a dull dough sours') he imagines the sinful and selfish spirit as a yeast which makes the 'dull dough' of his body sour. Instead of being nourished by bread, he finds its taste disgusting. (Compare this to the bread of Holy Communion which nourishes the soul.) The imagery suggests that **an overpowering, oppressive weight** has settled on his spirit. This idea is reinforced in the final two lines, where the speaker compares himself to the damned souls in Hell ('the lost'). Hopkins sees the real misery of the damned as the torture of facing the reality of what they are: 'their sweating selves'.

It can scarcely be said that the poem ends on a hopeful note, but there is a slight withdrawal from total despair in its last two words: 'but worse'. While sharing in kind some of the experiences of the damned, the speaker sees a difference in degree between their miseries and his: theirs extend into eternity; the speaker is not in hell, and therefore the damned are worse off than he is because their torment, unlike his, is endless.

Hopkins on Hell

Hopkins wrote a sermon on Hell, a common practice in his day, in which he emphasised the absolute self-isolation of the damned, left alone to torment themselves with the guilt of their sins. In imagery similar to that employed in 'I wake and feel', Hopkins wrote of the damned in Hell eternally confronting the bitter taste of their sins: 'no worm but themselves gnaws them, and gnaws no one but themselves'. The worm here is the worm of conscience, 'which is the mind gnawing and feeding on its own miserable self'.

Theme and imagery

The sonnet is a powerful account of spiritual desolation, mental torment and physical sickness.

The theme of the **relationship between the dutiful priest and his God** is to the forefront of this sonnet. The speaker's cries for help do not reach God, their intended recipient. At the same time the poem suggests that his suffering was decreed from God. The decree is described as 'deep', which is different from being understandable. (In one draft of the poem, Hopkins adjusted 'deep' to 'just' but changed it back to his original choice.)

The **symbolism of light and darkness** reinforces the main idea here. Light (**endlessly delayed**) signifies hope and reassurance, while darkness signifies spiritual desolation. This symbolism is in tune with the common description of this kind of spiritual despair as 'the dark night of the soul'.

The **taste** of bitterness and sourness as a reflection of his spiritual desolation is a powerful image. Here the **physical mirrors the spiritual**. In 'As kingfishers catch fire', Hopkins celebrated the idea that the purpose of the self is to become most itself, in all its individuality and uniqueness. In this sonnet, the self, tainted by original sin, tastes bitter in his own mouth. **The self is a source of loathing and self-hatred**. Given the importance of bread in Catholic ritual, where the bread of the Eucharist nourishes the soul, the image of the self as a bread that is sour and dull is striking.

Hopkins on hope

'There is a happiness, hope, the anticipation of happiness hereafter; it is better than happiness, but it is not happiness now. It is as if one were dazzled by a spark or star in the dark, seeing it but not seeing by it ...'

The end of the poem in which the speaker compares his suffering to the suffering of the souls in hell is startling. What distinguishes Hopkins's despair from the despair of the souls in hell is that he retains hope that he will go to heaven. In his periods of darkness, this hope did not comfort Hopkins, but it may have prevented him from surrendering completely to his despair.

Gerard Manley Hopkins

Form and language

The poem is a Petrarchan sonnet, with an octave and sestet, rhyming *abba abba ccd ccd*.

The rhythm is smoother and the language simpler than in the nature sonnets of 1877. While there is compression of meaning, these are more mature and thoughtful poems, **more direct** and emotionally powerful. The poem is less heavily alliterative than many of the other poems we look at. Instead, the sonnet uses **long vowel sounds and repetition** to convey the speaker's sense of weariness and despair, as in: 'What hours, O what black hours we have spent' (line 2). At moments it seems as if the words barely raise above a whisper: 'With witness I speak this' (line 5).

Questions

1	Comment on the symbolism of darkness and light in the poem.
2	In the second line, the speaker refers to 'black hours we have spent'. What is the significance of 'we' here?
3	What kind of intervention would help to ease the speaker's misery?
4	The speaker is being racked by two kinds of suffering. What are these, and how are they suggested?
5	Do you think that the speaker derives any consolation in thinking that the plight of souls in hell is similar to his own, 'but worse'? How does his plight differ from theirs?
6	What is the speaker's explanation of his suffering?
7	Explore the imagery of taste in the poem and comment on its effectiveness.
8	Compare Hopkins's view of selfhood in this poem with his view in 'As kingfishers catch fire'.
9	'The poem paints a portrait of a lonely, friendless person.' Discuss.
10	What view of God emerges from this poem?
11	The word 'I' is used eight times in the poem. What is the effect of this? Does it, for example, make the poem an intensely personal statement? Does it make the speaker seem preoccupied with himself? Explain your answer.
12	Where in the poem is the intensity of the poet's experience most vividly expressed?
13	Write a short poem or poetic monologue inspired by the title 'Dead Letters'.
14	*Groupwork* — The sonnet has many of the elements of a horror movie. With this in mind, discuss the colour scheme, the images, the sound effects and music you would use in making a film to illustrate the words of the poem.

HIGHER LEVEL

Before you read

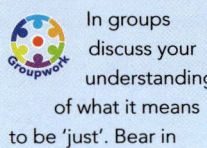 In groups discuss your understanding of what it means to be 'just'. Bear in mind your discussion when you read the sonnet.

Thou art indeed just, Lord

Justus quidem tu es, Domine, si disputem tecum; verumtamen justa loquar ad te: Quare via impiorum prosperatur? &c.

Thou art indeed just, Lord, if I contend
With thee; but, sir, so what I plead is just.
Why do sinners' ways prosper? and why must
Disappointment all I endeavour end?
Wert thou my enemy, O thou my friend,   5
How wouldst thou worse, I wonder, than thou dost
Defeat, thwart me? Oh, the sots and thralls of lust
Do in spare hours more thrive than I that spend,
Sir, life upon thy cause. See, banks and brakes
Now, leavèd how thick! lacèd they are again   10
With fretty chervil, look, and fresh wind shakes
Them; birds build – but not I build; no, but strain,
Time's eunuch, and not breed one work that wakes.
Mine, O thou lord of life, send my roots rain.

Glossary

Epigraph	*Justus… prosperatur:*	the Prophet Jeremiah (Book of Jeremiah, 12:1) wonders why God permits the good to suffer and the wicked to prosper; the Latin is translated in the first lines of the poem
1	*contend:*	argue, dispute, debate
7	*thwart:*	obstruct, frustrate
7	*sots:*	drunkards
7	*thralls:*	slaves
9	*banks:*	hedgerows, riverbanks
9	*brakes:*	areas where plants grow in abundance
10	*leavèd how thick:*	how thick they are with leaves
11	*fretty chervil:*	chervil is a kind of wild parsley, with delicately fringed ('fretty' or fretted) leaves
13	*Time's eunuch:*	the 'time' here is the present, when he feels so unproductive; a eunuch is a man incapable of having children; the usage echoes a verse in Matthew's gospel which suggests that some eunuch's make themselves so 'for the kingdom of heaven's sake'
13	*work that wakes:*	a living work; Hopkins may be referring to his priestly work or to his poetry

Gerard Manley Hopkins

Guidelines

'Thou art indeed just, Lord' was written in Dublin on St Patrick's Day 1889, in the last year of the poet's life. The year before, Hopkins had written:

> 'What is my wretched life? Five wasted years almost have passed in Ireland. I am ashamed of the little I have done, of my waste of time. All my undertakings miscarry. I am like a straining eunuch. I wish then for death, yet if I died now I should die imperfect, no master of myself, and that is the worst failure of all. O my God, look down on me.'

Hopkins on being in Ireland

'Tomorrow morning I shall have been three years in Ireland, three hard wearying wasting wasted years. … In those I have done God's will (in the main) and many many examination papers.'

Like the other 'dark' or 'terrible sonnets' ('No worst, there is none' and 'I wake and feel the fell of dark'), this one is largely autobiographical. The speaker is Hopkins himself and the subject matter is his despair that he has accomplished so little in his life, which he has dedicated to God. His feelings of failure were heightened by his unhappiness and personal circumstances. He disliked his job as a Professor of Greek in Dublin and his health was poor. He believed that he had little of worth to show for his sincere efforts as a priest to achieve something for those around him. He was also conscious that his poetic inspiration had largely failed and dried up. His old notebooks were filled with 'the beginning of things', like 'ruins and wrecks' which might well have been completed but for the fact, as he put it, that 'every impulse and spring of art seems to have died in me'.

These frustrations are reflected in 'Thou art indeed just, Lord'. In the year before he wrote the poem, he made some nightmarish entries in a notebook, describing his utter despair and self-contempt. In one of his entries, Hopkins recorded that 'I began to enter on that course of loathing and hopelessness which I have so often felt before, which made me fear madness'. It is little wonder that Hopkins described this, and the other 'Terrible Sonnets', as having been 'written in blood'.

Commentary

Lines 1–2
The unhappy, frustrated speaker, who is a priest and a creative artist, is **putting difficult questions to God**. He states in the opening line that God is just, but he has questions, and he feels those questions are also 'just'. The questions he goes on to ask are similar to those found in the Old Testament when good people, like the prophet Jeremiah, are shocked that the wicked are permitted to prosper, while the good endure hardship and disappointment. **For the good person, God's justice is incomprehensible.** This is the problem at the heart of this sonnet.

Lines 3–4
The speaker asks God why it is that people who spend their lives doing evil deeds enjoy success and prosperity while, at the same time, everything he, a faithful servant, attempts ends in failure.

Lines 5–7
He wonders how God, whom he acknowledges as his friend, could treat him any worse, if he were his enemy. As things stand, God seems to obstruct and defeat the poet's best efforts.

HIGHER LEVEL

Lines 7–9
The poet now moves to direct statement. Drunkards and those who are slave to their sexual appetites have more success in their spare time than he who devotes his life to the service of God.

Lines 9–12
There is a **shift of focus** beginning in line 9. Hopkins urges God to look on nature coming alive again in spring. There is energy in the wind and the birds are building their nests.

Lines 12–14
In mid-sentence, the speaker contrasts his situation with nature. Nature may be full of new life, but he is barren, dry and unproductive, and has nothing worthwhile to show for all his efforts. He opened the poem with a challenging, complaining question and **closes with a prayer**, asking God to nourish his talent and make him productive.

Themes and imagery

The poem is born out of a sense of bafflement with divine justice. The sonnet is a carefully composed expression of despair made by a faithful servant who questions whether his life of devotion has been wasted. The poem expresses a deep sense of personal failure and confusion. Hopkins portrays himself as existing in a state of spiritual and artistic paralysis: his **central image for this is sexual impotence**; he resents the fact that he cannot share in the teeming growth of nature, since **he cannot beget anything**. All around him, he sees growth, renewal and new life. But he is 'Time's eunuch' who cannot 'breed one work that wakes', i.e. one work that comes alive. The poem ends on a prayer: Hopkins prays that his sterility may be relieved by the God, who, as Hopkins put it in 'Pied Beauty', 'fathers-forth' everything in creation: 'Mine, O thou lord of life, send my roots rain'.

Underlying the structure of the poem and the language of the courtroom is the **image of God as the ultimate judge of human life**. The problem for Hopkins is that he sees no evidence of God acting justly, that is, giving people, including himself, what they deserve.

Form and language

The poem follows the rhyming scheme of a Petrarchan sonnet, *abba abba cdc dcd*, but the poem does not fall into the neat division of octave and sestet, with **new ideas beginning mid-line**. The poem can be divided loosely into **four movements**. In the first four lines, the theme (God's justice) is stated and the speaker outlines his case, arguing with God that he is being unfairly treated. In lines 5–13, **he brings forward the evidence** in favour of his argument. The first part of this evidence has to do with the success of others and his own failures: those who succeed are sinners whereas he, a virtuous man, is a failure (lines 5–9). The second part of the evidence consists of contrasting pictures of fertile nature and his own sterile, unproductive life (9–13). In the final line, the speaker moves from complaint to prayer as he seeks relief from his condition.

As the poem develops, there are **changes of tone**, which at the beginning is calm and controlled as the speaker addresses God, as a lawyer might address a judge in a courtroom. The **sense of control wavers** in line 7. The words 'Defeat' and 'thwart' suggest a personal and deliberate campaign waged by God against the speaker. The **speaker's emotion spills over** in his use of **judgemental and expressive language**, 'the

Gerard Manley Hopkins

sots and thralls of lust'. The speaker regains his composure across lines 8 and 9: '… than I that spend, / Sir, life upon thy cause.' Midway through line 9, there is further change of tone.

The imperatives 'See' and 'look', the exclamation mark after 'thick' (line 10), and the adjective 'fretty' (line 11) reveal an **excitement and pleasure in nature**, and a corresponding **quickening in the language** of the poem. The tone of these lines is more emotionally open and positive than at any other point in the poem. This hymn of praise to nature ends on the optimistic 'birds build' (line 12). Continuing the **zigzag in the poet's thought**, this phrase is immediately followed by the negatives 'not', 'no'. The **twisted syntax, punctuation and the repeated stresses** across lines 12 and 13 – 'but nót Í búild; nó, but stráin, / Tíme's éunuch, and nót bréed óne wórk that wákes.' – enact the speaker's struggle to accept his predicament. The poem ends with a quiet and dignified prayer to God to send rain to nourish the dry roots of his life.

Questions

1	In what sense does the speaker find God's ways difficult to understand?
2	How does the speaker's life differ from the life of nature all around him?
3	In your own words, summarise the argument outlined by the speaker.
4	What is the effect of the use of 'sir' (lines 2 and 9) in the poem?
5	How does this poem differ in mood and tone from 'No worst, there is none'?
6	What, do you think, is the speaker's main grievance?
7	How do the images used by the speaker help to advance his argument?
8	Where in the poem is it evident that the speaker's emotions threaten to break through the calm and logical arguments he is making?
9	a) On the evidence in the sonnet, what kind of person do you think the speaker to be? b) On the evidence in the sonnet, what kind of person does the speaker imagine God to be?
10	'For all its logic and controlled arguments, the sonnet is an expression of hurt, confusion and frustration.' Discuss.
11	This poem conveys the speaker's deep sense of being treated unfairly by God. Write a short piece, poetry or prose, about your own experience of being treated unfairly.

SNAPSHOT GERARD MANLEY HOPKINS

- Religious faith is at the heart of his poetry
- Range of human interest is relatively narrow
- Remarkable descriptive powers
- A profoundly gifted nature poet
- Celebrates the activity of God in the world
- An important experimenter and innovator
- Reveals his compassion for others
- Strives to express the essence and uniqueness of each individual thing
- Highly distinctive use of language
- 'Terrible Sonnets' explore spiritual desolation and psychological conflicts
- Sees God as the unchanging source of the diversity in nature

Exam-Preparation Questions

1. Having studied the poems of Hopkins, what kind of person, do you think, might have written them? Illustrate your answer with relevant details from the poems.

2. Hopkins was deeply conscious of the individuality and uniqueness of each created thing. How is this reflected in his poetry?

3. In his poetry, Hopkins reveals a profound understanding of the dark corners of the human mind. How is this reflected in his poetry?

4. 'Everything in Hopkins is influenced by his belief in God.'
   Consider Hopkins's poems in the light of this statement.

5. The poems of Hopkins alternate between gladness and dejection. Explain how this is so.

6. 'Hopkins's innovative style expresses both his joy in nature and his struggles as a priest.'
   Discuss this view of the poet, supporting your answer with reference to the poetry of Hopkins on your course.

7. Using the evidence provided in the poems, discuss Hopkins's understanding of God and his own relationship with him.

8. Discuss the elements of conflict in the poetry of Hopkins.

9. Hopkins is sometimes described as a difficult poet, fond of obscure language, unfamiliar ideas, and eccentric ways of expressing his meaning. Would you agree?

10. Write an essay on Hopkins as a nature poet. You might consider some of the following:
    - His view of the natural world as a reflection of God
    - His description of natural things
    - The happiness he derives from contemplating nature
    - How human beings relate to the natural world

11. Write a piece in which you explain why you like or dislike Hopkins's poetry. Support your points by reference to, and/or quotation from, the Hopkins poems on your course. The following are reasons you might give for liking Hopkins's poetry:
    - The poems are original and distinctive
    - Hopkins's descriptions make us see and feel what is being described, often in new and surprising ways
    - Hopkins is a fine nature poet
    - Hopkins's poems deal with important issues, such as humanity's place in the universe, our relationship with God, the reflection of God in nature
    - Hopkins is one of the great masters of language

    The following are reasons you might give for not liking Hopkins's poetry:
    - The poems are extremely odd
    - Many of the poems are baffling, and slow to yield up a meaning
    - Hopkins has invented a new kind of language, which is difficult to learn
    - Hopkins does not deal with subjects that interest me
    - The poems seem to have been written for learned readers, mainly adults, and not for young students

Gerard Manley Hopkins

Sample Essay

Write about those aspects of the poetry of Hopkins that appeal to you.

Introductory paragraph refers to the question and indicates areas that will be discussed

I admire Hopkins's originality, especially his use of language. No other poet I know uses language in the same way as Hopkins does. His originality lies mainly in his diction and rhythm, as well as in his strong reliance on alliteration.

Gives clear signpost to discussion of language

All of the ten poems on our course suggest that Hopkins was consistent in his use of alliteration, not for its own sake, but because it helped to give an effect of rhythmic energy and emphasis to his poetry. In 'The Windhover', for example, we can see how effective alliteration can be:

'how he rung upon the rein of a wimpling wing
In his ecstasy! then off, off forth on swing,
As a skate's heel sweeps smooth on a bow-bend; the hurl and gliding
Rebuffed the big wind.'

Uses details and quotation to support points

'The off, off forth on swing' is an example of how Hopkins can deploy a combination of alliteration and urgent rhythm to suggest the surging, swooping flight of the kestrel. In the same poem, he accents every syllable to express the idea that mere plodding effort causes a plough to shine in its progress through a furrow: 'shéer plód makes plough down sillion shine'. Another example of the same kind of effect is found in the opening of the sonnet, 'I wake to feel the fell of dark, not day', and again in 'Pied Beauty': 'Landscape plotted and pieced, fold, fallow and plough'.

Refers to more than one poem in discussion

I admire Hopkins's choice of words. In 'Pied Beauty', he conveys the endless variety of nature using the plainest words ('with swift, slow; sweet, sour; adazzle, dim'). A further dimension to the use of these six plain words is that their sounds echo their meanings. For example, the short vowel in 'swift' and the long vowel in 'slow' serve to enact the meanings. In the passage from 'The Windhover' above, the onomatopoeia – sound echoing meaning – of 'Rebuffed' is perfect in its context. I find Hopkins's experiments with words and groups of words fascinating. In 'The Windhover', he chooses a dialect word for furrow ('sillion') because it makes an appropriate rhyme for two other words suggesting intensity: 'billion' and the vibrant colour 'vermillion'. He also adds a depth of resonance and suggestiveness to his poems by using words with double or multiple meanings, as he does in 'I wake and feel the fell of dark'. In this context 'fell' can suggest 'malevolent' or 'evil' and also 'the hairy skin of a beast'.

Shows detailed knowledge of poem

Expresses personal response to the poems

Another aspect of his language that lends variety to his poetry is his resort to new coinages and sometimes obsolete dialect words. His coinages include 'groins of the braes' for hillsides, 'wiry heathpacks' for clumps of heather, and 'flitches' for clumps – all from 'Inversnaid'. His numerous obsolete and dialect words include 'Degged' for sprinkled in 'Inversnaid', 'tucked' for plucked in 'As kingfishers catch fire', and 'brinded' in 'Pied Beauty'. I particularly like the use of 'twindles' in 'Inversnaid', which incorporates 'twists', 'twitches' and 'dwindles'.

Introduces new area of discussion

HIGHER LEVEL 2021

HIGHER LEVEL

Returns to question → I also admire the way in which Hopkins, within the fourteen lines of a sonnet, can compress so much meaning, and achieve such variety of tone. In 'Felix Randal', for example, we see Felix the blacksmith in his feeble final days, no longer **Introduces new poem**

Uses short quotations → 'big-boned and hardy-handsome' but 'pining, pining' as a result of 'fatal four disorders'. He is 'impatient' at first and then, having been anointed by the priest (Hopkins himself), achieving peace ('a heavenlier heart'). Hopkins manages to include a spiritual reflection on the power of the sacraments of the Catholic Church to heal troubled souls, and the mutual love and respect that can grow between the sick person and the priest. In addition, he conveys his satisfaction that he has comforted and consoled Felix, and quenched his fears. Having expressed all these thoughts, Hopkins still manages a magnificent ending to the sonnet. This ending looks back to the mighty Felix as he was in his prime: 'When thou at the random grim forge, powerful amidst peers, / Didst fettle for the great grey drayhorse his bright and battering sandal!' **Emphasising the compression of meaning**

Opens up a new line of argument → A different sort of achievement of Hopkins's poetry is his deep understanding of depressive states of mind, as expressed in the dark sonnets he wrote towards the end of his life. The most impressive of these, 'No worst, there is none', gives a moving account of what a state of depression really feels like to someone who has experienced it: 'O the mind, mind has mountains; cliffs of fall / Frightful, sheer, no-man-fathomed. Hold them cheap / May who ne'er hung there...' In these 'depressive' sonnets, Hopkins is also able to give the reader a powerful sense of what a person with a deep faith in God experiences when the God in whom he believes and whom he trusts seems to repay this belief and trust by making him suffer constant agony and despair. This is especially so when he thinks all those around him are blessed with success, even when they have no time for God: 'Why do sinners' ways prosper? and why must / Disappointment all I endeavour end?' The poem from which these lines come, 'Thou **Quotation sums up argument**

Clear account of argument of the poem → are indeed just, Lord', dramatises the feelings of abandonment and despair that many good people feel when their best efforts end in total failure: he, Hopkins, cannot 'breed one work that wakes'.

Even more impressive than this sonnet is 'I wake and feel the fell of dark', which describes what a person in the depths of depression feels on waking in the dark of night, having had his or her sleep constantly interrupted by nightmarish thoughts and feelings. Worse still, the sufferer knows that further terrors await before morning comes: 'And more must, in yet longer light's delay'. One such night is bad enough, with its 'black hours', but there is worse: this suffering lasts a lifetime: 'But where I say / Hours I mean years, mean life'. This sonnet and others do not merely talk about **Effective summary of strength of the poem** → suffering: they use strong rhythm, condensed syntax and tortured language to act it out, and make us feel as if we are sharing it: 'My cries heave, herds-long; huddle in a main, a chief / Woe, world-sorrow; on an age-old anvil wince and sing –'

Another aspect of Hopkins's work that I admire is his treatment of the natural world, which he constantly sees as an expression of God's power and majesty. This is the joyful side of his achievement. One of his nature poems, 'God's Grandeur' is particularly relevant for the modern age. I find the description of what human beings have done to spoil the beauty of the natural world very moving: 'Generations have trod, have trod, have trod; / And all is seared with trade; bleared, / smeared with toil.' What I admire about this poem is that Hopkins, who **Discussion balances the depressive side of Hopkins's achievement** deplores the destruction of God's work by countless generations of people, can still express faith that God will restore what humans have devastated, because 'Nature is never spent' and 'Because the Holy Ghost over the bent / World broods with warm breast and with ah! bright wings.'

As well as identifying and discussing the aspects of Hopkins's poetry that appeal to me, I have tried to indicate why I find those aspects particularly impressive. I am struck by the range and variety of Hopkins's work, in form, subject matter and use of language, and by the fact that a poet whose work was completed well over a century ago can have the significance it does for a reader in the twenty-first century.

Concluding paragraph returns to question and summarises argument

ESSAY CHECKLIST		Yes √	No x
Purpose	Has the candidate understood the task?		
	Has the candidate responded to it in a thoughtful manner?		
	Has the candidate answered the question?		
Comment:			
Coherence	Has the candidate made convincing arguments?		
	Has the candidate linked ideas?		
	Does the essay have a sense of unity?		
Comment:			
Language	Is the essay written in an appropriate register?		
	Are ideas expressed in a clear way?		
	Is the writing fluent?		
Comment:			
Mechanics	Is the use of language accurate?		
	Are all words spelled correctly?		
	Does the punctuation help the reader?		
Comment:			

John Keats
1795–1821

To one who has been long in city pent	384
On First Looking into Chapman's Homer*	387
When I have fears that I may cease to be	392
La Belle Dame Sans Merci*	396
Ode to a Nightingale	404
Ode on a Grecian Urn	414
To Autumn	422
Bright Star	429

Biography

John Keats was born in London on 31 October 1795. In his lifetime he was sometimes attacked as a 'Cockney' poet, implying that he was a working-class Londoner. In fact, his family was not as poor as that word would suggest. His father had married the daughter of the owner of a busy coaching inn and stables near the City of London, and soon took over running it. John Keats was the eldest of five children, one of whom died as an infant.

When Keats was eight his father died in a riding accident, and soon afterwards his mother abandoned the family, leaving the children to be brought up by their grandmother in Edmonton. John Keats and his brothers, George and Tom, were sent to Clarke's School, a private boarding school run by a man of strong but unorthodox, free-thinking Christian beliefs. The school was in Enfield, close to Edmonton, now districts of north-east London, but then villages surrounded by fields, so Keats grew up knowing and loving the countryside.

At school Keats didn't show any great intellectual ability, but he got a good education, even though it was not in the old-fashioned classical tradition. He did not study Greek, but he learned to read Latin, and his education benefited greatly from his friendship with Charles Cowden Clarke, the son of the headmaster, who was eight years older than Keats, and acted as a mentor or guide, encouraging his interest in poetry, music, theatre and classical myths. Though he was sensitive and imaginative, he also had a pugnacious streak, and developed a reputation for fighting.

He was thirteen when his mother returned to be with her children. She was gravely ill with tuberculosis (TB), but far from rejecting her, her eldest son made it his job to nurse her when he was at home. She died when he was away at school, leaving him an orphan at fourteen.

His life was now under the control of his guardian, Richard Abbey, who seemed more concerned to curb his enthusiasms and ration his money than nurture or protect him. It was decided that Keats should become a doctor. The decision does not seem to have been forced on him; he had already shown compassion in the way in which he nursed his mother. He was apprenticed to a surgeon shortly before his fifteenth birthday. His childhood was over.

> **Tuberculosis**
>
> Tuberculosis, or TB, was the killer disease of earlier centuries, and is often compared to HIV/AIDS. It was known as consumption because it consumed or ate up the person who was infected and they wasted away. It was usually associated with coughs and breathing problems. In the nineteenth century, the disease killed tens of thousands every year in Britain and Ireland, especially among the urban poor. John Keats's mother and youngest brother died of the disease, and it is more than likely that he himself was infected while nursing Tom. The discovery of antibiotics in the mid-twentieth century finally provided a cure for TB.

His apprenticeship gave him freedom. He moved out of his grandmother's house and lodged with the surgeon. In some ways, it was the happiest period of his life. He had time for reading and writing and making friends. He gradually became more and more convinced that poetry was his true destiny.

After his apprenticeship, he went on to study medicine at Guy's Hospital in London from 1815. Although he qualified as an apothecary (in effect, a junior doctor) in 1816, he had made friends in the literary world and had started to have his poems published. He finally abandoned his medical studies at the end of 1816, at the age of twenty-one. He now dedicated his life to poetry.

Keats had formed strong friendships with men who gave him some access to London's artistic world of the time. There was Leigh Hunt, the poet and radical thinker, who edited the *Examiner*, the magazine which published some of Keats's early poems. There was William Hazlitt, a powerful literary figure of the day. There was also Benjamin Haydon, a painter who guided Keats around the ancient Greek artworks in the British Museum.

The years 1817 and 1818 saw Keats moving around in north London, living mostly in Hampstead, an expanding, increasingly fashionable suburb. It was an unsettled time, but a creative one. His first book of poetry was published in 1817, and the following year he published his first long poem, *Endymion*, on a mythological subject. It was hugely ambitious, but Keats knew he had not achieved what he had set out to do. It was savaged by the critics, and some commentators believe that the reviews destroyed him. His contemporary, the much-admired and very successful poet Lord Byron, claimed that he was 'snuffed out by an article'. But Keats was not really so feeble. As he wrote in a letter, 'I was never afraid of failure; for I would sooner fail than not be among the greatest.'

In any case, there were other things than bad reviews on his mind. His youngest brother Tom had developed TB, the same disease that had killed their mother, and Keats spent a lot of time and energy looking after him. In 1818, his other brother, George, to whom he had always been closest, got married and decided to emigrate to America. Keats went to see him off from Liverpool, and then went on a walking tour with his friend Charles Armitage Brown to the Lake District and then Scotland. They often walked for more than twenty miles a day in all sorts of weather, and it was after a trudge in the rain across the Isle of Mull that Keats showed the first symptoms of the illness that was to kill him.

On his return from Scotland he devoted himself to nursing his brother Tom in his final illness. At the same time, however, he applied himself with renewed energy to his writing, conscious that his imagination was becoming more and more powerful and that he was mastering his craft as a poet. As he wrote in a letter in October, 'The faint conceptions I have of Poems to come brings the blood frequently into my forehead.'

This was the beginning of an extraordinary year. Between the autumn of 1818 and the autumn of 1819 he wrote almost all the poetry for which he is now remembered, and which gives him the place he craved among the great English poets. The work of this period, completed by the time Keats was twenty-four, includes 'The Eve of St Agnes', 'La Belle Dame Sans Merci', and the great odes 'On a Grecian Urn', 'On Melancholy', 'To a Nightingale' and 'To Autumn', as well as the epic fragment 'The Fall of Hyperion'.

Tom died in December 1818, his brother John by his side. At much the same time Keats met for the first time Fanny Brawne, an eighteen-year-old girl. Although he had vowed to avoid women so that they did not distract him from his art, and although he fought against it and concealed his feelings from his friends, who thought her unworthy of him, he was falling in love.

This was a tortured yet intensely creative time for Keats. He was in love but was always battling his feelings. Not only did he lack the financial means to marry Fanny, but by early 1819 he knew, with his medical training and personal experience, that his persistent sore throat was a sign that he had contracted the same disease that had killed his mother and younger brother: tuberculosis. These days a course of antibiotics could easily cure the illness, but there was no good treatment two hundred years ago. It was a death sentence. He could not feel easy marrying Fanny when he knew that he would soon leave her a widow.

He knew all this but could not fully accept it. He alternated between devoting himself to Fanny and pushing her away. His love for her was mixed up in his mind with his approaching death. He wrote in one letter to her:

> I have two luxuries to brood over in my walks, your Loveliness and the hour of my death. O that I could have possession of them both in the same minute.

Perhaps the knowledge of his approaching death concentrated his mind. He knew he had little time to turn himself into the great poet he wanted to be, so he wasted none of it. The spring and early summer of 1819 produced most of the great odes in which he meditated on joy and suffering and the creative imagination, but by the end of the year he was exhausted, and would write little more.

In February 1820 Keats started coughing up blood. It was, as he declared, his 'death warrant'. He knew that he could have no more than a year to live, and that he had no hope of marriage to Fanny, although they were engaged. In September he sailed to Italy, persuaded that the mild climate of that country might improve his health. He described the last few months of his life as 'a posthumous existence'. He lingered only until 23 February 1821, when he died painfully in Rome.

Social and Cultural Context

Romanticism

Keats is usually grouped with the **English Romantic poets**. They were writers who reacted against the very rational, often witty, but primarily public poetry of the so-called Augustans, such as Alexander Pope. William Wordsworth and Samuel Taylor Coleridge had led the way with the publication of their *Lyrical Ballads* in 1798. Lord Byron, Robert Southey, William Blake and Percy Bysshe Shelley (see 'Ozymandias', page 566) were among the other poets associated with the movement.

Their politics were often radical, and they put ordinary people and their everyday language at the heart of what they wrote. Their poetry tended to focus on **the individual soul, the passions and the creative imagination**. As Shelley wrote, the imagination 'lifts the veil from the hidden beauty of the world'.

The **natural world** was a great inspiration and source of metaphors for their poetry. Wild landscapes and wild weather were appreciated for the emotions they could stir or suggest. Wordsworth did a great deal through his poetry to make fashionable the rugged grandeur of the Lake District in north-west England, where he came from and which he wrote about.

Keats lived through times of great political unrest, in the aftermath of the French Revolution, and had himself been brought up as a freethinker. He cared deeply about social justice and the plight of ordinary people. His first chief mentor in the literary world was Leigh Hunt, who co-founded and edited the radical magazine the *Examiner*, which published some of Keats's early poems. Keats believed that poetry could and should do some good in the world, and a great deal of the hostile reaction to his long poem *Endymion* came from conservative critics who disliked its **challenging political ideas**.

Little of this radical politics, however, is evident in the poems on your course. What is apparent is his love of the natural world, the high value he placed on the imagination and the truths it could reveal. His comment on Newton's scientific explanation of the colours of the rainbow reveals a great deal about his way of thinking. He said that Newton had 'destroyed all the Poetry of the rainbow by reducing it to a Prism'. He praised the 'sensual life of verse' and looked back to the older English poetic tradition of Chaucer, Spenser and Shakespeare rather than the Augustans of the previous century.

Classicism

Romanticism and Classicism are usually regarded as opposite poles, one representing passion and imagination, the other reason and order. Keats, however, was a great admirer of the **culture, art and literature of ancient or 'classical' Greece**, which is where this sense of the word 'classical' comes from.

The sonnet 'On First Looking into Chapman's Homer' takes as its subject his discovery of the beauties of Homer, the first and most revered of Greek poets. The 'Ode on a Grecian Urn' is fuelled by his love for classical visual art and sculpture. He spent many hours in the British Museum looking at its collection of ancient Greek and Roman objects. He responded above all to the pure, joyful beauty of classical form in Greek art, and if there are hints in the ode that he saw something cold in its perfection, his admiration of it was extremely passionate. His friend George Felton Mathew said that he 'invited comparison with the Greeks in that one of the main endeavours of his poetic career was to grow more Grecian'.

He loved **Greek mythology** too, and knew the stories intimately. Many of his poems use images and stories from Greek myths.

The letters

As well as his poems, Keats left us many long, thoughtful, passionate and spontaneous letters in which he revealed a great deal about his most private self, and also **discussed his beliefs about art, beauty, and the role of the poet**. They were written to his friends and family and often contained copies of his latest verses. In particular, he wrote long letters over extended periods to his brother George and his wife, Georgiana, in America. They act as a diary of his actions and inner life, and help us to understand his character, what he was thinking and what he was trying to achieve in his poetry.

One of Keats's central beliefs about poetry was that **the poet should be a sort of chameleon**, able to take on different personae or roles, and identify at the deepest levels with the subjects of his poems, human or otherwise. His model was Shakespeare. In a famous passage from a letter to his friend Benjamin Bailey, he discusses the power of the imagination and his capacity to lose his own identity entirely in the observation and contemplation of something outside himself: 'if a sparrow come before my window, I take part in its existence and pick about the gravel'. He also used the term **'negative capability'** to describe a similar capacity in the writer to suspend his judgement in order to let his imagination work. He described negative capability as 'when a man is capable of being in uncertainties, Mysteries, doubts, without any irritable reaching after fact & reason'.

In some ways his beliefs were a reflection of his personality. He always felt overwhelmed by other people. He wrote in a letter in 1818, 'When I am in a room with People … the identity of everyone in the room begins to press upon me.' But however difficult this was in his day-to-day life, he made this characteristic a virtue in his poetry. It meant that he was capable of exploring so much of life. As he wrote in a letter in October 1818, at the start of his greatest creative period, 'I feel more and more every day, as my imagination strengthens, that I do not live in this world alone but in a thousand worlds.'

Keats and women

Keats once wrote in a letter, 'I am certain I have not a right feeling towards Women'. As a boy, he said, he had idealised and idolised them. As a grown man he struggled with his feelings towards them. He was scared of letting them get too close in case they distracted him from his chosen destiny as a poet. He was scared of being humiliated or let down by them. He was also scared of letting them down. Despite his love for Fanny Brawne, he tried several times to break off the relationship or distance himself from it. He wrote to his brother George at one point, 'I feel I can bear any thing, any misery, even imprisonment – so long as I have neither wife nor child.' But he also wrote Fanny passionate love letters, one of which declared, 'Love is my religion – I could die for that – I could die for you.'

It is perhaps not surprising, given his early experiences, that he had **complicated feelings about women**. The first woman in his life was, of course, his mother, Fanny. She left her children after her husband died, and when she came back, Keats nursed her in her illness and lavished her with love. Then she abandoned him again by dying. His sister, also called Fanny, was much younger than him, and he never had a close relationship with her, a fact that sometimes made him feel guilty.

The conflicts in his attitude to women can be seen in 'La Belle Dame Sans Merci', where the lady is both bewitching and dangerous, and also in 'Bright Star', in which he seems to desire from his 'fair love' both sacred purity and the physical intimacy that might destroy that purity.

Themes

We have already touched on many of the themes of Keats's poetry. These include the **natural world** and, just as important, humankind's relationship with it. It is a theme that is present in many of the poems on your course, including 'To one who has been long in city pent', 'Ode to a Nightingale' and 'To Autumn'. Descriptions of the natural world abound in Keats's poetry, and where it is not the subject of the poem, the natural world is often a **rich source of metaphors and images**.

A closely related theme is **the relationship of life and art**, and the role of the artist in transforming one into the other. In both his letters and his poems, Keats focuses on the part played by the imagination that is needed for that transformation; and beauty, which is both the goal and the guarantee of the act of imagination, be it poem, painting, music or sculpture. He wrote in a letter to his friend Bailey in 1817:

> 'I am certain of nothing but of the holiness of the Heart's affections and the truth of Imagination – What the imagination seizes as Beauty must be truth – whether it existed before or not – for I have the same idea of all our Passions as of Love: they are all, in their sublime, creative of essential Beauty.'

HIGHER LEVEL

It is his notion of **the imagination as the most precious gift of the creative artist** that most clearly identifies Keats as a Romantic poet. Closely linked to this belief is his thirst for intense, transcendent experience. This can be the excitement at the discovery of beauty, as in 'On First Looking into Chapman's Homer', the destructive passion of 'La Belle Dame Sans Merci', the tender, erotic intimacy of 'Bright Star', or the vision-like experience of 'Ode to a Nightingale'.

This can be viewed as a sort of escapism, a sign of Keats's desire to be free of the miseries and suffering of life that he knew so well. As he wrote in his first letter to Fanny Brawne, 'I have never known any unalloy'd Happiness for many days together'.

But Keats's poetry turns this desire into something more than mere escapism. It is a way of seeing the world that was central to Keats's imagination. Intense experiences and emotions that are normally seen as very different are often closely related in his poetry: **suffering is close to joy; love is close to death**. It is most apparent in the 'Ode to a Nightingale', where the speaker's aching heart comes from 'being too happy', and he imagines death as a way of prolonging bliss:

> To cease upon the midnight with no pain,
>   While thou art pouring forth thy soul abroad
>   In such an ecstasy!

The knight's love for the lady in 'La Belle Dame Sans Merci' is intertwined with his suffering. The only imaginable alternative to the speaker's 'sweet unrest' lying blissfully in the arms of his beloved in 'Bright Star' is to 'swoon to death'.

You could argue that any intense experience in Keats's poetry contains an element of suffering, or a mixture of joy and suffering. This idea has a moral or philosophical dimension too. **Keats believed that suffering has a purpose.** In a letter to George and Georgiana, he wrote about the world as a school for the human soul, asking, 'Do you not see how necessary a World of Pains and troubles is to school an Intelligence and make it a soul?' Suffering is something to be faced and used rather than simply escaped.

John Keats

Timeline

1795	Born in London. Father ran a coaching inn
1803	Starts as a boarder at Clarke's school in Enfield
1804	Father dies
	Mother leaves the family home
	Children looked after by their grandmother
1810	Mother dies
	Leaves school to be apprenticed to a surgeon
1815	Becomes a medical student at Guy's Hospital in London
1816	First poems published
	Abandons medical studies for a life as a poet
1817	First volume of poems published
1818	Long mythological poem *Endymion* published, to hostile reviews
	Brother George leaves for America
	Nurses brother Tom, who is dying of tuberculosis
	Feels first symptoms of his own tuberculosis
	Meets Fanny Brawne
1819	Writes the five great odes, three of which appear in this anthology
1820	Publishes volume of poems including the odes
	Goes to Italy hoping to improve his health
1821	Dies in Rome

HIGHER LEVEL

Before you read

Do you prefer city or country life? Discuss in pairs, then share your thoughts with the class.

To one who has been long in city pent

To one who has been long in city pent,
    'Tis very sweet to look into the fair
    And open face of heaven,—to breathe a prayer
Full in the smile of the blue firmament.
Who is more happy, when, with heart's content,   5
    Fatigued he sinks into some pleasant lair
    Of wavy grass, and reads a debonair
And gentle tale of love and languishment?
Returning home at evening, with an ear
    Catching the notes of Philomel,—an eye   10
Watching the sailing cloudlet's bright career,
    He mourns that day so soon has glided by:
E'en like the passage of an angel's tear
    That falls through the clear ether silently.

Glossary

1	*pent*:	confined, imprisoned
4	*firmament*:	heavens, sky
7	*debonair*:	elegant, light-hearted
8	*languishment*:	pining, inactive unhappiness because of love
10	*Philomel*:	nightingale
11	*career*:	passing by
13	*E'en like*:	even like, just like
16	*ether*:	air, atmosphere; ether was believed to be an invisible element that filled all space

Philomel

According to the ancient Greek myth, Philomel (or Philomela) was a young woman who was raped by her sister's husband, King Tereus, who cut out her tongue to stop her telling. She was transformed into a nightingale, whose beautiful song is sometimes thought to express great sorrow.

Guidelines

This sonnet was written in June 1816 when Keats was still just twenty years old. At that time he was studying to be a surgeon at Guy's Hospital in the middle of London. According to his brother George, this poem was 'written in the fields' on one of his days off spent walking in the countryside around the city.

Keats was already considering a possible future as a poet rather than a surgeon, and he spent much of his spare time educating himself in classical literature and the great English poets of the sixteenth and seventeenth centuries, especially Spenser, Shakespeare and Milton. This poem's opening echoes some lines from Milton's

John Keats

Paradise Lost: 'As one who long in populous city pent, / Where houses thick and sewers annoy the air'. That vision of the city as a crowded, unhealthy place to be escaped from haunts Keats's poem, even though the city is never described in it.

Commentary

Octave (lines 1–8)

The first eight lines of the sonnet, the octave, express a simple thought and ask a simple question: in other words, it's great to get out in the open air on a nice day if you've been stuck in the city for a while (lines 1–4); and (lines 5–8) what could be better than lying back in the long grass with a good love story to read?

> **Guy's Hospital**
>
> Keats's studies at Guy's meant that he had to join crowds of other students pressing forward for a view of gruesome operations carried out with no anaesthetic except alcohol, or of dissections of dead bodies in suffocating and foul-smelling rooms. This was part of what he was escaping in his walks in the country celebrated in this poem, and what he would return to at the end of them. He gave up his studies at the end of 1816, determined to make his way as a poet.

Sestet (lines 9–14)

The second part of the poem evokes the mood at the end of the day in the countryside, 'Returning home at evening'. There is a pleasure in the evening's beauty – the 'notes of Philomel' (a nightingale), the little cloud sailing by – but there is also a strong sense of sadness at the day's ending: 'He mourns that day so soon has glided by'. The final image, which is the most striking and original one in the poem, focuses and deepens this doubleness: the angel suggests perfection of a kind, but the tear indicates sorrow. It is an image of heavenly, almost sacred sadness, made all the more poignant and magical because the tear falls 'silently'.

Themes

This is a simple yet charming sonnet without the depth or complexity of Keats's finest poems, but many of the themes and moods of those poems are foreshadowed in it.

There is, first of all, the **strong sense of fleeting beauty** – a beauty that is so vividly perceived because of the awareness that it is transient and will be gone all too quickly. This **connection between beauty and melancholy** (sadness) is central to the poem's effect. As well as the melancholy awareness that this day has to end, there is a close relationship between pleasure and suffering in other details. Though the 'face of heaven' (line 3) may be 'open' and the 'blue firmament' (line 4) is smiling, the pleasure of lying down to read is linked with exhaustion ('Fatigued he sinks', line 6) and the tale he reads mingles love and 'languishment' – the pining unhappiness that is conventionally associated with love. Do you think that it might also be significant that Philomel is not simply a Greek term for the nightingale, but has a story attached?

The mood of the poem also looks forward to the great odes, several of which we are studying on this course. There is a feeling of tiredness, heaviness and pleasant indolence, especially in lines 5–8, where the 'Fatigued' subject 'sinks' into the grass and even the story he reads involves 'languishment'. This mood is associated with sensual pleasures: the touch of the 'wavy grass', the sound of the nightingale, the sight of the passing cloud.

The poem also depends on the **contrast between city and country**. Though it is not directly described, life in the crowded, dirty city haunts the poem, making this day in the country so precious. The word 'pent' (line 1) does a lot of work, implying as it does that life in the city is a sort of imprisonment.

Imagery and language

The imagery of the poem is mostly **subtle but conventional**: the idea of heaven as a smiling face; a passing ('sailing') cloud like a ship in the sky. Only the final image, discussed above, is memorable. The language of the poem contains some rather archaic words and phrases, showing the influence of Keats's reading of Spenser and Milton: 'firmament', 'debonair', 'E'en like'. Elsewhere, the language is conventionally poetic: 'very sweet'; 'heart's content'; 'gentle tale'. Keats had not yet found a poetic language of his own.

Form

'To one who has been long in city pent' is a **Petrarchan sonnet**, divided into octave and sestet, with a rhyme scheme of *abba abba cdcdcd*. The argument of the poem fits neatly into the conventional divisions: the first two sentences occupy four lines each, and the third takes up the remaining six lines. Despite that, the poem never feels constrained by its form. Keats handles it with dexterity and skill with plenty of run-on lines (enjambment) to break up the rigid patterns of the sonnet form. Notice too how he uses rhyme words to highlight key ideas: 'ear' at the end of line 9 and 'eye' (line 10) remind us of the different senses that are evoked in the poem.

The final word of the poem, 'silently', is interesting in this respect. The word is emphasised by being placed out of its normal sentence position in spoken English ('falls silently through the clear ether') and by being only a half-rhyme, and that on an unstressed syllable; speak it aloud and you will hear that the stress falls on the first syllable of the word: *śilently*. What, do you think, is the effect of this?

Questions

1	What do you think is the main theme of the poem? ■ The contrast between city and country ■ The beauty of nature ■ The nature of pleasure ■ The transience of beauty Or what other response would you give? Explain your answer.
2	How would you describe the mood of this poem?
3	Comment on the form of the poem.
4	In what ways would this poem be different if Keats had written 'nightingale' instead of 'Philomel'?
5	Comment on the final image of this poem.
6	Are there any signs in the poem that suggest its writer was to become one of the most admired poets in the English language?
7	Suggest an alternative title for the poem. Explain your suggestion.
8	Write a short piece, either prose or verse, with the title 'The Pleasures of Exhaustion'.

John Keats

Before you read

Find out what you can about (a) Homer, the ancient Greek poet, and (b) George Chapman, who made an English translation of Homer's work.

On First Looking into Chapman's Homer

Much have I travell'd in the realms of gold,
    And many goodly states and kingdoms seen;
    Round many western islands have I been
Which bards in fealty to Apollo hold.
Oft of one wide expanse had I been told   5
    That deep-brow'd Homer ruled as his demesne;
    Yet did I never breathe its pure serene
Till I heard Chapman speak out loud and bold:
Then felt I like some watcher of the skies
    When a new planet swims into his ken;   10
Or like stout Cortez when with eagle eyes
    He star'd at the Pacific—and all his men
Look'd at each other with a wild surmise—
    Silent, upon a peak in Darien.

Glossary

Title	*Chapman's Homer*: George Chapman (c.1559–1634) was an English poet and dramatist whose verse translation of Homer's ancient Greek poems, the *Iliad* and the *Odyssey*, were published in 1616	
1	*realms*: territories, kingdoms	
2	*goodly*: fine, attractive	
4	*bards*: poets	
4	*fealty*: loyalty	
4	*Apollo*: Greek God of the sun, music and poetry	
6	*demesne*: territory, kingdom	
7	*serene*: clear, calm (air); normally an adjective, but here used as a noun	
10	*ken*: view, field of vision	
11	*tout*: brave	
11	*Cortez*: Spanish conqueror of Mexico; Keats is confusing him with Balboa, another Spanish adventurer, who discovered the Pacific in 1513	
13	*surmise*: thought, guess	
14	*Darien*: a neck of land joining North and South America; it is in present-day Panama, and has a chain of mountains running through it	

Guidelines

One day in October 1816, Keats's friend, Charles Cowden Clarke, showed him a copy of a rare old book, Chapman's translation of Homer's *Iliad* and *Odyssey*. Keats had never read Homer before, and they sat up all night reading the book. Keats left Clarke at six in the morning, excited by his night's reading, composed this sonnet in his head as he walked home, wrote it down when he got in, and sent it to Clarke by the early morning postal messenger.

The poem is full of the excitement with which it was written.

Commentary

As the title indicates, the subject of the sonnet is the experience of reading a great poem in translation, and yet books are never actually mentioned in the poem. Instead Keats uses an extended metaphor, speaking of his reading in terms of travel and exploration.

Lines 1–4

The 'realms of gold' with their 'goodly states and kingdoms' represent the world of the imagination as expressed in great literature. These include the old English poets Keats loved and also the classics of ancient Greece and Rome, as the reference to Apollo implies. These Keats knows. In the poem's central metaphor, he has 'travell'd' these areas.

Homer

The deep brows mentioned in the poem call to mind the busts of a serious-looking Homer. In fact, we know very little about the person who wrote the *Iliad* and the *Odyssey*. It is probable that both these works were composed to be recited aloud rather than read, and may not have been written down until long after they were composed. They may be the work of more than one person, and some have speculated that the poet was a woman.

The *Iliad* and the *Odyssey* are long, epic poems, full of heroes and gods and adventure. The *Iliad* tells the story of the Trojan War. The *Odyssey* tells the story of Odysseus, one of the Greek heroes returning from that war. It is a story of voyaging by sea among islands, and so is closely linked to the central metaphor of Keats's poem.

Lines 5–8

The metaphor is sustained, but the focus now narrows to one particular 'wide expanse', a 'demesne' or dominion greater than these others, 'ruled' by 'deep-brow'd Homer', most revered of all the ancient poets. Keats is referring to Homer's two great epic works: the *Iliad* and the *Odyssey*. He had 'been told' of this 'demesne', but had never visited it and breathed its 'pure serene' (i.e. read the poems) until now, when he 'heard Chapman speak out loud and bold' in his verse translation of Homer's works.

Lines 9–14

The rest of the poem describes Keats's feelings on reading Chapman's Homer ('Then felt I …'). He compares his thrill of discovery to that of an astronomer (a 'watcher of the skies') seeing a previously unknown planet in his telescope, and finally to that of a conqueror and explorer, 'stout Cortez' discovering the Pacific Ocean (though in fact he was thinking of Balboa: see Glossary).

John Keats

Notice how this reference to the conquest of Central and South America arises naturally out of the poem's opening metaphor of voyaging, especially its reference to 'realms of gold'. The Spanish *conquistadores* were both explorers and soldiers, drawn by the prospect of finding gold and discovering new lands – and conquering them.

The poem as a whole conveys the breathless excitement that Keats felt on reading Chapman's Homer. We know he wrote it quickly, and yet his poet's instincts for rhythm and phrasing keep his train of thought lucid. Notice how, in the final lines, the concluding image is held back by the aside about the soldiers ('and all his men / Look'd at each other …') so that the last line reaches a climax that is exalted (literally, high: 'upon a peak'), but also, after the rush of images in the poem, finally, magically, still: 'Silent'. Keats throws the emphasis on to this word by the line break before it, by the pause dictated by the comma after it, and also by the stress that falls on the first syllable of the word (*sílent*), breaking the iambic metre of the poem.

Themes

The clearest theme of the poem is **the world-changing joy and beauty to be found in great art** – in this case, the poetry of Homer. The 'realms of gold' stand for the domain of great art, which, like gold, is both beautiful and everlasting. Gold does not rust or tarnish so it is often associated with eternal or divine beauty. Think of gold leaf used on medieval religious paintings or on icons of the Greek or Russian Orthodox churches. Keats believed in the power of art, and of poetry in particular, to do good in the world, and this is a theme that runs through his poetry. He takes it up most directly in his 'Ode on a Grecian Urn', as we will see.

Beyond this simple celebration of timeless art, however, **this poem sees Keats reflecting on his own relationship with that art**. He was then a would-be poet who had not yet made the decision to commit his working life to poetry, and he was conscious that he was, to a great extent, an outsider in that world. He lacked the privileged background and classical education of Shelley or Lord Byron, who was at that time the most successful and widely read of the younger generation of poets. That meant, among other things, that he was unable to read Homer and other ancient classics in the original Greek. This sonnet acknowledges his shortcomings: he can read Homer only in translation, and can never know that 'demesne' directly. To some extent, he can only guess at the beauty of the original. The Pacific was distant and unknowable to Cortez/Balboa, just as Homer is to Keats. It is also surprising because the Spanish had expected to find Asia as they went west, not a vast ocean.

John Fuller has an interesting comment on this aspect of the sonnet:

> 'Keats's point is that just as Cortez (though Keats means Balboa, discoverer of the Pacific in 1513) discovers a continent through an ocean (i.e. that he is not in Asia after all), so Keats discovers Homer through Chapman's translation. This is what the 'wild surmise' of line 13 is all about: the discovery in each case is indirect.'

He was an outsider but he wanted to be an insider. You could see this sonnet as **Keats staking his claim to the poetic territory he wanted to occupy**.

Imagery

This poem works by means of its images. As discussed above, the **extended metaphor of voyaging and discovery**, including the discoveries of astronomy, is used to talk about discovering great poetry, even though books and poems are never actually mentioned. The explanation given by the poem's title is needed to interpret the metaphor. Though the same basic metaphor runs through the whole poem, notice how it develops from generalised travelling through the known world at the beginning to a specific, beautifully realised moment of discovery at the end, as 'Cortez' stands silent on a mountain peak, the first European to see the Pacific Ocean.

Form and language

Like 'To one who has been long in city pent', this is a **Petrarchan sonnet written in iambic pentameters**. Here, though, the form is treated a little more freely, conveying a great sense of urgency, especially in the sestet, the final six lines of the poem.

The sonnet is **beautifully constructed**. The octave divides neatly into two quatrains of four lines each. The first ends in a full stop, but the second concludes in a colon, which propels the reader into the sestet and helps create the sense of headlong excitement. The sestet divides unequally into two lines about the astronomer (9–10) and four about Cortez (11–14), so that the final four lines carry the impetus of the poem forward to the final, memorable and still final line: 'Silent, upon a peak in Darien'.

The language of the poem is conventionally poetic in some ways. It uses inversions in word order ('Much have I travell'd'; 'Yet did I never breathe'; 'Then felt I') and poetic diction (notably 'pure serene', line 7, where the adjective 'serene' is used as a noun). Yet some of its finest effects come from simple words used in a straightforward manner. The short words and hard consonants ('t', 'd', 'b') of 'Till I heard Chapman speak out loud and bold' (line 8) give us a feeling for the power of Chapman's verse, and the sheer simplicity of the final line, with its subtle repetitions of 'n' and 'p' sounds, is crucial to the atmosphere of breathless stillness.

John Keats

Exam-Style Questions

Understanding the poem

1. What actual experience is Keats describing with his images of voyaging in the first four lines of the poem?
2. Was the speaker acquainted with the work of Homer before reading Chapman's version? Explain your answer.
3. What experience is being conveyed in lines 7–8?
4. What do the speaker and the astronomer mentioned in line 9 have in common?
5. What do Cortez and the speaker of the poem have in common?

Thinking about the poem

1. Keats begins the sonnet with images of voyaging and discovery. Show how these images are maintained throughout the poem.
2. What impression of Homer do you get from the poem?
3. What purpose is achieved by the final six lines of the sonnet in relation to the first eight?
4. Describe the emotions of the speaker of the sonnet.
5. Show how indirect experience, rather than direct experience, is a theme of the sonnet.

Imagining

1. Imagine you were one of the soldiers with Cortez 'upon a peak in Darien'. Describe the scene in your own words, concentrating on the reactions of Cortez to seeing the Pacific.
2. Describe an exciting journey you have taken or a view that you love. You can use verse or prose, or just share your experience with a partner in class.

SNAPSHOT

- Petrarchan sonnet
- Rich poetic language
- Metaphors of voyaging and discovery
- Records a moment of intense experience
- Sense of wonder and delight
- Theme of indirect discovery

HIGHER LEVEL

Before you read

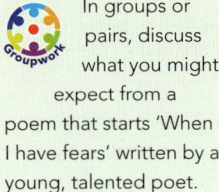

In groups or pairs, discuss what you might expect from a poem that starts 'When I have fears' written by a young, talented poet.

When I have fears that I may cease to be

When I have fears that I may cease to be
   Before my pen has gleaned my teeming brain,
Before high-pilèd books, in charactery,
   Hold like rich garners the full ripened grain;
When I behold, upon the night's starred face,   5
   Huge cloudy symbols of a high romance,
And think that I may never live to trace
   Their shadows with the magic hand of chance;
And when I feel, fair creature of an hour,
   That I shall never look upon thee more,   10
Never have relish in the faery power
   Of unreflecting love—then on the shore
Of the wide world I stand alone, and think
Till love and fame to nothingness do sink.

Glossary

2	*gleaned*:	picked out the best bits from; the image is from harvesting, where gleaning is the process of picking through the harvested field to find ripe grains that have been left behind
2	*teeming*:	filled with ideas, overflowing
3	*charactery*:	writing or print
4	*garners*:	granaries or barns, where the harvested grain is stored
11	*relish*:	enjoyment
11	*faery*:	magical, supernatural
12	*unreflecting love*:	love untroubled by uncertainty; spontaneous love

Guidelines

This poem was written in late January 1818. Keats had had his first volume of poems published the previous year, but it had received little attention. His self-belief was not diminished, but he had come to understand how difficult was the life he had chosen. It had also become clear that his youngest brother, Tom, was ill with tuberculosis.

In this poem Keats contemplates his hopes and ambitions and confronts the fear that he may not live long enough to achieve them.

John Keats

Commentary

The poem is a sonnet, but unlike the previous two poems, it is a Shakespearean sonnet, consisting of three quatrains (groups of four lines) and a final rhyming couplet.

The structure of the sonnet is simple. It is a single sentence. Each quatrain is a statement of a possibility (or conditional clause) introduced by 'when', and they are followed by a conclusion in the final two and a half lines, introduced by 'then'. The sentence's two main verbs do not arrive until line 13: 'I stand … and think'.

Lines 1–4
The first quatrain starts 'When I have fears …' and goes on to express those fears. The main fear is that he might die before he has been able to write and publish all the work he is capable of writing. The image here is of harvesting – his pen gleaning his 'teeming brain' as a peasant or farmer picks the ripe grains from the cut wheat (see Glossary), and then his words are turned into 'high-pilèd books', which Keats likens to stores of 'full ripened grain'.

He is confident that his imagination is rich and fertile enough for him to become a great poet and leave behind a significant body of work, if only he has time to write it.

Lines 5–8
The second quatrain, starting 'When I behold …', develops the main idea of the first. The speaker imagines looking up at the night sky and seeing in the stars the vague outline ('cloudy symbols') of a noble story ('a high romance'), and then he is struck by the thought that he may not live to compose this great work and turn those 'shadows' into poetic form. The 'magic hand of chance' is an ambiguous phrase. It seems to refer to the mysterious force of poetic inspiration, and yet at the same time it reminds us of the uncertain fate that hangs over the poet.

Lines 9–12
The third quatrain moves from poetry to love – another aspect of his life in which Keats had great, unfulfilled yearnings and also great fears. Perhaps the 'fair creature of an hour' is the woman he had glimpsed some years before in Vauxhall Gardens and wrote about then. Perhaps she is another woman he had met. But he is overwhelmed by the thought of never seeing her again and, more significantly, never experiencing 'the faery power / Of unreflecting love'.

Lines 12–14
The final thought – and the conclusion of the sentence – begins in the middle of line 12, before the last quatrain is complete: 'then on the shore …'. Keats has been thinking of how death can waste the talents of a poet like himself and how his dearest hopes and ambitions may be always unrealised. He imagines himself standing alone 'on the shore / Of the wide world', facing his hopes and fears, and thinking. If 'love and fame' are so vulnerable to time and death, they are nothing, he decides. You can read this as despair, but there is also a strength and determination to it. The speaker is not just a victim; it is in part his thinking that turns these worldly desires into 'nothingness'.

HIGHER LEVEL

Themes

Given that we know that Keats only had three more years to live when he wrote this poem, his anxiety that he might not live long enough to write what he knew was in him is deeply poignant, and feels prescient, as if he already knew he would die young. It is true that he expresses that fear in a number of poems, but it is important not to let the fact of his early death overwhelm our reading of the poem. It is worth remembering that Keats had quit medicine about a year before and decided to make his living as a poet. Poetry has never been an easy path to success, and very few poets manage to make a living from their writing. Keats never did. So it is not surprising that he was full of anxieties about the life he had committed himself to. The decision faced him with the possibility of failure, and the necessity, as he saw it, to prioritise his art over love. He believed – at least at times – that he would never be able to combine poetry with a loving relationship with a woman, and so he had effectively denied himself the 'faery power / Of unreflecting love' (lines 11–12).

Keats's **powerful sense of the transience of beauty** is something that we saw in 'To one who has been long in city pent', and an important element in the great odes that we will be looking at (see pages 404–428).

Imagery

The image of **harvest** in lines 1–4, discussed above, looks forward to Keats's late poem, 'To Autumn'. The image of the **starry sky** in lines 5–8 is another one that runs through his poetry, from the 'watcher of the skies' in 'Upon First Looking into Chapman's Homer' to the central image of the sonnet 'Bright Star'.

The poem's final image, of the speaker himself standing 'on the shore / Of the wide world' recalls 'stout Cortez' looking at the Pacific in 'Chapman's Homer'. The wide world is like an ocean into which 'love and fame' sink and disappear, and the 'I' is left alone facing the universe. What feelings does this image evoke for you?

Form and language

Keats had been rereading Shakespeare's plays and sonnets around the time he wrote this poem, and this was his first attempt at a **Shakespearean sonnet**. Like a Petrarchan sonnet, a Shakespearean sonnet has fourteen lines, but the rhyme scheme is looser (*abab cdcd efef gg*) and leads to a natural division of the sonnet into three quatrains (groups of four lines) and a final rhyming couplet.

The ideas of this sonnet follow this structure very closely, with one clause/statement ('when I …') for each quatrain, except that the final clause with its main verbs ('stand … think') starts in the middle of line 12 ('then on the shore …').

As well as using the Shakespearean form, this sonnet tackles a theme that Shakespeare wrote about in several sonnets: **the destructive power of time**.

The vocabulary, as ever with Keats, is **rich with adjectives and full of unusual and resonant words**. There is not enough space to look at all these in detail, so we will concentrate on the first quatrain. Notice how the idea of the abundant harvest is suggested by the abundance of adjectives relating to abundance: 'teeming', 'high-pilèd', 'rich', 'full ripened'. The effect is strengthened by assonance in 'gleaned … teeming' and 'high-pilèd', and double pairs of stresses in 'rích gárners', 'fúll rípened' and, again, 'hígh-pílèd'.

394 / DISCOVERY: POETRY ANTHOLOGY

John Keats

Keats is never afraid to use unashamedly poetic language full of unusual words and an order of words that is dictated more by the requirements of rhyme than the natural forms of spoken English. The richness of the language can occasionally become cloying, but it is tempered by the clarity of the thought that the language expresses. There is always a strong through-line, and he never stops to wallow in the rich language for its own sake. Keats is also capable of **moments of moving simplicity**, as in the final couplet of this poem, where the words are plain and the only 'effect' is the alliteration and long vowel sounds of 'wide world', which together suggest the vastness the speaker is contemplating.

Questions

1. In your own words, what fear is the speaker expressing in the first four lines of the poem?
2. What mode of composing poetry is suggested in the second quatrain (lines 5–8)?
3. What fears is the speaker expressing in the third quatrain (lines 9–12)?
4. What gifts does the speaker value most? Why do these seem less valuable to him at the end?
5. Describe the mood in the final three lines of this poem.
6. The poem conveys the speaker's sense of the power of his imagination. Explore this idea.
7. Comment on the significance of the repeated use of 'never' in the poem.
8. The words 'shore' (line 12) and 'sink' (line 14) suggest the ocean, a traditional image of fate or eternity. How does this idea throw light on what the speaker has been saying?
9. It has been suggested that the 'fair creature of an hour' was a woman Keats once saw in a public place in London, and perhaps never spoke to, but could never forget. Imagine the scene, and write your own account from Keats's point of view.
10. Respond to this poem by expressing your own fears for the future in a poem.

HIGHER LEVEL

Before you read

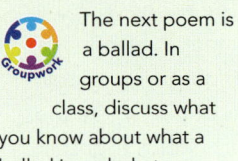

The next poem is a ballad. In groups or as a class, discuss what you know about what a ballad is and what you expect from a ballad.

La Belle Dame Sans Merci

O what can ail thee, knight-at-arms,
    Alone and palely loitering?
The sedge has wither'd from the lake
    And no birds sing!

O what can ail thee, knight-at-arms,   5
    So haggard, and so woe-begone?
The squirrel's granary is full
    And the harvest's done.

I see a lily on thy brow
    With anguish moist and fever dew,   10
And on thy cheeks a fading rose
    Fast withereth too—

I met a lady in the meads
    Full beautiful, a faery's child
Her hair was long, her foot was light,   15
    And her eyes were wild—

I made a garland for her head,
    And bracelets too, and fragrant zone:
She look'd at me as she did love
    And made sweet moan—   20

I set her on my pacing steed
    And nothing else saw all day long
For sidelong would she bend and sing
    A faery's song—

She found me roots of relish sweet 25
    And honey wild and manna dew
And sure in language strange she said
    'I love thee true'—

She took me to her elfin grot
    And there she wept and sigh'd full sore 30
And there I shut her wild wild eyes
    With kisses four.

And there she lullèd me asleep
    And there I dream'd—Ah woe betide!
The latest dream I ever dreamt 35
    On the cold hill side.

I saw pale kings and princes too,
    Pale warriors, death-pale were they all;
They cried 'La belle dame sans merci
    Hath thee in thrall.' 40

I saw their starv'd lips in the gloam
    With horrid warning gapèd wide
And I awoke and found me here
    On the cold hill's side

And this is why I sojourn here 45
    Alone and palely loitering;
Though the sedge is wither'd from the lake
    And no birds sing——

Glossary

Title	*La Belle Dame Sans Merci*:	Keats borrowed his title from a medieval poem by Alain Chartier; it means 'the beautiful lady without pity'
1	*what can ail thee*:	what is the matter with you?
3	*sedge*:	coarse grass which grows in wet places
6	*haggard*:	lean, hollow-eyed
10	*fever dew*:	the sweat of fever
13	*meads*:	meadows
18	*zone*:	belt or girdle (of fragrant flowers); 'zone' is used here with its original meaning, which was rare even when the poem was written
21	*set*:	put
25	*of relish sweet*:	sweet-tasting
26	*manna dew*:	sweet-tasting liquid; God provided manna as food for the Israelites in the desert
29	*elfin grot*:	fairy cave (grotto)
30	*full sore*:	very sorrowfully
35	*latest*:	last
40	*in thrall*:	in slavery
41	*gloam*:	twilight
45	*sojourn*:	stay for a while

HIGHER LEVEL

Guidelines

Keats wrote 'La Belle Dame Sans Merci', one of his best-loved and most haunting poems, in April 1819. A lot had happened in his life since writing the sonnets we have previously looked at. It had been an agonising year. His long poem *Endymion* had received hostile and wounding reviews. His brother George, closest to him in age and affection, had left England with his new wife for a new life in America. His youngest brother, Tom, had died of tuberculosis in December 1818. Keats had spent many weeks nursing him, and was with him at the end; he was also showing the first signs of the same disease, which was to kill him less than two years later. He had also met and fallen in love with the eighteen-year-old Fanny Brawne. All of these events are reflected in the emotional landscape of this poem.

The earliest text of the poem is known from a letter Keats wrote to his brother George. When it was published in the *Indicator* magazine in 1820, it was revised by his friend Leigh Hunt. It is generally accepted that the version printed here is the better poem.

Keats used minimal punctuation when he wrote it out for his brother, and though some adjustments have been made, and a few commas and hyphens added for clarity, this version is more lightly punctuated than those found in most modern editions.

Commentary

'La Belle Dame Sans Merci' is a ballad. Ballads were originally a popular form, using simple vocabulary, rhyme and repetition to tell stories that are memorable and create effects that are often mysterious. Keats's poem is a literary version of the popular form.

John Keats

Lines 1–12

The first three stanzas set the scene for the story: a solitary, unhealthy and unhappy-looking knight in a bleak, lifeless landscape. His forehead is white like a lily, and the rose-red in his cheeks is fading. The narrator asks what is wrong with him: 'O what can ail thee …?'

Lines 13–48

From the fourth stanza on, it is the knight who is speaking. He tells the story of meeting a beautiful, mysterious lady, 'a faery's child' (line 14), in the fields. He made her ornaments from meadow flowers and she seemed to love him, or so he thought. He put her on his horse and rode away.

At this point in the story she takes the initiative. She sang him songs and found delicious food for him and declared her love – or at least he thinks she did because it was 'in language strange' (line 27). She took him to 'her elfin grot' and, for reasons we are not told, 'wept and sigh'd full sore' so that he kisses her eyes, presumably to calm her down. But it is *she* who lulls *him* to sleep, and in his dream he sees kings and princes, presumably former doomed lovers of *la belle dame*. Their looks and their words warn him of his own fate, and when he awakes he is alone on 'the cold hill's side' (line 44).

The ending of the poem returns to its beginning, as the knight declares that the story he has told is the explanation for his being in this desolate place, 'Alone and palely loitering'.

Form and language

As noted above, 'La Belle Dame Sans Merci' is a **literary ballad**. It uses the common ballad form of four-line stanzas (quatrains) rhyming *abcb*. The metre is largely iambic, with four beats or stresses per line, except that the final line of each stanza is shorter, with just two main stresses. This creates a slightly deadened, **downbeat end to each stanza**, which adds to the melancholy mood of the poem.

Like many ballads, this poem makes much use of **direct speech**. Although Keats didn't use any quotation marks at all when he wrote out the poem, it is clear that the first three stanzas are not simply narration, but the narrator directly questioning the knight: 'O what can ail thee …?' The rest of the poem is the knight's reply.

The **syntax (word order) is straightforward and direct**, often using the simplest conjunction, 'and'. Look, for example, at lines 29–36, where the mysterious central events on the poem in the 'elfin grot' are narrated as a simple sequence linked by 'And there …'. The vocabulary is mostly plain, but it is heightened at times by obscure or unusual words that suggest the medieval and magical setting of the story: the 'fragrant zone' (line 18), the 'pacing steed' (line 21), the 'elfin grot' (line 29).

Another feature of the ballad, matching the simple narrative style, is **repetition**. Not only does the end of the poem echo the beginning, almost word for word, but there are many patterns of repetition with variation throughout. The second stanza mirrors the first, and they share an opening line: 'O what can ail thee, knight-at-arms'.

> ### Literary ballads
>
> The Romantic literary movement in Britain saw a revival of interest in ballads, a traditional popular form that used plain language and strong metre to tell stories that are often mysterious or tragic. Robert Burns and Walter Scott in Scotland wrote ballads, and the collection of poems by William Wordsworth and Samuel Taylor Coleridge that did so much to form the Romantic movement in England was called *Lyrical Ballads*. Coleridge's long poem *The Rime of the Ancient Mariner* is a ballad. They are known as literary ballads because they were written by poets who wanted to imitate and make use of the popular form, and because they were not meant to be sung, as most traditional ballads were.

HIGHER LEVEL

There is the simple repetition in 'wild wild eyes' (line 31) and the almost-repetition at a stanza's end at lines 36 and 44: 'On the cold hill side' / 'On the cold hill's side'. Read those two lines out loud. What difference does the added 's' make to the sound and mood?

This poem may not have the rich patterns of sounds and imagery that Keats employs in some of his poems, but it has a **haunting music of its own**. The repeated liquid 'l' sounds in the first lines of the poem – 'ail … / Alone and palely loitering' – are important in creating its seductive atmosphere. If you look through the rest of the poem you will find that Keats uses this letter prominently in every stanza.

Imagery

There is very **little use of metaphorical language in the poem**, except in the third stanza, where the 'lily on thy brow', standing for whiteness and sickness, and the 'fading rose' on the cheeks, standing for redness, blood and (fading) health, have an artful simplicity to them.

Otherwise **the imagery of the poem consists of the pictures the story paints**, and those are very vivid ones: the pale knight in the desolate landscape; the long-haired, wild-eyed lady; the flowers with which he adorns her; the foods with which she feeds him; the four kisses; the procession of ghoulish nobles and warriors.

The scene is given a certain glamour and distanced somewhat from everyday experience by the medieval trappings: the 'knight-at-arms', the 'steed', kings and princes and warriors. It is not surprising to learn that the poem was the inspiration for a number of paintings, especially later in the nineteenth century, when there was a revival of interest in the Middle Ages.

Interpretation and themes

The effect of the simple syntax, rhyme, metre and repetition is to create **clear, vivid impressions that are both mysterious and charged with emotion**. The mysteriousness of this poem is one of the glorious things about it. It can mean different things to different people. Nevertheless, a little information about what was happening in Keats's life at the time can provide hints of what emotions underlie the poem, and what he may have been writing about without even realising it.

Love is clearly central to the poem, and specifically a man's love for a woman. The story is seen from a male perspective, while the woman is mysterious, seductive, desirable, unpredictable and dangerous. What do we know about Keats's relationships with women?

The story of his childhood would suggest that he learned very early that they could let you down. His mother effectively abandoned her children after their father's death, when Keats was eight, and probably took up with another man. When she returned to the family several years later she was mortally ill with tuberculosis, and rather than looking after her children it was she who needed looking after. Keats appointed himself her carer, devotedly nursing her through her final illness until her death when he was fourteen. It has been pointed out that this pattern of loss–recovery–loss is mirrored in 'La Belle Dame Sans Merci', which starts and ends with the desolate, solitary knight.

John Keats

This early experience certainly affected his attitude to women, which was full of contradictions – desire and idealisation on the one hand; distrust and fear on the other. He understood this about himself. As he wrote in a letter in 1818, 'I am certain I have not a right feeling towards women.'

He could be strongly attracted to women, but did not think himself capable of having a conventional relationship. As a creative artist he often saw marriage and children as a threat to the freedom he believed he would need to be a true poet.

> **Love is my religion**
>
> 'Love is my religion – I could die for that – I could die for you. My creed is Love and you are its only tenet – You have ravish'd me away by a Power I cannot resist.'
>
> *Keats, letter to Fanny Brawne*

'La Belle Dame' was written a few months after Keats met Fanny Brawne, the last and greatest love of his short life. At first he was dismissive of his feelings for her, at least to his friends, but part of him wanted to yield himself utterly to them. This poem could be seen as his attempt to work out his contradictory feelings about her and about love: the beautiful lady is at the heart of a sublime experience, but her power is also destructive.

The encounter of knight and lady carries a strong sexual charge, hinted at in the lady's 'sweet moan' and underpinned by the masculine symbolism of the 'steed' and the feminine symbolism of the lady's 'grot' or cave.

HIGHER LEVEL

If love is one central theme of the poem, then surely **death** is the other. As in other poems, death is on Keats's mind. He had been with his brother when he died from tuberculosis, and must have been aware of the first signs of the disease in himself. The appearance of the knight – his fevered, white brow and flushed red cheeks – are those of a tuberculosis sufferer. Again, it is hard not to see a premonition of his own death in the pale, doomed knight.

Love and death are tightly bound together in the poem. The 'belle dame' promises love, but brings death. What does this mean? Should we read the poem as an expression of Keats's fear of women? Should we take it as his stark warning against love? And did Keats know what he was saying? It does not feel so simple as that. Whatever experience the knight has undergone, it has transformed him. He is not just a victim. When he awakens from his dream he doesn't run away, but chooses to remain or 'sojourn' on the 'cold hill's side'. He may be doomed, but he also seems to embrace his fate. Was this Keats's view of the poet's role – love as a form of suffering that would enrich his art?

In the end there is no one answer, and **different readers see different things in the poem**. As the poet Andrew Motion wrote in his biography of Keats, the poem 'creates surfaces of beguiling simplicity, through which readers peer into states of great emotional complexity'. We can only explore what those emotional states might contain.

SNAPSHOT

- Literary ballad
- Medieval setting
- Story told using two speakers
- Theme of the destructive power of love
- Theme of love and death
- Language simple, diction sometimes old-fashioned
- Simply told story with great emotional depth
- Natural world used to create mood

Exam-Style Questions

Understanding the poem

1. In your own words, describe what the first speaker sees in the first three stanzas?
2. From the fourth stanza onwards it is the knight who speaks. Tell his story in your own words.
3. What impression does the lady make on the knight to begin with?
4. How does this impression change later in the poem?
5. What is the knight doing at the end of the poem, and why?

Thinking about the poem

1. What kind of mood or atmosphere is created in the first three stanzas? How do the sounds of the words and the rhythms contribute to the mood?
2. The poem is divided between two speakers. Who are the speakers and what is achieved by dividing the poem between them?
3. How would you describe the knight's experience of love? What does the poem suggest about the relationship between love and happiness?
4. Consider the significance of nature images in the poem. How do these contribute to its overall meaning?
5. The poem features a most effective use of contrast. Examine the effects created by contrasting images throughout the poem.
6. The title of the poem suggests the contradictory nature of the lady. What does she represent?

Imagining

1. Write an account of what is described in the poem from the point of view of the woman ('la belle dame') mentioned in the title.
2. Imagine you are the first speaker. Tell your story of meeting the 'knight-at-arms' to a friend the next day.

HIGHER LEVEL

Before you read

Have you ever heard the song of the nightingale? Before reading the poem, find a recording of it online and listen to the sounds. Your teacher might be able to play you a clip in class.

Ode to a Nightingale

My heart aches, and a drowsy numbness pains
    My sense, as though of hemlock I had drunk,
Or emptied some dull opiate to the drains
    One minute past, and Lethe-wards had sunk:
'Tis not through envy of thy happy lot,   5
    But being too happy in thine happiness,—
        That thou, light-wingèd Dryad of the trees,
            In some melodious plot
Of beechen green, and shadows numberless,
    Singest of summer in full-throated ease.   10

O, for a draught of vintage! that hath been
    Cool'd a long age in the deep-delvèd earth,
Tasting of Flora and the country green,
    Dance, and Provençal song, and sunburnt mirth!
O for a beaker full of the warm South,   15
    Full of the true, the blushful Hippocrene,
        With beaded bubbles winking at the brim,
           And purple-stainèd mouth;
That I might drink, and leave the world unseen,
    And with thee fade away into the forest dim: 20

Fade far away, dissolve, and quite forget
    What thou among the leaves hast never known,
The weariness, the fever, and the fret
    Here, where men sit and hear each other groan;
Where palsy shakes a few, sad, last gray hairs,   25
    Where youth grows pale, and spectre-thin, and dies;
       Where but to think is to be full of sorrow
          And leaden-eyed despairs,
Where Beauty cannot keep her lustrous eyes,
    Or new Love pine at them beyond tomorrow.   30

Away! away! for I will fly to thee,
    Not charioted by Bacchus and his pards,
But on the viewless wings of Poesy,
    Though the dull brain perplexes and retards:
Already with thee! tender is the night,   35
    And haply the Queen-Moon is on her throne,
        Cluster'd around by all her starry Fays;
            But here there is no light,
Save what from heaven is with the breezes blown
    Through verdurous glooms and winding mossy ways.   40

I cannot see what flowers are at my feet,
    Nor what soft incense hangs upon the boughs,
But, in embalmèd darkness, guess each sweet
    Wherewith the seasonable month endows
The grass, the thicket, and the fruit-tree wild;   45
    White hawthorn, and the pastoral eglantine;
        Fast fading violets cover'd up in leaves;
            And mid-May's eldest child,
The coming musk-rose, full of dewy wine,
    The murmurous haunt of flies on summer eves.   50

Darkling I listen; and, for many a time
    I have been half in love with easeful Death,
Call'd him soft names in many a musèd rhyme,
    To take into the air my quiet breath;
Now more than ever seems it rich to die,   55
    To cease upon the midnight with no pain,
        While thou art pouring forth thy soul abroad
            In such an ecstasy!
    Still wouldst thou sing, and I have ears in vain—
        To thy high requiem become a sod.   60

Thou wast not born for death, immortal Bird!
    No hungry generations tread thee down;
The voice I hear this passing night was heard
    In ancient days by emperor and clown:
Perhaps the self-same song that found a path   65
    Through the sad heart of Ruth, when, sick for home,
        She stood in tears amid the alien corn;
            The same that oft-times hath
    Charm'd magic casements, opening on the foam
        Of perilous seas, in faery lands forlorn.   70

> Forlorn! the very word is like a bell
>   To toll me back from thee to my sole self!
> Adieu! the fancy cannot cheat so well
>   As she is fam'd to do, deceiving elf.
> Adieu! adieu! thy plaintive anthem fades   75
>   Past the near meadows, over the still stream,
>   Up the hill-side; and now 'tis buried deep
>   In the next valley-glades:
>   Was it a vision, or a waking dream?
>   Fled is that music:—Do I wake or sleep?   80

Glossary

Line	Term
2	*hemlock*: a poisonous plant, used as a powerful sedative
3	*opiate*: another sedative drug
3	*drains*: the dregs; the bottom of the bottle
4	*past*: ago
4	*Lethe-wards*: towards Lethe, the river of forgetfulness in the classical underworld
7	*Dryad*: a wood nymph
9	*beechen*: to do with beech trees
11	*a draught of vintage*: a drink of wine
13	*Flora*: Roman goddess of flowers and fertility
14	*Provençal song*: the reference is to a region in southern France, associated with music and romantic poetry
15	*warm South*: wine from the south
16	*Hippocrene*: the fountain on Mount Helicon whose waters inspired the Muses; Keats thought of its liquid as red wine rather than water, as is apparent from his calling it 'blushful'
23	*fret*: worry
25	*palsy*: a disease which causes limbs to tremble
32	*Not … pards*: not under the influence of wine; Bacchus, the god of wine, was traditionally shown in a chariot drawn by leopards ('pards')
33	*viewless*: invisible, because flying too high
33	*Poesy*: poetry
35	*tender*: mild
36	*haply*: perhaps
36	*the Queen-Moon*: Diana, the moon goddess
37	*Fays*: fairies; Keats imagines the stars as fairies in the service of Diana
40	*verdurous*: green, leafy, full of vegetation
43	*embalmèd darkness*: darkness steeped in scents, like the 'incense' of the previous line
46	*eglantine*: sweet briar
49	*musk-rose*: small rose with distinctive scent
51	*Darkling*: in the dark
52	*easeful*: comforting
53	*musèd*: thoughtful; also, perhaps, inspired by the Muses
59	*have ears in vain*: be unable to hear
60	*To thy … sod*: Keats is imagining the nightingale singing a requiem mass, which he will no longer hear, having returned to earth ('become a sod')
66	*Ruth*: in the Old Testament book which takes her name, Ruth is a lonely, unhappy exile, anxious to escape from her 'alien' environment
69	*casements*: window openings
70	*forlorn*: unhappy, lost
73	*fancy*: the imagination
75	*plaintive*: sounding sad or mournful
75	*anthem*: song, usually a setting of a religious text

John Keats

Guidelines

The 'Ode to a Nightingale' is one of a series of odes Keats wrote in 1819, which all throw light on one another, and some of which he probably worked on at the same time. Taken together, they are generally agreed to be his greatest achievement as a poet. As well as the poems on this course, the odes 'on Indolence', 'on Melancholy' and 'to Psyche' are worth reading to get a fuller idea of Keats's preoccupations and to appreciate how he uses the form of the ode.

This ode was written around the beginning of May 1819. According to Charles Armitage Brown, a friend of Keats, with whom he was staying when he wrote it, it was written very quickly. Brown recorded that Keats sat for some hours in his garden, listening to the nightingale's song, then came into the house with some scraps of paper in his hand that 'contained his poetic feeling on the song of the nightingale'. Brown claimed that he and Keats arranged the stanzas from Keats's fragments, and the result was 'a poem which has been the delight of everyone'.

That account is probably not the whole truth, but this ode, more than any of the others, has a sense of urgency to it, as if it was written quickly, while the excitement of the experience it describes was still present. The poem does not pursue an argument, but follows the shifting moods, the changing thoughts and imaginative processes of the speaker. His experience of listening and letting his imagination wander is the core of the poem. Indeed, a recent biographer of Keats, Nicholas Roe, who believes the poet was addicted to laudanum (a form of opium) at this time, describes this poem as 'one of the greatest re-creations of a drug-inspired dream-vision in English literature'.

Commentary

Stanza 1
Keats puts himself and his emotions at front and centre from the beginning of the poem: 'My heart aches'. The feelings he describes suggest dullness and dejection ('drowsy numbness'), as if he had been drugged into a stupor, but his heartache isn't altogether negative.

He explains, from line 5, the cause of these emotions. He is listening to a nightingale, and he is not feeling bad-tempered out of envy for the joy he hears in the nightingale's song; his heartache comes from being 'too happy' in the happiness of the nightingale. As elsewhere in Keats, joy and pain are close together. He goes on to describe the bird's 'happiness', like a Dryad or tree spirit singing among the trees 'in full-throated ease'.

Stanza 2
Though he has said he does not envy the nightingale, he wishes he could in some way unite himself with it, or with its song. The second stanza imagines that a drink of wine ('a draught of vintage') might enable him to 'fade away' with the nightingale 'into the forest dim'. He wants to prolong his ecstatic state of mind, and imagines a drink of wine that could do so. Not any ordinary wine, this, but something cooled deep in the earth, yet with the warmth of the 'South'. He imagines it as being infused with all sorts of qualities: flowers ('Flora') and dance and song and 'sunburnt mirth' – even the sacred spring of the ancient Greek Muses, the Hippocrene. It is not, in other words, just a glass of wine he wants, but the inspiration of all the cultural associations he invokes.

HIGHER LEVEL

Keats Listening to the Nightingale on Hampstead Health, Joseph Severn, 1949. Image courtesy of Keats House, City of London.

Stanza 3

The next stanza pursues the idea of fading away and elaborates on the reason for wishing to do so. Now it is less a matter of maintaining his rapt state of mind than of escaping from the world. The spontaneous joy of the nightingale's unthinking, untroubled song is set against the human experience of suffering, which is what 'thou among the leaves hast never known'. This misery is described in stark phrases with many monosyllables: 'Here, where men sit and hear each other groan'. Keats uses personification – 'palsy' stands for a feeble old person, 'youth' for a young one, 'Beauty' for a beautiful woman whose beauty will fade, and 'Love' for someone newly in love whose love will also fade.

But perhaps the most affecting and significant lines are the most direct: 'Where but to think is to be full of sorrow'. This is the heart of the contrast between the speaker and the nightingale: being conscious, the speaker is weighed down by the world's suffering, whereas the nightingale's song is unburdened by that knowledge.

Stanza 4

'Away! away!' at the opening of the fourth stanza takes up the desire at the end of the second stanza to fade away with the nightingale. Now, though, Keats dismisses the idea of getting drunk in order to achieve this. He will fly not by drinking wine, represented by 'Bacchus and his pards', but, despite his 'dull brain', 'on the viewless wings of Poesy'. Here he seems to mean the imagination that creates poetry (Poesy) as much as poetry itself, for with a thought he is 'Already with thee'. He conjures a comforting, beautiful image of the scene: 'tender is the night'. He thinks of the 'Queen-Moon' and the stars, as if in an allegorical painting, but makes clear that he is separate from this imagined scene. He is under a tree and in the dark, with no light except what 'is with the breezes blown' to the green ('verdurous') place where he sits or lies.

Stanza 5

In this stanza he explores this green place. He can see nothing, only smell the flowers and imagine what they must be. Lovingly and sensuously, he lists them. He revels in the 'embalmèd darkness', and yet there is also the haunting sense that all this beauty is short-lived and at the mercy of time: the violets are 'Fast fading', and the musk roses will become the 'haunt of flies' as summer comes.

The nightingale is not mentioned in this stanza, but the eradication of all senses except smell, and above all the removal of sight in the darkness, concentrates his mind on the listening. We know the song is continuing, and the stanza creates a sense of the listener's trance.

Stanza 6
The opening of the stanza returns us to that listener in the dark ('Darkling I listen') before reflecting on his state of mind, both now and in the past. The thought of death is now uppermost: 'I have been half in love with easeful Death' and 'Now more than ever seems it rich to die'. It is a special sort of death that he imagines: 'To cease upon the midnight with no pain'. It is as if death is the logical end point of the fading away and dissolving into the nightingale's song that he longs for, a way of partaking in the 'ecstasy' of that song. He imagines that death: the nightingale is still singing, but he, the listener, has turned into a 'sod' of earth, so that the song becomes a requiem over his grave.

Stanza 7
With the speaker's self obliterated, his attention turns back to the nightingale and its audience. By calling the nightingale an 'immortal Bird' he does not mean, of course, the particular bird he is listening to, but rather its song – the 'voice' that has been heard throughout history by all types of people, 'emperor and clown'. He thinks of the song as having the power to comfort, and imagines the biblical figure of Ruth, exiled and unhappy, being soothed by the nightingale's song. Then in the final three lines of the stanza he goes on to picture the song as an inspiration to the imagination, as if the music could cast a spell ('charm') on a view of a fantastical landscape. There is no human audience now, but the 'perilous seas' and 'faery lands' suggest tales of magic and adventure. It is clear that Keats is implying a relationship between the nightingale's song and the artist's or poet's imagination.

Stanza 8
The final stanza picks up the last word of the previous one: 'forlorn'. We are back with the listener, but the mood has changed, and so apparently has the nightingale's song. Where it was happy in the first stanza, singing 'in full-throated ease', now the feeling is sad and the song is a 'plaintive anthem'.

The word 'adieu' rings through this final stanza. The speaker is bidding adieu both to the bird flying off into the next valley and to his intense experience. Whatever experience that was is fading now, and Keats's imagination ('fancy') is not enough to keep it alive. It cannot 'cheat so well'. After all his rich imaginings he is left alone and lonely, his 'sole self'. He isn't sure what he has been through – a 'vision' of some essential truth or a 'waking dream', which sounds less significant. It sounds like waking up from a vivid dream when you are still half-asleep, caught up in the images of the dream and confused: 'Do I wake or sleep?' There is a sense of loss. The music is gone, 'fled' with the singing bird. The dream-vision is over.

Themes and imagery

The emotional landscape
On one level, the poem can be read as what it appears to be: **the account of an intense experience of listening in the dark to the beautiful singing of a nightingale**. As noted above, Nicholas Roe has suggested that Keats may have been addicted to laudanum, and the first stanza hints at the possibility that he may have 'emptied some dull opiate to the drains' (line 3); laudanum is an opiate.

But whether or not his intense and fluctuating emotions on listening to the nightingale were drug-inspired, **Keats lets his imagination roam, and pursues it where it takes him**. The emotional landscape it reveals is familiar from his other poetry. Suffering and joy are closely related: the happiness he feels in the nightingale's beautiful song makes his heart ache with an emotion that contains both **pain and pleasure**. His soul responds to the nightingale's – or that is how he sees it when he describes the song as 'pouring forth thy soul … / In … ecstasy' (lines 57–58).

This **ecstasy is at the emotional heart of the poem**. The speaker wants to prolong and intensify his trance-like state as he listens, and to share in the nightingale's 'ecstasy'. That is why he imagines 'a draught of vintage' (line 11) that would enable him to enter more deeply into that state of mind. Keats imagines that state in terms of transcendence (literally, rising above) in the imagery of the fourth stanza: 'I will fly to thee' (line 31). But more often he thinks of it in terms of **his own dissolution** (dissolving) or annihilation. He wants to 'fade away into the forest dim' (line 20), and in the next line, 'Fade far away, dissolve'. The word 'fade' or its variants occurs four times in the poem, and even the forest he wants to fade into is 'dim'. Read through the poem and notice the other words that have to do with blurring sight, half-light and semi-consciousness.

The furthest extension of the desire to dissolve is **the idea of dying** that Keats explores in the sixth stanza, and which we have seen before, especially in 'When I have fears that I may crease to be'. As he writes, 'for many a time / I have been half in love with easeful death' (lines 51–52). This death, however, is imagined as a sort of union with the nightingale. He wants to 'cease upon the midnight with no pain' while listening to the song.

In part this desire to fade, dissolve and 'quite forget' (line 21) is linked with **his desire to escape the troubles of the world**, as the third stanza makes absolutely clear. It is easy to understand this in the context of Keats's life. In the past year, his brother Tom had died from tuberculosis, and his memory haunts line 26: 'Where youth grows pale, and spectre-thin, and dies'. His other brother, George, to whom he was very close, had left for America; his poetry had received savage reviews, and his own health was fragile.

There is always a tension, however, between the urge to fade and die, and the vivid, joyful life that the speaker perceives in the nightingale's song. On the one hand, there is the imagery of dissolving, darkness and dimness; on the other, there is the world of 'sunburnt mirth' (line 14) and 'full-throated ease' (line 10). This is explored with great power in the fifth stanza, with its sensuous evocation of the unseen flowers and their sweet scents. Yet even here death is present: the darkness is 'embalmèd' like a body awaiting burial, and the violets are 'fading'.

The imagery of the poem is often richly sensual, and like the emotional journey it is complex and ambiguous. 'Ode to a Nightingale' is one of Keats's best-loved poems because of this complexity and intensity of emotions and images. It describes **elusive states of feeling** that readers often respond strongly to, especially if they have been touched by joy and sorrow, and know the way in which great beauty can stir those emotions.

Art and music

Thinking about the role of beauty brings into focus another important element of this poem. As the critic Helen Vendler has suggested, this ode is also an **exploration of the power of art**, and specifically of music.

The nightingale is not just a bird, it is an 'immortal Bird' (line 61). The bird has become its song, and its song is timeless in the way that great art is timeless. The association of the nightingale's voice with great music becomes more apparent as the poem goes on. At first it is simply birdsong, but later that song is described as 'pouring out thy soul', as a human musician might. Then its song is described as a 'high requiem' and a 'plaintive anthem' – both of which imply human composition – until in the final line it is simply 'music'.

The focus on music is strengthened by the poem's increasing **focus on the sense of hearing**. The visual images of the poem's opening – the 'beaded bubbles', the 'purple-stainèd mouth' – disappear as the speaker is lost in darkness, listening. In the fifth stanza the flowers are only guessed at by their scent, and by the sixth all senses but hearing have been left behind ('Darkling I listen', line 51), and the focus is all on the listening.

Keats's use of classical imagery – Lethe and the Dryad in the first stanza, Flora and the 'blushful Hippocrene', sacred to the Muses, in the second – reinforces the association of the nightingale's song with the values of ancient culture. So, in another way, does the mention of the Mediterranean culture represented by 'Dance, and Provençal song' and 'the warm South'.

Seen from this perspective, the poem becomes **an exploration of the powers and purposes of art**. It can, first of all, stir the emotions: the speaker's 'heart aches' because of the nightingale's song. It can be an **escape from the cares of the world**, a way of forgetting the suffering that comes with human consciousness, 'Where but to think is to be full of sorrow' (line 27). The bird and its music are free of that knowledge.

Art can also **console or comfort**. Keats said of his role as a poet, 'I am ambitious of doing the world some good.' The sort of good he meant is suggested by the story of Ruth in the seventh stanza: here music (the nightingale's song) provides a comfort for her as 'She stood in tears amid the alien corn' (line 67).

As noted in the Commentary, the next three lines touch on the nightingale's song as **inspiration for the artistic imagination** – music with the power to cast a spell on 'magic casements, opening on the foam / Of perilous seas' (lines 69–70). The image of casements (sets of windows) is a common one for the imagination, and the fact that here they look out on such a romantic landscape feeds the idea that Keats is thinking of the nightingale's song as poetic inspiration.

Music, at least as Keats views it in this poem, is all bound up with the senses, as opposed to thought. That is why it can be an escape from this world where 'men sit and hear each other groan' (line 24). The final stanza, as the nightingale flies away, its music fades and the vision dissolves, hints that art as escape from the world is of limited value.

Form

The 'Ode to a Nightingale' is the first of Keats's odes that we are studying. **An ode is a poem of praise for a person or thing, in which the subject is directly addressed**, as in line 61: 'Thou wast not born for death, immortal Bird!' There is no standard form for an ode, but Keats writes most of his in **ten-line stanzas**. The form bears some resemblance to a sonnet: the first four lines of each stanza rhyme *abab* like a Shakespearean sonnet, while the last six lines of this ode rhyme *cdecde* like the sestet of a Petrarchan sonnet. The metre is iambic, but in this poem Keats adds variety by introducing one shorter line (the eighth in each stanza) that has three stresses rather than the usual five. This form allows Keats more flexibility than would the tightly woven form of the sonnet, and though there is often a natural break between the first four lines and the last six (see, for example, the first stanza), this is not always the case; the fifth stanza has no clear division in it, a factor that contributes to the sense of being overwhelmed by impressions.

As well as flexibility within the stanzas, the links between them that move the train of thought from one to the next are also important. For example, the image of the poet dying and becoming a 'sod' to the nightingale's 'high requiem' (line 60) sparks the contrasting idea of the nightingale's immortality at the start of the following stanza: 'Thou wast not born for death' (line 61). Notice too how **Keats repeats key words** in order to make the links: 'fade away' at the end of stanza 2 is picked up in the opening words of stanza 3, and then again in 'Away! away!' at the start of stanza 4.

Language

The **richness of the language** is one of the great pleasures of reading this poem. Keats relishes the resources of poetic diction. These include the direct address to the nightingale using the intimate second-person 'thou', which was unusual in ordinary speech even two hundred years ago: 'Thou wast not born for death' (line 61). **Exclamations** (e.g. line 11: 'O, for a draught of vintage!'), **inversion** of word order (e.g. line 80: 'Fled is that music') and the use of **personification** in the third stanza (see Commentary) are other examples of poetic diction.

The language of the poem is **highly charged**. The use of the first person and the present tense from the first line ('My heart aches') contributes to the poem's emotional charge. So do the numerous, often richly resonant adjectives, which include many compound ones: 'light-wingèd', 'full-throated', 'deep-delvèd', 'purple-stainèd', 'spectre-thin', 'leaden-eyed'. There is a richness too, both of meaning and of sound, to many of the nouns and adjective–noun combinations. To take one example, the sensuality of 'sunburnt mirth' (line 14) is conveyed in part by the assonance of doubled vowel sounds in '—burnt mirth' and the three consecutive stresses that the phrase requires when spoken. (Try saying it.) The nouns often have their own richness, particularly in the flower names of the fifth stanza. There Keats uses the adjective–noun combinations to create the heady atmosphere of the sense impressions that accompany the nightingale's song in the 'embalmèd darkness' (line 43): 'soft incense', 'white hawthorn', 'pastoral eglantine', 'dewy wine', 'murmurous haunt'.

As already noted, the language is also rich with **musical effects**, including alliteration ('<u>d</u>eep-<u>d</u>elvèd'; '<u>b</u>eaded <u>b</u>ubbles') and assonance. Yet for all the richness of the language, it is never overwhelming. It always takes its place within a clear syntax which is never constrained by the rhymes and line endings, but always flows easily within them. Enjambment (run-over lines) is used a lot (see, for example, the poem's first two lines), but never draws attention to itself.

Also, for all the sensuous richness of the language, some of the poem's most powerful effects are achieved through **starkness and simplicity**: the plain **monosyllabic** epithets of 'a few, sad, last gray hairs' (line 25), for example.

The metre is iambic (unstressed, stressed), but Keats often varies it in subtle ways for effect. The monosyllables of line 25 quoted above require equal stresses and slow down the line, bringing out the bitter sadness in the words. The very opening of the poem, on the other hand, with its double stresses on the long vowels of 'heart aches', grab the reader's attention as well as conveying something of the speaker's anguish.

Questions

1. Describe the speaker's mood as this is conveyed in the first stanza.

2. The second stanza begins, 'O, for a draught of vintage!' Explain, in your own words, why the speaker wants a drink of wine, and what that 'draught of vintage' means to him.

3. In the third stanza, the mood of the poem changes. Explain.

4. Why, as the speaker expresses it in lines 27–8 ('Where but to think is to be full of sorrow / And leaden-eyed despairs'), does he suggest that thinking is the enemy of human happiness? What is his alternative?

5. What mood is created by the fifth stanza? How does Keats create this mood?

6. In stanza 6, the speaker's imagination surrenders to the attractions of an easy, painless death. Does this finally satisfy him? Explain your answer.

7. Line 61 ('Thou wast not born for death, immortal Bird!') is the focus for the main issues raised in the poem. Comment on the implications of this statement about the nightingale. In what sense is it true, and in what sense is it false?

8. What experience is being described in the final stanza? How would you describe the mood?

9. The poem is partly about the power of the poetic imagination, and of art in general, to transform human experience. Develop this idea.

10. Examine the tension between opposites found throughout the poem: between life and death, pleasure and pain, escapism and reality, life and art, mortality and immortality.

11. This poem has been described as a record of a 'drug-inspired dream-vision'. Is this a good description of the poem, do you think? Is it a complete one?

12. Choose one image or line from the poem that you particularly like (or dislike) and try to explain why. Comment on the sounds of the words if that is appropriate.

13. In his the draft of the poem, line 26 read, 'Where youth grows pale, and thin and old and dies'. Why do you think Keats changed it? Consider the rhythm and sounds of the line.

14. Imagine you are the poet. Write two or three diary entries dealing with the poem (for example, the inspiration behind it, your own assessment of its value).

15. Listen again to a recording of a nightingale, and decide for yourself whether the song is sad or happy. Give yourself ten minutes to write your own response, in prose or verse, as you listen.

HIGHER LEVEL

Before you read

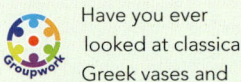 Have you ever looked at classical Greek vases and urns? Before you read the poem, find some pictures online of carved or painted vases to get an idea of what Keats was writing about in this poem.

Ode on a Grecian Urn

Thou still unravish'd bride of quietness,
   Thou foster-child of silence and slow time,
Sylvan historian, who canst thus express
   A flowery tale more sweetly than our rhyme:
What leaf-fring'd legend haunts about thy shape   5
   Of deities or mortals, or of both,
      In Tempe or the dales of Arcady?
   What men or gods are these? What maidens loth?
What mad pursuit? What struggle to escape?
   What pipes and timbrels? What wild ecstasy?   10

Heard melodies are sweet, but those unheard
   Are sweeter: therefore, ye soft pipes, play on;
Not to the sensual ear, but, more endear'd,
   Pipe to the spirit ditties of no tone:
Fair youth, beneath the trees, thou canst not leave   15
   Thy song, nor ever can those trees be bare;
      Bold lover, never, never canst thou kiss
Though winning near the goal – yet, do not grieve;
    She cannot fade, though thou hast not thy bliss,
   For ever wilt thou love, and she be fair!   20

Ah, happy, happy boughs! that cannot shed
   Your leaves, nor ever bid the spring adieu;
And, happy melodist, unwearièd,
   For ever piping songs for ever new;
More happy love! more happy, happy love!   25
   For ever warm and still to be enjoy'd,
      For ever panting, and for ever young;
All breathing human passion far above,
   That leaves a heart high-sorrowful and cloy'd,
      A burning forehead, and a parching tongue.   30

Who are these coming to the sacrifice?
    To what green altar, O mysterious priest,
Lead'st thou that heifer lowing at the skies,
    And all her silken flanks with garlands drest?
What little town by river or sea shore,   35
    Or mountain-built with peaceful citadel,
      Is emptied of this folk, this pious morn?
And, little town, thy streets for evermore
    Will silent be; and not a soul to tell
      Why thou art desolate, can e'er return.   40

O Attic shape! Fair attitude! with brede
    Of marble men and maidens overwrought,
With forest branches and the trodden weed;
    Thou, silent form, dost tease us out of thought
As doth eternity: Cold Pastoral!   45
    When old age shall this generation waste,
      Thou shalt remain, in midst of other woe
    Than ours, a friend to man, to whom thou say'st,
'Beauty is truth, truth beauty,' – that is all
    Ye know on earth, and all ye need to know.   50

Glossary

Line	Term
1	*unravish'd*: not broken or violated; virgin
3	*Sylvan*: to do with the woods and trees; the story on the urn takes place in a woodland setting
7	*Tempe … Arcady*: places in Greece traditionally associated with beauty and golden-age happiness
8	*loth*: reluctant, unwilling
10	*timbrel*: musical instrument resembling a tambourine
29	*cloy'd*: experiencing unpleasant feelings as result of overindulgence
30	*parching*: dried out; thirsty
36	*citadel*: stronghold; fortified building
41	*Attic*: Greek
41	*brede*: interwoven pattern
42	*overwrought*: very elaborately carved (by the artist), and also worked up to too high a pitch (with reference to the man and the maidens)
44	*tease us out of thought*: baffle us with its mystery; defy our attempts to think rationally about what the urn signifies

Guidelines

The 'Ode on a Grecian Urn' was written at much the same time as the 'Ode to a Nightingale', and the two can be viewed as a complementary pair, sharing many of the same concerns. Here, more obviously than in the nightingale ode, the subject is the nature and purpose of art, in this case visual art: an ancient Greek urn. Like the nightingale ode, this poem was first published in the *Annals of the Fine Arts*, a magazine aimed at readers interested in the visual arts in particular, and especially at those who valued ancient Greek art as the highest ideal of beauty.

HIGHER LEVEL

Keats had become more and more interested in classical Greek art and culture. He had spent a lot of time reading its literature in translation, and also looking at the Greek antiquities in the British Museum in London. According to his friend Mathew, 'one of the main endeavours of his poetic career was to grow more Grecian'.

This poem may have owed its immediate inspiration to some articles contributed to the *Examiner* in May 1819 by the painter and art critic Benjamin Haydon, a friend of Keats. In these articles, Haydon discussed some of the works of ancient Greek artists. These works included marble statues, marble ornamental decorations on buildings and beautifully decorated urns. Some of these artefacts depicted ancient Greek religious ceremonies, one in particular featuring a garlanded heifer and robed worshippers with dishevelled hair (see stanza 4), a boy flute-player wholly absorbed in the harmony of his own music (see stanza 2), and a city where 'all classes were crowding to the sacrifice' (stanza 4).

Commentary

Greek (or Grecian) urns were large vases, usually with handles and flat bases, used originally for storing the ashes of a cremated body. Although the painted clay vessels, often decorated with red and black figures, may be more familiar, Keats's urn is a marble one, decorated not by painting but by carving: 'with brede / Of marble men and maidens overwrought' (lines 41–42). Keats had looked at many, and had made a drawing of the Sosibios Vase (left) from a book about Greek art, but the urn he describes in the poem is his own invention, and does not match any actual vessel.

Stanza 1

Keats begins by addressing the urn, the subject of his ode. It is worth looking carefully at the first two lines and the words he uses to name the urn. The object is humanised, and thought of as female, a 'bride of quietness'. This phrase speaks to the literal silence of the urn, in contrast to the very vocal nightingale, but also to the sense of something tender, even sacred, in that silence. It is 'unravish'd', on one level, because although it is two thousand years old or so, it is undamaged, but the word also suggests both the femininity and purity of the object. The word 'still' carries a double meaning: 'not yet', after all this time, but also, simply, 'motionless'. The fact that it and all the scenes depicted on it are frozen in time is central to the poem.

The layers of meaning in the second line are equally rich and dense. The urn is a 'foster-child' because its original maker is long dead, and its foster parents are 'silence and slow time', embracing both the centuries during which the urn has survived, unchanging, buried or hidden, and the urn's own silence.

The urn is also called a 'Sylvan historian' that can tell a tale of the woods 'more sweetly than our rhyme'. Lines 5 to 10, following the colon at the end of line 4, question the nature of that 'flowery tale'. The speaker is trying to understand the story he sees carved into the urn. Are the figures gods or mortals? Where are they? What is happening? The maidens (plural) are 'loth'; there is a struggle; there are musicians. The scene conveys some sort of 'wild ecstasy'. Is this one of the stories of gods overpowering and raping mortal women that are so frequent in ancient Greek myths?

Stanza 2

The mood changes in the second stanza. The questions have stopped and instead there is an intense focus on the scene described, and clear statements about it.

The first four lines act as a transition between the stanzas, picking up on the pipes described in the first stanza. They start with a proposition: unheard melodies (like those we can imagine being played by the musicians on the urn) are 'sweeter' than heard ones, presumably because their beauty is limited only by the viewer's imagination. This unheard music plays to 'the spirit', not the senses.

The scene we see in this stanza seems to be different from that described in the first one: instead of the men, gods, maidens and struggle, there is one lover, one woman and one musician. Here Keats concentrates on the way the scene seems suspended in time because it is a carving of one moment: the trees always in leaf, the musician ('Fair youth') always playing. The lover will be always in love, always about to kiss the maiden, and she 'cannot fade' and will always be beautiful.

Stanza 3

Now the speaker begins to project emotions onto this frozen scene. The trees must be happy because they exist in an eternal spring. The piper never gets tired and plays songs 'for ever new'. Above all, the lovers are happy: 'more happy, happy love!' They are always young, always on the brink of enjoyment, never knowing disappointment or disillusion. They are 'far above' the reality of 'breathing human passion', which is always a let-down: 'That leaves a heart high-sorrowful and cloy'd, / A burning forehead, and a parching tongue.'

Do you find the repetition of 'happy' in this stanza convincing? Is the speaker responding with simple joy to what he sees on the urn, or does the reality of human passion weigh more heavily? Is he trying too hard to convince himself that the beauty of art can make up for the sad reality of human experience?

Stanza 4

The mood changes dramatically in the fourth stanza. The fevered excitement of stanza 3 is replaced by a solemn, questioning tone. The scene here is clearly a new one. Some sort of religious ceremony is taking place. A priest leads a heifer decorated with flowers to a sacrificial altar. As in the first stanza, the speaker questions the scene: 'Who are these …?'; 'To what green altar …?' From line 35, however, the questions have a different focus – not on what the urn shows, but on what it does not show. Keats imagines a 'little town' which must be empty because all its inhabitants have come out to take part in the ceremony. Like the urn, its streets will always be 'silent', the town 'desolate'. This unseen empty town casts a shadow over the poem.

Stanza 5

In the final stanza, Keats addresses the urn directly again. The language now is distancing, where it had been humanising ('bride' and 'child') at the start of the poem. It is an 'Attic shape', an 'attitude', a 'silent form'. The

> **Quotation marks?**
>
> The final two lines can be punctuated in different ways. In the original printing of the poem there were no quotation marks, but the fact that the words are addressed to 'ye', which is plural, strongly suggests that the urn is imagined as speaking to those looking at it, and through them to all humanity. In Keats's *Poems* of 1820 there were quotation marks around just 'Beauty is truth, truth beauty'. It has been suggested that those words were put in quotation marks because they are a quotation from an essay by the artist Joshua Reynolds. One solution, using modern conventions of punctuation, would be to put quotation marks around the whole of the final two lines, but the solution we have chosen leaves it open for the reader to interpret.

designs on it are 'Cold Pastoral'. There is admiration, but also perhaps a little frustration, even resentment, in the speaker's statement that the urn 'dost tease us out of thought / As doth eternity'. Thinking about the urn and its meaning is what the speaker has been doing, but thinking about it doesn't reduce it to something comprehensible, any more than thinking about the nature of eternity.

The final five lines, however, reassert the permanent value of the urn, as a positive force, 'a friend to man', and then, in an extraordinary reversal, the silent urn speaks to its human viewers/listeners ('ye') in the final two lines. What it says, and what exactly Keats meant by it, has been the subject of a great deal of controversy. Some critics, including the great poet T. S. Eliot, have regarded it as meaningless, but it would appear that the idea of beauty and truth being equivalent was not meaningless to Keats himself. As he wrote in a letter, 'I can never be certain of any truth but from a clear perception of its beauty'.

Themes and imagery

The 'Ode on a Grecian Urn' is **a meditation on the power and beauty of classical Greek art**, and through it on the purpose and place of art in general. Its imagery derives primarily from what is being contemplated: a marble Greek urn and the figures carved on it that suggest stories while being set in stone, as if frozen in time.

Despite an ending ('Beauty is truth, truth beauty') which sounds as though it summarises and clinches an argument, there is **no one simple, coherent argument** in what the poem says about art. There is, rather, an intense concentration on the object of contemplation and an engagement with it that is both intellectual and emotional, full of ambiguities of thought and feeling.

The poem's **central contrast is between the ideal and the actual**: the still and silent, utterly beautiful urn, and the messy realities of human life. This contrast comes to a head in the third stanza, where the 'happy, happy' trees and people, 'For ever panting, and for ever young' (line 27), are set against – and 'above' – the reality of 'breathing human passion'. This, on one level, is art as escape from life, and is familiar from the third stanza of the 'Ode to a Nightingale' and the desire to 'forget / … The weariness, the fever and the fret'.

One question to ask yourself in reading the poem is what makes the stronger impression on you, or feels more heartfelt – the exclamations at 'happy, happy love' or the description of human passion, 'That leaves a heart high-sorrowful and cloy'd, / A burning forehead, and a parching tongue'. Certainly there is tension. The silent, timeless perfection of the 'ditties of no tone' (line 14) or the eternal 'winning near the goal' (line 18) of stanza 2 are set against the human experience of time and the fact that 'old age shall this generation waste' (line 46).

The fourth stanza is interesting in this respect. It begins with questions about what is happening, where, and to whom. They resemble the questions in the first stanza aimed at understanding the story that is depicted on the urn. But from line 35, Keats's attention shifts. **Instead of using his intellect to try to understand the urn,**

John Keats

he uses his imagination, his 'negative capability', to enter into the scene, speculating on an imaginary 'little town' that must now be empty because all its inhabitants have gone to the sacrifice the urn depicts. This is an interaction of viewer and object which creates its own meaning for the work of art. It creates a mood too. The 'desolate' town resonates through the poem, perhaps reflecting Keats's own state of mind. In this ode, as in the nightingale ode, Keats's imagination is tormented by the spectre of time and change obliterating all mortal things.

The poem **plays with the idea that great art can triumph over time**. The beautiful figures carved into the urn are unchanging, immortal. But the speaker also discovers his doubts about the unmoving perfection of the ancient urn. It is a 'friend to man', but it is not an easy friendship.

The poem starts with an awed, spiritual response to the 'unravish'd bride of quietness' and the 'foster-child' in the first two lines. It moves, through questioning and speculation, to the more detached stance of the final stanza, where the urn is viewed with some uncertainty or suspicion as an object of cold marble saying something that may be profound, but which also sounds dismissive: 'that is all / Ye know on earth, and all ye need to know' might imply that humans are not capable of other kinds of knowledge.

As in most great poetry, **the tensions that give the poem its energy are never entirely resolved**.

> 'I am certain of nothing but of the holiness of the Heart's affections and the truth of Imagination – What the imagination seizes as Beauty must be truth – whether it existed before or not – for I have the same idea of all our Passions as of Love: they are all, in their sublime, creative of essential Beauty.'
>
> Keats, letter to Benjamin Bailey

Form and language

In this ode Keats uses much the same form that he used in 'Ode to a Nightingale', except that here there are no shorter lines, and the rhyme scheme of the last six lines varies somewhat. The layout of the poem will help you to see the rhyme patterns.

'Ode on a Grecian Urn' does not have the linguistic richness of 'Ode to a Nightingale'. Where the nightingale ode is sensuous and highly charged, **the language of this poem is, on the whole, much plainer**, lacking the profusion of adjectives of its companion piece. Despite the subtle and suggestive phrases used to address the urn at the start of the poem (see Commentary), the language of the poem is mostly to do with **interrogation** (questions) or **proposition** (statements). The syntax (sentence structure) is often repetitive, for example in the series of questions in the first stanza, or in the frequent use of phrases introduced by 'ever', 'never', and especially 'for ever' in the second and third stanzas.

Throughout the poem, Keats is trying to understand the meaning of the urn. Whereas listening to the nightingale is all about a sensory experience that takes him on an emotional journey, **contemplating the urn stimulates his mind to engage actively with what he sees**. Like the pipes in stanza 2, the urn appeals 'Not to the sensual ear' but 'to the spirit' (lines 13–14). As a result he asks questions about the figures on the urn in the first and fourth stanzas, or makes assertions about them in the second and third stanzas.

Naturally enough in a poem based on contrasts between the ideal and the real, art and life, time and eternity, stillness and action, those assertions are often framed as **paradoxes**, expressing truths through apparent contradictions. The most daring example of paradox is found in the opening of stanza 2, which states that unheard music is sweeter than music which is audible. This entire stanza is paradoxical. The action goes on although the actors are motionless. We have soundless sound ('ditties of no tone'), stationary growth (trees that can never be bare) and timeless time ('ever wilt thou love, and she be fair'). Can you find other examples of paradox in the poem?

The word music of this poem is less rich than that of 'Ode to a Nightingale', but there are **many subtle effects**. Notice, for example, how the double stress on 'slow time' (line 2) slows down the line to match its meaning. Notice, too, the play of sounds and rhythm in lines 13–14: 'Not to the sensual ear, but, more endear'd, / Pipe to the spirit ditties of no tone'. The key word 'ear' is echoed in 'endear'd', and in the next line the consonance of 'p' and 't' sounds, along with the short 'i' sounds in the first part of the line, creates a light, dance-like music that contrasts with the assonance of long 'o' sounds in 'no tone'.

John Keats

Questions

1. What impression is created of the urn in the first four lines of the poem? How does Keats create that impression?
2. In what sense can the urn tell a story 'more sweetly' than a poem ('rhyme') can?
3. What impressions do you get of the scene described in lines 5–10? Do you think it is the same scene as that described in the second stanza? Give reasons for your answer.
4. In the third stanza, why are the boughs, the musician and the lovers described as happy?
5. How do the speaker's questions about the scene he is looking at in stanza 4 differ from the questions he asked about the scene in stanza 1?
6. How would you describe the speaker's attitude to the urn in the final stanza? How does it differ from his initial attitude to it? Give reasons for your answer.
7. In what sense can the urn remain 'a friend to man'?
8. In stanza 3, do you think the speaker seems anxious to overcome whatever doubts might have been suggested in lines 15–20? Consider the significance of the repeated use of 'happy' in this stanza.
9. Why, do you think, does Keats dwell on the imaginary empty 'little town' in stanza 4? What mood does he create and what does the stanza add to the poem?
10. It has been said that this ode represents the triumph of Keats's imagination. Do you think that this comment is justified? Give reasons for your answer.
11. Is this an optimistic poem? Is the ending reassuring? Give reasons for your answer.
12. Comment on the language of this poem. How does it differ from that of 'Ode to a Nightingale'?
13. In stanza 4, the speaker wonders about the people coming to the sacrifice, and about the 'little town' they have deserted. Create your own version of the deserted town, of the people who have deserted it, and of the activities of those people on 'the pious morn' (line 37).
14. In stanzas 2 and 3 Keats imagines that the figures on the urn have feelings. Find a painting or sculpture that you like and imagine the thoughts and feelings of a character in it. Write them as a monologue.

HIGHER LEVEL

Before you read

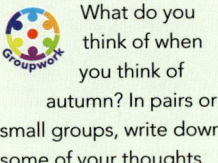

What do you think of when you think of autumn? In pairs or small groups, write down some of your thoughts.

To Autumn

Season of mists and mellow fruitfulness,
   Close bosom-friend of the maturing sun;
Conspiring with him how to load and bless
   With fruit the vines that round the thatch-eves run;
To bend with apples the moss'd cottage-trees,   5
   And fill all fruit with ripeness to the core;
     To swell the gourd, and plump the hazel shells
   With a sweet kernel; to set budding more,
And still more, later flowers for the bees,
Until they think warm days will never cease,   10
     For Summer has o'er-brimm'd their clammy cells.

Who hath not seen thee oft amid thy store?
   Sometimes whoever seeks abroad may find
Thee sitting careless on a granary floor,
   Thy hair soft-lifted by the winnowing wind;   15
Or on a half-reap'd furrow sound asleep,
   Drows'd with the fume of poppies, while thy hook
     Spares the next swath and all its twinèd flowers:
And sometimes like a gleaner thou dost keep
   Steady thy laden head across a brook;   20
   Or by a cyder-press, with patient look,
     Thou watchest the last oozings hours by hours.

Where are the songs of Spring? Ay, where are they?
   Think not of them, thou hast thy music too,—
While barrèd clouds bloom the soft-dying day,   25
   And touch the stubble-plains with rosy hue;
Then in a wailful choir the small gnats mourn
   Among the river sallows, borne aloft
     Or sinking as the light wind lives or dies;
And full-grown lambs loud bleat from hilly bourn;   30
   Hedge-crickets sing; and now with treble soft
   The red-breast whistles from a garden-croft;
     And gathering swallows twitter in the skies.

John Keats

Glossary

Line	Term
1	*mellow*: mature, ripe
4	*thatch-eves*: the part of the thatched roof that overhangs the wall
7	*gourd*: a large, fleshy fruit like the melon
7	*plump*: make fat
11	*o'er-brimm'd*: overflowed
14	*careless*: free from care
15	*winnowing*: to winnow is to expose grain to the wind or to a current of air, so that such lighter particles as chaff or other waste matter are separated or blown away; as Autumn is engaged in this work, her hair is blown in the wind
17	*poppies*: traditionally associated with sleep; the source of opium
18	*swath*: a width of grass or corn cut by a reaping-hook
19–20	*a gleaner … brook*: a gleaner is one who gathers grains of corn left by the harvesters
21	*cyder-press*: a cider-press is used to squeeze out the juice of crushed apples
25	*barrèd*: streaked
25	*bloom*: decorate like flowers
26	*stubble-plains*: the fields after the grain has been cut
27	*gnats*: small stinging flies
28	*sallows*: willows
30	*bourn*: land bounding the horizon
31	*treble*: high note
32	*red-breast*: the robin, the bird of winter
32	*croft*: an enclosed, cultivated patch of land near a house

Guidelines

'To Autumn' was written in September 1819, shortly after a walk Keats took in the stubble fields near Winchester in the south of England where he was then staying. We know this from a letter he wrote to his friend Reynolds two days later:

> 'I never liked stubble-fields as much as now – aye, better than the chilly green of spring. Somehow a stubble plain looks warm – in the same way that some pictures look warm – this struck me so much in my Sunday's walk that I composed upon it.'

Keats's poem, however, is much more than a simple description of what he saw on that Sunday walk. That was never his method. At about this time he described the essential difference between himself and the famous contemporary poet Lord Byron in these words: 'He describes what he sees – I describe what I imagine.' He added, 'mine is the hardest task'.

Commentary

Stanza 1

The dominant impression given by the first stanza is of the ripeness and abundance of autumn. The setting seems to be a cottage garden with a small orchard of old trees ('moss'd cottage-trees'). Everything is ripe and ready for harvesting, but harvesting has not begun. The verbs are important in creating the sense of ripe abundance: 'load and bless', 'bend', 'fill', 'swell', 'plump', 'set budding'. They have to do with actions involved in growth, filling and ripening. Everything is on the brink, ripe but not yet overripe. Only in the final image of the honey-making bees does this fullness overflow itself: 'Summer has o'er–brimm'd their clammy cells.'

HIGHER LEVEL

This 'mellow fruitfulness' is placed in a discreet semi-mythological framework, hinted at but undefined in the stanza's opening lines. Autumn is not just a season but a maternal figure, 'bosom-friend' to the sun (which is usually pictured as male, like the sun god Apollo in Greek mythology). Together, they 'conspire' to 'load and bless' the plants with their seasonal fruits. You could think of it as a marriage or sexual union, with the harvest as its offspring, but the language does not insist on that.

Stanza 2

The second stanza focuses on the figure of Autumn as a woman. She is the personification of the season, presumably a goddess of some kind, but it is her ordinary, humanity not her divinity, that is emphasised. She is treated as something everyday and normal, a familiar figure rather than an exotic one: 'Who hath not seen thee oft …?'

She appears in different guises – as a thresher sitting on the granary floor; as a reaper, asleep on the job; as a gleaner carrying her basket of grains on her head; as a cider-maker who is not turning the press but just watching the 'last oozings' of the cider. These are all roles involved in harvesting. The poem has moved on from the ripeness of what is ready to be harvested to the harvest itself: the grain from the fields and the cider from the orchard's apples.

The mood is sensuous, sleepy, satiated; concentrating not on the human efforts and actions involved in harvesting but on the feelings of satisfaction and deserved rest that come with a job well done (compare Frost's 'After Apple-Picking'). There is room for lazing, luxuriating, and a benign negligence: she spares 'the next swath and all its twinèd flowers', as if the grain harvest is so abundant that some corn can be left uncut in order to spare the flowers. The day is warm and sleepy, as if under the influence of 'the fume of poppies'. Time seems to have slowed down with the 'last oozings' of the apple juice.

John Keats

Stanza 3

The opening phrase of the third stanza – 'Where are the songs of Spring?' – raises for a moment a question that the poem does not pursue. It is put aside because it is this moment, autumn, that is being celebrated: 'thou hast thy music too'. The stanza goes on to describe some of that 'music' in the sounds made by the creatures: the 'wailful choir' of the gnats, the bleating of the lambs, the crickets singing, the song of the 'redbreast' (robin), and finally the twittering of the swallows.

The harvest is over now, and the figure of Autumn we saw in the second stanza is absent. The wheat fields have become 'stubble-plains'. The midday heat of the previous stanza has given way to evening, and a beautiful sunset, as 'barrèd clouds bloom the soft-dying day'. It is a lovely scene, as we move outwards from the fields to the 'river sallows' to the 'hilly bourn' and eventually up to the swallows in the sky.

There is a sense of things ending – the gnats are 'wailful' as if in grief; the lambs are 'full-grown', so no longer really lambs; and the swallows may be gathering for their migration south. But although winter may be around the corner, it is not here yet, and for now there is the music of autumn to listen to and enjoy.

Themes and imagery

Readers have always recognised the difference between this, Keats's final ode, and all the other odes he wrote, including the two we have already looked at. This poem feels **calmer, more accepting, less tortured** than the others. It is instructive to examine what is absent in 'To Autumn'.

It lacks, most obviously, the questioning and striving after meaning or truth of those other poems. **It lacks abstractions and abstract language**, like 'Beauty', 'Truth', 'Love', 'Youth'. Although Autumn herself is very present, she is imagined in entirely human terms. She is not an allegorical figure or a classical deity; though she owes something to the fertility goddess Ceres, and to Eve in Milton's *Paradise Lost*, she is a creature of Keats's own imagination. In fact, although, as we have seen, his imagination was filled with figures from classical mythology, there are no overt references to that mythology or culture in the poem.

Perhaps most significant of all, there is **no defined, personalised speaker**, no 'I' from whom we as readers can distance ourselves, whose emotions and ideas we can observe: no figure sitting in the dark under a tree listening to the nightingale and yearning to be dissolved into its song; nobody studying the urn and interrogating it until he can make it give up its secrets.

The effect of this is that we are not witnesses to a drama, but are absorbed into the speaker's viewpoint. No other perspective is offered. Instead of ideas, we are presented with images. Or, to put it another way, **the ideas in the poem are embodied in its sensuous images**. Let us examine some of those images.

One thing to notice is that **all the senses are involved in the poem**. As well as sight and hearing, taste is referenced in the 'sweet kernel' of line 8, touch in the bees' 'clammy cells' (line 11), and smell in the 'fume of poppies' (line 17). As noted in the Commentary, the first stanza makes much use of verbs of ripening and expanding that are almost **tactile**: 'fill', 'plump', 'swell'. The second stanza is primarily **visual**, as the figure of Autumn is presented in a series of tableaux (still scenes) like paintings. The third stanza is dominated by **auditory** images that follow on from the idea of the 'songs of Spring' and autumn's own music in the first two lines.

It has been suggested that the 'stubble-plains' mentioned in the third stanza (line 26), like those that Keats saw on his walk near Winchester, are the originating image of the poem. He saw them on that walk as 'warm', and his poem captures that warmth superbly. But stubble means that the harvest is over and winter is coming. And yet winter is the only season not mentioned in the poem, and traditional ideas about the cycle of the seasons, which tend to see autumn as a prelude to winter, are also absent.

Nevertheless, we should be sensitive to the nuances of the poem's mood. It was written at a time when Keats could no longer ignore the fact that he was seriously ill; when his ambitions to make a career as a writer seemed to be going nowhere; when he knew he had to make a decision about his relationship with Fanny Brawne (see Biography, page 381). The death of his brother Tom still haunted him, and he was anxious about his brother George in America. **'To Autumn' celebrates the beauty and abundance of the season, but it can't entirely shut out darker emotions.** It is impossible to read 'Until they think warm days will never cease' (line 10) without an awareness that they will, in fact, cease; or to hear 'last oozings' without being reminded that something is coming to an end. In the final stanza, the day is 'dying', albeit softly; the gnats 'mourn'; the wind 'lives or dies'; the lambs are 'full-grown'; the robin is often associated with winter (think Christmas cards); and those swallows will be flying away soon, even if not today.

> **Integrated imagination**
>
> 'Magnificent portrait of an integrated imagination, haunted by the fear of rejection, suppression and failure.'
>
> Andrew Motion on 'To Autumn'

The life and beauty that the poem so wonderfully conjures is all the more precious for the knowledge that it will not last forever, and we are aware of that without its being overtly stated. Unlike the other odes, the word 'adieu' (goodbye) is never used in 'To Autumn', and yet the poem can be read as one long, lovely goodbye.

One facet of the poem worth noticing is that it **explores the interaction of humans and nature**. The harvest of the cottage garden or the wheat fields is a result of humans' interaction with natural forces, as gardeners, beekeepers and farmers. It is **not a wild landscape but an agricultural, humanised one**, and the harvest is carried out and its products enjoyed by people. You can read this, as Helen Vendler does in her book on Keats's odes, as an image for the creative processes of art, and of writing poetry in particular. In Vendler's view, the voices of the creatures in the final stanza, the music of autumn, represent poetry. It is an image of art that focuses on its natural, organic processes – a counterbalance to the agonised debates in the nightingale and urn odes.

That is one person's interpretation. The marvellous thing about 'To Autumn' is how open it is to interpretation, but how little it insists on it. This has led some critics to dismiss it as lovely but meaningless. Others consider it Keats's greatest achievement. For them, it is complete in itself, its images fully realised, and the whole poem is holding in balance the different forces and emotions at play in it.

What do you think?

Form

'To Autumn' is written in iambic pentameters, all of which use end-rhyme. As always in his mature poetry, Keats handles the form with wonderful deftness, so that the thoughts flow easily within and between the lines. Each stanza is built on a single sentence, though the second and third stanzas pose a preliminary question before launching into theirs. In each case the syntax (sentence structure) works through a series of parallel phrases.

John Keats

The syntax and imagery of the first stanza all hinge on the third line, 'Conspiring with him how to …'. The verbs that follow – 'load and bless', 'bend', 'fill', 'swell … and plump', 'set budding' – all depend on that phrase and all follow the same pattern. In the second stanza the structure is built around 'Sometimes … Or … And sometimes … Or …'. In the third, the basic structure is: 'While' *x* (the sunset), 'Then' *a* (the gnats) 'And' *b* (the lambs) 'and' *c* (the robin) 'And' *d* (the swallows). In each case there is both **repetition and variation**, as the abundance of autumn is listed in all its variety. **The accumulation of phrases mirrors the abundance of the season.**

The poem is written in **eleven-line stanzas**, rather than the ten-line ones of the other odes. The first four lines rhyme *abab*, as in the others, but there is an extra line in the second part, meaning that there is always a rhyming couplet immediately before the stanza's final line. This in turn means that the final rhyme is delayed, and a greater tension is built up before it is released with the final rhyme that we know is coming. It is as if just one extra thing is always being crammed into the storehouse of the poem.

Language

As already noted, the language of the poem is sensuous and physical. It lacks the abstract elements that we find elsewhere in Keats's poetry, and is always working to create images. It also has a closely worked pattern of sounds that enrich the sensuousness of the images in multiple ways. These run through the entire poem, and are too numerous and complex to explore in any detail here. Nevertheless, look at how soft 'f' sounds (including in the word 'soft') run through the poem; or listen out for the vowel sound '–ore', not just in 'core' and 'more' and 'store' and 'floor', but also in 'warm', 'o'er-brimm'd', 'mourn', 'borne' and 'bourn', and also, of course, in 'or'.

We will finish by looking at some smaller-scale examples of word music, beginning with lines 15–16:

> Thy hair soft-lifted by the winnowing wind;
> Or on a half-reap'd furrow sound asleep …

Notice how the gentle consonants of 'soft-lifted', which imitate the action of the gentle wind, are taken up in 'half-reap'd furrow'; the alliteration of 'winnowing wind'; and the internal rhyme of 'reap' and 'asleep', as well as the half-rhyme of 'wind' and 'sound'.

In other examples, notice how the long vowels of 'last oozings hours by hours' slow down the rhythm to match the slow oozings; how the line break in 'keep / Steady' (lines 19–20) suggests the action of stepping carefully 'across a brook'; and how the reversed stresses on 'blóom the' (line 25) – *dúm*-di, instead of di-*dúm* – work with the alliteration on the initial 'b' and the long vowel ('–oom') that follows to emphasise 'bloom', and make it a verb of rich sensuous power in the line, as the setting sun catches the low clouds and lights them up like a great flower, a suggestion that is reinforced by 'rosy' in the next line.

Questions

1. In the first stanza, the richness and fullness of autumn's gifts are conveyed through tactile images (images that appeal to our sense of touch). Expand on this idea, drawing attention to the sounds of words and the rhythm and movement of the verse as the means of achieving sensuous effects.

2. In the second stanza Autumn is presented as an individual female figure. What are her main qualities as these are reflected in her activities? Are there suggestions that the figure of Autumn has some of the attributes of a goddess? Explain your answer.

3. Describe the mood of the second stanza. How does Keats create this mood?

4. How does the final stanza differ in mood and tone from the first two? What other differences are there?

5. In many poetic accounts of autumn, the emphasis is on decay and change. Is this true of Keats's poem?

6. In what sense is 'To Autumn' a more positive and optimistic poem than 'Ode to a Nightingale' or 'Ode on a Grecian Urn'?

7. Do you think that 'To Autumn' is the work of a poet at peace with the world? Explain your answer.

8. What view of nature is presented in 'Ode to Autumn'?

9. In what ways does the speaker of this poem differ from those of 'Ode to a Nightingale' and 'Ode on a Grecian Urn'? What are the effects of these differences?

10. Comment on the imagery of the poem. How does it differ from stanza to stanza?

11. Choose two examples of how Keats uses word music and rhythm to create effects, and describe how they work.

12. Your group wishes to make a short film of this poem. Describe what kind of setting, music, lighting, etc. you would use to convey the atmosphere of the poem to viewers.

13. What is your favourite season? Write a short piece about it, or some aspect of it, in verse or prose.

John Keats

Before you read

What qualities do you associate with a star? Read the poem and see if any of these qualities are present in it.

Bright Star

Bright star, would I were steadfast as thou art—
   Not in lone splendour hung aloft the night
And watching, with eternal lids apart,
   Like nature's patient, sleepless Eremite,
The moving waters at their priestlike task   5
   Of pure ablution round earth's human shores,
Or gazing on the new soft-fallen mask
   Of snow upon the mountains and the moors—
No—yet still steadfast, still unchangeable,
   Pillow'd upon my fair love's ripening breast,   10
To feel for ever its soft fall and swell,
   Awake for ever in a sweet unrest,
Still, still to hear her tender-taken breath,
And so live ever—or else swoon to death.

Glossary

1	*steadfast*:	constant
2	*aloft*:	high up in
4	*Eremite*:	an old word for 'hermit'
6	*ablution*:	cleansing

Guidelines

'Bright Star' was probably written in October 1819, and is one of Keats's last poems. It has always been associated with Fanny Brawne, the eighteen-year-old Keats had met and fallen in love with the year before. Their relationship is the subject of the 2009 film *Bright Star*. Keats presented her with a copy of this poem, and seems to have regarded it as a declaration of love. It certainly marked a new resolution in his attitude to her. Shortly after writing the poem, he and Fanny became formally, though secretly, engaged.

Commentary

The poem is a sonnet addressed to the 'Bright star' in the night sky, and expresses one fundamental wish, announced in the first line: 'would I were steadfast as thou art'.

HIGHER LEVEL

The next seven lines, up to the end of the octave of the sonnet, expand on the image of the star 'hung aloft the night', watching over the cleansing tides of the oceans (lines 5–6) or the snow-covered countryside (lines 7–8). However, the whole passage is governed by the 'Not' at the start of line 2. He does *not* want to be alone like the star, 'in lone splendour'. Because of that 'Not' it is unclear how much of this image he admires or desires.

What he does desire is the 'steadfast' and 'unchangeable' nature of the star (line 9). The 'No' at the start of line 9, introducing the sonnet's sestet (final six lines), refers back to 'Not' in line 2: he wants to be steadfast not in splendid isolation like the star, but in his relationship with his lover, his head 'Pillow'd upon my fair love's ripening breast'. He wants to be unchanging in his love, and the lines imply something in addition to that: he wants this moment, as he lies there, feeling the 'fall and swell' of her breathing, to last for ever. Either that or, he declares in the poem's final phrase, to 'swoon to death' in the midst of this intense, heightened state of being. The eroticism of the passage is subtly underlined in this last image, with its suggestion of a fulfilment other than death: the phrase *la petite mort* ('little death') has long been used in reference to orgasm.

Themes and imagery

The heart of the poem is the **contrast between the bright star in the octave and the lover resting on his beloved's breast in the sestet**. You could imagine that he can see the star from where he lies and compares his situation with that of the star.

Let us examine the image of the **star** to begin with.

The star is a traditional image of **steadfastness and constancy**. But though the speaker admires its constancy, other qualities of the star are just as prominent in this sonnet.

The star has a **remote grandeur**, 'in lone splendour hung aloft the night' (line 2). Keats imagines it as a 'sleepless Eremite' or hermit. Hermits are people who have withdrawn from the world to pursue a solitary life devoted to self-denial, dedicated to avoiding the temptations of the flesh. The watching Eremite is associated with two natural forces distinguished for their purifying influence – the sea and the snow. The star presides over these with constant watchfulness, like a hermit keeping a prayerful vigil. The action of the sea around the shores of the world is seen as a cleansing ('pure ablution'), ritually performed by a 'priestlike' agent. The freshly fallen **snow** is another image of **natural purity**. Together they suggest a passionless purity, free from disturbing desire.

What are we to make of these images of remoteness and purity? The description of the star is preceded by 'Not' (line 2), which applies grammatically to the entire passage, and yet despite that 'Not', there is an aching beauty in the description that suggests that the speaker is also attracted by it. Does the star represent Fanny, or how Keats imagined her, both pure and compassionate? Does it express the purity and compassion he wished to feel in his love for her? If he asks for steadfastness, is it because he has a passionate, unsteady temperament and is not as constant as he would like to be?

John Keats

Is the sonnet based on the ancient **conflict between lust and love**? This idea is supported by a comment Keats made on that subject at about the same time the sonnet was composed. He referred to 'lustful love' as 'the old plague spot and the raw scrofula' (a form of tuberculosis), and something that 'disgraces me in my own eyes'.

If the imagery of the octave represents perfect purity, the imagery of the sestet suggests another ideal, emphasising qualities the speaker finds lacking in the star. In contrast to the untouchable star is the image of the speaker with his head on his beloved's 'ripening breast' (line 10). It is **physically intimate and richly sensual**. The 'fall and swell' is now associated with his lover's breast rather than with the ebb and flow of the sea. The 'sweet unrest' of her embrace contrasts with the sexless, calm detachment of the star.

There is a **tension** between the two charged poles of purity and sensuality that the poem does not entirely resolve. Both are attractive in their different ways, and although the speaker chooses the holiness of physical love over the holiness associated with the star, the steadfastness or constancy he can experience in his lover's arms is of a very different sort from the steadfastness of the star. **He pictures it as an eternal continuation of his 'sweet unrest', and wants his heightened, aroused state to last for ever.** The word 'ever' is used three times in the last four lines.

That eternity is hard to imagine in the real world, which may be why he offers the alternative of swooning to death. Perhaps it was, in the end, unimaginable except as a sort of death, a dying into the moment, just as he had imagined in 'Ode to a Nightingale', prolonging a moment of happiness into eternity – 'to cease upon the midnight with no pain' while the nightingale sings.

Form and language

'Bright Star' is a **Shakespearean sonnet** with a rhyme scheme of *ababcdcd efefgg*, ending in a rhyming couplet. It divides naturally between the octave (first eight lines), which describe the star, and the sestet (last six lines), which describe the speaker lying in his beloved's arms. It consists of just **one sentence**, with the main idea announced in the first line, and the rest of the sentence stitched together by 'Not' in line 2, which introduces the image of the star, and 'No' in line 9, which links back to 'Not' and introduces the second image.

The ideas and images fit quite neatly into the lines. Although some of the images (e.g. lines 2–6) run over several lines, there is no jarring enjambment (run-on lines) to disrupt the flow. In the sestet, each element of the image fills a single line, with a comma at the end, until the final line, which contains the poem's only strong caesura (mid-line break), marked by the dash before 'or else swoon to death'.

The final rhyming couplet gives the poem a sense of completion or resolution that you could argue it does not quite deserve. Is the idea of swooning to death a natural completion, or is it a way out of a situation that cannot be resolved?

The language matches the subject matter. In the octave it has a restrained grandeur. The **paired stresses** of 'lóne splèndour' (line 2) and the pattern of 'l's and 'n's that is picked up in the words that follow, 'hung aloft the night', give a wonderful sense of the star's glory. The lines describing the 'sleepless Eremite' have a stately, unruffled rhythm.

HIGHER LEVEL

In the sestet the language is more sensual, and the sounds of the words and their rhythm respond to the new mood. In line 10, the three consecutive stresses on 'fáir lóve's rípening breast' make the reader linger on the image and relish in particular the striking word 'ripening'. In the next line, the play of 'f' and 'l' sounds in 'feel for ever its soft fall and swell' conveys the **gentle sensuality** of the image.

The sestet also uses a lot of **repetition** – of 'ever' and 'for ever', and of 'still' – to suggest the urgency of the speaker's desire to make the moment last. Notice in particular how the repetition of 'still' in line 13 almost stops the forward movement of the verse, as if he wants to stop time.

Questions

1	What impression do you get of the star in the first eight lines of the poem? What words and images are most important in conveying this impression?
2	The star is a traditional image of steadfastness or constancy, which is what the speaker of the poem desires. Why, in that case, does he not find in the star a satisfying image of his ideal?
3	What is the speaker's more perfect image of his ideal, as described in the final six lines?
4	The sonnet suggests that even the most satisfying human experience is imperfect. How does it do this?
5	Compare and contrast the language used in the second part of the poem with that used in the first. How does Keats use the sounds of the words to bring out this contrast?
6	In 'Ode on a Grecian Urn', Keats contrasts 'breathing human passion' (line 28) with the 'Cold Pastoral' of 'marble men and maidens' (lines 45 and 42). Consider the relevance of this kind of contrast to that on which 'Bright Star' is based.
7	Do you find this poem happy or sad? Explain your answer.
8	Based on your reading of the poem, what kind of person do you think the poet is? Discuss this in pairs or small groups.
9	Keats sent a copy of this sonnet to Fanny Brawne, the 'fair love' mentioned in line 10. Compose a letter that she might have written on receiving the sonnet.

Exam-Preparation Questions

1. 'In his poetry, Keats explores the relation between pleasure and pain, happiness and melancholy, imagination and reality, art and life, with brilliant poetic force.'
   Do you think this is a good description of Keats's poetry on your course? Refer in your answer to at least three of the poems.

2. 'John Keats presents abstract ideas in a style that is clear and direct.'
   To what extent do you agree or disagree with this assessment of his poetry? Support your points with reference to the poetry on your course.

3. Often we love a poet because of the feelings his/her poems create in us. Write about the feelings John Keats's poetry creates in you and the aspects of the poems (their content and/or style) that help to create those feelings. Support your points by reference to the poetry by Keats that you have studied.

4. 'While Keats's poetry celebrates life, it also acknowledges life's limitations.'
   Discuss this statement, supporting your answer by reference to the poems by Keats on your course.

5. 'In the poetry of Keats we see the poet striving towards a satisfying notion of permanence.'
   Discuss this view, supporting your answer by reference to the poems by Keats on your course.

6. 'Keats is one of the greatest descriptive poets.' Write a response to this comment.

7. You have been asked to give a talk with the title: 'An introduction to Keats's poetry'. Write out the text of the talk you would give.

8. Would you agree that after reading the poetry of Keats, we are left thinking that neither the beauty of nature nor the beauty of art can console us for the miseries of life?

9. Some readers may feel that Keats lays too much emphasis on the darker aspects of human experience, and that his poetry lacks joy. Basing your comments on the prescribed poems, say what you think of this idea.

10. 'Keats's poetry is essentially escapist. He is always trying to fly away from or forget the miseries of the world. For him, even death is a form of escape.'
    Is this a fair summary of Keats's poetry? Discuss the question with detailed reference to the poems on your course.

11. Explore the ways in which Keats uses rhythm and word music (alliteration, assonance and other techniques) to create effects that are central to the meaning of his poems. Use detailed examples from the poems on your course.

Sample Essay

'Keats uses sensuous language and vivid imagery to express a range of profound tensions.' To what extent do you agree or disagree with this statement? Support your answer with reference to the poetry of John Keats on your course.

Addresses the question immediately → It is hard to disagree with this description of Keats's poetry. Keats's language is not always sensuous, nor his images always vivid, but his poetry is full of both, and there are always tensions and ambiguities in what it is expressing. It is true too that a great range of tensions can be found in his poetry, but the ways in which his language and imagery express those tensions are varied. I will look at three of Keats's poems in some detail in order to explore this variety. *Adds qualification to first response*

Discussion of first poem uses key words from question → 'Ode to a Nightingale' is the poem which this quotation brings immediately to my mind. Here Keats's language is at its most rich and sensuous, the imagery vivid and varied. Here, too, the emotional tensions expressed by the speaker are at the heart of the poem. 'My heart aches', declares the speaker at the beginning, 'and a drowsy numbness pains my sense'. But this is a paradoxical heartache, brought on not by grief or envy but because he is 'too happy in thine happiness'. As so often in Keats, pain and pleasure are bound closely together, held in a tension that enriches them both and that is central to the poem's meaning. The sublime beauty of the nightingale's song provokes apparently contradictory responses in the speaker: a profound melancholy and a joyous exhilaration; a desire to let his imagination fly like the bird and a longing to die. The song itself can sound both happy, as the bird sings in 'full-throated ease' in the first stanza, and sad, in the 'plaintive anthem' of the final stanza.

Uses short quotations throughout

Addresses one element of the question (imagery) → The imagery has great variety – from the classical references to Flora and the Hippocrene in the second stanza, to the personifications of youth, love and beauty in the third, to the simple visual image, drawn from the Bible, of Ruth standing 'in tears amid the alien corn'. Perhaps the most vivid and sensuous imagery comes in the fifth stanza with Keats's description of the flowers that he can only guess at in the darkness. Their names – 'White hawthorn, and the pastoral eglantine' – help to convey an idea of the richness of the sensory experience, and of the abundance of the plant life, but Keats uses carefully chosen words to add an unease to that abundance. The darkness is 'embalmèd', and the scent of the flowers is described as 'incense', words that have overtones of death. All these details remind us of decay and death in the midst of luxuriant life. The texture of the language holds the tension between life and death that is set up earlier in the poem, with the strong contrast between the celebration of life in the 'draught of vintage' tasting of 'Dance, and Provençal song, and sunburnt mirth', and this death-haunted world 'Where youth grows pale, and spectre-thin, and dies'. *Detailed analysis of the words used*

Addresses the second element of the question (language) → And yet, for all its vivid imagery, it is the language of the poem that I find most remarkable. It is full of memorable phrases, and although it is often *Personal view* very sensuous, especially in its musical use of sounds, it has great delicacy and variety. Keats's language is acutely sensitive to the changing moods: the delighted relish conveyed by the alliteration of 'beaded bubbles winking at the brim', or the slow, dirge-like monosyllables of 'a few, sad, last gray hairs'. At the same time, the mood of the poem as a whole is created in part by the use of the soft initial 'f' that recurs throughout the poem in key words such as 'fade', 'forget', 'fly', 'forest', 'forlorn', 'Flora', 'flowers', 'faery', and 'Fled', which begins the final line with a strong stress. It is a gentle, breathy sound that suggests the idea of fading and dissolving that is central to this poem, and it is often accompanied by the similar 'v' and 'th' sounds, as in 'the fever, and the fret' or 'Fast fading violets cover'd up in leaves'.

[Use of quotation to analyse the sounds of words.]

But although Keats's use of sound is very sensuous, it seems to me that some of the most powerful effects in the poem are created by the simplest, plainest language. For example, 'Where but to think is to be full of sorrow' is a statement that is moving because it is so stark and simple. The beautiful description of the nightingale's disappearance in the final stanza is not sensuous, but merely a series of short phrases whose simple syntax seems to mirror the bird's journey: 'Past the near meadows, over the still stream, / Up the hill-side; and now 'tis buried deep / In the next valley-glades'.

[Returns to the terms of the question]

[Has there been too much discussion of one poem?]

A similar combination of simplicity and power is evident in 'La Belle Dame Sans Merci'. Here, though, it is the imagery rather than the language that is most striking.

[Link to next poem to be considered]

The poem is a ballad, and in keeping with the story-telling style of this genre, the language and syntax are simple, almost childish, with the repeated use of 'and'. For example, the knight's description of meeting the lady uses conventional language in a simple way: 'Her hair was long, her foot was light, / And her eyes were wild'. Carefully chosen details are used to build up vivid images. The bleak setting is established by the detail that the 'sedge has wither'd from the lake', and the solitary knight is depicted strikingly in white and red – a lily on his brow and a 'fading rose' on his cheeks. There is the 'lady in the meads' with her 'wild' eyes, and the description of their courtship: his gifts of the garland and bracelets, the journey on the 'pacing steed', her gifts of 'honey wild and manna dew'; her weeping, his kisses; and then the dream of the 'pale kings and princes'. The narrative is constructed from these vivid images.

[Continued use of short quotations]

Unlike the 'Ode to a Nightingale' there is no clearly defined 'I' at the centre of the poem whose shifting thoughts and emotions we are privy to. There is no description of motivation or the interior life of either of the two main 'characters', but everything is seen from the outside. We know 'she wept and sigh'd full sore', but we are not told why. We know that he 'shut her wild wild eyes / With kisses four' but we do not know what he was feeling. This creates a sense of mystery. There is a sense of the importance of the details – the possible symbolism of the lily and the rose, of honey and manna, of the 'pacing steed' or the 'elfin grot', but nothing is defined.

[Contrasts one poem with another]

What is certain is that there is a profound tension at the centre of the poem. The lady is beautiful and she seems to be loving, but her love is fatal. She is both vulnerable (weeping and sighing) and powerful, having the knight 'in thrall'. She is the object of love but also the bringer of death, something to be both desired and feared. This fundamental ambiguity reflects a powerful ambivalence in Keats himself, who remarked in a letter that he did not have 'a right feeling towards women'.

[Returns to the terms of the question]

[Use of biographical information relevant to the poem]

> **Introduction of third poem links it to the second**

The tension in 'Bright Star' also concerns a woman, and is focused on the two contrasting primary images – of the distant star in the octave and the intimate embrace of the lovers in the sestet.

The remote grandeur of the star is given an aura of purity and spirituality. It is a 'sleepless Eremite' or hermit, withdrawn from all the pleasures of the world, watching over the oceans and the fresh snow, whose whiteness also implies purity. Keats's language is in keeping with the austerity of the image. The vocabulary suggests spiritual purity: the star watches with 'eternal lids'; the oceans perform a 'priestlike task' of 'pure ablution'. The rhythm is measured and solemn, made stately by the long vowels and strong stresses in a line such as 'Like nature's patient, sleepless Eremite'.

The image of the speaker in his beloved's arms, however, is intensely sensuous. Whereas the image of the star is primarily visual, the sense of touch is primary here. The word 'Pillow'd' evokes a familiar physical sensation, and the experience of lying against her 'ripening breast' is conjured in the next line: 'To feel for ever its soft fall and swell'. The repeated 'f', 's' and 'l' sounds add a great deal to the sensuality of the image. The rhythm too responds to the emotional intensity, with the repetition of 'Still, still' at the beginning of the line seeming to prolong this intense moment.

> **Quotation and detailed analysis of language**

The tension of the poem hinges on the speaker's desire to bring those two images together – to have the 'unchangeable' steadfastness of the star while lying in his lover's arms, as if that moment could be extended for ever. At some level, he knows and the reader knows that that is impossible. I think that the poem's final phrase, 'or else swoon to death', is really an admission of that impossibility. The everlasting intensity of experience he desires can only be imagined as a sort of dying, just as Keats had imagined that he could 'cease upon the midnight with no pain' in the 'Ode to a Nightingale', and so make the ecstatic moment a final fulfilment.

> **Personal interpretation backed up by argument**

As a man, Keats was full of contradictions, and subject to impulses which pulled him in different directions: towards sensuality and towards purity; towards a celebration of life and towards a longing for death. The tensions between these different impulses give his poems their special power. Even when he celebrates life most, as in 'To Autumn', a sense of life's transience (the swallows gathering for their migration) ensures that the poetry is full of tensions, and all the richer for it. Keats was a master of poetic language, and although it is often sensuous in its vocabulary and in the music of the words, its power can also come from simplicity. Vivid images are sometimes evoked in the plainest language. I would say that the statement in the question is true, but it is not the whole truth.

> **Is this too vague? Could it have been developed?**

> **Brief mention of a fourth poem**

> **Final sentence summarises the answer to the question**

John Keats

ESSAY CHECKLIST		Yes ✓	No ✗
Purpose	Has the candidate understood the task?		
	Has the candidate responded to it in a thoughtful manner?		
	Has the candidate answered the question?		
Comment:			
Coherence	Has the candidate made convincing arguments?		
	Has the candidate linked ideas?		
	Does the essay have a sense of unity?		
Comment:			
Language	Is the essay written in an appropriate register?		
	Are ideas expressed in a clear way?		
	Is the writing fluent?		
Comment:			
Mechanics	Is the use of language accurate?		
	Are all words spelled correctly?		
	Does the punctuation help the reader?		
Comment:			

SNAPSHOT JOHN KEATS

- Poems display rare imaginative power
- Remarkable descriptive power
- Master of the musical use of language
- Lacking in wit and humour
- Poems often explore the significance of art
- Deep understanding of the tragic aspects of human experience
- Imagery often drawn from nature and country life
- Love of classical culture and art
- Poems reveal a troubled personality
- An escapist tendency in some poems
- Poetry is sensuous and passionate
- Drawn to intense, transformative experiences

HIGHER LEVEL

Sylvia Plath

1932–1963

Black Rook in Rainy Weather	446
The Times Are Tidy	451
– Morning Song	454
Finisterre	458
– Mirror	463
Pheasant	468
Elm	472
– Poppies in July*	479
– The Arrival of the Bee Box	484
– Child*	489

Biography

Parents and early childhood

Sylvia Plath was born in Boston, Massachusetts on 27 October 1932. Her father Otto Plath was a forty-six-year-old biology professor at Boston University when he met the twenty-two-year-old Aurelia Schrober, a student of his. Plath's father was from Grabow in Germany, a place Plath would refer to in her autobiographical novel *The Bell Jar* as 'a manic depressive hamlet in the black heart of Prussia'. He had been married before, to Lydia Clara Bartz, but this ended in divorce after only three weeks. Otto was a confirmed pacifist and left the Lutheran ministry where he was training when the beliefs he was studying became totally incompatible with his interest in Darwin's theories of evolution. This resulted in Otto being shunned by his family. He was investigated and cleared by the FBI of 'pro-German leanings' and became entranced by zoology while a student at Harvard University. He particularly enjoyed the study of bees and wrote a book on the subject called *Bumblebees and Their Ways*, showing a clear talent for creative writing: 'it is a delightful thing to pause and watch these queens clad in their costumes of rich velvet'. Plath would later dramatically recreate the queen bee image for herself in 'Lady Lazarus': 'With her lion-red body, her wings of glass? Now she is flying / More terrible than she ever was, red / Scar in the sky, red comet'.

Plath was later to write bee poems, including 'The Arrival of the Bee Box' and 'The Beekeeper's Daughter', as well as a short story entitled 'Among the Bumblebees'. Plath would write that Otto was a bad father and husband: he could be extremely tyrannical at home and was 'a stickler for order and a lover of logic', according to Plath's biographer Andrew Wilson; but she also talked of her idyllic childhood. Such seeming contradictions were typical of Plath.

Aurelia was extremely well read and interested in her children's education and progress. Plath became a sister with the birth of Warren in 1935. The two were fiercely competitive for Aurelia's love and approval. Aurelia recorded Plath's development in minute detail, a trait Plath would also develop. For example, while away at camp one summer Plath wrote down everything she ate and even the number of paces she walked.

Plath's father developed diabetes and later pneumonia and Plath cared for him continually at the time, even dressing in a nurse's costume. He became very depressed at his ill-health and died of an embolism in hospital on 5 November 1940. The young Plath announced, 'I'll never speak to God again'; she had been praying nightly for his recovery. The following day she wrote 'I promise never to marry again' on a piece of paper and made her mother sign it. Aurelia wouldn't allow her children to attend their father's funeral, something Plath never forgave. Plath explored this grief and anger in many poems, most famously 'Daddy': 'I was ten when they buried you. / At twenty I tried to die / And get back, back, back to you. /… A man in black with a Meinkampf look // And a love of the rack and the screw.'

A young writer and troubled youth

In 1942 the Plaths moved to Wellesley, away from Sylvia's beloved sea. 'Finisterre' and 'Morning Song' reference this. Her mother worked hard to send Plath to the prestigious Wellesley College. A friend recounts that she tried to cut her throat at age ten, and that 'achievement was central to her world'. Plath began avidly collecting girl scout badges, including one for creative writing, which led to the publication of a story she had

HIGHER LEVEL

Plath attended Smith College in Massachusetts.

written in *The Townsman*, a local newspaper. Plath was exhilarated to see her work and name in print and it was something she yearned for ever after; but even though she published many stories and poems, she was always deflated by the rejections she received. As Wilson says, 'her drive was phenomenal, her ego extreme, her vision quite clear'.

Plath was a **hugely sensitive youngster** and called herself 'an ugly introvert' in her journal, as she suffered from acne. Worries about popularity, money and fitting in with the wealthy social circles of her schoolmates plagued Plath, and she became obsessed with the poetry of Sara Teasdale, who had committed suicide by overdosing on sleeping pills. Her talent impressed her English teacher who advised she apply for an English scholarship. Her talent was further nurtured at Gamaliel Bradford High School where Mr Crockett, the English teacher, was a major influence on Plath, giving her vast reading lists and reciting her poems to the class. Upon reading her poem 'I Thought That I Could Not Be Hurt' he told her that she had 'a lyric gift beyond the ordinary', a comment that meant a huge amount to the young writer. She continued to publish poems and stories, finally having the short story 'And Summer Will Not Come Again' published in national teen magazine *Seventeen*. It was a landmark moment in the young writer's life.

In 1951 Plath won scholarships to the exclusive Smith College for Women in Massachusetts, and had work published in the upmarket magazine *Mademoiselle*, a publication she would later edit briefly. In 1953 Plath's application to attend a Harvard writing course run by Frank O'Connor was rejected, sending her into a tailspin of despair. The treatment for this was electroshock therapy, which only made things worse, culminating in a suicide attempt from which Plath took six months to recover: Plath took an overdose and hid in the crawl space beneath the porch; police and media were involved in the search and after two days Plath was discovered by her brother Warren. She had slipped into a coma and vomited the pills. Her biographer, Anne Stevenson, comments: 'brought up in a privileged society, protected by a tightly knit family that closed in about her (as families will) after her father's death, cosseted by her teachers, laden with scholarships and honours, **she rebelled in some deep part of herself against the very image she labored to create**'. This conflict and contrast is at the very heart of Plath's poetry: the **tension between how things seem and what is really happening**, between light and dark, hope and despair, love and hate. In 1954 Smith College awarded Plath a scholarship, allowing her to complete her degree, and she graduated with distinction. She relentlessly submitted her poetry and stories for publication and literary prizes. She was regularly successful but received many rejections also.

Sylvia Plath

Cambridge and Hughes

In 1955 Plath won the prestigious Fulbright and Woodrow Wilson scholarships, facilitating her move to Cambridge University, England. Plath had won first prize at the Glascock poetry competition which introduced her to the poet Marianne Moore, who was a friend and mentor of Elizabeth Bishop and who would later review some of Plath's poems as 'too grisly and unrelenting'. Plath wrote to her mother that she had earned four hundred and seventy dollars from awards and prizes for her writing.

Plath loved the relative freedom of Cambridge, unaware that many of her contemporaries there found her gauche and spoiled. The winter weather depressed her so much that she sought the help of the university psychologist and found she missed her mother terribly – 'someone to bring me hot broth and tell me they love me'.

Plath's poetry had received a negative review by Daniel Huws, a friend of Ted Hughes, some of whose poetry Plath had read and memorised. Plath met them at a party, 'dressed in the reds and blacks she favoured for sexual conquest'. She had drunk a lot of whiskey, and challenged Huws about his mocking review. She then noticed Hughes, 'that big, dark, hunky boy', and recited some of his poetry to him; 'then he kissed me bang smash on the mouth … when he kissed my neck I bit him long and hard on the cheek' (Hughes later said that Plath's account was exaggerated). The pair were soon in a relationship, sharing a passion for art and literature. Plath said that Hughes 'even fills somehow the huge, sad hole I felt in having no father'. They married secretly on Bloomsday, a tribute to James Joyce, the subject of Plath's thesis.

Plath taught in Smith College in Massachusetts for a year (instead of the minimum two years she was expected to complete) but found the pressure of the job and the faculty there hard to cope with. This negative experience inspired 'The Times Are Tidy'.

Ted's work was becoming successful largely thanks to Plath's support; she typed out and sent his poetry to various contests and publications. They began to move in increasingly literary circles in the US and England, meeting and entertaining the likes of Robert Frost, T. S. Eliot and Robert Lowell.

Before returning to England the couple lived at Yaddo, an artists' colony in Saratoga Springs, thanks to a five-thousand-dollar grant awarded to Ted by the Guggenheim. Here both wrote prolifically and explored the work of other artists and poets such as Elizabeth Bishop, whose work Plath said had a 'fine originality, always surprising, never rigid, flowing'.

Back in England Plath gave birth to the couple's first child, Frieda, on 1 April 1960. Only twenty days later, she brought her baby daughter to watch the Aldermaston anti-nuclear march – 'an immensely moving experience'. Plath had an increasing fear of nuclear war. Following a miscarriage in the spring of 1961, Plath wrote 'Morning Song' celebrating Frieda but also expressing the pain and loss Plath felt at the time. **She was plagued by nightmares** and many of her poems have a nightmarish quality. Ted seems to have been a doting husband but Plath was often overcome with intense and irrational jealousy. For example, when Hughes was late home from a meeting with a BBC producer which ran overtime, he arrived to find Plath had torn up his most precious books and his current writing projects. This seems to have been a

> **Ariel**
>
> Ariel is a character from Shakespeare's *The Tempest*, a play Plath's mother brought her to see when she was a child in Boston, and which influenced much of Plath's work, especially her poem 'Full Fathom Five'. Ariel is a spirit trapped in a pine tree until Prospero frees her. Read 'The Arrival of the Bee Box' for a similar scenario.

turning point for Hughes, who up until then seemed to have borne his wife's mood swings patiently. When asked why he didn't 'put his foot down' more with Sylvia by their friends the Merwins, Hughes answered 'she couldn't be helped that way'.

Final years

Plath wrote her autobiographical novel *The Bell Jar* between March and May 1961. She had her poetry collection *The Colossus* published in the UK and anticipated its US release in the spring of 1962. It contained a lot of the poetry she'd written at Yaddo and was the only collection of her poetry to be published in her lifetime. Sylvia and Ted decided to leave London and write in the idyllic setting of Devon. They sold their flat in Chalcot Square to David Wevill, and his wife Assia (who would later become Ted's lover), and bought an old thatched rectory near Dartmoor called Court Green with the help of a loan from Ted's mother. They moved in on 31 August 1961. Plath was pregnant with the couple's second child. Some of Plath's most disturbing poetry was written here, including 'Finisterre' and 'Mirror', with their underlying atmosphere of menace.

In January of 1962 Plath gave birth to Nicholas, but by the summer of that year her marriage to Hughes was in serious trouble. He'd become involved with Assia Wevill and moved out of Court Green; Hughes and Plath had taken a holiday in Ireland in an attempt to save their relationship, but it had failed. Plath's depression spiralled. She wrote forty of the poems that make up her most famous collection *Ariel* during this time, but her depression and ferocious work rate, coupled with raising two small children, took its toll on the poet's health.

Plath moved back to London in November and lived at 23 Fitzroy Road, the street where Yeats had once lived. Despite the publication of *The Bell Jar*, she was plagued by depression and illness and felt cut off from the world. The lack of a phone made this worse. January brought some of the worst weather London had seen for years and Plath wrote 'Child' during this time, revealing **a wish to die**. Plath saw a doctor, who arranged a session with a psychiatrist and a course of anti-depressants, but Plath took her own life on Monday 11 February 1963. She was expecting a nurse to call that morning and seems to have thought her neighbour would let the nurse in. However, the nurse, receiving no answer, enlisted the help of a builder working nearby to break into Sylvia's flat, where they discovered the poet sprawled on the floor with her head in the gas oven. The children were found upstairs in their room crying. Many think Plath meant to be discovered before the gas could fully take effect, and that her suicide was intended as a cry for help.

Plath with husband and fellow poet Ted Hughes.

Sylvia Plath

In response to his wife's poetry and suicide, Ted Hughes wrote a collection of poems, *Birthday Letters,* which were thirty years in the making. In the particularly moving 'Last Letter', he recollects the moment he heard of Sylvia's suicide: 'Then a voice like a selected weapon / Or a measured injunction, / Coolly delivered its four words / Deep into my ear: "Your wife is dead". Hughes died in 1998 and ten years later their son Nicholas took his own life. Their daughter Frieda is a poet and artist.

> **Letters Home**
>
> Her biographer Anne Stevenson says of the letters Plath wrote to her mother, which were published together in a volume entitled *Letters Home*:
>
> '*Letters Home* can be seen as one long projection of the 'desired image' (the required image) of herself as Eve – wife, mother, home-maker, protector of the wholesome, the good and the holy, an identity that both her upbringing and her own instinctive physical being had fiercely aspired to.'

Social and Cultural Context

The society into which Sylvia Plath was born in Boston, in 1932, was a **male-dominated** one. Her father ruled the family and her mother was wife and home-maker, although both were highly educated and passionate about learning and culture. **Plath wanted to achieve and be a perfect American girl. She put huge pressure on herself to do this.** Many feel this was to please her parents and Plath's letters to her mother, written throughout her life, attest to this. Magazines like the *Ladies' Home Journal* defined this ideal. A woman should be a wife, a home-maker and a mother, but she was not expected to be a professional or to have her own career. She was to be 'respectable'. In this middle-class culture there was a tolerance of male promiscuity but girls were expected to be modest and virginal; not to marry was to risk being labelled 'unfeminine'. Throughout her life, **Plath struggled to escape this ideal of perfection yet at the same time be seen to adhere to it**. This conflict led to much of Plath's anxiety and depression. Her letters to her mother are full of references to her attempts to make a home for herself and Ted Hughes and to win her mother's approval. She was conscious of this tendency in herself, noting in her journal: 'Old need of giving mother accomplishments, getting reward of love.'

Themes

Search for an identity

Much of Plath's poetry can be seen as **a struggle to create a new identity for herself that transcended the cultural limitations imposed upon women**. Given society's view of women, Plath found it difficult to find acceptance as a writer outside of women's books and magazines. In her lifetime, her work won serious admiration from only a small number of people. She was more famous for being the wife of the poet Ted Hughes than for being a talented, ambitious and dedicated poet, novelist and short-story writer in her own right.

Plath's desire to fit in at school and be an 'all-American girl' was deepened by her consciousness of her German ancestry. Plath's use of Holocaust imagery and her reference to her father as a Nazi in her poem 'Daddy' indicate a feeling of displacement, a fear that she might, somehow, be tainted by her origins. She also employed Holocaust imagery to speak of the suffering of women. More than is sometimes acknowledged by critics, **Plath was attuned in a personal way to the major historical issues of her time**. She lived during the period of the **Cold War** and the **threat of nuclear warfare** between America and Russia. She was conscious of the dangers of a nuclear conflict and concerned for the future safety of her children. In a letter to her mother in December 1961, Plath wrote of these fears:

From *Letters Home*

'Don't talk to me about the world needing cheerful stuff! What the person out of Belsen – physical or psychological – wants is nobody saying the birdies still go tweet-tweet, but the full knowledge that somebody else has been there and knows the *worst*, just what it is like. It is much more help for me, for example, to know that people are divorced and go through hell, than to hear about happy marriages.' 21 October 1962

'… I simply couldn't sleep for nights with all the warlike talk in the papers … I began to wonder if there was any point in trying to bring up children in such a mad, self-destructive world. The sad thing is that the power for destruction is real and universal.'

The fears expressed here are active in the terrifying imagery of her final poems. 'Elm' is a particularly strong example of this with its nightmarish litany of fear and suffering until the violent and very final ending: 'That kill, that kill, that kill.'

Displacement, feminism and Plath's legacy

For Sylvia Plath, the opportunity to live and study in England was a partly liberating experience. From England she could view with clarity the consumerism and militarism of American culture, something she criticised in 'The Times Are Tidy'. However, she did not always feel at home in England and disliked the shabby inefficiency which she saw in English life. By the end of her life, Plath was caught between the two cultures, feeling ambivalent towards both. Her feelings of displacement are important in shaping the poetry she wrote. There is often a **distance in her work** that reflects this displacement, especially in the poems which feature her children, such as 'Morning Song' and 'Child'.

Many feminists saw Plath's suicide as the result of patriarchal oppression, as manifested in her father's tyrannical nature and her husband's imagined selfishness; they championed Plath as a victim, but many biographies counter this view. Hughes in particular was certainly a patient and protective husband and father. Plath's daughter Frieda, herself a poet, said in an interview with the *Guardian* newspaper, 'It was quite a shock to find that she wasn't angelic because that was how my father presented her.' Frieda also hit out at representations of her mother in film and the media. In a poem called 'My Mother' she writes of 'Their Silvia Suicide Doll, / Who will walk and talk / And die at will'.

Plath's legacy is much more than being a famous suicide or a feminist icon; **she speaks to the dispossessed**, the depressed (often with a wry wit), **lovers of nature** and those **in love with words and sound**, as those who take the time to study and read her work will find.

Timeline

1932	Born 27 October in Boston, Massachusetts
1940	Father Otto dies; Sylvia declares: 'I'll never speak to God again'
1950	*Seventeen* magazine publishes her story 'And Summer Will Not Come Again'
1951	Wins a scholarship to the exclusive Smith College for Women to study English and Art
1953	Wins guest editorship at *Mademoiselle* magazine; attempts suicide after failing to gain a place on a writing course at Harvard
1954	Graduates with distinction from Smith College
1955	Wins prestigious Fulbright Scholarship and attends Cambridge; meets fellow poet Ted Hughes
1956	Marries Hughes on Bloomsday, 16 June
1960	Gives birth to Frieda Rebecca Hughes, the couple's first child; publishes first collection, *The Colossus*
1961	Moves to Devon; writes with great energy in her first months there; concerned by talk of nuclear warfare
1962	Gives birth to son Nicholas; Plath and Hughes separate; writes over 40 poems in October and November
1963	Publishes semi-autobiographical novel *The Bell Jar*; commits suicide in February
1965	*Ariel*, a collection of her last poems, is published

HIGHER LEVEL

Before you read

When you are feeling down, what things help to make you feel better? It might be a thought, a memory, something you do or see, or something else.

Black Rook in Rainy Weather

On the stiff twig up there
Hunches a wet black rook
Arranging and rearranging its feathers in the rain.
I do not expect a miracle
Or an accident   5

To set the sight on fire
In my eye, nor seek
Any more in the desultory weather some design,
But let spotted leaves fall as they fall,
Without ceremony, or portent.   10

Although, I admit, I desire,
Occasionally, some backtalk
From the mute sky, I can't honestly complain:
A certain minor light may still
Lean incandescent   15

Out of kitchen table or chair
As if a celestial burning took
Possession of the most obtuse objects now and then –
Thus hallowing an interval
Otherwise inconsequent   20

By bestowing largesse, honour,
One might say love. At any rate, I now walk
Wary (for it could happen
Even in this dull, ruinous landscape); sceptical,
Yet politic; ignorant   25

Of whatever angel may choose to flare
Suddenly at my elbow. I only know that a rook
Ordering its black feathers can so shine
As to seize my senses, haul
My eyelids up, and grant   30

Sylvia Plath

A brief respite from fear
Of total neutrality. With luck,
Trekking stubborn through this season
Of fatigue, I shall
Patch together a content   35

Of sorts. Miracles occur,
If you care to call those spasmodic
Tricks of radiance miracles. The wait's begun again,
The long wait for the angel,
For that rare, random descent.   40

Glossary

Line	Term
8	*desultory*: without pattern, randomly changing
10	*portent*: an omen, often a sign of something negative
12	*backtalk*: cheeky banter
13	*mute*: unable to speak, silent
15	*incandescent*: glowing, luminously shining
17	*celestial*: heavenly, to do with stars and planets, etc.
18	*obtuse*: annoyingly insensitive or slow to understand
19	*hallowing*: allowing a space for something holy or sacred
20	*inconsequent*: unimportant
21	*bestowing*: giving as a gift
21	*largesse*: generosity
23	*Wary*: careful, on the lookout
24	*sceptical*: suspicious, doubting
25	*politic*: sensible in a self-serving way
31	*respite*: a break; a rest from
32	*neutrality*: a feeling of nothingness, of being totally unimportant and worthless
33	*Trekking*: making a long, hard journey
37	*spasmodic*: in sudden brief spells that cannot be predicted

Guidelines

From *The Colossus* (1960), and first published in the English journal *Granta* while Plath was a student at Cambridge University.

Written in the mid-1950s, this poem explores **the randomness of poetic inspiration and the power of that inspirational moment to transform ordinary things**. The poem also describes the **bleakness of Plath's depression. Contrast, nature, weather and colour** are all used to great effect and will be regular features in Plath's work. The poem is **intense**: both nightmarish and dreamlike in its mood.

Commentary

Lines 1–10
'Stiff', 'hunches', 'rain', 'desultory', 'spotted'; these words set the tone for the opening of the poem: it is **bleak, constrained and low-key**. The speaker notices a black rook preening on a branch in the rain. It is at the mercy of the elements just as the speaker is at the mercy of her depression. There is **an air of resignation and fear**, the poet doesn't dare to hope that the light of inspiration will descend on her, she accepts the random nature of things: 'let spotted leaves fall as they fall'. Here 'spotted' suggests decay, while the leaves fall without 'ceremony or portent'. The word 'portent' implies **a bad omen**. A black rook was often perceived as such in superstition. The use of these words and images and their connotations give the poem an ageless feel. The poet must be passive and await her inspiration patiently.

> **Leaves and The Sybil**
>
> In book six of Virgil's epic poem The *Aeneid* the Sibyl appears. She made prophecies by arranging leaves, but the wind would blow and scatter them. The ancient Greeks also believed in watching the behaviour of birds as a way to predict the future.

Lines 11–22
The poet isn't totally resigned though; she 'admits' to hoping that the heavens may give her a sign: 'I desire, / Occasionally, some backtalk / From the mute sky'. She pokes gentle fun at herself here, and then the energy of the poem picks up as she tells us that she is inspired sometimes. She describes poetic inspiration as a 'certain minor light' that seems to make ordinary objects glow with significance, 'As if a celestial burning took / Possession of the most obtuse objects'. These moments when the muse is upon her give her a break from the 'inconsequent' dullness of everyday life, and she feels very blessed by these moments of **epiphany**, 'bestowing largesse, honour, / One might say love'. **Religious words filled with light and love** lift the mood dramatically from the darkness of the first two stanzas, but these moments are out of the poet's control.

Lines 23–32
Dark and light combine and contrast in the rest of the poem. The speaker is on the lookout for these moments as she passes through the bleakness of her days, 'this dull, ruinous landscape'. However, she is also suspicious of and oblivious to 'whatever angel may choose to flare / Suddenly at my elbow'. What she is sure of is that when she is inspired, the transformation which occurs makes her look up, be alive and awake to the beauty of the world, momentarily feeling good about herself, and energised: 'seize my senses, haul / My eyelids up, and grant / A brief respite from fear / Of total neutrality'. She momentarily escapes her depression. This poem is the product of one of those moments; she has seen a wet rook and the 'shine' of its feathers has lifted her into the **rapture of creativity**.

Lines 33–40
The mood falls a little here as the poet expresses a half-hearted hope that she might be able to bear the slog of waiting for the next moment of inspiration. The line 'Trekking stubborn through this season / Of fatigue' sums up the **determination of the speaker to persevere**, but also expresses how hard life is for her when she is not writing poetry. As she nears the end of the poem she settles down to wait for the next 'miracle': 'The wait's begun again, /… For that rare, random descent.' The **alliteration** of the 'r's and **assonance** of the 'g', 'n' and 'm' sounds ('–gun', '–gain', 'ran–', '–dom', '–ent') **emphasise the possibly long wait ahead**. Without these moments of creativity her life would be intolerable; she is overcome by fatigue yet tentatively optimistic.

Sylvia Plath

Themes

Depression, which manifests as **a fear of feeling 'total neutrality'**, i.e. nothing, is a strong theme. This contrasts sharply with the theme of **poetic inspiration**, the **exhilaration** the speaker feels when moved to create art. **Fear and hope** are major themes intrinsically linked to these first two. The poet fears that she will have to wait a long time to be inspired and creative, but is hopeful about this also. The speaker's existence seems a worryingly random mix of the two and she feels she lacks any control over her life.

Imagery

The exterior world is strongly connected to the poet's interior world, her psyche. The darkness and light she perceives and interprets around her affect her mood profoundly. Plath uses **contrast** effectively: words such as 'black', 'rain', 'fall', 'minor', 'inconsequent', 'dull', and 'ruinous' convey the **struggle** and **desperate dullness** of her life, which thankfully is punctuated by 'sporadic' moments of light – 'fire', 'miracle', 'celestial', 'incandescent', 'angel'. Nature and religion are used extensively as important symbols. The pathetic fallacy of **the dark rainy day sets the background mood of despondency**. Obviously the **rook** is an important symbol here, a token of ancient superstition but also symbolic of how nature's beauty can comfort and inspire. The rook could also be Plath herself as a poet, someone battered by the rain of depression, yet she continues to put a brave face on things and keeps going just as the rook preens despite the rain.

Language and form

The **personal pronoun 'I' pervades the poem**, creating an **intensely personal and intimate atmosphere**, which can seem **claustrophobic** at times. **Internal rhyme** is used effectively in the echo of 'ow' in stanza 6: 'Suddenly at my elb<u>ow</u>. I only kn<u>ow</u>' – the effect created by this rhyme and assonance emphasises the speaker's yearning for the moment of poetic inspiration to occur again. There is much uncertainty in her world but what she does know is that moments of beauty, though rare, are deeply moving for her.

The poem is constructed of eight **unrhymed stanzas, a form Plath used often** ('The Times Are Tidy' has three; 'The Arrival of the Bee Box' consists of seven). This form allows for **flexibility in rhythm and pacing**, and this poem is full of **intricate sound patterns** which reflect the mood of the speaker.

The stanzas consist mostly of short lines, but in each there are one or two long lines, **as if the emotion felt by the speaker has slipped from the rigid grasp of the strict format and spilled over**. The overwhelming feeling is of someone **on the edge** of breaking down, who is holding on to whatever she can to keep her from this fate, yet **feigning detachment**. Look at this pattern in the poem: do you agree with this analysis or do you have a different opinion?

HIGHER LEVEL

Religious words signal relief and elation, while an almost post-apocalyptic landscape is created by the use of phrases such as 'dull, ruinous', 'total neutrality' and 'season of fatigue', giving us a representation of the poet's general state of mind. **Archaic words mix with much more modern ones** ('Portent' / 'backtalk') to emphasise the **randomness** of it all and the never-endingly relentless cycle of depression punctuated by brief moments of epiphany. This combination of old and new gives the poem a **timeless quality**. Plath's language also creates a middle ground of doubt and sceptical optimism: these moments of light might be 'miracles' or they might be 'tricks'; she is fearfully **non-committal**. A hidden rhyming scheme perhaps suggests that life may not be as random and unpredictable as the speaker first thinks it is. Look for words ending in 't' for this.

Questions

1	Describe the setting created in the first two stanzas. What strikes you as the overall mood of this section of the poem? What details create this mood?
2	Do you agree that the next two stanzas are more positive? Back up your opinion with reference to this part of the poem.
3	What is happening to ordinary objects in stanzas 3 and 4? What is causing this transformation in your opinion? Look especially at references to light.
4	Why does the poet 'now walk / Wary' (lines 22–23)?
5	What effect does the light shining on the rook's feathers have on the poet's mood (stanzas 6 and 7)?
6	'A brief respite from fear / Of total neutrality' (lines 31–32). What is the speaker's opinion of herself judging by this phrase?
7	Read stanza 7. What are the speaker's hopes for the future? Do you find this viewpoint optimistic or pessimistic in the light of what she has said so far?
8	'Miracles occur' (line 36). What, do you think, might these miracles be?
9	'The wait's begun again' (line 38). What is the poet waiting for? What is her tone here?
10	Comment on the poet's use of contrast in the poem. Focus especially on references to light and dark, hope and despair.
11	*Groupwork* Following the death of her father, Plath said, 'I'll never speak to God again'. List the references to religion or a higher power in the poem and, in pairs or groups, discuss them in the light of this statement.
12	In this poem Plath seems to believe that the poetry she creates has nothing to do with her own talent and intelligence. This tells us a lot about her self-esteem. Read her biography and timeline up to 1955. Now write a letter to Plath where you respond to the persona she portrays in this poem.

Sylvia Plath

Before you read

Who, do you think, are the heroes of today and why? Was the past a more heroic place than now? Explain.

The Times Are Tidy

Unlucky the hero born
In this province of the stuck record
Where the most watchful cooks go jobless
And the mayor's rôtisserie turns
Round of its own accord.   5

There's no career in the venture
Of riding against the lizard,
Himself withered these latter-days
To leaf-size from lack of action:
History's beaten the hazard.   10

The last crone got burnt up
More than eight decades back
With the love-hot herb, the talking cat,
But the children are better for it,
The cow milks cream an inch thick.   15

Glossary

2	*stuck record*	when a vinyl record is scratched and the needle keeps skipping to play the same part of the music over and over again; metaphor for something that is not moving on/making progress
3	*watchful cooks*	from the Middle Ages onwards the poisoning of food was common in attempts on the lives of the powerful, thus cooks had to be vigilant
4	*rôtisserie*	an apparatus consisting of a rod upon which meat is impaled and then rotated over heat to cook it
7	*lizard*	dragon
10	*hazard*	risk, adventure
11	*crone*	witch, hag

HIGHER LEVEL

Guidelines

From the 1960 collection *The Colossus,* and written in the summer of 1958 after Plath had resigned from her job teaching in Smith College. Plath was disenchanted with her former teachers and the pressure of the job pushed her physical and mental health to its limit: 'they deal in inference, hint, threat, double entendre, gossip, I'm sick of it'.

Unusually for Plath, there is no 'I' persona here. It is a **straightforward social commentary** on the sameness of modern culture compared with the more magical fairy-tale world of the past. Plath's German background was important to her and her family, who read German fairy tales and studied much of German culture, for example *Grimm's Tales* and the composer Wagner. She and Hughes were interested in ouija boards, tarot cards and horoscopes linking to the notion of magic in the poem.

Commentary

The title is **laced with irony**; modern times are too neat and safe for the poet.

Stanza 1
Plath uses the **metaphor of a stuck record** to convey the blandness of the world she lives in and suggests that those born into it are 'unlucky', as there is so little opportunity for adventure. Plath's **tone is scathing** when she contemplates how the best people are unrewarded: 'the most watchful cooks go jobless', while society is repetitive and boring: 'the mayor's rôtisserie turns / Round of its own accord'. In this prosperous 'province', the hero and the skilled cook have been replaced by the lazy mayor and his automated rôtisserie.

Stanza 2
More **dark wry criticism dominates** the second stanza as Plath asserts that knights battling dragons would be idle today; the dragon is reduced to a 'lizard, / Himself withered'. With 'History's beaten the hazard', Plath **laments** that time has moved on and daring, heroic deeds are no more. At the time Plath wrote this poem, America was a wealthy and powerful nation, the only world super-power, and had possibly grown comfortable and complacent.

Stanza 3
Plath says that the last witch was burned eighty years before, along with superstitious beliefs in magic such as 'the love-hot herb, the talking cat'; she is **sarcastic** when she says 'the children are better for it'. The thick cream is a reference to a superstition that if the cow's milk wasn't creamy a witch had cursed it. It's obvious that Plath doesn't think modern sanitised consumer culture is any match for the more heroic mystical times past. Like the dragons, the witches are no longer a threat to the province's cattle and children.

Themes and imagery

Mystery and wonder have disappeared for the young. Plath is **frustrated and bitter** about the lack of imagination and heroism in modern life. She may have believed Hughes' Yorkshire background, where superstition and folktales were still going strong, was preferable to the urban culture of the USA.

Sylvia Plath

The **monotonous circular images** of the stuck record and constantly rotating rôtisserie are symbolic of the banal safe world the poet sees around her, and **contrasts sharply with images of the fantastic past such** as dragons, heroes, witches, magic spells and talking animals. This contrasting imagery suggests the theme of a better, more heroic past and an unexciting present. It seems Plath's experience of teaching at Smith College made her cynical about education and American society in general. Interestingly, Plath would later describe teaching as 'a public-service Vampire that drinks blood and brain without a thank-you'.

Language and form

The poem shows **Plath's attention to the craft of poetry**. In each of the three five-line stanzas there are interesting patterns of sound. Look, for example, at how the **assonance of 'o' and 'u' sounds are woven into stanza 1**. The **alliterative 'k'** sound in the first word of the poem is **repeated at intervals** and concludes the poem. The stanzas and rhymes are carefully worked. Some do not rhyme fully, for example 'hazard' / 'lizard'. Listen to these rhymes as you read stanza 2 fully. Does this rhyme work? If not, why not? The **regular structure reflects the regular, predictable society** that is being satirised in the poem. Plath's voice here is quite different to her other poems; the surreal imagery and intensity of her work is absent here in this dry, witty critique of American 1950s society.

Questions

1	Where or what is the 'province of the stuck record' (line 2), and why does Plath use this metaphor here?
2	Why is the 'hero' born in this province unlucky?
3	What details in the poem suggest that the past was better than the present?
4	'The venture / Of riding against the lizard' (lines 6–7). What does the poet mean here, do you think?
5	What has happened to the lizard in 'these latter-days'?
6	What, do you think, does Plath mean in the line 'History's beaten the hazard' (line 10)?
7	In your opinion, does the speaker believe that the gains referred to in the last two lines of the poem compensate for the losses mentioned in the rest of the poem? Support your answer by reference to the poem.
8	Choose the two images that appealed to you most in the poem and give reasons for your choices.
9	Suggest an alternative title for the poem and justify your choice with reference to the poem.
10	Describe the tone and mood of the poem and the attitude it expresses towards the contemporary world. You may wish to consider some of the following options, or your own choices: frustration, anger, amusement, sarcasm, pessimism, disillusionment.
11	How does this poem differ to others you have studied by Plath?
12	Write a personal essay where you agree or disagree with Plath's opinion in this poem, or hold a class debate on the issue.

HIGHER LEVEL

Before you read

Think of some similes you could use to describe a new baby: 'A new baby is like a …'

Jot down three or four and explain why you think they are suitable.

Morning Song

Love set you going like a fat gold watch.
The midwife slapped your footsoles, and your bald cry
Took its place among the elements.

Our voices echo, magnifying your arrival. New statue.
In a drafty museum, your nakedness
Shadows our safety. We stand round blankly as walls.

I'm no more your mother
Than the cloud that distills a mirror to reflect its own slow
Effacement at the wind's hand.

All night your moth-breath
Flickers among the flat pink roses. I wake to listen:
A far sea moves in my ear.

One cry, and I stumble from bed, cow-heavy and floral
In my Victorian nightgown.
Your mouth opens clean as a cat's. The window square

Whitens and swallows its dull stars. And now you try
Your handful of notes;
The clear vowels rise like balloons.

Glossary

2	*midwife*:	nurse who helps to deliver a baby
3	*elements*:	earth, air, water and fire, something fundamental
9	*effacement*:	gradual erasing of something
11	*flat pink roses*:	patterned wallpaper

Guidelines

Plath wrote this poem in the spring of 1961, ten months after her daughter's birth. She had recently suffered a miscarriage. The poem was published in the *Observer* newspaper that year, and after her death in her collection *Ariel*.

In these six unrhymed three-line stanzas or tercets Plath examines the mix of feelings she is experiencing as a mother; there is **deep love and affection** for the child but at the same time a feeling of **disorientation and distance**. The title refers to the early morning cries of her child. By using the word 'song' Plath seems **to celebrate** her baby.

Sylvia Plath

Commentary

Stanzas 1 and 2
The poem opens on a positive note with the word 'Love'. Love is what created the child, who is compared to a 'fat gold watch', suggesting a chubby, precious baby. Gold watches are often given as presents so perhaps Plath feels the child is **a gift**. The ticking of the watch is like the heartbeat of the child; it is now a living person who will live and then die. At the child's birth the midwife slapped her feet and she cried for the first time. This cry seemed so raw and honest that Plath describes it as 'bald', pure enough to be elemental; as if being, or perhaps having, a baby is the most natural and fundamental thing possible to humanity.

Plath now imagines her baby is a museum exhibit, like a 'New statue' around which people stand discussing it like a work of art, at a loss to explain it: 'We stand round blankly as walls.' '… your nakedness / Shadows our safety' is ambiguous, suggesting how vulnerable and innocent the child is, but that it also casts a shadow on the security of the adults present; a new baby will always mean worry and a duty to protect where before life may have been more carefree. The second stanza has a **stilted feeling** to it; lots of punctuation emphasises this effect and suggests the speaker is finding aspects of being a new parent hard.

Stanzas 3 and 4
Plath feels **estranged** from her baby: 'I'm no more your mother / Than the cloud'. She feels that she is now reduced, less of a real person; she likens herself to a cloud reflected in the puddle it has created, and made smaller by this act of creation: gradually what remains is blown away by the wind. Feelings of inadequacy are a feature of many of Plath's poems. She strove to be perfect in her academic and personal life, putting on a show of coping admirably, but her journals and poems tell a very different tale. Many of Plath's friends and relatives were shocked by her suicide and her struggle with depression, saying that they had no idea she was so tormented.

> **Baby brother**
>
> **When Plath's brother Warren was born she resented him deeply, and later wrote about this saying, 'A baby, I hated babies … I would be a bystander, a museum mammoth. Babies!'**
>
> **Does this correspond to the tone or imagery in the second stanza?**

The poet is a reflection of her child but she feels distant and drained. She feels that motherhood is slowly erasing the essence of who she was before. This sensation is not uncommon in new mothers who are often overwhelmed by caring for an infant. A similar feeling, a fear of disappearing, is described in 'Black Rook in Rainy Weather'. **Mirrors, reflections and pools are recurring images** in Plath's poetry.

The narrator lies awake listening to her child breathe. The use of the word 'moth' effectively captures the soft quiet breathing of the child, and combined with 'Flickers' suggests fragility, like the flame of a candle that could easily be snuffed out. The sound reminds Plath of the gentle waves of the sea (Plath grew up by the sea and missed it terribly when the family moved after her father's death). Thus the baby calms and worries her at the same time.

Stanzas 5 and 6
The distance Plath has been feeling closes as her child cries out. Straightaway Plath is up to tend to the infant. She is self-deprecating here as she describes herself as 'cow-heavy and floral / In my Victorian nightgown', wryly referring to her milk-heavy breasts and frumpy night attire. The pattern on her nightdress echoes the rose-patterned wallpaper in stanza 4 and the simile at the end of stanza 2. Plath seems to feel that she is in the **background rather than the central figure** in this child's new life. She dehumanises herself further with

the phrase 'cow-heavy'; she has lost her femininity, her sexuality, but there is a light-hearted tone here too, and the poet is **able to poke fun at herself**.

The child's open mouth as it wails is 'clean as a cat's', the **crisp alliteration** here suggesting the urgency of the infant's cries, and the image conveys that the poet is engaged with and **fascinated** by her child. It is as if activity has broken the dark spell of her night-time fears. Dawn breaks as Plath feeds the baby; 'The window square // Whitens and swallows its dull stars' as the child swallows her mother's milk. The mood lifts further at the poem's end as Plath admires her daughter's seemingly deliberate attempt to sing, to make herself heard: 'you try / Your handful of notes; / The clear vowels rise like balloons.' As the room becomes lighter so does Plath's heart, and it seems to swell with love for the child in this final uplifting celebratory simile.

Themes

The **emotional rollercoaster of being a new mother** is central to the poem as the poet tries to deal with the negative effects it has had on her self-image and self-esteem. She is **disoriented by** the experience and struggles to come to terms with being secondary, with feeling different physically, and with the responsibility of parenthood. This is countered, however, by the clear love and affection Plath feels for her little girl. The imagery in the final stanza – 'stars', 'notes' and 'rise like balloons' – coupled with 'Song' in the title make the poem ultimately a **celebration** of motherhood.

Imagery

Unusual comparisons give this poem energy. Plath needs to find utterly new ways to describe this infant and how it makes her feel: 'fat gold watch', 'New statue', 'moth-breath', 'clean as a cat's'. **Aural images** permeate the poem – the 'bald cry'; the poet hears a 'far sea'; **the child's 'moth-breath', 'handful of notes' and 'clear vowels' combine to create the 'Song' in the title.** The **cloud image in stanza 3 is complex** and reflects effectively the evolving mother–daughter relationship. The imagery is vivid and symbolic: the balloons are a particularly strong representation of celebration. In stanza 5 the personification of the window swallowing stars as the infant feeds shows Plath in harmony with her surroundings; physical contact with the child has dispelled the emotional estrangement she had felt earlier.

Language and form

There is a strong, steady metre in stanza 1 emphasising the ticking of the 'fat gold watch' and the rhythmic breathing of the baby. 'Bald' is an adjective Plath was using in many of her poems at the time. It works on various levels here, an adjective describing the head of the baby, the starkness of the sound the baby's cry makes, and how elemental and pure our first noise is, unchanged through the ages. **Plath controls the pace of this poem rigidly.** It is halting and stilted when she feels disoriented and distant: 'Than the cloud that distills a mirror to reflect'; and becomes smoother when the poet connects with her child: 'your moth-breath / Flickers among the flat pink roses.' The alliteration of the 'f' and 'th' sounds creates a harmonious flow. The word 'Love' begins the poem and, despite the poet's struggles with motherhood, love is the prevailing mood.

The poem is written in three-line unrhymed stanzas, creating a more immediate and narrative tone. The first line has ten syllables, which is the standard line length in English poetry (e.g. Shakespeare's iambic pentameter). What is interesting in the poem is **how Plath breaks the line to achieve certain effects**. Look, for example, at how the short line 10 creates a space that is filled by 'flickers' on line 11, so that we almost hear the child's breath in the sound and rhythm of the stanza.

Questions

1	What is the mood of the first stanza and how is this mood created?
2	Why, do you think, does Plath compare the child to a 'New statue'? How do the adults seem to feel in this stanza?
3	'Your nakedness / Shadows our safety' (lines 5–6). What do you think Plath wants to convey here?
4	Explain the image of the cloud reflected in the puddle in stanza 3.
5	Plath feels distant from her child at times in the poem. Find examples of this.
6	Trace the mood of the speaker as the poem progresses. Overall do you find the mood positive? Why or why not?
7	The poem contains a number of unusual comparisons. Choose the two you like most, explaining what they represent and why you like them.
8	'Although tender in tone, the poem is clear-sighted and unsentimental.' Discuss this view of the poem.
9	The opening and closing stanzas are more positive than the others. In pairs or groups, discuss, offering an opinion, if you agree, as to why this may be so.
10	'The tenderness "Morning Song" evinces for the baby acts at a distance … [a] chill, beautiful poem'. Do you agree with Anne Stevenson's opinion of this poem? Explain.
11	Imagine you are a friend of Plath, and write the dialogue of a conversation you both have about motherhood.
12	Frieda Hughes, Plath's daughter, is also a poet. Assuming her voice, write an answering poem using details from 'Morning Song'. You could begin with the line: 'You were the first to hear my handful of notes'. What title would you give your poem?

Before you read

As part of a scene in a horror or sci-fi film, you are to imagine and describe a place that is 'Land's End' – the last place in the world. What would it look like? What atmosphere would you create and how?

Finisterre

This was the land's end: the last fingers, knuckled and rheumatic,
Cramped on nothing. Black
Admonitory cliffs, and the sea exploding
With no bottom, or anything on the other side of it,
Whitened by the faces of the drowned.   5
Now it is only gloomy, a dump of rocks –
Leftover soldiers from old, messy wars.
The sea cannons into their ear, but they don't budge.
Other rocks hide their grudges under the water.

The cliffs are edged with trefoils, stars and bells   10
Such as fingers might embroider, close to death,
Almost too small for the mists to bother with.
The mists are part of the ancient paraphernalia –
Souls, rolled in the doom-noise of the sea.
They bruise the rocks out of existence, then resurrect them.   15
They go up without hope, like sighs.
I walk among them, and they stuff my mouth with cotton.
When they free me, I am beaded with tears.

Our Lady of the Shipwrecked is striding toward the horizon,
Her marble skirts blown back in two pink wings.   20
A marble sailor kneels at her foot distractedly, and at his foot
A peasant woman in black
Is praying to the monument of the sailor praying.
Our Lady of the Shipwrecked is three times life size,
Her lips sweet with divinity.   25
She does not hear what the sailor or the peasant is saying –
She is in love with the beautiful formlessness of the sea.

Gull-colored laces flap in the sea drafts
Beside the postcard stalls.
The peasants anchor them with conches. One is told: 30
'These are the pretty trinkets the sea hides,
Little shells made up into necklaces and toy ladies.
They do not come from the Bay of the Dead down there,
But from another place, tropical and blue,
We have never been to.   35
These are our crêpes. Eat them before they blow cold.'

Sylvia Plath

Glossary

3	***admonitory***: warning, reprimanding, advising
10	***trefoils, stars and bells***: wildflowers, identified by shape rather than name
13	***paraphernalia***: miscellaneous items, bits and pieces
30	***conches***: large seashells
30	***one***: as in, a person

Guidelines

This poem comes from a group of poems Plath wrote in autumn 1961. It was inspired by a trip the poet took with Ted Hughes during which they stopped at Berck-Plage on the Normandy coast, a seaside resort where they saw the sanatoria for soldiers who had been wounded in the Algerian war (referred to in line 7 of the poem). Many were amputees, which resonated with Plath, whose own father had had a leg amputated due to diabetes.

There is a famous statue there called 'Our Lady of the Shipwrecked' (line 19) which commemorated those lost at sea. A companion statue depicting a sailor kneels at her feet. Finisterre is located at the westernmost part of Brittany, France. Its name means 'land's end', from the ancient belief that the horizon marked the end of the created world. Its dangerous waters were the scene of so many shipwrecks that locals came to call it 'The bay of the dead'.

Commentary

Stanza 1

The poem opens on a statement – 'This was the land's end' – referring to the meaning of Finisterre, but also perhaps foreshadowing the **destructive erosion** of the coastline by the crashing waves of the sea. This process is described by the poet in terms of a **military conflict**, and the rocks that lie in the seabed are likened to **casualties of war**. The description of the landscape creates a 'gloomy', bleak atmosphere from the first line which contains the words 'end', 'last' and 'rheumatic'. The 'admonitory' cliffs warn of the **dangers of the sea** and perhaps scold it for its relentless attack. The cliffs and submerged rocks are depicted as victims of this conflict; they are gnarled arthritic hands or stubborn casualties of war hiding their 'grudges under the water'. A chilling note is struck with Plath's mention that in the past the water was 'Whitened by the faces of the drowned'. Finisterre was a notorious place for shipwrecks. The power of the sea is clear; it explodes and the crashing of the waves is like the roar of cannons which further **torment** the rocks it has hacked from the ever-diminishing coastline. The **sea beyond seems endless** as if the world ends here, forever. 'With no bottom, or anything on the other side of it'. The overall effect is of a post-apocalyptic wasteland reminiscent of the 'dull ruinous landscape' Plath spoke of in 'Black Rook in Rainy Weather'.

Stanza 2

Nothing thrives in this godforsaken place; even the little clifftop flowers Plath describes as 'trefoils, stars and bells' are so small they could be something 'fingers might embroider', and they are 'close to death'. The 'mists'

that hardly bother with the flowers consist of the souls of the drowned coming from the dark past of this place, 'part of the ancient paraphernalia'. These mists obscure and then clear away as if they have a godly power: 'They bruise the rocks out of existence, then resurrect them.' **Despair pervades** as 'They go up without hope'. The **nightmarish imagery** now takes a surreal turn as the speaker enters the mist as if she wishes to be a formless dead soul too. The experience produces the terrifying feeling that 'they stuff my mouth with cotton'. Perhaps Plath is remembering the electroshock therapy she endured, which involved having a sponge placed in her mouth. She is left with remnants of the mist condensing as drops on her face, which she describes as 'beaded with tears'. She is clearly deeply upset.

Stanza 3

Plath now describes the statues: 'Our Lady of the Shipwrecked', who seems to be 'striding toward the horizon' oblivious to the 'marble sailor' praying for protection from the sea; and the 'peasant woman in black' (the colour of mourning) kneels there also. Despite her holy nature, 'Her lips sweet with divinity', Our Lady doesn't listen to the woman's prayers; she is too mesmerised by the 'beautiful formlessness of the sea', much as Plath was **entranced** by the ghostly mists in the previous stanza.

Stanza 4

The locals have set out their stalls for tourists like Plath, displaying white 'Gull-colored' lace, postcards, shell necklaces and little effigies of women also made of shells. Are these 'toy ladies' like the statue in stanza 3 or like Plath herself in any way? The locals weigh down their wares with conch shells. One stall-holder is anxious to distance the merchandise from 'the Bay of the Dead down there', assuring the narrator that originally these shells came from a warmer, prettier place that is 'tropical and blue'. There is a note of regret as the peasant admits 'We have never been to' this faraway paradise. Thus the note of hope we feel when hearing that there is a happier realm is tempered by its far distance from this bleak and unforgiving place. All the trader can offer now is sustenance from their local food: 'These are our crêpes.' The swirling wind will soon chill them, so Plath is advised to 'Eat them before they blow cold'. The message here is **ambiguous**: on the surface the meaning is a simple 'hurry up and eat before it's cold', but could there be other connotations? Perhaps the message is to embrace life because death comes soon. The image also links to that of the souls that earlier filled the speaker's mouth 'with cotton'.

Themes and imagery

Plath once wrote in her journal of 'the potently rich sea of my subconscious'; the stormy sea and windy coastline **reflect the speaker's inner turmoil. Terror and mental anguish are forcefully conveyed** in the bleakness of the setting, the violence of the sea and the nightmarish image of dead souls cramming the speaker's mouth. Against this terror there is little or no consolation. Does religion provide any comfort? 'Our Lady of the Shipwrecked' is deaf to the prayers of those she should protect, her pink 'marble skirts' blown back by the wind as she seems to stride determinedly towards the sea. (Remember eight-year-old Plath's declaration 'I'll never speak to God again' upon her father's death.)

Our Lady is supposed to be the supreme mother in the Catholic faith, yet here she neglects her flock to pursue what fascinates her. Does Plath identify with this statue? Does she feel she has neglected her duties as a mother to pursue her art? The image of the shell dolls – literally the shell of a woman – may contribute to this idea also.

The **central image is the sea**, representing the **themes of decay and destruction**. The effect is twofold: to convey death and war. As a twelve-year-old, Plath saw Shakespeare's 'The Tempest', a play that begins with a shipwreck. Later she associated Ariel's song – 'Full fathom five thy father lies; / Of his bones are coral made' – with her own dead father. **Plath often used the sea as a metaphor** and it was often **strongly linked to her father**, whom she regularly depicted as a sea-god. Plath would have seen many wounded soldiers on her trip to 'Finisterre', perhaps inspiring this comparison. The **personification of the sea** and rocks emphasises the idea of 'messy wars' as they battle eternally; 'messy' dismisses these conflicts as ultimately futile yet harmful. It is worth remembering that Plath was terrified of nuclear conflict, which loomed large as the USA and Russia engaged in the Cold War.

The **surrealist** imagery is in part influenced by Plath's interest in art, particularly the paintings of Giorgio de Chirico.

Language and form

At one level, 'Finisterre' is a description of a seaside resort: the rocky shoreline and the cliffs that surround the bay known as the Bay of the Dead, the mists that rise from the sea, the statue of Our Lady of the Shipwrecked, a memorial to the sailors who died at sea; the poem concludes with a description of the stalls and the trinkets sold by the local peasants. On another level, 'Finisterre' is a symbolic poem, in which the **meeting of ocean and land is presented in terms of the recurrent drama of death and rebirth**, of **entrapment and freedom**, and of **form and formlessness**. These **contrasts** pervade the language of the poem. As with other Plath poems, the symbolic language sends the reader's thoughts in many directions. Thus, 'Finisterre' can support different interpretations.

HIGHER LEVEL

The poem consists of four nine-line stanzas. This gives the poem a definite shape, **a form to contrast with the 'formlessness' that is strongly represented in the imagery** of the poem. The structure of the poem, like the cliffs and rocks, seems **firm and fixed**. However, the notion of permanence is undermined as these structures are eroded by the elements which ravage them, and the fragility of the flowers that 'fingers might embroider'. Perhaps there is a message that what we imagine to be solid and permanent may not be quite so; everything is subject to change.

The language of the poem is **rich in sound effects**. Plath **plays with rhyme**; for example 'budge' and 'grudges' in stanza 1 create an echo, the halting sound of 'dge' emphasising the stubbornness of the rocks. **Alliteration** is used effectively also: 'Her marble skirts blown back into two pink wings'. The alliterative 'b' and 't' sounds suggest the power of the wind. Look for examples of sibilance also, and note the internal rhyme between 'pink' and 'wing'.

Questions

1	Plath describes the cliffs as 'Admonitory'. Look at the glossary for the poem, and choose which meaning of admonitory you think Plath intends. Give reasons for your choice.
2	Describe the setting created in stanza 1. What atmosphere is created here?
3	How are the flowers and mists in stanza 2 linked to death?
4	What, do you think, is happening to the speaker in the last four lines of stanza 2?
5	Look at the depiction of 'Our Lady of the Shipwrecked' in stanza 3. What impression do you get of her? What is her relationship to the sea?
6	What representations of the sea are conveyed in the final stanza? How is it personified here and in the poem as a whole?
7	Do you find the ending of the poem hopeful or despairing? Explain. What is your understanding of the last line?
8	In your view, is the speaker of the poem attracted to the sea? Plath regarded the sea as an image of the artist's subconscious. What does the description of the sea in the poem suggest about Plath's subconscious and its concerns?
9	In pairs or groups, choose the two images you found most striking in the poem and explain your choices.
10	Comment on the poet's use of sound effects in the poem.
11	Contrast the notions of permanence and chaos in the poem.
12	Does the tone of the poem change as it progresses? Trace the poet's tone through the poem.
13	Describe a contrasting place – somewhere full of life and joy and growth. How would it look? What might the statues there depict? What might the stalls sell?

Sylvia Plath

Mirror

Before you read
Write a riddle where the answer is 'a mirror'. As you read the poem look for any similarities with the description of the mirror in the poem.

I am silver and exact. I have no preconceptions.
Whatever I see I swallow immediately
Just as it is, unmisted by love or dislike.
I am not cruel, only truthful –
The eye of a little god, four-cornered.   5
Most of the time I meditate on the opposite wall.
It is pink, with speckles. I have looked at it so long
I think it is a part of my heart. But it flickers.
Faces and darkness separate us over and over.

Now I am a lake. A woman bends over me,   10
Searching my reaches for what she really is.
Then she turns to those liars, the candles or the moon.
I see her back, and reflect it faithfully.
She rewards me with tears and an agitation of hands.
I am important to her. She comes and goes.   15
Each morning it is her face that replaces the darkness.
In me she has drowned a young girl, and in me an old woman
Rises toward her day after day, like a terrible fish.

Glossary

1	*preconceptions*:	ideas or opinions formed in advance without basis in real knowledge or experience
3	*unmisted*:	not fogged up, unobscured
14	*agitation of hands*:	hand-wringing; a similar symbol of distress is used in 'Child' (page 489) to convey the speaker's anguish

Guidelines

Plath wrote 'Mirror' in 1961 just before her twenty-ninth birthday, while pregnant with her second child, Nicholas. The Hughes family had recently moved to Court Green in Devon where Plath would write some of her most intense and surreal poetry. Mirrors and reflection are **recurring images** in Plath's work. She had become fascinated with the work of the artist Leonor Fini who exhibited a collection full of paintings of **masks, doubles and divided selves**. Plath often spoke about finding her double or other self in her close friendships (these often failed after a time due to Plath's high standards, moodiness and possessiveness).

HIGHER LEVEL

Commentary

Stanza 1

The mirror describes itself: it is 'silver and exact'. 'Exact' is ambiguous; it may mean 'precise' or have a darker connotation: 'to exact', meaning to elicit payment forcibly. The mirror tells of its unbiased and faithful nature, but **the reader must decide how accurate or truthful the mirror is**. The mirror becomes like a mouth, swallowing whatever it sees and internalising this. It presents back an 'unmisted', unobscured mirror image without emotion, 'love or dislike', or bias: 'I am not cruel, only truthful –'. Consider why Plath places the dash here. Does it imply deception? Look at the slightly smug statement in the very next line: 'The eye of a little god'. Is a god impartial or unbiased?

The mirror passes most of its time observing the 'pink', speckled wall opposite, which it has become so familiar with that now 'it is a part of my heart'. The mirror's assertion that it has a heart not only further develops this **personification** but suggests that it is **subject to emotion and bias**, despite its earlier statements to the contrary. The only 'flickers' that obscure the pink wall are the darkness of the night and the faces which look into it; both of these images will be explored further in the second stanza.

Stanza 2

The mirror becomes more fanciful in its description of itself: 'Now I am a lake.' A lake can reflect just like a mirror but often **distorts** that reflection, as its surface is not always even. The faces mentioned in stanza 1 become a woman who 'bends over me'. The woman is 'Searching' the mirror to find out 'what she really is', **just as poets often use their poetry to explore and interpret the deepest parts of their own psyche**.

Plath felt enormous pressure throughout her life to maintain a double-standard of the outer socially acceptable mother/wife/daughter, and the inner poet/independent woman/depressive. Perhaps unhappy with the reflection she sees in the mirror, or **divided by this double life**, the woman often turns to the night, 'those liars, the candles or the moon' to examine herself. Is she afraid of the harsh light of day, preferring the softer more flattering 'flicker' of candles? Note Plath's use of this word in

'Poppies in July' (page 479). The mirror sounds stung by the woman's disloyalty; 'those liars' sounds vitriolic, full of jealousy and bitterness. However, the mirror stays true, and when the woman returns it reflects her 'faithfully'. She 'rewards' the mirror by honestly showing her distress: 'tears and an agitation of hands'. Is this an ironic use of the word 'rewards'? The mirror concludes that it is 'important to her'.

Every morning the woman notes the changes in her wrought by time: 'In me she has drowned a young girl'. There are a number of interpretations possible here. In one sense the poet might think of her bygone youth as a drowned girl. She herself could be responsible for the drowning, or it could be the fault of her mother; Plath often blamed her mother for her father's death and for not allowing her to grieve properly for him: she wouldn't let Sylvia attend his funeral. Plath often depicted her father as 'drowned' and part of the water-world, like a sea-god. She also used water regularly as a symbol for her mental state; in this sense the **young girl drowns in the anxiety of the woman**. The image could also refer to the toll motherhood has taken on Plath. The image of the lake is continued here as old age looms inexorably, 'like a terrible fish', a frightening creature of the deep which lurks beneath, ready to rise up and destroy or devour.

Themes

Mental anguish and the woman's attempts to explore this are central in the poem; her 'tears' and 'agitation of hands' convey deep suffering, which in her own life Plath kept hidden from her friends and family. She tried to deal with her depression by writing about it in her journals and her poetry; these were her **confessionals**. Like Elizabeth Bishop, Plath was influenced by Robert Lowell and attended a seminar given by him; he was one of the 'confessional' poets where the poet's real experiences and fears are dealt with directly or indirectly in their poetry.

> **Confessional poetry**
>
> **The confessional poetry movement was a largely American literary phenomenon where often a persona at the heart of the poem shares a personal experience (usually a negative one). The tone is confidential and confessional and the poetry tends to be deeply personal in subject, but set apart from the poet, providing distance through the use of this persona.**

Creating poetry may itself be a theme also. Plath attended psychiatrists during her life and became fascinated with the ideas of Freud and Jung, who examined the depths of the subconscious in the belief that by releasing repressed memories and anxieties they could help the sufferer cope with their current depression. Perhaps the relationship between the poet and the mirror is **a reflection of the relationship between analyst and patient, or writer and poem**.

The poem deals with relationships on a number of levels. The mirror's relationships dominate the poem: with the wall, the night and the woman. The wall inspires a feeling of kinship and affection – 'part of my heart' – while the mirror seems jealous of the night and 'those liars, the candles or the moon'. The relationship with the woman is more complex: she uses the mirror to search herself but at other times neglects it, and yet the mirror is always there, faithful and unswerving in its loyalty. Reading the image another way, there is the sinister idea of **the mirror swallowing and drowning its subjects**, and the future it presents for the woman, 'like a terrible fish', is a frightening one. On a deeper level, the poem explores **the way in which we relate to ourselves**, through the act of examining ourselves in a mirror; the implication that we can see through the reflection into the inner self (the psyche, the emotions) make this poem far more complex than it seems on the surface.

Imagery

Water

Water is a recurring image in Plath's poems and often represents her subconscious. In 'Finisterre' the poet's deepest fears are powerfully evoked by the sea; she is almost suffocated by its mists. It batters the cliffs like Plath's depression has battered her emotionally. In this poem the mirror likens itself to a lake that drowns the speaker's youth and threatens her future like a 'terrible fish'. It 'swallows' her as she desperately searches its reaches to find out who she truly is. Plath in her poetry seems to be enacting just such a desperate search for identity coming up with multiple personas all speaking to and of different aspects of her psyche. Her poem 'Full Fathom Five' is a deep meditation on this and is worth reading for comparison.

Reflection

Plath's poetry is a *reflection* of herself encompassing the different sides of this complex poet: wife, mother, depressive, creative, nature-loving, fearful, anguished, etc. In 'Black Rook in Rainy Weather' the rook *mirrors the poet*, battered and beleaguered by rain and self-doubt. 'The Times Are Tidy' reflects her dissatisfaction with teaching and American society. In 'Morning Song' the poet imagines she is a cloud disappearing while being reflected in the puddle (her baby daughter) it has 'distilled'. Similarly, in 'Child' her son's eye is a 'pool in which images should be grand' and she worries about what sights her child's eye will *reflect* as it grows. She is reflecting herself as a nervous mother who feels totally inadequate. The image of herself at the end of this poem reflects her deep depression and lack of self-worth and in it she fears she will block her child's reflection of what is good and worthy in life, she is a 'dark / Ceiling without a star'. 'Mirror' centres on reflection, like her poetry the mirror sees and interprets her, often bleakly and unkindly.

Water in Plath's poetry is an important image. It often suggests death or escape, as in 'Finisterre', and Plath uses the sea, **a lake and even a puddle** ('Morning Song') to **convey reflection, self-doubt, fear and longing**. The mirror is clearly symbolic and it reflects a **dense complex of associations: the dark and fearful** inner life of the poet, the **deep act** of making poetry itself, or even those females closest to Plath, her mother and daughter. The world the mirror and woman inhabit is **unstable** – the exactness of the mirror's action contrasts with the darkness, the unstable sources of light such as 'candles or the moon', and the wallpaper that 'flickers'. The 'speckles' suggest the pink wall is mildewed; this idea of decay may echo the images of ageing at the end of the second stanza.

Language and form

Two nine-line stanzas reflect each other much as the mirror reflects the woman in the poem. The structure of the poem is therefore catoptric, i.e. it reflects itself. If indeed the mirror symbolises poetry and how poems reflect their writer, it is doubly reflective. The speaker of the poem is the mirror which describes itself and its relationships. As in 'Elm' (page 472), **the poet gives voice to an object and dramatises its situation to convey her own fears and insecurities**. In 'Finisterre', Plath also used nine-line stanzas, their length giving room to explore an image or concept in detail. The opening line of this poem sounds like an old-fashioned riddle, where an object describes itself and we must guess the answer. Without the title, do you think you would guess that a mirror was the speaker here?

Harsh consonant sounds in the first stanza, as well as the words themselves, create a coldness: 'exa<u>c</u>t', 'disli<u>k</u>e', '<u>c</u>ruel', 'spe<u>ck</u>les', 'dar<u>k</u>ness'. The **terseness** in the short, complete lines creates a **controlled accuracy**, suggesting someone who is afraid to unleash their emotions freely. There is a sense that, just as under the lake a threat awaits, **under the surface of the poem dark and violent emotions lurk**. An 'atmosphere of weird threat' is something several critics have noticed in Plath's poetry, one of Plath's biographers ascribed this to 'the deep self full of violence and fury she was suppressing under her poised and capable appearance' (Stevenson). This is countered by the tenderness the mirror feels for the wall, which is undemanding, constant and stable.

Questions

1	What details are we given about the mirror in lines 1–5?
2	Describe the relationship between the wall and the mirror.
3	What are the only things which obscure the mirror's view of the wall? How, do you think, does the mirror feel about these interruptions?
4	'I am not cruel, only truthful'. Is the mirror as unbiased and neutral as it suggests in stanza 1?
5	Why and how does the woman use the mirror? Describe the relationship between the woman and the mirror in stanza 2.
6	How can we tell that the woman is suffering? Why, do you think, does the mirror call her display of 'agitation' a 'reward'?
7	What is your interpretation of the last two lines of the poem?
8	Read the poem aloud. Look for examples of rhyme in the poem. Which words echo each other and what is the effect of this? For example, consider the rhyming effect of 'I see' and 'immediately' (line 2). Keep in mind the rhymes are not necessarily at the end of the lines.
9	Comment on the symbolism of the mirror, the wall, the night and the lake. What interpretations are possible for these images?
10	Comment on how the form and structure of the poem echo its subject and theme.
11	Discuss the voice of the mirror: what personality is conveyed? Is it masculine or feminine, caring or cruel? Is it the woman's inner voice, and is the voice of the poem an aspect of Sylvia Plath's own voice? Or should we keep a distance between the poet and the speaker of the poem? Explain.
12	Do you agree that this poem has an 'atmosphere of weird threat'? Explain.
13	Write an answering poem or narrative paragraph entitled 'Woman' or 'Wall', where the one you choose describes themselves and their relationship to the mirror.
14	Find pictures to accompany and illustrate the various ideas and images in the poem, and set these to music that you think suits the mood.

HIGHER LEVEL

Before you read

Describe an experience you have had (real or imaginary) when you were able to observe a rare or unusual animal at close quarters.

Pheasant

You said you would kill it this morning.
Do not kill it. It startles me still,
The jut of that odd, dark head, pacing

Through the uncut grass on the elm's hill.
It is something to own a pheasant,   5
Or just to be visited at all.

I am not mystical: it isn't
As if I thought it had a spirit.
It is simply in its element.

That gives it a kingliness, a right.   10
The print of its big foot last winter,
The tail-track, on the snow in our court –

The wonder of it, in that pallor,
Through crosshatch of sparrow and starling.
Is it its rareness, then? It is rare.   15

But a dozen would be worth having,
A hundred, on that hill – green and red,
Crossing and recrossing: a fine thing!

It is such a good shape, so vivid.
It's a little cornucopia.   20
It unclaps, brown as a leaf, and loud,

Settles in the elm, and is easy.
It was sunning in the narcissi.
I trespass stupidly. Let be, let be.

Sylvia Plath

Glossary

3	*jut of that odd, dark head*	description of the jerking fashion in which the pheasant moves its head as it walks about
12	*our court*	Court Green is the name of the house in Devon where the poem is set; also suggests a royal court, picking up on the reference to the kingliness of the bird
13	*pallor*	an unhealthy pale appearance
14	*crosshatch*	shading effect in art using intersecting lines; here used to describe the pattern of the prints left by the pheasant overlapping on those left by other birds
20	*cornucopia*	a Roman symbol of plenty depicting a horn out of which limitless food tumbles; here, it represents treasure
23	*narcissi*	daffodil-like plants, but smaller and highly scented, with white or yellow flowers; they were planted in their thousands around Court Green

Guidelines

Sylvia Plath wrote 'Pheasant' in April 1962, during a period of enormous creativity in which she wrote a number of fine poems within days of each other. The poem had its origins in Plath's glimpse of a pheasant standing on a hill at the back of her house. Some critics read the poem in terms of the relationship between the speaker of the poem and the person she addresses. The poem expresses Plath's love of nature as the speaker becomes fascinated with a pheasant seen in her garden.

Commentary

Stanzas 1 and 2

Stanza 1 **opens dramatically**: 'You said you would kill it this morning.' The repeated 'you' is sharply accusatory. This is quickly followed by the speaker's command, 'Do not kill it', but she gives a strange reason for wanting to keep it alive: 'It startles me still'; 'still' suggests that the bird has been seen before. Plath was often **fascinated by things that shocked her**, such as the mist in 'Finisterre' and the flowers in 'Poppies in July' (page 479). She finds the movement of the bird – 'the jut of that odd, dark head' – captivating, and feels privileged to 'be visited at all' by such a beautiful creature as it paces through the long grass on the hill where an elm tree grows. She feels it is hers: 'It is something to own a pheasant'.

> **Hunting**
> Ted Hughes was a keen hunter and once likened the act to writing poetry, saying, 'This is hunting and the poem is a new species of creature, a new specimen of the life outside your own.'
> *Poetry in the Making*, 1967

Stanzas 3, 4 and 5

With 'it isn't / As if I thought it had a spirit', the speaker denies that she believes there is a magical or special relationship between herself and the bird, or that it has a soul, but this denial could be a defence against accusations of irrationality. The speaker **appreciates how the bird fits into its setting**; it belongs in nature: 'It is simply in its element.' The pheasant has 'a kingliness, a right'. This is its **territory**; it was in the garden 'last winter' and she recalls the impressions its feet and tail made in the snow. What amazes her most is how 'rare' it is to see the pheasant, compared to more common birds like 'sparrow and starling'. She is struck by its larger, more majestic footprints through the tiny crosshatch pattern the footprints of these more ordinary birds create in the snow's 'pallor'.

Stanzas 6, 7 and 8

The tone grows in excitement as she imagines 'a dozen', even 'A hundred' pheasants 'on that hill – green and red' as they cross and re-cross the grass. This would be 'a fine thing!' The **exclamation mark here emphasises her joy** at this imagined scene. The shape of the pheasant reminds the poet of 'a little cornucopia', an ancient symbol of nature's plenty, as it 'Settles in the elm' tree to safety. Just before this 'It was sunning in the narcissi', until the poet had disturbed it. She seems annoyed at herself for having disturbed the bird, 'stupidly'. The final line may be an admonishment to herself to leave the bird alone or a repetition of her instruction to her husband not to kill the bird: 'Let be, let be.'

Themes

The **beauty and wonder of nature** is clearly a theme here. Plath celebrates the rarity of the pheasant and ends by asserting its right to inhabit her garden. Plath is also saying that **what is rare is wonderful**; the sparrows and starlings don't fascinate the poet like the pheasant does because they are common, everyday birds. The effect of the pheasant on the speaker is reminiscent of 'Black Rook in Rainy Weather', where the poet is fascinated by the beauty of the rook preening on the branch of a tree.

For some critics, the plea is not for the pheasant but for the poet herself. Plath wrote 'Pheasant' during a tense period in her relationship with Ted Hughes. In this reading, Plath is the narrator and Hughes is 'you'. The pheasant represents the marriage itself, under threat from the male. It is he who is intent on destroying it. The female **pleads** for it; she pleads **for its beauty and wonder**, and **for the life and passion which animate it**. The fact that it's the female who makes the plea suggests that the relationship of power is an unequal one, with the male possessing the authority to take or spare life as he wills. (In 'The Arrival of the Bee Box' (page 484), the narrator says she will be sweet god and spare the lives of the bees.) For the critic Linda Wagner-Martin, 'Pheasant' rests on the fear that the male will not listen to the female's plea for the life that deserves to exist.

Imagery

The image of the pheasant dominates the poem, symbolising what is rare and beautiful in nature. It has lifted the poet's spirit, and her excitement grows as she continues to observe it and then imagine many of them in her garden. Although a positive poem in many ways, the **rapturous description** of the bird is **framed by a threat** to it: 'Do not kill it /… Let be'. There is a loneliness despite the admiration the poet feels for the kingly pheasant; the bird, the poet and even the elm tree **seem solitary figures**. The elm tree is explored deeply in Plath's next poem, 'Elm'.

Language and form

'Pheasant' is a **beautifully achieved poem**. It has a conversational quality. Plath uses a nine-syllable line, and there are **subtle rhymes and half-rhymes** throughout the poem. The rhyme scheme is a version of **terza rima**, a form in which the last word in the middle line of each stanza provides the rhyme for the next stanza. What is so impressive about 'Pheasant' is the way **Plath follows a strict form while never losing the conversational feel** of the poem.

Sylvia Plath

The **use of 'You' and 'I'** in the poem **creates a distance** between them; **there is no 'we'**. In her language about herself Plath is defensive and self-critical: 'I am not mystical', 'I trespass stupidly'. This contrasts strongly with the effusive praise she gives the pheasant: 'rare', 'kingliness', 'The wonder of it'. Can you find other examples of Plath being self-deprecating in her poetry?

The repetition at the end of the poem is often a feature in Plath, and can be compared to 'colourless' in 'Poppies in July' and 'that kill' in 'Elm'. Observe, too, the effect of the extra syllable in the final line. What is achieved by this elongation of the line?

Questions

1	What is happening in the first two lines of stanza 1? What scene do you imagine when you read it? Imagine the tone, body language and facial expressions of the speaker as they speak these lines.
2	What are the speaker's feelings towards the pheasant in the first two stanzas?
3	Reading stanzas 3 to 5, what attributes does the pheasant have? What are the speaker's reasons for wanting the bird to be spared?
4	Read lines 15 and 16: 'Is it its rareness then? It is rare. / But a dozen would be worth having'. How does the poet contradict herself here?
5	Write a description of the pheasant based on the information given in the poem.
6	Has the position of the speaker and the bird switched as the poem moves from the opening to the end? Think in terms of who the 'intruder' seems to be.
7	'The difference between "Pheasant" and "Black Rook in Rainy Weather" is that in the former there is no movement from the outside to the inside. It is the bird, rather than the poetic persona, who is the centre of the poem.' OR 'In "Pheasant", the poetic persona pleads for herself in pleading for the bird.' Which of the above readings of the poem is closest to your own? Support the points you make by reference and quotation from the poem.
8	In writing about 'Pheasant', Ted Hughes speaks of Sylvia Plath achieving a 'cool, light, very beautiful moment of mastery'. Write a note on the kind of mastery achieved by Plath in 'Pheasant'. You might like to consider some or all of the following in your answer: ■ The choice of verbs and their effect ■ The descriptions of the pheasant ■ The dramatic language ■ Line length and syllable count ■ The stanza form In considering the above, be alert to the sounds of the poem and their effect.
9	If, as some critics suggest, the poem describes the relationship between the poet and her husband, what kind of relationship is portrayed? Does the poem support this reading?
10	Write a dialogue between the 'you' and 'I' where the fate of the pheasant is decided.
11	Have a class debate on the rights and wrongs of hunting.

HIGHER LEVEL

Before you read

What are the different sounds a tree makes? Think of the different parts of a tree and how different kinds of weather can affect it. Share your ideas with the class and see if any of the sounds are similar to the ones described in the poem.

Elm

for Ruth Fainlight

I know the bottom, she says. I know it with my great tap root:
It is what you fear.
I do not fear it: I have been there.

Is it the sea you hear in me,
Its dissatisfactions? 5
Or the voice of nothing, that was your madness?

Love is a shadow.
How you lie and cry after it
Listen: these are its hooves: it has gone off, like a horse.

All night I shall gallop thus, impetuously, 10
Till your head is a stone, your pillow a little turf,
Echoing, echoing.

Or shall I bring you the sound of poisons?
This is rain now, this big hush.
And this is the fruit of it: tin-white, like arsenic. 15

I have suffered the atrocity of sunsets.
Scorched to the root
My red filaments burn and stand, a hand of wires.

Now I break up in pieces that fly about like clubs.
A wind of such violence 20
Will tolerate no bystanding: I must shriek.

The moon, also, is merciless: she would drag me
Cruelly, being barren.
Her radiance scathes me. Or perhaps I have caught her.

I let her go. I let her go 25
Diminished and flat, as after radical surgery.
How your bad dreams possess and endow me.

Sylvia Plath

I am inhabited by a cry.
Nightly it flaps out
Looking, with its hooks, for something to love.   30

I am terrified by this dark thing
That sleeps in me;
All day I feel its soft, feathery turnings, its malignity.

Clouds pass and disperse.
Are those the faces of love, those pale irretrievables?   35
Is it for such I agitate my heart?

I am incapable of more knowledge.
What is this, this face
So murderous in its strangle of branches? –

Its snaky acids hiss.   40
It petrifies the will. These are the isolate, slow faults
That kill, that kill, that kill.

Glossary

Line	Term	Meaning
1	*the bottom*	the bottom is the furthest point that can be reached; in this context, it is the subterranean world
1	*tap root*	the main root that goes deep into the soil
6	*voice of nothing*	absence of inspiration
15	*arsenic*	a deadly poison
16	*atrocity*	an extremely wicked, violent or cruel act or event, often causing death on a large scale
18	*filaments*	fine wires like those in a light bulb or electric wire
19	*clubs*	stout-ended sticks used as weapons
33	*malignity*	evil

Guidelines

The elm of the title is a wych elm, a large deciduous tree with convoluted branches which Plath described as an 'Intricate nervous system'. It was often used to make coffins. One grew on a prehistoric mound in the garden of Court Green in Devon and is the tree described in 'Pheasant' where the bird roosts at the end of the poem. The 'ease' described at the end of 'Pheasant' is replaced by deep anguish and unease in this poem.

HIGHER LEVEL

Ruth Fainlight

Ruth Fainlight was a close friend of Plath's in the final years of her life and a fellow poet with similar ideas and themes. A. S. Byatt said her poems 'give us truly new visions of unusual and mysterious events'. Fainlight said of herself, 'I am a poet who is a woman, not a woman poet.'

Plath wrote the poem in April 1962 as her marriage to Ted Hughes was breaking up. **Plath often gave voice to inanimate objects to describe her emotions and thoughts.** The 'You' persona is addressed by the 'I' of the tree, but their **voices become tangled** towards the end of the poem, like the branches of the elm tree.

Commentary

Stanzas 1 and 2

The elm tree addresses the 'You' persona, telling her 'I know the bottom'. The tree has **dark, deep knowledge** and **knows the very essence of things**; it knows that 'the bottom' is what 'You' fears most. Perhaps this 'bottom' is the deepest darkest recess of the true self. The poem explores various fears and traumas, perhaps suggesting that our deepest fears and the pain we have suffered are what truly define us. The tree asserts that it has explored this and is unafraid.

In stanza 2 the tree wonders whether the sound of the wind in its leaves reminds 'You' of the sea and 'Its dissatisfactions'. Plath used the sea extensively in her poetry to represent her childhood before her father's death (as in 'Morning Song'), and also to symbolise **formlessness and death** as we saw in 'Finisterre'. The sea seems to **frighten and fascinate Plath in equal measure**. The tree suggests that it may remind 'You' of 'the voice of nothing, that was your madness'. The **mocking, dispassionate tone echoes the voice of the mirror** in the poem of the same name. Silence – the absence of inspiration – was the cause of severe depression in Plath. She constantly feared that her poetic gift would desert her; this was eloquently written about in 'Black Rook in Rainy Weather'.

Stanzas 3 and 4

Here the focus turns to the heartbreak 'You' has endured, with the elm asserting that 'Love is a shadow', something intangible and dark that cannot be captured. As night comes, the elm continues to mock, saying, 'How you lie and cry after it'. **Note the pun on the word 'lie'.** The elm compares the harsher sound of the wind in its branches to the noise of hooves, in a metaphor likening the poet's love life to a bolting horse which will 'gallop' away from the listener. Plath's marriage break-up could be the theme here, and perhaps the comparison of the head to a stone conveys the numbing, heavy despair she was feeling at the time. The **sound of fleeing love** seems to haunt the listener in the effective repetition of 'Echoing, echoing'.

Stanza 5

The third sound made by the elm may remind 'You' of 'the sound of poisons' as the rain falls through its boughs. The movement of thought from unattainable love to poison and oblivion is similar to the movement in 'Poppies in July' (page 479) whereby numb nothingness is presented as an alternative to a life of intense feeling. It is a **quiet but insidious** sound, 'this big hush', and the white berries on the tree are like deadly arsenic, suggesting death.

Stanzas 6 and 7

The **intensity** of the elm's descriptions is **heightened further** as it boldly states 'I have suffered the atrocity of sunsets', which is reminiscent of the flash and blast of an atomic bomb exploding. The experience has scorched its roots, burning them. Plath had a dread of nuclear warfare, and the reference to 'red filaments' and 'wires' reminds us of the botched ECT (electroconvulsive therapy) Plath suffered in her early twenties, which led to a suicide attempt. The elm now seems to suffer as much as the 'You' persona, unlike earlier in the poem when it seemed aloof and unscathed by suffering. It is attacked by a storm, which seems to have been gathering as the poem has progressed, and it is broken into 'clubs' which will harm any 'bystander'. Maybe the poet is saying that the intense heartbreak and rage that her mental health issues have caused threaten those closest to her. The **violence** of these two stanzas reaches **a climax** in the elm's anguished plea 'I must shriek'. The imagery, with its **references to suffering** – 'scorched', 'wires', 'violence', 'shriek' – suggests the suffering endured by Sylvia Plath's body in the electric shock treatment she received. From this point on, the narrator seems identifiable with the poet herself.

Stanzas 8–11

Night is just as difficult for the elm as the sunset; the moon 'drags' it, mocking its lack of fertility with its lunar glow, and its 'radiance scathes me'. Notice the moon is referred to as 'Her'.

> **The Moon**
>
> There are sixty-one references to the moon in Plath's poetry and none are benevolent.

The elm seems confused and its **voice becomes increasingly confused with the 'You' persona**. It thinks it may have caught the moon and so releases her, leaving her 'Diminished and flat, as after radical surgery'. This shocking image seems to imply a double mastectomy. Line 27 is an important one. Here **the elm accuses the narrator**, asserting that it is her nightmares which **possess** the tree and make her what she is: 'How your bad dreams possess and endow me.' From this point on, the voices of elm and narrator **merge**. In 'The Moon and the Yew Tree', Plath says that the trees of the mind are black. The elm is black and expresses some of the dark, incomprehensible fears that occupy the narrator's mind.

The speaker continues to list her nightmares: at night something awakens inside her, trying to get its claws into her, 'Looking … for something to love'; but this love is twisted and dark and it terrifies her. She feels it sleep in her like a roosting bird, possibly an owl given its nocturnal nature, and she can feel its evil 'malignity' like a cancer inside of her.

> **Bad Dreams**
>
> 'your bad dreams possess and endow me'
> In classical mythology the underworld had an entrance hall called 'Orcus' where all of the evils of mankind dwelled. At its centre was a huge elm tree where nightmares slept beneath the leaves waiting to fly out at night to haunt the dreams of sleeping people.
>
> Virgil, *Aeneid* Book VI

Stanzas 12–14

There follows a brief moment of calm (perhaps wrung out exhaustion following the intensity of emotion that has gone before). Time goes by: 'Clouds pass and disperse', their pale forms reminding the speaker of the faces of those she's loved, 'those pale irretrievables'. She feels she'll never recover their affection, for they have 'disperse[d]' like the clouds. The **sense of loneliness and abandonment** is striking. She wonders whether their fickle attentions were worth her spent passion – 'Is it for such I agitate my heart?' Suddenly she notices a face, 'So murderous in its strangle of branches'. This is a sinister image that seems to contain a paralysing and ultimately deadly poison.

The final sound of the tree is a 'snaky … hiss' that 'petrifies the will'. This reminds us of Medusa in classical mythology, a gorgon monster who had snakes for hair and eyes that turned people who gazed upon her to stone. The **numbing** poison is like the oblivion-bringing opiates in 'Poppies in July'. All of these fears and terrible traumas are 'the isolate, slow faults' which act like poisons to eventually destroy the speaker – 'That kill, that kill, that kill'.

Themes

Mental anguish in an uncaring world is the theme here. The speakers in the poem express their deepest fears and sufferings with **no sense or hope of escape**. It is **incredibly dark and dramatic**. The fears expressed include true self-knowledge, insanity, rejection and lost love, the poisoned atmosphere of nuclear fall-out, violence, cancer, nightmares, infertility and night terrors.

Suffering and **rejection** are at the heart of the surreal set of images used by Plath to convey these themes. The **cruel and taunting voice of the elm** offers no consolation, empathy or understanding – 'I do not fear it', 'How you lie and cry after it' – reflecting a world that doesn't care about the mental torment the 'You' persona endures, and even jeers her for it. Is this how Plath felt the world viewed her poetry or herself, with disdain and a lack of compassion?

The need for love, its absence, and a destructive inner force dominate the theme of the second part of the poem where the **voices meld into a single anguished lament**. The speaker has been **abandoned**; the dispersion of 'those pale irretrievables' is the final straw in this **litany** of grief. With 'I am incapable of more knowledge', she declares that she can take no more, and yet another horror lurks, the murderous face in the 'strangle of branches'. The shocking imagery of violent death, and the darkness and suffering endured, is relentless.

Imagery

Each set of torments is associated with a sound made by the effect of the weather on the tree: the sea in rustling leaves, horses' hooves in the strong wind, a hush of poisons in rain, and the sharp hiss of 'snaky acids'. The final image is reminiscent of the **serpent in the Garden of Eden**, as well as the Medusa reference mentioned previously. The **'shriek'** of the elm in line 21 becomes **all-encompassing** seven lines later – 'I am inhabited by a cry'. We get the sense that reality, fear and nightmare are **blurring** into one tormented existence. (Read Emily Dickinson's 'I Felt A Funeral in My Brain' for a similar experience.)

A sunset and night that grow steadily stormier and stormier dominates the imagery, causing the tree to eventually break into 'clubs' that will hurt anyone near, perhaps a reflection of Plath's state of mind and how it may affect others. Part of the night imagery concerns **the moon**, which is associated with women but does not harbour life. 'Barren' is an adjective Plath uses often to suggest a strong dislike or horror of someone. A barren woman is, Plath suggests in another poem, like an empty museum.

Language and form

Artemis and Owl

Artemis was the Greek goddess of the moon, night and chastity. She was a hunter whose sacred bird was the owl, a creature suggested in lines 28 to 33: 'this dark thing / That sleeps in me; / All day I feel its soft, feathery turnings'. Artemis was often cruel and vengeful, particularly to women who fell in love.

The poem is written in fourteen **tercets** of **irregular length**. It becomes darker and more upsetting until the **black finality** of the final line: 'That kill, that kill, that kill.' The **triple repetition mirrors the tercets** that comprise the poem.

Repetition and internal rhyme are used effectively to create the nightmarish, surreal atmosphere of the poem. **Look at how 'I' and 'know' are repeated in stanza 1** and think about the effect this has. Is it sinister, arrogant, or something else?

Sylvia Plath

Questions

1. What impression of the elm is created by the statements in the first stanza? How would you describe the tone here?

2. Why, do you think, did Plath make the persona of the elm female?

3. Examine the questions posed by the elm in stanza 2. What do they suggest about the elm and the person she addresses?

4. What image of love is created in stanzas 3 and 4? Is the elm comforting or cruel in these stanzas? Explain your answer.

5. Stanzas 5 to 9 describe the elements of rain, sun, wind and moon in their relationship to the elm. What aspect of each is emphasised? How does each affect the elm? What, in your view, is the most striking image in these stanzas? Why?

6. What is the elm's attitude to the moon? Where is this attitude most apparent? Comment on the images of infertility and disfigurement in this part of the poem.

7. What do stanzas 5 to 9 suggest about the nature of the elm's existence? Select the words or phrases that strike you most forcefully.

8. 'How your bad dreams possess and endow me' (line 27). What relationship is suggested between the elm and the 'You' of the poem, in this statement? The line can be read as either the elm addressing the woman or the woman addressing the elm. What is the effect of each reading? Which do you agree with?

9. The last five stanzas are rich, complex and difficult. How does the speaker view herself? What images strike you as particularly disturbing or vivid?

10. What is your reaction to the use of the word 'faults' in the final stanza? What is the tone of the poem's extraordinary last line?

11. 'In "Elm", the boundary between outside and inside is blurred. It is as if the "You", the poetic persona, takes the elm into herself.' What effect does this create in the poem? If we read the poem as a description of Plath's mental state, what is revealed to us?

12. Plath's choice of words and phrases in the poem are especially striking and startling. Take, for example, 'atrocity of sunsets'. Explain what you think she means by this phrase and choose three others that particularly caught your attention, explaining the reasons behind each choice.

13. '"Elm" vividly conveys suffering, self-doubt and despair.' Give your response to this assessment of the poem, supporting the points you make by quotation from the poem.

HIGHER LEVEL

14 There is no single reading of 'Elm' that will do justice to its rich complexity. Here are three of the many readings proposed for the poem. Working in small groups, share your opinion of each.

a) 'The poem's narrator confesses that she is searching desperately for someone to love. Because of this hysteria, she realises that some deadly force within her has been triggered into action by the loss of love. The disintegration of love, the poem says, is a sure death warrant for the speaker.' Paul Alexander

b) '"Elm" describes the effects of nuclear and chemical damage upon a tree and a woman. "I have suffered the atrocity of sunsets", the speaker explains, and further, "My red filaments burn and stand, a hand of wires." … "Elm" is one of the many poems in which Plath explores the consequences of isolation, and argues against the impulse to hold oneself as separate from the rest of the world.' Tracy Brain

c) 'In the poem, originally titled "The Elm Speaks", wych elm becomes witch elm, a frightening mother-double of the poet, who offers death as the only possible love substitute. Between the taproot of the tree and the murderous face of the moon, the poet, "incapable of more knowledge", is forced into a terrible acknowledgement of "faults" – suddenly a new word in Sylvia's poetic lexicon. The poem suggests them as somehow built into her nature, bent like a crooked tree by traumatic childhood events: "These are the isolate slow faults / That kill, that kill, that kill."' Anne Stevenson

15 'Elm' is a poem with many striking visual images. You might like to offer your own creative response to, or interpretation of, the poem, in visual form.

Sylvia Plath

Before you read

Brainstorm the title 'Poppies in July'. What do you expect a poem with this title to be about? What general mood and atmosphere would you expect to encounter?

Poppies in July

Little poppies, little hell flames,
Do you do no harm?

You flicker. I cannot touch you.
I put my hands among the flames. Nothing burns.

And it exhausts me to watch you   5
Flickering like that, wrinkly and clear red, like the skin of a mouth.

A mouth just bloodied.
Little bloody skirts!

There are fumes that I cannot touch.
Where are your opiates, your nauseous capsules?   10

If I could bleed, or sleep! —
If my mouth could marry a hurt like that!

Or your liquors seep to me, in this glass capsule,
Dulling and stilling.

But colourless. Colourless.   15

Glossary

10	*opiates*	a class of drug; heroin and morphine are opiates; opium comes from an unripe poppy seed
10	*nauseous capsules*	tablets causing the taker to feel they want to vomit
13	*liquors*	a liquid solution of a drug or chemical
13	*glass capsule*	a bell jar, the kind used in scientific experiments or to hold a specimen; Plath wrote an autobiographical novel called *The Bell Jar*

HIGHER LEVEL

Guidelines

Plath's marriage to Ted Hughes was breaking up, and Hughes was having an affair, when she penned this poem in 1962. In the poem Plath **subverts** the usual symbolism associated with poppies – remembrance, peace and the warmth of summer – and instead makes the poppies a **dark and threatening presence** that might hurt or numb the poet.

Between the end of September and 1 December 1962, Plath wrote forty of her 'Ariel' poems in an 'astonishing blaze of creativity' (Stevenson). In a letter to her friend Ruth Fainlight she wrote, 'the muse has come to live here, now Ted has gone'. Stevenson says 'Poppies in July' is Plath 'At the manic extreme' where there were 'great storms, projected outwards in vituperative exorcism of ferocious tirades'.

The Bell Jar

Writing under the pseudonym 'Victoria Lucas', Plath published her autobiographical novel *The Bell Jar* in 1963. The protagonist Esther Greenwood (representing Plath) becomes a guest editor, has ambitions to be a published poet, is rejected when she applies to join a creative writing class, has a breakdown and undergoes electroshock therapy. These experiences lead to suicide attempts and closely mirror Plath's life.

Commentary

Couplet 1

The affectionate 'Little' at the beginning of the poem describing the poppies quickly darkens as 'Little poppies' become 'little hell flames', suggesting **suffering and torment**. When the speaker asks, 'Do you do no harm?' the accusatory tone suggests that the poppies have deceived her. They seemed harmless and sweet, but they are actually destructive 'little hell flames'. The poet's anguish is clear; perhaps they have **deceived** her like she felt her husband had. The vibrant red poppies were in abundance in the English countryside during July, and the poet **projects** her torment and pain onto them. She is going through 'hell' and so sees the world around her in these terms.

Couplet 2

The speaker **extends the flame image** by comparing the movement of the poppies' delicate, papery petals flapping in the breeze to the flickering of flames, but when Plath tries to touch these 'flames', 'I cannot touch you' and 'Nothing burns'. These last two words should be a positive thing, yet they sound rueful, as if she is disappointed not to be burned. Perhaps she is so numb that she is **incapable of feeling**. This is a state Plath feared above all else, as far back as 'Black Rook in Rainy Weather', with the poet's fear 'Of total neutrality'.

Couplets 3 and 4

The speaker can only watch the poppies 'Flickering' and even this 'exhausts' her. The broad vowel sounds in this part of the poem **emphasise this extreme lethargy**: listen to the 'au', 'ou' and 'oo' sounds of these four lines. This lethargy soon turns to vitriol when Plath rails against the poppies as if disgusted by them, for they are like 'the skin of a mouth'. Is the sensual connotation of a red mouth negated or simply twisted by the next line; does 'A mouth just bloodied' suggest that the mouth has been punched? The shape of the poppy flower when upside down is like 'Little bloody skirts!' This disturbing image is **ambiguous**; it could allude to Hughes' lover Assia, Plath herself, menstrual blood or even miscarriage. **Sexuality and suffering in women combine** in this **metaphor** just as blood and fire combine in this stanza to produce dramatic and unsettling images.

Sylvia Plath

Couplet 5

Plath next considers the product of the unripe poppy seed, opium, a drug that is 'Dulling and stilling'. Just as the flames don't 'touch' her, neither do the fumes of the burning poppy seeds. Nothing brings relief or release. Her tone in the questions of line 10 is manic in its desperate yearning: 'Where are your opiates'. She is prepared to suffer the 'nauseous' side-effects of the drug if it will help her.

Betrayal

Plath had recently discovered love letters from Assia Wevill, her husband's lover, in Hughes' attic study, and had intercepted a call from Wevill to Hughes. She took the letters to the garden where she burned them on a bonfire, relating directly to the imagery of flames in the poem. She declared that she had 'given her heart away and could never get it back'.

Couplet 6

The speaker's anguished state becomes even more intense in her futile plea for pain or oblivion: 'If I could bleed, or sleep! –'. The **exclamation mark and dash** here **intensify** the desperation and despair expressed in this wish for some extreme of agony or unconsciousness. 'If my mouth could marry a hurt like that!' increases her desperation further. It is a startling line combining the rage, violence and sexuality pervading the poem. Perhaps Plath is reminded of her first meeting with Hughes at a Cambridge party where she famously bit him on the cheek, drawing blood. She wrote in her journal that she left him with, 'a swelling ring-moat of tooth marks'. It is as if she is **both fascinated and appalled by the intensity of the raging passion** she is feeling. The poem reaches its **emotional climax** here.

Couplet 7

The speaker's mood **deflates** as she becomes exhausted and more passive in her desires – 'Or your liquors seep to me'. She addresses a 'glass capsule' which, if the contents are ingested, she hopes will be 'Dulling and stilling'.

Line 15

The last line stands alone as if she is too exhausted to complete the couplet. What she craves is to be 'colourless. Colourless'. Is this a death wish where the speaker rejects the blood and fire in favour of a colourless fume which will bring on oblivion? Consider the manner of Plath's suicide described in the biography.

HIGHER LEVEL

Themes and imagery

The poppies of the title are clearly the central image in the poem and take on **very original and powerful symbolism** at the hands of the poet. They represent the relief she longs for, but this 'relief' is destructive. The poppies are the fire, blood and numbness she desperately craves to escape her unbearable reality.

Blood and fire dominate the first part of the poem inspired by the vivid red of the poppies' petals. Poppies are a very delicate flower with petals so fragile they are almost transparent – 'clear red' – but Plath's poppies are fierce and powerful 'flames', a 'bloodied mouth' and a powerful drug. By addressing them directly – 'Do you do no harm?' – Plath personifies the poppies. Colour is often an important aspect of Plath's symbolism; red is the colour of danger and passion, 'the blood and pain of continuing life' according to one biographer, but the poet is done with these things. What she longs for most by the end, with 'colourless. Colourless', is to be **nothing**, to feel nothing.

Bell jars

The image of the 'glass capsule' (bell jar) is a recurrent one in Plath's work. References to bell jars and liquor suggest hospital and museum specimens kept in chemical solutions. Plath witnessed such specimens when she posed as a medical student and observed an anatomical dissection. The experience proved traumatic. In this case, the imagery suggests that the speaker sees herself as trapped in a glass jar, like an exhibit in a museum or a laboratory.

Language and form

Short statements create drama; there is a **bare, terse effect** as if the poet is struggling to express her pain. The balance of short and long lines in unrhymed couplets, and careful punctuation, emphasise this **struggle** further and contrast all the more starkly with the lone last line. Look at how **question and exclamation marks are used to intensify the drama** and longing the speaker wishes to convey, for example 'If I could bleed or sleep!' For such a short poem **the range in tone is broad**: at first affectionate, then harsh, accusatory, observant, longing, exhausted, fascinated, disgusted, repulsed, frustrated, anguished and, at the end, a mix of resignation and yearning. Examine the use and effect of sound, for example the soft **sibilance** and long vowels emphasise the longing in the line, 'Where are your opiates, your nauseous capsules?'

This poem is **a lyric**, which is a formal type of poetry **expressing personal emotions or feelings**, usually written in the **first person**. Carrying the image of the mouth from the third to the fourth couplets makes this the most passionately intense section of the poem – 'Little bloody skirts!' The pun here on 'bloody' means Plath can express a lot in a short line. Think about the variety of interpretations this line might have.

SNAPSHOT

- Misleading title
- Unusual symbolism of poppies
- Short dramatic statements and questions
- Personification
- Contrast between strong emotion and exhaustion
- Startling imagery
- Colour and lack of it
- Intricate sound patterns
- Concludes with wish for annihilation

Exam-Style Questions

Understanding the poem

1. How are the poppies personified in the first couplet and how does the speaker feel towards them?
2. Despite thinking that the poppies will burn her, the speaker longs to touch them. Why, do you think, is this?
3. Read lines 5–8 again and explain the comparisons Plath uses here. What is your interpretation of each comparison/image?
4. Why, do you think, does the speaker question the poppies about their 'opiates'?
5. Explain the wishes the speaker expresses in the sixth and seventh couplet.
6. What is the wish expressed by the speaker at the end of the poem? How does the wish make you feel? Comment on the effect of the repetition here.

Thinking about the poem

1. Choose the two images from the poem which you found most striking and explain why you chose them.
2. What sound effects did you notice in the poem; briefly comment on the effect of some of them.
3. Complete the statement below that is closest to your own feelings for the speaker of the poem and explain your choice:
    - I admire the speaker because …
    - I pity the speaker because …
    - I am fascinated by the speaker because …
    - I can or cannot relate to the speaker because …
4. In your opinion, what is the theme of this poem?
5. Find and read Plath's poem 'Poppies in October' and compare it to this poem.

Imagining

1. Imagine you are Plath's friend or husband and have read the poem. Write a letter to her in response to it.
2. Find, describe or draw images to accompany each couplet and combine them into a format for display.

HIGHER LEVEL

Before you read

 What things are you most afraid of? Do you think people should face their fears? Why or why not? Have you had experience of this? Discuss this with a partner and feed back your ideas to the class.

The Arrival of the Bee Box

I ordered this, this clean wood box
Square as a chair and almost too heavy to lift.
I would say it was the coffin of a midget
Or a square baby
Were there not such a din in it.   5

The box is locked, it is dangerous.
I have to live with it overnight
And I can't keep away from it.
There are no windows, so I can't see what is in there.
There is only a little grid, no exit.   10

I put my eye to the grid.
It is dark, dark,
With the swarmy feeling of African hands
Minute and shrunk for export,
Black on black, angrily clambering.   15

How can I let them out?
It is the noise that appals me most of all,
The unintelligible syllables.
It is like a Roman mob,
Small, taken one by one, but my god, together!   20

I lay my ear to furious Latin.
I am not a Caesar.
I have simply ordered a box of maniacs.
They can be sent back.
They can die, I need feed them nothing, I am the owner.   25

I wonder how hungry they are.
I wonder if they would forget me
If I just undid the locks and stood back and turned into a tree.
There is the laburnum, its blond colonnades,
And the petticoats of the cherry.   30

They might ignore me immediately
In my moon suit and funeral veil.
I am no source of honey
So why should they turn on me?
Tomorrow I will be sweet God, I will set them free.   35

The box is only temporary.

Glossary

Line	Term
5	*din*: loud noise
13	*swarmy*: moving together in large numbers
15	*clambering*: climbing awkwardly
29	*laburnum*: tree with long bunches of yellow flowers
29	*colonnades*: rows of columns
30	*petticoats of the cherry*: tree with full pale pink blossoms which are compared to a type of old-fashioned underclothing
32	*moon suit*: astronaut's space-suit, which looks like a beekeeper's protective clothing

Guidelines

In 1962, Plath and Hughes had decided to take up bee-keeping, but they split shortly before this poem was written. Hughes had had an affair, and although the couple tried to repair the damage done with a holiday in Ireland in September, by October they had separated. Plath was devastated and felt deep anger, confusion and depression. Her father, Otto, was an expert on bees and had even written a book on the subject. This is one of a sequence of five bee poems which **explore themes of fear, identity, entrapment, freedom and control**.

> **Pandora**
>
> The poem reminds us of the legend of Pandora's Box which Pandora was told never to open, but driven by curiosity she opens the box and releases all of mankind's evils onto the world. The only thing which remained inside was hope.

Commentary

Stanza 1

'I ordered' opens the poem with an integral concept: control or the lack of it. Plath has ordered a bee box, though now it has arrived she seems surprised and hesitant about it, as conveyed in the repetition of 'this, this clean wood box'. The language and imagery is at first straightforward and conversational; 'Square as a chair' makes the box seem **ordinary, domestic, a simple object**. The poet imagines what this might be – 'the coffin of a midget / Or a square baby' – giving the poem a nightmarishly surreal quality. **Death** is clearly suggested here – the death of someone small. 'Din in it' has an onomatopoeic quality, conveying the **furious buzzing** of the confined bees. **This noise builds as the poem progresses**, forcing the poet to make a decision.

HIGHER LEVEL

Stanza 2
The speaker is conflicted, and she dances between **fear and fascination**. 'The box is locked, it is dangerous', with 'no exit', creating a hugely claustrophobic sense of **confinement** like a windowless prison cell, yet she 'can't keep away from it'. The poet is captivated by the noise and by curiosity much like Pandora.

Stanza 3
A dark sense of **desperation** dominates here. The bees are like exported African slaves, 'angrily clambering', their entrapment causing them to panic and trample each other. The repetition of 'dark' and 'black' emphasises this mood. She has ordered the bees to make honey for her just as slaves were forced to work by their white American 'owners'. Plath had an interest in African sculpture and folktales but has been criticised by some commentators for using this metaphor.

Stanzas 4 and 5
Now the bees are compared to a 'Roman mob', which was a powerful force in classical times. Mobs often rioted causing mayhem and killing those in power – 'How can I let them out?' Plath is most disturbed by the noise, which might represent the thoughts swarming in her own mind. **She'd like to release this noise** (these thoughts), but knows she cannot control them once they're out; she fears their wrath and collective force: 'Small, taken one by one, but my god, together!' 'Unintelligible syllables' echoes how impossible it is for Plath to interpret the 'furious Latin' of the bees. 'I have simply ordered a box of maniacs' is wryly **humorous**; although she's growing more **exasperated** she sees the funny side. She realises she cannot command them, so her only alternatives are to return them or starve the bees to death. The box will become the coffin she imagined in stanza 1. Only for a moment does she consider adopting the role of becoming Caesar or slave owner, with the power of life or death.

Stanzas 6 and 7
'I wonder how hungry they are.' Immediately Plath's humane, nurturing side rejects the idea of starving the bees. Calmer now, **she begins to explore how to release the bees** without incurring harm to herself: 'If I just undid the locks and stood back and turned into a tree.' Here she evokes the myth of Daphne, who in Greek mythology was turned into a tree after begging the gods to save her from the god Apollo's relentless amorous pursuit. The pretty feminine description of the laburnum and cherry trees contrasts with the much darker imagery used earlier, and **lightens** the previously heavy atmosphere. The speaker hopes the bees 'might just ignore me', as she is 'no source of honey'. She makes her decision: 'Tomorrow I will be sweet God, I will set them free'. Despite the air of determination here there is also hesitancy as the speaker postpones any immediate action.

Final line
The last line is left on its own, emphasising its significance – the bees will not remain in the box for long. There are a number of possible interpretations in terms of the poem as a whole:

486 / DISCOVERY: POETRY ANTHOLOGY

Sylvia Plath

- The speaker will soon release the bees but fears they will harm her.
- **We cannot repress our feelings forever, they must be released – Plath does this by writing the poem.** Does she plan a more final release for her inner turmoil?
- The beekeeper opening the box is like someone venting their inner turmoil, like a poet exploring painful and dark themes: the process may be harmful to the poet. Thus the poem is about **the kind of poetry Plath writes – deeply personal and often exploring difficult memories and experiences**. She is appalled by what she has been through, but is compelled to investigate it further.
- If poetry is 'the box' that Plath uses to express her emotions, its cathartic effects do not last. Soon the darkness will come again. This is an idea explored in 'Black Rook in Rainy Weather' also.

Themes

On the surface the poem explores the arrival of the bee box and the speaker's mixed emotions of fear and fascination. She explores ideas of power and control over the bees while seeing herself in different roles: as a Caesar, owner, a tree, an astronaut, a mourner and even God, thus exploring identity. The poem is not only about control and entrapment, but also **poetry itself**, which is **an attempt to master and shape an outpouring of thoughts and emotions**. In this reading, the bees are the speaker's heart and mind while the box is her outer self, and the poet explores **how the inner world takes form through communication**, sometimes to create a socially acceptable 'I'. On this deeper level we can interpret the poem as **highly symbolic**. The **'swarmy' bees represent the tumultuous emotions and thoughts inside the speaker** who is trying to decide how best to deal with her feelings.

> **The Forge**
>
> **Compare the imagery in this poem with that in Heaney's 'The Forge'. How do the two poems explore through metaphor the craft of poetry?**

Imagery

Plath uses highly original imagery rooted in nature. The box itself is described with surreal dark humour as 'the coffin of a midget / Or a square baby'. The bees are **personified**: they are tiny Africans, and then a Roman mob conveying their angry sound. The **trees** too are metaphorically a 'colonnade' (linking them to the simile of a Roman mob) and 'petticoats', as if the frilly blossoms of the cherry tree are underwear! The poet juxtaposes two ideas when she compares her bee-keeping attire to a 'moon suit' and 'funeral veil', suggesting adventure and exploration on one hand, and death on the other.

Questions

1. How is the bee box described and what is the speaker's initial attitude towards it in the first two stanzas?
2. The bees are compared to tiny Africans and a Roman mob. What does each comparison demonstrate about the bees?
3. The speaker is unsure what to do with the bees. What options does she consider in stanzas 5 and 6?
4. 'I am the owner.' Are you convinced by the speaker's determination here? Explain.
5. What decision is made in the last stanza?
6. Why does Plath leave the last line on its own, do you think?
7. In your opinion, is the ending of the poem a positive one?
8. Which of the following statements best describes the theme of the poem?
   - It is a poem about bees
   - It is a poem about inner turmoil
   - It is a poem about writing poetry

   Explain your choice with reference to the poem as a whole.
9. Trace the tone of the poem as it progresses. Where does the tone change? How does it change and why?
10. Write a note about the imagery the poet uses and the effect these images have.
11. Plath once said, 'I think I would like to call myself "The girl who wanted to be God." … But, oh, I cry out against it'. Discuss Plath's statement in response to 'The Arrival of the Bee Box'.
12. What impression of Plath have you formed from reading this poem? What aspects of the poem created this impression for you? In pairs or groups, share your thoughts.
13. Write two diary entries for the speaker, one on the day that the bee box arrives and another for the following day.

Sylvia Plath

Before you read

Imagine you are the parent of a newborn baby. What hopes and dreams do you think you would have for the child?

Child

Your clear eye is the one absolutely beautiful thing.
I want to fill it with colour and ducks,
The zoo of the new

Whose names you meditate –
April snowdrop, Indian pipe,
Little   5

Stalk without wrinkle,
Pool in which images
Should be grand and classical

Not this troublous   10
Wringing of hands, this dark
Ceiling without a star.

Glossary

Line	
4	*meditate*: reflect upon, think deeply about
5	*snowdrop*: small plant with drooping bell-like white flowers, often the first flower of spring
5	*Indian pipe*: small woodland flower that feeds on rotting plants
10	*troublous*: agitated, unsettled, disturbed

Guidelines

From the collection *Winter Trees* (1971), published eight years after Plath's death. The poem was written at the end of January 1963, just after her son's first birthday and less than two weeks before Plath's suicide at the age of thirty.

The poet expresses her **hopes and dreams for her child** and describes her **own feelings about being a mother**.

Commentary

Stanza 1
The opening line of the poem is **a statement of pure love and adoration**. To the speaker, the child's eye is perfection: it is 'clear', in other words pure, untainted and full of innocence. It is the 'one absolutely beautiful thing'. The speaker wants the child to see only beauty in the world, to 'fill' the eye of her child with 'colour and ducks, / The zoo of the new'. Perhaps the speaker means the beauty of nature here or may even be thinking of the toys and teddy-bears a child would have. Either way, the child should see only lovely things that will entertain and inspire them.

Stanzas 2 and 3
The speaker imagines the child becoming fascinated by the names of things in the natural world – 'April snowdrop, Indian pipe' – which are both woodland flowers. It is worth noting that snowdrops are delicate and pretty white spring flowers that suggest birth, purity and innocence. 'Indian pipe', however, lives in darker parts of the woods and feeds on the rotting matter of other plants. The name is unusual though and will perhaps be amusing for the child. Plath clearly would like her own fascination with words and her love of nature to pass onto her child, who is a 'Stalk without wrinkle'; like the delicate snowdrop it **is fresh, new and beautiful**, unspoiled by life's trials and tribulations.

The **child's eye** is a 'Pool in which images / Should be grand and classical'; the speaker wishes her child to see only beauty and culture, not the 'dark Ceiling' that is his mother. The last stanza is the opposite of the hope-filled first three in its despair and negativity. 'Should' here is less certain than 'I want to fill it' from line 2. There is an **uncertainty** here and a **foreshadowing of the darkness to come**.

Stanza 4
The speaker sees herself reduced to a 'troublous / Wringing of hands', a gesture of deep agitation and hopelessness. The speaker feels that her presence will only bring darkness to her son's life, and he **would be better off without her**. It is deeply sad that such a gifted poet with a brilliant mind felt this way about herself. That she sees herself as a 'dark / Ceiling without a star' is an absolutely desolate statement which is heart-breaking for the reader.

Themes

Motherhood is a recurring theme in Plath's poetry. 'Morning Song' is another example. Both poems celebrate the child but have a darker side where **the mother feels displaced, or in this case considers herself an obstacle to her child's happiness**. The further tragedy is that Nicholas took his own life (at the age of 47) just as his mother had.

The theme of **hope** is expressed; the first three stanzas list the speaker's **hopes and dreams for the child**. The wishes expressed are for the child's eye to be filled with colour, nature, culture and everything that is beautiful and edifying in the world. The theme of love is strong and the first three stanzas are an outpouring of this fierce love, which contains her hopes and dreams for the child as it grows. **Then there is the absolute lack of love or regard the speaker** has for herself, which is a strong and heart-breaking contrast in the poem.

Sylvia Plath

Imagery

The child's eye is the key image here. It is 'clear'; in other words, absolutely **new and free from any taint** the challenges of life could cause; there is a **strong sense of potential and possibility** as the speaker tells the infant all of the things she wants them to experience. They are **compared to a pool to be filled with beauty**. Pools and mirrors that reflect are featured in many of Plath's poems; in the poem 'Mirror', the eye or pool can absorb what it reflects and be affected by that. For this reason the speaker doesn't want herself to be reflected. 'Colour and ducks' are childlike, fun and carefree, while 'grand and classical' images are more grown up. Thus the two sets of images communicate the speaker's hopes both for the younger child and a more grown up person.

'This troublous / Wringing of hands' is a **startling image**; the speaker has reduced her whole being to a single anxious gesture. She describes herself as a 'dark ceiling', in sharp contrast to the bright and colourful imagery of the previous stanzas. This suggests that **the speaker sees herself as blocking the child**, hindering their enjoyment of life. To further emphasise this, the final words 'without a star' convey utter despair. There is no ray of hope. If we go back to 'Black Rook in Rainy Weather', the fear that the 'light' of relief and inspiration may strike at any time seems to have been replaced with the certainty that the 'light' has disappeared forever.

Language and form

The poem's title, language and form are **stripped back** to brief simplicity. 'Child' is at once an affectionate dedication of the poem to her son but the title conversely suggests distance too, unlike for instance if she'd used 'My Child' or the baby's name. Is Plath just making the title more universal, accessible and therefore more relevant to her readers, or does this reflect the distance she feels in terms of her emotional connection to the child? The **language is straightforward and even playful**, for example the 'zoo of the new' rhyme, which could be from a children's verse. It is as if the speaker really wants the child to understand what she's saying.

This simplicity is echoed in the structure of the poem, which consists of four unrhymed tercets. The first line is the longest, effusive in its enthusiasm for the striking beauty of the child's 'clear eye'. The first line is a contained sentence while the rest of the poem forms the second sentence; **the speaker becomes carried away by the list of things she is eager for this child to experience**, until she turns her gaze inward and regards herself, which brings the poem to an abrupt end.

The phrase 'agitation of hands' from Plath's poem 'Mirror' closely echoes 'Wringing of hands' here. It is perhaps a gesture she associates closely with herself. It also suggests the idea of the **child as a mirror of the mother** – this would explain the poet's fear of becoming a 'dark / Ceiling without a star' in the child's eyes.

SNAPSHOT

- Mother caught between love and despair
- Simple yet lyrical language
- Lack of confidence that speaker can create joy for child
- Hopes and dreams for child
- Carefully phrased and controlled poem
- Playful humour in imagery
- Troubled ending

Exam-Style Questions

Understanding the poem

1	What is the tone of the first line?
2	List in your own words the things the speaker wishes the child to experience. Are they typical of what most parents would wish for their baby? Explain.
3	Comment on the effect of the references to flowers and plants in lines 5–7.
4	What is the effect of the metaphor where Plath compares the child's eye to a pool? Have you seen this idea elsewhere in Plath's work? Where?
5	'Clear', 'zoo' and 'Little'. Comment on Plath's use of these words in the context of the poem.
6	How did reading the last stanza make you feel?
7	What is the speaker trying to say through the imagery she uses in the last stanza?

Thinking about the poem

1	'The poem presents a speaker who has lost confidence in her ability to create joy.' Do you agree with this interpretation of the poem?
2	Compare the end of this poem to the endings of 'The Arrival of the Bee Box' and 'Poppies in July'. How is the end of each poem similar or different?
3	Choose two images that you particularly like or dislike in the poem. In pairs or groups, explain why you chose them.
4	Which of the following statements is closest to your own view of the poem? ■ It is a poem about love ■ It is a poem about despair ■ It is a poem about innocence Explain your choice with reference to the poem as a whole.

Imagining

1	Imagine and write the letter or poem the grown-up child might write in response.
2	If this poem were depicted as a photograph, what would it look like? Where would the child and mother be? In what place? In what position?

Exam-Preparation Questions

1	Andrew Wilson said, 'Plath, as a child, as a woman and as a poet, was constantly in search of an overarching metaphor that would capture her strange complexity.' Do you agree with this assessment of Wilson's in the light of the poetry on your course by Sylvia Plath?
2	'Most of us who knew Sylvia knew a different Sylvia.' How true is this assessment by her friend Clarissa Roche when applied to the different voices, personas and perspectives you have encountered in Plath's poetry? Did you find that her poetry is a reflection of her different 'selves'?
3	Plath's biographer Anne Stevenson said of Plath, 'Haunted by a fear of her own disintegration, she kept herself together by defining herself, writing constantly about herself, so that everyone could see her there, fighting and conquering an outside world that forever threatened her frail being.' Discuss this analysis in the light of the poetry you have studied by Plath.
4	What aspects of Plath's style most captured your attention and why? In your answer you may refer to some of the following or other aspects you have chosen: ■ Form and structure ■ Recurring images ■ Sound effects ■ Use of personas ■ Contrast
5	If you had to choose one poem which you found to be most typical of Plath to include in an anthology, which would it be and why is it typical of her work? You should refer to her other poems on your course to back up the points you make.
6	Write a personal response to Sylvia Plath's poetry with regard to the effect her work has had on you, your opinion of her as a person and a poet, and which poems you liked or disliked most and why.
7	In your opinion is Plath a feminist poet, a political poet, or neither? Explain your views with reference to at least five poems by Plath on your course.
8	Do you agree with Plath's teacher who said she had 'a lyric gift beyond the ordinary'? Explain your answer with reference to the poems you have studied.
9	'Conflict and contrast is at the very heart of Plath's poetry: the tension between how things seem and what is really happening, between light and dark, hope and despair, love and hate.' Discuss the above statement with reference to the poems of Sylvia Plath which you have studied.
10	Analyse images of water and reflection in the poetry of Sylvia Plath.

SNAPSHOT SYLVIA PLATH

- Use of personas
- Confessional poet
- Central image highly symbolic and indicative of poet's inscape
- Importance of water and reflection
- Love of nature evident
- Struggles with self-doubt and depression
- Balance of opposites; hope and despair, light and dark, etc.
- Explores extreme emotions and states of mind
- Influence of childhood experiences and break-up of marriage
- Original and powerful imagery

HIGHER LEVEL

Sample Essay

'Plath's provocative imagery serves to highlight the intense emotions expressed in her poetry.'

To what extent do you agree or disagree with this assessment of her poetry? Support your answer with suitable reference to the poetry of Sylvia Plath on your course.

> **Defines terms of question by listing reactions provoked by imagery**

The startling imagery I encountered in the poetry of Sylvia Plath provoked many strong reactions in me including sympathy, shock, admiration, amusement and fear, because her images powerfully convey her intense feelings. '… This dark / Ceiling without a star' is a good example of this. In 'Child', Plath is expressing her immense despair and fear. In this powerful image she depicts herself as an obstacle to her young son's happiness. She feels that she obstructs her child's chance of seeing beauty and having a happy life.

> **Intense emotions mentioned in response to image and reaction provoked explained**

I found this image striking; I felt deep sympathy for the speaker in the poem as she uses this simple yet thought-provoking metaphor to convey her sense of inadequacy and her self-loathing. I pitied this talented woman and longed to tell her how gifted she clearly was and how much I had enjoyed studying her work. In her poetry Plath's imagery was extremely provocative and highlighted clearly the intense emotions she expresses in her work, the most common of which I found to be fear.

> **Stance in response to question clearly taken**

> **Link to previous point clearly made as new poem introduced and point developed**

Fear is overwhelmingly present in Plath's imagery – fear of not being a good enough mother, in 'Child'; fear of losing her poetic gift, which is at the very heart of the beautiful poem 'Black Rook in Rainy Weather'. Here Plath is apprehensive about inspiration deserting her though she is inspired at the time to write this poem. I felt frustrated that she was so full of self-doubt and really pitied Plath her insecurity. In the poem she nervously wonders when her next inspired moment will occur and uses the beautiful image of a 'wet black rook / Arranging and rearranging its feathers in the rain', which can 'so shine' that they lift her senses and make her feel alive, thus giving her 'A brief respite from fear / Of total neutrality'. I found this image provoked a strong reaction in me. Like Plath I am struck by the beauty of nature and the transformative power of light, 'As if a celestial burning took / Possession', but I felt an undercurrent of fear, and I worried for Plath too. The bleakness of the poet's world when not inspired seemed frightening to me in its almost apocalyptic emptiness – 'this dull, ruinous landscape', 'season / Of fatigue'. Plath uses images of light and dark skilfully in the poem to convey the same contrast in her life, the 'celestial burning' she feels when the muse is upon her contrasts starkly with the pathetic fallacy of the rainy, dull day, the 'desultory weather' and its decaying 'spotted leaves'. These descriptions speak so strongly of how bleak her world is when she does not feel inspired. My admiration for her beautiful writing and sympathy for this tortured soul were provoked.

> **Personal response**

> **Like the 'rook' image earlier in the paragraph, imagery of light and dark explored**

> **Consistency of approach**

'Finisterre' is another poem expressing Plath's intense fear, and her imagery reflects this. She depicts the cliffs of this dangerous French bay as 'knuckled and rheumatic, / Cramped on nothing. Black'. As in 'Black Rook …' the landscape is bleak. Perhaps Plath is using descriptions of nature to convey her inner landscape, which seems to be fearful, anguished and stark. A ghostly mist, possibly the souls of drowned sailors, 'stuffs' the poet's mouth 'with cotton', and she is deeply shaken by the experience – 'beaded with

> **Intense emotion conveyed through imagery**

494 / DISCOVERY: POETRY ANTHOLOGY

Sylvia Plath

Provocative – student's reaction provoked by image addressed

tears'. I was startled by this frightening image. Plath seems to fear and yet be fascinated by the sea in equal measure. In 'Finisterre' Plath comments on 'the beautiful formlessness' of the sea and I was interested to see Plath again use water as an image to convey her intense feelings of fear and her thoughts of death and annihilation. In 'Morning Song', Plath compares herself to a cloud whose dispersal into nothingness is reflected in the puddle it has distilled. In 'Mirror' she uses the persona of a silver mirror which compares itself to a lake in which has 'drowned a young girl'; 'an old woman / Rises … day after day, like a terrible fish'. It seems to me that in these images Plath fears she will disappear unnoticed and in awful pain. I felt great sympathy for her; if only she knew just how successful she would become after her death and how much comfort her work has given to fellow sufferers of depression.

Personal response

In all of the poems so far there is a nightmarish intensity to many of the images, especially those involving water, and I feel that Plath is conveying panic and fear. The effect on me was startling. Her poems are so intense the reader cannot help but be captivated and affected deeply. I was filled with admiration for her poetic talent and her honesty. This empathy and intensity is perhaps strongest in the poems 'Poppies in July' and 'Elm'. In 'Poppies …', Plath compares the vibrant red flowers to 'hell flames', 'A mouth just bloodied' and 'bloody skirts'. I found her imagery here hugely original, such a different take on pretty, delicate summer flowers. Plath uses these images and comparisons to express her anger and hurt at her husband's affair and his desertion of her. Plath's rage and longing to escape from her emotions struck me. The intensity she builds up in the poem dissipates abruptly as she instead yearns for oblivion, symbolised by the narcotic effect of the poppies – she longs for their 'nauseous capsules' to dull and still her torment. She ends the poem on almost an 'anti-image', longing to be 'colourless. Colourless'. I found this poem captivating in its passion and heart-breaking in that Plath was so hurt that she wished to be nothing. It struck me that the 'fear / Of total neutrality' she so feared in 'Black Rook …' has become an anguished longing for just that. This is a tragic idea, as if Plath has totally given up on herself, and leading eventually to her image at the end of 'Child', where she reduces her whole self to a 'troublous / Wringing of hands' and a 'dark / Ceiling without a star'.

Intense emotions

Strong engagement as response provoked by image explained

Use of personas acknowledged and effective synopsis of poem

'Elm' is equally disturbing and its imagery is arguably the darkest of any of her poems. The elm tree and the 'You' persona in the poem list their fears and suffering in a litany of surreally nightmarish images to convey the intense despair and fear Plath feels. The poem made me feel I had an insight into why someone so gifted might feel compelled to loathe themselves and wish to take their own life. Love is compared to a bolting horse – 'How you lie and cry after it / Listen: these are its hooves'. The image that most struck a chord with me was quite obscure; 'I am terrified by this dark thing' is an effective way to represent that indefinable gnawing anxiety most people suffer at one time or another, like a feathery creature inside us which twists and turns, poisoning us with 'its malignity'. The fear of not being good enough has reduced Plath to seeing herself as a collection of 'isolate, slow faults' which will ultimately destroy her: 'That kill, that kill, that kill'. Plath's imagery here shocked me. I wished she had never suffered as she did; she should have seen how talented she was. I felt deeply that a terrible irony was at work – if Plath had not suffered from such mental torments, would her poetry have been as powerful? Her true legacy, however, is to have written honest, original and unsettling poetry with consummate skill. She is so much more than a 'dark / Ceiling without a star', and I am grateful that that star shone on after her death enough to allow me to explore and admire her work.

The imagery in this poem could have been expanded on in much more detail

Final statement conveys strong engagement with poems and poet and 'star' comment sums up overall reaction provoked by Plath's poetry on the course

HIGHER LEVEL

ESSAY CHECKLIST			Yes √	No x
Purpose	Has the candidate understood the task?			
	Has the candidate responded to it in a thoughtful manner?			
	Has the candidate answered the question?			
Comment:				
Coherence	Has the candidate made convincing arguments?			
	Has the candidate linked ideas?			
	Does the essay have a sense of unity?			
Comment:				
Language	Is the essay written in an appropriate register?			
	Are ideas expressed in a clear way?			
	Is the writing fluent?			
Comment:				
Mechanics	Is the use of language accurate?			
	Are all words spelled correctly?			
	Does the punctuation help the reader?			
Comment:				

Robert Browning
1812–1889

Meeting at Night 498

Biography

Robert Browning was born in Camberwell, a suburb of London, in 1812. He lived with his parents and his sister until 1846, when he married the poet Elizabeth Barrett. Browning's parents supported him in his ambition to be a writer and he and his sister, Sarianna, gained a liberal education from their parents and the family library of more than six thousand books. By the age of fourteen Browning was fluent in five languages.

In 1845, Browning read the poetry of Elizabeth Barrett and wrote to her declaring, 'I love your verses with all my heart.' Soon he told her that he loved her, too. Barrett was 36, six years older than he was, and invalided with a mysterious illness. She lived in London, ruled over by her strict father. During their courtship, conducted largely through letters, Barrett wrote a series of celebrated love sonnets. Knowing that her father would not agree to his daughter marrying a poor poet, the couple eloped to Florence in Italy where Elizabeth's health improved. The couple had a son. For fifteen years they lived and worked together side by side until Elizabeth's death in 1861.

By the time of Browning's death in 1889, he was considered one of England's greatest poets and philosophers. He is probably best remembered today for his poem 'The Pied Piper of Hamelin', a work that he himself did not rate very highly.

ORDINARY LEVEL

Before you read

 Share with a partner the most exciting journey you ever undertook and the circumstances that made it exciting.

Meeting at Night

I

The grey sea and the long black land;
And the yellow half-moon large and low;
And the startled little waves that leap
In fiery ringlets from their sleep,
As I gain the cove with pushing prow,   5
And quench its speed i' the slushy sand.

II

Then a mile of warm sea-scented beach;
Three fields to cross till a farm appears;
A tap at the pane, the quick sharp scratch
And blue spurt of a lighted match,   10
And a voice less loud, thro' its joys and fears,
Than the two hearts beating each to each!

Glossary

4	*ringlets*: ringlets were fashionable in Victorian times
5	*cove*: small sheltered bay on a rocky coast
5	*prow*: the front part of a boat
6	*quench*: (in this context) to bring to a stop

Guidelines

'Meeting at Night' was originally part of a longer poem called 'Night and Morning' first published in 1845. However, in the 1849 collection *Dramatic Romances and Lyrics*, Browning divided the poem into two. The first part became 'Meeting at Night' and the second 'Parting at Morning'. Browning often stated that his poetry was **dramatic rather than confessional** and refused to identify himself with the speaker in his poetry. However, it is surely no coincidence that he wrote a poem about a secret meeting between lovers in the year in which he eloped with Elizabeth Barrett.

Commentary

Stanza 1

The first stanza is purely descriptive. It describes a boat coming ashore in a cove at night.

There is one metaphor, which involves a word play on 'waves'. The little waves disturbed by the boat are described as leaping in fiery ringlets. 'Fiery' presumably relates to the light from the large, low moon. The description has a cinematic feel. The 'I' of line 5 seems almost incidental. We are given no clue to the identity of the person in the boat, or his motivation or purpose. (Browning identified the speaker of the poem as male, though there is nothing in the poem to establish this.)

Stanza 2

In the second stanza, the narrator continues his journey on foot. He does not have far to go. We learn that the destination is a farm. The final lines describe two lovers meeting in what appears to be a secret or forbidden act. The second stanza is narrated in the third person and has a similar cinematic feel as the first.

Themes and imagery

The poem describes a secret meeting or rendezvous between two lovers. The focus is on the journey of the man to reach the destination and the joy that both lovers feel when they meet. **Love is presented as an adventure**, with the man portrayed as the adventurer, the one undertaking the journey. The implied feelings that surround the adventure are excitement and anticipation. The stated feelings are fear and joy. The meeting of the lovers is surrounded in mystery. We know nothing of the two people involved, or the reason for meeting at night and the fear of discovery that surrounds the rendezvous. The narrator does not dwell on the virtues of the beloved or reflect on his own feelings. The poem is pure story. **It involves separation and reunion.** It is a love story charting a particular moment in the relationship. The drama comes from the fact that the love affair is conducted in secret. The unanswered questions add to the **sense of mystery**.

The imagery is simple and conventional and appeals to the senses. In the tradition of love poetry, the night-time and the moonlight are emphasised in 'the grey sea', 'the long black land', 'the yellow half-moon'. The movement of the boat disturbs the surface of the water and this leads to the most elaborate description in the poem: the personified waves are startled from their sleep (lines 3–4) and their movement is compared to 'fiery ringlets' (line 4). The 'pushing prow' (line 5) suggest the energy and eagerness of the lover to reach his destination.

In the second stanza, the beach is described in simple, effective terms, as 'warm sea-scented'.

In three onomatopoeic words, 'tap', 'scratch', 'spurt', the poet describes the sounds that signal the arrival of the lover and **the secrecy of the visit**, when each small sound might lead to discovery. **The imagery has a cinematic quality.** There is a change from the sweeping landscape imagery of stanza one to the intimacy of the match being struck and the two hearts beating 'each to each!' (line 12) in the second stanza. The imagery of the flaring match suggests the flame of love between the lovers, a love concealed in the darkness in which they meet.

ORDINARY LEVEL

Language and form

The poem takes the form of **a dramatic lyric**. The narrative is a simple one told in two stanzas of six lines each. Each stanza is composed of a single sentence. The punctuation of each sentence is closely paralleled, with enjambment occurring between lines 3 and 4 in both cases, which speeds up the movement of the poem. Apart from the punctuation, both stanzas follow a similar pattern of rhyme, the rhyming sounds repeated in reverse order: *abccba* (stanza 1) and *deffed* (stanza 2). Each stanza is enclosed by the rhyme between the first and last line of the stanza.

The poem is written in a loose form of iambic tetrameter; lines of four iambs (an iamb is a metrical foot consisting of an unstressed syllable followed by a stressed one, which creates a trotting, ta-TUM rhythm). This metre is associated with **songs and story-telling poetry**, where the action moves forward at pace. The use of this metre, the phrasing and the use of numerous monosyllabic words combine to create **a strong rhythm and sense of narrative propulsion**. The use of 'and' and 'then', and the clever use of punctuation, create the sensation of things happening in quick succession. The sense of drama is aided by the sound effects of the poem. Browning uses alliteration, consonance, assonance, rhyme and onomatopoeia to create **a lively soundscape**. The consonant 'l', for example, occurs ten times in the first three lines. The phrase 'pushing prow' (line 5), with its plosive sounds, catches the effort of the boatman, as the boat comes to shore. The onomatopoeic 'quench' (line 6) mimics the scrunching sound as the boat makes contact with the beach. The wonderful phrase 'slushy sand', and the full stop that follows it, brings the boat and the first part of the narrative to a complete stop.

In the enjambed lines 9–10, the drama and movement are intensified. The command of language is superb. Browning uses consonance, alliteration, punctuation, rhyme, onomatopoeia, phrasing and rhythm to create the **drama and excitement** of the lovers on the point of reuniting. The three stressed syllables and the 'scr' sound capture the scraping noise of the match being struck in the phrase 'the quick sharp scratch' (line 9).

The frantic pace is slowed in the final two lines of the poem. Line 11 is the longest in the poem. The long vowel sound of 'loud' and the comma that comes after it slow the line, as does the long stressed vowel in 'joys'. The repetition of 'each' in the final line brings the narrative to a satisfying conclusion.

Robert Browning

Exam-Style Questions

Understanding the poem

1. Describe the scene painted in the opening lines of the poem.
2. From the evidence of stanza 1, does the lover seem eager to reach his destination?
3. Describe the second part of the lover's journey, as described in the opening lines of the second stanza.
4. What sounds are emphasised in the second stanza?
5. What details in the second stanza suggest that the lovers fear discovery?

Thinking about the poem

1. What do you learn about the lovers from the poem?
2. What questions remain unanswered?
3. Which of the following statement is closest to your own reading of the poem?
   - The poem is about love
   - The poem is about adventure
   - The poem is about secrecy

   Explain your choice
4. Identify a striking phrase from the poem. Explain your choice.
5. The poem has real sense of pace and forward motion. How, in your view, is this achieved?
6. 'The descriptions in the poem have a cinematic feel.' Discuss.
7. 'The poem has nothing new to say about love, but it is an exciting poem.'
   Discuss this view of the poem.
8. Suggest an alternative title for the poem.

Imagining

1. Imagine you are the woman in the poem. Write a diary entry in which you describe the day of the meeting and your thoughts and feelings after your lover departed.
2. In small groups, prepare a reading of the poem that fully exploits the rich sound effects created by Browning.

SNAPSHOT
- Love as adventure
- Secret meeting
- Narrative drive
- Conventional imagery
- Cinematic
- Dramatic
- Carefully structured
- Rich-sounding

ORDINARY LEVEL

Kate Clanchy

b.1965

Driving to the Hospital — 503

Biography

Born in Glasgow, Scotland in 1965, Kate Clanchy is a poet, print and broadcast journalist, teacher, playwright and novelist. Educated in Edinburgh and, later, Oxford, Clanchy moved to London for a few years before settling in Oxfordshire, where she now lives.

She has won numerous awards, including the Somerset Maugham Award for her 1995 collection Slattern and the Scottish Arts Council Book Award for Samarkand (1999). She was awarded an MBE and was poet-in-residence for the UK Red Cross.

The poet Carol Ann Duffy taught her at Arvon (a charitable organisation in the UK that promotes creative writing) and was a major influence on Clanchy, whose poetry regularly tackles social and cultural issues, but often with a very personal slant. She has been criticised for describing the lives of women in overly traditional terms, but others see her differently. Jules Smith wrote that Clanchy is 'a sympathetic chronicler of female lives and experiences — her own and those of other women'.

She is married to Oxford academic Matthew Reynolds, and this poem details the journey to the hospital for the birth of their first son, Michael.

Kate Clanchy

Driving to the Hospital

We were low on petrol
so I said let's freewheel
when we get to the hill.
It was dawn and the city
Was nursing its quiet   5
And I liked the idea
Of arriving with barely
A crunch on the gravel.
You smiled kindly and
eased the clutch gently   10
and backed us out of
the driveway and patted
my knee with exactly
the gesture you used
when we were courting,   15
remember, on the way
to your brother's: I like
driving with my baby,
that's what you said. And
at the time I wondered   20
why my heart leapt and leapt.

Before you read

When you hear the phrase 'driving to the hospital', what thoughts come to mind? Do you have a specific experience relating to this? Does this phrase have positive or negative connotations for you?

Glossary

2	*freewheel*: using the slope of a hill to propel a vehicle rather than using the power of the engine
5	*nursing*: tending to, breast-feeding, looking after someone who is ill
15	*courting*: an old-fashioned term for dating

Guidelines

This poem comes from the collection *Newborn*, published in 2004, the same year in which Clanchy also edited *The Picador Book of Birth Poems*. *Newborn* chronicles pregnancy and birth in a sequence of poems. 'Driving to the Hospital' mixes the present with memories from the past to create a simple yet evocative poem full of love, hope and possibility, and it is one of a pair of poems from the collection that describe this momentous journey in the life of a couple.

Commentary

Lines 1–8
The couple in the car seem either to be lacking funds or ill-prepared for this important journey, 'we were low on petrol', but the speaker seems unruffled by this and calmly suggests 'let's freewheel / when we get to the hill'.

The setting is dawn, approaching a sleeping city. The idea that this couple are on their way to have a baby is reinforced by the image of the city 'nursing its quiet' like a mother nurses her infant. The speaker appreciates this tranquillity and hopes to arrive at the hospital with little fuss, 'with barely / a crunch on the gravel'. She seems to savour this calm and quiet, as these first lines show.

Lines 9–21
The attention now shifts to the speaker's partner, who is similarly calm and reassuring. He is driving the car and eager to show his partner affection and consideration. Words like 'kindly' and 'gently' demonstrate this. His loving pat on her knee evokes a memory from when they first dated, 'when we were courting'. She recalls a specific journey to his brother's when he had said to her 'I like / driving with my baby'. Recalling this moment now of course takes on a whole new significance. 'My baby' is no longer just a term of endearment for her; it has become literal now.

As they carry on their journey to experience the birth of their child she finally recalls the passion she felt in the early stages of their relationship and how this had taken her by surprise, 'at the time I wondered / why my heart leapt and leapt'.

Themes and imagery

The dawn setting is a fitting one. Dawn is often an image of new beginnings, of **birth and hope**. The unusual personification of the city as a nursing mother adds to this idea. The city is 'nursing its quiet' much like a new mother breastfeeds her baby. The theme of **birth** combines with the theme of **love** and this union can be seen clearly in the remembered phrase 'I like / driving with my baby'. The word 'baby' now has a twofold meaning; it was an affectionate term for the partner's girlfriend in the past, but now takes on a new significance as it refers to the child about to be born to the couple.

An underlying theme and image in the poem is also of a **journey**, both the physical journey the couple are taking to the hospital and also the metaphorical journey they embarked upon many years before as a couple in love. Becoming a family is the next stage of this journey and it is one they are now approaching. Time becomes fluid, a mixture of memories of the past; the now – their current situation; and also the future, when they will become parents.

The overall atmosphere is one of **calm affection** embodied by the partner's gentle pat on the woman's knee and how he always seemed to call her 'my baby'. Not having enough fuel for their journey doesn't mean they aren't prepared and ready to share their deep love, trust and affection with their new child.

Kate Clanchy

Form and language

'Driving to the Hospital' is a **lyric of 21 lines** using simple and straightforward language. The tone is calm and conversational: 'I said let's freewheel'. The speaker addresses her partner directly: 'You smiled kindly'. Calmness is conveyed though images and sounds relating to peace and quiet; the city nurses its quiet and the couple hope to arrive soundlessly, 'with barely / A crunch on the gravel'.

The couple's affection for one another is demonstrated repeatedly through the language using verb and adjective phrases like 'smiled kindly' and 'eased … gently'. Clanchy's use of the word 'courting' is an old-fashioned one and adds **a quaintness and sense of nostalgia** to the poem, while specifying that the past journey they took was 'to your brother's' lends authenticity to the account.

The repetition of 'leapt and leapt' at the end of the poem lifts this lyric from its calmness and quiet affection by introducing **a note of passion**; at once nostalgically recalling falling in love but simultaneously perhaps relating to the excitement and nervousness an expectant mother feels on this journey.

SNAPSHOT

- Journey to hospital to give birth
- Personification
- Affection between couple
- Calm and peaceful tone
- Repetition in last line
- Mix of past and present
- Love poem
- Birth
- Literal and metaphorical journey

ORDINARY LEVEL

Exam-Style Questions

Understanding the poem

1. What does the information that the car was 'low on petrol' suggest to you about this couple? How do they deal with this potentially worrying situation?

2. Describe the setting of the poem – time and place.

3. What sort of arrival does the speaker wish to make at the hospital (lines 6–8)? Why, do you think, is this so?

4. Read lines 9–15 again. How is the care and affection the couple share conveyed in this section?

5. In lines 17 and 18 the speaker recalls her partner saying 'I like / driving with my baby'. What, do you think, did this originally mean to the couple? Might the meaning of 'baby' have changed in their current situation? Explain. In your answer identify the physical gesture made by the poet's partner that triggered this memory.

6. In the last sentence of the poem the speaker recalls the reaction she had all those years ago to her partner saying, 'I like / driving with my baby'. Re-read this last sentence. Did she seem to fully understand why her 'heart leapt and leapt' at the time? Do you think she understands now? Explain.

Thinking about the poem

1. How is the city personified in lines 4 and 5: 'It was dawn and the city / was nursing its quiet'? How does this image relate to the theme of birth in the poem?

2. The poem has a calm and gentle tone. Show how Clanchy creates this through her language and imagery.

3. How would you describe the relationship between the couple? Use details in the poem as you answer.

4. Past, present and future shift and merge as the poem progresses. Trace and describe this.

5. Which of the following best describes what you feel to be the main theme of the poem: falling in love, birth, memory? Justify your choice through specific quotation and reference.

Imagining

1. Write about the same journey from the driver's point of view in any format you like – a diary entry, poem, descriptive passage, etc.

2. Clanchy said: 'People think, oh, that's about mothers and babies, that's very nice, then put the poem away. People do that to women poets – they minorise them.' Do you agree that poems about birth and motherhood seem less important than poems dealing with other themes? Discuss in pairs or groups, perhaps referring to other poems you have studied.

3. Write a descriptive piece about a real or imagined important journey.

Thom Gunn

1929–2004

Considering the Snail — 508

Biography

Born Thomas William Gunn in Kent, England on 29 August 1929, Gunn moved around England a lot with his father, Bert, after his journalist parents divorced. He credits his mother with fostering his love of words and was inconsolable when she took her own life. He was fifteen years old. He said, 'I was devastated for about four years … I read … very much as an escape.' Gunn spent two years in the army before going to Cambridge University, where he met his partner, Michael Kitay.

Fighting Terms, his first collection of poetry, was published in 1954 and was well received. Gunn won the Levinson Prize, a Guggenheim and McArthur Fellowship and a Rockefeller award. He was associated with a group called the Movement, a typically English group of poets including Larkin and Kingsley Amis, who wrote with dignity and avoided modernism in their work. They were nostalgic for a more rural England at a time when urbanisation was sweeping the land. Gunn's 1992 collection, *The Man with Night Sweats*, explored the effects of the HIV virus.

He moved to San Francisco with Kitay in 1960 and died there in 2004 from a drug overdose.

ORDINARY LEVEL

Before you read

What do you feel about snails? Do they disgust you, or do you like them? What adjectives and verbs come to mind when you think of or see a snail?

Considering the Snail

The snail pushes through a green
night, for the grass is heavy
with water and meets over
the bright path he makes, where rain
has darkened the earth's dark. He   5
moves in a wood of desire,

pale antlers barely stirring
as he hunts. I cannot tell
what power is at work, drenched there
with purpose, knowing nothing.   10
What is a snail's fury? All
I think is that if later

I parted the blades above
the tunnel and saw the thin
trail of broken white across   15
litter, I would never have
imagined the slow passion
to that deliberate progress.

Guidelines

Published in Gunn's third collection, *My Sad Captains* (1961), this poem looks at the humble snail with a keenly observant and original eye. It skilfully examines the unseen forces that govern nature.

Thom Gunn

Commentary

Stanza 1

As the poem opens the snail is pushing his way through a dark tunnel created by blades of grass heavy with droplets of water. He lights this darkness by forging a path through the wet, green dark.

The tiny grass tunnel is compared to a 'wood', reminding us of the **importance of perspective**. To us this may be a tiny scene, the snail, grass and droplets of water minuscule, but from the snail's perspective the blades of grass are like trees and forging through them requires force, determination and a passionate desire to move forward: 'He / moves in a wood of desire'.

Stanza 2

Stanza 2 opens in a run-on line. **Enjambment is used extensively** in this poem. The tentacles on the snail's head are likened to antlers, thus developing the 'wood' metaphor by comparing the snail to a male deer. The tentacles or 'antlers' are 'pale' and barely move as the snail 'hunts'. At this point the speaker interjects, placing himself in the poem, as he keenly observes the path of the snail and meditates on the mysteries it suggests to him: 'I cannot tell / what power is at work'. The snail is not just 'drenched' by the water (which of course is ideal for the snail as he can move about far more freely in wet conditions) but he is also 'drenched there / with purpose'. The snail's determination to continue his journey, perhaps to find food ('hunt'), is driving his every fibre.

'What is a snail's fury?' This question is ambiguous. Is it mocking or sincere? How could this creature possibly communicate such intensity? How could we tell from its behaviour, from its movements, what a snail might feel? (Perspective is important here again; because of the huge difference in scale, things look totally different from the snail's and its human observer's points of view.) This question raises many interesting possibilities and we will revisit it later.

The speaker wonders what he might have thought about if he were to come upon the same scene after the snail had been and gone, and this is developed in the final stanza.

Stanza 3

The speaker pictures parting 'the blades' of grass through which the snail had earlier travelled, uncovering its distinctive trail of slime, 'the thin / trail of broken white across / litter'. Had this been the only evidence of the snail's path, the speaker acknowledges that he could 'never have / imagined' the determination and tenacity of the snail in his journey, 'the slow passion / to that deliberate progress'. The poem seems to end on a note of admiration for the snail, which has left little behind to disturb the landscape after his ardent hunt.

Themes and imagery

Gunn said, 'as humans we look at things and think about what we've looked at. We treasure it in a kind of private art gallery.' This certainly pertains to the themes and imagery in this poem. Gunn has taken a relatively everyday sight, a snail moving through grass, and meditated deeply on it, exploring through detailed and evocative images themes about **nature and the forces within it**. From the outset **light and darkness** dominate the imagery and theme. The tunnel of grass creates for the snail 'a green / night', yet through it he forges a

ORDINARY LEVEL

'bright path'. The 'rain / has darkened the earth's dark', yet the snail's passion transforms this into a 'wood of desire'. The drive of this creature, its strenuous single-minded exertion, illuminates the dark. Even after he has gone the snail has left a 'trail of broken white' on the dark earth. Through these images Gunn shows us that if we don't take things for granted, if we really look and wonder at the world, the darkness of **ignorance can be brightened with knowledge**.

The speaker realises that the snail is not an insignificant creature on a random path – it has intention and focus; 'he hunts', 'what power is at work, drenched there / with purpose'. Knowledge enlightens the darkness of ignorance. To understand we must explore, we must question as the speaker does. We must wonder.

The personification of the snail as a 'he' is interesting as land snails are hermaphrodites (they have both male and female reproductive organs). Why might Gunn want to portray the snail as male? Does this fit the powerful hunter/stag image more accurately? What do you think?

The **importance of perspective** looms large in the imagery and theme of the poem. In an extended metaphor, the grass resembles a dark wood to the tiny snail and within it the snail is a stag with 'pale antlers'. The tentacles of the snail (which are actually its eyes) inspire this image. Is comparing a snail to a majestic stag gently mocking in tone or is it sincere in its admiration? If we see the grassy tunnel as a microcosm of what we would consider to be a wood, surely the snail in that scale is as mighty a hunter as any deer?

Could this poem be a metaphor for how we live? The 1960s was a time of huge social, cultural and technological change. Gunn may be telling us to **look at the world from other perspectives**, not just our own. We may discover wonderful things if we do, and bring light and knowledge to the darkness of fear and ignorance.

The notion of nature as an entity of unseen forces and powers is also a possible theme here. The snail has real purpose and intent as he pursues his 'desire' with 'power' and 'purpose'. Despite our possible perception of the snail as slow and rambling we might now see him as the speaker does; a creature with 'slow passion' and 'deliberate progress'. There is a **tension at work** here. Is nature a dormant force or a sentient entity? This depends on our perspective. Rukhaya MK commented:

'What the poet read in the purposeful trail was its inherent passion to succeed, divorced from external factors and extraneous implications. To the snail all that mattered was resolution, and not the result; action and not intention and finally, the journey in itself and not the destination.'

Do you agree with this analysis?

Thom Gunn

Form and language

The language here is deceptively simple yet contains **verbs of great power and energy**; 'pushes', 'makes', 'hunts', 'drenched' and so on. We are made aware of the 'power', 'purpose' and 'fury' of the snail as he forges a 'bright path' through his 'wood of desire'. 'What is a snail's fury?' What does Gunn mean here? Is he asking how we can possibly know what emotions this creature feels from our distant and lofty perspective? Is the notion of a snail's fury comical, powerful or something else?

The language is almost sexual in its intensity. His 'passion' and 'desire' suffuse the poem with intensity and might lead us to see this humble and much-maligned creature in a totally new light.

The poem's structure has a subtle intelligence; its pattern becomes visible only upon close scrutiny and what seems like free verse is actually something adhering to strict rules of form. In much the same way, the snail's slow progress may seem free and random but in fact is deliberate and careful. Almost every line has seven syllables, but the odd line breaks and enjambment might distract us from this at first. Look at the first stanza, for example. The lines are short and every one uses enjambment, 'The snail pushes through a green / night, for the grass is heavy / with water and meets over / ...' Look at the extensive use of enjambment here, allowing Gunn to masterfully control the pace and flow of the poem. Each line (with one exception) has seven syllables. Each stanza has six lines. Reading it aloud, we hear a very **deliberate tone** which moves along steadily albeit slowly. This **syllabic metre** reminds us of the deliberate and steady path of the snail. What on the first couple of readings might seem like a simple poem is actually written with **great skill and precision**. Look at the next two stanzas now. Does the poem follow this strict pattern throughout? Is there any deviation at all? If so, where and why?

Why is the form hidden here? Gunn's discovery of the snail's passion and intent is hidden in the dark tunnel. It takes effort and deep thought to see the passion in his actions. This is the same for Gunn's poem. One must look closely at it and strive to see the **patterns and deliberate nature** of its metre and rhymes, not visible to the reader who just casually glances through it. In the same way, the speaker in the poem slowly realises the steady and intentional yet passionate journey of the snail. Like him, we must part 'the blades above / the tunnel' to gain a new knowledge and understanding illuminating the world anew for us.

Exam-Style Questions

Understanding the poem

1	Describe in your own words the landscape the snail travels through in stanza 1. You could also sketch this.
2	Look at the metaphors in stanzas 1 and 2. What is the grass tunnel and the snail compared to? Are these effective comparisons?
3	'I cannot tell ...' (line 8). What puzzles the speaker in stanza 2?
4	Look at the words used to describe the snail in stanza 2: 'antlers', 'hunts', 'power', 'drenched', 'purpose' and 'fury'. What impression of the snail do you form from these words?
5	What does the speaker imagine himself doing at the end of stanza 2 and the beginning of stanza 3?

ORDINARY LEVEL

6	The word 'litter' can have different meanings. Look it up in a dictionary or thesaurus. Which meaning do you feel most closely fits with that of the poem's in line 16?
7	What, do you think, does the poet mean in the final two lines when he talks about the snail's 'slow passion' and 'deliberate progress'?

Thinking about the poem

1	Trace and comment on images of light and dark in the poem.
2	The language of the poem is deceptively simple but on closer inspection is full of strength, intention and intensity. Find examples of this throughout the poem.
3	The Movement, a literary term coined by J. D. Scott (literary editor of *The Spectator*), described poets like Gunn who strived for their poems to be '**simple, sensuous**' with '**traditional content** and **dignified form**'. Is this statement true of this poem? Look at the four elements in bold here and work in pairs to identify any two of them in this poem.
4	Look back at your response to the 'Before you read' exercise. Has this poem altered your impressions of the humble snail in any way? Compare your verbs and adjectives with Gunn's. Discuss with your classmates.
5	On the surface the poem doesn't seem to rhyme, but there is in fact a subtle and hidden rhyming scheme consisting of an *abc abc* pattern. Work in pairs to see if you can find this.
6	How is the rhyming scheme and metre of the poem hidden by Gunn? What is the effect of this and why, do you think, does he do this?
7	Give two or three examples of enjambment in the poem and comment on their effect.

Imagining

1	Think of another creature that most people might consider small, weak or insignificant and describe it with a new perspective, as Gunn has here. Alternatively, take a creature considered powerful and do the opposite.
2	Write a letter to the poet outlining your personal response to this poem and asking any questions you may have about it.
3	Write a short stream of consciousness piece using the inner voice of the snail on his journey. What is he seeing, feeling and thinking as he moves forward? Alternatively create a cartoon strip-style piece showing this visually with thought bubbles and/or a brief commentary beneath each image.

SNAPSHOT

- Speaker's admiration for the snail
- Importance of perspective
- Light and dark
- Enjambment
- Hidden metre and rhyme
- Rigid form
- Nature as a force
- Knowledge
- Intense feelings
- Strong verbs
- Metaphors
- Snail personified as male

Randolph Healy
b. 1956

Frogs — 514
Primula veris — 520

Biography

Randolph Healy is an Irish poet, publisher and teacher who was born in Irvine, Scotland in 1956 and moved with his family to Dublin aged eighteen months. His father was a postman who wrote ballads; his mother was 'well read' and 'had a store of folk songs'. He left school at fourteen and worked in many different jobs before returning to education, attending Trinity College, Dublin, where he studied maths and science before graduating and becoming a secondary-level teacher in these subjects.

Healy has become part of the modern poetry movement Another Ireland, a group that rejects being defined as 'Irish poets', as this so often means referencing history, colonisation, etc. Peter Riley says of Healy, 'he doesn't trade in that substance: nationality'. Healy prefers to use scientific data and logic rather than 'tribal memory'. His style is experimental and innovative, for example 'writing a computer program that will write itself part of your poem'.

He married Louise McMahon in 1983 and they have two daughters, one of whom is deaf, which inspires him to examine issues around language, exploring deafness and sign language. He lives in Co. Wicklow.

ORDINARY LEVEL

Before you read

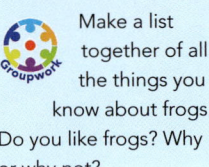

Make a list together of all the things you know about frogs. Do you like frogs? Why or why not?

Frogs

On a grassy hill, in a luxury seminary in Glenart,
I found, screened by trees,
a large stone pond.
The waters of solitude.
Friends.   5

Patriarchs,
ten thousand times older than humanity,
the galaxy has rotated almost twice
since they first appeared.

They get two grudging notices in the Bible: 10
Tsephardea in Exodus,
Batrachos in the Apocalypse.
I will smite all thy borders with frogs.
I saw three unclean spirits, like frogs.

Their numbers have been hugely depleted,   15
principally by students.

Sever its brain.
The frog continues to live.
It ceases to breathe, swallow or sit up
and lies quietly if thrown on its back.   20
Locomotion and voice are absent.
Suspend it by the nose,
irritate the breast, elbow and knee with acid.
Sever the foot that wipes the acid away.

It will grasp and hang from your finger.   25

There is evidence that they navigate
by the sun and the stars.

This year, thirty-two, I said
'I'll be damned if Maureen has frogs'
and dug a pond.   30
Over eighty hatched, propped up with cat food.
Until the cats ate them.
It was only weeks later we discovered
six shy survivors.

> The hieroglyph 35
> for the number one hundred thousand
> is a tadpole.
>
> Light ripples down a smooth back.
> *La grenouille.*
> Gone. 40

Glossary

Line	Term
1	*seminary*: institution for training priests
1	*Glenart*: place in County Wicklow, location of seminary
6	*Patriarchs*: male heads of a family or tribe; in the Bible a patriarch is a figure regarded as a father of the human race, such as Adam, Noah and Abraham
11	*Tsephardea in Exodus*: *Tsephardea* is the Hebrew word for frogs (literally meaning 'marsh-jumper'); it appears in the Old Testament Book of Exodus (8:12–24)
12	*Batrachos in the Apocalypse*: *Batrachos* is the Greek word for frogs from the New Testament Book of Revelations, which describes the end of the world, which we know now as the Apocalypse (16:13)
13	*smite*: to strike with a violent blow
21	*Locomotion*: movement
35	*hieroglyph*: Egyptian symbol
39	*La grenouille*: French word for frog

Guidelines

From the collection *Green 352. Selected Poems 1983–2000*. Randolph Healy is an innovative modern poet who uses science, data and logic in his work. He has spoken of how evolution fascinates him, how patterns arise, yet he comments that evolution is 'by no means green', referring to the waste and death that occurs in the natural world. 'Frogs' explores this idea and looks at the human contribution to the decline of the frog population in Ireland, as well as **exploring the existence of frogs through the ages, and mankind's changing attitude towards them**.

Commentary

Lines 1–9

The speaker describes the setting: 'Glenart' is a 'luxury' training college for priests in Co. Wicklow and in its grounds on a 'grassy hill' there is a secluded pond, 'screened by trees'. In its 'waters of solitude' the speaker finds 'Friends'. The first description of frogs here is a **positive** one, they are the 'Friends' of line 5 and seem shy creatures who live in 'solitude', peacefully.

In keeping with the **religious allusion** in the first line the speaker then calls the frogs 'Patriarchs'. In biblical terms this refers to the founders of the first tribes of mankind (see Glossary, above). He sees the **frogs as our**

forebears, perhaps because of how long they have been in existence compared to us – 'ten thousand times older than humanity'. The speaker then measures this time in another way, astronomically; our galaxy, the Milky Way, has 'rotated almost twice / since they first appeared'.

Lines 10–14

In **contrast** with this respectful and positive view of frogs, the speaker goes on to describe how the two mentions of frogs in the Bible express something quite different. He uses one example each from the Old Testament and the New Testament – 'They get two grudging notices in the Bible'. In the first, from the Book of Exodus, a plague of frogs is sent to punish Egypt for its enslavement of the Jews: 'I will smite all thy borders with frogs'; *tsephardea* is the Hebrew word for frog (this is the language the Bible was originally written in). The New Testament reference comes from the Book of Revelation: 'I saw three unclean spirits, like frogs'. **In the Bible, frogs symbolise spiritual impurity.** In this instance the three spirits emanate from the mouth of a dragon during the apocalypse, the end of the world. *Batrachos* is the Greek word for frog (Greek was the first language the Bible was translated into). Frogs are therefore seen in religion as something malign, **a curse or punishment**.

Lines 15–25

The huge decline in the frog population in Ireland is the next subject on the speaker's 'list'. He accuses science students of being 'principally' at fault for this, and goes on to describe in vivid detail how the dissection of a frog is carried out. The speaker seems very familiar with this procedure and the description **sounds like a set of instructions**. We are told that even if its brain is severed, the frog will still be alive. He notes that even though it stops breathing and ceases moving, if it is hung 'by the nose' and acid is rubbed onto its 'breast, elbow and knee', once its foot is cut off it will 'grasp and hang from your finger'. The reaction expected from us is unclear at this point, **the tone of the speaker is so matter-of-fact that it's difficult to know whether we are supposed to be horrified, fascinated or merely informed** by this.

Lines 26–27

The next two lines suggest that frogs have **an innate wisdom and a harmony with the universe**. The lines 'There is evidence that they navigate / by the sun and the stars' remind us of lines 7 and 8, where the speaker commented on how long frogs have been on Earth, using the age of our galaxy to explain this. Placed just after the description of a frog being scientifically dissected, this account of frogs (as in tune with the universe) suggests that these wise creatures don't deserve to be treated so callously. Just like the first sailors and explorers, frogs use the heavens to find their way and were doing this long before we were.

Lines 28–40

The speaker now brings the poem back to his **personal experience** of frogs. He describes how, at age 'thirty-two', having found that 'Maureen has frogs', he undertook to dig a pond to encourage their numbers, feeding with cat food the 'Over eighty' which subsequently hatched. This unfortunately led to the cats eating all but six of the frogs. Like the frogs in stanza 1, these were 'shy' and had evaded discovery for weeks. His misguided efforts to help them had been almost in vain. **Perhaps this is a commentary on the damage we frequently do to the natural world, often despite our best efforts and intentions.**

Juxtaposed with this tiny number of just six surviving frogs, the speaker notes that the signifier for the number one hundred thousand in ancient Egypt 'is a tadpole'. Something that once symbolised a teeming multitude, an abundance, now exists in a tiny number. Frogs were once an ancient symbol of fertility due to their **vast numbers**, particularly when depicted as spawn and tadpoles.

Randolph Healy

The final stanza **focuses on the beauty of the frog and its looming extinction**. 'Light ripples down a smooth back' – the light acts like the watery conditions the frog lives in and the frog is not slimy but smooth. The French word for frog is used here: *'La grenouille.'* Could this be a reference to the French delicacy of frogs' legs? The last word is simple yet startling – 'Gone'. All of this history, these fascinating snippets of information about this shy, mysterious ancient species culminates in the terrible possibility of their extinction.

Themes

Man's fickle attitude to these gentle creatures is explored by the poet here and, in a wider sense, perhaps **our attitude to nature** is under scrutiny too. This relationship is one-sided; frogs are depicted as shy, solitude loving creatures and 'Friends'. They are far older than us and in an evolutionary sense are our forebears – 'Patriarchs'. All life began in a primordial swamp, therefore amphibious creatures like frogs were near the very beginning of life on Earth. **Mathematical and scientific ideas** feature in Healy's poetry and they are prominent in this poem, from **measurements** of time and astronomy to **scientific experimentation**. Religion is a theme also: the poem opens in the grounds of 'a luxury seminary in Glenart' and references to the Bible fill the third stanza. The **depiction of religion** is ultimately a negative one in terms of how it views this ancient species as a curse, impure and unclean.

Humanity is depicted as a callous, invasive and ultimately destructive presence in the world of frogs. We dissect them, use them to symbolise evil and impurity (as the Bible references show), and even when we try to help them we often do more harm than good, as shown in the comical effort to build a pond and feed the frogs.

Language and imagery

The form of the poem seems at first to be a **lyric**. There is **a list-like accumulation of facts, figures and anecdotal stories about frogs** in unrhymed stanzas which vary in length from one to eight lines. In fact the poem is much more than a list of interesting snippets about these creatures. It **builds steadily** to the final stark prediction 'Gone'. Frogs through the ages, and our changing relationship with them, is **explored in a series of scientific, mathematical, religious and anecdotal ways.**

Religion

The first image shows the secluded pond in the seminary grounds. 'Luxury' is an interesting adjective here – why would an institution for training priests be luxurious? Is this sarcasm? This suggests an already antagonistic attitude towards religion which the speaker elaborates on in stanza 3. The references to frogs in the Old and New Testament both depict them negatively: first as a punishing plague on Egypt; second, used in a simile comparing them to 'unclean spirits'.

ORDINARY LEVEL

Language
Healy's interest in language is evident in the Biblical references; he is known as **a poet who explores language in various ways**. This poem uses the words for frogs in **three different languages besides English**: Hebrew, Greek and French. Healy also recognises that language can be more than words. **Hieroglyphs** also convey meaning. The form of a tadpole is the signifier, as the symbol for a vast number (one hundred thousand). The mention of hieroglyphs connects us back to the reference in stanza 3 to the biblical story of the plague of frogs in Egypt.

Number
Data like **numbers and measurements** feature in the language of this poem. Frogs are: '**ten thousand** times older than humanity'; 'the galaxy has rotated almost **twice** /' since they first appeared'; they get '**two** grudging notices in the Bible'; they are compared to '**three** unclean spirits'; '**thirty-two**' may be the age of the speaker when he dug them a pond; 'Over **eighty** hatched' but only **six** survived; the 'hieroglyph / for the number **one hundred thousand** / is a tadpole.' All of these numbers lead the reader to the final word – 'Gone'.

Dissection
One of the most **vivid series of images** in the poem concerns the dissection of a frog. The poet is a science teacher and clearly knows this process intimately. The instructions given are related dispassionately like **instructions in a manual**, but at the same time seem cruel: 'Sever its brain'; 'Suspend it by the nose, / irritate the breast, elbow and knee with acid. / Sever the foot'. The **sibilance here creates an uneasy, sinister effect**. The image of the frog's foot trying to wipe the acid away during this process is disconcerting to say the least. There is a clear sense of the animal being tortured. The astronomical reference that directly follows this: 'they navigate / by the sun and the stars' – suggests an ancient wisdom in these creatures which puts them in harmony with a universe where they have existed for millennia. This makes their dissection all the more uncomfortable to dwell on, making us **question whether we have the right** to do this to these animals.

Mystery and beauty
The overall image of the frogs is of ancient, shy creatures who just want to be left alone. They live in 'The waters of solitude', they are 'Friends' and 'Patriarchs' who have amazing physical mysteries, as explored in stanzas 5, 6 and 7. The 'six shy survivors' in the speaker's homemade pond represent the few frogs that remain, largely due to our variously bungling, unkind and callous treatment of these gentle amphibians. The **image of light rippling** down the smooth back of the frog is a final testament to their **beauty** and innate right to survive in nature, but then quick as a flash that pleasant image is snatched from us as the speaker predicts their extinction – 'Gone'.

Exam-Style Questions

Understanding the poem

1	What details do you learn about the frogs in the first two stanzas?
2	According to stanza 3, how does the Bible depict frogs?
3	Why might students be responsible for the huge depletion in the numbers of frogs?
4	Explain in your own words the process of dissection outlined by the speaker. How did you feel reading this?

Randolph Healy

5. What happened when the speaker tried to encourage frogs to breed (lines 28-34)? What might this anecdote say about man's attempts to preserve nature?

6. 'Gone.' Has the frog here simply hopped away out of sight or is a larger point being made?

Thinking about the poem

1. What picture of frogs emerges from the poem as a whole? What details in the poem help to create this picture?

2. Examine and comment on the religious references in the poem.

3. How is humanity's relationship with frogs through the ages depicted by the poet?

4. Examine the references to science and maths. What do these bring to the poem as a whole?

5. 'I'll be damned'. Why might the poet have chosen this phrase? Could it link back to the religious references in the poem as well as having a more colloquial meaning?

6. Which of the following is closest to what you think the main theme of this poem is?
   - Frogs are fascinating creatures
   - People have been very cruel to frogs
   - The complex relationship between humanity and nature

   Discuss with reference to the poem.

Imagining

1. Make two lists, one cataloguing the positive references to frogs in the poem and the other listing the negative references. Which list is longer? Does this reflect the poet's opinion in your view? Does it reflect your own?

2. Write up the dissection section of the poem as a scientific experiment; list the equipment you will need, the reason for the experiment and the process. What are your findings at the end?

3. Write three diary entries describing and expanding on the 'cat massacre' anecdote (lines 28–34). You might add details from elsewhere in the poem to your account.

SNAPSHOT

- Shy, solitude-loving nature of frogs
- Scientific, astronomical and mathematical data
- Anecdote
- Religion's attitude towards frogs
- Different translations of word for 'frog'
- Varying styles of language including religious to scientific and everyday speech
- Alliteration and sibilance
- Humanity's complex relationship with these creatures
- Decline in frog population and their possible extinction

Before you read

 Look at the picture of the cowslip flower on page 523. Describe each part of this plant using a simile or metaphor for each section; leaves, stem and flowers.

Primula veris

Clustering atop a leggy stem
ten elf green bodices tapered down
to blown about yellow pinafores.

Near the ground a mob of blotched leaves,
belching and gulping, stiff with liquor,   5
watched constellations kink and bend
and languages drift from grammar to grammar.

Sister Mary's favourite flower
cast a light on all the gougers
that she coaxed, effing and blinding,   10
to various degrees of joined-up writing.

One great arching cadence
glosses the world as a double spiral
speaks to itself with epochs for clauses

root shoot and flower   15
stitching together the heavens and the earth

Glossary

Title	*Primula veris* is the botanical name for the cowslip – a type of primrose. Translates from the Latin as 'first thing of spring'
1	*atop*: on top of
1	*leggy*: long, thin
2	*bodices*: the part of a dress (excluding the sleeves) which is above the waist
2	*tapered*: becoming narrower towards one end
3	*pinafores*: a collarless, sleeveless dress worn over a blouse or jumper
4	*blotched*: marked with irregular spots
5	*liquor*: a thick liquid (like sap); an alcoholic drink
9	*gougers*: Irish colloquial term for louts or thugs
10	*coaxed*: gently persuaded to do something
10	*effing and blinding*: swearing
12	*cadence*: the flow or rhythm of events, especially the pattern in which things are experienced; a change in the pitch of speech or music
14	*epochs*: long specific periods of time in history which mark a particular age
14	*clauses*: the basic units of a sentence

Randolph Healy

Guidelines

This poem comes from the 1997 collection *Rana Rana!* and, typically of Healy, combines a scientific view of the natural world with a love of language and history. This combination can also be seen in Healy's poem 'Frogs'.

Commentary

Stanzas 1 and 2
'Leggy' is the word used to describe how long and thin the cowslip's stem is. At its top are flowers which have yellow blooms with a green base. These remind the speaker of dresses made from 'elf green bodices', which narrow like a waist until they meet the 'blown about yellow pinafores' that are the skirt-like bright yellow petals of this spring flower.

The crinkled leaves below are less pretty and are nearest the ground. They are mottled, 'blotched' and twisted, seeming like gluttonous, belligerent drunks lying there 'belching and gulping, stiff with liquor'. The three different parts of this plant – leaves, stem and flower – remind the speaker of the constellations of stars, watched by astronomers, that undulate, 'kink and bend'. They are also **like languages, changing, forever evolving**, as they 'drift from grammar to grammar'.

We can already see Healy's passion for science and language, which are subjects explored in much of his work.

Stanzas 3–5
The cowslip reminds the speaker of his old teacher, 'Sister Mary', as they were her 'favourite flower'. Language is again referenced as the speaker remembers how she gently 'coaxed' the difficult students in her class to learn to write in cursive script, 'gougers / that she coaxed, effing and blinding, / to various degrees of joined-up writing'. The bright yellow of the cowslip seemed to illuminate, 'cast a light' – perhaps the light of knowledge – on this scene.

The final five lines are **complex in language and concept**. The image of light in stanza 3 is repeated, this time as a shine, a gloss brought to 'the world' like a great arching sentence or change in tone. 'Cadence' often refers to a rhythm in speech or a phrase in music. Perhaps here the poet is talking about how language (and learning) has been fundamental in the development of humanity and how its various elements combine to make sense of us and our history. The DNA helix is alluded to here – this 'cadence' takes the form of a 'double spiral'. It 'speaks to itself' as if all of life or language and its various stages become part of one sentence which has vast ages of time – 'epochs' as 'clauses' in this sentence.

This idea is reflected in this simple flower, one of the first of spring. Its 'root shoot and flower' could be like the parts of language, perhaps noun, adjective and verb. The imagery of clothing from stanza 1 finds an echo here as the three parts of this one flower combine to bring all of 'the heavens and the earth' together as if 'stitching' them. Everything is connected and the **microcosm** (the small version of a much bigger world) reflects the **macrocosm** (the bigger world).

ORDINARY LEVEL

> **DNA is an extremely long chain of molecules which contains the information necessary for all cells to develop and function. These are the building blocks of life. The individual molecules that make up DNA are called nucleotides. The pattern is a ladder-like twisting spiral. A strand of DNA is much like an extremely long sentence which uses only four letters.**

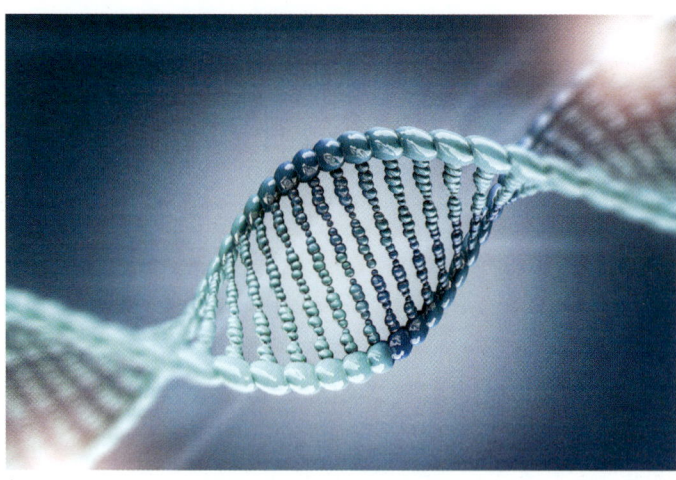

Just as time and language have separate elements which are also part of one entity, so the simple cowslip has leaves, stem and flowers which, although different (ugly, 'leggy' and pretty), are part of one organism. The **infinite variety of nature and life** is also one unified entity. Patterns in nature repeat, from the smallest plant to our language and beyond to the universe itself. Think, for example, how the veins in a leaf reflect the structure of the tree's trunk and branches.

Themes and imagery

The central image is, of course, the plant itself but, typically for Healy, **science is also central to the poem**. Instead of simply using the common name 'cowslip', he uses its Latin botanical name, *Primula veris*, literally 'the first thing of spring'. Before moving on to far more complex ideas, Healy begins by simply describing the plant's appearance using some **original and quirky comparisons**. The stem is 'leggy' as it's slender and tall,

> **Cowslips were associated with protection for fairies and also featured in Norse mythology – they were dedicated to the goddess Freya.**

almost gangly in appearance. The flowers at the top of the plant are counted carefully. There are 'ten elf green bodices'. The image of elves is a pretty one; the tiny mischievous **mythical woodland creatures** are perhaps at odds with the **scientific bent** of the poem in later stanzas.

The speaker seems to admire these flowers whose green bases 'tapered down' until they burst into pretty yellow blooms. The **clothing imagery is expanded** upon by comparing the flowers to 'blown about yellow pinafores', and this is picked up again in the last line, where the three parts of the cowslip are 'stitching together the heavens and the earth'. The leaves at its base, however, are a different story. These are ugly and seem almost like drunken figures passed out on the ground after binging on alcohol. They are a 'mob', personified as angry figures who lie 'belching and gulping'. The leaves of the cowslip are quite thick and rigid, and seem 'stiff with liquor'. The flowers of the cowslip are renowned for producing a delicious wine, which also has analgesic (pain-killing) qualities.

From here the imagery and theme of the poem become more **abstract and complex**. Elements of **language** and **astronomy** are introduced. The leaves are 'watched constellations'. The minutely crinkled nature of their leaves seem like clusters of stars observed by an astronomer, which 'kink and bend' like space. They are like languages, changing almost arbitrarily as they travel around the world with their differing grammars. All are stars, all are languages, all different, yet ultimately the same thing.

Randolph Healy

The **teaching of language** is mentioned in stanza 3, embodied in the figure of 'Sister Mary', who patiently 'coaxed' the skill of 'joined-up writing' from 'gougers' who used a very different language than the one this teaching nun was attempting to promote – they are 'effing and blinding', perhaps reminding us of the drunken mob in stanza 2. Here we see the variety of language; there are **different types for different people**, yet they all have the same purposes – expression and communication. This reminds us of the cowslip, which has different elements – roots, stem, flowers and leaves – yet is one plant.

Science, time and language continue in the poem's themes and imagery in the most complex fourth stanza, where DNA, vast eras in time and speech ('double spiral', 'epochs for clauses' and 'arching cadence') **combine**, just as the stem, flowers, roots and leaves combine in the plant. These things unite to stitch the 'heavens and the earth'. It is difficult to know exactly what the speaker is conveying through this image. Perhaps he marvels at **how disparate the elements of our world and universe are** and yet they are all connected and reflected. As in Thom Gunn's poem 'Considering the Snail', it depends on our perspective. A simple plant, a language, a constellation of stars or even a garment has patterns and elements that are repeated on an ever bigger scale as our point of view expands, so that **a simple clause in a sentence is like an epoch in time**. This big idea may help make us see the little cowslip in a very different light, like the light it has cast on Sister Mary's reluctant pupils.

> We may be reminded of the ideas of W. B. Yeats, who meditated on the same concept using a tree and a dance as images. The tree is made up of leaf, flower and trunk. The dance must have music and a dancer. These are one, yet must combine different and various elements which cannot be separated:
>
> O chestnut tree, great rooted blossomer,
> Are you the leaf, the blossom or the bole?
> O body swayed to music, O brightening glance
> How can we know the dancer from the dance?

Form and language

Beginning the poem with the scientific name for the cowslip lends the speaker's voice an air of authority. He knows what he is talking about. We may be surprised then at the quirky and less than scientific language used to draw comparisons; 'leggy' is hardly a scientific adjective, while elves, 'bodices', 'pinafores' and an angry drunken mob form the metaphors used to describe the various sections of the plant. The repetition of 'o' sounds in the third line reflect the effect of the wind blowing the flowers and stem about.

'Bodices' and 'pinafores' are quite old-fashioned garments, words not much used these days, lending the tone a nostalgic quality. Perhaps the speaker recalls a time when cowslips were plentiful; they have sadly become a rarity in the Irish countryside. But according to the Wildflowers of Ireland website, 'The good news is that this little plant, noticeably absent for some time, is now starting to make a come-back. Its spread declined as a result of intensive farming and even over-picking, but now it is beginning to reappear on some roadsides and pastures.'

'Gougers' is similarly an old and now rarely used term for the rough and ready students Sister Mary seeks to enlighten. What terminology would be used for these characters today?

A cowslip.

ORDINARY LEVEL

Of course, much of the **language is very specific and technical**, for example 'cadence' and 'epoch'. This combination of colloquial, archaic and scientific is very much in the style of Randolph Healy's work. He seeks to examine these ideas and is happy to combine such **disparate elements**, just as the parts of the cowslip seem to differ wildly yet form a coherent whole. The free verse makes the poem seem more accessible, perhaps, but some difficult concepts demand deep thought and much exploration.

The punctuation and form seem partly rigid at first. Stanzas 1 and 4 are each three lines long; stanzas 2 and 3 are four lines each; and each of the first three stanzas ends on a full stop. This changes in stanza 4, which has no punctuation. Why abandon the rules of language? As the speaker has pointed out earlier in the poem, 'languages drift from grammar to grammar' (line 7). The rules of speech and writing change and evolve from place to place and through time. **Language is always evolving and changing** and Healy reflects this in his deliberate lack of punctuation at the end, which might also convey the speaker's excitement and enthusiasm for the connections he has made in the poem and leaves these ideas open for further discovery and development.

SNAPSHOT

- Science and language
- Clothing imagery
- Difference and unity
- Personal anecdote
- Universal themes
- Complex language and ideas
- Patterns in nature
- Colloquial and old-fashioned language
- Quirky metaphors and personification
- Yellow and green – spring colours

Exam-Style Questions

Understanding the poem

1	To what does the poet compare each part of the flower – the stem, flowers and leaves? Which comparison did you like best? Why?
2	What do (a) the constellations and (b) the languages seem to do in the second stanza? How does this echo the description of the leaves and the plant as a whole in the poem?
3	What did 'Sister Mary's favourite flower', the cowslip, cast a light on in stanza 3?
4	What impression of Sister Mary's class is given in stanza 3? Did you find this description amusing, sad or offensive? Explain.
5	What, do you think, does the poet mean in stanza 4 of the poem? Use the glossary to help you formulate your answer.
6	How do the different parts of the cowslip bring 'the heavens and the earth' together in the final two lines of the poem?

Randolph Healy

Thinking about the poem

1. Look back at your response to the 'Before you read' exercise. Were your images and descriptions of this flower similar to or different from the poet's? Compare your ideas and his.

2. Which of the following most closely matches your view of the theme of this poem?
   - The wonder of nature
   - The importance of language
   - The vastness of the universe
   - The repeated patterns all around us
   - Something else?

3. Healy mixes scientific language with old-fashioned and colloquial words. Find examples of this in the poem. Why, do you think, does he combine these styles?

4. Trace the imagery of language, clothing and science in the poem. What, if anything, do they have in common?

5. Why, do you think, does the poet not punctuate the final four lines of the poem?

6. Compare this poem to Healy's poem 'Frogs'. What similarities can you identify between these poems? Which did you prefer? Give reasons.

7. The last stanza seems a line short if we take the rest of the poem as having a pattern. Suggest a final line or two which you feel might work to end the poem.

8. This might seem a difficult poem. Write out a list of four or five things about it that puzzle you. Share them as small groups and finally as a class and hopefully this discussion will help you with your understanding of it.

Imagining

1. Imagine you are Sister Mary. Write your diary entry after an eventful day in class.

2. What is your favourite plant, animal or natural feature? What is it you admire so much about it? Describe it using aesthetic language.

3. Do some research into DNA. What is the 'spiral' Healy refers to? Perhaps some students in your class do biology and could be of help to the rest of the class. You may also refer to the notes above.

ORDINARY LEVEL

George Herbert

1593–1633

Easter Wings   527

Biography

George Herbert was born in Wales in 1593 into a rich and powerful family. His father was a member of parliament, and after a good education in England at Westminster School and Trinity College, Cambridge, Herbert too became an MP. He gave up his political ambitions in order to be ordained a priest in the Church of England, and spent the rest of his short life as the rector of a parish church in the county of Wiltshire in southern England. He had always suffered from poor health, and died of consumption in 1633 at the age of 39. His poems in English (he also wrote poetry in Latin and Greek) were published as *The Temple* shortly after his death. All the poems are on religious themes, and are remarkable for their wit and wordplay as well as the piety they show. He is usually associated with the Metaphysical poets of the seventeenth century, known for their inventive use of metaphors.

George Herbert

Before you read

Look at the shape this poem makes on the page before you read it. In pairs or small groups, discuss why a poet might want to make a poem look like this. In the first publication of this poem it was printed sideways across two facing pages. Can you suggest why?

Easter Wings

Lord, who createdst man in wealth and store,
  Though foolishly he lost the same,
    Decaying more and more,
      Till he became
        Most poore: 5
      With thee
     O let me rise
    As larks, harmoniously,
  And sing this day thy victories:
Then shall the fall further the flight in me.   10

My tender age in sorrow did beginne
  And still with sicknesses and shame.
    Thou didst so punish sinne,
      That I became
        Most thinne.   15
      With thee
     Let me combine,
    And feel thy victorie:
   For, if I imp my wing on thine,
Affliction shall advance the flight in me.   20

Glossary

Line	Term
1	*store*: abundance, plenty
8	*larks*: birds known for their beautiful singing as they fly
10	*further*: here, a verb meaning lengthen, extend
11	*tender*: young, vulnerable
19	*imp*: to repair a damaged wing feather by attaching part of a new feather (a term from hawking: hunting with trained hawks)
20	*Affliction*: pain or harm
20	*advance*: increase, improve

Guidelines

This poem was first published in *The Temple* in 1633. As its title indicates, it was written for Easter, the most important festival in the Christian calendar.

Easter is when Christians celebrate the resurrection of Jesus Christ, who is God in human form. According to Christian theology, his death and resurrection redeemed mankind from the original sin of Adam and Eve in the Garden of Eden. This reconciliation of God and humanity is called atonement. A knowledge of these beliefs and the stories associated with them is important for a full understanding of 'Easter Wings'. These stories are well known in our society today, and would have been very familiar to everybody when the poem was written.

In the original printing of the poem the reason for the other element of the title (Wings) was even clearer than it is now. The poem was printed sideways across two pages of the book, making the poem's lines look very much like two butterflies or birds, or the wings of two angels as they are often drawn or painted. Turn this book sideways and you will get an idea of how it looked, though in the original great care had been taken to create the outline of wings in the way the poem was printed.

This shape is not just decorative. The visual form of the poem and the changing lengths of the lines contribute to its meaning, so it is impossible to appreciate it fully without considering the way the lines look on the page. The form is discussed in detail below, but we need to take it into account as we look at what the poem says.

Commentary

Lines 1–5

The poem starts by addressing God ('Lord'), and uses the intimate second-person form of address ('thou', 'thee', 'thine'), and the old-fashioned verb forms that match them: 'createdst' (line 1) and 'didst' (line 13). This is a form of language appropriate to a prayer, and that is in part what this poem is: the speaker's prayer at Easter asking for God's help to rise above his sinful state and become closer to God.

The first five lines refer to the story of Adam in the Garden of Eden, who was given all he needed ('wealth and store') but 'foolishly' lost it all by eating the forbidden fruit from the Tree of Knowledge. As a result he declined 'more and more', 'Decaying' like rotting fruit, until he became 'Most poore': not just materially poor but spiritually poor because he had cut himself off from God by his action.

Lines 6–10

Whereas lines 1–5 get shorter and shorter as Herbert describes man's decline until he became 'Most poore', in the second half of the stanza the lines become longer and longer as the mood becomes more hopeful.

Where the first half of the stanza was a third-person, past-tense account of the Fall, the second half is a first-person plea for the speaker's future: 'let me rise / … / And sing'. He wishes to rise 'with thee' (God) like larks, which are known for their beautiful singing as they fly higher and higher. He wants to sing 'this day thy victories'. Since, as the title tells us, 'this day' is Easter, the victories are Christ's triumph over death by resurrection on Easter Sunday.

The stanza's final line needs a little theology to understand fully. Here, 'the fall' is both Adam's fall and the speaker's own, since according to Christian doctrine Adam's fall affected the whole human race, and so you could say that Adam lives on inside us all. The line is optimistic, even joyful. In a central paradox of the Christian story, the Fall was often thought of as a good thing because it meant that God had to become human in Jesus in order to redeem mankind. This paradox is known by the Latin term *felix culpa*, which is translated as 'fortunate fall' or 'happy fault'. In the terms of the poem, that means that the speaker has to fly further and higher because he has fallen so low.

Lines 11–15

The second stanza follows the pattern of the first – not just as it appears on the page but in its movement from a downward spiral in the first half to an upward spiral in the second. Here, however, the fall is personal.

The stanza starts, 'My tender age in sorrow did beginne'. This is a reference to the pains of childbirth, which is traditionally associated with sin in the Christian tradition because God's punishment of Eve in the Genesis story of the Garden of Eden was painful childbirth. In the words of the King James version of the Bible that Herbert would have known, 'in sorrow thou shalt bring forth children'.

Sorrow is followed by 'sicknesses and shame', further punishments for 'sinne'. Rather than the speaker saying he is a particularly wicked person, this is another acknowledgement of the doctrine that Adam's 'original sin' has infected and affected the whole human race. When he says that he became 'most thinne', that is an indication of his spiritual rather than his physical state.

Lines 16–20

Line 16 exactly repeats line 6, at the equivalent stage in the first stanza: 'With thee' – 'thee' being, of course, God. Here the speaker's desires are more intense and dramatic: he wants to 'combine' with God, and 'feel thy victorie' – the victory of Christ's resurrection on Easter Sunday. His dependence on God is still closer. In a metaphor taken from hawking, he wants to 'imp' his wing on God's, as if he were a hawk with a damaged wing feather who could fly only with the help of feathers taken from God's wing. In that way, his 'Affliction', meaning both the damaged wing and the original sin which it represents, will enable him to fly further and higher ('advance the flight in me').

> 'For as in Adam all die, even so in Christ shall all be made alive.'
>
> 1 Corinthians 15, v. 22

In simpler terms, he is praying for God's help in rising above his own sinfulness to be closer to God. That help is what the Easter story of Christ's suffering and resurrection promises.

Themes and imagery

As already noted, this poem is a **prayer or meditation at Easter**, the festival that celebrates the suffering, death and resurrection of Christ, who in the Christian story came to save mankind from sin. Adam may have lost the 'wealth and store' God gave mankind, but Easter means that humans can still be saved. Even though, as lines 11–15 indicate, the speaker, like all people, is sinful, he can still rise above his sinfulness with the help of God.

Underlying the poem is **the paradox of *felix culpa*** or the fortunate fall: the idea that what happened in the Garden of Eden (Adam eating the fruit of the Tree of Knowledge), often known as the Fall of Man, was in fact a good thing because it meant that God had to be born as a man in Jesus Christ in order to redeem humanity. As a result, in the poem's central metaphor of flight, the speaker can fly higher and further: 'Then shall the fall further the flight in me' (line 10).

The **image of flying**, indicated by the poem's title and by its resemblance to wings on the printed page, appears in the second half of both stanzas. In the first stanza the wings belong to larks, in the second to a hawk. The different birds give the two images different flavours. The larks are harmonious, and their song is a song of praise to God for 'thy victories'. **The image of the hawk does more to suggest the sensation of flying.** The idea of 'imping' your wing on God's is an intimate one involving close physical contact. It also implies that if God has wings, then flying is a bit like being God, and it is notable that in these lines the speaker does not just want to sing, but 'feel' God's victory.

Form

'Easter Wings' is a **pattern poem**: one whose shape on the printed page is part of its meaning. There are examples of these poems dating back to ancient Greece, and they were first written in English in the early sixteenth century, but this is one of the finest.

It is clear from the Commentary above that the **wing shapes** of the two stanzas are not merely decorative. Most obviously, they **reinforce the central metaphor of the poem: flying**. Not only that, but the word 'wing' is mentioned in the penultimate line, along with the idea of God having wings. The outline of the poem in its original printing emphasised the resemblance to angels' wings as they are often depicted in medieval art.

That shape is created by lines that get shorter and shorter in the first half of each stanza and longer and longer in the second half. In fact, they do so in a very specific way. The poem is written in an **iambic metre**, where each measure or 'foot' consists of an unstressed syllable followed by a stressed one (dĭ-dúm). In the first line of each stanza there are five feet and five stresses; in the second there are four; and in each line that follows there is one less until in the fifth line there is just one. The second half of each stanza repeats the process in reverse, adding a foot with each line, until by the final line there are five stresses, as in the first line. The pattern of each stanza is reinforced by a rhyme scheme that falls neatly into two halves: *ababa cdcdc*.

Not only does this form create the shape of the poem on the page, it also reflects what it is saying and contributes to the emotional impact of the poem. In the first half of each stanza the decline and decay of, first, 'man' and then the speaker are described in lines which get increasingly short, reflecting the decline and creating a sense of constriction as the line breaks come more and more frequently. Then, in the second half of each stanza, the lines lengthen as they describe a sense of rising and taking wing, becoming more optimistic. **The increasing line lengths create a feeling of opening out and gaining freedom that matches the imagery of taking flight.**

Language

Although the ideas that underlie the poem may be unfamiliar to you, and require you to grasp a paradox that may seem difficult, **the language in which the poem is written is simple and direct**, even though it does contain one word ('imp', line 19) used in a sense you probably hadn't heard before.

The words are carefully chosen and shaped so that, for instance, 'With thee' is positioned at the start of the second part of each stanza, in lines 6 and 16. Where the natural word order in speech would be 'O let me rise with thee' and 'Let me combine with thee', shifting 'With thee' to the beginning places a special emphasis on the phrase, and so on the central relationship in the poem – the relationship between the speaker and God. There are other close parallels between the stanzas, most notably the matching fifth lines: 'Most poore' and 'Most thinne'. Notice that just as the whole poem revolves around the paradox of the 'fortunate fall', there is a paradox within the words of each of those lines. 'Most' could be glossed as 'very', but it carries the sense of largeness and abundance, just as it does in modern English, so the idea of abundance is put up against words that speak of absence or lack: 'poore' and 'thinne'.

Although the diction is plain, Herbert uses the sounds of the words to add to the elegance of the poem and highlight key lines. There is plenty of **alliteration and assonance**. Let's take one example of each. The repetition of 'f' and 'l' sounds in line 10, 'Then shall the fall further the flight in me', does a lot to help create the sense of soaring flight that the line expresses. Two lines before, the assonance of the 'ar' vowels in 'larks, harmoniously' reflects the **harmony** that it describes.

The poem relies on the **language of prayer**, with its intimate address to God ('thou' and 'thine'). It is personal and heartfelt in its simple wish to rise above sin and fly. It feels sincere, but the emotion never overwhelms the clarity of the thought that is expressed. The speaker is not characterised in any particular way. It is **the voice of someone speaking to God**. It is easy to imagine it as the voice of George Herbert, a devout seventeenth-century priest, but the words could be spoken by anyone with a belief in the Christian God, even a partial belief. It is the voice of someone who knows he needs God's help to reach God.

ORDINARY LEVEL

Exam-Style Questions

Understanding the poem

1	Who is the poem addressed to?
2	Who is the subject of the first five lines? What is the story that they refer to?
3	Why are larks an appropriate bird to choose for the image in lines 7–9 ('O let me rise / As larks …')?
4	What impression do you get of the speaker in lines 11–15?
5	In your own words, explain what the speaker wants to do in line 19 ('if I imp my wing on thine').

Thinking about the poem

1	How would you describe the mood of this poem? ■ Serene ■ Yearning ■ Optimistic ■ Ecstatic Or what other word would you use? Give reasons for your answer.
2	Why, do you think, does Herbert write 'the flight *in* me' (lines 10 and 20) rather than, for example, 'the flight *of* me'?
3	Comment on the way in which the form of the poem contributes to its meaning.
4	Comment on the way in which the sounds of the words contribute to the poem's meaning.
5	What do you learn, if anything, about the speaker of the poem?

Imagining

1	Write your own pattern poem on any subject you like, using the shape of the words on the page to match your subject in some ways. You can use rhyme and metre if you like, but you don't have to.
2	In groups of four or five, experiment with ways of performing this poem. Can you find ways of using different speakers, ways of speaking, volume and pitch, physical shapes and actions, to bring out the form and meaning of the poem? Show what you have come up with to the other groups.

SNAPSHOT

- Pattern poem
- The form contributes to the poem's meaning
- Prayer or meditation at Easter
- Based on the Christian stories of the Fall and
- Christ's resurrection
- Paradox of *felix culpa*
- Imagery of flying
- Simple but intimate language
- Use of alliteration and assonance

Andrew Hudgins

b. 1951

The Glass Hammer

Biography

Andrew Leon Hudgins was born on 22 April 1951 in Killeen, Texas. His strict father was a soldier, and during Andrew's childhood the family moved between different military bases in the Southern states of America and abroad. After Huntington College, where he was an average student but a 'voracious reader', Hudgins attended the University of Alabama, where he achieved a BA in English and history in 1974 and an MA in English in 1976, and later studied at Syracuse University in New York. His first collection of poetry, *Saints and Strangers* (1986), was shortlisted for the prestigious Pulitzer Prize. His poems have a strong narrative voice and are often quirky and amusing, while his style has been described as modern American Gothic. This genre often features characters who seem unable to use logic to overcome their perversity and tends to use grotesque, nightmarish imagery to explore themes including history, religion and family.

Hudgins has completed several residencies, including some at the artists' colony in Yaddo (in Saratoga Springs, New York State), and has been awarded a Guggenheim fellowship. He has also won the Harper Lee Prize. As well as poetry, Hudgins has published essays and literary criticism. He currently teaches at Ohio State University. He lives in Ohio with his wife, the writer Erin McGraw.

ORDINARY LEVEL

Before you read

 Why do we have ornaments in our homes? Do you have any? Ponder and discuss these questions with your classmates.

The Glass Hammer

My mother's knickknack crystal hammer
shone on the shelf. 'Put that thing down.
It's not a play-pretty'. Tap, tap,
against my wooden blocks. 'I said,
PUT   THAT   THING   DOWN!'   5

But when she wasn't looking – ha! –
I'd sneak back to the hammer, and heft it.
Enchanted, I held it to my eyes
And watched, through it, the living room
Shift, waver, and go shimmery – haloed   10

with hidden fire. Our worn green sofa glowed
and lost its shape, as if some deeper shape
were trying to break loose. The chairs,
the walls, the cross-stitched pictures all
let go, smeared into one another.   15

I scrounged a rust-flecked nail and hit it.
The hammer shattered in my hand.
Blood spattered on my shorts. I screamed,
was snatched off my fat bloody feet,
rushed to the doctor, stitched, cooed at, spanked,   20

embraced, told never, never, never
do that again, and pondered how
I could, the hammer having burst,
and not, therefore, a proper hammer
despite the gorgeous world it held.   25

Glossary

1	*knickknack*:	an ornament
3	*play-pretty*:	a decorative toy
7	*heft*:	lift something heavy
10	*waver*:	to move in a wave-like motion
10	*haloed*:	ringed with light
14	*cross-stitched*:	a popular form of embroidery using x-shaped stiches to form words and images, which is usually framed and hung

Andrew Hudgins

Guidelines

This poem comes from the fourth of seven poetry collections by the Texas-born poet. The collection's full title is *The Glass Hammer: A Southern Childhood* (1994) and contains sixty-five short lyrical poems exploring Hudgins' life in Texas and Alabama as the eldest son in a military family. The mix of grotesque imagery combined with a strong sense of family root this poem in the American Gothic tradition (see the biography). This is the first poem in the collection, which includes lots of playful poems with equally playful titles; 'Grandmother's Spit', 'Biff Burger' and 'James Bond Considers Career Opportunities in Library Science' are some examples.

Commentary

Stanzas 1 to 3

The crystal hammer of the title is clearly prized by the speaker's mother, who keeps it 'on the shelf'. The object is purely decorative and is certainly not a toy. Despite his mother's vehement demands for the boy to stay away from the hammer, he persists in fiddling with it, 'Tap, tap, / against my wooden blocks'. Having ignored her twice the boy gleefully defies her again and '– ha! –' sneaked it from the shelf.

At first it is the view of the room through the hammer which 'Enchanted' the boy so much; he marvels at how it transforms their shabby home. The crystal distorts the room with a kaleidoscopic effect and as the boy peers through it the room seems to shimmer and become suffused with light, 'haloed / with hidden fire'. The 'worn green sofa' now glows. Ordinary objects like the chairs and cross-stitch pictures seem to abandon their rigidity, 'let go' and melt into one another, 'smeared'.

Stanzas 4 and 5

Soon, however, the decorative aspect of the hammer becomes secondary to the practical use the young speaker feels it should have. Resourcefully, he 'scrounged a rust-flecked nail' and, perhaps predictably, hit it with the hammer, which just as predictably 'shattered in my hand'. A scene of confusion and carnage follows. There is blood, screaming and stitching as the boy is rushed 'off my fat bloody feet' to the doctor by his frantic mother, who seems torn between concern for her injured child – 'embraced', 'cooed at' – and outrage at his disobedience. He is 'spanked' and warned 'never, never, never / do that again'. This command puzzles our young speaker, who, with the innocent and literal mind of a child, puzzles at how that would be even possible since the hammer in question has been obliterated.

Themes and imagery

Family and childhood are obvious themes here. Hudgins writes extensively about his mother, father and siblings in this collection. The mother seems to try her best to be strict, 'PUT THAT THING DOWN', but is no match for her tenacious child: ' – ha! – / I'd sneak back to the hammer, and heft it.' The frustration of parenting is clearly displayed in the mother's divided reaction to the child's injury at the end of the poem, where she spanks and embraces him almost simultaneously.

ORDINARY LEVEL

The value of a thing is a more abstract theme. **Is something decorative more or less worthwhile than something practical?** The hammer is pretty and also prettifies the room: 'the living room / shift, waver, and go shimmery'. However, it does not function as a utile (practical/useful) object. A hammer should bang in a nail, as far as the speaker is concerned, but this one does not: 'I scrounged a rust-flecked nail, and hit it. / The hammer shattered in my hand.' We might just put this down to childhood naivety and yet if we ponder this idea more deeply we might ask ourselves why have such an object? What is the point of a crystal hammer anyway? Is the fact that the hammer lifts the very ordinary room out of its tired shabbiness into a glowing and shifting wonder something that informs this debate? Note the image of the light being like a halo around the room. There is an almost **sacred dimension** to this image. Yet consider also that the hammer ultimately injures the boy when he seeks to do something practical with it. What, then, does the crystal hammer symbolise? Does it show that art lifts us out of the ordinary? Is it representative of the **gulf between how adults and children see the world**? Or something else? Perhaps the hammer is like the poem; it is not the real thing but an artistic reflection or **representation of a real experience**. But how useful or practical is poetry or art in general? The hammer might also represent justice.

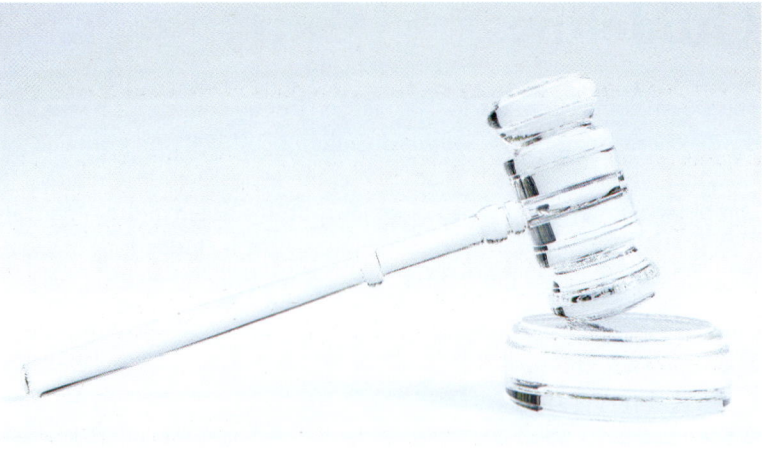

> A hammer-like object, a gavel, is used by a judge in a courtroom to keep order. Is the injury received by the boy a sort of natural justice for disobeying his mother?

Form and language

> 'Despite a highly developed technique, his voice has a rough veneer' said one critic of Hudgins's work. Do you agree with this statement in the light of this poem?

This narrative poem has a rigid form consisting of five five-line stanzas, but **dialogue, enjambment and playful language** soften this rigidity. Contrasts such as this are a feature of the poem; the hammer as toy or ornament, the mother's conflicting reactions to her son's injury, the shabby room and its transformed state all contain **vivid contrasts**.

The words 'knickknack' and 'play-pretty' add to the quick rhythm of the first four lines, with one nine- and then three eight-syllable lines. The repetition in 'tap, tap' also emphasises this playful mood. The rhythm and mood are broken by the repeated exhortation of the mother, now capitalised to show her frustration: 'PUT   THAT   THING   DOWN', with four short, forceful syllables. Hudgins leaves significant gaps between each word. We might all recognise **the cadence** of a parent about to lose their temper; the words are almost punctuated by gaps of trying to hold on to whatever patience remains while anger builds, and the volume increases! The playful '– ha! –' in stanza two shows the mischievous nature of the boy, who is comically unaffected by his mother's growing ire. The repetition of 'h' sounds in these lines softens the language and shows the wonder

Andrew Hudgins

of the boy enchanted by not only the hammer but by his success in outwitting his mother, 'I'd sneak back to the hammer, and heft it. /Enchanted, / … and watched … / shift…and go shimmery – haloed'. Note Hudgins' **clever use of gaps and dashes to create mood and immediacy** in these first two stanzas.

Enjambment (run on lines) is used repeatedly, which adds to the flow of the action, for example 'haloed / with hidden fire'. The past-tense verbs in the final three stanzas create great energy and imagery in the poem. The sofa 'glowed', the objects in the room 'smeared into one another', he 'scrounged' a nail, the hammer 'shattered' and he 'screamed', was 'snatched', 'stitched' and 'spanked' before being 'embraced'. These one- and two-syllable verbs lend power and energy to the poem. You might also have noticed **the sibilance** of some of these words, speeding up the rhythm of the poem in the panicked section where the boy is hurt. See if you can find others.

We can see lots of sibilance in the verbs above and Hudgins uses **alliteration** effectively too. One particularly strong example is 'fat bloody feet' (line 19). The image is at once visceral and cute; the 'f' sounds give the phrase force, yet we can also picture the chubby feet of a child lending a cuteness and vulnerability to the image.

The poem is narrative in style – a childhood memory is recounted and brought vividly to life – but Hudgins lifts the poem from mere anecdote by **exposing the dilemma** at the heart of the imagery and the story; he 'pondered how' this shattered hammer, 'having burst', was 'not … a proper hammer / despite the gorgeous world it held'. We are invited to ponder this too.

Exam-Style Questions

Understanding the poem

1	What does the speaker's mother tell him to do with the hammer? Why, do you think, does she order him to do this?
2	Does the child heed her? Give evidence for your answer.
3	What does the child do when his mother is not looking?
4	What does the capitalisation and gaps in the mother's demand in line 5 show us about her tone and mood?
5	What about the glass hammer seems to entrance the speaker so much?
6	What does the boy do to cause the hammer to shatter?
7	Describe in your own words the scene that follows the breaking of the hammer.
8	In the final stanza, what puzzling idea is 'pondered' by the speaker? Does he admire or dismiss the hammer at the end?

ORDINARY LEVEL

Thinking about the poem

1. The glass hammer is placed 'on the shelf'. Why, do you think, is it placed in this position?
2. 'Knickknack' and 'play-pretty' are words used in stanza 1. What, do you think, do these words mean? What sort of words are these?
3. Describe the character of the boy. Does he seem mischievous, curious, poor, naughty or something else? Use three words to describe him. Perhaps discuss your ideas with a classmate.
4. Read over lines 9–15 of the poem, which describe the 'shimmery' prismatic effect the hammer has, distorting the shabby room. What details did you like best in this section? Explain.
5. What is the theme of the poem, in your opinion? You may choose the one you feel best describes the theme or you can choose your own: childhood nostalgia; the consequences of disobedience; ornament versus utility; justice.
6. Trace the tone of the poem as it changes through the stanzas. Where, how and why do changes in tone occur?
7. Would you consider the overall general viewpoint of the poem to be positive or negative? Explain.

Imagining

1. Write a descriptive passage about how you imagine the hammer looks. Use lots of aesthetic language.
2. With a classmate, write a dialogue in which the mother of the child tells his father about the incident. Each take the part of a parent. Include lots of stage directions to convey mood, reactions, etc.
3. Write or talk about an object that is treasured in your home. Is it useful or decorative or both?
4. The English artist William Morris once said, 'Have nothing in your house that you do not know to be useful, or believe to be beautiful.' Do you agree with this statement? Perhaps its ideas could form the basis of a class debate.

SNAPSHOT

- Anecdotal style
- Rigid form
- First-person narrative
- Contrast
- Sound effects
- Childhood
- Transformation
- Practicality/ utility
- Symbolism of hammer
- Humour
- Forceful verbs

Francis Ledwidge

1887–1917

Lament for Thomas MacDonagh   540

Biography

Francis Ledwidge was born near Slane, Co. Meath, in 1887, the eighth of nine children in a farmworker's family. He was five when his father died, leaving the family in poverty. He left school at thirteen, and worked as a farmhand, a road mender, a copper miner and a shop assistant. Meanwhile, he read widely and wrote poems for local newspapers. Lord Dunsany, a local landlord and writer, allowed him to use his library and helped him with money and advice. Although Ledwidge was a nationalist and a member of the Irish Volunteers, he enlisted in the Royal Inniskilling Fusiliers, Lord Dunsany's regiment, and fought on the British side in the First World War. His first volume of poems, *Songs of the Fields*, was published in 1915 when he was in the Balkans. He was killed by a stray shell near Ypres in Belgium on 31 July 1917.

ORDINARY LEVEL

Before you read

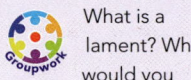 What is a lament? What would you expect to find in a poem with 'lament' in its title? Share your knowledge and ideas in small groups.

Lament for Thomas MacDonagh

He shall not hear the bittern cry
In the wild sky, where he is lain,
Nor voices of the sweeter birds
Above the wailing of the rain.

Nor shall he know when loud March blows   5
Thro' slanting snows her fanfare shrill,
Blowing to flame the golden cup
Of many an upset daffodil.

But when the Dark Cow leaves the moor,
And pastures poor with greedy weeds,   10
Perhaps he'll hear her low at morn
Lifting her horn in pleasant meads.

Glossary

Title	**Thomas MacDonagh**: (1878–1916) teacher, poet and playwright from Co. Tipperary, who became one of the Easter Rising leaders and a signatory of the Proclamation and who was executed by firing squad at Kilmainham Gaol on 3 May 1916
1	*bittern*: marsh bird of the heron family known for its booming call
6	*Thro'*: through
6	*fanfare*: short ceremonial tune or flourish, usually played on a trumpet or other brass instruments
9	*Dark Cow*: traditional poetic symbol of Ireland
11	*low*: moo
12	*meads*: meadows; fields

Francis Ledwidge

Guidelines

This poem was written to commemorate Ledwidge's friend and fellow poet Thomas MacDonagh, who had been executed in May 1916 for his part in the Easter Rising. Ledwidge shared MacDonagh's nationalist beliefs, but they found themselves on different sides: Ledwidge with the British Army in the First World War and MacDonagh with the Irish Volunteers against the British. Although he remained a loyal soldier, Ledwidge became disillusioned with the war, and on his final leave home he told his brother that he would not choose to fight at that stage even if the Germans were coming over their garden wall. In this, his best-known poem, Ledwidge makes clear his republican sympathies.

Commentary

Title

When it was first printed in the collection of Ledwidge's poetry assembled by Lord Dunsany after the poet's death, this poem was entitled simply 'Thomas McDonagh'. Without that indication of who 'he' in the poem is, there would be no way of knowing its subject. Later editors made it clearer exactly what sort of poem this is by adding 'Lament for' to the title. **A lament is a poem expressing grief for someone who has died.**

> **'The Yellow Bittern'**
>
> Thomas MacDonagh wrote a translation of an old Irish poem called 'The Yellow Bittern', which contains the lines: 'It's not for the common birds that I'd mourn, / The blackbird, the corn-crake, or the crane, / But for the bittern that's shy and apart / And drinks in the marsh from the lone bog-drain.' Ledwidge's mention of the bittern in the first line of his poem is probably a tribute to MacDonagh's poem, which mentions the bittern in a context of grief.

Stanzas 1–2

The first two stanzas create a **bleak, sorrowful atmosphere** appropriate to a lament, with the 'wild sky' and 'wailing' rain, the 'slanting snows' and the 'upset' daffodils. The sentence structure can be a little confusing: 'In the wild sky' (line 2) belongs with line 1, so it is the bittern's cry that is heard in the wild sky, not that 'he is lain' in the wild sky. In other words, MacDonagh will not be able to hear the bittern, with its deep booming call, nor the 'voices of the sweeter birds' from his grave (the place where 'he is lain') in Dublin. Notice that the word 'bittern' contains the word 'bitter', which makes the contrast with the 'sweeter' birds all the more pointed.

The second stanza imagines another scene MacDonagh will not experience: the March gales at the end of winter blowing the snow sideways and knocking over the daffodils. Should we look for symbolic significance here? Is March's 'fanfare' a military call to arms? Perhaps those 'upset' daffodils might stand for the rebels who fell in the Easter Rising of 1916, and the wind, by 'Blowing to flame' their 'golden cup', is breathing new life back into them, or into their cause? Certainly some sort of rebirth is being hinted at here.

Stanza 3

In the final stanza the **symbolism – and politics – comes to the fore**. We can read the daffodils simply as daffodils blown by the March winds, but the 'Dark Cow' with its ominous capital letters clearly stands for something else. Were that not so, it would be hard to find meaning in the words. Why should it be any more important to hear a cow mooing than wind blowing or a bird singing? The fact that **the dark cow is an old symbol for Ireland**, used by the Jacobite poets in the eighteenth century, and possibly with its origins in ancient Irish legends, gives you the key. Once you have that key, the symbolism of the rest of the stanza

ORDINARY LEVEL

becomes clear. The moor with its 'pastures poor' stands for the impoverished state of Ireland, choked by the 'greedy weeds' of British occupation. Ledwidge is looking forward to a time when Ireland is free and prosperous, in 'pleasant meads', and he imagines that perhaps MacDonagh will be able to hear the 'Dark Cow' and be comforted, knowing that what he had fought for, Ireland's freedom, has been accomplished.

There is, perhaps, **a question of consistency** here. The first two stanzas tell us that MacDonagh, as he lies in the grave, will not be able to hear the bittern or the 'sweeter birds' (stanza 1) and that he will not even know when the winds of March are blowing (stanza 2). This would suggest that in the afterlife, MacDonagh's spirit has no consciousness of what is happening in this life. Then, in stanza 3, Ledwidge leaves open the possibility that MacDonagh will be able to hear the 'Dark Cow' lowing when Ireland has won her freedom. Is this a problem with the poem, do you think?

Dunsany's explanation

Ledwidge's patron, Lord Dunsany, understood quite well what Ledwidge was saying in this poem, even though he himself was strongly opposed to the 1916 Rising. Commenting that 'some may wonder' that Ledwidge could have written such a poem in the circumstances, he suggested that 'rather than attribute curious sympathies to this brave young Irish soldier I would ask his readers to consider the irresistible attraction that a lost cause has for almost any Irishman'.

Themes and imagery

As well as mourning for his dead friend, Ledwidge is making **a political statement** in this poem. The **rain, snow and wind** imagery of the first two stanzas creates a bleak atmosphere that corresponds with the feelings of **grief** he is expressing. As discussed above, there are undertones of **symbolism** that are made overt in the final stanza.

It is worth asking why Ledwidge expressed his thoughts indirectly, through symbolism that has to be unlocked for the poem to be understood. Although he had strong nationalist sympathies, he was a soldier in the British Army when he wrote the poem. Perhaps he felt he needed to be secretive about what he wanted to say.

Form and language

A great part of the poem's impact comes from the music its words make. Its rhymes are the central part of that music. The rhyming scheme of the poem is influenced by that of Gaelic poetry, in which rhyming is not simply between end-words, but also between a word at the end of a line and a word in the middle of the next line, so that there are **two interconnected rhyming schemes**. In the third stanza, for example, as well as the end-rhymes of 'weeds' and 'meads' on the second and fourth lines, 'moor' at the end of the first line rhymes with 'poor' in the middle of the line after, and 'morn' at the end of the third line rhymes with 'horn' in the fourth. The second stanza works in the same way, except that one rhyme is 'hidden' inside a word, as 'cup' rhymes with '*up*set'. The only difference in stanza 1 is that nothing in line 4 rhymes with 'birds' in line 3.

The rhyming is reinforced by **strong assonance** that is often close to internal rhyme. It tends to fall on long vowel sounds, such as 'wild sky' (line 2), 'wailing of the rain' (line 4), which together suggest the wild weather in an almost onomatopoeic way. There is a lot of alliteration and consonance too. Look at the way the 'f' sound repeats itself through the second stanza, and how 'l' and 'p' intertwine through the third.

The language of the poem is largely **clear and simple**, although the syntax can be a little confusing. It is not, however, conversational or casual, and Ledwidge uses poetic devices such as personifying the March wind as a woman blowing a fanfare. He also sometimes **inverts the natural word order**, a device that is common in poetry, especially when rhymes need to be found. For example, he writes 'fanfare shrill' (line 6) instead of 'shrill fanfare', and 'pastures poor' (line 10) instead of 'poor pastures'.

SNAPSHOT

- Poem in tribute to a dead hero
- A patriotic poem
- Imagery drawn from nature
- Interpretation depends on background information
- Symbol of the 'Dark Cow'
- Language of poem is simple and familiar
- The sounds of the poem echo its meaning

ORDINARY LEVEL

Exam-Style Questions

Understanding the poem

1	What mood is created in the first stanza? How does Ledwidge create this mood?
2	What impression do you get of 'loud March' in the second stanza? Is it all negative or are there any positives? Explain.
3	Describe the tone of the first two stanzas. For example: ■ Mournful ■ Angry ■ Bitter ■ Heroic Or would you choose a different word? Give reasons for your answer.
4	How does the final stanza differ from the other two?
5	Comment on the imagery of the final stanza.

Thinking about the poem

1	Ledwidge chose an unusual rhyming scheme for his poem. Do you think it works well? Explain your answer.
2	In your opinion, which of the following words best describes the effect of this poem: depressing, optimistic or mournful? Or would you choose a different word? Give reasons for your answer.
3	Some critics have argued that the reader would not know that this poem is a lament without that information in the title. Do you agree? Give reasons for your answer.
4	How do the sounds of the words contribute to the effect of this poem?
5	Would it be possible for any reader to know what this poem is about without a good deal of background information? Explain your answer.

Imagining

1	 Your group has been asked to make an audio-visual presentation to accompany a reading of this poem. What images, music, sounds or other effects would you use? You will probably need to make different choices for each stanza.
2	Imagine you were Lord Dunsany, who was a great admirer and supporter of Ledwidge but was strongly opposed to the 1916 Rising. You have been sent this poem after Ledwidge's death. Write a letter to a friend explaining your reaction to the poem.

Richard Murphy
1927–2018

Moonshine   546

Biography

Richard Murphy was born in Milford House, his family home in Galway. His father, Sir William Lindsay Murphy, was in the British Colonial Service, and Murphy spent his childhood in Ceylon (now Sri Lanka) and the Bahamas. He was educated at boarding schools in Ireland and England, and won a scholarship to Oxford at the age of seventeen, where he studied English under C. S. Lewis. He also studied at the Sorbonne in Paris. Murphy returned to Ireland in the early 1960s. He set up home on the island of Inisbofin, making his living from an old sailing boat, which he restored. His 1963 collection *Sailing to an Island* won wide acclaim.

Murphy's book *The Price of Stone* (1985) charts his colourful life through the houses and buildings he has known. His 1968 long poem *The Battle of Aughrim* is of interest for many reasons, not least because his ancestors fought on both sides. Among Murphy's most famous literary friends were the poets Ted Hughes and Sylvia Plath who visited him in September 1962, a short time before Plath's death. Richard Murphy was poet-in-residence at a number of American universities. For many years he divided his time between Dublin and Durban in South Africa, where his daughter Emily lives. His *Collected Poems* was published in 2000 and in 2002 he published a memoir, *The Kick: A Life among Writers*. In later years he returned to Sri Lanka and died there on 30 January 2018.

ORDINARY LEVEL

Before you read

 The word 'Moonshine' has a number of different meanings. What do you expect from a poem entitled, 'Moonshine'? Share your thoughts with a partner and then read the poem to see if your expectations are fulfilled.

Moonshine

To think
I must be alone:
To love
We must be together.

I think I love you   5
When I'm alone
More than I think of you
When we're together.

I cannot think
Without loving   10
Or love
Without thinking.

Alone I love
To think of us together:
Together I think   15
I'd love to be alone.

Glossary

Title **Moonshine**: the word has a variety of meanings, including: moonlight; foolish talk or thoughts; illicitly distilled whiskey or spirits

Guidelines

Murphy's short, clever poem brings a lightness of touch to the age-old conflict between the need for love and the artist's need to be alone. Witty and elegant, the poem hovers between nonsense and distilled wisdom, as suggested in its brilliant title. The clever arrangement of words (especially the last word of each line) suggests the nature of the conundrum. For admirers of his work, 'Moonshine' is an example of Murphy's poised and dazzling style.

Richard Murphy

Commentary

Stanza 1
The speaker sets out his dilemma in the first stanza in the form of two witty formulations. The first emphasises the need for the 'I' to be alone: 'To think / I must be alone'. The second emphasises the necessity of the 'We' to be together: 'To love / We must be together.'

Stanza 2
In the second stanza, the speaker makes an admission that, however playful, may sound insulting to the lover to whom it is addressed. He admits that 'I think I love you / When I'm alone / More than I think of you / When we're together.' It is hardly an admission that a lover would want to hear.

Stanza 3
In stanza three, the speaker considers the relationship between loving and thinking and thinking and loving. He declares that, for him, one cannot happen without the other.

Stanza 4
The fourth stanza, which risks exasperating the beloved to whom it is addressed, declares that when he is alone, he wants to be together and when they are together, he wants to be alone! Significantly, the poem ends with the line, 'I'd love to be alone.' Add this to the nine 'I's in the poem and you might be forgiven for concluding that that the speaker is more than a little self-obsessed.

Form and language

This is a light-hearted poem that is composed in a careful, witty way. Each short stanza is **perfectly balanced**. The arrangement of the final word in each stanza **echoes** the meaning of the entire poem. The phrasing of each line is elegant and formal. Each statement is clear and direct.

Theme

The poem is a playful meditation on four terms: 'I', 'We', 'think' and 'love'. In the manner of a mathematical equation, the terms are moved around in an attempt to make them balance.

The poem sets up a conflict between the romantic idea of the artist's **need for solitude and detachment versus the need for love and intimacy**. The detached treatment of the theme suggests that the speaker will come down on the side of detachment.

The poem has no imagery. It is a poem of direct statement, an accurate and witty record of the speaker's thoughts on a subject that could, in the hands of a different poet, be treated in a personal and emotional way. However, the speaker seems unwilling to surrender his educated, detached self for the more exciting, if unpredictable, state of loving intimacy.

> **High Island**
>
> Richard Murphy bought the uninhabited monastic island High Island, three miles off the coast of Connemara, in the 1960s. For one critic, the island served as a symbol of artistic solitude and Murphy's commitment to the craft of poetry. The poet said of the purchase: 'I got excited at the thought of buying this inaccessible holy island, restoring the beehive cells and oratory of its derelict hermitage and preserving the place from destruction either by tourists or by sheep.'

ORDINARY LEVEL

Exam-Style Questions

Understanding the poem

1	When does the speaker think he is in love?
2	The four lines in the first and last stanzas end with the same four words. Comment on the significance (or otherwise) of the change in order from stanza 1 to stanza 4.
3	What, in your view, is the tone of the poem? ■ Playful ■ Loving ■ Teasing ■ Selfish ■ Other Explain your choice.
4	Which **one** of the following statements best describes your view of the speaker of the poem? ■ The speaker is really clever ■ The speaker is really annoying ■ The speaker is really confused ■ The speaker is really charming Explain your choice with reference to the text.
5	Experiment with reading the poem in different ways and mark the words that need to be stressed as well as any pauses and hesitations.

Thinking about the poem

1	Using the glossary, consider the various meanings of the word 'moonshine' and the relevance of each to the poem.
2	'The most important word in understanding the poem is the word "must", as it is used in lines two and four.' Do you agree with this point of view?
3	The last line of the poem is 'I'd love to be alone.' Is this an appropriate line on which to end? Explain your answer.
4	Which of these three statements is closest to your own reading of the poem? ■ This is a silly playful, poem and should not be taken seriously ■ Although it is light-hearted, the poem deals with a real dilemma ■ For all its cleverness, this is a really insulting poem Explain your choice.

Imagining

1	Using the same range of words as used by Richard Murphy, write your own poem on a similar theme.
2	Imagine you are the person addressed in the poem. Write your response to the poem, choosing what you consider an appropriate tone.

SNAPSHOT

- Suggestive title
- Theme of the writer's need for love and the need to be alone
- Light treatment of themes
- Clever word play
- Witty and playful tone
- Balanced phrases and stanzas
- Presents the dilemma of the speaker
- More emphasis on 'I' than 'We'

Julie O'Callaghan
b. 1954

The Net 550
Problems 554

Biography

Julie O'Callaghan was born in Chicago in 1954 into an Irish-American family. She was the oldest girl and the second oldest in a family of seven children. Her family lived five minutes from the beach at Lake Michigan and the children spent the summer swimming and playing in the sand. In school, English was her favourite subject and she enjoyed writing stories, articles and poetry. Julie came to Ireland as a student in 1974. She was to spend a year studying at Trinity College before returning home. However, she met her future husband, the poet, essayist and critic Denis O'Driscoll (who died in 2012), and never left. She works in the library at Trinity College. Julie O'Callaghan has published several collections of poetry for children and young adults as well as her work for adults. She has earned numerous distinctions and awards for her work, including a number of Arts Council Bursaries. She is a member of Aosdána, the national academy of arts. On being a poet in Ireland, she says: 'Poetry in Ireland comes from an ancient tradition and is part of the culture. You don't have to apologise for it. I can't think of a better place to be writing.' Julie is known for her humorous, sly take on the absurdities of ordinary life.

ORDINARY LEVEL

Before you read

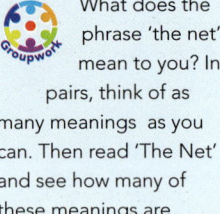 What does the phrase 'the net' mean to you? In pairs, think of as many meanings as you can. Then read 'The Net' and see how many of these meanings are relevant to the poem.

The Net

I am the Lost Classmate
being hunted down the superhighways
and byways of infinite cyber-space.
How long can I evade the class committee
searching for my lost self?   5

I watch the list
of Found Classmates
grow by the month.
Corralled into a hotel ballroom
festooned with 70s paraphernalia,   10

bombarded with atmospheric
hit tunes, the Captured Classmates
from Sullivan High School
will celebrate thirty years
of freedom from each other.   15

I peek at the message board:
my locker partner,
out in California, looks forward
to being reunited with
her old school chums.   20

Wearing a disguise, I calculate
the number of months left
for me to do what I do best,
what I've always done:
slip through the net.   25

Glossary

3	*infinite*: vast, limitless	
3	*cyber-space*: here, the internet; more generally, the environment or space in which communication takes place over computer networks	
9	*Corralled*: herded in and confined as if in a corral or animal enclosure; it can also mean 'captured'	
10	*paraphernalia*: trappings, accessories	
13	*Sullivan High School*: the secondary school in Chicago that Julie O'Callaghan attended	

Julie O'Callaghan

Guidelines

'The Net' was inspired by a real event, when Julie O'Callaghan saw that Sullivan High School was organising a thirtieth anniversary reunion for her class. In her words, 'It gave me the creeps having people hunting for me in the cyber-world.'

The poem is humorous and deals with two interesting themes. The first is the sinister nature of the internet and its powers of surveillance, which can track and locate individuals even when they wish to remain invisible and live a private life. The second is the pressure on people to celebrate school reunions and subscribe to the myth that schooldays are the best days of your life, especially if, like the poet, you are shy and retiring by nature.

Commentary

Stanza 1
In the first stanza, the speaker presents herself as 'the Lost Classmate' being hunted down by the class committee. She wonders how long she can evade detection.

Stanzas 2 and 3
On the Internet site set up for the reunion, the speaker watches the list of 'Found Classmates' grow as more and more of her fellow students are contacted. She imagines the celebration: the former students 'herded' into a hotel that is decorated with 'paraphernalia' from the 70s and where hit songs from the time are played.

Stanza 4
The speaker takes a look at the message board on the internet site set up for the reunion. She sees that her locker partner is looking forward to the reunion.

Stanza 5
In the final stanza, the speaker calculates the number of months she has to evade detection and slip through the net.

Themes and imagery

The poem works by playing on the meaning of the word 'net'. The internet (the 'Net') is not viewed as an exciting worldwide form of communication, but as a sinister worldwide form of surveillance, entrapment and tyranny. The Net **catches people**. However, the speaker of the poem does not wish to be caught and hopes, as she says in the last line of the poem, 'to slip through the net'. The net imagery is used in a humorous way to describe the **oppressive nature** of school reunions, where individuals are forced to celebrate their time in school. For the speaker, the thirty years that have elapsed since she left school has been a period of freedom. To go to the reunion would be **a form of recapture**. She and the other 'Captured Classmates' (line 12) would be 'Corralled into a hotel ballroom' (line 9) and 'bombarded' (line 11) with hit tunes from the period.

The imagery in the poem suggests that the speaker is a character in an espionage thriller, trying to evade detection. In this world, the class committee take on a sinister role, chasing down and capturing 'lost

ORDINARY LEVEL

classmates' like the intelligence service of a totalitarian state. For the speaker of the poem, the growing list of 'Found Classmates' is not a cause for rejoicing. Like an escaped prisoner reading that her fellow escapees have been recaptured, the Lost Classmate feels **the net tightening**. However, she is determined to stay in hiding and slip through the net. 'Wearing a disguise', the speaker keeps an eye on the internet site that tells her what is happening.

As portrayed in the poem, the internet creates a **nightmarish society** in which the individual never feels safe and secure. There is the constant fear of being discovered and subject to unwelcome attention.

Form of the poem

The poem is written in five five-line stanzas. The stanzas are unrhymed and irregular and follow the pattern of speech. This gives a conversational feel to the poem. However, part of the pleasure of reading the poem is recognising the many sounds that repeat and echo through it. See, for example, how the 'c' and 'l' sounds feature throughout the poem. Look at the rhyme between 'superhighways' (line 2) and 'byways' (line 3); or the echo between 'corralled 'and 'ballroom' in line 9.

Exam-Style Questions

Understanding the poem

1	What does the speaker mean when she says she is 'The Lost Classmate' (line 1)?
2	Who is hunting her down?
3	Which of the following best describes the feelings of the speaker as she watches the list of found classmates? ■ She is alarmed ■ She is determined ■ She is flattered Explain your choice.
4	What, according to the speaker in stanza 3, will the captured classmates have to celebrate?
5	What is the attitude of the speaker's 'locker partner' to the proposed reunion?
6	How can the speaker 'wear a disguise' in relation to the internet?

Julie O'Callaghan

Thinking about the poem

1. Comment on the phrase 'the Lost Classmate' and suggest what it means to you.
2. Comment on the use of the verbs 'corralled' and 'bombarded' in the poem.
3. What do the following verbs suggest about the life and attitude of the speaker: 'hunted', 'evade', 'peek', 'calculate'?
4. The poem is written in five-line stanzas. Why, do you think, has Julie O'Callaghan broken the lines in the way that she has? You might find it helpful to read the poem aloud a number of times before answering the question.
5. Trace the imagery of escape and capture, flight and pursuit in the poem. Do you think the imagery is effective? Explain your answer.
6. Having read the poem, what do you imagine were the speaker's feelings on leaving Sullivan High School?
7. The poem suggests that the internet is part of the technology of surveillance and tracking. Do you agree with this point of view? Explain your answer.

Imagining

1. Write a letter to Julie O'Callaghan in which you either: a) encourage her to attend the class reunion; or b) offer support for the point of view she expresses in the poem.
2. Compose a short poem inspired by the phrase 'infinite cyber-space'.
3. 'Even if you want to, the social network sites on the internet make it impossible to stay invisible and private.' Prepare a contribution to a class discussion on this statement.
4. You have been asked to make a short film version of the poem. Describe the atmosphere you wish to create. Outline the images, the shots and camera angles and the soundtrack you would use to create this atmosphere.

SNAPSHOT

- First person narrative
- Sounds echo and repeat
- Imagery of flight and pursuit
- Fear of discovery
- Symbolism of the net
- Interesting use of verbs
- Tyranny of media and internet
- Dislike of school reunions

ORDINARY LEVEL

Before you read

 Working with a partner, consider the most challenging problems ordinary people face in their lives. When you have read and discussed the poem, compare the issues you identified with those listed in the poem.

Glossary

4	*obliterate*: wipe out, destroy completely
15	*discoloration*: staining, fading of the original colour
21	*knuckleheads*: idiots, fools

Problems

Take weeds for example.
Like how they will overrun
your garden and your life
if you don't obliterate them.
But forget about weeds   5
– what about leaves?
Snails use them as handy
bridges to your flowers
and hordes of thuggish slugs
will invade – ever thought about that?   10
We won't even go into
how leaves block up the gutters.
I sure hope you aren't neglecting
any puddles of water in your bathtub
– discoloration will set in.   15
There is the wasp problem,
the storms problem, the grass
growing-between-the-bricks-in-the-driveway problem.
Then there's the remembering to
lock-all-the-windows problem.   20
Hey, knuckleheads!
I guess you just don't appreciate
how many problems there are.

Guidelines

Julie O'Callaghan got the idea for the poem when she and her husband moved into their new house in the 1990s and each had a different attitude to the minor problems that go with settling into a new home, with one wanting to solve all the problems and the other happy to ignore them. From this starting point, O'Callaghan portrays a person having a rant. The speaker sees many problems but is frustrated that the 'you' doesn't share his or her concern. In the speaker's world the glass is always half empty. For the reader, the rant seems comical, absurd and touching. O'Callaghan writes many of her poems in an American speaking voice. In an interview, she said:

> 'Americans have this wacky way of looking at things which I did not notice until I came here [to Ireland]. It's just so funny. Every time I go back I'm just listening. Because they say the funniest things.'

You might bear this in mind when reading 'Problems'.

The poem comes from O'Callaghan's 2005 collection of the same name, *Problems*.

Julie O'Callaghan

Commentary

Lines 1–4
Problem 1: weeds.
The poem is written as a dramatic monologue, like something we might hear in a play or a film. The opening line brings the reader right into the middle of the action: 'Take weeds for example.' It seems we are overhearing a casual conversation on gardening. The conversation could be between a couple of friends or neighbours. The tone seems easy-going: 'Like how they will overrun / your garden' (lines 2–3). We can imagine the speaker of the poem as a reasonable person making the kind of comment that people make all the time on subjects such as gardening or the weather, the kind of everyday subjects that allow people to connect with each other without anything being at stake or in dispute. However, when the speaker says that the weeds will overrun 'your life' (line 3), alarm bells begin to sound.

The suspicion that the speaker might lack a sense of proportion or reasonableness is confirmed in line 4 by the use of the verb 'obliterate'. When reading the poem, it is as if we, the readers, take a step back from the speaker at that point. We do not want to be drawn into an unbalanced and absurdly negative view of the world, even if we are fascinated to know why the speaker is getting so worked up, and are amused by the ridiculousness of his or her comments.

Lines 5–12
Problem 2: leaves.
The speaker is on a roll now. There is energy in line 5 – 'But forget about weeds' – and the speaker turns to another 'problem', that of leaves and how they act as bridges to allow 'hordes of thuggish slugs' (line 9) to invade the garden and attack 'your flowers' (line 8). The language is striking, the speaker feeling the need to warn 'you' to be on the lookout for snails and slugs in the garden. However, the tone seems aggressive: 'ever thought about that?' (line 10). This tone implies that the listener (the 'you' of the poem) is not paying enough attention to these problems, or that the speaker has been left to face them alone.

Lines 11 and 12 refer to another 'problem' caused by leaves: they block gutters. Up to this point, we can see a logic in the ideas of the speaker: weeds, garden, snails, slugs, flowers, leaves, gutters. The next movement of thought is less predictable.

Lines 13–15
Problem 3: puddles.
The reference to gutters may account for the sudden mention of the problem of 'puddles of water', but the reader has not been prepared for the location of these puddles: 'in your bathtub' (line 14). There is no logic to this and it seems a bit daft. As in the earlier part of the poem, the tone suggests that the speaker does not trust the 'you' to do what is required: 'I sure hope you aren't neglecting / any puddles …' (lines 13–14).

Lines 16–20
Four more problems.
Lines 16–20 present a list of 'problems' delivered in quick-fire succession. The 'problems' mentioned by the speaker (the wasps, the storms, the grass growing in the driveway, remembering to lock the windows) suggest someone who sees nothing but problems.

ORDINARY LEVEL

Lines 21–23

Problem 8: knuckleheads.
Having worked him or herself up into an agitated state, the speaker now turns to the biggest problem of all: all the 'knuckleheads' (line 21) who do not 'appreciate' all the problems there are, and who, by implication, do not appreciate the speaker who has tried to make 'you' aware of them. The last two lines can be read as the speaker dismissing 'you'; or they may suggest that the speaker has used up all his or her energy and is now overcome by the 'many problems there are' (line 23).

Language and form

The poem is dramatic and captures the voice of the speaker. It uses many of the words and phrases of everyday speech to shape the thought: 'Like how'; 'I sure hope'; 'Hey'; 'I guess'. The use of hyphens between the words, such as 'the grass / growing-between-the-bricks-in-the-driveway problem' (lines 17–18), creates a sense of energy and movement, as does the use of run-on lines or **enjambment**. The poem is not rhymed and is written in lines of varying length. The tone is negative, with the speaker expressing different degrees of excitement, alarm, accusation, frustration and contempt.

A notable feature of the poem is the strength in the language and the sounds of words, as in the phrase 'thuggish slugs', with its **internal rhyme and consonance**. If you read the poem aloud you will hear many sounds that require a physical effort to create them. These harsh guttural and explosive sounds add to the energy and expressiveness of the speaker's voice and capture the tones of disgust, anger or fear.

There are many examples of **repetition** in the poems, both of words and sounds. Look, for example, at the alliteration in 'thuggish', 'thought', 'that' or how the sounds echo across words, as in 'gutters', 'puddles', 'bathtub'. Contributing to the sense of an energetic speaker is the imagery of war in words like 'overrun', 'obliterate', 'hordes' and 'invade'.

Themes

One theme that emerges from the poem is **perspective**. One person's problem is often another person's delight; Gerard Manley Hopkins, for example, speaks of the beauty of spring 'When weeds … shoot long and lovely and lush'. Another theme is a person's ability to cope with the minor stresses of life. It is hard to decide whether the speaker is simply obsessed with order or is completely overwhelmed by the small 'problems' of everyday living. Another theme that emerges is **intolerance** – the speaker is so certain that his or her perspective is correct that everyone else is dismissed with contempt. The fact that the 'you' does not share the concerns of the speaker might be the very thing that provokes the increasing sense of anger and frustration.

Julie O'Callaghan

Reader's response

The reader might be amused by the speaker's **lack of balance**, by the sheer absurdity of what is said. The reader might feel sympathy for the speaker and his or her inability to cope with everyday problems. On the other hand, a reader might be irritated by the way the speaker dismisses as 'knuckleheads' everyone who does not share his or her point of view.

If readers see the speaker as addressing them directly, they might feel exhausted by the relentless identification of 'problems' or alarmed by the aggression in the speaker.

Exam-Style Questions

Understanding the poem

1	Consider the title of the poem. Does it make you want to read the rest of the poem? Explain your answer.
2	How does the opening of the poem suggest that the speaker is partway through a conversation?
3	In lines 2 and 3, what does the speaker suggest is the problem with weeds? How, in line 4, does s/he suggest this problem might be solved?
4	What is the speaker's problem with leaves (lines 5–10)?
5	What is the additional problem that the speaker identifies in line 12?
6	Do you think that any of the things mentioned by the speaker in lines 16–20 are, in fact, problems? Explain your answer.
7	Who, do you think, is the speaker addressing when s/he says 'Hey, knuckleheads!'? Give a reason for your answer.
8	How do you interpret the last two lines of the poem?

Thinking about the poem

1	In your view, what is the effect of the verb 'obliterate' in line 4?
2	Comment on the effectiveness of the description 'hordes of thuggish slugs' (line 9).
3	If you were to list the biggest problems in your life, would you include any of those mentioned by the speaker in lines 16 to 20? Explain your answer.
4	In line 21 the speaker calls his or her listeners 'knuckleheads'. What does this name tell you about the speaker?
5	Choose the two words from the following list that best describe the tone of the poem: frustrated, unreasonable, fearful, aggressive, alarmed, anxious. Explain your choice.

ORDINARY LEVEL

6	Select two examples of interesting sounds in the poem and say why you chose them.
7	Which of these two statements is closer to your reading of the poem? ■ The speaker of the poem is more pitiful than scary ■ The speaker of the poem is frustrated because people do not take things seriously Explain your choice.
8	'The theme of the poem is that of perspective and tolerance.' Give your view of this assessment of the poem.
9	Based on your reading of 'Problems', suggest an alternative title for the poem.
10	'"Problems" is not a poem that we should take too seriously. It's just a humorous representation of a person having a rant.' Give your opinion of this view of the poem.

Imagining

1	Imagine you are the 'you' of the poem. Write a monologue in which you have your say. You can begin the monologue with the words, 'Now, wait a minute'.
2	The poem is being dramatised as part of a television series entitled *I'm as Mad as Hell*. You are the director. Write notes to the actor on how you want him or her to play the part of the speaker.
3	Imagine the situation in which the speaker might have said these things. Write a short paragraph describing the scene.
4	Experiment with reading the poem in different accents and spoken by a man and then a woman. Which reading is most interesting? Explain your answer.

SNAPSHOT

- Dramatic monologue
- Humorous
- Clear picture of speaker's character emerges
- Language is vigorous and energetic
- Litany of problems
- Movement of thought becomes less predictable
- Speaker alienates listeners/readers
- Theme of perspective
- Repetition of words

Mary O'Malley

b.1954

Caoineadh Mháire   560

Biography

Mary O'Malley was born in Connemara in 1954 and educated at University College, Galway where she would later teach an MA course in writing. As she is the daughter of a fisherman, the sea features prominently in her work. She is also an active marine conservationist who has spent time aboard the *Celtic Explorer* vessel. She has taught creative writing in prisons and schools and the universities of Villanova in Pennsylvania, Lisbon (where she lived for eight years), Paris, Belfast, Derry and New York. O'Malley has also worked as an editor including on two books for children. She writes for and broadcasts regularly on RTÉ. A member of Aosdána, she has won a number of awards and is in demand as a reader of her own work both here and abroad. She lives in Moycullen, Co. Galway.

Caoineadh Mháire

Before you read

This poem is a lament. What do you understand by this term? What would you expect a lament to be about?

Why do we love men that are bad for us –
are we that weak? Hardly the kisses,
fruit in the mouth soon melts.
His Spaniard's eyes never settled on me right
but the mouth music lured me.   5

There was something old about his voice
that took the city ground from under me
and brought little yellow shells
scattering up the back streets of Glasgow.
Oh he was handsome, though, like a stag.   10

When I felt the fine sand
between my toes I should have run
to the nearest forgettable city boy
and chanced the ordinary,
but he sang and I was caught.   15

I listened as the hook eased in,
listened for the blas he put on my name
until all I could hear was my own breath
like the tide in a cave, echoing, going out
and the children crying.   20

A grey crow settled on my chest
and took his time.
A high price for a slow song:
'A Pheadair, a Aspail, an bhfaca tú mo ghrá bhán?
Ochón agus ochón ó'.   25

Glossary

Line	Term	Meaning
Title	*Caoineadh Mháire*	Marie's lament
5	*mouth music*	singing
17	*blas*	accent, can also mean taste or flavour
21	*grey crow*	grief
21	*chest*	heart
24/25	*'A Pheadair, a Aspail, an bhfaca tú mo ghrá bhán? / Ochón agus ochón ó'*	Peter, Apostle, have you seen my bright love (or radiant boy)? / Alas and alas o!)

Mary O'Malley

Guidelines

The poem refers to a well-known religious lament, 'Lament of the three Marys' 'Caoineadh na dTrí Mhuire' in which Mary searches for Jesus, asking Peter the Apostle where he is. Peter replies that he has been crucified. This poem is from O'Malley's 1997 collection *The Knife in the Wave* and is one of a suite of poems commissioned by RTÉ for a documentary by Michael Davitt on the Sean-nós singer Joe Heaney called 'Sing the Dark Away' (1996).

According to O'Malley, '**The poem is a persona poem**, where the poet uses the voice of a real or imaginary woman, in this case the wife of a singer.'

Joe Heaney

Joe Heaney was an Irish Sean-nós singer born in Carna, Galway in 1919. One of the most famous of the over five hundred songs in his repertoire is the 'Caoineadh na dTrí Mhuire'. 'The poem uses lines from this, 'one of the great laments, sung especially at Easter. In the song, 'Mo ghrá bhán' is Jesus, but in the poem it is the woman's husband'.

He lived in Glasgow with his wife Marie and travelled a lot, working and singing. In another poem in this collection, 'Geis', O'Malley writes, 'He was a singer … A thousand songs! Oh he was fine / my young king of the sky … I was the woman with red hair/watching his black eyes quench'. Marie died of TB after only six years of marriage. Heaney died in 1984 having moved to America where he felt Irish traditional music was more appreciated.

Commentary

Title

'Marie's Lament' is a reference to Joe Heaney's wife Marie and is linked to his famous rendition of the 'Caoineadh na dTrí Mhuire', but it's important to remember that the speaker is a persona and the content of the poem is not a faithful biography of her. It is not supposed to be – **she represents any woman who suffers the grief of lost love. Her tears and regret fill the poem.**

Stanza 1

The speaker wonders why women often fall for 'bad men' and questions whether the answer is weakness. She doubts the kisses they share explain this as kisses are fleeting and the sensation is soon forgotten: 'fruit in the mouth soon melts'. It seems this Spanish-looking man she loved did not reciprocate the intensity of her ardour: his 'eyes never settled on me right'. The stanza ends by answering the question which began it; in her case it was this Spaniard's singing which made her fall in love with him, his 'mouth music lured me'.

Stanza 2

The alluring voice of the speaker's beloved is further described; it had 'something old' about it (Heaney sang old, traditional Irish songs). His voice transported her from 'the city ground' of Glasgow to a beach somewhere far more exotic 'and brought little yellow shells / scattering up the back streets of Glasgow' – note how the alliteration of the 't's here sounds like the clattering of shells on a hard surface. Her lover is also manly, commanding and handsome, 'like a stag'. This man sounds like an alpha male, talented, strong and utterly captivating to the speaker.

Stanzas 3 and 4

She recalls how he made her feel 'the fine sand / between my toes', continuing the imagery of being on a sandy shore from stanza 2.

Regret is expressed here as she muses in hindsight that she should have 'run / to the nearest forgettable city boy / and chanced the ordinary', but she didn't stand a chance: 'he sang and I was caught.' **His voice and its spellbinding effect on the speaker is the lure that causes her to be caught in his magic like a fish on a hook.** The way he said her name, the 'blas' he used to say it, distracted her as 'the hook eased in' and before she knew it, she was his. All else except her own breathing seems to disappear under his spell and we are back to the seashore again as the sound of her inhale and exhale is 'like the tide in a cave, echoing, going out'. This has the quality of a surreal dream or an out of body experience emphasised by the repeated 'c' and 'ch' sounds, but the magic does not last forever. **The spell is broken by the sound on the edge of her consciousness, of 'the children crying'.** We are back to the reality of a hard life in urban Glasgow.

Stanza 5

Loneliness and grief descend on the speaker then like 'A grey crow' which 'settled' on her 'chest / and took his time'. **The poet says that 'the grey crow is grief and heartbreak, she is settled 'on the chest' in the sense of the heart, as sorrow and augur of death. Marie Heaney died of TB, the great scourge of that time**. Her suffering was a 'high price for a slow song'. Two lines of this song complete the poem wherein another woman grieves for a love she has lost. This may be the subject of the song that was the original 'mouth music' which so captivated the speaker in stanza one, and of course reflects her own loss and sorrow now. The poem ends on the long sad-sounding 'o's of the Irish for 'alas': 'Ochón agus ochón ó'.

Themes and imagery

Regret and lost love dominate the poem as the speaker rues falling for this handsome, talented Spaniard singer and not some more ordinary 'forgettable city boy' who wouldn't have broken her heart. Imagery of kisses, 'little yellow shells' and a handsome 'stag' soon change to 'children crying' and a 'grey crow' of grief sitting on the speaker's heart. **The contrast in these images conveys how exciting the relationship was at first, but how devastating its end was for her.** The **power of music and song** is very important here. We can be transported by a wonderful voice to different places and someone who sings traditional songs ('There was something old about his voice) keeps important history and culture alive, just as Joe Heaney did. O'Malley says, 'biography is only incidental to a poem, the starting point, but the real story is in what the singer puts into the song. **That is really what the poem is about – what makes a singer great.**'

Mary O'Malley

O'Malley's **imagery is very sensual**. We can imagine seeing the 'yellow shells', feeling 'fine sand' between our toes, hearing the tide go in and out or the crying children. The most sensual images centre on the mouth. The kisses are compared to 'fruit that soon melts' evoking our sense of taste. The voice of the singer is 'mouth music', 'old' and alluring, when she hears the 'blas' he puts on her name she is hooked and focuses on her breathing as if captured by an intense, aroused passion for him. Sound is evoked by these images.

A sense of place is created by the singer in the poem and within the poem itself. Glasgow is the setting for the relationship and the Spanish-looking singer seems to transport the speaker with his song to beaches and caves there. O'Malley grew up by the sea in the West of Ireland and explains, 'Spain featured largely in our imaginative lives in the West, whether because of the wreck of the Armada, the history of trade with Spain, or the strong images of a seafaring nation that was Catholic, loved singing and had sunshine and gold.' **The notion of seafaring is reinforced by the fishing imagery in the poem, she is 'lured' by his music and 'caught / … as the hook eased in'.**

Form and language

The poem consists of five unrhymed stanzas yet has a musicality and very Irish phrasing which reflects the Sean-nós tradition celebrated in its title and final lines. For example, 'the mouth music lured me' sounds Irish in its cadence and Irish words like 'blas' add to this effect.

The lament form is a very ancient one and O'Malley has created a modern version of this while incorporating a more traditional one, where the female voice (laments were traditionally sung by women keening at funerals in Ireland) mourns the loss of her true love.

Of the final two lines and the lament O'Malley says, 'I use it because it is the first line of the lament, beautiful and austere and I wanted the poem to take its cadence.' The repetition of 'A' in 'A Pheadair, a Aspail' convey yearning, while **the beautiful, haunting assonance of 'Ochón agus ochón ó' brings the poem to a plaintive close**.

SNAPSHOT

- Provocative question begins poem
- The exotic versus the ordinary
- Use of Irish language and syntax
- Central notion of song and music
- Intimate tone
- Locations – Spain, Ireland and Glasgow
- Evocative imagery – similes and metaphors
- Lament for lost love
- Sensual

Exam-Style Questions

Understanding the poem

1. What question does the speaker ask in the first line and how does she answer this? Do you agree with her? Explain.
2. Describe what we learn about the voice of the singer and the effect it has on the speaker.
3. What sort of setting is evoked by 'little yellow shells' and 'fine sand' and how do these contrast with the impression created of Glasgow?
4. In stanza 3 what does the speaker say she should have done? Why do you think she says this?
5. What, do you think, happens to the speaker in stanza 4? Give details and reasons.
6. What might the 'grey crow' represent? Why might it be on her chest and why is it there for so long?
7. 'A high price for a slow song'. Explain what you think the speaker means here.
8. What do the final two lines mean in English and why do you think the poet adds them here?

Thinking about the poem

1. How does the question asked and examined in the first stanza, coupled with the title, foreshadow the events the poem goes on to describe?
2. Identify examples of internal rhyme and alliteration in stanza 2 and comment on their effect.
3. List the references to mouths and music in the poem. Comment on them.
4. Do you think the alternative 'city boy' the speaker talks about in stanza 3 would have been a better match for the speaker? Explain your answer with reference to what you have learned about her in the poem.
5. Find examples of imagery connected with the sea in the poem and comment on their effect.
6. Do you agree that the syntax and phrasing in the poem sounds very Irish? Give a reason for your answer and back it up with examples from the poem.
7. 'And the children crying'. Why, do you think, has the poet added this detail in line 20? Overall is the tone of the speaker in the poem reminiscent of someone 'crying' for her past? Explain.
8. Which of the following options is closest to the main theme of the poem in your opinion?
    - It is a poem about heartbreak
    - It is a warning to women to avoid men that are too charismatic
    - It is a poem about the power of song

Imagining

1. Read the full text of the translation of the original lament or listen to Joe Heaney sing it online. What did you think of it?
2. Write the text of a brief talk about the importance of music in your life. Share with your class.

Percy Bysshe Shelley

1792–1822

Ozymandias — 566

Biography

Percy Bysshe Shelley was born into wealth and privilege in southern England in 1792, but from his boyhood he held radical opinions that set him apart. He was bullied at Eton College and expelled from Oxford University after co-writing a pamphlet called 'The Necessity of Atheism'. He was a radical thinker, not only atheist but anti-monarchist, and an enemy of the abuse of power wherever he found it. In 1812 he travelled to Ireland and published *An Address to the Irish People* condemning the Act of Union which deprived Ireland of its parliament. He was unconventional and controversial in his personal life too. After a short-lived first marriage, he eloped with Mary Godwin, daughter of the radical thinker William Godwin. Mary became famous as the author of *Frankenstein*. They spent most of their time in Europe, especially Italy, and it was there, in 1822, that he was drowned when the boat he was sailing sank. Shelley wrote some of the finest lyric poems in the language, among them 'Ode to the West Wind' and 'To a Skylark'.

ORDINARY LEVEL

Before you read

Who or what was Ozymandias? Find out what you can and think what the poem with that title might be about before reading it.

Ozymandias

I met a traveller from an antique land
Who said: Two vast and trunkless legs of stone
Stand in the desert … Near them, on the sand,
Half sunk, a shattered visage lies, whose frown,
And wrinkled lip, and sneer of cold command,   5
Tell that its sculptor well those passions read
Which yet survive, stamped on these lifeless things,
The hand that mocked them, and the heart that fed:
And on the pedestal these words appear:
'My name is Ozymandias, king of kings: 10
Look on my works, ye Mighty, and despair!'
Nothing beside remains. Round the decay
Of that colossal wreck, boundless and bare
The lone and level sands stretch far away.

Glossary

1	*antique land*: a country which boasted an ancient civilisation
2	*trunkless*: without a body
4	*visage*: face
9	*pedestal*: base of the statue
10	*Ozymandias*: another name for Ramesses II, the Egyptian pharaoh
14	*lone*: lonely; also single, unchanging

Guidelines

This poem was written in 1817, at a time of growing British interest in the antiquities of the Middle East, particularly Egypt. It may have been inspired by the announcement that the British Museum had acquired a large fragment of a colossal statue of Ramesses II, ruler of Egypt in the thirteenth century BC. The fallen colossus can still be seen in the Egyptian desert in Thebes, the severed head wearing a double crown. Ramesses built more temples and more gigantic statues of himself than any other pharaoh before or since. He vigorously promoted the cult of his own personality.

In the poem, Shelley calls him Ozymandias. This was the name used by the ancient Greek historian Diodorus, who described a huge statue in the desert that had an inscription like the one Shelley quotes.

Commentary

The speaker of the poem is recording the experience of a traveller who has been in a foreign land with an ancient civilisation. After 'Who said' in the second line, everything else in the poem is his story. He states that there are two enormous legs of stone in the desert. They are the remains of a great statue still standing after thousands of years. The trunk of the statue is missing. On the desert sand, half-buried, is the damaged head of the statue.

The traveller does not say that he has seen these things, but we assume he has, to judge by his description of the face ('visage') of the statue. Its expression is not pleasant. The frown, 'wrinkled lip' and sneer are those of a tyrant, used to giving commands and having these commands obeyed. The face suggests a cold heart and a pitiless nature.

Now the attention turns to the sculptor who made the statue. He could read the heart of the tyrant, and understand his passions: the cruelty, the anger, the lust for power and authority. He was also highly skilled. His carving still shows those passions etched in the stone ('stamped on these lifeless things'). By depicting them so accurately, the sculptor was exposing or mocking them. His is 'The hand that mocked them'; the 'heart that fed' is the tyrant's.

The next three lines describe the inscription on the base of the statue. Ozymandias boasts of being not merely a king, but a 'king of kings'. The inscription invites other great men ('ye Mighty') who look at the statue, and the other great works found throughout the kingdom, to despair, because they have no hope of ever achieving such magnificence. The tyrant would like to be the envy of the world.

However, as we are told in the final three lines, nothing now remains for anyone to envy. The once awe-inspiring statue is a 'colossal wreck'. The tyrant's kingdom, with all its splendours, has vanished, buried under an endless stretch of desert.

Themes and imagery

The **central theme of the poem is embodied in its central image**: the ruins of an enormous statue that was originally erected as a symbol of overwhelming power, but which now symbolises the vanity of all earthly glory. Instead of striking awe into those who saw it because of the power it represented, it now demonstrates to all who see it that time will destroy the greatest hopes and achievements of the most powerful men.

There is a **fundamental irony at the heart of the poem**. Irony arises from the contrast between what is being said, implied or suggested by somebody, and what is actually the case. The irony here is centred on the inscription on the pedestal: 'My name is Ozymandias, king of kings: / Look on my works, ye Mighty, and despair!' (lines 10–11). When he ordered this inscription, Ozymandias meant it as a means of impressing other rulers ('ye Mighty') with his power, so that they would 'despair' of ever rivalling it.

Now, however, the ruined statue and its inscription take on **a second meaning that Ozymandias never intended**. Anybody looking at them (or reading the poem) will now apply them to Ozymandias himself. He was the mightiest of the mighty, but his works have been reduced to rubble. He would have good reason to despair if he could see this scene now, and the present rulers of the world could learn a lesson: even if they achieve the greatness of Ozymandias, their greatest achievements are doomed to meet the same fate as that which has befallen Ozymandias and his empire.

ORDINARY LEVEL

The poem was first published in Leigh Hunt's magazine the *Examiner*, which also published some of Keats's early poems (see page 378). Leigh Hunt was a friend of Shelley, and his magazine was known for its radical views. In that context, knowing Shelley's hatred of monarchy, it is easy to see that the poem has a more contemporary meaning. Ozymandias could stand for any tyrant, and the poem is, in part, a veiled attack on George III, the unpopular king at the time.

The poem's final image of the 'boundless and bare' desert sands that half bury the statue and that 'stretch far away' could be seen as an emblem of **the destructive power of time**.

There is another theme more subtly present, but which is a favourite among poets: **the immortality and power of art**. Here, although Ozymandias and his great civilisation have been dead for thousands of years, this broken statue, a work of art, survives. Not only that, but it still retains its power. According to the traveller in the poem, the sculptor's skill is still evident in the 'shattered visage'. Not only has his art survived, but it still has the power to give us an insight into the passions of the tyrant, even to mock them down the centuries.

Form

'Ozymandias' is written in **iambic pentameters**: lines with five beats or stresses with a basic rhythm of an unstressed syllable followed by a stressed one (dĭ-*dúm*). The poem is a **sonnet**, although the rhyme scheme is very unusual, and does not fit neatly into the normal sonnet structure. The first five lines rhyme *ababa* and the last nine *cdcedefef*. Nevertheless, there is a broad division between the first eight lines (the octave) and the last six (the sestet).

In the first eight, the emphasis is on **description**. We are asked to imagine a huge, broken statue in the desert, especially the expression on its face. The final six lines hinge on the words on the pedestal. Although these lines are also descriptive, the boastful inscription and the image of the endless desert encourage us to **reflect** on what has been described.

Language

Although the images of the wrecked statue and the endless desert are powerful and memorable, the language Shelley uses to create them is plain, precise and unadorned. The diction is not poetic, but is drawn from ordinary speech. The language of the sonnet is mainly descriptive, using well-chosen adjectives and common nouns to create a vivid picture: 'shattered visage', 'wrinkled lip', 'colossal wreck'.

The final image is the most striking:
> Round the decay
> Of that colossal wreck, boundless and bare
> The lone and level sands stretch far away.

Here the **sounds of the words echo their meanings**. The alliteration of the hard 'b' in 'boundless and bare' suggests the bleakness of the desert landscape. The slow rhythm and the long vowels in the final line, along with the repeated 'l' and 's' sounds, help to evoke the lifeless, unending desert.

Percy Bysshe Shelley

Exam-Style Questions

Understanding the poem

1. What do we learn about the 'traveller' the speaker mentions in the first line?
2. In your own words, describe the scene the traveller describes.
3. What do we learn about the sculptor in the poem?
4. Whose is 'the heart that fed' (line 8)? What does the phrase suggest about him?
5. Why did Ozymandias have the words in lines 10 and 11 inscribed on the pedestal?
6. What do those words mean to the viewer or the reader thousands of years later?

Thinking about the poem

1. What motive, do you think, did Shelley have in writing this poem?
2. On the evidence supplied by this poem, what impression do you form of Ozymandias?
3. Explain the way that irony works in this poem.
4. Choose two lines from the poem that you find particularly impressive and give reasons for your choice.
5. What is the purpose of the last three lines of the poem?
6. Is it possible to feel pity for Ozymandias?

Imagining

1. *Groupwork* Your group has been asked to make an audio-visual presentation to accompany a reading of this poem. What images, music, sounds or other effects would you use?
2. Imagine a scene in the future when the civilisation we know has long since disappeared. Imagine you are a traveller in that future coming across some remains of our civilisation. Describe what you see and how you feel about it.

SNAPSHOT

- Sonnet with unusual rhyme scheme
- Plain, precise, descriptive language
- Vivid images of decay and destruction
- A thought-provoking poem
- Use of irony
- Contrast between glorious past and desolate present
- Commentary on the nature of earthly power
- Theme of the power and permanence of art

Penelope Shuttle
b.1947

Jungian Cows

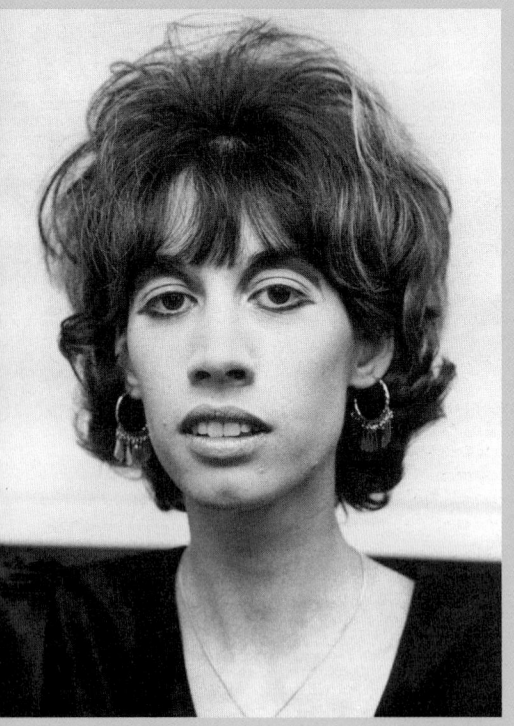

Biography

Penelope Shuttle was born in Middlesex, England in 1947. Since 1970 she has lived by the sea in Falmouth in Cornwall, in the southwest of England. The weather, the landscape and the history of Cornwall have inspired her work. She was married to the poet Peter Redgrove, who died in 2003. With her late husband she wrote two books on women's menstrual cycle, which combine anthropology, poetry and Jungian psychology.

Since 1980, Penelope Shuttle has published eight collections of poems, all highly regarded. 'Jungian Cows' is taken from her 1988 collection *Adventures with My Horse*. One of her most celebrated collections is *Redgrove's Wife* (2006), a book of lament on the deaths of both her husband and her father, as well as a celebration of her husband's life and work. More recent collections are *Sandgrain and Hourglass* (2010) and *Unsent: New and Selected Poems* (2012). In 2016, she published a pamphlet of travel poems. In a recent interview she said: 'I follow my dreams as a poet, and draw from the deep reservoir of the images I find there and the places of the collective unconscious to which dreams lead'. She has a keen interest in yoga and has remarked on the importance of breath in determining the shape and form of a poem: 'For me it is the way the poem breathes that gives it form.'

Penelope Shuttle

Jungian Cows

In Switzerland, the people call their cows
Venus, Eve, Salome, or Fraulein Alberta,
beautiful names
to yodel across the pastures at Bollingen.

If the woman is busy with child or book,   5
the farmer wears his wife's skirt
to milk the most sensitive cows.

When the electric milking-machine arrives,
the stalled cows rebel and sulk
for the woman's impatient skilful fingers   10
on their blowzy tough rosy udders,
will not give their milk;

so the man who works the machine
dons cotton skirt, all floral delicate flounces
to hide his denim overalls and big old muddy boots,   15
he fastens the cool soft folds carefully,
wraps his head in his sweetheart's Sunday-best fringed scarf,
and walks smelling feminine and shy among the cows,

till the milk spurts, hot, slippery and steamy
into the churns,   20
Venus, Salome, Eve, and Fraulein Alberta,
lowing, half-asleep,
accepting the disguised man as an echo of the woman,
their breath smelling of green, of milk's sweet traditional climax.

Before you read

Do you keep a pet? Does your pet have dreams? Has your pet ever behaved in a way that made you think, 'How did he or she know to do that?' Do animals inherit memories from their ancestors? Share your thoughts and experiences with your classmates.

Glossary

Title	*Jungian*:	relating to the theories of Carl Gustav Jung (1875–1961), the Swiss psychologist who developed the concept of the collective unconscious and its archetypes or inherited mental images and symbols. The collective unconscious is the part of the unconscious mind that stores symbols, memories, instincts and experiences common to all humans and inherited from our ancestors. Some of the universal symbols of the collective unconscious include the Great Mother, the Wise Old Man, the Hero, the Warrior, the Tree of Life. This poem makes the light-hearted suggestion that cows have a collective memory of the milkmaid
1	*Switzerland*:	Jung's birthplace. There is a strong tradition of farming and herding in Switzerland
2	*Venus, Eve, Salome*:	all three names are associated with female power. Eve exercised her power over Adam; Salome persuaded her stepfather Herod to give her the head of John the Baptist; Venus was the Roman goddess of love
2	*Fraulein*:	a form of address or a title similar to 'Miss' in English
2	*Alberta*:	a common girl's name
4	*yodel*:	a style of singing or vocalisation that was developed in the Swiss Alps as a way of communicating between one mountain valley and another. When yodelling, the singer changes from the ordinary voice to falsetto and back again
4	*Bollingen*:	a small village on the northern shore of Lake Zurich in Switzerland, where Carl Jung built a country retreat and where he completed much of his writing
11	*blowzy*:	in this context, flushed and full with milk
14	*flounces*:	frills
24	*climax*:	the high point or culmination of an experience or sequence of events

ORDINARY LEVEL

Guidelines

'Jungian Cow' is taken from Shuttle's 1988 collection, *Adventures with My Horse*.

A recurring feature of Penelope Shuttle's poetry is her humour and playfulness. Many of her poems deal with the extraordinary (myth, magic or fantasy) as it is found in ordinary life. Thus, the narrative of a Shuttle poem often has a fantastical or surreal quality delivered in a deadpan tone.

Together with her late husband Peter Redgrove, Penelope Shuttle pursued an interest in Jungian psychology. 'Jungian Cows', which is set in Bollingen, where Jung did most of his writing, is a humorous application of Jung's ideas to that most Swiss of Swiss animals, the dairy cow.

Commentary

Stanzas 1 and 2
The poem has a gentle conversational tone with the speaker offering us some information on Switzerland. The speaker says the Swiss give names to their cows and remarks that the names are beautiful ones to call across the mountain pastures. In the second stanza the speaker tells us another piece of information: that a Swiss farmer will put on his wife's skirt to milk the most sensitive cows if his wife is busy. The information is given as fact, though we are not sure how seriously we are to take it.

Stanzas 3–5
In stanza three, the speaker tells us that the cows are not happy when the milking machine replaces milking by hand. The cows sulk for a woman's touch and will not give their milk. So the man who works the machine dresses in his 'sweetheart's' good scarf and wears her cotton skirt and walks 'smelling feminine' among the cows until the milk comes because the cows accept the man 'as an echo of the woman' and are content.

Themes and imagery

'Jungian Cows' may be read as a playful suggestion that the physical process of milking is linked to an image of a milkmaid that is deeply rooted in the unconscious of the cows. In order that the cows respond to 'the man who works the machine' he has to take on the feminine persona of the milkmaid. Once the cows accept the man as an echo of the traditional milkmaid, they are content and give their milk happily, their breaths smelling sweetly of fresh milk and grass as the process of making milk comes to a climax. This is a humorous version of an idea that occurs in different guises in Penelope Shuttle's work, that various forms of healing come not from masculine solutions but from an openness to **feminine experience, know-how and wisdom**.

In addressing the theme of milking, the poem explores the relationship between humans and their domesticated animals. It

Penelope Shuttle

points to the traditional relationship between cows and women and the need for a feminine touch in milking the sensitive cows. There is a reminder, in an era of milking parlours, of the need to stay in touch with traditional ways of relating to animals. The modern world might learn from the example of the Swiss, who give their cows beautiful names and respect the cows' preference for a feminine presence, or a trace of that presence, in the milking parlour.

The imagery in the first two stanzas is not particularly visual or detailed. However, Shuttle offers enough information to enable the readers to visualise the scene for themselves. Thus, we supply the details as we imagine the cowherd yodelling the names of the cows across the pastures at Bollingen. In stanza 3, the verbs 'rebel' and 'sulk' give us enough information to form an image, without controlling what it is we see in our mind's eye. In stanza 4, the description of the man dressing up in his sweetheart's clothes is the fullest description in the poem. It is **as if the clothes alter his persona** – he walks 'shy among the cows' (line 18). The language used to describe the udders of the cows, 'blowzy tough rosy' (line 11) and the milk spurting into the churns 'hot, slippery and steamy' (line 19) is as much tactile as it is visual.

Form and style

The poem is written in **irregular, unrhymed stanzas**. The whole poem flows, aided by the run-on lines, the soft sounds, the **alliteration** and the **long vowels**. The poem is written in the present tense, which gives the impression of unhurried timelessness. The humour in the poem comes from the straight-faced recounting of stories that sound like tall tales. The final word of the poem, 'climax', suggests that the milk spurting into the churns is the high point of the agricultural process. The word also relates to literature and to human psychology and sexuality, two of the concerns of Carl Jung.

Exam-Style Questions

Understanding the poem

1	What kinds of personalities are suggested by the names given to the cows?
2	Do you think the names are given because the people like to sing them across the pastures or because they like their cows?
3	What is your reaction to the information that the farmer puts on a skirt if his wife is busy 'with child or book' (line 5)?
4	What is the cows' reaction to the arrival of the milking machine?
5	How does the man 'who works the machine' (line 13) make himself feminine so that he is accepted by the cows 'as an echo of the woman' (line 23)?
6	'… walks smelling feminine and shy among the cows …' (line 18). What does this line tell you about the farmer?
7	What happens when the cows accept the man 'as an echo of the woman' (line 23)?
8	Penelope Shuttle has said: 'I've got quite a sense of the ridiculous.' Is this evident in the poem?

ORDINARY LEVEL

Thinking about the poem

1. What, in the context of the poem, do you understand by the phrase 'the most sensitive cows' (line 7)?

2. Comment on the phrase, 'the woman's impatient skilful fingers' (line 10).

3. Do you think the adjectives 'blowzy tough rosy udders' (line 11) are well-chosen?

4. In the last line of the poem the breath of the cows is described as 'smelling of green and of milk's sweet traditional climax.' How do you interpret this line?

5. Which two of the following statements best describe your view of the poem?
   - It is a poem about cows
   - It is a poem about getting in touch with one's feminine side
   - It is a poem about the ingenuity of farmers
   - It is a poem about modern and traditional ways of farming
   - It is a poem about the importance of the feminine

   Explain your choices with reference to the text.

6. In your view, what is the connection between the title of the poem and the men dressing as women?

7. '"Jungian Cows" is an amusing and humorous poem.'
   Discuss this statement. Support the points you make with reference to the poem.

8. Penelope Shuttle has written on the relationship between breath and the shape and form of a poem. Read 'Jungian Cows' aloud, noting the relationship between breath and the shape of the poem on the page.

9. 'Behind the humour, the poem reminds us of the need for openness to the feminine in life.'
   Give your response to this reading of the poem.

10. What, in your opinion, is a Jungian cow?

Imagining

1. Imagine you are one of the cows named in the poem. Write your views on the ideal conditions for giving milk.

2. Write a short letter to Penelope Shuttle, telling her about your thoughts and feelings on the poem. Refer to the text of the poem in your letter.

3. 'If cows could dream …' Write a short piece, in prose or poetry, inspired by this title.

SNAPSHOT

- Humorous and playful poem
- Factual narrative voice
- Straight-faced account of an unlikely story
- Applies the ideas of Carl Jung to cows
- Creates amusing scenes
- Stresses the importance of the feminine
- Sensuous and suggestive language
- Poem concludes on the word 'climax'

Gary Soto

b.1952

Oranges 576

Biography

Gary Soto was born on 12 April 1952 in Fresno, California to Mexican-American parents, Manuel and Angie Soto. His father died when Soto was just five years old and the family struggled to make ends meet. He worked in the fields picking crops to supplement the family's meagre income. Crime and poverty seemed the norm for the community where Soto grew up and he said he'd always imagined a future of poverty and hardship for himself.

Soto was at best an average student until high school, where he began to fall in love with poetry. Robert Frost, Pablo Neruda and Gabriel Garcia Marquez are all major influences.

He enrolled in college to avoid being drafted into the army and studied geography, but after reading an anthology of American poetry he was convinced that he had found his true calling. He transferred to California State University, where he achieved his MA and joined a group of poets known as the Fresno School. In 1977 he published *The Elements of San Joaquin*, which won the United States Award of the International Poetry Forum.

Soto's poetry has always focused on his own experiences. His books have sold over half a million copies and he has published almost twenty poetry collections. His eighteenth, *Meatballs for the People*, was published in 2017.

In 1999, Soto received the Hispanic Heritage Award for Literature.

He has a wife and daughter and lives between Berkeley and Fresno, California. He writes every day.

ORDINARY LEVEL

Before you read

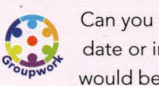

Can you recall your first date or imagine how it would be? Think of three words that describe the experience. Share them with the person beside you. Were there any similarities? Discuss with the class.

Oranges

The first time I walked
With a girl, I was twelve,
Cold, and weighted down
With two oranges in my jacket.
December. Frost cracking   5
Beneath my steps, my breath
Before me, then gone,
As I walked toward
Her house, the one whose
Porchlight burned yellow   10
Night and day, in any weather.
A dog barked at me until
She came out pulling
At her gloves, face bright
With rouge. I smiled,   15
Touched her shoulder, and led
Her down the street, across
A used car lot and a line
Of newly planted trees,
Until we were breathing   20
Before a drug store. We
Entered, the tiny bell
Bringing a saleslady
Down a narrow aisle of goods.
I turned to the candies   25
Tiered like bleachers,
And asked what she wanted—
Light in her eyes, a smile
Starting at the corners
Of her mouth. I fingered   30
A nickel in my pocket,
And when she lifted a chocolate
That cost a dime,
I didn't say anything.
I took the nickel from   35
My pocket, then an orange,
And set them quietly on
The counter. When I looked up,
The lady's eyes met mine,
And held them, knowing   40
Very well what it was all
About.

Gary Soto

>   Outside,
> A few cars hissing past,
> Fog hanging like old   45
> Coats between the trees.
> I took my girl's hand
> In mine for two blocks,
> Then released it to let
> Her unwrap the chocolate.   50
> I peeled my orange
> That was so bright against
> The gray of December
> That, from some distance,
> Someone might have thought   55
> I was making a fire in my hands.

Glossary

Line	Term
15	*rouge*: blusher – a type of make-up to add colour to the cheeks
18	*used car lot*: where second-hand cars are sold
25	*candies*: sweets and chocolate bars, confectionery
26	*Tiered*: in ascending rows
26	*bleachers*: benches, usually found in sports grounds for spectators to sit on
31	*nickel*: a five-cent coin
33	*dime*: a ten-cent coin

Guidelines

'Oranges', published in Soto's 1985 poetry collection *Black Hair*, was written in June 1983 and remains one of Soto's most famous and well-liked poems. It is a fine example of his unique style and authentic voice. The narrator of the poem describes his first romantic encounter with a girl when he was twelve years old. The subject matter is easy to relate to, as most people can remember the excitement and anxiety they experienced on their first date. Soto once remarked that to him 'the finest praise is when a reader says, "I can see your stories".'

Commentary

Lines 1–17

The speaker sets the scene for the reader: it is a cold, frosty December day and he is on his way to meet a girl. It is his first date, 'The first time I walked / With a girl, I was twelve'. The description of him being 'weighted down' is interesting. He may be 'weighted down' with nerves about the impending date as well as the physical weight of the oranges in his jacket. The light in her porch 'burned yellow', contrasting with the bleak winter surroundings, 'Frost cracking', and at first there is tension: 'A dog barked at me, until / She came out'. Her appearance dispels the aggression of the dog and, like her porch and the hidden oranges, she is glowing, 'face bright / With rouge'. He is glad to see her, 'I smiled', lightly touches her shoulder and they set off on their 'walk'. Despite this being his first date, he understands how to behave around girls.

ORDINARY LEVEL

Lines 18–42
A 'used car lot' may not be the most romantic setting for a first date but it indicates to the reader the type of urban environment that the speaker occupies. The mention of the 'newly planted trees' (line 19) suggests that this is an area that is making an effort to improve its surroundings.

They stop outside the drugstore. It is cold outside; their breath is visible in the air. The 'narrow' aisles overflowing with goods create a cramped and claustrophobic atmosphere. The poem reaches its climax when the speaker generously invites the girl to choose a candy. He anxiously fingers the nickel in his pocket. He sees the joy in her face as she chooses the candy, which costs more than he can afford, 'Light in her eyes, a smile / Starting at the corners / Of her mouth'. At this point it could all go terribly wrong, but his response is that of a confident young boy. To avoid her disappointment and his embarrassment, he remains silent, takes the nickel and an orange out of his pocket and catches the saleslady's eyes. Within this gaze is a tacit understanding between the saleslady and the boy. On some level she understands what is going on and sympathises with the speaker. She graciously accepts his unspoken offer. This is all conveyed with great subtlety by Soto, 'When I looked up, / The lady's eyes met mine, / And held them, knowing / Very well what it was all / About.' We don't know why she does this; perhaps she is won over by their innocence, perhaps he reminds her of her younger days or maybe she is impressed by the speaker's ingenuity and kindness. Whatever the reason, the speaker gets away with it. He makes his girl happy and it was worth the risk.

Lines 43–56
The second section starts as the young couple go back 'Outside'. Note how Soto places the first word of the second section at the end of the last line of the first section. There is a clear division yet a connection. It marks a change of setting and mood. There is a physical closeness between the speaker and the girl that wasn't there before: they are now holding hands. The boy has a renewed sense of confidence. He calls her 'my girl'; he 'takes' her hand, and then 'releases' it to 'let' her unwrap her candy.

The dreary, cool, damp weather has no effect on the boy. It is the brightness of the orange in his hands that captures how he feels; something inside him was set alight, something 'was making a fire' (line 56).

Gary Soto

Themes and imagery

The imagery surrounding the boy, 'cold', 'December' and 'frost cracking' is contrasted with the warmth of the girl's rouged face and the brightness of her yellow porchlight. Throughout the poem she is associated with images of light: 'porchlight', 'light in her eyes'. This is contrasted with the gloom of the setting: 'Fog hanging' and 'gray of December'.

Contrast is used repeatedly in the poem, particularly the contrast between light and dark. Images of nature, such as the 'newly planted trees' and the 'frost cracking', are set against the urban backdrop, the 'used car lot' and the 'drug store' where the 'candies' are 'Tiered like bleachers'. This is a very original simile and adds authenticity to the American town setting of the poem, as does the couple's entrance into the drugstore, which is heralded by a little bell ringing. This **sensory detail** makes the experience very real for the reader. Another striking simile describes the pervading fog which hangs 'like old / Coats between the trees'. The fog, gloom and frost may represent the poverty of the boy and of this town, but like the 'newly planted trees' there is hope, there is an effort to be better and brighter. **New beginnings**, the growth of something natural and beautiful like their relationship may be suggested here. The boy is determined to win his girl's approval and the budding romance between them is possibly symbolised in the imagery of light which lifts the poem throughout, 'I was making a fire in my hands.' So we see the themes of love, romance, beginnings and hope communicated through the cinematic description in the poem.

Poverty is also a theme. The boy only has a nickel to spend on this date and must be resourceful because it is only half the amount required to buy the girl her preferred candy bar, 'I fingered / A nickel in my pocket … she lifted a chocolate / That cost a dime'.

It seems that love, or at least romance, is the light that will lift this twelve-year-old boy out of the 'gray of December' (which may be an image for his poverty) into a brighter world of **hope and possibility**. The passion ignited by the girl shines as sweetly and brightly as an orange on a grey December day.

Form and language

The poem is written in unrhymed short lines with two or three stresses: 'December. Frost cracking'. This gives the impression of natural speech and also helps the poet to give the story pace and atmosphere. The line length and frequent use of **enjambment** (line breaks in the middle of a sentence) create short phrases, and add a sense of breathlessness or nervousness in keeping with the situation: 'my breath / Before me, then gone' (lines 6–7). It also helps to give the poem momentum.

Soto said of his work, 'as a writer, my duty is not to make people perfect, particularly Mexican Americans. I'm not a cheerleader. I'm one who provides portraits of people in the rush of life.' Do you agree that this is a very realistic poem, or has Soto romanticised the account of this date? This might be an interesting question to discuss in groups.

ORDINARY LEVEL

Exam-Style Questions

Understanding the poem

1. What does the speaker mean when he says, 'I walked with a girl'?
2. Why is the barking dog included? Is it important that the barking stops when the girl comes out?
3. Why does the speaker describe the candies as 'tiered like bleachers'? Is this an effective simile? Find and comment on another simile in the poem.
4. Why is he 'fingering' the nickel in his pocket?
5. In your opinion, why didn't the boy say anything to the lady in the drugstore?
6. How would you describe the speaker in this poem? Is he resourceful, romantic, considerate or something else? Explain with reference to the poem.
7. Trace and explain how the connection/relationship between the boy and girl deepens as the poem progresses.
8. 'The setting of the poem is vividly created and conveyed.' Discuss this statement with reference to the language and imagery in the poem.
9. Is the final line a suitable one for the poem? Explain.

Thinking about the poem

1. Compare the depiction of oranges at the beginning, the middle and the end of the poem.
2. Though there is only one point in the poem when someone speaks, there is a lot of communication between characters. Do you agree or disagree?
3. Explain the phrase 'knowing / Very well what it was all / About.'
4. Read the section on themes and choose the one you feel most closely fits what you felt was the theme of the poem.
5. What atmosphere is created by the descriptions of weather in the poem?
6. Joyce Carol Oates has said, 'Gary Soto's poems are fast, funny, heartening, and achingly believable, like Polaroid love letters, or snatches of music heard out of a passing car; patches of beauty like patches of sunlight; the very pulse of a life.' Discuss this statement, giving your opinion in the context of this poem.
7. Would you like to read more poetry by this poet? Explain why or why not.
8. Write about the effect of one of the following in the poem, using quotation and reference: enjambment, imagery, contrast.
9. Trace the imagery of hands and touching in the poem. How do they add to the poem's mood and meaning?

Gary Soto

Imagining

1.  Imagine that the lady in the drugstore didn't accept the orange as payment for the candy. With the person beside you, write out the dialogue that follows.

2. Imagine you are the boy in the poem but it is fifteen years later and you are marrying the same girl. Write the part of the wedding speech where you describe the first time you went out.

3. Write one diary entry for each of the three characters on the day featured in the poem; the boy, the girl and the lady.

4. This poem has a very cinematic quality. Divide the poem into sections and in groups create a story board for your group's section. Then collate them and discuss the results.

SNAPSHOT

- Images of light and colour
- Nostalgic
- Winter
- Similes
- Short lines
- Narrative poem
- Highly visual and sensory appeal
- Rich in imagery
- Theme of youth and first love
- Accessible language
- Poverty
- Urban setting

ORDINARY LEVEL

David Wheatley
b.1970

Chronicle

583

Biography

David Wheatley was born in Dublin and grew up in Bray, Co. Wicklow. He studied English at Trinity College and edited the magazine *Icarus*. He went on to do a doctorate on the poetry of Samuel Beckett and now teaches English at the University of Aberdeen. Wheatley reviews for a wide range of newspapers and journals, including *The Guardian*, the *Times Literary Supplement* and the *Irish Times*.

David Wheatley is still writing about Wicklow. A sequence of sonnets in his last collection is set in the village of Kilcoole and he has written a long prose memoir on growing up in Bray. Wheatley is married to the writer and editor Aingeal Clare, and the couple have a son, Felix and live in rural Aberdeenshire.

Wheatley has published five collections: *Thirst* (1997), *Misery Hill* (2000), *Mocker* (2006), *A Nest on the Waves* (2010) and *The President of Planet Earth* (2017). With fellow poet Justin Quinn he founded the poetry journal *Metre*, which ran from 1995 to 2005. His work features in various anthologies, including *The Penguin Book of Irish Poetry*.

Critics have praised Wheatley's intelligence, humour and technical daring. A trained musician, Wheatley is interested in the rhythm and movement of a poem.

Chronicle

David Wheatley

My grandfather is chugging along the back roads
between Kilcoole and Newtown in his van,
the first wood-panelled Morris Minor in Wicklow.
Evening is draped lazily over the mountains;
one hapless midnight, mistaking the garage door   5
for open, he drove right through it, waking my father.

The old man never did get to farm like his father,
Preferring to trundle his taxi along the back roads.
Visiting, I stand in his workshop door
and try to engage him in small talk, always in vain,   10
then climb the uncarpeted stairs to look at the mountains
hulking over soggy, up-and-down Wicklow.

Cattle, accents and muck: I don't have a clue,
I need everything explained to me by my father.
Clannish great-uncles somewhere nearer the mountains   15
are vaguer still, farming their few poor roods,
encountered at Christmas with wives who serve me oven-
baked bread and come to wave us off at the door.

My grandfather pacing the garden, benignly dour,
a whiskey or a Woodbine stuck in his claw,   20
a compost of newsprint in the back of his van.
You're mad to go live in Bray, he told my father,
somewhere he'd visit on rare and timorous raids,
too close to 'town' to be properly Cill Mhantáin.

All this coming back to me in the mountains   25
early one morning, crossing the windy corridor
to the Glen of Imaal, where schoolchildren read
acrostics to me of 'wet and wonderful Wicklow',
and driving on down to Hacketstown with my father
we find grandfather's grandfather under an even   30

gravestone gone to his Church of Ireland heaven,
and his grandfather too, my father maintains,
all turned, long since turned to graveyard fodder
just over the county line from their own dear Wicklow,
the dirt tracks, twisting lanes and third-class roads   35
they would have hauled themselves round while they endured,

before my father and I ever followed the roads
or my mountainy cousins first picked up a loy
or my grandfather's van ever hit that garage door.

Before you read

In pairs, take turns to share a story that is part of the folklore of your family.

Glossary

Line	
Title	*Chronicle*: a history of events in the order in which they happened. Most chronicles date from the medieval period and were written by monks. There was little attempt to separate fact from fiction and local events were given as much importance as national ones
2	*Kilcoole and Newtown*: villages in east Co. Wicklow
3	*Morris Minor*: a popular make of car in the 1950s and 1960s
5	*hapless*: unfortunate
8	*trundle*: move slowly
12	*hulking*: large, towering
15	*Clannish*: closely united through family ties
16	*roods*: an old measurement of land, about 400 square metres
19	*benignly*: kindly
19	*dour*: serious and sad
20	*Woodbine*: a brand of cigarette
21	*compost*: decaying mixture
22	*Bray*: a seaside town in Co. Wicklow
23	*timorous*: timid
24	*Cill Mhantáin*: the Irish name for Wicklow, literally 'church of the toothless person'. The toothless person was a follower of Saint Patrick who had his teeth knocked out in an attack by locals. Undeterred, he built his church
27	*Glen of Imaal*: a scenic valley in west Wicklow
28	*acrostics*: poems in which the first letters of each line spell a word or sentence. Wheatley was writer-in-residence for Wicklow County Council (1997–1998) and edited an anthology of writing by schoolchildren
29	*Hacketstown*: town in east Co. Carlow
33	*fodder*: food, usually for cattle
34	*line*: border
38	*loy*: long, narrow spade for digging peat

ORDINARY LEVEL

Guidelines

'Chronicle' is from the collection *Misery Hill*, published in 2000. The poet's experience of working as writer-in-residence in Co. Wicklow brings to mind stories and memories of his father's family, long-established in County Wicklow.

Commentary

Stanza 1
The poet describes his grandfather as he drives along 'the back roads' of Wicklow in his van. The present tense makes the past seem alive. There is family pride in the claim that the car is the 'first wood-panelled Morris Minor' (line 3) in the county. The verb 'chugging' (line 1) and the description of the evening as 'draped lazily over the mountains' suggest a slow pace of life. The stanza concludes with a story that has clearly become part of family lore: how his grandfather drove his van straight through the closed garage door, waking the poet's father. The first stanza establishes the key relationships in the poem: grandfather, father and son.

Stanza 2
The poet returns to his grandfather, 'the old man' of line 7. His grandfather did not follow his father into farming, preferring to 'trundle' his taxi along the 'back roads'. The word 'trundle' and the phrase 'back roads' suggests someone who takes life slowly, someone who is not ambitious; someone who has no desire to be in the limelight. Using the present tense, the poet describes visiting his grandfather. The grandfather is something of an enigma. The image of the poet's younger self standing in the workshop door suggests a distance between them. The boy is unable 'to engage him in small talk' (line 10). The stairs being uncarpeted implies that the grandfather lives modestly. The image of the 'hulking' mountains and the 'soggy' landscape suggests that the narrator is not captivated by the landscape he observes. This may be a reflection of his frustration with his visit to his grandfather.

Stanza 3
Three words sum up the poet's experience of farming: 'Cattle, accents and muck' (line 13). He is a townie who, by his own admission, hasn't a clue about farming. Just as he remained on the margins of his grandfather's workshop, so the poet remains distant from his farming relatives, his grand-uncles who farm poor land near the mountains. He describes them as 'clannish' and his understanding of them is as vague as his understanding of farming. They are relatives he sees at Christmas. He remembers the oven-baked bread served by their wives. He remembers his uncles waving them off at the door. Interestingly, he uses the word 'wives' rather than 'aunts' (line 17). This is very much a patriarchal chronicle of the family, focusing on the male line of his father's family.

Stanza 4
This stanza presents an image of his grandfather that is stored in the poet's mind: walking in his garden with a glass of whiskey or a Woodbine cigarette 'stuck in his claw' (line 20). He is described as 'benignly dour', a phrase that returns to the idea of a man of few words, not inclined to small talk, who keeps his thoughts to himself. It is a measure of the strength of his feelings that he tells his son he is 'mad to go to live in Bray' (line 22). What are we to make of the image of the newspapers rotting in the back of his van (line 21)? Does it suggest a man lost in his own world, a word of small towns and back roads, and ill at ease in a busy town like Bray, a place he does not regard as really belonging to Wicklow?

David Wheatley

Stanzas 5–7

The opening lines of stanza 5 explain the circumstances that prompt the memories outlined in the previous four stanzas: the narrator is driving to a school in west Wicklow to hear the children's poems on 'wet and wonderful Wicklow' (line 28), and afterwards he drives with his father to Hacketstown, just over the border in Co. Carlow. There, in a Church of Ireland churchyard, they view the grave of his grandfather's grandfather (line 30) and, according to the poet's father, 'his grandfather too' (line 32). His ancestors have now turned to soil, food or fodder for worms. There is a gentle irony in the fact that these men are buried 'just over the county line from their own dear Wicklow' (line 34). Interestingly, in the last line of stanza 6, the poet uses the past tense to describe these distant ancestors hauling themselves round 'the dirt tracks, twisting lanes and third-class roads … while they endured' (lines 35–36). The **memories** in the first four stanzas seem to be **alive in the poet's imagination**, but these ancestors and their lives belong to the distant past.

The last three lines of the final stanza emphasise the **sense of time long past** in the use of 'before' (line 37) and 'ever' (lines 37 and 39). And yet there is a connection between the poet and his long-dead ancestors, in the roads they have travelled and in the family line they share. Moreover, the events the poem chronicles owe their origins to these men 'long since turned to graveyard fodder' (line 33).

Themes and imagery

The most obvious theme of the poem is the connection but also the distance between the **generations of a family**. The poet is **connected** to his ancestors by living in Wicklow and travelling many of the same roads they have travelled. But he is also **distant** from them: finding it impossible to engage in small talk with his grandfather; having only the vaguest of connections with his uncles who farm in the mountains; living in Bray. Interestingly, this is a chronicle of the Wheatley family, the name inherited from the poet's father and traced back through seven generations of the male line. It is no coincidence that the word 'father' is a key one in the poem. And this male line has 'endured' (line 36).

'Wicklow' is another key word. This is a poem about **belonging and attachment** to a place, to his ancestors' 'own dear Wicklow' (line 34). The use of place names (Kilcoole, Newtown, Bray, Glen of Imaal, Hacketstown) adds texture and specificity to the poem. The landscape of Co. Wicklow is a backdrop to the lives of everyone mentioned in the poem, including the children the poet meets during his work. It is as if Wicklow has its own spirit and nature. The evening is 'draped lazily over the mountains' (line 4); the mountains hulk over the soggy fields (line 12); the midnight is 'hapless' (line 5).

However, to be rooted in a place is not the same as being rooted to a spot. The imagery of the poem is one of motion and transit: roads, back roads, lanes, tracks, journeys, van, taxi, car, crossing, visits. In fact, the impression is one of unending motion. The road imagery also speaks to the idea of **connection**. Within the

ORDINARY LEVEL

family, there is a system of alliances and connections, some strong (father and son), some unfathomable (grandson and grandfather), and some weak (nephew and uncles) but all part of the network that is family.

This network exists within a space, the county of Wicklow, but dispersed along the roads, tracks and lanes, that stretch from the mountains to the sea. It also exists across time, from ancestors, remote and unknown, to the poet's immediate family, all linked by ties of blood, lived within a geographical region and a county.

The history described in the poem is not history with a capital 'H'. It is not a history of public events or violent uprisings but of small stories and trips to relatives. Like all family histories, it contains its small dramas: family members moving away to start a new life but staying connected. The speaker is clearly at peace with his family even if he is partly disconnected from some members of his extended family. The use of the present tense avoids nostalgia and suggest that **history is a living thing**, present in the moment and in memory.

Structure and language

The poem is written in the form of a **sestina** – a poem of six stanzas of six lines each, followed by a three-lined seventh stanza. The sestina follows a set pattern. The main feature is that the poet uses six words as the end words of each line, but in a different order in each of the six stanzas. In the final last three lines, all six words are repeated, two in each line with one serving as the end word of the line. The six main words in this poem are: roads, van, Wicklow, mountains, door, father.

These are the end words of the six lines in the first stanza. However, as the poem proceeds, Wheatley plays with the form by using words which sound like the original ones. For example, 'roads' (line 1) becomes 'roods' (line 16), 'raids' (line 23), and 'read' (line 27). 'Van' (line 2) becomes 'vain' (line 10), 'oven' (line 17), 'even' (line 30), and 'heaven' (line 31). 'Mountains' (line 4) becomes 'Cill Mhantáin' (line 24), 'maintains' (line 32), and 'mountainy' (line 38). 'Wicklow' (line 3) is echoed in 'clue' (line 13), 'claw' (line 20), and 'loy' (line 38). 'Door' (line 5) becomes 'dour' (line 19), 'corridor' (line 26) and 'endured' (line 36). The word 'father' (line 6) remains the same, with the exception of 'fodder' (line 33). The poem is rich in other verbal textures too, and with many lines containing alliterative phrases. This interweaving of sounds mirrors the way in which individual lives are woven together to form a family history.

Note how the first four stanzas are each written as one sentence, while the last three stanzas, spread over 15 lines, constitute one sentence. The enjambment across the final three stanzas creates a sense of forward motion, reflective of the way in which history moves relentlessly. This sense of constant motion is also reflected in the use of the present participle of verbs: 'chugging', 'waking', 'farming', 'pacing', 'crossing', 'driving' and 'twisting'. The repetition of words and imagery reinforces the idea of family connection and continuity. The idea that history repeats itself is embodied in the complex repetitions of the poem.

SNAPSHOT

- Family history and lore
- Traces the male line
- Character of the grandfather
- Rooted in Wicklow
- Themes of connection and distance
- Sestina form
- Richly patterned poem
- Imagery of transit and motion
- Vivid details
- Use of present tense
- Poet as visitor and outsider

David Wheatley

Exam-Style Questions

Understanding the poem

1	What impression of the poet's grandfather do you form from the first four stanzas of the poem?
2	The poet tries to engage his grandfather in small talk, 'always in vain' (line 10). What does this tell us about each of them?
3	What kind of people are the great-uncles described in stanza 3? Explain your answer.
4	Why, do you think, might the grandfather have considered his son 'mad' to move to Bray?
5	What prompts the memories described in the first four stanzas of the poem?
6	What do the poet and his father find in Hacketstown?
7	Comment on the phrase 'Church of Ireland heaven' (line 31).
8	The poem ends on the word 'door'. In what way might the poem be described as a door?
9	Is the poem a chronicle – a family history told in the order in which events happened?
10	What is the biggest event in the history recounted here?

Thinking about the poem

1	Discuss the idea that the poet presents himself as a visitor and an outsider in the poem.
2	'The connection with place is an important part of a person's identity.' Discuss.
3	Comment on the absence of women in the chronicle.
4	'This is a poem about the backroads of history.' Discuss this view of the poem.
5	Take a stanza and identify the various patterns of sound it contains.
6	Images of transit and motion occur throughout the poem. What purpose do they serve? Explain your answer.
7	Select two details that you think are particularly effective. Explain your choice.
8	What, in your view, are the main themes of the poem?

Imagining

1	Imagine you have left Ireland to live abroad. Describe the journey or excursion you miss most. You can use the prompt: 'I really miss …'
2	Write a short poem or prose piece in which you describe your feelings for the place from which your family originates.
3	Write an acrostic poem where the first letter of each line spells out the name of your county, city, town or village.

Reading Unseen Poetry

Reading the Unseen Poem

Reading a poem is **an activity in which your mind, your beliefs and your feelings are all called into play**. As you read, **you work to create the poem's meaning from the words and images offered to you by the poet**. This process takes a little time, so be patient. However, the fact that poems are generally short – much shorter than most stories, for example – allows you to read, and re-read, a poem many times over.

As you read a poem, **jot down your responses**. These notes may take the form of words or phrases from the poem that you feel are important, although you may not be able to say at first why this is so. Write questions, teasing out the literal meaning of a word or a phrase. Write notes or commentaries as you go, expressing your understanding. **Record your feelings. Record your resistance to, or your approval of, any aspect of the poem:** its statements; the choice of words; the imagery; the tone; the values it expresses.

Begin with the title. What expectations does it set up in you? What does it remind you of?

Next, read the poem and jot down **any ideas or associations brought to mind** by any element of the poem, such as a word, a phrase, an image, the rhythm or the tone.

Be alert to **combinations of words** and **patterns of repetition**. Look for those words or images that carry emotional or symbolic force. Try to understand their effect.

Note other poems that are called to mind as you read the unseen poem. In this way, you create a territory in which the poem can be read and understood.

Poems frequently work by way of **hints, suggestions or associations**. The unstated may be as important as the stated. Learn to live with ambiguity. Learn to **enjoy the uncertainty of poetry**. Don't be impatient if a

Reading Unseen Poetry

poem does not 'make sense' to you. Most readers interpret and work on poems with more success than they know or admit! Learning to recognise your own competence, and trusting in it, is an important part of reading poems in a fruitful way. Remember that **reading is an active process** and that your readings are provisional and open to reconsideration.

Do not feel that you have to supply all the answers asked of you by a poem. In a class situation, **confer with your fellow students**. Words and images will resonate in different ways for different readers. Readers bring their own style, ideas and experiences to every encounter with a poem. **Sharing ideas and adopting a collaborative approach** to the reading of a new poem will open out the poem's possibilities beyond what you, or any individual, will achieve alone.

In an examination situation, of course, you will not be able to talk with your fellow students or return to the poem many times over a couple of days. **Trust yourself.**

The poem may be new to you, but you are not new to the reading of poems. **Draw on your experience of creating meaning.**

Poetry works to reveal the world in new ways. D. H. Lawrence said, 'The essential quality of poetry is that it makes a new effort of attention and "discovers" a new world within the known world.' In an examination answer, you are looking to show how a poem, and your reading of it, presents **a new view of the world**. Read the poem over, noting and jotting as you do so, and then focus on different aspects of the poem. **The questions set on the poem will help direct your attention.**

Possible Ways into a Poem

There are many ways to approach a poem; here are some suggestions.

The words of the poem

Remember that every word chosen by a poet suggests that another word was rejected. In poetry some words are so charged with meaning that everyday meaning gives way to **poetic meaning**. Often there are one or two words in a poem that carry a weight of meaning – these words can be read in a variety of ways that open up the poem for you. Think, for example, of how the words 'rocks' and 'sea' come to signify fixed forms and formlessness in Sylvia Plath's poem 'Finisterre'.

Here are some questions you might ask yourself:

- Are the words in the poem simple or complex, concrete or abstract?
- Are there any obvious **patterns of word usage**, for example words that refer to colours, or verbs that suggest energy and force?
- Is there a pattern in the descriptive words used by the poet?
- Are there **key words** – words that carry a symbolic or emotional force, or a clear set of associations? Does the poet play with these associations by calling them into question or subverting them?
- Do patterns of words establish any **contrasts or oppositions**; for example, night and day, winter and summer, joy and sorrow, love and death?

The music and movement of the poem

In relation to the sounds and rhythms of the poem, **note such characteristics as punctuation, the length of the lines, or the presence or absence of rhyme**. A short line can create a feeling of compressed energy; a long line can create an impression of unhurried thought.

Look carefully at the punctuation in a poem and the way in which it affects your reading. Think of G. M. Hopkins's 'The Windhover' and the way in which the punctuation works with the alliteration to control the flow and energy of the poem.

Consider how sound patterns add to the poem's **texture and meaning**. For example, do the sound patterns create a sense of hushed stillness, or an effect of forceful energy?

Ask yourself the following questions:
- What is the pattern of **line length** in the poem?
- What is the pattern of rhyme?
- Is there a pattern to **vowel sounds and length**? What influence might this have on the rhythm of the poem or the feelings conveyed by the poem?
- Are there patterns of consonant sounds, including **alliteration**? What is their effect?
- Are there changes in the poem's **rhythm**? Where and why do these occur?
- What part does **punctuation** play in controlling or influencing the movement of the poem?

The voice of the poem

Each poem has its own voice. When you read a poet's work, you can often recognise a distinctive, poetic voice. This may be in the poetry's rhythms or in the viewpoint the poems express. Sometimes it is most evident in the **tone** of voice.

Sometimes you are taken by the warmth of a poetic voice, or its coldness and detachment, or its tone of amused surprise.

Try to catch the distinctive characteristic of the voice of the poem, as you read. Decide if it is a man's voice or a woman's voice and what this might mean. Try to place the voice in a context; for example, is it the voice of a child or an adult? This may help you to **understand the assumptions in the poem's statements, or the emotional force of those statements**.

The imagery of the poem

Images are the descriptive words and phrases used by poets to speak to our senses. They are mostly visual in quality (word pictures) but they can also appeal to our sense of touch, smell, taste or hearing.

Images, and patterns of imagery, are key elements in the way that poems convey meanings. They **create moods, capture emotions and suggest, or provoke, feelings** in the readers.

Reading Unseen Poetry

Ask yourself these questions:

- Are there patterns of images in the poem?
- **What kind of world is suggested** by the images of the poem: familiar or strange; fertile or barren; secure or threatening; private or public; calm or stormy; generous or mean? (Images often suggest contrasts or opposites.)
- What emotions are associated with the images of the poem?
- What emotions might have inspired the choice of images?
- What emotions do the images provoke in me?
- If there are images that are particularly powerful, **why do they carry the force they do**?
- Do any of the images have the force of a **symbol**? What is the usual meaning of the symbol? What is its meaning in the poem?

The structure of the poem

There are endless possibilities for structuring a poem, for example:

- The obvious structures of a poem are the **lines and stanzas**. Short lines give a sense of tautness to a poem. Long lines can create a conversational feel, and allow for shifts and changes in rhythm.
- Rhyme and the **pattern of rhyme** influence the structure of a poem.
- The **poem is also structured by the movement of thought**. This may or may not coincide with line and stanza divisions. **Words such as 'while', 'then', 'and', 'or' and 'but' may help you to trace the line of thought**, or argument, as it develops through the poem.
- In narrative poems, a simple form of structure is provided by **the story itself** and the sequence of events it describes.
- Another simple structure is one in which the poet describes a scene, and then records his or her response to it.
- A poem may be built on a comparison or a contrast.
- A poem may be structured around a question and an answer, or a dilemma and a decision.
- The structure may also come from a series of parallel statements, or a series of linked reflections.

The structure of a poem can be quite subtle, perhaps depending on such things as word association or changes in emotions. **Be alert to a change of focus or a shift of thought or emotion in the poem.**

Quite often there is a **creative tension** between the stanza structure (the visual form of the poem) and the emotional or imaginative structure of the poem. Think, for example, of the three-line stanza form of Sylvia Plath's 'Elm', which gives the impression of neat tidiness, and the alarming changes of tone that occur within the structure. For this reason, **look out for turning points in poems – these may be marked by a pause, a change in imagery or a variation in rhythm.**

If the poem is in a conventional form such as a sonnet, consider why the poet chose that structure for the subject matter of the poem. Also note any departures from the traditional structure and consider why the poet has deviated from the convention.

On the following pages you will find some **sample unseen poems** and questions for you to try.

'Blessing' by Imtiaz Dharker

Read the following poem by Imtiaz Dharker and answer **either** Question 1 **OR** Question 2 which follow.

Blessing

The skin cracks like a pod.
There never is enough water.

Imagine the drip of it,
the small splash, echo
in a tin mug,
the voice of a kindly god.

Sometimes, the sudden rush
of fortune. The municipal pipe bursts,
silver crashes to the ground
and the flow has found
a roar of tongues. From the huts,
a congregation: every man woman
child for streets around
butts in, with pots,
brass, copper, aluminium,
plastic buckets,
frantic hands,

and naked children
screaming in the liquid sun,
their highlights polished to perfection,
flashing light,
as the blessing sings
over their small bones.

---

1 (a) From your reading of this poem, explain your understanding of the title, 'Blessing'. (10)

(b) Choose one image from the poem that appealed to you. Explain your choice. (10)

OR

2 Write a personal response to this poem, highlighting the impact it makes on you. Your answer should make close reference to the text. (20)

Reading Unseen Poetry

'The Envoy' by Jane Hirshfield

Read the following poem by Jane Hirshfield and answer **either** Question 1 **OR** Question 2 which follow.

The Envoy

One day in that room, a small rat.
Two days later, a snake.

Who, seeing me enter,
whipped the long stripe of his
body under the bed,
then curled like a docile house-pet.

I don't know how either came or left.
Later, the flashlight found nothing.

For a year I watched
as something – terror? happiness? grief? –
entered and then left my body.

Not knowing how it came in,
Not knowing how it went out.

It hung where words could not reach it.
It slept where light could not go.
Its scent was neither snake nor rat,
neither sensualist nor ascetic.

There are openings in our lives
of which we know nothing.

Through them
the belled herds travel at will,
long-legged and thirsty, covered with foreign dust.

---

1 (a) Based on your reading of the poem, explain what you think the poet means when she says, 'There are openings in our lives.' (10)

(b) Choose two images from the poem that appeal to you and explain your choice. (10)

OR

2 Discuss the effectiveness of the poet's use of language throughout this poem. Your answer should refer closely to the text. (20)

'Darling' by Jackie Kay

Read the following poem by Jackie Kay and answer **either** Question 1 **OR** Question 2 which follow.

Darling

You might forget the exact sound of her voice
or how her face looked when sleeping.
You might forget the sound of her quiet weeping
curled into the shape of a half moon,

when smaller than her self, she seemed already to be leaving
before she left, when the blossom was on the trees
and the sun was out, and all seemed good in the world.
I held her hand and sang a song from when I was a girl –

Heel y'ho boys, let her go boys –
and when I stopped singing she had slipped away,
already a slip of a girl again, skipping off,
her heart light, her face almost smiling.

And what I didn't know or couldn't say then
was that she hadn't really gone.
The dead don't go till you do, loved ones.
The dead are still here holding our hands.

---

1 (a) What do you believe is the central message of this poem? Support your answer with reference to the poem. (10)

(b) Identify two phrases or images which you find interesting in the poem. Explain your choices, supporting your answer with reference to the poem. (10)

OR

2 Based on your reading of the poem, identify the emotions expressed by the poet and explain how these emotions are conveyed in the poem. (20)

Reading Unseen Poetry

'Saint Francis and the Sow' by Galway Kinnell

Read the following poem by Galway Kinnell and answer **either** Question 1 **OR** Question 2 which follow.

Saint Francis and the Sow

The bud
stands for all things,
even for those things that don't flower,
for everything flowers, from within, of self-blessing;
though sometimes it is necessary
to reteach a thing its loveliness,
to put a hand on its brow
of the flower
and retell it in words and in touch
it is lovely
until it flowers again from within, of self-blessing;
as Saint Francis
put his hand on the creased forehead
of the sow, and told her in words and in touch
blessings of earth on the sow, and the sow
began remembering all down her thick length,
from the earthen snout all the way
through the fodder and slops to the spiritual curl of the tail,
from the hard spininess spiked out from the spine
down through the great broken heart
to the sheer blue milken dreaminess spurting and shuddering
from the fourteen teats into the fourteen mouths sucking and blowing
    beneath them:
the long, perfect loveliness of sow.

---

1 (a) What, according to the poem, does the bud stand for? Support your answer with reference to the poem. (10)

(b) Identify two images that you find interesting in this poem. Explain your choices, supporting your answer with reference to the poem. (10)

OR

2 Discuss the poet's use of language in the poem. Your answer should make close reference to the text. (20)

'For a Five-Year-Old' by Fleur Adcock

Read the following poem by Fleur Adcock and answer **either** Question 1 **OR** Question 2 which follow.

For a Five-Year-Old

A snail is climbing up the window-sill
into your room, after a night of rain.
You call me in to see, and I explain
that it would be unkind to leave it there:
it might crawl to the floor; we must take care
that no one squashes it. You understand,
and carry it outside, with careful hand,
to eat a daffodil.

I see, then, that a kind of faith prevails:
your gentleness is moulded still by words
from me, who have trapped mice and shot wild birds,
from me, who drowned your kittens, who betrayed
your closest relatives, and who purveyed
the harshest kind of truth to many another.
But that is how things are: I am your mother,
and we are kind to snails.

1 **(a)** What in your view is the dominant tone of the poem? Refer to the text in support of your answer. (10)

(b) Identify one interesting use of language in the poem. Explain your choice. (10)

OR

2 Write a personal response to the poem, highlighting the impact it made on you. Your answer should make close reference to the text. (20)

Reading Unseen Poetry

Exam Advice from the Department of Education and Skills

The Department of Education and Skills published this advice to students on answering the unseen poem questions in the Leaving Certificate Examination.

As the Unseen Poem on the paper will more than likely be unfamiliar to you, you should read it a number of times (at least twice) before attempting your answer.

You should pay careful attention to the introductory note printed above the text of the poem.

The Department has also issued an explanation of the following phrases, which may be used in the exam questions on poetry:

'Do you agree with this statement?'

You are free to agree in full or in part with the statement offered. But you must deal with the statement in question – you cannot simply dismiss the statement and write about a different topic of your choice.

'Write a response to this statement.'

As above, your answer can show the degree to which you agree/disagree with a statement or point of view. You can also deal with the impact the text made on you as a reader.

'What does the poem say to you about …?'

What is being asked for here is your understanding/reading of the poem. It is important that you show how your understanding comes from the text of the poem, its language and imagery.

Last Word

The really essential part in reading a poem is that you **try to meet the poet halfway**.

Bring your intelligence and your emotions to the encounter with a poem and **match the openness of the poet with an equal openness of your mind and heart**. And when you write about a poem, give **your honest assessment**.

In responding to the unseen poem in the exam, **never lose sight of the question you have been asked**. Make sure that you **support every point** you make **with clear references to the poem**. Your answers do not have to be very long, but they must be **clearly structured** in a coherent way. For this reason, **write in paragraphs**. Write as **clearly and accurately** as you can.

Guidelines for Answering Questions on Poetry

Phrasing of Examination Questions

Questions may be phrased in different ways in the Leaving Certificate English examination. In the earlier years of the examination, questions were usually phrased in a general way. Some examples include:

- Poet V: a personal response.
- What impact did the poetry of Poet W have on you as a reader?
- Write an introduction to the poetry of Poet X.

However, in recent years students have been presented with more specific statements about a poet, to which they are then invited to respond. Some examples include:

- 'Boland makes effective use of symbols and metaphors to explore personal experiences and deliver penetrating truths about society.' To what extent do you agree or disagree with this statement? Support your answer with reference to the poetry of Eavan Boland on your course. (2017)
- From your study of the poetry of Robert Frost on your course, select the poems that, in your opinion, best demonstrate how the poet helps us to understand the darker aspects of his poetic vision through this effective use of poetic narrative and dramatic scenes. Justify your selection, demonstrating how Robert Frost helps you to understand the darker aspects of his poetic vision through his effective use of poetic narrative and dramatic scenes in the poems you have selected. (2018)
- 'Durcan takes a narrative approach to explore a variety of issues in poems of great emotional honesty.' Discuss this statement, supporting your answer with reference to the poetry of Paul Durcan on your course. (2016)

Answering the full question

You will notice that these questions refer to more than one aspect of the poet's work. For example, the questions ask you to consider the **themes** (i.e. **the subject matter**) of the poems as well as the poet's **style**, i.e. **how he or she expresses these themes**.

Pay special attention to the guidelines that follow the opening statement. Examiners will expect discussion of both aspects of the question (e.g. observation and experience; subject matter and style; themes and language) although it is not always necessary to give exactly equal attention to both.

Do not neglect the final aspect of the questions asked: 'Support your points with suitable reference to the poems on your course.' This may take the form of **direct quotation or paraphrasing** of the appropriate lines.

Whatever way the question is phrased, you will need to **show that you have engaged fully with the work of the poet** under discussion.

Marking criteria

As in all of the questions in the examination, you will be marked using the following criteria:

- *Clarity of purpose* (30% of marks available). This is explained by the Department of Education and Skills as 'engagement with the set task' – in other words, **are you answering the question you have been asked**? Is your answer **relevant** and **focused**?
- *Coherence of delivery* (30% of marks available). Here you are assessed on your 'ability to **sustain the response over the entire answer**'. Is there **coherence** and **continuity** in the points you are making? Are the **references** you choose to illustrate your points **appropriate**?
- *Efficiency of language use* (30% of marks available). This concerns your 'management and control of language to achieve clear communication'. Aspects of your writing such as **vocabulary**, use of **phrasing** and **fluency** will be taken into account – in other words, your writing style.
- *Accuracy of mechanics* (10% of marks available). Your levels of **accuracy in spelling and grammar** are what count here. **Always leave some time available to read over your work** – you are bound to spot some errors.

Preparing for the Examination

In order to prepare well for specific questions such as those above, it is necessary to examine different aspects of the work of each poet on your course.

The poet's choice of themes

Be familiar with the issues and preoccupations of each poet on your course. In **writing about themes** in the examination, you will need to **know how the poet develops the themes, what questions are raised** in the poems and **how they may or may not be resolved**. Bear in mind that the themes may be **complex and open to more than one interpretation**.

Write about **how you responded to the poet's themes**. In forming your response, questions you should ask yourself include:

- Do the poet's themes appeal to me because they **enrich my understanding of universal human concerns** such as love or death?
- Do the themes offer me an **insight into the life of the poet**?
- Do I respond to the themes because they are **unusual or unfamiliar**?
- Do the themes appeal to me because they **reflect my personal concerns** and interests?
- Do I respond to themes that **appeal to my intellect as well as to my emotions**, for example politics, religion or history?

The poet's style or use of language

Any discussion of a poet's work will involve his or her style or use of language. In preparing for the examination you should study carefully the **individual images** or **patterns of imagery** used by each of the poets on your course.

When you write about imagery, try to analyse **how the particular poet you are discussing creates the effects he or she does** (i.e. what the poet's unique or distinctive **style** is). Ask yourself the following questions:

- Do the images appeal to my **senses** – my visual, tactile and aural senses, and my sense of taste and of smell? **How do I respond?** Do I find the images effective in conveying theme or emotion?
- Are the images **clear and vivid**, or **puzzling** in an **unusual or exciting** way?
- Are the images created by the use of **simile** and **metaphor**? Can I say why these particular **comparisons** were chosen by the poet? Do I find them surprising, precise, fresh, painterly …?
- Has the poet made use of **symbol** or **personification**? How have these devices added to the poem's **richness**?
- Does the poet **blend poetic and conversational language**? Has language been used to **denote** (to signify) and/or to **connote** (to suggest)?
- Does the poet use **simple expression** to convey his or her ideas **or complex language** to express complex ideas? An exploration of language may include **style**, **manner**, **phraseology** and **vocabulary**, as well as imagery and the techniques mentioned above.

The sounds of poetry

Many people find that it is the sound of poetry that they respond to most. It is an ancient human characteristic to respond to word patterns like **rhyme** or musical effects such as **rhythm**. This may be one of the aspects of a poet's work that makes it **unique or distinctive**.

Sound effects such as **alliteration**, **assonance**, **consonance** and **onomatopoeia** may be used for many reasons – some thematic, some for emotive effect, some merely because of the **sheer pleasure of creating pleasant musical word patterns**.

Look carefully at **how each of the poets** you have studied **makes use of sound**. Your response will be much richer if it is based on **close reading** and **attention to sound patterns and effects**.

The poet's life, personality or outlook

Since poems are often written out of **a poet's inner urgency**, they can **reveal a great deal about the personality of the poet**. An examination question may ask you to discuss this aspect of a poet's work. For example, in 2016, a question referred to Paul Durcan's 'emotional honesty'.

Poems can be as revealing as an autobiography. Read the work of each of the poets carefully with this in mind. Ask yourself the following questions:

- Can I build up **a profile of the poet** from what he or she has written, from **his or her personal voice**?
- Is this voice honest, convincing, suggesting **an original or perceptive view of the world**?
- Do I find the personal issues revealed to be **moving**, **intense**, **disturbing**? What reasons can I give for my opinion?

It may also be that you like the work of a particular poet for a contrasting reason: that he or she goes beyond personal revelation to create other voices, other lives. Many poets adopt a different **persona** to explore a particular experience. Might this enrich our understanding of the world? Your response may also take this aspect into account.

Poetry and the emotions

At their best, poems celebrate **what it is to be human**, with all that being human suggests, including confronting our deepest fears and anxieties. Very often it is **the emotional intensity of a poem** that **enables us to engage with it most fully**.

Questions to consider include:

- What is the **tone** of the poem? **Tone conveys the emotions that lie behind the poems.** All of the elements in a poem may be used to convey tone and emotion. Each stylistic feature – such as the poet's choice of imagery, language and sound patterns – contributes to the tone of the poem. Look at the work of the different poets with this in mind.
- **What corresponding emotions does the work of each poet on the course create in you as a reader?** Do you feel consoled, uplifted, disturbed, perhaps even alienated?
- Does the poet succeed in conveying his or her feelings effectively, in your view?

These are issues you should consider in preparing to form your response to a specific question in the examination.

Conclusion

It is worth remembering that you will be rewarded for your attempts to come to terms with the work of the poets you have studied in **a personal and responsive way**. This may entail a heartfelt negative response, too. But even a negative response must **display close reading** and should **pay attention to specific aspects of the poems mentioned in the question**. Do not feel that you have to conform to the opinions of others – even the opinions expressed in this book!

Read the question carefully. Some questions may direct your attention to specific aspects of a poet's work – make sure you deal with these aspects in your answer.

Some questions may simply invite you to include some aspects of a poet's work in your response. **It would be unwise to ignore any hints** as to how to proceed!

You will be required to **support your answer by reference to or quotation from the poems chosen**. The Department of Education and Skills has published the following advice to students on answering the question on poetry:

> It is a matter of judgement as to which of the poems will best suit the question under discussion and candidates should not feel a necessity to refer to all of the poems they have studied.

Remember that long quotations are hardly ever necessary.

Good luck!

Glossary of Terms

allegory A story or poem in which the characters and events represent ideas about the world.

alliteration Repetition of consonants, especially at the beginning of words. The term itself means 'repeating and playing upon the same letter'. Alliteration is a common feature of poetry from every period of literary history. It is used mainly to reinforce a point or enhance the music of a poem. Consider the alliteration from Eavan Boland's 'The Shadow Doll': cards… coffee pots… clocks … case… cotton.

allusion A reference to a person, place or event or to another work of art or literature. The purpose of allusion is to get the reader to share an experience that has significant meaning for the writer. The title of Paul Durcan's poem, 'The Arnolfini Wedding', alludes to the celebrated fifteenth century painting by the Dutch painter Jan van Eyck.

ambiguity Ambiguous words, phrases or sentences are capable of being understood in two or more possible senses. In many poems, ambiguity is part of the poet's method and is essential to the meaning of the poem.

assonance The repetition of identical or similar vowel sounds, especially in stressed syllables, in a sequence of words. Assonance can contribute significantly to the meaning of a poem. Keats's poetry is full of assonance, as in his description of the nightingale 'pouring forth thy soul abroad' in 'Ode to a Nightingale'.

ballad A poem or song that concentrates on telling a story. Ballads are usually composed in quatrains with the second and fourth line rhyming.

caesura The pause which occurs in most lines of poetry of any length. Sometimes it is marked by a punctuation mark, though not always. Possibly the most famous caesura in all literature occurs in Shakespeare's *Hamlet*: 'To be, or not to be, that is the question.' You might like to recite the line and decide how long to hold the caesura on the comma between 'be' and 'that' in the middle of the line.

colloquialism Using the language of everyday speech. The colloquial style is plain and relaxed. In much poetry of the twentieth and twenty-first centuries, there is an acceptance of colloquialism, and even slang, as a medium of poetic expression. 'She'd put her boot through the screen' is an example of colloquialism from Durcan's 'Wife Who Smashed Television Gets Jail'.

connotation The additional meanings that words have beyond their basic or dictionary meaning. In using the title 'The Underground' for a love poem, Seamus Heaney plays upon the association between underground and underworld and the story of Orpheus and Eurydice.

Glossary

consonance Repetition of consonant sounds within as well as at the beginning of words. You can hear consonance in Frost's 'After Apple-Picking' in the repeated 's', 'n' 't' and 'p' sounds in 'Essence of winter sleep is on the night, / the scent of apples'.

convention Any aspect of a literary work that author and readers accept as normal and to be expected in that kind or genre of writing. For example, it is a convention that a sonnet has fourteen lines that rhyme in a certain pattern.

diction The vocabulary used by a writer – his or her selection of words and word combinations. Until the beginning of the nineteenth century, poets wrote in accordance with the principle that the diction of poetry had to be clearly different from the diction of current speech. There was a certain sort of 'poetic' diction, which, by avoiding commonplace words and expressions, was supposed to lend dignity to the poem and its subject. This is entirely contrary to modern practice.

elegy A poem written to commemorate someone who has died. An elegiac poem is one which has a mournful or sad tone. Eavan Boland's 'Child of Our Time' is an example of a modern elegy.

enjambment Also referred to as a **run-on line**, this is when the meaning carries over from one line of poetry into the next, almost without a pause, often creating an extra burst of energy, as in Boland's 'War Horse' 'This dry night, nothing unusual / About the clip, clop, casual / Iron of his shoes as he stamps death …'.

epigraph A quotation from another piece of literature that is placed beneath the title at the beginning of a poem. The Latin epigraph used by Hopkins at the start of 'Thou art indeed just, Lord' introduces the theme of despair.

free verse Poetry that does not rhyme and does not have a regular **metre**. That does not mean that it lacks musical qualities, but it does not follow any conventional form. Some of Durcan's poetry is written in free verse.

genre A particular literary species or form. Traditionally, the important poetic genres were epic, tragedy, comedy, elegy, satire, lyric and pastoral. Until modern times, critics tended to distinguish carefully between the various genres and writers were expected to follow the rules prescribed for each.

iamb The most common metrical 'foot' in English poetry, consisting of one unstressed syllable followed by one stressed one (˘ ´), as in the words 'bĕcáuse' and ' ŭnléss'. Iambic verse has a natural connection to the beat of the heart or the rhythm of walking.

iambic pentameter A line of verse consisting of five iambs (dĭ-dúm, dĭ-dúm, dĭ-dúm, dĭ-dúm, dĭ-dúm), used by Shakespeare in all his plays and sonnets, and one of the most common metres in English-language verse.

image A descriptive word or phrase used by poets to speak to our senses. The poet Cecil Day Lewis puts the matter well when he describes an image as 'a picture made out of words'.

imagery This is a term with a very wide application. When we speak of the imagery of a poem, we refer to all its images taken collectively. Often the imagery of a poem has a certain theme or other quality in common.

lament A poem expressing deep sorrow and grief. A lament can express private grief at the death of a loved one or communal grief, such as that which follows the death of a leader. Boland's 'Child of Our Time' laments a victim of the Dublin bombings in 1974.

lyric Any relatively short poem in which a single speaker, not necessarily representing the poet, expresses feelings and thoughts in a personal and subjective fashion. Most poems are either lyrics or feature lyrical elements.

metaphor A comparison between two elements that is implied by the words, rather than by using 'like' or 'as'. (See also **simile**.) If in a simile someone's teeth are like pearls, in a metaphor they are pearls. A metaphor is capable of a greater range of suggestiveness than a simile and its implications are wider and richer. For example, in Heaney's 'The Forge', the forge becomes a metaphor for the creative imagination.

metonym A word or expression that stands for something with which it is closely associated. For example, in Heaney's 'Sunlight' baking can be seen as a metonym for nurture and care and for the idea of family love.

metre The rhythm or pattern of stressed and unstressed sounds in a line of poetry. Especially in traditional and rhyming forms, a line of poetry consists of a number of 'feet', and each foot is made up of two or three syllables in a specific pattern. For example, if you say 'incy wincy spider' aloud, you can see that it has three feet of one stressed followed by one unstressed syllable (´ ˘); 'hickory dickory dock' has two feet of one stressed syllable followed by two unstressed syllables (´ ˘ ˘), and then the final word 'dock'. The different types of foot have names. The most common one is the **iamb** (˘ ´), which has its own entry above. Others include: trochee (´ ˘), anapaest (˘ ˘ ´), dactyl (´ ˘ ˘) and spondee (´ ´). The **metre** of a line of verse can be given a name according to the number and type of feet in a line. A line with four feet is called a tetrameter; a line with five feet is called a pentameter. So a line made up of five iambs would be called an **iambic pentameter** (see separate entry on page 603).

ode A poem written in praise of something or someone. The subject often allows the poet to express his/her emotions. Odes are written in an exalted (high-flown) style using complex stanza forms. The poem is usually addressed to the source of the poet's inspiration.

onomatopoeia The use of words that resemble, or enact, the very sounds they imitate. In 'Felix Randal' Hopkins uses the verb 'battering' to describe the sound of the horse's shoe striking the ground.

paradox An apparently self-contradictory statement, which, on further consideration, is found to contain an essential truth. Paradox is so intrinsic to human nature that poetry rich in paradox is valued as a reflection of the central truths of human experience. 'Frost's poem 'Design' turns on the paradox that the scene he describes in the poem suggests that design in nature might be controlled by an evil force rather than hand of God.'

persona Sometimes a poet adopts the mask or character of another person, or even an object, as the speaker in a poem.

personification The attribution of human qualities to an animal, concept or object.

quatrain A stanza form of four lines, which can be rhymed or unrhymed. The most popular rhyme schemes are: *abab* and *abba*. Boland's 'The Black Lace Fan' is written in quatrains.

refrain A repeated line or lines (often a couplet) at the end of a series of stanzas.

rhetoric Language which is designed to persuade or impress the reader or listener. We call such language rhetorical. Traditionally, rhetoric involved a range of techniques, but the only one commonly recognised now is the rhetorical question, which is a question that makes a point but does not expect an answer. 'Frost's poem 'Provide, Provide' uses rhetorical language, though not rhetorical questions.'

run-on line See **enjambment**.

sestina A poem with six stanzas of six lines each, followed by a three-line seventh stanza (known as an envoy). The poet uses six particular words throughout the poem as the end words of each line, but in a different order in each stanza. Elizabeth Bishop's 'Sestina' is a celebrated example. David Wheatley's 'Chronicle' is also a sestina.

Glossary

sibilance The hissing sound associated with certain letters such as 's', 'sh'. The sound is used to good effect by Robert Frost in 'Birches': 'Soon the sun's warmth makes them shed crystal shells, / Shattering and avalanching on the snow crust'.

simile A comparison between two things that uses a comparative word ('like' or 'as'). In Eavan Boland's 'War Horse' there is a striking simile describing the horse's iron hooves striking the ground: 'as he stamps death / Like a mint on the innocent coinage of earth'.

sonnet A rhymed lyric poem of fourteen lines. These fourteen lines are long enough to make possible the fairly complex development of a single theme, and short enough to test the poet's gift for concentrated expression. English poets have traditionally written one of two kinds of sonnet – the Petrarchan and the Shakespearean. The Petrarchan sonnet, named after the Italian poet who made the form popular, and favoured by Keats, falls into two divisions – the octave (eight lines rhyming *abba, abba*) and the sestet (six lines generally rhyming *cde, cde*). The octave usually presents a problem, situation or incident; the sestet resolves the problem or comments on the situation or incident. In contrast, the Shakespearean sonnet consists of three quatrains (groups of four lines rhyming *abab, cdcd, efef*) and a rhyming couplet (*gg*). Keats's 'To one who has been long in city pent' is an example of a Petrarchan sonnet.

style A writer's manner of expression – that is, his or her particular way of saying things. Consideration of style involves an examination of the writer's diction, use of figures of speech, order of words, tone and feeling, rhythm and movement. Traditionally, styles were classified as: high (formal or learned), middle, and low (plain). Convention required that the level of style be appropriate to the speaker, the subject matter, the occasion that inspired the poem, and the literary genre.

symbol Any word or image that stands for something else. In this sense, all words are symbols. Literary symbolism, however, comes about when the objects signified by the words stand in turn for things other than themselves. Objects commonly associated with fixed ideas or qualities have come to symbolise them, for example the cross is the primary Christian symbol, and the dove is a symbol of peace. Colour symbols have no fixed meaning but derive their significance from the context: green may signify innocence or Irish patriotism or envy; red may signify anger or love or Communism. In Seamus Heaney's poem 'The Pitchfork', the simple farm implement of the title becomes a symbol for the imagination's capacity to travel beyond the limits of the real.

tercet A stanza form of three lines.

tone Every speaker must inevitably have an attitude to the person or object being addressed or talked about. The tone expresses this attitude. When one is trying to describe the tone of a poem, it is best to think of every poem as a spoken, rather than a written, exercise. A poem has at least one speaker who is addressing somebody or something. In some poems, the speaker can be thought of as meditating aloud, talking to himself or herself; we, the readers, overhear the words.

Poets Examined at Higher Level in Previous Years

2018
Robert Frost
Eiléan Ní Chuilleanáin
John Montague
Philip Larkin

2017
Eavan Boland
John Donne
John Keats
Elizabeth Bishop

2016
Emily Dickinson
T. S. Eliot
Elizabeth Bishop
Paul Durcan

2015
John Montague
Robert Frost
Eiléan Ní Chuilleanáin
Thomas Hardy

2014
W. B. Yeats
Emily Dickinson
Philip Larkin
Sylvia Plath

2013
Elizabeth Bishop
G. M. Hopkins
Derek Mahon
Sylvia Plath

2012
Thomas Kinsella
Adrienne Rich
Philip Larkin
Patrick Kavanagh

2011
Eavan Boland
Emily Dickinson
Robert Frost
W. B. Yeats

2010
T. S. Eliot
Patrick Kavanagh
Adrienne Rich
W. B. Yeats

2009
Derek Walcott
John Keats
John Montague
Elizabeth Bishop

2008
Philip Larkin
John Donne
Derek Mahon
Adrienne Rich

2007
Robert Frost
T. S. Eliot
John Montague
Sylvia Plath

Elizabeth Bishop Revision Chart

Poem	Theme	Tone	Imagery	Language	Form	Mood	Effect
The Fish	Surviving adversity and second chances	Admiring, curious, respectful, joyful	Nature, lots of colour and unusual comparisons	Conversational; musicality brought through sound effects	Long, descriptive narrative, fable	Celebratory, elation	Allegorical – teaches a lesson; uplifting
The Bight	The creative process, how the subconscious mind works	Regretful; realistic yet hopeful	Extremely detailed; links exterior world to poet's interior thoughts	Lots of sound effects, very detailed description	Personal lyric	Regret, acceptance, optimism	Personally revealing, celebratory
At the Fishhouses	Explores the nature of knowledge and imagination	Curious, tentative; sadness, sense of loss	Symbolism, the sea a central image, similes and metaphors	Very descriptive and metaphorical; moves from external to internal	Personal lyric, meditation	Deeply analytical, philosophical	Mysterious, thought-provoking
The Prodigal	Debasement, addiction and redemption	Resigned, fretful, nervously hopeful	Religious, agricultural, light and darkness, squalor	Highlights dehumanisation of Prodigal; religious, descriptive	Double sonnet; last line doesn't fully rhyme emphasising theme	Resignation and acceptance moves to tentative optimism	Disturbing, evoking sympathy, biographical
Questions of Travel	Travel – why people do it and how it should be undertaken; home	Curious, weary, critical, admiring	Vivid descriptions of sights and sounds	Blend of poetic and conversational, use of tourist persona, questions	Long stanzas work through the questions and ideas	Wryly humorous, quirky, playful	Thought-provoking, exotic
The Armadillo	Adverse effect of mankind on natural world	Admiring, horrified, angry	Similes, animals, fire	Lots of sound effects; modern to more archaic in last stanza	Allegory	Indignant horror, sympathy	Evokes empathy for suffering animals
Sestina	Childhood loss, family, home, power of imagination	Sadness, naivety	Personification of domestic objects, child's drawing, tears, pathetic fallacy	Childlike, repetitive	Archaic poetic seven stanza form with strict rules	Grief, incomprehension	We feel we know the poet more deeply; moving
First Death in Nova Scotia	How children try to make sense of the world and of death	Confusion, curiosity; observant	Key details anchor poem – loon, body in coffin, pictures, white and red	Childlike, repetition, mix of fantasy and domestic reality	Biographical narrative	Mixture of innocence and awareness	Moving, naïve, honest
Filling Station	Family; a mother's love	Playful: feigns confusion and disapproval	Multisensory, domestic, detailed	Conversational, descriptive, questioning	Narrative account, allegorical effect of lesson at the end	Wryly humorous, curious and enquiring	Entertaining, evokes sympathy for poet at the end
In the Waiting Room	Identity, cultural awareness, femininity	Shocked, disoriented, questioning	Descriptive, exotic, symbolism of waiting room	Moves from realistic to surrealistic description	Personal narrative	Philosophical, pondering deep questions of identity and belonging	Thought-provoking, complex, intense

Eavan Boland Revision Chart

Poem	Theme	Tone	Imagery	Language	Form	Mood	Effect
The War Horse	Violence, history, indifference	Thoughtful, questioning	Conflict, horse, suburban order	Metaphorical, symbolic	Rhyming couplets	Reflective, ominous	Thought-provoking
Child of Our Time	Childhood, responsibility	Sorrowful, angry	Childhood, language, music	Uses antithesis	Sestet, with tight rhyme scheme	Regretful, determined	Disturbing
The Famine Road	Suffering, marginalisation, women's experience	Detached, cold	Building of famine road; infertile woman	Terse, sometimes awkward	Two distinct elements: monologue; rhyme	Grief, bitterness	Unsettling, thought-provoking
The Black Lace Fan My Mother Gave Me	Love and relationships; female sexuality	Hesitant, regretful, yet sensuous	The fan; the blackbird; stormy weather	Plain, descriptive, increasingly metaphorical	Quatrains with occasional rhyme	Troubled, tense, then celebratory	Troubling, then thrilling
The Shadow Doll	Marriage, women's experience	Thoughtful	The doll: whiteness, passivity, imprisonment	Precise, considered	Unrhymed tercets	Reflection	Thought-provoking, ominous
White Hawthorn in the West of Ireland	Nature, superstition, unspoken history	Meditative	Nature, water, language	Intimate, metaphorical	Unrhymed four-line stanzas	Reflective	Mysterious, thought-provoking
Outside History	Myth and history; landscape and belonging	Mournful	Light and dark; time and space	Intimate but controlled, precise	Unrhymed tercets; meditative lyric	Regretful, determined	Moving, thought-provoking
This Moment	Time; preciousness of the moment	Delicate, reflective	Mother and child; nature	Simple, sensuous	Free verse, lyric	Celebration	Uplifting
Love	Love and marriage; time and loss	Celebratory; anguished	Dark and light; speech; myth of Aeneas	Plain and direct, but evocative	Unrhymed stanzas; meditative lyric	Reflective, regretful	Troubling, thought-provoking
The Pomegranate	Mother–daughter relationship; time and loss	Loving, restrained	Pomegranate; Ceres–Persephone myth	Direct, intimate	First-person narrative/reflection	Troubled but accepting	Moving

Revision Charts

Paul Durcan Revision Chart

Poem	Theme	Tone	Imagery	Language	Form	Mood	Effect
Nessa	Journey of a relationship	Excited, nostalgic, regretful	Water	Repetition, use of a refrain	Lyric, aisling	Honest, open	Romantic
The Girl with the Keys to Pearse's Cottage	Emigration, first love, erosion of Irish identity	Fascinated, regretful	Colour, rural Ireland	Accessible, contrast	Lyric	Regretful, admiring	Sad
The Difficulty that is Marriage	Estrangement, marital discord	Confessional, tender	Permanence, transience	Speaks directly to beloved	Sonnet	Yearning	Evokes sympathy
Wife Who Smashed Television Gets Jail	Family dysfunction, justice	Pseudo-journalistic, satirical	Violent	Judicial, journalistic, misogynistic	Free verse	Angry	Amusing, thought-provoking
Parents	Estrangement, parenthood	Deeply anxious	The sea, separation	Repetition, contrast	Free verse	Helpless	Unsettling
En Famille, 1979	Childhood	Yearning	Darkness	Repetition, alliteration	Couplet	Nostalgic	Enigmatic
Madman	Stigma of 'madness'	Seems glib	Street	Accessible	Couplet	Darkly funny	Joke-like, shocking
'Windfall', 8 Parnell Hill, Cork	Home and family life	Range of emotions	Art, domestic, urban	Varied, direct, repetition	Long lyric	Moving	Poignant
Six Nuns Die in Convent Inferno	Religious faith	Cheerful	Surreal, detailed, contrast	Religious, colloquial	Lyric	Lively, upbeat	Surprising
Sport	Father–son relationship	Proud, regretful	Gaelic match	Accessible, conversational	Free verse	Brooding	Very revealing
Father's Day, 21 June 1992	Marital discord	Regretful	The axe, train journey	Dialogue used	Lyric	Regretful, anxious	Amusing
The Arnolfini Marriage	Romantic love, marriage	Arrogant	Bedroom	Direct, standoffish, assured	Lyric in tercets	Confident	Distances reader, ambiguity
Ireland 2002	Affluence, emigration	Flippant	Travel	Conversational	Couplet	Humorous	Witty
Rosie Joyce	Joy at becoming a grandfather	Elated	Travelling through Ireland, flowers	Repetition, speaks to child	Lyric in tercets	Jubilant, prayer-like	Uplifting, affirming
The MacBride Dynasty	Family, ageing	Gently mocking	Ageing, reptilian	Conversational, Yeats-like opening	Lyric	Reflective	Revealing, anecdotal

Robert Frost Revision Chart

Poem	Theme	Tone	Imagery	Language	Form	Mood	Effect
The Tuft of Flowers	Human fellowship, relationships	Reflective, optimistic	Mowing grass, flowers, butterfly	Descriptive, mostly conversational	Rhyming couplets	Celebratory	Uplifting
Mending Wall	Barriers to human understanding	Considered, humorous	The wall, farm work	Straightforward, conversational	Blank verse narrative	Questioning	Thought-provoking
After Apple-Picking	Exhaustion, physical labour, the imagination	Peaceful yet uneasy	Apple-picking, dreams, sleep	Sensuous, metaphorical	Rhymed iambic lines of varying length	Suspended between wakefulness and sleep	Celebratory but uneasy
The Road Not Taken	Choices, remembering	Rueful, yet humorous	Roads in wood, autumn	Simple, descriptive	Rhymed five-line stanzas	Regretful, wistful	Moving or amusing
Birches	Conflicted feelings about life	Nostalgic, reflective	Swinging birches, nature	Conversational, sometimes richly sensuous	Blank verse	Celebratory	Uplifting
"Out, Out—"	Realities of rural life; fate	Detached, almost cold	Farm work, the buzz saw	Straightforward, simple	Blank verse narrative	Ominous, dark	Disturbing
Spring Pools	Transience of life; creation and destruction	Regretful	Water, flowers, trees	Metaphorical, rhetorical	Tightly structured lyric	Sombre	Troubling
Acquainted with the Night	Alienation, depression	Hopeless, weary	Urban life	Neutral, repetitive	Fourteen lines, tightly rhymed, but not a sonnet	Resigned, melancholy	Chilling
Design	Purpose in nature	Questioning	Spider, moth, flower, whiteness	Descriptive, precise	Sonnet with just three rhyme sounds	Cynical	Thought-provoking
Provide, Provide	Need for self-reliance	Cynical, ambiguous	Poverty, power	Plain but rhetorical	Rhyming triplets	Bitter, disillusioned	Ambiguous

Revision Charts

Seamus Heaney Revision Chart

Poem	Theme	Tone	Imagery	Language	Form	Mood	Effect
The Forge	Craft, imagination	Wonder, lament	Light and dark, sacred	Strong, rich in sound	Sonnet	Celebration	Transforming
Bogland	Landscape, memory, poetry	Assured, confident	Bogs and prairies	Spare, musical	Lyric meditation	Excitement	Opening up possibilities
The Tollund Man	Violence, ancestry, imagination	Sadness, longing	Burial, sacrifice, germination, pilgrimage	Simple, clear, prayer-like	Lyric meditation	Sombre contemplation	Raising questions
Mossbawn: Two Poems in Dedication (1) Sunlight	Love, family, nurture	Affectionate, loving	Baking, warmth	Flowing, descriptive	Lyric description	Tenderness	Warming
A Constable Calls	Fear, power, alienation	Fearful, guilty	Precise, inhuman	Clear, impersonal, harsh	Narrative	Oppression	Threatening
The Skunk	Married love, erotic intimacy	Humorous, ironic, affectionate	Unusual metaphors; sensuous, sacramental	Descriptive, full-sounding, symbolic	Lyric meditation	Love	Amusing, startling
The Harvest Bow	Father–son relationship, hope	Nostalgic, loving, harmonious	Craft and making	Richly descriptive	Lyric addressed to poet's father	Admiration	Inspiring
The Underground	Marriage, love	Playful, celebratory, erotic, honest	Classical allusions, flight and pursuit	Allusive, energetic	Love lyric	Celebration, perseverance	Energising
The Pitchfork	The real and the marvellous	Uplifting, admiring	Visionary; weight, weightlessness	Light, sensuous, symbolic	Lyric meditation	Trust	Transforming
Lightenings, viii: 'The Annals Say'	The real and the marvellous	Tolerant, understanding, definite	Flight, anchorage	Clear, matter-of-fact	Narrative	Lightness	Freeing of the spirit
A Call	Love, death	Fearful, apprehensive, relieved	Silence, waiting	Clear, dramatic	Dramatic narrative	Relief	Involving
Postscript	Openness, the unexpected	Thoughtful, excited	Land and sea, light and air	Conversational, descriptive, symbolic	Sonnet-like	Openness	Being in two worlds
Tate's Avenue	Love, influence of place	Intoxicated, cautious	Rugs, picnics, home and abroad	Descriptive, sensuous	Love lyric	Fond remembrance	Revealing of the lovers

Gerard Manley Hopkins Revision Chart

Poem	Theme	Tone	Imagery	Language	Form	Mood	Effect
God's Grandeur	World filled with the grandeur of God; human activity degrades nature	Praising; regretful, then hopeful	Religious then industrial, then drawn from nature	Descriptive	Sonnet	Varies from celebratory to disillusioned to optimistic	Inspirational
Spring	Celebration of spring; spring a reflection of the innocent springtime of the world	Celebratory	Nature, Christian story	High descriptive, alliterative	Sonnet	Celebratory, then pleading	Convincing affirmation of the divine purpose in creation
As kingfishers catch fire	Uniqueness of every created thing	Affirmative, celebratory	Natural world, Christianity	Descriptive then philosophical	Sonnet	Optimistic, celebratory	Reassuring, inspirational
The Windhover	Splendour of the falcon reflects the greater splendour of Christ	Celebratory	Falconry, crucifixion	Powerfully descriptive, devotional	Sonnet	Happy, reverential	Joyful, reassuring
Pied Beauty	Unchanging God created a highly varied world	Affirmative	Natural world	Close and accurate description	'Curtal' (shortened) sonnet	Celebratory, joyful	Heartening
Felix Randal	Spiritual relief of suffering	Sympathetic	Catholic, bodily suffering and physical strength	Alliterative, descriptive, devotional	Sonnet	Nostalgic, devotional, sympathetic	Inspirational, deeply moving
Inversnaid	Joy in wild nature	Celebratory	Nature	Descriptive	Lyric	Enthusiastic	Happy
No worst, there is none	Horrors of despair	Desolate	Religious, literary, natural	Descriptive, narrative, reflective	Sonnet	Deeply despairing	Deeply disturbing
I wake and feel the fell of dark, not day	Horrors of depression and spiritual desolation	Deep despair	Darkness, illness	Descriptive use of plain words	Sonnet	Dark, depressive	Frightening
Thou art indeed just, Lord	Questioning divine justice	Despairing, pleading	Biblical, nature	Reflective, interrogative	Sonnet	Questioning, disillusioned, disappointed, pleading	Stimulating

John Keats Revision Chart

Poem	Theme	Tone	Imagery	Language	Form	Mood	Effect
To one who has been long in city pent	Natural beauty; city and country	Joyful but poignant	Nature; the angel	Descriptive; conventionally poetic	Sonnet	Pleasurable indolence	Touching
On First Looking into Chapman's Homer	Discovery; great art	Enthusiastic	Voyaging; adventure; astronomy	Poetic, metaphorical	Sonnet	Excited, awestruck	Thrilling
When I have fears that I may cease to be	Fear of premature death	Anxious, reflective	Agriculture; nature; the ocean	Rich and poetic	Sonnet	Troubled	Moving
La Belle Dame Sans Merci	Love and death	Deadpan, innocent	Nature; medieval adventure	Simple syntax; some archaic vocabulary	Literary ballad	Sombre, disillusioned	Disturbing
Ode to a Nightingale	Intense experience; beauty and transcendence	Emotional: ecstatic and grieving; celebratory	Nature; classical mythology	Descriptive, sensuous, musical	Ode	Melancholy	Thought-provoking; saddening
Ode on a Grecian Urn	Art and beauty; time and eternity	Questioning; celebratory	Classical art and life	Interrogative, analytical	Ode	Pensive, troubled	Thought-provoking; moving
To Autumn	Autumn; natural abundance	Celebratory	Nature: tactile, visual, aural	Descriptive, sensuous	Ode	Sensuous, calm	Ravishing; restful
Bright Star	Ideal love; the ideal and the real	Yearning	Distant star and human intimacy	Austere and sensuous by turns	Sonnet	Intense desire	Moving

Sylvia Plath Revision Chart

Poem	Theme	Tone	Imagery	Language	Form	Mood	Effect
Black Rook in Rainy Weather	Inspiration	Fearful, hopeful, cautious	Light and radiance; transformation	Heightened, metaphorical, controlled	Lyric meditation	Hesitantly hopeful	Evokes sympathy
The Times Are Tidy	Blandness of contemporary culture	Dismissive, satirical	Fairy tale	Clear, patterned	Lyric, confident statements	Irony	Low-key, amusing
Morning Song	Motherhood, birth	Joyful, amazed, protective	Museum, separation, baby's cry	Clear, direct, musical	Lyric, expressive	Elation, celebration at end	Surprising, elevating
Finisterre	Life and death	Anxious, calm	Surreal images of the ocean, war, fog, rocks	Detailed, symbolic	Lyric description and meditation	Heightened emotion	Fascinating, unsettling
Mirror	Judgement, fear, ageing	Detached, cold	Personification, rising, fish	Precise, accurate	Dramatic monologue	Darkness	Disturbing
Pheasant	Preciousness of life, fear of destruction	Accusing, pleading, admiring	Visual, descriptive	Intense	Dramatic monologue in terza rima	Anguish	Revealing of the poet
Elm	Fear, love, self-hatred	Mocking, fearful, threatening	Subconscious, dreams, nightmares	Powerful, symbolic, rich	Dramatic monologue	Terror	Overpowering
Poppies in July	Fear and longing	Dramatic, disturbed, emotional	Sickness, violence, annihilation	Intense, passionate, onomatopoeic	Concentrated lyric	Darkness	Unsettling
The Arrival of the Bee Box	Personal fears	Frightened, fascinated	Entrapment and freedom	Direct, powerful	Present-tense narrative	Triumphant optimism	Entertaining
Child	Love and despair	Frustration, longing	Whimsical, images of reflection	Inventive, composed	Short lyric	Anguish	Heart-breaking

NOTES

NOTES

NOTES

NOTES